Palgrave Macmillan Transnational History Series

Series Editors

This distinguished series seeks to develop scholarship on the transnational connections of societies and peoples in the nineteenth and twentieth centuries; provide a forum in which work on transnational history from different periods, subjects, and regions of the world can be brought together in fruitful connection; and explore the theoretical and methodological links between transnational and other related approaches such as comparative history and world history.

Gregor Benton

Chinese Indentured Labour in the Dutch East Indies, 1880–1942

Tin, Tobacco, Timber, and the Penal Sanction

palgrave
macmillan

Gregor Benton
Cardiff, UK

ISSN 2634-6273 ISSN 2634-6281 (electronic)
Palgrave Macmillan Transnational History Series
ISBN 978-3-031-05023-7 ISBN 978-3-031-05024-4 (eBook)
https://doi.org/10.1007/978-3-031-05024-4

Cover illustration: Art World / Alamy Stock Photo

This Palgrave Macmillan imprint is published by the registered company Springer Nature Switzerland AG.
The registered company address is: Gewerbestrasse 11, 6330 Cham, Switzerland

Praise for *Chinese Indentured Labour in the Dutch East Indies, 1880–1942*

"Gregor Benton is a veteran researcher and a prolific author on Chinese revolutionary history, Chinese migration, and overseas settlement. In this rich and widely ranging study, he explores Chinese labour migration to Sumatra under Dutch rule, the iniquities of the Dutch recruitment system, and the penal sanction with which Dutch indenture became synonymous. He also offers profound reflections on the contrasts between Chinese labour indenture and its Indian and Javanese equivalents. Benton proposes a novel and highly innovative explanation of the special features of Chinese labour migration and identifies its social, cultural, and economic causes in China's modern crisis and international weakness. The study benefits from its author's virtuoso linguistic skills and the breadth of his knowledge of Chinese society and politics."

—Hong Liu, *Tan Lark Sye Chair Professor of Public Policy and Global Affairs, Nanyang Technological University, Singapore*

"Gregor Benton has written a most impressive work, a highly original contribution to the study of the Chinese labour diaspora. His pioneering study of Chinese 'coolies' (Huagong) and their descendants in the late-colonial Dutch East Indies builds on Chinese, Dutch, and other sources, and offers a convincing blend of fine description and careful analysis."

—Marcel van der Linden, *International Institute of Social History, The Netherlands*

"This book is much more than a beautifully written social history of Chinese indentured labour in the Dutch East Indies in the nineteenth and twentieth centuries. It is a thoughtful, rigorous, and comparative analysis of how and why Chinese differed from Indian and Javanese indenture. Based on sources in several languages, this fascinating study has much contemporary relevance and makes an invaluable contribution to Chinese diaspora studies, indenture studies, and the interdisciplinary field of migration studies."

—Min Zhou, *Distinguished Professor, University of California, Los Angeles, USA*

"Finally, a pioneering study of Chinese labour migration and a cohesive narrative of colonial indenture in comparative perspective. Painstakingly researched and using an impressive array of Chinese, English, and Dutch sources, this study provides a fresh look at the complex multi-layered phenomenon of unfree labour. This is a book that captures the horrors of this dehumanising form of labour diaspora so well that we see it for what it really was—indenture slavery."

—Edmund Terence Gomez, *Professor Emeritus of Political Economy, University of Malaya*

Acknowledgements

I wrote this book as my contribution to a collective research project on indentured Chinese labour in Asia and the Pacific in the early twentieth century. The project was run from the School of Humanities and Social Inquiry in the Faculty of Arts, Social Sciences and Humanities at the University of Wollongong, Australia, by Julia Martínez and Claire Lowrie, and was funded by the Australian Research Council (ARC DP180100695). Julia and Claire were ideal and energetic partners in our collaborative effort, which they initiated and led. I was aided in organising my part of the study by them and by colleagues in the School of History, Archaeology and Religion at Cardiff University, where I am an Emeritus Professor. I am grateful to Leila Hughes, Emma Fisher, Ann-Marie Morgan, David Watkinson, and Shaun Tougher for helping to administer my travel and funding. I would like to thank all these people, in New and old South Wales, for their help, support, tolerance, and kindness. In the course of my research, I visited libraries, museums, and archives in Leiden, Hong Kong, Nanjing, Kuala Lumpur, Singapore, Miri, Jakarta, Belitung, and Bangka and historic sites in Bangka-Belitung. I would especially like to mention Bangka's Tin Museum in Pangkal Pinang and Belitung's Tanjung Pandan Museum. In all these places, I owe a great debt of gratitude to staff and local people, who received me with patience and goodwill. At Palgrave Macmillan, Tikoji Rao Mega Rao coordinated the book's publication and Sam Stocker looked after its editing, following the departure of Meagan Simpson, my initial contact at Palgrave Macmillan. Akira Iriye and Rana Mitter, by agreeing to host the book in their Transnational History series, gave me an additional stimulus to persevere with the project and organised a very helpful review of the manuscript, as well as helping me to solve various practical problems. Again, I am deeply grateful to all these people. At Nanyang Technological University in Singapore, my friends Liu Hong and Zhang Huimei were in many ways an inspiration for the book, which followed on naturally from the research that the three of us did in the mid-2010s on *qiaopi* (migrants' remittances), leading to conferences, workshops, and several books, including *Dear China*, and articles. Hong and Huimei not only procured much of the archival material on which parts of this book (in particular in Ch. 5) depend but helped by producing the map that graces its front matter.

Others helped with scholarly advice and guidance, technical assistance, and other forms of material or spiritual support. They include, in alphabetical order, Sunlie Thomas Alexander (Bangka-Belitung), Rebecca Urai Ayan (Sarawak), Zvi Ben-Dor Benite, Daniel Fanxi Benton, Jan Breman, Sebastian Budgen, Feng Chongyi, Margo Groenewoud (Curaçao), Danny Hayward, Gregory Jany, Daniel Wan Jonathan, Kaan Kangal, Paul Key, Arun Kumar, Toby Lincoln, Marcel van der Linden, Fiona Middlebrook, Budiman Minasny, Josie Pollentine, Christopher Reinhart (Jakarta), Lomarsh Roopnarine, Shen Yuanfang, Willie Xue (Bangka-Belitung), Kevin Yang, and Taomo Zhou. To all of them, my heartfelt thanks.

This detail of Liu Yi in close-up shows that he is wearing spectacles, suggesting that he was not necessarily an ordinary miner but might have been an educated man, perhaps one of the Chinese teachers who turned up on Bangka at around this time

The arrest of the rebel miners' leader Liu Yi on Bangka, 1900

This cartoon, published in a Chinese magazine at the time, depicts the imagined life and death (by suicide) of an indentured Chinese labourer. Leaving home for the Nanyang, he aims to return with wealth and in glory. He digs tin under the hot sun; loses his job when the market collapses; is forced to roam the streets as a beggar; and comes to a sorry end

A museum representation of a Chinese miner on Bangka-Belitung working under Dutch supervision

Tin lakes left behind on former Huagong mining sites on Bangka-Belitung

Contemporary plaster statue of a Huagong miner, situated on an out-of-town roundabout on Bangka

Village shop on Bangka run by Huagong descendants

The Chung Hwa School, established on Bangka in the Huagong years

The author at the recently renovated Fude Taoist temple (Fuk Det Che), established at Pangkal Pinang on Bangka in the Huagong years

Chinese graves on Bangka-Belitung from the Huagong years

A Note on Language

Chinese words are given where appropriate in the Hanyu Pinyin transcription, except for names and terms given in another transcription in the original source and in the case of personal and place names better known in other spellings—for example, Sun Yat-sen and Hong Kong, which are left in their more familiar form. Indonesian and Malay words are generally given in the spelling adopted in Malaysia and Indonesia in 1972, except in direct quotations from sources that use other transcriptions, including the Van Ophuijsen system used to write Indonesian words between 1901 and 1947. Chinese, Indonesian, Indian, and other loan-words from non-European languages that have become embedded and nativised (usually in modified spelling) in European languages (for example, laukeh and kongsi) are given in Roman font, whereas non-embedded words imported into the study in their original form and spelling (like *xinke* and *laoke*) are given in italics.

Contents

List of Tables

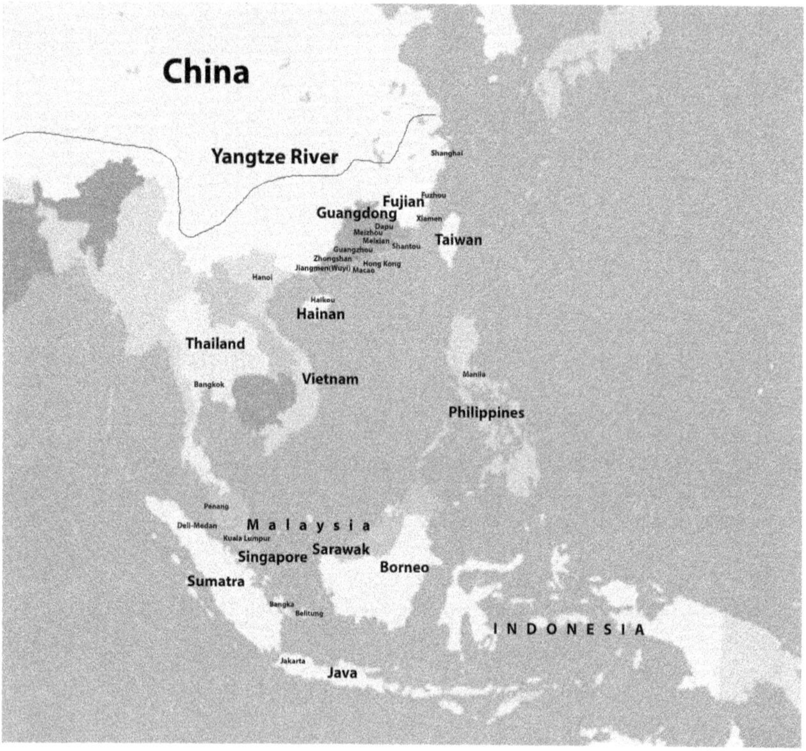

China and Southeast Asia

CHAPTER 1

Introduction

This book has two aims, complementary and of equal weight. One is to tell the story of Chinese labour migration to Sumatra in the Netherlands East Indies in the late-colonial period. The other is to contribute to the study of colonial indenture in comparative perspective, in particular in Asia and the Atlantic world, by looking at Chinese indenture in the light of Indian and Javanese indenture. Indenture studies are a relatively new addition to the field of migration studies, but more and more have begun appearing, both descriptive and theoretical, starting in the late twentieth century. Dutch scholars writing about the East Indies have contributed richly to this work. They are, in most cases, specialists in Indonesian studies, including many who work with sources in Indonesian. This study, in contrast, is written by a specialist in Chinese studies and uses sources in Chinese as well as in Dutch and other languages. Its main focus is on the Chinese labour diaspora and only marginally on Javanese migration to Sumatra.

Under Dutch rule in the Indonesian Archipelago, indenture was realised in the form of the penal sanction. It was a Dutch-inflected strain of the Nanyang or Southeast Asian variant of the Asian form of an imagined archetype of colonial indenture. Colonial labour indenture happened mainly in the tropics and sub-tropics—in South Asia, Southeast Asia, the New World, Africa, Australia, and Oceania. A migrant contracted, in theory freely, to work for an employer in exchange for a loan, usually to cover

G. Benton, *Chinese Indentured Labour in the Dutch East Indies, 1880–1942*, Palgrave Macmillan Transnational History Series, https://doi.org/10.1007/978-3-031-05024-4_1

the cost of his or her ticket overseas. The resulting debt, which bound the migrant for a fixed or indeterminate term, grew as a result of interest charges and other costs. Indenture is one among several forms of unfree labour in which the labourer is bound by debt, by contract or informally, to a particular employer. The debt was hard to repay and the cause of a lengthy, sometimes unending, period of servitude. Despite the appearance of choice, indenture entailed a strong element of coercion—not just poverty but brute force. It differed from slavery in that indentured labourers had rights that could, in principle, be adjudicated in law, and they were supposed to be in thrall for a set time rather than a lifetime. Even so, indenture had much in common with slavery—it was dehumanising, unfree, life-cheapening, life-shortening, often violent, sometimes interminable. Seen by many as slavery under another name, indentured paraslavery is an appropriate coinage for it.[1]

The East Indies was a main destination in Southeast Asia of Chinese indentured labour, alongside British Malaya and the Straits Settlements, Thailand, and French Indochina. In China, the labourers were known as Huagong,[2] and as "coolies" to their foreign employers. Chinese migrants were the biggest minority in the East Indies from outside the archipelago. They arrived even before the Dutch and remained indentured for longer than any comparable group. Today, Indonesia's ethnic Chinese, including Huagong descendants, are the world's largest ethnic-Chinese population and 20 percent of the world's overseas Chinese.[3]

Despite their worldwide spread, in scholarship labour indenture and the plantation economy were for a long time best known in their "Atlantic" form. Brij Lal dates the "first real advance towards a new indenture historiography" (after some anthropological accounts mainly in the 1960s and Hugh Tinker's seminal *A New System of Slavery* in 1974) to the conference on "Colonialism and Identity" held in Trinidad in 1975 and addressed by V. S. Naipaul. Lal also notes the later opening of a literary and autobiographical dimension in "coolie" writing that "seeks to understand migration and indenture across the globe as a transcultural process in non-essentialist ways through poetry, art and prose, both conventional

[1] Kuhn 2008, 116.
[2] The term is explained in Chap. 2.
[3] Citing the estimate of Taiwan's Overseas Community Affairs Council for 2014.

and experimental."[4] These genres feature more rarely in Chinese than in Indian writing on the subject.

Before these changes, "Asian" indenture was generally less studied, Chinese indenture less still. In the twenty-first century, however, work on indentured labour outside the Caribbean has begun to flourish. The Indian Ocean now rivals the Atlantic and the New World in studies as a littoral space and epicentre of intense and transformative contacts.[5] The focus of this work has largely been on Indian labour migration round the British Empire and Javanese migration within the East Indies. Few studies in any language look at the Chinese labour diaspora. Even studies on Asian indenture have rarely taken Chinese as their focus, and instead look nearly always at the Indian case. Chinese indenture has therefore been neglected first as Asian and then as Chinese. In China, despite the Communist injunction on scholars to give voice to the voiceless, the indentured proletarian or peasant seems to have figured less in scholarship than the multiclass Chinatowner. In Indonesia, Chinese indenture has been even more severely neglected, even though it preceded and was, until the twentieth century, more numerous than indenture fed by transmigration from Java to Sumatra. This neglect has perhaps been due in part to echoes in the academic world of Sinophobia—the stigmatisation of Chinese as alien and "disloyal."[6] Only in the Netherlands has scholarship on forced labour in the East Indies thrived, but mainly as the work of Indonesianists.[7]

In India, south China, and Java, the cultural perception of migration and labour migration evolved in step, from anathema and ordeal to celebration. Ocean travel in pre-modern times was discouraged and often banned in all three places, as a wilful act of self-separation from the ancestral hearth and culture. In India, *kala pani* or "black waters" warned against embarking on "life-changing journeys" into the unfamiliar and deadly seas beyond the *mare clausum*, potentially breaking the cycle of reincarnation and leading to ostracisation and excommunication at home and social death at the Middle Passage. In Java, the legendary spirit Nyai Roro Kidul ruled the waves from her underwater palace in the Indian Ocean and, as Queen of the Southern Sea, "was greatly feared by

[4] Lal 2021, 10-12.

[5] MacDonald 2008, 109.

[6] Lindsey and Pausacker, eds, 2005.

[7] Even the work on Bangka by Heidhues, rich and authoritative, generally lacks references to Chinese-language sources (Heidhues 2003, 13-14).

fishermen of the southern coast." China, its ocean deeps populated by demons, ghosts, and monsters, imported the *kuhai* or "bitter sea" metaphor from Indian Buddhism, and Chinese applied it as a literary trope to ocean crossings.

But the fear of crossing seas, anyway stronger in the Indian and Javanese than in the southern Chinese mind, weakened with time and seaworthiness became a migrant's badge of pride. China's Mazu, the Tian Hou or Heavenly Empress, typically pictured captaining a boat, served as the Daoist matron deity of fishers, seafarers, migrants, and maritime traders. Starting in the seventeenth century, she sailed brandishing her divine lantern from Fujian across the Sinophone to guide ships and save those lost at sea.[8] In recent years, as we shall see in Chap. 3, historians of Guangdong and Fujian have laid claim for their provincial forebears to an "oceanic" nature of the sort posited by Hegel (familiar in China as the forebear of Karl Marx) as a universal precondition for freedom of spirit and progress to modernity. Copying him, they cock a daringly unorthodox ideological snook at the imperial Chinese north, a landlocked, bureaucratic place where liberty and enterprise were, according to oceanism, impossible. In India and the Indian diaspora, the *kala pani* narrative has been similarly reclaimed by the coolitude literary movement, "to stamp a distinctive and dynamic reinterpretation of indenture, avoiding essentialist connections with an idealised Mother India and anchoring migration experiences in a discourse of the global South." It suggests a new sense of Indian identity[9] and, for the labourers, a new status as "brothers of the [indenture] ship," *jahajibhai*, on the high seas, whatever their caste or religion. For Indians in Mauritius, the indenture journey turned "from [ocean] trauma to pilgrimage" as displaced Hindu labourers sacralised Lake Ganga Talao as a Mauritian Ganges and Mauritius as "Hindu diasporic land."[10] In Java, too, "the myth of the sacredness of the Southern Sea" faded in the twentieth century.[11]

This study puts China at centre stage in the history of indenture, using Dutch colonial reports, official Chinese reports, the Dutch, Chinese, and English-language press of the time, and oral-history sources. Chapter 2 sets the historical and geographical scene and explains terms and concepts.

[8] Benton 2013.

[9] For China, see Chapter 3; for the Indian case, Bates and Carter 2021, 53.

[10] Claveyrolas 2018; Lal 2021, 4.

[11] Susanto 2014, 105-106. See also Andayani and Jupriono 2019.

Chapter 3 explores the implications of Chinese indenture for the comparative study of indenture and for our understanding of the role played by colonial states in labour migration and the plantation economy. Chapter 4 looks at indenture as a legal matter, in the form of the penal sanction, with which it became synonymous in Dutch. Chapter 5 looks at the recruitment of indentured Chinese labour and the changes in it over time. Chapter 6 looks at Chinese indenture in the East Indies in the round, and returns to the question of its place in the general study of indenture and of plantation economy and society.

Given that a Chinese focus is relatively uncommon in writing on labour indenture and a focus on labour indenture is uncommon in studies on Chinese diaspora, exploring the Chinese labour diaspora in one of its historic strongholds will help to dismantle the view of indenture and the colonial labour system as monolithic. Identifying special features of Chinese indenture will help overcome the reduction of the plantation complex to a fixed type. It will also throw light on general questions in the study of worldwide indenture.

Indenture in the East Indies evolved differently from other systems of indenture, as suggested by its special lexicon, much of which remained specific to the East Indies. The ubiquity of the term penal sanction in Dutch colonies is a case in point, as is the prominence of generic terms derived from Chinese dialects but rendered in other colonial lexica by words from other languages. The longevity of the Chinese labour diaspora in the East Indies permits a longer, broader view of indenture's transformations, from a system partly based on imported Chinese forms to the emergence of modern colonial forms and the start of mechanisation, anything but static and unchanging.[12]

Chinese labourers in the Nanyang had a reputation for being hard to handle but they were also prized as strong and industrious, more so than Javanese and (in Malaya) Indians. However, they were unable to fulfil the long-term needs of the colonial labour regime, which, being overwhelmingly labour-intensive, depended on the constant and ready availability of a cheap workforce. The Dutch state planned to solve this problem by establishing self-reproducing workers' colonies, but the Chinese sojourner mentality and alien status clashed with such a thought. The planters in the East Indies were also unable to resolve the problem of how to achieve a steady inflow of Chinese labour, because of their own bad reputation

[12] Houben (1999, 8) notes the lack of "temporal and spatial differentiations" in studies.

among potential migrants and Chinese official disapproval. They generally resisted the idea of labour colonisation in whatever form and evaded or overrode it wherever they could.[13] The critical problem of delivering labour to the plantations was increasingly solved by an ever greater reliance on Javanese recruitment, which led to the eclipse of Chinese indenture.

This study looks in greatest detail at the years 1917 to 1942. Indenture all but vanished from most colonial settings after the First World War. Its survival in the East Indies, staining the Dutch reputation, has often gone unremarked in discussions that tend to focus on the far greater volume of indentured labour trafficked around the British Empire until the late 1910s. In the latter years of Dutch rule, in the 1930s, more Javanese worked as labour migrants, most of them free of indenture, than Chinese. However, more Chinese remained under contract in Sumatra in 1931 than not. Chinese indenture did not entirely end until the wartime collapse of Dutch rule in 1942.

Chinese labourers played a central role in building the economy of the East Indies. Without their contribution, the Dutch would never have achieved global prominence in tin, tobacco, and cash crops. However, knowledge of their impact remains limited. They bequeathed to their descendants a legacy of occasional defiance and resistance. On the whole, though, they either got on with their main job, to save for a glorious return to China—or frittered away their lives and savings in the opium den or the gambling shed. Certainly less is known about them in China than is known in India about the Indian plantation labourers, who figured more centrally in the nationalist movement and whose history apparently matters more to Indian scholars. The repatriation of thousands of Huagong survivors after 1945 was largely passed over in silence in China, apart from a little-remarked academic investigation in 1963 (see Appendix A). Only in more recent times have Huagong migrations, including to the Nanyang, begun to attract greater attention in Chinese scholarship and the popular imagination. In Indonesia, they are more likely to be noticed since the relaxation of constraints on migrant-Chinese history-writing and the greater recognition of Chinese-Indonesian ethnicity in the post-Suharto

[13] De Kat Angelino 1931, 305, said that emigration followed by agricultural or labour colonisation "has been too insignificant to bring the solution of this big problem in that direction much nearer."

era.[14] In Sumatra and on the tin islands, the story of the Huagong is today celebrated more than in the past, including in local museums. A colourful plaster statue of a Huagong miner stands, somewhat isolated and forlorn, on an out-of-town roundabout on the road to Manggar in Belitung. Politically, however, Chinese ethnicity and a China tie remain potentially dangerous in Indonesia,[15] where the conditions are still not ripe for a full exploration of the Huagong episode.

Several recent studies combine to suggest a theoretical framework that can help to explain the special features of indenture and their refusal to conform to a single pattern. Where previous analyses have treated dependency and the integration of rural societies into the global market and the transformations wrought in them by global capitalism as a homogenising process, the new approaches suggest a more decentralised view of the mobilisation of marginalised peasants to migrate abroad. They draw attention to the precolonial and indigenous roots of labour migration and the numerous ways in which indentured labour was organised and recruited, both across and within different ethnic and national groups. Where much previous scholarship understood labour diaspora as a one-way passage into other histories and geographies, the new studies stress the mutual and interdependent constitution of migrants and sending states in "diaspora time." This produced, in China, an "ever more fragmented and more networked" homeland.[16]

Kerry Ward's study on the Dutch East India Company (Vereenigde Oost-Indische Compagnie or VOC) focuses on the VOC's nodes and networks, which amalgamated over time into a web of empire. Ward rejects a simple binary opposition of metropole to periphery, thus chiming with the methods and spirit of the radical style of writing history from below and focusing on the active role played by "colonial subjects" in the colonial project. This approach, as Tonio Andrade points out in a review, is especially relevant to the history of the Chinese networks of traders, labourers, and seafarers that sailed the routes of the VOC and both contested and helped sustain them. Far from controlling the web of Chinese networks, the Dutch heavily depended on it and were secretly, silently, and subtly undermined by it.[17] However, Ward does not deny the role played by networks in helping the imperial apparatus of the VOC manage its affairs and

[14] Kitamura 2007.
[15] Zhou 2019, 217.
[16] Chan 2018, 12, cited in Jany 2021, 51.
[17] Tonio Andrade, in Reviews 2009.

assert its primacy. Her study can therefore be read, beyond networks, as a history of the VOC's imperial rise through "conquest and forced migration" and its creation of an entire range of primary "structures of governance."[18]

China and other countries consigned by the actions of European states to a periphery or semi-periphery of the world economy retained their own independent network structures and managed their own peripheries. What looked from a European point of view to be a periphery was a centre from another angle. The networks emanating from "peripheralised" centres were able in many instances to restrict the extent to which the VOC took over and monopolised regional trade. Because of their resilience and the political and economic challenges they presented to globalising capitalism, the VOC had no choice but to compromise and negotiate with them, or even in some cases to give in. A good example of a clash of Dutch and Chinese centres from which the former came out worst is the short war on Taiwan in 1661-1662, when a colony founded by the VOC in 1624 was ousted by the Ming-loyalist Zheng Chenggong (known to the Dutch as Koxinga).[19] Ward's approach is particularly helpful for understanding the part played in the East Indies economy by Chinese, whose relations with colonial powers differed from those of the two other main streams of migrant labour, Indian and Javanese.

Ulbe Bosma makes a related argument for the decentering of labour history in island Southeast Asia. His study on its incorporation into the global capitalist economy looks at Indonesia, Malaysia, and the Philippines. Why did a once prosperous region become a periphery engaged primarily in the export of cheap labour? Unhappy with dependency theory and world-systems explanations, which divide the world into an early-industrialising core and a periphery and semi-periphery reduced by the core to commodity exporters of tropical crops, Bosma argues the need to differentiate between countries and parts of countries and to explore their historical specificities. This is because peripheralisation is complex and path-dependent rather than homogenising, unilinear, and unidimensional. Bosma also distinguishes between different groups of migrant workers in a single region: Chinese, for example, were all along more likely to be recruited along patron-client ties and more likely because of the greater

[18] Diogo Ramada Curtu, in Reviews 2009.

[19] Ward 2009, 62, citing Andrade 2006.

resilience of their institutions and the relative stability and autonomy of their migration systems to make the transition to smallholding and sharecropping. Such differences were likely to curtail peripheralisation and render it "incomplete," by limiting the appropriation of cultivation by colonial powers. Bosma's main conclusion is that peripheralisation can best be understood in the context of differences in population density and modes of labour control. Its homogenisation in world-systems scholarship is "fundamentally ahistorical."[20]

Philip Kuhn's *Chinese Among Others* provides concepts and terminology more directly related to Chinese labour migration to Southeast Asia in late-colonial times. In a global sweep, Kuhn magisterially synthesises the state of Chinese diaspora studies at the start of the twenty-first century and enriches it with terms and approaches borrowed from other contexts. One key term is compatriotism, the native-place bonds—local rather than national—between migrant kinsmen sojourning elsewhere in China or overseas. Another is migration corridor, the hometown extension that linked, and to some extent continues to link, both physically and culturally, those at home and those away from home. The sojourners had access to institutions that served both as hostels or lodges and mutual-aid or social clubs and reinforced their home ties. Migration chains carried same-dialect compatriots back and forth along the corridors linking their native places to Chinese towns and cities and to foreign lands. The corridor was "the architecture of their lives" and the essence of their sojourning. It preserved modes of economic and cultural belonging and of kinship, so that "in certain respects the migrant has never left home."[21]

The concepts and approaches embodied in these three studies anticipate many of the findings of this book and strengthen its conclusions. They offer a new perspective on the centre-periphery debate and the mobilisation of indentured labour by industrial and agricultural capitalism to plant and mine in tropical colonies. They help greatly in reconceptualising the recruitment and employment of indentured labour and its long-term trajectory, by demonstrating the inadequacy of a single focus on whole regions and even on whole nations.

[20] Bosma 2019, 103-106 and 181.
[21] Kuhn 2009, 43-53 and 185.

References

Andayani, Ambar, and D. Jupriono. 2019. "Representation of Nyi Roro Kidul in Myth, Legend, and Popular Culture." In *Anaphora: Journal of Language, Literary, and Cultural Studies*, vol. 2, no. 1, 28-36.

Andrade, Tonio. 2006. *How Taiwan Became Chinese: Dutch, Spanish and Han Colonization in the Seventeenth Century*. New York: Columbia University Press.

Bates, Crispin, and Marina Carter. 2021."Kala Pani Revisited: Indian Labour Migrants and the Sea Crossing." *Journal of Indentureship and Its Legacies*, vol. 1, no. 1, 36–62.

Benton, Gregor. 2013. "San Fancón and the Goddess of Mercy: Two Chinese Folk Gods in Cuban Transfiguration." *Cultural & Social History: The Journal of the Social History Society*, vol. 10, no. 1, 93-108.

Bosma, Ulbe. 2019. *The Making of a Periphery: How Island Southeast Asia Became a Mass Exporter of Labor*. New York: Columbia University Press.

Chan, Shelly. 2018. *Diaspora's Homeland: Modern China in the Age of Global Migration*. Durham: Duke University Press.

Claveyrolas, Mathieu. 2018. "From the Indian Ganges to a Mauritian Lake: Hindu Pilgrimage in a 'Diasporic' Context." In Simon Coleman and John Eade, eds., *Translating the Sacred: Pilgrimage and Political Economy in Transnational Contexts*, New York: Berghahn, 21-39.

De Kat Angelino, A. D. A. 1931. *Colonial Policy*, vol. 2, *The Dutch East Indies*. Translated by G. J. Renier. The Hague: Martinus Nijhoff.

Heidhues, Mary F. Somers. 2003. *Golddiggers, Farmers, and Traders in the "Chinese Districts" of West Kalimantan, Indonesia*. Ithaca, NY: Cornell University, Southeast Asia Program Publications.

Houben, Vincent J. H. 1999. "Introduction: The Coolie System in Colonial Indonesia." In Vincent J. H. Houben and J. Thomas Lindblad, eds, *Coolie Labour in Colonial Indonesia: A Study of Labour Relations in the Outer Islands, c. 1900–1940*, Wiesbaden: Harrassowitz Verlag, 1999, 1-24.

Jany, Gregory. 2021. *Imperial Crossings: Chinese Indentured Migration to Sumatra's East Coast, 1865-1911*. Council on East Asian Studies, Yale University.

Kitamura, Yumi. 2007. "Museum as the Representation of Ethnicity: The Construction of Chinese Indonesian Ethnic Identity in Post-Suharto Indonesia." *Kyoto Review of Southeast Asia*, issues 8-9, 2007.

Kuhn, Philip A. 2008. *Chinese among Others: Emigration in Modern Times*. Lanham: Rowman and Littlefield.

Lal, Brij V. 2021. "Indian Indenture: History and Historiography in a Nutshell." *Journal of Indentureship and Its Legacies*, vol. 1, no. 1, 1-15.

Lindsey, Tim, and Helen Pausacker, eds. 2005. *Chinese Indonesians: Remembering, Distorting, Forgetting*. Monash: ISEAS.

MacDonald, Andrew. 2008. "The View Across the Ocean: Indian Ocean Worlds and the Question of Power over the Long Nineteenth Century." *Journal of Natal and Zulu History*, vol. 26, no. 1, 108-129.

Reviews. 2009. Kerry Ward, *Networks of Empire: Forced Migration in the Dutch East India Company.* With a Response by Kerry Ward. *International Journal of Maritime History*, vol. 21, no. 1, 297-340.

Susanto Zuhdi. 2014. *Nasionalisme, Laut, dan Sejarah* ("Nationalism, the sea, and history"). Jakarta: Kobam.

Ward, Kerry. 2009. *Networks of Empire: Forced Migration in the Dutch East India Company.* Cambridge: Cambridge University Press.

Zhou, Taomo. 2019. *Migration in the Time of Revolution: China, Indonesia, and the Cold War.* Ithaca: Cornell University Press.

CHAPTER 2

The Setting

In the colonial heyday, between 1846 and 1940, fifty million people left East and South Asia for European colonies in Southeast Asia, on the Indian Ocean rim, and in the South Pacific, far surpassing the estimated 2.5 million Europeans who left for the Americas. Most were labourers bound for workshops, mines, and plantations. They included around 30 million Indians and 19 million Chinese,[1] many of them under indenture.

In the seventeenth and eighteenth centuries, indenture had been a common way to recruit European labourers to work in the United States, but it came into its own in the nineteenth. Where the abolition of slavery produced labour shortages, indenture became a normal way of recruiting non-white labour for the tropics. Denounced as a modern form of the slavery that it supplemented and then replaced, it declined rapidly in the early twentieth century, for economic and political reasons, but more rapidly in some places than in others, and least rapidly (with one or two small exceptions, including in the British Western Pacific Territories) in the Netherlands East Indies.

This study looks chiefly at bonded Chinese labour in the East Indies in the twentieth century, between the two world wars, and at China as its

[1] On the distribution of Chinese labour migrants, see Wang Qimin (1982) and McKeown (2004).

G. Benton, *Chinese Indentured Labour in the Dutch East Indies, 1880–1942*, Palgrave Macmillan Transnational History Series, https://doi.org/10.1007/978-3-031-05024-4_2

place of recruitment. At the destinations, it looks chiefly at the tin islands of Bangka and Belitung (now a province in their own right) off Sumatra's eastern coast and the Deli region of northeastern Sumatra (the *cultuurgebied* or "plantation belt"),[2] major sites of Chinese labour diaspora. The islands were known for tin, Deli for planting.

The mines preceded the plantations chronologically, but it makes sense to treat mines and plantations together, for they later existed side by side and were organised in a similar way (along primitive factory lines). Imported Chinese worked in both industries and circulated between the islands and Deli. Usually owned by corporations, both industries produced for the world market, applied force to their workers, and had bad reputations. Chinese indenture started earlier, was more extensive, and lasted longer in the East Indies than in most other places, and was outlived only in parts of Africa and on some Pacific islands.

Sources

Archival sources in Dutch and Chinese on Chinese labour in the East Indies are richer than those on other Chinese labour diasporas elsewhere outside China but poor by comparison with those on other groups. Sources in cognate disciplines like archaeology are even poorer.[3] Major problems of evidence face historians of indenture almost everywhere, but this is particularly true of Chinese indenture.

Brij V. Lal, discussing the historiography of Indian indenture, points out that much of the writing on it remains at a general level, because of the infancy of the field and its reliance on "conventional" archives and quantification. As an antidote, he recommends a "bottom-up" approach, including interviews with survivors and oral sources. Quantification can answer only a certain type of question. But while historians of Indian indenture have access to census reports and statistical data, oral-history sources are far from plentiful, and the last generation of indentured labourers in the early twentieth century is now dead. So even the Indian record, despite its comparative richness, is incomplete and irretrievable.[4]

[2] Deli incorporated the *cultuurgebied* from Acheh to Asahan, a plain crossed by rivers and joined after 1883 by a railway to transport tobacco.

[3] On the potential uses of archaeological evidence in the study of colonial indenture, see Allen (2021).

[4] Lal (1983).

Historians of Chinese indenture face similar if not worse problems. Even "top-down" investigation and quantification is harder than in the case of Indian indenture, which was more closely policed and therefore better documented. Since 1949, there has been a concentrated effort to record the oral history of China's toilers, at home and abroad, consonant with the Marxist-inspired intention to create a mass-based story of "the people without history," but China's labour diaspora has been less studied than its domestic workers or general diaspora.

The first collection of oral materials on Chinese labour migrants dates back to 1873, when Chin Lan-pin went to Cuba on behalf of the Qing to investigate the scandal of Chinese indenture and collected more than one thousand depositions by Chinese "coolies." Chin's report was an exemplary work of verbatim testimony, not incompatible with the idea of oral history.[5] This affinity with oral history, which treats the lives of men and women otherwise undocumented, is a paradox, for the Qing government was a secretive regime unconcerned with the fate of Chinese labourers anywhere, especially overseas, where emigrants were excoriated as traitors in line with a ban by the imperial court on emigration. That the Cuba Report was compiled had more to do with the Qing Emperor's worries about China's poor image in the world and the effect of the "coolie traffic" on his negotiations with the British and others than with any concern about the trafficked labourers.[6]

The second oral-history cache is more directly relevant to this study, with its focus on the early twentieth century. It concerns Chinese labourers in Sumatra between 1910 and 1942, and was part of China's effort after 1949 to develop "mass history" and a "native" or insider anthropology in which the objects of research appear as its subjects. Its practitioners at Xiamen University in the early 1960s collected scores of interviews from labourers who had retired to state farms in China. The interviews were edited by those who took them (though with little indication of the criteria) and they cleave closely to the political line propagated by state ideology after 1949, so they are not necessarily an authentic rendering of "the native's voice" in all respects. Even so, they are rich in detail of a sort generally unavailable about late-nineteenth- and early-twentieth-century non-white labour diasporas anywhere in the world.

[5] García Triana and Eng Herrera (2009, Appendix 1).

[6] Yen Ching-hwang (1985, 81–82).

A major source on the global history of Chinese labour migration in the colonial period is the 12-volume set of edited historical materials compiled by Chen Hansheng, a pioneer of modern social science in China, and published in 1981–1985. The compilation covers Chinese labour migration on all continents in the late Qing Dynasty and the Republic, and includes official reports, press reports, and excerpts (some in translation) from contemporary studies on Chinese labourers in Southeast Asia and the East Indies.

The most recent and prolific addition to scholarship and archival study on Chinese labour migration emerged in the twenty-first century as the newly invented genre of *qiaopi* studies, whose focus is on the remittances sent home to the *qiaoxiang* (emigrant regions) and the two-way correspondence they engendered. Chinese scholars in the old migrant-sending regions of South China have used interviews, letters, and unconventional sources to write histories and edit documentary collections of the "people without history" that shed light from unfamiliar angles on the nature of labour migration. In the first two decades of the People's Republic, few Chinese scholars worked on ethnic and migrant Chinese communities abroad or in the sending regions, because of the stigmatisation of groups with "foreign" ties. However, the rise of Overseas Chinese studies in China after the 1970s led to the discovery in *qiaoxiang* villages of huge hoards of migrants' letters that have now been collected and published in many volumes and led to the production of dozens of books and hundreds of articles in Chinese and a few in other languages. The letters depict the everyday life of transnational labour migrants in Southeast Asia and their social and economic organisation and their feelings and aspirations, as well as the mechanics of their recruitment, shipment south, and (in some cases) eventual repatriation. These migrants letters are more plentiful, absolutely and proportionately, than those of any other nationality and add an affective dimension to the study of Huagong history, sociology, and economics.[7]

The Meaning of Indenture

Indentureship was integral to early globalisation, when it served as the main remedy for the labour shortages that plagued plantation-based capitalism. The evolution of capitalism was pictured by classical economists as

[7] Benton and Liu (2018).

a peaceful product of the interplay of free labour and free markets, but in reality the primitive accumulation of capital was rooted in violence at home and abroad in the age of colonial expansion.

According to neoclassical economic theory, free labourers sell their own labour, on a competitive market that can bring prosperity to both them and the buyer, but this was least the case with indentured labourers, over whose labour power the employer could claim an exclusive right. As a form of bondage, indenture is close in nature to the older system of peonage, where the peon was legally bonded to an employer by the receipt of an advance. The difference between "traditional" debt bondage and twentieth-century indenture was thin and there was much overlap.[8] The main difference was that whereas indenture could be legally enforced, payment of a "traditional" debt usually depended on pressure from kin or community. Because of the thinness of the line between indenture and other types of bondage, which continued to include more or less disguised forms of indenture even where it was formally abolished,[9] it is wise to avoid a strict distinction. The imprecision of the idea of indenture is evident from the early twentieth-century debate on it, where the terms indentured labour, forced labour, bonded labour, contract labour, and "coolie" labour were used interchangeably.[10]

Even before the abolition of slavery, starting in the British Empire in 1833, indentured Indian and Chinese labourers were traded to British and other colonies, despite Britain's ostensible commitment to abolishing the traffic. In the nineteenth century, Britain was "both the leader of the anti-coolie trade movement and at the forefront of establishing indentured labour as a replacement for African slaves in their Caribbean colonies."[11] Both the British and the Dutch colonial states shaped the geographic spread of labour diaspora. Indians worked in the tropics either side of the equator and the prime meridian, but nearly always in places colonised by the British.[12] In the years between Britain's Slavery Abolition Act of 1833

[8] Derks (2010, 841–842). Mònica Ginés-Blasi (2020, 4–5) says the credit-ticket system that bonded Chinese labourers in the Philippines was tantamount to or worse than indenture, being less visible.

[9] Stanziani (2014).

[10] On the forms, linkages, and commonalities of bonded labour, see Tappe and Lindner (2016).

[11] Young (2015, 132).

[12] In this book, "Indian" is a generic term that includes people from places now known as Pakistan, Bangladesh, and Sri Lanka.

and its abolition of indenture in the 1910s, millions of Africans, Chinese, Indians, Indonesians, and other colonial subjects went to work on plantations and down mines in British, Dutch, and other European colonies. Although only a small minority—perhaps fewer than 10 percent—were literally indentured, many more were under a debt that carried much the same implications.

Up to 11 million Chinese went to the Straits Settlements, whence more than one third were transhipped to the East Indies, Borneo, and other places. Others were shipped to the Indonesian Archipelago directly, from Hong Kong, Shantou, and other ports in China. Estimates of the number of Chinese working under indenture between the eighteenth and twentieth centuries, mainly in Southeast Asia, range from three to seven million. In the later period, between around 1890 and 1940, up to one million Javanese were contracted to work on the Outer Islands of the East Indies,[13] also under indenture or conditions that amounted to it.[14]

Indentured labour dominated colonial labour politics after the abolition of slavery. However, indenture did not merely succeed slavery but preceded and accompanied it. Before the nineteenth century, indentured servitude was widespread among poor whites in North America, where up to two thirds of white immigrants between the 1630s and the American Revolution were indentured servants, redemptioners, or convicts.[15] In the course of the eighteenth century, however, white indenture declined and largely disappeared.

Forms of labour bondage also featured within the empire run between 1602 and 1799 by the VOC.[16] In places under its rule, the VOC established for Dutch colonialism a legacy of slavery and forced labour that was generally absent from the Dutch Republic, which lacked a homeland slave

[13] The Outer Islands, also known as the Outer Possessions or Outer Provinces, was an official term for islands outside the colonial heartland of Java, Bali, and Lombok. A better term would be "other Indonesian islands," to dispel the colonial Java-centric bias, but this study retains the old term to chime with sources (Nitisastro 2006, 2, fn. 2).

[14] McKeown (2004, 156–158 and 162). See also Behal (2013, 1), Pan (1998, 61), and Termorshuizen (2008, 278), who points out that some labelled "Javanese" were recent immigrants to Java. A standard Chinese source says that 3 million Huagong went overseas between 1800 and 1925, of whom one third died abroad (Lu Wendi et al. 1981b, 172). Fix (2018, 20–22) finds that emigration from Xiamen to the Straits Settlements grew nearly six-fold, from 13,418 to 79,270, between 1875 and 1900, totalling 1,023,960 "native" passengers, and four-fold between 1875 and 1894.

[15] Galenson (1984, 1–2), Batsha (2017, 3).

[16] Hoefte (2017, 364).

tradition. The VOC developed a system of penal transportation, debt bondage, forced migrations, and criminal laws and a slave code that influenced the system of indenture that developed in the East Indies in the nineteenth century and bequeathed to the colony methods of disciplining and securing the workforce. However, the historiography of Dutch slavery in the East Indies and of forced migration in the early colonial period is weak, so it difficult to identify the precise link between the VOC and the emergence of the penal sanction.[17]

English writing about Cape colonial society in the VOC era used the term "indentured" to describe the so-called "Bastaard-Hottentots," the children of Khoikhoi mothers and slave fathers, creating the appearance of a continuity between indenture under the VOC and in the later Dutch colonial empire. However, the link is spurious and the terminological association misleading. Khoikhoi "indenture," known in Afrikaans as the *inboekstelsel*, was essentially a form of child labour or apprenticeship, legally enforceable only until the age of twenty-five and only with the agreement of the Khoikhoi mother.[18] The VOC's decline and the conquest of its territories by the British at the end of the eighteenth century put an end to its imperial autonomy and led to its incorporation into the Dutch state and its system of law. This transition widened the hiatus between early and late forms of labour bondage under the Dutch, even though the British initially supported slavery and the *inboekstelsel* at the Cape.[19]

In fact, the general system of indenture in its second phase, starting in the nineteenth century, differed in more than one way from the first, not just under Dutch rule but worldwide. Indentured labourers in the second phase were less likely to become free at the end of their indenture and more likely to renew it, or to return home. From another point of view, their status was more clearly demarcated from other forms of labour bondage, especially slavery, and their labour increasingly took the form of a commercialised commodity.[20]

In British Malaya and other British colonies, most Indian and Chinese labourers before the twentieth century arrived under a system that put contractual obligations on both parties but more particularly on the

[17] Ward (2009, 18–26 and 50–51).

[18] Literally, *inboeking* meant "registration" (of the personal details of the child, parents, and master). On the *inboekstelsel*, see Viljoen (2005, 59–60) and Delius and Trapido (1982). Morton (2005, 202) says that the term was a euphemism for slavery.

[19] Ward (2009, 301–305).

[20] Stanziani (2014, 22–28).

worker. Colonial employers preferred such a system to free migration, believing that state regulation was the best way to guarantee the availability of sufficient labour.[21] The worker's reproductive costs were borne by the worker, as a massive subsidy to the employer, and the worker could even be worked to death. Replacing this system with on-the-spot family reproduction, known in Dutch colonies as "colonisation," would encumber the planters with the extra costs entailed in caring for the workers' families. Such a system did begin to evolve in Southeast Asia, first in Malaya (in around 1910) and then in the East Indies (in the 1920s), as we shall see—but not before important shifts in the ways in which contract labour was recruited and not in relation to Chinese labourers.[22]

In Dutch colonies, indenture and debt bondage was inextricably tied to the penal sanction, deemed necessary in a system lacking positive financial incentives to encourage effort. Penal sanctions were also used in the age of the transportation of convicts from Britain and Ireland, between 1788 and 1868. The notion of penal sanction was dealt a seemingly fatal blow by its removal from labour contracts in the French Revolution and the abolition in 1875 of Britain's Master and Servant Acts.[23] However, it was resurrected to regulate the recruitment of workers in situations of severe labour shortage in Europe's tropical colonies, and the term became particularly associated with Dutch indenture. Penal sanctions could take one of two forms, or a combination of them—physical punishment of the sort used under slavery and imported (in the form of arrest, imprisonment, and beatings) into the system of indenture; and financial penalties, including fines, wage cuts, and deductions.[24]

In the 1910s, indenture was formally abolished in most British colonies and a new variant of labour recruitment came to prevail, whereby "native" contractors recruited labourers on behalf of European firms, a system analysed in Chap. 5. However, in many respects such systems perpetuated indenture, by preserving the element of debt bondage and putting obstacles in the way of labourers absconding.[25]

Indenture was the subject of intense moral debate throughout the world, and pressure grew for its reform or abolition. Some saw it as a new

[21] Mishra (2015, 371).
[22] Gordon (2004).
[23] Stanziani (2018).
[24] Hui and Kambhampati (2020, 22–23).
[25] Jomo (1988, 188–189).

slavery, because indentured workers could not withhold their labour or bargain over contracts.[26] Others persevere with a strict distinction between chattel slavery, in which slaves could be traded or inherited, and free wage labour, and say that ending the former leads to the latter. Indenture and contract labour, in the positive view, widened the choices available to those who entered it—its benefits outweighed its defects, and it offered an "escape route" out of poverty.[27] Some talk of intermediate forms of labour seemingly free but actually incorporating elements of slavery, and argue that indenture was designed "not so much to provide economic opportunities for the labourer as to secure for the planters a labour force whose wages were determined outside the labour market," for it made the worker liable to criminal prosecution for breach of contract.[28] Some accept the distinctions between slavery and indenture but see the dissimilarities as technical,[29] a view that is hard to rebut, since indenture in some respects served the planter even better than slavery, by landing labourers with their own reproductive costs.[30] Some argue that the idea of indentured labour has been reified as a "grand narrative," a separate stage in the transition to capitalism proper, whereas in fact there was no fundamental distinction between it and free labour under capitalism.[31] Finally, a recent essay classes indentured labourers, "retrospectively, as archetypal precursors of the contemporary global precariat, [...] 'an emerging global mass class' characterised by precarious employment, debt and insecurity."[32]

The Staged Abolition of Indenture

The abolition of indenture happened at different rates in different countries, even within one colonial empire and in different parts of one colonial state. The reforming intentions of states that exported labourers could be frustrated by importing countries refusing to cooperate.[33]

[26] Tinker (1974). Conflating slavery and bonded labour continues into the present (Derks (2010, 840).
[27] Varma (2005, 49).
[28] Mohapatra and Behal (1991, 142–143).
[29] Pande (2013, 61).
[30] Gordon (2004, 528).
[31] Knight (2011, 419–432).
[32] Rajasinghamsenanayake (2017, 69).
[33] E. g., Chatterji and Washbrook (2013, 104).

In India, indenture was banned in 1916–1917 due, in part, to pressure from Indian nationalists and a decline in profits on colonial investments. Known as "the second abolition," after that of Atlantic slavery, it took several years to implement across the board.[34] Chinese indenture continued in some British colonies even after 1917. In British Malaya as in British India, ending indenture was driven at top levels by the British state and was staggered in its implementation. In Mauritius, where indenture ended in 1923, 6475 Huagong arrived in 1921.[35] Indenture mattered less in Indian nationalist circles than the rights of free migrants, and only became the target of a concerted drive for abolition in the 1920s.[36]

In 1919, the International Labour Organization (ILO) was set up, in the aftermath of the First World War, to ensure universal and lasting peace by legislating for social justice. The ILO made a core part of its mission the eradication of forced labour.[37] Its activities resulted in the establishment in 1929 of an internationally recognised definition of forced labour as work or service "exacted from any person under the menace of any penalty and for which the said person has not offered himself voluntarily." The Forced Labour Convention was adopted in June 1930 and brought into force in May 1932.

The ILO's definition of indenture as "life and work under duress" has been criticised on the grounds that it was not necessarily involuntary or forced in all respects and at every stage (from entry to his exit). Others, however, insist on the element of compulsion—Marcel van der Linden, for example, finds only one "actually voluntary" reason (out of ten) why a person should enter into a coerced labour relationship, and even exit can be forced, conditional, or impeded.[38] Most commentators now agree that the divide between free and unfree labour is less clear than previously assumed and many therefore disagree with the ILO's conceptualisation of indenture in a rigid binary with "voluntary" labour.[39]

The establishment of international norms did not lead to a synchronous abolition. The ILO's 1930 convention has never been universally ratified. Ten countries, including Japan and Spain, ratified it before the end of

[34] Bates et al. (2017).

[35] Extract (1912), Wu Fengbin (1988, 429–436).

[36] Kumar (2014).

[37] Maul (2007).

[38] Van der Linden (2016, 311–312). See also the discussion of Indian tribal indenture in Bates (1992, 205–245).

[39] Lewis et al. (2015, 588).

1932 and the Netherlands ratified it in 1933, Italy in 1934, and France in 1937, but all five countries continued to allow indenture.[40]

The Netherlands preserved indenture longest, save for a few minor exceptions in other colonial empires. In the East Indies, indentured labour was confined to the Outer Islands, i.e., islands other than Java, for Java was densely populated and had no need to import labour from elsewhere in the archipelago or abroad.

Up until the 1880s, most labourers recruited to the Outer Islands were Chinese, who had started migrating to the region in large numbers in the eighteenth century. Indenture continued to meet the labour needs of the Dutch colonial economy through until the 1930s. In time, the hundreds of thousands of indentured Javanese brought to Sumatra came to outnumber the Chinese, whose labour diaspora shrank, first proportionately and then absolutely. As some Chinese left for home, however, others continued to arrive in their thousands, to join the long-established labour settlements.

Naming the Labourer

What to call the labourers who left China to work under contract overseas? The word "coolie" was widely used of Asian labourers (including Chinese) at home or abroad. Tamil or Gujarati in origin, "meaning to hire, and usually referring to coloured workers in general,"[41] in China the word was transliterated (as *kuli*) with characters meaning "bitter strength." It became embedded in the Chinese language, where it expresses the idea of hard work performed under miserable conditions. It had pejorative connotations from the start. In 1872, a British official said:

> There is no doubt the term is galling, and a source of annoyance. We would suggest that the term "Indian Immigrants" be substituted for that of Coolie in all official documents, and that the designation of "Coolie Agent" be changed to that of "Protector of Indian Immigrants."[42]

Today, the word is still likely to cause offence, because of its association with passivity and submission (although some seek to reclaim it[43]). Now

[40] ILO, Forced Labour Convention, 1930 (no. 29).
[41] De Graaf et al. (1918, vol. 2, 360).
[42] *Report* (1872, 14).
[43] Yun (2008, xix).

seen universally as offensive, for obvious reasons, is "piglet", used in colonial times of Chinese labourers and perhaps coined after the "pigtails" worn under the Manchus by Chinese, whose trafficking abroad was likened to selling pigs.[44] The term entered into colonial parlance and official discourse, even in China, and labourers even used it of themselves.

The term generally used in labour legislation and reports was and remains contract worker. However, this term has a wide range of applications. Having survived until today, it has acquired a neutral ring and lost its connotations with indenture. It suggests reciprocal or even employer-only obligations, whereas indenture is historically specific and focuses one-sidedly on the employee's debt.

The term favoured by Chinese observers since the late nineteenth century is Huagong, where *Hua* is an elevated word for China and *gong* means work. Chinese historians still use it even now. The term applied chiefly to Chinese labourers abroad, but it also applied to members of labour gangs in Hong Kong and the Treaty Ports, in the docks and on the railways, and in Japanese-annexed parts of China and in Taiwan. This coincidence mirrors a real connection, for gangs working the "China ports" were the source of some overseas migrant labour; and the port workers' internal organisation matched that overseas.

The term Huagong covered not just indentured labourers but the extensive class of semi-indentured and non-indentured labourers and declassed peasants who worked overseas or along the coast for Chinese or foreign capitalists, usually in gangs. The same goes for coolie, a name applied to casual or seasonal labour in ports throughout Asia. The term Huagong was well suited to a situation in which the distinction between free and unfree labour and between the proletarian and petty-business sectors of the Chinese diaspora was blurred, for there are many gradations of indentured labour—many indentures had ties to Chinatown and many became free, whereupon they returned to China or took another job abroad.

At around the time of the dispatch of Huagong to Europe in the First World War, the term *qiaogong* was sometimes used in official Chinese documents. This word belongs to a cluster around *qiao*, as in the word Huaqiao (Chinese sojourner overseas). The word Huagong, and even more so *qiaogong*, chimed with China's attempt in the 1910s to encourage Chinese overseas, including labourers, to identify with the motherland

[44] Yap and Man (1996, 29).

and to extend the new nationalist awareness to diasporans previously reviled as traitors. This concern for Chinese overseas began in the 1870s, with efforts to protect Chinese in Cuba and Peru.[45] By the twentieth century, overseas Chinese featured centrally in China's international relations. So this book favours the term Huagong, a word that highlights labour migrants' specificity, embraces their distinctions, and is not offensive.

Chinese Labour in the East Indies

The search for cheap, easily replaceable labour to work in tropical enterprises was a very early focus of Dutch officials. The import of Chinese "to people the islands and exploit their riches" began between 1619 and 1795 under the rule of the VOC, whose traders, according to the Dutch liberal Jan de Louter, "with profits as their lodestar and greed as their compass, obtained, through the chance of events, absolute control of one of the most beautiful and fertile regions of the earth, and unhesitatingly sacrificed it to their low ideals." Jan Pietrszoon Coen, Governor of the East Indies, thought the best way to obtain

> the very great number of people necessary [was] to send another fleet to visit the coast of China and take prisoner as many men, women, and children as possible, [for] no people in the world do us better service than the Chinese. [...] As trade cannot be gotten by friendly means, it is requisite [...] if the war proceed against China [that] an especial foresight must be used to take a very great number of Chinese especially women and children for the peopling of Batavia, Amboyna, and Banda. [...] By no means you must suffer any women to return to China, or any other part out of the Company's jurisdiction, but with them to people the same.

In the early 1620s, more than one thousand Chinese prisoners taken by the Dutch during the seizure of the Penghu (Pescadores) Islands were shipped to Batavia as slave labour. The great majority died of thirst and other causes on the journey south.[46]

In the early years, the VOC's Chinese victims were left to their fate by China's Qianlong Emperor, who "was little solicitous for the fate of

[45] Yen Ching-hwang (1985, 122).
[46] Groeneveldt (1898, 219–221).

unworthy subjects who, in the pursuit of lucre, had quitted their country and abandoned the tombs of their ancestors."[47]

Alongside Dutch fleets, most of the early recruitment was by Chinese merchants, who dominated the region's foreign trade and worked in concert with sultans in the archipelago. Starting in the late eighteenth century, tens of thousands of Chinese worked as labour migrants in Borneo and the Malay Peninsula, and by 1800 their numbers are thought to have grown to between 156,000 and 193,000, who were in turn just a small part of the total ethnic-Chinese population.[48] For much of the nineteenth century, recruitment depended mainly on kongsis, self-governing brotherhoods practising mutual aid and prized for their mining and farming skills.[49] An early Dutch history of Bangka noted that "the recruitment originally happened by way of the mine kongsi, without any intervention by the [Dutch] Tinwinning Company."[50]

Starting in the 1840s, with the further rise of indenture and migration, Asian labour migration to the East Indies began to change. By the 1860s, recruitment was carried out by agents representing Dutch interests. The new system coincided with the start of a plantation economy in Sumatra, where tobacco farming started to flourish in what became the island's main agricultural belt, followed in around 1910 by rubber and tea plantations. At first, concessionaries[51] imported indigenous workers, but in 1870 they started using the services of Chinese recruitment brokers in Penang and Singapore.[52] Kongsi recruitment fell and the kongsis changed in nature, as we shall see in a later chapter. By the 1920s, kongsis played little further role, except as labour bodies that served Dutch companies by administering the workforce and enabling local Chinese powerholders to control it, or by hiring gangs to clear jungles and burn charcoal.

By the twentieth century, half a million Chinese lived under Dutch rule, mostly in Java and Sumatra, rising to 700,000 by the mid 1920s and around 1.2 million in the 1930s.[53] By the 1930s, some half a million Chinese had entered East Sumatra on contracts, peaking at 58,516 in 1900, during the tobacco boom, and falling to 25, 934 in 1929, on the

[47] Cited in MacNair (1924).
[48] Bosma (2019, 30–32).
[49] For a fuller account, see Chap. 3.
[50] Kort historisch overzicht (1928).
[51] Concessionaries included those granted land tenure in the Deli Sultanate (Manan 2019).
[52] Stibbe et al. (1927, 229).
[53] Bosma (2019, 76).

eve of the Great Depression.[54] The majority arrived in the sixty years up to the 1920s, and lived in the cities. They included a substantial group of prosperous merchants who engaged in import and export or acted as middlemen between Europeans and the local market. Some became millionaires and ran sugar estates in Java. Other city-based Chinese worked for the colonial government in the dockyards or in private engineering works and factories, or ran workshops.[55]

China and the *Qiaoxiang* in the Early Twentieth Century

Up until the late 1970s and China's post-Mao re-opening to the West, most Chinese going overseas were from Fujian or Guangdong and their destinations were in Southeast Asia. In modern times, most Huaqiao came from a small number of *qiaoxiang* in China's southeastern littoral. These rural counties were inhabited by emigrants' kin and dependants (*qiaojuan*) and returned sojourners (*guiqiao*). The ancestors of most Chinese in Indonesia came from these *qiaoxiang* or from provinces (especially Guangxi) abutting Fujian and Guangdong.

Mainland Chinese studies emphasise the forces in class society that drove migration. These included the economic devastation wreaked by landlordism, warlordism, and imperialism, the destructive forces that foreign economic and military intrusion unleashed, and the interplay between overpopulation and land-hunger and the economic pull of colonial economies in the tropics, where an indigenous labour force was hard to come by.

Western studies too focus on the role played by hardship, famine, and overpopulation in migrant-sending areas, with population densities up to ten times those in migrant-receiving countries. The Dutch Sinologist De Groot noted that "when the elderly indicate to the youngsters the wish that they should emigrate, because there is not enough food for all, those young people leave the country in groups."[56] Studies speak of an integrated labour market "stretching from South India to Southeastern China, with Southeast Asia at its centre," wherein the former served as "hinterlands" of surplus labour and the latter as a centre driven by international trade, so that "surplus natural resources and surplus labor were

[54] Reid (1979, 43–44).

[55] MacNair (1924).

[56] Cited in De Bruin (1918, 10).

complementary." The unlimited availability of immigrants in India and China meant that real wages in Southeast Asia remained stagnant between the 1880s and the late 1940s.[57]

Other Western studies focus more on migration as a way of life, created over centuries and practised along corridors through to the ports and extending across the sea. In south China, what Kuhn has called the "maritime interest" arose, sustained by migrants' strategic calculation.[58]

Pathways along the corridors were created by associations based on lineage and other ties of affinity or geography and realised (for example) in provincial or county guilds (*huiguan*), boarding houses, and temples. Such associations served migrating villagers along the way. Alongside this self-generating migration, economic interests and colonial states in Southeast Asia set up their own supply lines, which fed the "coolie ships," with foreign recruiters and their Chinese agents working in tandem.

At the height of mass Chinese emigration, Huagong made up the great majority of migrants, alongside a much smaller number of merchants, teachers, domestic servants, entertainers, prostitutes, etc. Some—the "piglets"—were kidnapped or trapped into contracts that deprived them of freedom for up to eight years.[59] Crimps and passage-brokers went out to the villages and made recruits, under the credit-ticket system. In some cases overseas-Chinese business interests paid the fares, did the paperwork, arranged accommodation, and found the migrants jobs.[60]

Rates of emigration from south China were comparable in size to those from emigrant regions of Europe. The average annual rate of overseas emigration from Guangdong in the 1920s was 9.6 per 1000, compared with 10.8 per 1000 from Italy and 7 per 1000 from Ireland.[61] In China, migrants came from a small number of counties where up to one third of the rural population lived off emigration, as dependants of emigrants or returners. This concentration was far greater than in Europe, where most emigrants came from scattered towns and cities.[62]

[57] Huff and Caggiano (n.d., 6 and 25–26).

[58] Kuhn (2008, ch. 1).

[59] On the distinction between "piglets" and credit-ticket Huagong, see Mei and Zhang (2001, 40–41).

[60] Williams (1999, 21–23).

[61] McKeown (2004, 160).

[62] For Europe, quantitative analysis of regional differences is lacking, but it would seem that provenance was less dominated by local groups than in China (Baines 1994, 530 and 538).

The Sending Places

The decrease in migration from South China to Southeast Asia organised by the migrant communities themselves and its capture by agents of foreign capitalism raises questions about basic assumptions concerning Chinese migration. In the past, studies pictured migration in push-and-pull terms, with an interaction between pressures at home and opportunities abroad. However, Dutch observers noted the limits of the analogy. The early Sinologist A. G. de Bruin wrote that migration was not

> a jungle torrent that with irresistible force forces through a path for itself but rather [...] a smooth stretch of water that must be protected with all kinds of measures against drying out and silting up. [...] Whoever thinks that when opening companies in the Indies one can have unlimited access to a workforce in South China is wrong.[63]

In the 1980s, scholars in the West criticised the push-pull view as reductive and stressed the part played by social networks. In the Chinese case, they focused on vectors such as clans, lineages, and native-place associations, including their transnational extensions, and their role in transmitting social and cultural capital. At the root of the particularism of the sending regions was Kuhn's "compatriotism."[64]

Networks have always played a major role in transnational Chinese migration. In the East Indies, membership of a speech group gave migrants an advantage. Early migrants included Hakkas, Hokkien, Cantonese, Teochiu, and Hainanese. Diasporic communities formed on the basis of ties of clan, native place, and dialect, institutionalised in *huiguan*, kongsi, and temples and replenished along sub-ethnic networks.[65] After 1842, Cantonese migrants dominated Chinese communities in the New World Anglophone, where the great majority of Chinese migrants originated in the Siyi and Sanyi regions and Zhongshan. Migrants from these places ruled Chinatowns through arrangements that reached back to the sending places. This migration conformed to the theory of migration systems and networks, with its emphasis on clustered, circular movement along corridors.

[63] De Bruin (1918, 11).
[64] Kuhn (2008, 43).
[65] Miles (2020, 64–78).

Migrant chains and networks run by informal labour brokers continued to operate between south China and the Nanyang into the twentieth century. The brokers were celebrated in folklore for shepherding migrants across the sea and for running a remittance trade on a scale unmatched by any other people.[66]

During the chaos and breakdown of rural institutions in the nineteenth and early twentieth centuries, however, old migrant ways fell into disuse and Huagong were increasingly managed by professional recruiters. Lower-class migrants became more dependent on the "ungrounded empires"[67] formed by Chinese power-brokers. In the ports, many without the support of networks fell foul of predators. Instead of arriving in an organised flow, they came in dribs and drabs from many places. Stray individuals were picked up along the way or in hostels, whose managers doubled as commercial crimps.[68] Unlike Chinese in the Anglophone, those in Southeast Asia came from a wide range of places, including some not previously known as migrant-sending, and were less likely to enjoy the support of fellow villagers, while Cantonese from places without an established tradition of migration came to match in numbers the better organised Hakkas.[69]

The diverse composition of the new migratory stream worked partly to the employers' detriment. It made a constant replenishment of the pool of labour by serial recruitment less likely and put a stop to the vetting of new migrants by earlier arrivals. That employers regretted the lack of self-sustaining ties to sending villages is clear from their efforts to restore a link by paying time-expired labourers to convince new cohorts of recruits to repeat the cycle, and from state attempts to create (among Javanese migrants) self-reproducing labour colonies. But above all it worked to the detriment of the migrants, who lost old protections.

So the systems approach that has become orthodox in migration studies is less helpful for explaining Chinese labour migration in the chaos of the early Republic. The same was true of the 1920s and 1930s, when inequalities of power and the weakening of rural institutions led to a steeper decline in cohesion.

[66] Benton and Liu (2018).
[67] Ong and Nonini (1997).
[68] Pastor (1927, pp.41–42).
[69] Heidhues (1992, 113).

An obvious comparison is with the nineteenth-century "piglet trade" to Cuba and Peru, which was marked by violence, abduction, and deception. The "piglets" were socially, geographically, and linguistically heterogeneous and registered under many prior occupations (in Cuba, fewer than 20 percent were thought to be peasants).[70] In 1873, Portugal was forced by international pressure and fear of "national disgrace" to close down the labour trade through Macao, after which it began to take a less abusive form. After the Revolution of 1911, however, China's collapse into ever greater chaos disrupted patterns of migration. The role played by lineage and speech groups diminished. Much of the migrant flow became a floating mass of the uprooted. The inflow of Hakkas, noted for their self-organisation, was overtaken in parts of the East Indies by Cantonese. By 1930, only 35 percent of local-born and only 13 percent of foreign-born Chinese on Bangka identified as Hakka.[71] Of the 124,712 Chinese left on the tin islands in 1930, the relative majority (69,824) were from seven other provinces north of Guangdong and Fujian.[72]

Language and Labour Migration

The motor of Chinese emigration to the Nanyang was poverty, but its vehicle was dialect or sub-dialect. Dialect was an essential marker of ethnicity in the *qiaoxiang*, as generally in China. Speech groups continued to form the basis for ethnic identification overseas, including in the labour diaspora. New recruits sought out fellow-speakers on arrival in the Nanyang, while old hands waiting at the dockside welcomed newcomers into a kindred setting.

But despite their linguistic diversity, diasporic Chinese identified collectively as Chinese. Where speakers of different dialects mixed, one dialect usually came out on top as a lingua franca, acquiring new words and sounds from other dialects and non-Chinese languages.[73] However, groups of mixed provenance were less stable.

Where Malay was widely spoken on a plantation or encampment, it rather than Chinese tended to become the lingua franca. This was a role

[70] Yun (2008, 60–70), García Triana and Eng Herrera (2009).

[71] Belitung, however, remained firmly Hakka: Hakkas comprised 64 percent of the local-born and 75 percent of the China-born (Heidhues (1992, 179).

[72] Yang Tongling et al. (2004, 82).

[73] Tan Chee-Beng (2000, 37–70).

to which it was well suited, given that Bazaar Malay was widely used throughout the archipelago and had evolved a highly effective pidgin.[74]

The main dialect divides were between speakers of Min, Yue (Cantonese), and Hakka (Kejia). In Fujian, speakers of the Min supergroup predominate, whereas in Guangdong and Guangxi dialects of the Yue supergroup are most widely spoken. Hakka is spoken in northeastern Guangdong and western Fujian. Varieties of southern Min (Hokkien), Yue, and Hakka are the main Chinese languages in Southeast Asia. Some dialects of Min and Yue were and are seen as rustic and unpolished, while Hakka, spoken mainly in hilly uplands, was stigmatised as a marker of low class, backwardness, and clannishness.

Distinctions can be made between Hokkien-speaking parts of the Fujianese *qiaoxiang* and the inland Hakka-speaking regions, and between speakers of major and lesser dialects of Fujian's Southern Min linguistic supergroup.[75] Up until the mid-nineteenth century, most Chinese migrants in the East Indies were from Hokkien-speaking parts of Fujian, notably Quanzhou and Zhangzhou, but after 1850 larger number of Cantonese and Hakka-speakers began arriving. Hakka access to the coastal cities was often mediated through non-Hakkas, and many Hakka remittance houses were branches of non-Hakka firms.[76]

Guangdong, like Fujian, was remote from the centre of imperial power in Beijing. Its best-known emigrant communities were in Siyi and Sanyi. Siyi was poor, overpopulated, and ravaged by a cruelly suppressed peasant rising, wars between "native" Punti and "immigrant" Hakkas, a long string of natural disasters, and endemic banditry.[77] Sanyi was more prosperous, due to its richer farmland, access to waterways and markets, and proximity to Guangzhou and its linguistic affinity with standard Cantonese.[78] Some Siyinese and Sanyinese ended up in Southeast Asia, but most went to America and Australia, so their migration dominates Western scholarship.

Guangdong's Min-speaking region was similarly marked by divisions between rich and poor. The wealthier Chaozhou-Shantou (Chaoshan) region abuts to the north onto Guangdong's Hakka heartland,

[74] Pastor (1927, 48–50).
[75] Ding (2016).
[76] Xia Shuiping and Fang Xuejia (2004, 183), Xiao Wenping (2004, 257).
[77] Mei Weiqiang and Zhang Guoxiong (2001, 29–32).
[78] McKeown (2001, 62–63), Yong Chen (2002, ch. 1).

impoverished due to its restless history, rugged terrain, and remoteness. The Chaoshan element preponderated demographically and in the remittance trade and Huagong recruitment.[79] Better-off merchant groups and officials formed relationships with foreign capitalists to the disadvantage of the poorer regions, which became reservoirs of cheap labour.

Ethnic differences within the Chinese population resulted in the creation of an emigrant hierarchy among Huagong, who were divided into two classes, depending on their provenance. At the top, in class one, were migrants from Chaozhou, Lufeng, and Haifeng and Hokkiens, while class two comprised Hakkas and Hainanese. The latter two groups were considered unsuitable for work (like tobacco farming) requiring careful and persistent effort, and were therefore valued more lowly than the former. This led to a disparity in the purchase price of each class—in 1910, a class-one and a class-two Huagong cost f93 and f69 respectively.[80]

The Political Context of Recruitment for Indenture

The three main sending-places of indentured labour, China, India, and Java, were all shaped by imperialism but in different ways. India and Java were under direct rule by the British and the Dutch, who promoted emigration within their respective empires—in the Dutch case, mainly from Java to Sumatra and other parts of Indonesia—and occasionally beyond them. China was in a condition designated by Lenin as semi-colonial, a pathology that combined "feudalism" with incomplete and fragmentary colonialism.[81] For migrants, being a semi-colony was in some ways an even greater handicap than full colonialism, for despite the atrocities colonialists vented on their subjects, the British were forced in time by nationalism in India and public opinion at home to improve the treatment of Indians overseas as "sons of empire." They were later followed in this by the Dutch in the East Indies. Chinese migrants, in contrast, lacked a homeland-based administration capable of mitigating their problems.

Treaties signed between Britain and China in 1842 and 1860 appeared to protect Chinese emigrants, but their prime purpose was to protect foreigners in China. Starting in the United States in the late 1860s, Chinese

[79] Benton and Liu (2018, 84).
[80] Pelzer (1935, 92).
[81] Shih (2001, 34).

diplomats sought guarantees for Chinese emigrants and gradually extended consular representation, including to the East Indies. However, the consuls' focus was on promoting trade and harnessing merchants, students, and intellectuals to the national cause rather than on migrant labourers.

In the early days of the Chinese Republic, some of the measures taken by Beijing to protect nationals overseas applied to Huagong, particularly during the negotiations to provide Huagong contingents to help the Allies in the First World War, which led to the adoption of an institutional framework to supervise overseas-Chinese affairs. The arrangements might have provided a template for the later treatment of Huagong, but few survived into the peace. Neither the Beijing government up to 1928 nor the Nanjing government that succeeded it were more than minimally able to translate the new norms governing the wartime recruitment of Huagong into measures to improve their postwar recruitment in Southeast Asia and elsewhere. Where Beijing campaigned against the maltreatment of Chinese abroad, it did so to promote China's "national interest" and "national sovereignty"—the labourers' plight remained secondary. Such was the case, for example, at the time of the massacre of Huagong in Japan after the Kantō earthquake in 1923, when Beijing denounced the atrocity as a violation of Chinese national sovereignty.[82]

Both before and after the Kuomintang established the second Chinese Republic in Nanjing in 1927, Kuomintang leaders sought to incorporate Chinese overseas into their foreign policy. In 1921 in Guangzhou, they tried to ban labour migration. Employers in the East Indies condemned this "act of revolutionary dictatorship" but later interpreted it as an attempt by Chinese officials to increase the "squeeze" on buyers of Chinese labour and did their best to circumnavigate it.[83] Planters in Malaya ignored Sun Yat-sen, whose government was not recognised by Britain, and instead favoured the Beijing government, considered "benevolent,"[84] i.e., malleable. In 1927, the Kuomintang set up an Overseas Chinese Affairs Bureau which became a ministry in 1932, with offices in the ports and in migrant-sending regions.[85] However, Chinese overseas lacked

[82] Shen (n.d.); Academia Sinica archive, Jilin Province to Foreign Ministry, 03-331-007-02-011, November 30, 1923; Academia Sinica archive, Beiyang Foreign Ministry to Chinese Ambassador in Japan, January 11, 1924, 03-31-008-03-042, September 1, 1924.

[83] Mollema (1922, 153).

[84] *Malaya Tribune*, July 12, 1922.

[85] Zhuang Guotao (1998).

strong representation even in the 1930s, when world opinion swung behind China during the Japanese invasion. In the early 1940s, Nationalist China became the West's wartime ally but lost its consulates in Southeast Asia.

Outside China, care for its nationals' wellbeing was far from China's primary concern. Few Huagong registered with the local colonial authorities or a Chinese consul.[86] Chinese consular representation in the East Indies was small and under pressure, for the Dutch feared "the China threat" and the dangers of "Chinese imperialism," especially after the Revolution of 1911. Forming consulates was constrained by the chaos in China. According to an agreement reached between the Netherlands and China in 1914, Chinese consuls could only pursue commercial matters. The Dutch decision to grant Dutch subjectship to Chinese residents was in part to combat activities viewed as subversive, after a series of visits by Chinese officials starting in 1906.[87] Chinese representatives in the colony did not always stick to the agreements struck, but the shortage of consuls in remote regions where Huagong worked meant that consuls could rarely tackle labour grievances. In some places, Chinese chambers of commerce acted as unofficial consulates, but they lacked the weight of an accredited diplomat.[88]

China's chronic weakness in the age of the great migrations and its preoccupation at home with its very survival ruled out a systematic defence of its migrants. The West took full advantage of China's weakness to press for ever more privileges, even when China began negotiating the West's relinquishment of extraterritoriality in 1929. In the East Indies, Chinese consuls were criticised in the 1930s for "interfering" in local affairs or intervening to protect the interests of local-born Chinese. The supine Chinese Consul-General, Fartsan T. Sung, sided not with the local Chinese but with the Dutch, telling Nanjing that a Chinese book criticising Dutch abuses was "ridiculously untrue" and written "by an old man without a brain."[89]

The Chinese community in the East Indies was divided into Malay-speaking Peranakans, descendants of early waves of Chinese settlement in the Malay Peninsula and the Indonesian Archipelago, and Totoks, new

[86] Guowuyuan [May] (1920b, 47).
[87] Liem and Tjiook-Liem (2009, 472–478).
[88] On Chinese consuls in the East Indies, see Nugteren (2016) and Liu (2014).
[89] Alg. Sec, Grote bundel, TZG Agenda 9035, 1933, Jakarta, Arsip Nasional.

immigrants and their offspring who spoke Chinese and saw China as their homeland.[90] On Java, for example, 69.9 percent of Chinese in 1920 were Peranakans.[91] The presence in the East Indies of the strong and long-established Peranakan community did not necessarily work to the advantage of newly arrived labourers. Some Peranakans opposed Chinese labour immigration and called for its restriction. Huagong could sometimes find common ground with Peranakans on issues concerning China, and many paths led from the mines and estates into Chinatown, where traditional associations had ties to the labour diaspora. However, not all Peranakans were happy with the Totok presence. Some said that the newcomers would become "Indos" in a generation and contribute to economic progress, but others thought that they lowered the tone.[92]

Unlike in British India, where nationalist politicians helped bring about the abolition of indenture, and even in Java, where Javanese labourers gained political support from the anti-colonial movement, the Huagong found few champions. Although the colonial system in the East Indies threw up a few pro-Huagong whistle-blowers, the eventual abolition of indenture (just before the Japanese invasion in 1942) was more a result of external triggers (actions by the ILO and the threat of hostile US tariffs) than of internal opposition, as we shall see. When abolition finally came, the Japanese invasion prevented its full implementation.

Three Sites of Chinese Indenture in Sumatra

The Dutch first established a presence in the Indonesian Archipelago at the turn of the seventeenth century, when the VOC was established as a chartered company. The VOC quickly became active across most of Asia. In the eighteenth century, it gained political dominance over Java and ran bases throughout the region, including in Sumatra. Its collapse at the end of the century led eventually to the transfer of its possessions to the Dutch state. In the nineteenth century, Java was at the heart of the East Indies economy. Dutch colonial administrators focused almost exclusively on Java and left the other islands largely to themselves. In Sumatra, Dutch

[90] Skinner (1963, 105–106).

[91] Coppel (2013, 348). In 1917, 563,449 Chinese lived in the Netherlands East Indies, including 99,236 on Sumatra's East Coast and 43,723 on Bangka (Paulus 1919, vol. 1, 487).

[92] Arsip Nasional, Jakarta, Algemene Secretarie, Grote Bundel, TZG Agenda, file no. 9243, Overzicht van de Inlandsche en Maleisch-Chineesche Pers, no. 35, 35, August 30, 1935.

power was contested throughout the nineteenth century. By 1900, however, the Dutch campaign to subjugate the island was almost complete.

While laying the basis for a unified administration of the East Indies, the Dutch in Sumatra presided over the creation of a plantation belt in Deli, known in the late nineteenth century as Medan-Deli after its new capital in Medan. Private concessions occupied a swathe of land 40 miles deep and 150 miles long, financed by Dutch and other foreign investors, and specialised in growing rubber, tobacco, and other cash-crops. As an exporter, Sumatra soon eclipsed Java and the other islands.

This study looks chiefly at the three main sites of Chinese labour on Bangka and Belitung and in Deli. Bangka and Belitung today have a population exceeding 1.4 million, around one third of whom are ethnic Chinese descendants of immigrant labourers and merchants, compared with the 40 percent Chinese share of the islands' then population of around 265,000 in the 1920s.[93] Deli, to the west, was ruled until the 1940s by sultans who developed close relations with Dutch officials and Dutch and Chinese planters. In 1891, the Sultan of Deli moved his capital to Medan, which in 1918 came under direct Dutch rule. The Chinese presence in Deli is, and was, proportionately far smaller than on the tin islands. In the 1860s, Deli began to flourish as a tobacco-producing centre and commercial hub. Today, Chinese form around ten percent of Medan's population of around 2.2 million, compared with around 50,000 Chinese labourers in Deli in 1914 and 25,000 in 1920.[94] Besides mining, the Bangka-Belitung economy in colonial times included a large number of plantations.

Most early labourers in Sumatra were Chinese imported through the Straits Settlements or from China.. Chinese settlement in Sumatra dated back to the late thirteenth century. Tin-mining kongsis were operating as early as 1710, as territorial administrations and companies nominally under the Sultan of Palembang.[95] Initially, they employed Malay and Chinese miners from West Kalimantan.[96] In 1852, rich tin deposits were discovered on Belitung,[97] whose small population of just 28 Chinese was quickly joined by 250 Chinese miners, one quarter of whom died of tropical diseases and leg ulcers. Large-scale recruitment of Chinese began only

[93] Heidhues (1991).
[94] Lindblad (1999, 52).
[95] Wazar (2004 [1956], 209).
[96] Heidhues (1992, 37–39), Shimada (2014, 207–210).
[97] On the history of tin mining on Belitung, see Mollema (1922).

after the establishment of the Billiton Maatschappij mining company in 1860. Between 1862 and 1863, tin production doubled,[98] using a mainly Chinese workforce. When tobacco farming started up in Deli, again the workforce was at first predominantly Chinese.[99]

According to a later Chinese account,[100] the population of Bangka had grown from 24,000 in 1840 to 70,000 in 1917, while the number of Chinese had grown to 96,500 by 1930 (and to around 100,000 out of 310,000 by 1963). In 1920, the population of Bangka was 190,000, of whom 90,000 were Chinese—45,000 miners and 45,000 plantation workers. Belitung, on the other hand, had a population of 40,000, half of whom were Chinese, of whom 80 percent were miners and 20 percent traders. According to the same source, in 1930, 88,806 Chinese (66,215 males, 29,883 females[101]) lived on Bangka and 35,906 on Belitung (including 6023 females). The Chinese mining community on Bangka then entered a steep decline, with only 1454 left by 1934.

Towards the end of the nineteenth century, the planters began to recruit more and more Javanese to meet the needs of the booming rubber, tobacco, and coconut-palm plantations, and by the 1920s the Chinese, more expensive to employ and considered insufficiently docile, had become a minority.[102] Between 700,000 and one million Javanese went to Sumatra in the late nineteenth and early twentieth centuries.[103] By 1910, Javanese arrivals outnumbered Huagong by 12,000 to 9000, and by the late 1910s Javanese immigration was increasing by more than 40,000 a year, compared to just 11,000 Huagong.[104] Even so, by 1905 more than half a million Chinese lived in the archipelago, rising in 1917 to 700,000, with 400,000 in Java and 200,000 in mainland Sumatra and the rest scattered across Bangka, Belitung, and other islands.

The Huagong lived in rural areas, whereas most Chinese in the East Indies lived in cities. Many were merchants, with a smaller number of landowners. By the 1920s, Chinese in the cities had progressed from being middlemen, mid-way between Europeans and Indonesians, to an

[98] *Gedenkboek* (1927, pt 1, 1–2, 9–10 and 20–21).
[99] Vleming (1992 [1926], 203), Wang Linqian and Wu Kunxiang (2002, 167–168).
[100] Yang Tongling et al. (2004, 79 and 102–103).
[101] These sets of figures for Bangka and Belitung do not add up.
[102] Houben (1999, 25).
[103] Termorshuizen (2008, 287).
[104] Lu Wendi et al. (1984a, 256).

independent role, as owners and managers of businesses and estates, alongside a large number of Chinese mechanics.[105]

Between 1888 and 1931, 305,000 Chinese landed in Belawan (the main port for Deli) and were taken off to plantations run by members of the DPV.[106] Of this group, 246,500 were *xinke*, nearly all of them direct arrivals from the Chinese mainland.[107] The number of Huagong on the plantations peaked at 58,516 in 1900, from a starting point of 4476 in 1884, but had dwindled to 27,113 in 1926. By 1937, their numbers had fallen even further, to just 12,000. The number of Javanese, in contrast, rocketed, from 859 in 1874 to 150,392 in 1920 and around 200,000 in 1937. However, the Chinese population as a whole kept growing.[108] In 1930, Chinese accounted for 11 percent of the population of East Sumatra and 47 and 42 percent of that of Bangka and Belitung.[109] The Chinese population of the East Indies as a whole was 1,190,014 in 1930, of whom just 433,842 were first-generation.[110]

Bangka and Belitung are the two main islands in an equatorial provincial archipelago of nearly one thousand islands. The Dutch interest in tin in the East Indies started in the eighteenth century under the VOC, which began exporting it to China even before large-scale Western expansion into the region. The mining was administered and the tin marketed by Chinese merchants in collaboration with the Sultanate. After the dissolution of the VOC in 1799 and the French and British occupation, in 1816 Bangka was returned to the Dutch, who elbowed out the Sultanate but left the mining in Chinese hands, until around 1850.[111]

Bangka is 136 miles long and 69 miles wide, separated from the Sumatra mainland by ten miles of water across the Bangka Strait, while Belitung is 55 miles from north to south and 43 miles from east to west. The two islands are in turn separated by the Gaspar Strait, which connects the Java Sea and the South China Sea. Chinese envoys in 1920 noted that 80

[105] MacNair (1924).

[106] The Deli Planters' Association—see Chap. 4. A few other planters not belonging to the DPV imported labourers from the Straits Settlements.

[107] Pelzer (1935, 93).

[108] Reid (1970, 319). Wong Yee Tuan 2015 gives different but compatible statistics. For the 1920s, see *Xianggang gongshang ribao*, November 26, 1921. For 1937, see "Nu en vroeger" and "Het ronselen," *Soerabaijasch Handelsblad*, February 13.

[109] Heidhues (1996).

[110] Bosma (2019, 113).

[111] Heidhues (2007, 63–66).

percent of the surface was jungle, "inhabited by fierce animals, including tigers."[112]

In 1905, Bangka's population of 115,000 included 43,700 Chinese, said by Dutch officials to "belong to the crudest and most uncivilised" parts of the Chinese population. Chinese not in tin worked on plantations or traded in gambier and pepper, raised vegetables and pigs, or lived by fishing.[113] Commenting on the lack of agriculture, a Chinese report said the natives "are too stupid to know how to produce."

By 1920, Bangka's population had passed 190,000, including 90,000 Chinese, 100,000 Malays and indigenous people, and 600 Dutch merchants, soldiers, and officials. The miners numbered 22,302, alongside 20,000 "miscellaneous workers" who were self-employed or unregistered or traders. More than 32,000 Chinese and Chinese-associated women and children lived on the island, a far larger proportion than on other Huagong sites in the region, a reflection of Bangka's long Chinese settlement and diversification.[114]

In 1920, Chinese inspectors described Belitung as similarly tiger-infested, with a small indigenous population. Its tin deposits were mined by companies on 25-year extendable government contracts that paid three eighths of their profits to the government. The companies mined more than 800,000 *dan*[115] of tin a year, bringing in an income of fl6 million and a profit of f6 million. In 1915, the population of Belitung was 58,000, including 400 Europeans and around 20,000 Chinese. Some Chinese ran brickyards and lime-kilns or lived by hunting, fishing, etc.[116]

Belitung in 1920 was far less developed than Bangka, and local people likewise practised slash-and-burn farming, while rice for the Chinese was imported from Singapore. Eighty percent of the Chinese on Belitung were labourers, 16,715 of them miners, proportionately far more than on Bangka, and 20 percent "miscellaneous workers" and merchants.[117] Between 1888 and 1931, around 305,000 Huagong arrived in Belitung and, in most cases, subsequently left.

[112] Guowuyuan [January] (1920a, 1, [May] b, 3).

[113] Paulus (1919, vol. 1, 159–163).

[114] Guowuyuan [May] (1920b, 1–5).

[115] One *dan* equals 450 kilos.

[116] Paulus (1919, vol. 1, 303–306).

[117] Guowuyuan [January] (1920a, 1–5). Heidhues (1992) gives a gender ratio on Belitung of 1.6 men to 1 woman.

Towards the end of the colonial period, the Chinese population of the two islands became more equal. According to a Chinese account, 28,614 Huagong lived on Belitung in 1930 and by 1939 Bangka and Belitung had only 20,000 Huagong between them. Chinese numbers collapsed even more dramatically during the Japanese occupation.[118]

Chinese labour was differently organised on Bangka and Belitung, mostly because Bangka mining was under state control while mining on Belitung was in private hands.[119] The miners on Belitung were more independent and nominally free. Because Chinese settlement on Belitung was more recent, Chinese institutions were stronger, and the kongsis, rather than decay, evolved into numpangs, teams that worked cooperatively and shared profits. (They are described in greater detail in a later chapter.) On Bangka, the miner was a wage worker, whereas on Belitung he was still a shareholder, as on Bangka in earlier times.[120] Colonial officials found that Chinese labourers on Belitung were happier than on Bangka and enjoyed better health and welfare.[121] Huagong were even said to hate the larger island, whereas on Belitung there was "no need for a recruiting drum" and recruits turned up of their own accord.[122] Working and living conditions were better than on Bangka because of the numpang system, and because workers were more homogeneous in origin and therefore more united.[123] In 1927, the Dutch Parliament rejected a proposal to put Belitung under state management, like Bangka.[124]

Most trade and shops on the two islands were in Chinese hands. Some Chinese companies on Bangka traded on a massive scale. During a rice shortage in 1919, for example, they imported f15 million worth of rice from Java. The island had five ports, the biggest of which, Tanjung Pandan, had around 200 shops, 80–90 percent of them Chinese-owned. Even so, Chinese businesses on the islands were far less prosperous than elsewhere in the Nanyang.[125]

[118] Wang Linqian and Wu Kunxiang (2002, 169 and 221), Lu Wendi et al. (1984a, 64–68). It is not clear how many were under indenture.

[119] Heidhues (1992, 117), Guowuyuan [January] (1920a, 1).

[120] Rapport (1905, 13), *Gedenkboek* (1927, pt 1, 60).

[121] Heidhues (1991, 4–8, 1992, 80 and 126).

[122] *Gedenkboek* (1927, pt 1, 20–29, and pt 2, 60).

[123] Erman (2017, 514–539, 1999).

[124] *Gedenkboek* (1927, pt 1, 65).

[125] Guowuyuan [May] (1920b, 1–5).

The islands' Chinese population was segmented into an urban commercial class and rural workers. In the early nineteenth century, the rural element predominated, but not by much—in 1816, the 2528 Chinese miners on Bangka were almost matched by 2123 other Chinese. By 1930, a "settled element" of urban Peranakans dominated the community on Bangka, at a time when ethnic Chinese were 47.5 percent of a total population of 205,432. Local-born Chinese outnumbered China-born Totoks by around 56,000 to 40,000, while two out of five of the former were born of fathers themselves born on Bangka (compared with just 19 percent on Belitung). Heidhues comments that, in this respect, Bangka was "more Peranakan than any other major Chinese settlement outside Java,"[126] for other Chinese settlements outside Java had relatively small Peranakan populations.[127] Almost everywhere, however, Peranakans dominated the lower administration of enterprises employing Chinese because of their knowledge of Dutch and Malay as well as of Chinese and because they were considered "more civilised."[128]

On Bangka, the nativisation of the Chinese population had started early but took a different form from that in Java. In 1823, miners and local-born Peranakan Chinese living in the kampungs numbered around 4000 and 3000 respectively. Unlike in Java, however, these Peranakans spoke Malay-inflected Hakka creole rather than a local language.[129] Miners in the camps had close ties to the kampung Chinese and the shopkeepers and merchants. Belitung's Chinese were similarly divided into urban, rural, and mining segments and were more likely to include China-born Chinese, again because of the shorter length of settlement.[130] In 1871, when Belitung's Chinese mining population was only around 3000,[131] the island's general population already included 790 Chinese non-miners.[132]

Even the China-born who formed families, by importing brides or marrying local women or local-born Chinese or mixed-race women, remained attached to China, as evidenced by the popularity of Chinese-language schooling on the islands. Most Huagong were illiterate, but they valued

[126] Heidhues (1992, 176–178).
[127] *Gedenkboek* (1927, pt 2, 78).
[128] Rapport (1905, 12), Heidhues (1992, 119).
[129] Heidhues (1992, 43 and 145).
[130] Guowuyuan [January] (1920a, 44–49).
[131] *Gedenkboek* (1927, pt 2, 60).
[132] De Groot (1887, 358).

education as an avenue of social mobility. A Chinese-schools movement survived despite competition from Dutch-language schools, which the authorities privileged financially. The Dutch hoped to assimilate Chinese children and used sabotage and bribes to win the battle of the classrooms. Official Chinese representatives in the islands' ports countered with a campaign to "console" the Chinese schools, though to less effect.[133]

In 1920, more than 1000 Chinese labourers worked in a variety of trades with few ties to the European sector of the islands' economy. There were no special restrictions on the Chinese merchants, who dominated most trades.[134]

Chinese officials in the East Indies knew little about the islands until their 1920 visit. They reported that the archipelago was "remote and virtually unknown in China, and not a focus of concern," and regretted that "there is no basis for the Chinese Government to protect the workforce. [...] Having Huagong in the Nanyang is nothing new, nor is their abuse new. In the past, the government sighed but did nothing. The Dutch behave unscrupulously. Bad habits die hard. Unfortunately most Huagong are ignorant. Our government negotiates but never gets justice."[135]

The Islands after the Dutch

The Japanese occupation of Indonesia led, during the war, to slavery for many Chinese. Heidhues recounts the failure of the Japanese to rehabilitate the mines after their wrecking by the tin companies, but says that little is known about the occupation.[136] Food was scarce, China-bound sea traffic was policed by the Japanese or destroyed by the Allies, and relations between Chinese and Japanese were tense.[137]

After the Japanese surrender in 1945, the Republican leaders Sukarno and Hatta proclaimed Indonesian independence. The Dutch reinstalled some administration but granted the new Republic de facto recognition. Dutch forces retook Bangka in February 1946, after which mining resumed. Bangka Tinwinning remained the biggest tin mining company in Indonesia, and continued under the same name until 1961.[138] In

[133] Lu Wendi et al. (1985a, 420–421), Guowuyuan [May] (1920b, 51).
[134] Guowuyuan [January] (1920a, 44–49), Lu Wendi et al. (1985a, 451–453).
[135] Guowuyuan [May] (1920b, 62).
[136] Heidhues (2018, 83).
[137] Xu Guanxi and Wu Zikai (n.d.).
[138] Yuniarti et al. (2020).

December 1949, Sukarno and others negotiated formal independence at the company's Bangka headquarters.

In the first two years after the surrender, Huagong on Bangka and Belitung suffered further losses. Many were forced back to China and denied compensation. In Hong Kong, they were suspected of harbouring Communist sympathies, especially after reports of strikes by Huagong on the tin islands.[139]

Meanwhile, thousands more Huagong sailed in the opposite direction, to the Nanyang, as recruits or returners. In March 1947, however, Southeast Asian governments began imposing new restrictions.[140] Chinese on Bangka and Belitung strove to gain acceptance into local society. The islands avoided the extremes of ethnic conflict witnessed elsewhere in Indonesia. Indenture shrank almost to nothing and a socially more balanced Chinese population formed. A string of Chinese associations "sprang up, matured, and stabilised." They included a Chinese Association[141] in each port, together with a Chinese Chamber of Commerce, study associations, an influential General Association, women's organisations, welfare clubs, sports associations, and reading clubs.

Chinese labour organisations formed and Chinese political groups began supporting Indonesian independence.[142] Most Huagong stayed in Indonesia to work on plantations or become farmers. Deli, Bangka, and Belitung became industrial regions, and Huagong played a role in that transition.[143] In the first postwar years, the Chinese Foreign Ministry reported a wave of labour unrest on Belitung.[144]

Despite the maturation of the Chinese community and its assertion of local belonging, anti-Chinese measures by the new Indonesian rulers deepened the rift between Chinese and local people and led to a Chinese exodus. The measures included discriminatory laws and the imposition of a system of permits controlled by an extortionary bureaucracy.

In the twentieth century, separate waves of indentured labourers returned to China, where they were accommodated by the government

[139] Foreign Ministry 02-010807-0009. October 23, 1946-January 3, 1948 (Academia Sinica).

[140] Wang Linqian and Wu Kunxiang, eds (2002, 50), Xu Guanxi and Wu Zikai (n.d.).

[141] *Zhonghua huiguan*, comprising leaders of various *huiguan*.

[142] Yang Tongling et al. (2004, 109 and 113).

[143] Zhu Jieqin (1984, 242–243).

[144] Foreign Ministry file 020000001585A. June 1946–December 1948 (Academia Sinica).

(including the Kuomintang before 1949) or found their way back home. At the start of the Depression in 1929, at the end of the Second World War, and in 1950 thousands returned. A fourth wave started in 1959 and included many China-born Chinese, who were suffering increasingly at the hands of the new authorities, resentful of the Chinese "stranglehold" on trade. The outflow peaked in 1959–1961, when Beijing encouraged the return of Huagong and traders. Others left after the troubles of the mid 1960s—most went to China, but some settled in other parts of Southeast Asia or left for Europe, North America, and Australia.[145]

Only a minority of the 80,000 Huagong Chinese said to have gone to Indonesia between 1931 and 1940 returned to China. The great majority died abroad. Some speak of hundreds of Huagong repatriates, others of thousands, "falling as leaves to the root of the tree." Most were above sixty, physically or psychologically scarred. Some were blind, maimed, deaf, or mute, and appeared depressed or broken, "unwilling to speak as a result of forty years of silent suffering."[146]

Many Huagong who had become addicted to opium or hopelessly indebted cut their home ties and became waifs and strays of the diaspora. They too suffered during the pogroms in Indonesia in the 1960s.

Among the repatriates, Huagong were outnumbered by tens of thousands of better-off urban Chinese. The migration was portrayed as a "return," but many had never set foot on ancestral soil. Most student "returners" ended up in the countryside and led a life of hardship, for their overseas links rendered them suspect during the Cultural Revolution. Unlike richer repatriates, many of whom enrolled in schools and universities, the Huagong were assigned to state farms.[147] Up until 1966, 200,000 Chinese from Indonesia and elsewhere in Southeast Asia were received in China.[148] Even most of the educated returnees ended up in the villages in the 1960s, an outcome they resented. However, returned labourers, including miners from Belitung, complied and voiced their gratitude.[149]

[145] Heidhues (1992, 219). For Meixian, see Xia Yuanming (2008, 374–375).

[146] "'Qiyue Huagong' huidao zuguo" (Indentured labourers return to the motherland), *Renmin ribao* (People's Daily), July 3, 1960.

[147] Godley and Coppel (1990, 179–180), Zhou (2019, ch. 10).

[148] Wang Cangbai (2013, 69). Zhou (2019, 191), says "at least 164,000."

[149] Zhou (2019, 202).

The "return" was quite unlike that of earlier returners, who went as private individuals. Instead, it was a "national return," bureaucratically conceived and collectively organised. Not all went as refugees. Some left to do business or to "save China."[150]

Little has been written in Western studies about the labourers who returned to China in the 1960s, partly because "exile studies" tend to focus on writers and political leaders rather than on "ordinary" refugees.[151] The scores of interviews with retired labourers recorded shortly after their repatriation and translated in Appendix A are a rare exception and perhaps unique in Huagong annals.

Despite the repatriations, huge numbers of ethnic Chinese now live on the tin islands. After a sharp decline in the mining population, only 1454 Huagong miners remained on Bangka in 1934, but the Chinese community grew as a result of an inflow of traders and others and the emergence of a second generation. In 1930, 96,500 ethnic and migrant Chinese lived on Bangka. In 1963, just under one third of the total population of 310,000 were Chinese, a proportion that still holds.[152]

References

Allen, Richard B. 2021. "The Poverty of Archival Riches: Reconstructing Eighteenth- and Nineteenth-Century Mauritian History." *International Journal of Historical Archaeology*, https://doi.org/10.1007/s10761-021-00639-y.

Baines, Dudley.1994. "European Emigration, 1815–1930: Looking at the Emigration Decision Again." *The Economic History Review*, vol. 47, no. 3, 525–544.

Bates, Crispin. 1992. "Tribal Migration In India and Beyond." In Gyan Prakash, ed., *The World of the Rural Labourer in Colonial India*, Delhi: Oxford University Press, 1992, 205–245.

Bates, Crispin, Marina Carter, and Vishwanaden Govinden. 2017. The Abolition of Indian Indentured Migration to Mauritius. Unpublished paper.

Batsha, Nishant. 2017. The Currents of Restless Toil: Colonial Rule and Indian Indentured Labor in Trinidad and Fiji. PhD, Columbia University.

[150] Hui Yew-Foong (2013, 109).

[151] Hill (2020, 339).

[152] Yang Tongling et al. (2004, 103).

Behal, Rana. 2013. *Coolies, Recruiters and Planters: Migration of Indian Labour to the Southeast Asian and Assam Plantations during Colonial Rule*. Crossroads Asia, Working Paper series no. 9.

Benton, Gregor, and Hong Liu. 2018. *Dear China: Emigrant Letters and Remittances, 1820–1980*. Oakland, CA: University of California Press.

Bosma, Ulbe. 2019. *The Making of a Periphery: How Island Southeast Asia Became a Mass Exporter of Labor*. New York: Columbia University Press.

Chatterji, Joya, and David Washbrook. 2013. *Routledge Handbook of the South Asian Diaspora*. London: Routledge.

Coppel, Charles A. 2013. "Diaspora and Hybridity: *Peranakan* Chinese Culture in Indonesia." In Chee-Beng Tan, ed., *Routledge Handbook of the Chinese Diaspora*, Abingdon: Routledge, 2013, 345–358.

De Bruin, A. G. 1918. *De Chineezen ter Oostkust van Sumatra*. Issued by Het Oostkust van Sumatra-Instituut. Leiden: Brill.

De Graaf, S., and D. G. Stibbe, with W. C. B. Wintgens, eds. 1918. *Encyclopaedie van Nederlandsch-Indië*, second edition. 2 vols. The Hague: Martinus Nijhoff.

De Groot, Cornelis. 1887. *Herinneringen aan Blitong, Historisch, Lithologisch, Mineralogisch, Geographisch, Geologisch en Mijnbouwkundig*. The Hague: H. L. Smits.

Delius, Peter, and Stanley Trapido. 1982. "Inboekselings and Oorlams: The Creation and Transformation of a Servile Class." *Journal of Southern African Studies*, vol 8, no. 2, 214–242.

Derks, Annuska. 2010. "Bonded Labour in Southeast Asia: Introduction." *Asian Journal of Social Science*, no. 38, 839–852

Ding, Picus Sizhi. 2016. *Southern Min (Hokkien) as a Migrating Language: A Comparative Study of Language Shift and Maintenance Across National Borders*. Singapore: Springer.

Erman, Erwiza. 1999. Miners, Managers and the State: A Socio-Political History of the Ombilin Coal-Mines, West Sumatra, 1892–1996. PhD thesis, University of Amsterdam.

Erman, Erwiza. 2017. "Chinese *Taukeh*, Labourer, and State Control: Case Study of *Panglong* in Eastern Region of Sumatra (1890–1930)." *Wacana*, vol. 18, no. 2, 514–539.

Extract from the Proceedings of the Imperial Legislative Council, India. March 1912. In *Speeches and Writings of Gopal Krishna Gokhale*, vol. 1, Asia Publishing House, 1962, 349–368.

Fix, Douglas. 2018. "Xiamen: Emigrants' Portal to a Broader World." Chinese Studies Research Center Working Paper, June.

Galenson, David W. 1984. "The Rise and Fall of Indentured Servitude in the Americas: An Economic Analysis." *The Journal of Economic History*, vol. 44, no. 1, 1–26.

García Triana, Mauro, and Pedro Eng Herrera. 2009. *The Chinese in Cuba, 1847-Now.* Edited and translated by Gregor Benton. Lanham: Lexington Books.

Gedenkboek Billiton, 1852–1927. 1927. 2 pts. The Hague: Martinus Nijhoff.

Ginés-Blasi, Mònica. 2020. "A Philippine 'Coolie Trade': Trade and Exploitation of Chinese Labour in Spanish Colonial Philippines, 1850–98." *Journal of Southeast Asian Studies*, 1–27.

Godley, Michael R., and Charles A. Coppel. 1990. "The Pied Piper and the Prodigal Children: A Report on the Indonesian-Chinese Students who went to Mao's China." *Archipel*, vol. 39, 179–198.

Gordon, Alec. 2004. "Dynamics of Labour Transformation: Natural Rubber in Southeast Asia." *Journal of Contemporary Asia*, no. 34, 523–546.

Groeneveldt, Willem Pieter. 1898. *De Nederlanders in China.* The Hague: Nijhoff.

Guowuyuan qiaogong shiwu ju, eds. [January] 1920a. *Nanyang He shu Wanlitong dao Huagong qingxing diaocha shu* (An Investigation into the Situation of Huagong on Dutch-ruled Belitung Island in the Nanyang). Beijing: Guowuyuan qiaogong shiwu ju.

Guowuyuan qiaogong shiwu ju, eds. [May] 1920b. *Nanyang He shu Wangjia dao Huagong qingxing diaocha shu* (An Investigation into the Situation of Huagong on Dutch-ruled Bangka Island in the Nanyang). Beijing: Guowuyuan qiaogong shiwu ju.

Heidhues, Mary F. Somers. 1991. "Company Island: A Note on the History of Belitung." *Indonesia*, no. 51, 1–20.

Heidhues, Mary F. Somers. 1992. *Bangka Tin and Mentok Pepper: Chinese Settlement on an Indonesian Island.* Pasir Panjang : Institute of Southeast Asian Studies.

Heidhues, Mary Somers. 1996. "Chinese Settlements in Rural Southeast Asia: Unwritten Histories." In Anthony Reid, ed., *Sojourners and Settlers: Histories of Southeast Asia and the Chinese,* Sydney: Allen and Unwin, 1996, 164–182.

Heidhues, Mary Somers. 2007. "Poor Little Rich Islands: Metals in Bangka-Belitung and West Kalimantan." In Greg Bankoff and Peter Boomgaard, eds, *A History of Natural Resources in Asia: The Wealth of Nature.* Houndmills: Palgrave, 2007, 61–80.

Heidhues, Mary Somers. 2018."When We Were Young: The Exile of the Republic's Leaders in Bangka, 1949." In Daniel S. Lev and Ruth T. McVey, eds, *Making Indonesia: Essays on Modern Indonesia in Honor of George McT. Kahin.* Ithaca, NY: Cornell University Press, 2018, 81–95.

Hill, David T. 2020. "Cold War Polarization, Delegated Party Authority, and Diminishing Exilic Options: The Dilemma of Indonesian Political Exiles in China after 1965." *Bijdragen tot de Taal-, Land- en Volkenkunde*, no. 176, 338–372.

Hoefte, Rosemarijn. 2017. "Indentured Labor." In Karin Hofmeester and Marcel van der Linden, eds, *Handbook Global History of Work*, Berlin: De Gruyter, 363–376.

Houben, Vincent J. H. 1999. “Before Departure: Coolie Labour Recruitment in Java, 1900–1942.” In Vincent J. H. Houben and J. Thomas Lindblad, eds, *Coolie Labour in Colonial Indonesia: A Study of Labour Relations in the Outer Islands, c. 1900–1940*, Wiesbaden: Harrassowitz Verlag, 1999, 25–42.

Huff, Gregg, and Giovanni Caggiano. N.d. Migration and Elastic Labour in Economic Development: Southeast Asia before World War II. Unpublished paper.

Hui, Neha, and Uma Kambhampati. 2020. The Political Economy of Indian Indentured Labour in the 19th Century. Economics Discussion Papers 2020–16. Department of Economics, Reading University.

Hui, Yew-Foong. 2013. “The Translocal Subject between China and Indonesia: The Case of the Pemangkat Chinese of West Kalimantan.” In Siew-Min Sai and Chang-Yau Hoon, eds, *Chinese Indonesians Reassessed: History, Religion and Belonging*, New York: Routledge, 2013, 103–120.

Jomo Kwame Sundaram, 1988. *A Question of Class: Capital, the State and Uneven Development in Malaya*, Singapore: Oxford University Press.

Knight, Roger. 2011. “Indenture, Grand Narratives and Fragmented Histories: The Dutch East Indies, c. 1880–1940.” In Marcel van der Linden, ed., *Humanitarian and Changing Labor Relations: The Long-term Consequences of the Abolition of the Slave Trade*, Leiden: Brill, 2011, 419–432.

Kort historisch overzicht van de werving voor de Bankatinwinning buiten Banka, benevens van de maatregeln in verband met die werving getroffen, bijgewerkt tot 1 juli 1928. Arsip Nasional, Jakarta, Algemene Secretarie, Grote Bundel, TZG Agenda, file no. 8436, 1–3.

Kuhn, Philip A. 2008. *Chinese among Others: Emigration in Modern Times.* Lanham: Rowman and Littlefield.

Kumar, Ashutosh. 2014. “Indian Nationalists and the End of Indentured Emigration.” NMML, Occasional Paper, History and Society New Series, no. 48.

Lal, Brij V. 1983. “Indian Indenture Historiography: A Note on Problems, Sources and Methods.” *Pacific Studies*, vol. 6, no. 2, 33–50.

Lewis, Hannah, Peter Dwyer, Stuart Hodkinson, and Louise Waite. 2015. “Hyper-Precarious Lives: Migrants, Work and Forced Labour in the Global North.” *Progress in Human Geography*, vol. 39, no. 5, 580–600.

Liem, Giok Kiauw Nio, and Patricia Tjiook-Liem. 2009. *De rechtspositie der Chinezen in Nederlands-Indië 1848–1942: Wetgevingsbeleid tussen beginsel en belang.* Leiden: Leiden University Press.

Lindblad, J. Thomas. 1999. “Coolies in Deli: Labour Conditions in Western Enterprises in East Sumatra, 1910–1938.” In Vincent J. H. Houben and J. Thomas Lindblad, eds, *Coolie Labour in Colonial Indonesia: A Study of Labour Relations in the Outer Islands, c. 1900–1940*, Wiesbaden: Harrassowitz Verlag, 1999, 43–78.

Liu, Oiyan. 2014.“Countering ‘Chinese Imperialism’: Sinophobia and Border Protection in the Dutch East Indies.” *Indonesia*, no. 97, 87–110.

Lu Wendi, Peng Jiali, and Chen Zexian, eds. 1981b. *Guanyu Dongnan Ya Huagong de siren zhuzuo* (Private individuals' writings about Huagong in Southeast Asia). In Chen Hansheng, ed., *Huagong chuguo shiliao huibian* (A compilation of edited historical materials regarding going abroad by Huagong), Beijing: Zhonghua shuju, 12 vols, vol. 5.

Lu Wendi, Peng Jiali, and Chen Zexian, eds. 1984a. *Guanyu Dongnan Ya Huagong de siren zhuzuo* (Private individuals' writings about Huagong in Southeast Asia). In Chen Hansheng, ed., *Huagong chuguo shiliao huibian* (A compilation of edited historical materials regarding going abroad by Huagong), Beijing: Zhonghua shuju, 12 vols, 1981–1985, vol. 5.

Lu Wendi, Chen Zexian, and Peng Jiali, eds. 1985a. *Zhongguo guanwen shu xuanji* (A selection of official Chinese documents). In Chen Hansheng, ed., *Huagong chuguo shiliao huibian* (A compilation of edited historical materials regarding going abroad by Huagong), Beijing: Zhonghua shuju, 12 vols, vol. 1, pt 1.

MacNair, H. F. 1924. "The Chinese in the Dutch East Indies." *The China Weekly Review*, September 20.

Manan, Tarmizi Abdul. 2019. "Legal Implication of Plantation Concessions during the Dutch Colonialism on the Contemporary Land Governance and Civil Rights." *Journal of Legal, Ethical and Regulatory Issues*, vol. 22, no. 2.

Maul, Daniel Roger. 2007. "The International Labor Organization and the Struggle against Forced Labor from 1919 to the Present." *Labor History*, vol. 48, no. 4, 477–500.

McKeown, Adam. 2001. *Chinese Migrant Networks and Cultural Change: Peru, Chicago, Hawaii, 1900-1936*. Chicago, University of Chicago Press.

McKeown, Adam. 2004. "Global Migration, 1846–1940." *Journal of World History*, vol. 15, no. 2, 155–189.

Mei Weiqiang and Zhang Guoxiong, eds. 2001. *Wuyi Huaqiao Huaren shi* ("A history of Wuyi's overseas and ethnic Chinese"). Guangzhou: Guangdong gaodeng jiaoyu chuban she.

Miles, Stephen. 2020. *Chinese Diasporas: A Social History of Global Migration*. New York: Cambridge University Press.

Mishra, Amit Kumar. 2015. "Sardars, Kanganies and Maistries: Intermediaries in the Indian Labour Diaspora During the Colonial Period." In Sigrid Wadauer, Thomas Buchner, and Alexander Mejstrik, eds, *The History of Labour Intermediation: Institutions and Finding Employment in the Nineteenth and Early Twentieth Centuries*, International Studies in Social History, vol. 26, New York: Berghahn, 368–387.

Mohapatra, Prabhu, and Rana Behal. 1991."'Tea and Money versus Human Life': The Rise and Fall of the Indenture System in the Assam Tea Plantations, 1840–1908." *Journal of Peasant Studies*, vol. 19, nos. 3–4, 142–172.

Mollema, J. C.. 1922. *De ontwikkeling van het eiland Billiton en van de Billiton-Maatschappij*. The Hague: Nijhoff.
Morton, Fred. 2005. "Female *inboekelinge* in the South African Republic, 1850–1880." *Slavery & Abolition*, vol. 26, no. 2, 199–215.
Nitisastro, Widjojo. 2006. *Population Trends in Indonesia*. Jakarta: Equinox Publishing.
Nugteren, Bastiaan. 2016. The Impossible Colonial Border: Chinese Migration and Immigration Policies in the Netherlands East Indies, 1880–1912. MA thesis, Leiden University.
Ong, Aihwa, and Donald Nonini, eds. 1997. *Ungrounded Empires: The Cultural Politics of Modern Chinese Transnationalism*. New York: Routledge.
Pan, Lynn, ed. 1998. *The Encylopedia of the Chinese Overseas*. Singapore: Archipelago Press.
Pande, Amba. 2013. "Conceptualising Indian Diaspora Diversities within a Common Identity." *Economic & Political Weekly*, December 7, 2013, vol. 48, no. 49.
Pastor, G. 1927. *De panglongs*. Weltevreden: Landsdrukkerij.
Paulus, Jozlas, compiler. 1919. *Encyclopaedie van Nederlandsch-Indië*, second edition, 2 vols. The Hague: Martinus Nijhoff.
Pelzer, Karl J. 1935. *Die Arbeiterwanderungen in Südostasien: Eine wirtschafts- und bevölkerungsgeographische Untersuchung*. Würzburg: Konrad Triltsch.
Rajasinghamsenanayake, Darini. 2017. "Precarious Citizens, Cyber-Nationalism: South-South Asia's Diasporas." *IIC Quarterly*, vol. 44, no. 2, 66–82.
Rapport betreffende Chineezen-Werving op Billiton. 1905. BrRG-33 = 16072 KIT.
Reid, Anthony. 1970. "Early Chinese Immigration into North Sumatra." In Jerome Chen and Nicholas Tarling, eds, *Studies in the Social History of China and South-East Asia: Essays in Memory of Victor Purcell, 1896–1965*, Cambridge: Cambridge University Press, 1970, 289–320.
Reid, Anthony. 1979. *The Blood of the People: Revolution and the End of Traditional Rule in Northern Sumatra*. Kuala Lumpur: Oxford University Press.
Report of Coolie Commission, Appointed to Inquire into the Condition of the Indian Immigrants in the Colony of Natal. 1872. Pietermaritzburg: Keith & Co.
Shen, Jiaying. n.d. "A Great Convergence: The Mass Killing of Chinese in the 1923 Kantō Massacre." https://doi.org/10.1080/10371397.2020.1771175.
Shih, Shu-mei. 2001. *The Lure of the Modern*. Berkeley: University of California Press.
Shimada, Ryuto. 2014. "Hinterlands and Port Cities in Southeast Asia's Economic Development in the Eighteenth Century: The Case of Tin Production and its Export Trade." In Tsukasa Mizushima, George Bryan Souza, and Dennis O. Flynn, eds, *Hinterlands and Commodities: Place, Space, Time and the*

Political Economic Development of Asia over the Long Eighteenth Century. Leiden: Brill, 2014, 197–214.

Skinner, G. William. 1963."The Chinese Minority." In Ruth McVey, ed., *Indonesia*, New Haven, CT: Yale University Southeast Asia Studies, 1963, 97–117.

Stanziani, Alessandro. 2014. *Bondage: Labor and Rights in Eurasia from the Sixteenth to the Early Twentieth Centuries*, New York: Berghahn Books.

Stanziani, Alessandro. 2018. *Labor on the Fringes of Empire: Voice, Exit and the Law*. New York: Palgrave Macmillan.

Stibbe, D. G., and C. Spat, with E. M. Uhlenbeck, eds. 1927. *Encyclopaedie van Nederlandsch-Indië*. Second edition. 8 vols. The Hague: Martinus Nijhoff, vol. 5.

Tan Chee-Beng. 2000 "Socio-cultural Diversities and Identities." In Lee Kam Hong and Tan Chee-Beng, eds, *The Chinese in Malaysia*, Shah Alam: Oxford University Press, 37–70.

Tappe, Oliver, and Ulrike Lindner. 2016. "Introduction: Global Variants of Bonded Labour." In Sabine Damir-Geilsdorf, Ulrike Lindner, Gesine Müller, Oliver Tappe, and Michael Zeuske, eds, *Bonded Labour: Global and Comparative Perspectives (18th-21st Century)*, Bielefeld: Transcript Verlag, 9–34.

Termorshuizen, Thio. 2008. "Indentured Labour in the Dutch Colonial Empire, 1800–1940." In Geert Oostindie, ed., *Dutch Colonialism, Migration and Cultural Heritage: Past and Present*, Leiden: Brill, 2008, 261–314.

Tinker, Hugh.1974. *A New System of Slavery: The Export of Indian Labour Overseas 1830–1920*. London and New York: Oxford University Press.

Van der Linden, Marcel. 2016. "Dissecting Coerced Labor." In Marcel van der Linden and Magaly Rodríguez García, eds, *On Coerced Labor: Work and Compulsion after Chattel Slavery*. Leiden: Brill, 2016, 293–332.

Varma, Nitin. 2005. "Coolie Acts and the Acting Coolies: Coolie, Planter and State in the Late Nineteenth and Early Twentieth Century Colonial Tea Plantations of Assam." *Social Scientist*, vol. 33, no. 5–6, 49–72.

Viljoen, Russel. 2005. "Indentured Labour and Khoikhoi 'Equality' before the Law in Cape Colonial Society, South Africa: The Case of Jan Paerl, c. 1796." *Itinerario*, no. 29, 54–72.

Vleming, J. L., ed. 1992 [1926]. "The Chinese Business Community in Netherlands India." In M. R. Fernando and D. Bulbeck, eds, *Chinese Economic Activity in Netherlands India: Selected Translations from the Dutch*, Singapore: Institute of Southeast Asian Studies, 1992, 90–260.

Wang Cangbai. 2013. "*Guiqiao* as Political Subjects in the Making of the People's Republic of China, 1949–1979." In Biao Xiang, Brenda S. A. Yeoh, and Mika Toyota, eds, *Return: Nationalizing Transnational Mobility in Asia*, Durham: Duke University Press, 2013, 63–82.

Wang Linqian and Wu Kunxiang, eds. 2002. *Zaoqi Huaqiao yu qiyue Huagong (mai zhuzai) ziliao* (Early materials relating to overseas Chinese and indentured Huagong [piglet trade]). Chaoshan: Chaoshan lishi wenhua yanjiu zhongxin, Shantou shi wenhua ju, Shantou shi tushu guan.

Wang Qimin. 1982. "Qiyue Huagong zhi de lishi fenqi wenti" ("The issue of the historical stages of indentured Huagong") *Fujian shida xuebao (zhenxue shehui kexue ban)*, no. 1, 95–101.

Ward, Kerry. 2009. *Networks of Empire: Forced Migration in the Dutch East India Company*. Cambridge: Cambridge University Press.

Wazar, R. M. 2004 [1956]. "Tinnen Munten van Bangka." *Erts: Maandblad der Billitonbedrijven*, October 1956, no. 10. Reprinted in Yang Tongling, Lin Zhang, Li Xinyun, Tan Enli, and Li Ensi, *Hunqian mengrao de guxiang – Bangjia dao* ("Lost in a reverie about one's native place: Bangka Island"), Beijing: Zhongguo youyi chuban gongsi, 2004, 209–211.

Williams, Michael. 1999. *Chinese Settlement in NSW: A Thematic History*. A Report for the NSW Heritage Office.

Wong Yee Tuan. 2015. *Penang Chinese Commerce in the 19th Century: The Rise and Fall of the Big Five*. Singapore: ISEAS.

Wu Fengbin. 1988. *Qiyue Huagong shi* (History of indentured Chinese labour). Nanchang: Jiangxi renmin chuban she.

Xia Shuiping and Fang Xuejia. 2004. "Meizhou keshu diqude shuike ye shulüe" ("Discussion of the shuike trade in the Meizhou Hakka region"). In Wang Weizhong, ed., *Shou jie qiaopi wenhua yanjiu hui lunwen ji* (Papers from the First Qiaopi Cultural Symposium), Shantou: n.p., 2004, 179–186.

Xia Yuanming 2008. "Meizhou keshu diqu de shuike yu qiaopi ye shulüe" ("Short Account of the Shuike in the Meizhou Hakka Region"). In Wang Weizhong, ed., *Di erjie qiaopi wenhua yantao hui lunwen xuan* ("Selection of Papers from the Second Qiaopi Culture Symposium"), N. p.: Gongyuan chuban youxian gongsi, 2008, 370–390.

Xiao Wenping. 2004."Kejia shancun de shuike, qiaopi, yu qiaoxiang shehui" ("Shuike, qiaopi, and qiaoxiang society in the Hakka mountain villages"). In Wang Weizhong, ed., *Shou jie qiaopi wenhua yanjiu hui lunwen ji* (Papers from the First Qiaopi Cultural Symposium), Shantou: n.p., 2004, 253–263.

Xu Guanxi and Wu Zikai. n.d. "Shiliao cong: Zhongguo Yue xinan dao Heshu dong Yindu: Yifen zhuzai zhi xikuang laogong shi yuan cang" (Historical Materials: From Southwestern Guangdong Province to the Dutch East Indies: A Historical Record of Labour in the Tin Mines as Seen in a Piglet Identity Card"). *Guangzhouwan Historical Research Bulletin*.

Yang Tongling, Lin Zhang, Li Xinyun, Tan Enli, and Li Ensi. 2004. *Hunqian mengrao de guxiang – Bangjia dao* ("Lost in a reverie about one's native place: Bangka Island"). Beijing: Zhongguo youyi chuban gongsi.

Yap, Melanie, and Dianne Long Man. 1996. *Colour, Confusion and Concessions: The History of the Chinese in South Africa*. Hong Kong: Hong Kong University Press.

Yen Ching-hwang. 1985. *Coolies and Mandarins: China's Protection of Overseas Chinese During the Late Ch'ing Period (1851–1911)*. Singapore: Singapore University Press.

Yong Chen. 2002. *Chinese San Francisco, 1850–1943: A Trans-Pacific Community*. Stanford: Stanford University Press.

Young, Elliot. 2015. "Chinese Coolies, Universal Rights and the Limits of Liberalism in an Age of Empire." *Past & Present*, vol. 227, no. 1, 121–149.

Yun, Lisa. 2008. *The Coolie Speaks: Chinese Indentured Laborers and African Slaves in Cuba*. Philadelphia, PA: Temple University Press.

Yuniarti, Dewi Santoso, Jasmine Amelia Ulfah, and Iman Prihandono. 2020. "Buyer's Role in Improving BHR Practices in Indonesian Mineral Mining Industry." *Advances in Economics, Business and Management Research*, vol. 130, 285–299.

Zhou, Taomo. 2019. *Migration in the Time of Revolution: China, Indonesia, and the Cold War*. Ithaca: Cornell University Press.

Zhu Jieqin. 1984. "Shijiu shiji zhongqi zai Yindunixiya de qiyue Huagong" ("Indentured Huagong in Indonesia in the mid nineteenth century"). In Chen Hansheng, ed., *Huagong chuguo shiliao huibian* (A compilation of edited historical materials regarding going abroad by Huagong), Beijing: Zhonghua shuju, 12 vols, vol. 5, 217–243.

Zhuang Guotao. 1998. "Relations with China." In Lynn Pan, ed., *The Encylopedia of the Chinese Overseas,* Singapore: Archipelago Press, 1998, 98–103.

CHAPTER 3

Indenture in Three Keys: Chinese, Indian, and Javanese

Reviewers of the studies on indentured labour that began appearing in greater numbers in the late twentieth century have criticised them on two main counts: their compartmentalism and their failure to frame their arguments in a historical context. These two criticisms are seemingly at odds but actually compatible, for a proper understanding of indenture in the round requires a comparative perspective based on the richness of what the geographer and sociologist Nicholas Entrikin called "place as context," as distinct from "place as location."[1]

Richard Allen has criticised studies of indenture for failing to develop "a more fully rounded and sophisticated understanding of [it] in all of its complexity" and for submitting to the "tyranny of the particular," not just geographic but conceptual and chronological. Unhappy with the "Atlantic centrism" of early migrant labour histories, he notes that Asian indenture rarely figured in them; while indenture rarely figured in work on Asian diasporas. He criticises scholars for neglecting indentured migrants' agency and their interaction with other groups; for neglecting the comparative study of indenture; for neglecting the links between different forms of unfree labour; and for writing studies that are ahistorical and overlook the "complex chronologies" of indenture.[2]

[1] Entrikin 1991.
[2] Allen 2017, 1 and 6.

G. Benton, *Chinese Indentured Labour in the Dutch East Indies, 1880–1942*, Palgrave Macmillan Transnational History Series,
https://doi.org/10.1007/978-3-031-05024-4_3

Indians, Javanese, and Chinese were the three main "racial" migrant groups employed as indentures in the colonial economies of Southeast Asia. Political developments in the sending places, the role played in recruitment by states, and other factors structured each group differently. In this chapter, I try to meet current criticisms of the field by asking what light studies on the Indian and Javanese labour diasporas throw on the understudied topic of Chinese indenture.

Historically, the Chinese labour diaspora was second only to the Indian in size,[3] and the two migrations happened more or less simultaneously and shared destinations.[4] The two diasporas are strikingly similar in some respects, so the case for setting Chinese indenture against its Indian counterpart makes sense, especially given the many studies on the latter. So too does the case for including Javanese migration in the comparison, to the extent that it coexisted with the Chinese labour diaspora in Sumatra.

The Diversity of Indenture

That there is no "grand narrative of indenture"[5] should by now be obvious. Indenture in the Caribbean differed from that in Latin America, and even in the Caribbean it varied from place to place.[6] As Lisa Yun comments, contrasts arise in "coolie systems" due to "demarcations of empire, economy, and local developments in emigration."[7] Indenture differed not just across national groups but within them, even in one place. These differences are sometimes neglected in general studies, which often approach the subject as just one among many manifestations of globalisation.

Even so, many features of indenture were repeated across national groups. Indentured migrants everywhere perpetuated pre-existing patterns of migration. In the Indian and Javanese cases, the manner of recruitment evolved from a system controlled by the state to one in which employers used time-expired contract workers as recruiters. In the Chinese case, the domestic state was far less active, except to the extent that it sought, in the early years, to ban migration.

[3] McKeown 2004, 156-158. See also Amrith 2015, 13; and Look Lai 2009, 28-54.
[4] This comparison draws for the South Asian case on Bates 2017.
[5] Knight 2011, 419.
[6] Look Lai 1993, xi.
[7] Yun 2008, 8-10.

Contracts were similar in all three cases, as were the punishments and abuses. South Asian labour migration was, like its Chinese equivalent, largely regional, with workers coming from a small number of places and often drawn to this or that destination by pioneers. The maintenance of home ties was a practically universal feature.

Indenture and the State

Most Indian migration was controlled from above, first by the sultanates and then by the British, whereas Chinese migration was often spontaneous and autonomous, even though the British tried to establish a recruiting system in China. Chinese society below county level remained relatively cohesive, bound together by kinship networks, local identity, and communal norms and generally free from official interference, despite state efforts after 1911 to modernise its institutions. The official presence was smaller in rural China than in rural India,[8] where local society changed greatly under the British.

The places of provenance and destinations of Indian and Javanese labour were policed by colonial armies, whereas in China Huagong recruitment was far less subject to state intervention. In India and Java, and in destination territories like British Malaya and Sumatra, professional soldiers helped maintain the colonial order.[9]

South Asians, as residents of British colonies and British subjects, were freer in theory than Chinese to move around within their destinations. In practice, however, the Chinese were more mobile, for reasons explained later. Indian migration to Malaya was at first organised by Indian shipping merchants, who advanced the passage money and directed migrants to employers, and by the East India Company. Later, the British started monitoring migration. In the 1870s, they established a monopoly on the supply of labour[10] and subsequently set up a system of contracts to ensure a steady supply of workers to their and (less commonly) other countries'

[8] Li 2005, 9-20. The author says his findings also apply to other areas of southeastern China.

[9] Bosma 2009.

[10] Amrith 2009, 556-559.

colonies.[11] The passing of the Immigration Fund Ordinance led to new ways of recruitment, including free passage, fewer debt obligations, and an end to crimping.[12]

Indians in Malaya thus "became one of the most intensively governed migrant populations in all of South-East Asia."[13] They left on British ships from British-controlled ports under increasing regulation. Although under contract and, until 1921, penal sanction, new legislation improved their position somewhat. Their imperial status gave them greater access than Chinese to various practices that allowed a small degree of participation in "the politics of empire," including an array of petitioning practices. Although these practices were generally ineffective even in the case of imperial subjects, because of the arcane workings of the system and the racial hierarchy, they were even less effective in the case of Chinese petitioners,[14] who were usually without any form of external support.

The British prided themselves on the vigilance with which they monitored Indian migration to Dutch colonies, with which were competing for a limited pool of labour. Having at one point let Indian labourers go to Surinam under Dutch rule, they suspended the project because of "alarmingly high" mortality.[15] There were similar confrontations in the 1880s, between British officials in Singapore and the Dutch in Sumatra.[16] Dutch recruiting missions to India failed when the Dutch forbade the British to station monitors in Deli.[17] (Indians in places not under British rule could claim help from the British consul, who reported on conditions and helped resolve disputes.[18])

In Malaya and the Straits Settlements, Indian wages were pegged after 1929 to the cost of living. Indians worked not just on plantations but in public works and utilities and on the railways, which widened the government role in their recruitment. Javanese workers' wages in British Malaya

[11] Mishra 2015, 372.

[12] Mongia 2018, 1-2 and 17; Rengasamey and Sunda 2012, 38-49; Rengasamey and Raja 2020, no. 1, 115–133.

[13] Amrith 2010.

[14] Huzzey and Miller 2022; Kynoch 2005.

[15] Termorshuizen 2008, 296-297.

[16] Paragraphs 21-27 of the Report of the Chinese Protectorate, Singapore and Penang, for 1881, signed by W. A. Pickering with Statement of Labour Contracts in Singapore appended, in *The Deli Coolie Question* 1881-1882.

[17] Breman 1989, 52.

[18] Hoefte 2017, 370.

were structured along lines similar to those of Indian workers, whereas Huagong wages were set by employers. These differences generally ruled out joint action by the different groups, and the authorities used "racial" antagonisms to play them off against each other.[19]

At the start of the Depression, the Immigration Fund was used to repatriate jobless Indians, more of whom returned home than Chinese. Between 1834 and 1937, 30 million Indians left India and around 24 million returned,[20] compared with 60 percent of Indians in Malaya between 1821 and 1934.[21] In the early twentieth century, Chinese returned at a lesser rate. In the first quarter, more returned than left. In some years, a balance was achieved between returners and leavers, but in crisis years (like 1931) the former outnumbered the latter.[22] In later years, most time-expired Huagong stayed in Indonesia.[23]

In the Depression, 82.1 percent of the 200,000 Indians who left Malaya did so at government expense, while only "decrepit and destitute" Chinese were repatriated free of charge. In Malaya, Chinese were more likely to be jobless and their welfare and security ranked far below that of Malays and Indians.[24] Similarly in the Caribbean, Huagong were denied the free return passage available to Indians.[25]

Between 1888 and 1931, nearly three times as many Chinese landed in Deli as left—305,000 compared with 117,800. (The figures cover only the plantations.) On average, 6,930 arrived each years while 2,670 returned to China, a far smaller proportion than of Indian returners.[26]

Ironically, in some respects the difference in treatment gave the Chinese an advantage. As a result of state monitoring, non-Chinese labour migration in Southeast Asia was less anarchic than Chinese migration, for which

[19] Kaur 2004, 40-1, 64-5, 74, 78-9, and 154-5.

[20] Davis 1951, 99.

[21] Singh 1969, 158. Others give higher figures (Thampi 2015, 189). The Indian return from Mauritius, Fiji, South Africa, the Caribbean, and South America was far smaller. Only around one third returned, a figure borne out, for the Caribbean, by Walton Look Lai (Roopnarine 2006, 308-324; Roopnarine 2010; and Look Lai 1993, 37).

[22] [Hong Kong] Administrative Reports for the Year 1931 record the collapse in emigration and the extent of the return. The shipping companies made a killing, but that did not stop them raising the ticket prices for Huagong awaiting repatriation (*Shen bao*, October 16, 1931).

[23] Zhu Jieqin 1984, 242-243.

[24] Huff 2001, 310-12.

[25] But only 30 percent of Indians took advantage of it (Look Lai 1993, 202 and 218).

[26] Pelzer 1935, 93.

there was no Indian-style supervising power. This lack of a shield could leave Chinese at risk, but it sometimes left them freer to act in their own interests and profit from the absence of control. During the Depression, when Indians were repatriated from Malaya free of charge and the Chinese were left to fend for themselves, the colonial state licensed thousands of Chinese squatters to raise chickens and vegetables, with the Chinese as a future reservoir of labour to be tapped when the time came. The licences were revoked in 1934, when many Chinese were able to side-step controls and return to work with a head-start on the Indians.[27]

Even so, huge numbers of Chinese were repatriated from Malaya and the East Indies during the Depression. In 1931, 28,637 Huagong left Penang, in batches of 1,000, and were sent back to the countryside from Hong Kong with the help of the Tung Wah charity.[28] In 1932, 60,000 Huagong left East Sumatra.[29] Between 1931 and 1933, there was a net outflow from British Malaya of 442,951 Chinese.[30]

The return was not risk-free. In Hong Kong and other ports, repatriates were subjected to extortion by corrupt officials, by members of the gangs that infested the docks, or by the crews of the small boats that ferried them ashore. Criminals posing as officials ambushed the sampans and motorboats dropping passengers off at the customs office and demanded fake landing fees.[31] In the interwar years, parts of the *qiaoxiang* were controlled by officials who preyed on men returning home, by illegal militias, and by village powerholders.

The British role in creating an Empire-wide labour diaspora distinguished Indian from other forms of indenture, particularly Chinese, in which states—Chinese or otherwise—played a far lesser role. Even so, Indian labour migrants could still use informal networks of support.[32] As for Javanese, most went to Sumatra, although more than 30,000 went to Surinam,[33] which continued to receive indentured Javanese until the late 1920s.[34] Initially, only sixty thousand Javanese went to British and other colonies, mostly under indenture (25,000 returned). Like Indians, they

[27] Rengasamey and Raja 2020, 119.

[28] [Hong Kong] Administrative Reports for the Year 1931.

[29] *Nanyang shangbao*, January 20, 1932.

[30] *Malaixiya Huaren shi xinbian*, vol. 1, 208.

[31] *Xianggang Huazi ribao*, April 25, 1930.

[32] Bates and Carter 2012, 67-92; Mahase 2021, 12-16.

[33] Hoefte 1998, 19.

[34] Stibbe and Spat 1927, at 230; Hoefte 2012, 259.

therefore remained largely within their colonisers' Empire. Later, however, greater numbers crossed into Malaya, where 300,000 lived at the start of the Depression, as the third-largest immigrant group.[35]

In the course of time, the Dutch stepped up their regulation of labour migrants to protect them from abuse and to improve their own supply of workers. In 1877, the Dutch withdrew punitive police regulations for natives (pribumi[36]) but not for "workers imported from elsewhere." Subsequent decrees were routinely applicable only to immigrants, mainly Chinese.[37]

In the early twentieth century, the old Dutch system of recruitment acquired a new framework,[38] in which the colonial authorities played a greater role in exporting Javanese. New ordinances in 1909 and 1914 called for the registering of migrants from Java, regulated aspects of their recruitment, and forbade embarkation by those without work permits.[39]

In the late nineteenth century, indigenes in the East Indies were classified as Dutch subjects or *onderdanen* (unlike the white Dutch citizens or *staatsburger*). Huagong, although China-born, were also subjects, but like all classes of Chinese, they were also foreigners. As part of the lowest class of Chinese aliens, they suffered even greater restrictions than "native" subjects.[40] In 1860, the Dutch on Bangka established a single category of "natives," erasing the distinction between Javanese and groups such as the Bangkanese.[41] This trend gathered pace after the introduction at the turn of the twentieth century of the Ethical Policy, designed to improve the position of indigenes at the expense of Chinese.[42] Commenting on the relationship between Javanese and Dutch, Anthony Reid suggested that "with the Javanese came a paternalistic involvement of the colonial government, and a less speculative spirit among the powerless contract labourers."[43] Chinese merchants and labourers complained that the courts discriminated against them in favour of local people when adjudicating

[35] Bosma 2019b, 112 and 125.

[36] On pribumi, see Indrayana 2017.

[37] Heijting 1925, 16-22.

[38] Termorshuizen 2008, 287-301.

[39] Houben 1999a, 16; Houben 1999b, 32. Changes in the legislation over time were documented in the *Staatsblad van Nederlandsch-Indië*.

[40] Mededeling no. 20, Deli Planters 1929, 6-7.

[41] Heidhues 1992, 95.

[42] Siddique and Suryadinata 1981, 668.

[43] Reid 1979, 44.

clashes of interest. This is said to have happened as a matter of course in mining areas, which were more cut off from outside scrutiny.[44]

Chinese born in the East Indies rarely enjoyed the same rights as Straits-born Chinese in Malaya,[45] even though they had intermarried with the native population to a far greater extent than Chinese in Malaya and greatly outnumbered China-born Chinese in the early 1940s (by 750,000 to 450,000)—in Malaya, most Chinese were China-born.[46] In 1920, of 900,000 Chinese in the Dutch colony, only 528 were said to be *Staatsblad-Europeanen*, i.e., "equated" (*gelijkgesteld*) to Europeans.[47] In later years, the legal position of Chinese in the East Indies came to look more like that of Europeans, but equivalence rather than equality was the main direction of reform. The Chinese were to become equal not with Europeans but with the "natives."[48]

Differences in the role played by states combined with other circumstances to put the Chinese labour diaspora at a disadvantage. Once the Chinese state began encouraging labour emigration, its endemic corruption led it to surrender control of the flow to foreign interests. Foreign consuls in China, working in theory to protect their citizens and facilitate commerce, became part of the predatory apparatus. In the Treaty Ports, foreign courts and consuls strong-armed their way to ever greater rights, winking at actions deemed illegal by the Chinese state.

Among the worst offenders were the Spanish, whose consuls acted as middlemen in the "coolie traffic" despite Spain's marginal standing in the world. Spain was notorious for the abuses committed by its consuls and by at least one Spanish minister, who benefited personally from the trade.[49]

The British were even better placed to exploit China's weaknesses. Their biggest advantage was Hong Kong, a deep-water port astride key shipping lanes and served by recruiting agencies that supplied the indenture trade. Adventurers joined in the free-for-all. Spain and other countries appointed British merchants as their vice-consuls, to serve non-British

[44] Lu Wendi et al. 1985, 454-456.

[45] Chinese born in the Netherlands East Indies were not automatically citizens, and Straits-born Chinese were British subjects but not British nationals (Suryadinata 2015, 44).

[46] British Foreign Office, FO 371, Far Eastern, 1943, China File No. 2539.

[47] "Het Vreemde Element in Ned.-Indië," *Bataviaasch Nieuwsblad*, August 24, 1926. *Staatsblad* was the publication in which *gelijkstelling* (putting on an equal footing, here of Asians with Europeans) was recorded, hence *Staatsblad-Europeanen*.

[48] Liem and Tjiook-Liem 2009, 579-581.

[49] Ginés-Blasi 2021, 1-24.

business interests while personally waxing rich. European missionaries played their part, ostensibly to mitigate the suffering, though the outcome was often far from benign.[50] British consular staff in Xiamen turned a blind eye to the exportation of Chinese labourers to Australia.[51] British consuls everywhere expedited the recruitment of indentures and thwarted attempts to ban it.[52]

The Dutch too used consuls to acquire cheap labour. A special feature of Dutch recruiting was the role played in it by pioneers of Dutch Sinology, who moonlighted from their books or consular duties to act as labour crimps. (Their activities are described in a following chapter.)

The crisis of the Chinese state put the Chinese diaspora, including the labour diaspora, at greater potential risk than migrants from other places backed by a state capable of supporting them. The latter included not only whites but non-Chinese and non-colonial "coloured races" like the Japanese. Because of its international degradation, China was less able to protect its nationals from persecutions during the "Yellow Peril" scare. "The Chinese has no government to pamper him, to run after him with the promise of little schools and nice laws," according to one Dutch reporter.[53]

For decades the Qing Dynasty had tried to stop emigration and shown no sympathy for emigrants. Theoretically, Article V of the Beijing Treaty of 1860 between Britain and China should have led to the laying aside of the prohibition on emigration. The Treaty also took the first steps towards regulating emigration for the purposes of developing colonial mining and plantations. However, the envisaged change did not begin to happen until 1879, when the Treaty midwifed a new style of Chinese diplomacy[54] marking the start of the Chinese quest for "parity with all nations" and of China's engagement with international law.[55]

China also took steps to set up permanent diplomatic representation overseas. This included consuls in countries with large Chinese populations, to protect them and extract financial benefit. In 1911, a consular convention was struck with the Netherlands that gave China the right to

[50] Lutz 2009, 133-154; Wong Tze-ken 2000.

[51] Darnell 1999, 3.

[52] Richardson 1977; Reid 1970, 311.

[53] "Oost- en West-Indie. Uit de Indische Bladen," *Haagsche Courant*, October 28, 1922.

[54] Benton 2010, 162.

[55] Suryadinata 2015, 44; Le Moli 2021.

representation in the East Indies (although like all consuls in Dutch colonies they lacked diplomatic jurisdiction). However, the convention benefited the Dutch more than the Chinese, for despite the law of *jus sanguinis* embodied in the 1909 Chinese Nationality Law, an understanding was reached that Dutch subjects (even of Chinese descent) would be recognised as such in China if they registered with the Netherlands consul.[56] In any case, the strengthening of Chinese representation overseas did not necessarily mean that the new embassies would back Chinese nationals, especially labour migrants. The neglect continued under the Republic.[57]

In Southeast Asia, Chinese born in China had Chinese nationality. Chinese born in one of the Malay States were theoretically British Protected Persons, but only a minority acquired this status before the late 1930s, partly because Nanjing claimed them as Chinese subjects. Only Chinese born in a Straits Settlement qualified as British subjects, for the Settlements were under direct British rule. A foreign-born Chinese could acquire British subjectship through naturalisation, but this rarely happened. As a result, the great majority of Chinese in Malaya had far fewer rights than Indians in Malaya and Javanese in Sumatra and could be deported.[58]

When China's wartime alliance in the late 1910s with Britain and France failed to lead to lasting changes in the treatment of Chinese labour migrants, a handful of reformists in the new Republican government established after 1911 renewed their efforts to protect overseas Chinese, who had been to the fore in supporting China's revolutions. Special bodies were set up to represent them and the plight of the Huagong was debated in parliament and with leaders of the diaspora. However, few decisions of note ensued.

As a result, Chinese overseas—especially Huagong—were in much the same boat as Jewish people, who lacked diplomatic protection as Jews and were the target of an anti-Semitism that looked a lot like Sinophobia. In

[56] Paulus 1919, vol. 1, 486; Tsai 1910.

[57] See, for example, Benton and Gomez 2008, 308.

[58] Lee Hock Guan 2013, 169-171. In Taiwan, the Japanese tried to disadvantage indentured labourers from the Chinese mainland by redefining them as foreigners and temporary migrant workers and refusing them benefits and the right to settle. However, the manoeuvre backfired. Taiwanese Chinese rejected the practice and the "temporary" migrants were assimilated into local society (Douw 2012). In 1931, 41.6 percent of Chinese in Malaya lived in Federated Malay States, 38.8 per cent in the Settlements, and 19.6 percent in Unfederated Malay States (Pelzer 1935, 75).

some places, Chinese migrants were even worse off, for they lacked Jewish people's cohesion around old communities and their phenotypical invisibility. Unlike Indians and Javanese, who migrated around a single imperial system, Huagong were scattered across several. In China, foreign recruiters copied each other's excesses, often with impunity. Only occasionally did the central authorities crack down on the more egregious predators, especially the Spanish and Italians who tried to take Huagong to Africa—but Spain and Italy were among the weakest powers and the softest targets.

The deadliest blow to Huagong in the East Indies in the early twentieth century was the steady switch in Sumatra to a Javanese workforce. Between 1905 and 1922, the number of Huagong fell from 49,664 to 27,400, while that of Javanese men rose from 27,452 to 113,640 and of Javanese women from 6,209 to 36,990.[59] By 1932, Javanese outnumbered Chinese in Sumatra by 300,000 to 170,000. Although Javanese were "seen as no less foreign by Bataks and Malays," they counted as Dutch subjects, had freedom of movement, and did not suffer the same restrictions as Chinese.[60]

But there was an upside to Chinese migration summarised by Walton Look Lai, with reference to the Caribbean. It was more complex than Indian migration, for it could happen in more ways—migrants could pay their own fare, get a ticket from a sponsor, or travel under state-supervised indenture. Having more options, Chinese were more self-directing and enterprising, and ended up in more destinations. If Indians migrated within the British Empire, Huagong went to countries with "a wide variety of political jurisdictions and widely divergent legal and labor traditions." In the Caribbean, no more than 11-12 percent of Chinese arrived under indenture. They had "much greater self-awareness" and greater "discrimination between destinations."

The downside was that China was weak and ailing. Although Huagong were in some respects freer than Indians and Javanese to branch out independently, in other ways they were often more open to interference by foreign interests,[61] and they lacked the securities, however arbitrarily enforced, to which migrants from more stable countries could in principle lay claim.

[59] For these figures, see Heijting 1925, 106.

[60] Mededeling no. 17 (1926?), *De vrije emigratie van Java. Deli planters vereeniging*, 3 and 9; *Mededeling no. 22 (1932), DPV, Een en ander over Javanenkolonies en arbeidersvetigingen ter Oostkust van Sumatra*, 6-7. It is not clear whether the figure of 170,000 refers to Huagong or to all Chinese.

[61] Look Lai 2009, 32, and Look Lai 1993, 37-8, 44-5, and 71.

Self-organisation Among Labourers

Huagong have often been portrayed as victims of class and national oppression, weakened by interconnected troubles at home and abroad. At the time and on the ground, however, they had a reputation in the colonial world for being "too demanding" and particularly hard to handle.[62] Some even saw them as an *imperium in imperio*[63] representing an incipient "Chinese imperialism." Recent scholarship on the labour corridors to the Nanyang has added to the perception of labour migrants as capable given the chance of asserting their collective interests, a characterisation perhaps best supported by the Chinese case. How can one account for the apparently greater assertiveness and self-confidence of the Chinese labour diaspora?

According to Amarjit Kaur, Indians were the preferred workforce in Southeast Asia. Huagong worked harder but cost more, and were thought to pose a social and political threat. They could only be hired in gangs and were known for their solidarity, so employers preferred more biddable recruits. Chinese and Javanese employment normally increased only when Indians were unavailable.[64]

Huagong social organisation is key to explaining the perception of Chinese workers as a threat. The high degree of Chinese self-organisation was due in part to the weakness of the imperial Chinese state and the prevalence of "free" labour that resulted from China's relative overpopulation. This tradition of self-reliance and self-organisation created tensions between Chinese labourers in the Nanyang and their colonial employers, but it also helps to explain the employers' grudging admiration of Huagong, whose hard work and collective effort set them apart from the supposedly "lazy" natives.

As for Indians overseas, various distinctions continued to undermine group solidarity. These included differences of caste (of which there were hundreds), language, and provenance. It is true that such differences melded over time into a new collective identity, said (in South Africa) to have started to form immediately Indians boarded the indenture ship.[65] According to Goolam Vahed, "the experiences of Muslims and Hindus

[62] Pelzer 1935, 94.
[63] Amrith 2010, 233.
[64] Kaur 2004, 65.
[65] Mahmud 2012, 239; Vahed 1995, 28-33.

were closely intertwined, partly a legacy of syncretic and eclectic rural Indian Islam but more importantly a consequence of the indenture experience and imperial context in Natal. Indenture bound Hindu and Muslim together, and the broad identity 'Indian' superseded all others in relations with whites and Africans."[66] However, although caste hierarchies and the caste structure were weakened by the plantation economy, especially for low-caste workers, caste prejudices and sentiments survived and regional origins continued to matter.[67]

The villages from which Javanese migrated to the Outer Islands, by contrast, had a weak sense of cohesion. They tended towards atomism and mutual indifference founded in strong, self-contained nuclear families, especially after the weakening by monetisation of mutual aid. Jan Breman has challenged the view of the "traditional" Javanese village as autonomous, self-regulating, and harmonious and believes that it was instead the product of *domeinverklaring* (territorial demarcation) done by the colonial state for the purposes of taxation.[68]

Ann Stoler notes that Javanese "contract coolies" were disencumbered by their migration of cultural ties that nurtured passivity, but she shows that they were less inclined to engage in collective action than Chinese, who in 1925 committed one third of assaults on supervisors while forming just one tenth of the work force. Javanese were more likely to rebel by slipping away to form clandestine squatter communities, much like maroons. Between one third and one half of Javanese absconded in the 1920s and 1930s, but Chinese seem to have done so less.[69] This absconding perpetuated a form of resistance found in Java, where attachment to home and land was slighter.[70]

In an essay contrasting the housing conditions of Indians, Chinese, and Javanese in British Malaya, Amarjit Kaur shows how the different ways in which they lived and were accommodated reflected differences in their culture and internal social organisation and in their relationship to colonial society and the state, and sees the Indians as the sorriest of the three groups:

[66] Vahed 1995, 222.

[67] Moore 1977, 96-107; Look Lai 1993, 254-255; Vahed 1995, 34.

[68] Breman 1996, 3-28. This approach has been criticised for ignoring resistance (see Hjorleifur Jonsson's review in *Indonesia*, no. 63, 1997, 201–204).

[69] Stoler 1985, 35, 47, 67, and 86-7. Note, however, that of 30 coolie attacks recorded in 1921 and 21 in 1922, most attackers were Javanese (Heijting 1925, 58).

[70] Breman 1996, 25.

> Whereas Indians were housed in permanent lines (compound housing) in the central section of the plantation, Chinese contract workers lived outside the plantations in their own kongsi accommodation (communal housing) or in separate huts. Javanese also lived in compound housing but they had greater opportunities for interaction with Malays due to language and religious connections. [...] The Indians were the most marginalised of workers. They resided in closed plantation societies in frontier zones and the plantation symbolised the boundary of their existence. The isolation of plantations and colonial vagrancy laws also prevented them from leaving the plantation. In any case, the Indian workers' low caste backgrounds and inability to speak either Malay or English intensified their isolation and vulnerability. They were trapped in an unending cycle of dependency and poverty on the plantation. According to one writer, the provision of housing and other amenities by planters had a built-in mechanism for social control. Labourers living in estate housing were not charged rent (which was included in the wage calculation). Consequently if they were dismissed, they faced eviction. They were thus effectively tied to the estates and the low-wage structure inherent in the plantation system.[71]

There is scant evidence of a Communist influence, directed by external agitators, on the Javanese plantation workers, whose constant moving and rotating worked against the emergence of a sense of solidarity. However, when Javanese plantation workers did engage in collective action after the turn of the twentieth century, it was as a result of intervention by political movements.[72] The campaign to abolish Indian indenture also drew on political connections and was transcontinental in nature. Movements in different parts of the British Empire created a transnational flow of information to and from India.[73]

Communists were active among Huagong, but far less so than Indonesian agitators among Indonesians, for their overwhelming focus was inevitably on the political and military struggle in China. Wang Gungwu pointed to the strict limits to what Chinese who sought to heighten political consciousness in Southeast Asia could do. They had few material resources and received none from China—on the contrary, they were expected to help finance Chinese parties. They were helpless when arrested. Their organisations were closed down and they had to seek

[71] Kaur 2013, pt 2.
[72] Stoler 1985, 53-65 and 85-6.
[73] Mahase 2021, 12-16.

sanctuary in the conservative faction in charge of urban trade and community associations in Chinatown.[74] Chinese workers were the main force in the Nanyang Federation of Labour in 1926, but the Federation was crushed after the defeat of a Communist rising in Java.[75] Only in Malaya, in the 1930s, did Huagong influenced by developments in China respond to Communist-inspired trade unions.[76] (Indians in Malaya also failed to set up workers' organisations until after the 1920s.[77])

Language and Labour Diaspora

The multilingualism associated with the underdevelopment from which labour diasporas spring has often been a major hindrance to attempts to promote communal unity among migrant workers. The linguistic segmentation of diasporic labour in Southeast Asia was used by employers to divide and rule their workers. However, the diversity of languages and identities within multi-ethnic diasporic communities could be reduced by pidginisation and translanguaging or (in Southeast Asia) by resorting to Malay.[78]

Dialect (akin, in the Chinese case, to language) was a main principle of Chinese identification and by nature divisive. Most speech groups among overseas Chinese are mutually unintelligible and an obstacle to pan-Chinese solidarity. Segmentation along dialect lines was cemented by employers' using existing employees to recruit new ones. Speech-group rivalry plagued Chinese mining districts in parts of Southeast Asia, especially in the late nineteenth century and after, when Huagong were increasingly drawn from different places.

However, dialect differences did not preclude wider identities among Huagong. A dialect, even bastardised Malay, could become a lingua franca. On Bangka, for example, non-Hakkas learned Hakka and Hakka itself creolised in the direction of Malay, so that even local Bangkanese could pick it up. This was a tiny foreshadowing of the domination of parts of Malaysia by a dialect group like Hokkien in Johore and Cantonese in Kuala Lumpur.[79] So although dialect divisions could hamper fellow-feeling, they

[74] Wang Gungwu 1970.
[75] Turnbull 1977, 143-4; McVey 1965, ch. 13.
[76] Kaur 2004, 155.
[77] Southall 1988, 141.
[78] De Bruin 1918, 34.
[79] Tan Chee-Beng 2000.

were not insurmountable. On Bangka, the consolidation of a pan-Chinese society was even promoted by the Dutch, who in 1913 set up *gemeenten* (municipalities) that performed on behalf of the whole Chinese community tasks carried out elsewhere by *huiguan*.[80]

Indian indentured labourers were also divided by language. The ancestral languages spoken overseas, including Hindi, Tamil, Telugu, and Marathi, belonged to different language families (unlike the Chinese ones), which sharpened intra-ethnic boundaries still further. However, the divisions were muted by the fact that most Indians overseas also spoke Hindi, exported versions of which ("Overseas Hindi," "Bazaar Hindustani") developed as compromise dialects.[81]

Linguistic studies on transmigrant Javanese in Sumatra are apparently lacking.[82] However, the three main dialects of Javanese are mutually intelligible, which lessened the grounds for disunity. Adrian Vickers has argued that "up until the late nineteenth century, 'Malay' was a fluid category [...] frequently combined with or used alternately with 'Javanese,'" and the two languages were not exclusive.[83] Although Malay was rarely spoken as a first language in colonial times, Low or Bazaar Malay had been a lingua franca for centuries. Javanese labourers shared not just a linguistic affinity with Malay speakers but a religion, and could mix with them. So linguistic divisions were less likely to affect Javanese. However, speakers of different forms of Chinese and of Indian dialects and languages could also communicate using compromise languages.

As a result of its speech-groups, the Chinese labour diaspora preserved primeval allegiances that were transnational in character, but these allegiances lessened when the recruitment of Chinese labour became more random. In time a new variety of Mandarin, known as Huaqiao Guoyu (Overseas Mandarin), grew up as a result of the spread of Chinese schools across Indonesia, though not among generations born before the 1940s.[84]

The Indian labour diaspora was, from a linguistic point of view, less variegated, while the Javanese diaspora also had fewer language divisions and could, through its exposure to Malay, become more easily embedded. But it is hard to say in the absence of tailored studies.

[80] Heidhues 1992, 43, 75, 155-56, and 175-176.
[81] Siegel 1988, 2-5.
[82] Kartomi 2012, 373.
[83] Tirtosudarmo 2005, 3.
[84] Hoi Ying Chen 2016, 246.

Gender and Indenture

Most Huagong were single men of prime working age. Settled urban communities of Chinese migrants and their womenfolk and descendants did not generally include indentured labourers, who saw themselves as sojourners. However, some Indian, Javanese, and Chinese women were recruited under indenture, and some married and had children.

Studies on the effect of British rule on India divide into those that praise its effects and those that say that it increased poverty and disruption, but most agree that it transformed the rural economy. Critics argue that it destroyed communal forms of ownership, increased landlessness and social stratification, destroyed clan structures that had underpinned village community, and led to economic depression and decline, attended by "novel strains."[85]

One outcome of the transformations and disruption in India was a leap in domestic and international labour migration. Although in most of colonial India the peasantry remained introverted and immobile, international migration became an unstoppable trend.[86] Jan Breman noted that although this migration seemed to be tidal and haphazard, in reality it was "prestructured by highly personalised control mechanisms that bridge the distance between home area and destination."[87] In many respects, however, it differed radically from pre-colonial migration—it was more permanent and the migrants went further.

Another important outcome was a reshaping of rural women's role. A woman's place in traditional India was in the village, observing purdah. Male migrants remained tied to the village, to which they remitted and returned in sickness or old age.[88] However, women in British India migrated far more than in the past. Family groups migrated to tea plantations and coal-mining regions, where they worked in gangs. Not all women left in family units—one third of females in the mines were single. After the turn of the century, migration by single women outstripped men's in much of India. A quarter of mill workers in Bombay and a fifth in Calcutta were female. In 1920, women made up more than one third of coal-miners.

[85] Stokes 1978, 44. See also Karmakar 2015, 277-288; and Metcalf 1979, 111–119.

[86] Look Lai 1993, 26.

[87] Breman 1985, 328–329, cited in Bates and Carter 2017, 463.

[88] Bates 2000.

On the whole, however, migration by single women was considered deviant, and women migrated less than men. Organisations like the Anti-Slavery Society condemned the skewed sex ratio on the plantations and demanded a "due proportion" of women, to end violence and promiscuity by promoting marital stability. Planters too saw women as a means to control the estates, by recreating "ethnic hearths," and to reproduce the labour force.[89] Eventually, the colonial authorities agreed to remove obstacles to a more equal sex-ratio. Female migration remained a source of controversy and laws aimed at limiting it often proved ineffective,[90] yet Indian women were for years far likelier than Chinese women to leave home to work, in India or abroad.

In British India, officials began in 1842 to promote female emigration with the aim of rendering the Indian labour diaspora more settled. The aim was that 40 percent of migrants should be women. That figure was rarely reached, and Malaya was exempted from the rule stipulating that no more than one-fifth of assisted migrants could be single males.[91] Yet far more South Asian labourers in Malaya in the colonial era lived in families than Chinese. This shaped the way in which the community developed and was one reason why Indian labourers were less trouble. Indian women comprised up to 45 percent of the Indian labour force in Malaya up to the 1940s, and more than 80 percent of the Indian agricultural labour force there. Most were married to plantation workers, with whom they shared cottages.[92]

The changes in women's role in India are important for understanding differences between Indian and Chinese labour migrants. The emigration of women weakened Indian migrants' ties to their native places. Millions returned from abroad, especially during downturns. However, a settled labour diaspora developed earlier among Indians in Malaya than among Chinese.[93] Only in the 1930s, during the Depression, did the government try to stabilise the Indian and Chinese populations, while banning further labour immigration (in 1938).

[89] Faruqee 1996, 61-76. Chatterjee (1997, 160) borrows the term "ethnic hearth" from Sidney Mintz.

[90] Sen 2004a and Sen 2004b, 32-35.

[91] Bates 2000, 10; Lee 1989, 315.

[92] Lee 1989, 321-324. Other sources give lower estimates for Indian women in agriculture in British Malaya.

[93] Guilmoto 1993, 115.

In Sumatra, female Javanese were imported in small numbers at around the turn of the century, when they comprised 10-12 percent of Javanese. Paid half the male rate and denied housing, many became prostitutes. Labourers on the estates would not reproduce unless their conditions of existence improved, so colonial officials and companies began to encourage female and family emigration. When in the 1910s and 1920s coercive policies towards Javanese began to be phased out, the emphasis switched to creating a labour reserve based on working families gathered together in settlements or agricultural colonies, formed artificially rather than naturally.[94] This policy began in 1905 with the creation of colonies in southern Sumatra and the granting to migrants of a small premium, free transportation, housing, and a patch of land.[95]

The programme got off to a slow start because of planters' resistance, but it gradually picked up. In Deli in 1913, 1,793 family members accompanied 1,410 workers, whereas in 1918, 6,265 family members accompanied 5,296 workers.[96] By 1920, the number of Javanese women leaving for the Outer Islands had begun to soar, after planters realised that Javanese males worked better when accompanied by women. In 1922, around one third (36,990) of Javanese on Sumatra's East Coast were women, compared with around one fifth (5,805) in 1906.[97] Starting in 1929, recruitment focused increasingly on couples. This coincided with a decline in Javanese unrest.[98]

Tea plantations in Sumatra, unlike rubber and tobacco plantations, which employed mainly single men, had a large female workforce all along and recruited couples, seen as more likely to foster a stable and secure environment.[99] Some Javanese migrants to Malaya took their families with them, but most left home as single men. However, after a few years, having procured a piece of land, they returned to fetch their families.[100]

Javanese men were more likely than Chinese, though less likely than Indians, to migrate with their womenfolk and to form families or reunite with their families after migration. This difference was in part a result of Dutch encouragement. According to Rosemarijn Hoefte, writing about

[94] Stoler 1985, 11 and 31-32.
[95] Oekan Soekotjo Abdoellah 1987, 184-185.
[96] Fruin 1923, 62-63.
[97] Heijting 1925, 88 and 106.
[98] Stoler 1985, 38-44 and 206.
[99] Lamb 2014, 536-537.
[100] Shamsul Bahrin 1967.

Surinam, sometimes more women than men arrived from Java between 1918 and 1940 and there were proportionately more women even than among Indian migrants, usually said to have the least distorted ratio.[101] In 1920, on Sumatra's east coast, women made up more than 35 percent of the Javanese labour force.[102] Between 1927 and 1931, many Javanese families moved spontaneously to Sumatra in search of free land and to join kin. Fewer than hoped joined sponsored settlements on the Outer Islands (a total of 189,938 went), but family migration transformed the Javanese diaspora.[103] Although family-formation was encouraged chiefly in order to help solve the labour shortage, it was also aimed at binding the workers to their companies and helping to calm a turbulent population.[104]

Some Huagong in the East Indies formed relationships with Javanese women working on the plantations, but most "coolie contract marriages" failed. In other colonies, too, Chinese set up families with women of other ethnic groups, in the absence of Chinese women,[105] ending in their estrangement from the community or the abandoning of the women.

Huagong society was overwhelmingly male, but not everywhere. In places where Huagong had lived for decades, a substantial minority lived together with local-born wives and children. In Bangka, at the end of the nineteenth century, 3,000 of 15,000 Chinese miners and their families lived in small houses with their own gardens and the wives and children helped with tin-washing.[106] On Belitung, the Dutch brought over 137 Javanese women in 1864 to "marry" Huagong.[107] As for Chinese women, only a couple of hundred a year settled, compared (in 1896) with more than three thousand Chinese arrivals overall.[108]

On the whole, few Chinese women emigrated before the late 1920s, despite efforts to lure them with false promises or with monetary incentives and free passage. Between the 1870s and the 1890s, women made up only 6-10 percent of Chinese migrants passing through Hong Kong. In 1920, there were 26,020 Chinese women in East Sumatra compared with 107,730 men. By 1930, the number of women had more than doubled,

[101] Cited in Termorshuizen 2008, 283.
[102] Kaur 2004, 93.
[103] Oekan Soekotjo Abdoellah 1987.
[104] Heijting 1925, 157.
[105] Chatterjee 1997, 161.
[106] Heinoldt 1897, 4.
[107] Heidhues 1991, 10, fn. 45.
[108] Heidhues 1992, 60.

to 57,670, as against 134,220 men. However, most of them were the wives of artisans, traders, and tandils. Almost none were labourers' wives.[109] In 1939, just 15 percent of migrants from Fujian were women, and most returned to China in times of financial difficulties. The great majority stayed at home to till the fields, keep the household intact, rear children, look after the senior generation, and perform religious rites.[110] Many women who did go overseas lived tragic lives. Of 1,385 Chinese women in San Francisco in 1877, 567 were prostitutes, 761 were concubines, and only 57 married.[111]

In the 1930s, colonial officials and some employers again went to great lengths to persuade Chinese women to emigrate. Planters in Deli provided facilities for women, but a mere 129 women and children arrived in 1915, most of them wives of tandils or laukehs (overseers), against an overall total on Sumatra's East Coast of 132,000 Chinese.[112] In the early 1920s, Chinese women who went to work in the East Indies were far likelier than men to lose their jobs during the economic malaise, when they comprised 11,000 of the 24,000 workers made redundant.[113] Fewer than 7 percent of Chinese working on the Deli estates at the start of the twentieth century were women, but by 1930 the male-female ratio had narrowed to 3:2[114] and the rest of the decade saw a brief boom in Chinese female emigration, coinciding with a clamp-down on male immigration. Between 1934 and 1938, 190,000 Chinese women left for Malaya and the proportion of Chinese female to male migrants overtook the Indian proportion, though not by much. Restrictions on entry were extended to Chinese women in 1938.[115]

A far larger proportion of Chinese than Indian women ended up in towns in Malaya. In 1931, 16 percent of Chinese women worked in domestic service and another 4 percent in personal services, proportionally eight times more than Indian women. By the 1940s, Chinese women

[109] Pelzer 1935, 94.

[110] Shen 2012, 5-37.

[111] Gong Kai 2016, 7-9; Zhenggang and Liwa 2008, 11-15.

[112] De Bruin 1918, 3 and 91. Of the 99,236 Chinese on Sumatra's East Coast, 92,646 were men. In Belitung and perhaps in other places where the labour diaspora was predominantly Chinese, tandils were also known as tai-kung (Rapport 1905, 3).

[113] Heijting 1925, 30.

[114] "Nanyang Huagong weiji ribi" ("The Huagong crisis in the Nanyang intensifies daily"), *Shen bao*, September 14, 1930.

[115] Stoler 1985, 31; Lee 1989, 316; Kaur 2004, 58.

accounted for nearly 70 percent of urban domestic servants. Many single Chinese women—building workers as well as domestic servants—formed spinster sisterhoods and shared communal quarters. In 1931, far fewer Chinese than Indian women worked in agriculture (53 and 89 percent respectively) and far more in manufacturing, commerce, and finance (8.3 and 0.9 percent respectively). This meant that fewer Chinese than Indian women joined the rural labour diaspora.

Even so, a surprising number of Chinese women in Malaya worked in tin mining, an industry that Chinese dominated. In 1901, women made up 16 percent of the Chinese workforce in mining areas, rising to 36 percent in 1931. They were either miners' wives or single women who performed overground operations for less pay and no board or lodging. Chinese women also worked on the rubber estates in Malaya, where in 1934 they formed 20 percent of the Chinese labour force, but as casual workers on temporary contracts rather than, like most men, fixed employees. A smaller number owned rubber smallholdings. Unlike the Indian women, they had not been specifically recruited to work on the plantations but were drawn from the squatter settlements.[116]

We have no clear picture of what it meant to be a woman migrant worker in the Nanyang. However, we can draw some tentative conclusions from available descriptions of migrant women in Malaya. Until the 1930s, there were more Indian women to Indian men than Chinese women to Chinese men. The migration of Indian women was relatively regular and supervised. Indian women worked mainly in agriculture alongside men, with whom they shared accommodation. Chinese women migrants in rural areas lived in squatter settlements. A large number of Chinese women lived in towns and cities, many of them in sisterhoods. These differences suggest that Indian conjugal relationships in migration were more stable and that male Huagong had less access to Chinese women than Indian labourers to Indian women.

The absence from the labour diaspora of women mattered in two ways. Male migrant communities focus on the sending places, a focus that shapes their behaviour. Chinese male migrants traditionally left their women behind to look after house and home. Migrants living as bachelors were more likely to be restless, to identify collectively, and to engage in violence.

In China, the ancestral home generally remained intact and the male migrant's womenfolk less mobile. His native place remained his emotional

[116] Lee 1989, 320-26.

and material focus, at least until the late 1920s, when Chinese women started emigrating on the same scale as Indians.

Communities with a more balanced gender ratio, like the Indians and Javanese, were more likely to orient towards the place of settlement, especially after having children. Married migrants were less likely to see themselves as sojourners, while bachelors were more likely to be marginalised and disaffected.[117]

Remittance and Letter-writing

A measure of the home-belonging of Chinese in the Nanyang was the Chinese remittance trade. This trade was linked to the transport of migrants overseas, taking migrants' children to China and old migrants back to China, and managing migrants' homeland affairs. Thousands of people were employed in remitting and couriering. Agents of the remittance houses poured into the countryside on paydays to collect money from workers and sent it back on their behalves to China, when banks and postal services were beyond the reach of most Huagong. The trade matured into a massive, stable industry, based on networks of blood, place, and dialect.[118] Chinese remittance and couriering from the Nanyang was largely conducted independently of employers or officials.

Heidhues noted the practice of remittance on Belitung, but found no evidence of it among Bangka labourers.[119] But it is inconceivable that the millions of guilders accumulated by miners stayed on Bangka while on Belitung remittance flourished, and more likely that it remained invisible to Dutch observers. Bangka was well connected and relatively close to China. More than one thousand couriers travelled between China and the island each year, and up to one thousand Chinese labourers left Bangka annually with their savings. Others (estimated at 3,000 out of a total in 1897 of 15,000 miners) had settled on Bangka and lived prosperous lives with local-born wives and children.[120]

By 1905, Huagong who had achieved *laoke* status and avoided addiction were repatriating substantial sums to China. From Belitung, between

[117] Wickramasekara 2015.

[118] For this trade, see Benton and Liu 2018.

[119] Heidhues 1991,10, and Heidhues 1992, 129. On Belitung, see also Rapport 1905, 11.

[120] Heinoldt 1897, 3-4. Bosma 2019, 127, quotes sources claiming that 78 percent of Bangka miners "returned to China penniless," and explains that the miners were squeezed dry by the truck and usury system. Heinoldt's account suggests otherwise.

800 and 1,000 Huagong returned to China annually (usually at their own expense, except in the case of invalids) taking with them a total of f200,000, on top of f75,000 remitted by *shuike* (couriers) on behalf of others who had not yet returned.[121] In 1915-1916, Huagong in Deli remitted f89,180.50.[122] In 1928, Chinese workers in Sumatra remitted f176,000, four times as much as the far more numerous Javanese.[123]

The contrast with remittance by Indians and Javanese is striking, and can be summed up in six points. (1) While Indians too remitted money and wrote home, sometimes with the help of returners,[124] much of their remittance (and the associated money-lending) was in the hands of Chettiars, a Tamil caste. Chettiars provided similar services to those provided by Chinese remittance traders—they gave credit, helped migrants settle, and booked sea passages.[125] (2) Indians apparently made greater use of professional letter-writers than Chinese. (3) In China, there were no postal services in most Huagong villages, making an independent remittance system indispensable. In India, the post office penetrated to the remotest villages, and the half-an-anna post put sending letters within many people's reach. (4) Where officials often transmitted Indian workers' letters, Chinese letters tended to be handled by remittance houses.[126] (5) Chinese wrote home more often. In British Guiana in 1882, when eighty-eight thousand Indians were employed in Demerara, the labour recruiting agency in Calcutta recorded just 702 letters home, itself a record.[127] (6) Chinese letters ended up in family archives, where many have remained intact, whereas Indian letters have not been preserved as carefully. This explains the greater attention to Chinese letters and remittances in Chinese scholarship.

So the suggestion by Hamashita Takeshi that the Chinese and Indian remittance systems were similar ignores the fact that whereas Chinese remittance happened along ties of native place, much of Indian remittance was conducted by a merchant-banking caste that stood outside the community. Moreover, the Indian correspondence was on a smaller scale.[128]

121 Rapport 1905, 8-11.

122 De Bruin 1918, 47.

123 De Kat Angelino 1931, 559.

124 Bates and Carter 2012, 86.

125 On the Chettiars, see Rudner 1994. Afghans also provided Tamil labourers with credit services, perhaps including remittance (Warner 2020).

126 Bates 2000, 142 and 144. Indian migrants also remitted through returners.

127 But the agency counted only letters that passed through it (Kumar 2015).

128 Hamashita 2015. For the scale of Chinese letters, see Benton and Liu 2018.

In the East Indies, the Planters' Association provided a remittance service as part of their campaign to recruit more Javanese, at a time when Chinese recruitment was drying up. The planters spent lavishly on remitting and writing letters for Javanese.[129] However, the Javanese sent far fewer letters and remitted far less per worker,[130] while the Chinese used remittance houses in preference to the channels provided by planters. Again, the contrast with the self-sufficient, self-contained, entrepreneurial Chinese is telling.

Explaining the Differences

Why did Huagong in Southeast Asia retain a greater distance from authority? Chinese and Indian migration to Southeast Asia began centuries before its colonisation by the West. In the Ming Dynasty (1368-1644), waves of migrants headed south as part of the so-called Huashang (or Chinese merchant) migration, which led to the establishment of settled businesses in the region. In the eighteenth century, Southeast Asia was home to thriving Chinese and Indian diasporas. However, Chinese economic influence prevailed in "the Chinese century," 1740-1840,[131] when Chinese junks swarmed over the Nanyang. This early migration set the scene for a huge transfer of Chinese population. Indian trade with the archipelago began declining in the late seventeenth century, after which British merchants dominated.[132] The East India companies largely withdrew from the China Seas trade, except for that with Guangzhou, and China's influence in Southeast Asia eclipsed India's.[133] Indian ties remained intact, but fewer Indians frequented the region.[134]

Javanese migrants had begun to spread across the archipelago centuries before the modern era, but they tended to lose their distinctiveness and

[129] *Mededelingen uitgegeven door de Deli Planters Vereeniging*, jaargang II, no. 7, 5-15, and *Mededeling*, no. 17 [1926?], *De vrije emigratie van Java der Deli Planters Vereeniging*, 11-12; Heijting 1925, 134.

[130] In 1917, 1918, and 1919, Javanese in specified enterprises sent 4,438, 4,557, and 8,118 letters containing f22,225, f15,475, and f24,677, whereas Chinese, although by then many times fewer, sent more letters (13,394, 12,084, and 9,975) and remitted more money (f115,600, f86,000, and f71,740) (Heijting 1925, 102-103).

[131] Reid 1997.

[132] Om 1998, 31-42.

[133] Blussé 1999, 113-123.

[134] Sandhu 1993, 151.

become Malay. After the founding of the Straits Settlements, Javanese gathered in them, before the introduction of Javanese labour, but their communities remained small.[135] In the nineteenth century, Chinese outnumbered indigenous traders even in Java's northern ports, and played a far greater economic role than Java's South Asian merchants.[136]

Colonial officials in Southeast Asia attributed the small proportion of Indians going from rags to riches to a lack of entrepreneurial spirit. However, Sunil Amrith believes that the closer tying of Indians in Malaya to plantations, where the design of production was more likely than in the mines to hinder mobility, meant that Indians had fewer options than Huagong other than to engage with the colonial state.

The greater social mobility of Huagong had other causes, too, including the opportunities afforded by Chinatown. Chinese could much more easily join enterprises run by members of their own dialect group.[137] Traffickers helped them escape bad employers by hiding them in safe houses, a practice that the Dutch tried unsuccessfully to forbid. Huagong were less encumbered than Indians by the colonial administration and had access to a far denser network of associations.[138] Even in the Caribbean they "showed no lasting affinity for life as plantation laborers [...] and seized the opportunity to move into occupations that gave them a fuller measure of independence and control over their own destinies." The Indians, in contrast, farmed on even after indenture.[139]

Indian trading communities have been active in Southeast Asia since antiquity, second only to the Chinese. Tamils moved back and forth across the Bay of Bengal in a constant stream, engendering transnational communities of traders and labourers. Outside Malaya, however, their presence was overshadowed by the Chinese. In the East Indies, Indian trading was insignificant compared with trading by Chinese, who numbered more than half a million in 1900 and "were as necessary to Dutch rule" as Dutch rule was to them.[140] In 1880, Chinese already owned more than one third of factories and plantations in the East Indies.[141]

[135] Lockard 1971.

[136] Claver 2014, 18-19.

[137] Amrith 2015, 15.

[138] Kaur 2004, 57.

[139] Look Lai 1993, 188-89 and 220-21.

[140] Furnivall 1939, 48

[141] Pabottingi 1991, 62. There was no Indian labour diaspora to speak of in the colony (Fokkens 1896 [1992], 71).

Few Indian diasporic settlements had much to do with labour migration. As Sunil Amrith points out, low-caste migrants "lived and worked a world away from the openness of the port cities, enclosed and isolated on plantations." Out of this immobilised community grew a new sense of diaspora, but it did not immediately take shape in institutions. Indian merchants later played some part in it, but caste differences divided them from labour migrants.

Previously established urban Chinese communities had an older and more organic tie to the labour diaspora, whose quitters and absconders could end up working for them. The free Chinese population grew steadily through the accretion of "vanished coolies."[142] After the 1870s, free Chinese, including traders and artisans, outnumbered contract migrants by six to one in Malaya.[143]

Indian migrant labourers had less contact with the urban Tamil elite partly because of the role played by officials in recruiting them. Tamil leaders in the towns had few of the institutional ties that linked Huagong with Chinatown. Not until the 1920s did Indian associations regard the labour diaspora as a target of their political project, sparking a debate that did not take off until the late 1920s. This disconnection was, in part, because the "ambivalent place of the mass of Tamil plantation labor within the political imagination of the Tamil diaspora in urban Southeast Asia proved a constant limitation on the reach of Tamil diasporic consciousness."[144]

Even remote sites of Chinese labour diaspora in the East Indies acquired a big fringe of free migrants and officials working for the Dutch, as we saw in Chap. 2. Bangka's Chinese pioneers were not just miners but included what later generations prochronistically described, in Maoist terms, as "enlightened personalities" and their descendants, who had resisted "feudal" rule under the dynasties. Chinese miners started migrating to Bangka as early as 1812, and in 1840 the Chinese community (including local-born) numbered around 10,000, of which miners made up more than half.[145]

Although the Malay-speaking Peranakan descendants of earlier waves of Chinese settlement tended to look down on the Totoks,[146] in the 1920s

[142] Breman 1989, 58.
[143] Look Lai 2009, 47.
[144] Amrith 2009, 547-548 and 560-562.
[145] Yang Tongling et al. 2004, 96-102.
[146] Paulus 1919, vol. 1, 481.

many Peranakans were beginning to identify with the nationalist cause espoused by Totoks and a greater sense of ethnic unity came about, heightened by Japan's aggression against China.[147] This was especially the case in places like Belitung and Bangka, isolated sites where Peranakans and Totoks interacted vigorously. Chinese trading communities flourished side by side with deep-rooted communities of workers. The 16,000 Huagong on Belitung in the 1920s lived close to a 10,000-strong trading community Peranakan at the top and Totok at the bottom, including former miners. By that time, the distinction between ethnic Chinese and Totok miners had blurred somewhat. The trading communities supplied labourers' daily needs and were a magnet for their runaways. The Peranakans' Chinese identity owed much to their ties to the Totoks—the traders, with whom they cooperated, and the miners, whose needs they served.[148]

Also different were the types of work that Chinese and Indians performed. Whereas Indians in Malaya worked largely on rubber plantations, many Chinese were miners.[149] Studies on miners throughout the world note their collectivism. G. D. H. Cole attributed their "intense solidarity" to their isolation, which "ministers to their own self-sufficiency and loyalty to one another."[150] Unlike plantations, mines have a permanent location, for minerals are mined where they are found.[151] Mining communities were therefore more settled than those based on plantations. Remote from the mainstream, stable, and mutually dependent in a dangerous industry, miners are more likely to be collectivists.[152]

So the largely Indian labour force on the plantations in Malaya was for several reasons more regulated and controlled than the Chinese. So were the Javanese employed on Sumatra's rubber plantations. Tobacco and rubber were grown in a long cycle of shifting cultivation.[153] Workers moved from estate to estate and their ties were not necessarily long-lived,

[147] Wang Gungwu 2018, 81-82; British Foreign Office, FO 371, Far Eastern, 1943, China File No. 2539.

[148] *Gedenkboek* 1927, pt 2, 86 and 141-2.

[149] Amrith 2015.

[150] Cole 1923, 7.

[151] Thompson 1932, 603-611.

[152] Heidhues 1992, 41, discusses mining in Bangka and Malaya in the context of the history of European mining activity.

[153] Pelzer 1957, 155, says this is the sole instance in which swidden has been practised in the plantation system, but Jackson 1969, 39, refutes this claim..

inhibiting their solidarity.[154] As miners, Chinese bonded better. In Deli, they too worked on plantations and shifted around, but usually in fixed teams that were therefore less atomised.

The Chinese Kongsi

Chinese who had left China clandestinely, despite the Qing Dynasty ban on leaving, dominated mining in the Nanyang as early as the mid eighteenth century. Indigenous rulers welcomed the traditional technologies and communal sources of finance these Chinese commanded. In the two hundred years that followed, their community underwent deep changes. Early miners set up kongsis,[155] described as "a kind of Republic" of shareholders organised in territorial administrations, which distributed earnings equally. The kongsis were speech-group based brotherhoods of related and unrelated males that held elections (often boisterous), rotated officials, pursued common goals, and had some egalitarian features. They harked back to the Confucian organisations set up in China to avoid conflict among villagers and were a bedrock of village government. The word kongsi eventually switched to the kongsi's leader, the *primus inter pares.* Initially, the kongsi arranged labour recruitment, in which for a while Dutch mining companies played no role.[156]

In time, the kongsi crumbled. At first, colonial administrators used it as a form of indirect rule, but later its powers were further curbed and it became a target for investment by outsiders and forfeited its democracy. Even in the early years, newly arrived labour migrants worked for wages rather than as shareholders, a status they acquired only after paying off their passage. Kongsi bosses held more shares than ordinary members, and some shareholders (including traders) hired others to work in their stead. When Dutch administrators took over from the original headmen, the former bosses became non-working shareholders and mine employees, and invested in importing labourers who had to work for years before becoming eligible to join a kongsi.

[154] Stoler 1985, 85.

[155] In Pinyin, gongsi. The following paragraphs on the kongsis and *hui* and on the origins of Chinese forms of indenture draw on Heidhues 1992, Ownby 1993, Heidhues 1993, and Trocki 1993.

[156] Kort historisch overzicht 1928.

This polarisation of the kongsi into classes happened at the same time as fundamental changes in the general Chinese diaspora in the East Indies: from a society of immigrants into one in which descendants of early settlers, speaking Dutch and Malay as well as a Chinese dialect and perhaps Mandarin, had grown in influence. These people used their local ties and other advantages to control the workers.

Despite this mutation, which was completed in the nineteenth century, the kongsi distinguished Chinese indenture from other forms of indenture. Indenture was generally imposed on colonised peoples by colonial powers, but Chinese indenture preceded colonisation and was rooted in a form of primitive communism. Other countries, including in Asia, also knew indenture before its colonial transformation, but it was not exported in the same way and did not create the same potential for contestation.

The old, romantic view of the kongsi as a political challenge to colonialism never had much basis in fact, and kongsi leaders exploited the rhetoric of brotherhood to increase their own power. In time, kongsi leaders came to act more and more openly as oppressors, while assuming administrative functions for the colonialisers. Kongsi shareholding became concentrated, and eventually many kongsis had just one shareholder.[157]

However, the decline of the kongsi was offset by the emergence of the *hui* or "secret societies," which used egalitarian rhetoric and served as a vehicle for dissent. Like the kongsi, most *hui* formed around speech, native-place, or surname groups, and were hierarchical as well as particularistic. Others even shed old loyalties. A. G. de Bruin observed that

> secret connections with a local goal are very common, and in those associations the [local] goal is to the fore. They are sometimes so hybrid that father and son belong to different hostile alliances and tribesmen oppose each other, so that the tribal spirit has been replaced by a spirit of association.[158]

The *hui* practised many kongsi rituals, secretly retained its symbols and paraphernalia, and staged rebellions led in some cases by ritual specialists from China. The colonial state tried to stamp them out, but they constantly resurfaced.

[157] Bosma 2019, 108-111, has a different view of the kongsis, which he sees as part of the explanation of the "resilience of the smallholder in the Outer Islands and as structures of self-governance that "operated entirely beyond the purview of the colonial state." However, this view is based on sources (chiefly, Chew 1990, 27-33) that relate to the special circumstances of Sarawak under James (Rajah) Brooke between 1841 and 1868.

[158] De Bruin 1918, 42.

Slavery and Indenture

Early scholarship on indenture, stirred by moral revulsion and influenced by Hugh Tinker's classic study, called it a "new slavery," a characterisation that came to be known as the Tinkerian paradigm. Today, scholars find a more complex relationship between chattel slavery and other forms of labour. To accept this distinction is not to deny that colonial indenture inherited many features of the system run by the slave-based plantocracy in the West Indies, including its legal sanctions and racial hierarchy.[159] However, the relationship between slavery and indenture took different forms in different contexts. Whereas it was in part direct in the Indian and Javanese cases, in the Chinese case it was indirect and incidental.

Indentureship bestowed on the master or mistress a transferable property right in the servant. It originated in thirteenth-century Europe, centuries before the birth of modern capitalism. Despite its feudal ring, it was essentially non-feudal, since it required neither homage nor fealty, was usually voluntary (at least superficially), and money and mutual need were at its crux. Even so, it grew out of fief-rent, with which it coexisted for centuries, so it was sometimes known as bastard or new feudalism.[160]

The idea of indenture and other forms of unfree labour, "the mainstay of global accumulation during the phase of emergence and consolidation of capitalism as a mode of production,"[161] was exported to the colonies from the capitalist metropole, but in many cases it displayed features of precolonial indigenous labour systems. To understand capitalism, with its culture of speculation, abuse, and acquisition of wealth without work, we are told "to start on the plantation."[162] To understand the plantation, we should first study its precedents. These included not just an "umbilical link" to African slavery[163] but its Asian setting and the pre-colonial roots in Asia of colonial structures.

Fifty years ago, Benedicte Hjejle found structural links between praedial slavery on the one hand and nineteenth-century agricultural debtor bondage and the Indian labour diaspora in Ceylon on the other, a relationship in which slave owners retained their power and where serfs (padiyals) and their descendants continued to work under old masters and were

[159] Belle 2015, 167. See also Reddock 2017 in her review of Jayawardena and Kurian 2015.
[160] Compton Reeves 1972.
[161] Mahmud 2012, 243.
[162] Desmond 2019.
[163] Vahed and Desai 2012, 197.

bound to them by loans.[164] The antecedent arrangements that shaped Indian indenture therefore included slave-like features.

Other authors agree that Indian indenture cannot be fully understood outside past slave systems. Richard Allen notes that Europeans' export of Indian slaves laid the foundations for the trade in indentured labour, while Look Lai says that slavery in South India shaped the colonial export of labour and the shipping firms that trafficked labour out of China also transported African slaves.[165] Jayawardena and Kurian show how slave-like systems were imposed on pre-existing forms of "oriental slavery."[166] Lasker concludes that "it is not difficult to show the organic relation of the indentured labor of the nineteenth century to the serf and slave labor that preceded it."[167]

The British practice of settling Indian convicts in penal colonies to build roads was another form of slavery that shaped the early history of Indian indenture. Tens of thousands of convicts were transported to Malaya to do jobs later performed by indentured labourers.[168]

Some practices in sending societies protected migrants overseas, enabling them to forge links, resolve conflicts, and establish patron-client ties.[169] The role played in recruiting Indian labourers by intermediaries went far beyond collecting them for export. It extended to acting as their spokespersons, moneylenders, and bankers, and in other social roles. The labourers' relationship with the intermediaries was a strategy for survival. The jobbers' relations with planters and officials were often conflictual, for they both facilitated and mitigated the labourers' exploitation.[170] However, patron-client relations in the Indian countryside were markedly more hierarchical than in China.[171]

Javanese had fewer collective resources on which to draw, and the settlements they built around the plantations lacked the security of Indian labourers and the strengths of Chinese. The planters' strategy pivoted

[164] Hjejle 1967. Hjejle's argument is confirmed by the registers recording the arrival of indentured Indian immigrants in Mauritius in the late 1830s, some of whom were identified explicitly as of the "slave" caste (Allen 2022, 28).

[165] Allen 2012, 6; Allen 2014, 330; Look Lai 1993, 24-25; Look Lai 1989, 124.

[166] Cited in Reddock 2017, 192-193.

[167] Lasker 1950, 210.

[168] Lal 2017, 17-18.

[169] Singh 2019, 12.

[170] Bates and Carter 2017, 468 and 473.

[171] Mishra 2015.

(says Ann Stoler) on welding "the semblance" of peasant life to the reality of labour-colonies. Many Javanese communities on the plantation periphery were squatter camps that the planters saw as a source of labour but also as a threat to order. As elsewhere in the world, the plantation poor were no "full proletariat" but retained peasant features and some self-sufficiency. Elsewhere, this led to the reconstitution of peasant communities, but less so in Sumatra. Javanese contract labour was a potential hotbed of unrest. Confrontation happened in different ways, and sometimes led to the establishment of maroon-style settlements. After 1920, the proportion of former labourers in such communities, where some lived undetected for decades, had gone up to a half. Many joined a new proletariat working for Chinese. Not until after the start of the Depression in 1929 was the associated unrest dissipated by weeding out trouble-makers and encouraging families, a strategy the planters had previously opposed. (After the war, collective actions included strikes and land seizures.)[172]

Javanese indenture was also genetically related to precolonial slavery. Slavery had a long history in Southeast Asia and lasted into the twentieth century, despite its official abolition on Java and Madura in 1860.[173] *Pandelingschap* (debt-slavery) also persisted well into the twentieth century—its abolition was still under discussion in The Hague in 1927. Indigenous slavery, having preceded indentureship, was among its matrices, in Java as in India.[174] Bosma estimates the slave population at between 701,500 and 970,500 in the early nineteenth century, most of it in the Indonesian Archipelago, and argues that servile relationships allowed the incorporation of labour into colonial commodity production throughout the region and that the spread of international market relations "imbued the entire institution of slavery."[175]

The *cultuurstelsel* (a state-sponsored forced cultivation system), introduced in 1830, had its origins in the rice deliveries that the VOC exacted from the regencies in Java, copying the local chiefs' previous role as underlings of the Javanese emperors.[176] Based supposedly on mutual agreement, it yielded one third of Dutch income in 1860. Village heads had, on pain of punishment, to deliver labourers for compulsory cultivation, and later

[172] Stoler 1985.

[173] For a narrative history of slavery and forced labour in the East Indies, see Baay 2015, chs 5-6.

[174] Reid 1983.

[175] Bosma 2019b, 55-57, 63, and 68.

[176] Palmier 1960, 206.

to secure labour for official and private colonial projects and provide corvee labour for the colonial state. This continued, well into the 1920s.[177]

Due to the government's lack of control and the population's ignorance, this system remained widely in force even after its formal abolition. A corvee system continued in parts of the Outer Islands until the war, enforced by punishments. The Europeans and their indigenous administrators later made use of the traditional *pandjar* (Dutch *bindsom*) system, a form of financial bondage whereby the holder of a bond had to work for its provider and village heads had to punish recalcitrant workers and hunt down run-aways.

In 1880, indenture in the East Indies was subjected to special regulations set out in the first colonial ordinance, analysed in the next chapter. This ordinance imposed conditions that seemed, on paper, a step forward. It required the registering of labour contracts, a three-year limit on indenture, better working conditions and methods of payment, the right to complain to officials, and a ticket home for time-expired labourers.[178] However, it preserved the penal sanctions attached to labour contracts, which led the Dutch Social Democrats to denounce it as a form of slavery. The penal sanction was retained into the 1930s, as we shall see. Even outright slavery continued until around 1930 and was probably never completely abolished. However, just as Indian sardars and kanganis sometimes acted to protect their charges against their employers, so too in the East Indies local officials sometimes tried to persuade managers to redress workers' grievances.[179]

Slavery and Indenture in China

In China, indenture lacked a direct antecedent in slavery.[180] By the eighteenth century unfree labour had given way in China to tenancy and wage labour, as a result of the labour surplus created by population growth.

[177] Tjandra 2016, 27, fn.

[178] Reid 1970, 301.

[179] Ingleson 1986, 63.

[180] Richard Allen (2022), in a book that came out after the completion of this study, reminds us that international slavery studies are characterised by a continuing "tyranny of the Atlantic," and that studies on Asian slavery mainly concern the Indonesian archipelago and colonial India, while studies on China remain sparse, weakly defined, and focused mainly on women and girls. He also asks to what extent the trade in Asian slaves influenced forms of overseas migration, including the export of indentured labour, and what role the migration not only of Indian slaves but of free Indian artisans and craftsmen to the Mascarenes between 1770 and 1810 played, questions that remain to be settled.

Extreme forms of bonding largely ceased. Even wage labour was less common than self-sufficient farming, and state-managed or tributary labour relations were rarer still.[181] Although human trafficking was not uncommon in north China, even after its abolition in 1910, it was generally confined to household bondage, unlike in India and Java, where it was both domestic and state-sponsored or praedial.[182]

Labour indenture was spread across India and Java by Westerners and their agents. In China, however, the export of indentured labour to the Nanyang preceded the "coolie traffic." It grew out of indigenous labour systems, including the kongsi. In the nineteenth century, the management of Chinese labour fell into colonial hands, but Chinese-managed indenturing was in existence as early as the eighteenth century, after the discovery of gold in Borneo.[183] The kongsi imported newcomers under debt bondage, but the recruits were eligible to join the kongsi after working off their passage. The kongsi later metamorphosed into a tool of the colonial ruling class. However, a residue of the kongsi ethos and ideology clung on in collective memory and in the *hui*, its final refuge The *hui* eased the pain of indentureship in imagination and in practice. Its survival even after the erosion of the kongsi helps explain the Chinese reputation for assertiveness and rebellion.

The development of Chinese indenture overseas was different in that it was not directly associated with a pre-existing domestic form of slavery. Instead, it was a perpetuation in new circumstances of a non-servile Chinese practice tied to complex and multi-functional institutions with deep rural roots. Although the Chinese labour diaspora in its eventual form ended up under colonial control and was therefore subject to abuses indirectly shaped by a heritage of colonial slavery, it continued to bear traces of its non-servile Chinese origins—not just the kongsi, the numpang, and the *hui* but the corridors and the networks of couriers and associations with which it had long been linked.

Short of slavery, however, other forms of unfree labour, including indenture, were common in China and looked a lot like Chinese indenture overseas. As Wai Kit Choi said of unfree labour in Shanghai between 1927

[181] Moll-Murata 2016.

[182] Chevaleyre 2013, 271; Ransmeier 2017.

[183] De Groot 1887.

and 1937, "pre-existing institutions of domination such as the state, criminal gangs, and family patriarchy mediated the capitalists' exercise of power over workers."[184] I discuss this issue further in the chapter on recruitment.[185]

Indentured Labour and Narratives of Nationhood

Asian indentured labourers rarely confronted employers and authorities openly and were more likely to resist passively.[186] The labourers' protests, noted Rosemarijn Hoefte, were "responsive and had short-range goals."[187] In at least this regard, the Chinese, Indian, and Javanese experience of indenture was much the same.

With few exceptions, Asian indentured labourers united behind collective interests only briefly or not at all. In the East Indies, the struggle against the penal sanction was waged less by its victims than by Dutch and colonial politicians, by the ILO, and even (self-interestedly) by US opponents of the "contract coolie" system, seen as inimical to US economic interests. Where conditions in Sumatra improved in the 1920s and 1930s, it was because of the actions of "progressive" employers and officials designed to ensure a dependable inflow of labour, create a stable environment, lessen labour seepage, and increase output. It was not, like welfare capitalism elsewhere, a response to pressure from trade-unions, which were banned by the colonial state.[188]

[184] Choi 2018.

[185] Some argue that the lack of references to slavery in Chinese studies on early modern China may be due to the influence of the Marxist-inflected view that only ancient Chinese society had slaves, that the Chinese nationalist preoccupation with Qing oppression overshadowed enslavement in the Ming and earlier dynasties, and that Chinese historians are currently more interested in explaining China's earlier commercial achievements than in slavery (Zurndorfer 2022, 131-132). Chevaleyre (2022, 176-177) points out that the shipping of Chinese slaves to Southeast Asia may have happened along the same routes as indentured labourers beginning in the eighteenth century, and asks to what extent the Chinese slave trade might have been intertwined in the nineteenth century with other migrant labour trades. This seems to me to be a question that it is not yet possible to answer given the current state of knowledge. However, it is important to note that most of those trafficked in late imperial China were women and children, and that Chinese enslavement, unlike enslavement in other Asian countries, was never sufficiently extensive to be economically important (Lovins 2022, 186).

[186] Adas 1986.

[187] Hoefte 1998, 35.

[188] Yacob 2007.

The exceptions mainly concerned Indian labourers mobilised by nationalist campaigners. After the petering out in the 1870s of the campaign against indenture waged by the London-based Anti-Slavery Society, the movement remained dormant until 1913, when Indian workers in South Africa went on strike. Before then, even Indian nationalists had described indenture as potentially beneficial. The strikes built on a pre-existing tradition of struggle, but the real catalyst was Gandhi's denunciation of indenture. The new attention in India to the plight of its migrant workers led in 1914 to the founding by intellectuals in India of a journal, *Indian Emigrant*, "advocating the cause of Indians abroad [...] and safeguarding their interests in the Colonies."[189] Despite appearances, however, Gandhi was generally indifferent to the labourers' fate and his eye was on the political capital he hoped to accrue. The Anti-Slavery Society has been criticised for sympathising more with the West Indies freedmen threatened by indenture than with the labourers.[190]

The end of Indian indenture resulted from an effort that transcended caste and class, created by players with distinct agendas who came together, "probably unintentionally," in a movement that started as humanitarian and then became anti-colonial. Although labourers agitated against indenture, they rarely called for an end to it, and the anti-indenture movement was driven by a mixture of nationalist indignation at the inhumanity of the system and middle-class self-interest.[191]

The next big challenge to the system of indenture came with rebellions on the Assam tea plantations in 1921-1922, which led to its dismantling. These events were also influenced by Gandhians—their launching of a campaign of civil disobedience, without which the rebellions might not have had the same outcome.[192]

Chinese historians point to a number of explosions of Huagong wrath in the East Indies, most notably the "Liu Yi war" of 1900. The latter fell far short of the Indian rebellions. Even so, the Chinese are generally portrayed as a people less subject. Even Tinker, who called indenture a "new

[189] Das 2019.

[190] Heartfield 2017, ch. 13; Desai and Vahed 2015. Kumar 2015, 38-39, notes the role played in the anti-indenture movement by Calcutta's Marwari community, to whose sources of cheap labour emigration as a threat.

[191] Mahase 2021, 12-16.

[192] Behal 2014, 290-291 and 332. However, "[t]here was no effort to connect Gandhi with the labour communities in Assam Valley tea gardens at the height of their struggle in 1921" (ibid, 309-310).

slavery," distinguished between the rebellious Chinese and the stoical, tractable Indians.

But Huagong resilience very rarely stretched to Liu Yi-style resistance. One reason was their lack in China of the backing of a state.[193] Another was the persistence among Chinese of sub-ethnic identifications. In China, too, the heterogeneity of the workforce hampered the spontaneous emergence of class solidarity. Where mass strikes did happen, they were often only possible because Chinese authorities supported or connived at them as a way of weakening the foreign capitalists.[194]

As for the Javanese, resistance was mainly confined up until the late 1910s to actions such as setting fire to canefields. After the First World War, a wave of strikes and social unrest took place, again stimulated by outside organisers, but it subsided in the 1920s.[195]

So acts of collective and strategic resistance, as opposed to individual and reactive resistance, were rare. This, said Goolam Vahed, speaking of Indian indenture but in terms applicable to Huagong, was

> because of such factors as the monopoly of armed violence by settlers, restrictions on the movement of the indentured and their freedom of association, absence of leadership, dispersal across the colony, and differences of caste, region and ethnicity among the indentured. These practical constraints made joint resistance difficult. Academics searching for heroic acts of defiance may be disappointed in not finding too many instances of these.

Rather than fight back openly, victims were more likely to practise minor arts of resistance. Some engaged in "absenteeism, insubordination, foot-dragging, legal challenges, theft, flight, malingering, feigning illness, destruction of property, and neglect of duty." Others survived as best they could, with an eye to life after release.[196] So the calendar of migrant labour in Asia was largely empty of heroic risings. At most labourers wielded weapons of the weak, including songs, jokes, stories, petitions, pilfering, minor acts of sabotage, and an occasional beating or murder.

As Jayawardena and Kurian point out,[197] in this respect Asian plantation workers differed from their Caribbean counterparts, who had a longer his-

[193] Tinker 1974, 168 and 218.
[194] Choi 2018, 107-132.
[195] Wertheim 1993, 277-281.
[196] Vahed and Desai 2012, 314-316.
[197] Jayawardena and Kurian 2015.

tory of resistance and in some cases entered the national imaginary as symbols of the anti-colonial struggle. In Cuba, this elevation included the Chinese, who played a big role across three decades (1868-1898) in Cuba's wars of liberation.[198] In Asia, however, Indian and Chinese "coolies" remained perpetual aliens, a "metonym of negation and a symbol of cultural and national lack," and both they and the Javanese represented the antithesis of a peasantry pictured as the repository of national "authenticity." Uprooted by the colonialists, they were marginalised and even persecuted by nationalists, who preferred settled farmers over transnational labourers as their emblems of nationhood.[199]

Far from being champions of their own fate, they were the "colonial being," naïve victims tricked into bondage by poverty and their assumed backwardness, poor, uneducated, and unskilled. The words used to label them often became racist slurs designed to dehumanise them.[200] The marginalisation of indentured labourers was practically worldwide—not even Marx and Engels were immune to it.[201] The term "coolie" was incorporated into all the world's languages as a badge of shame. It featured as a curse on the banners of white sinophobic labour activists and provided a title for Abraham Lincoln's "anti-coolie bill." For historians keen to find radical agency in the history of indentured labour, there are, sadly, few stories of revolt.

Chinese Migration in Comparative Perspective

In exploring the ways in which Chinese labour migration differed from other national forms, what if one widens the angle of view to include Europe? By looking at China's labour migrations in the light of Europe's "great migrations," new issues come into view that further clarify its features. European migration implies movement from one place to another with the aim of settlement, by individuals or families, ending in integration and assimilation. These aims and outcomes bore little resemblance to the actions of Chinese labour migrants. Their decision to migrate was communal rather than individual. Few aimed at personal liberation, and even fewer took their families in tow. In the early days, nearly all Chinese

[198] García Triana and Herrera 2009.
[199] Manjapra 2018, 21-22.
[200] Lamb 2014, 530-556, citing Amrith 2011, 47.
[201] Benton 2007, 6-7.

migrants were unaccompanied males who served their kin and lineage from a distance. They lived as bachelors, but their orientation was collective, their goal to save for a return in triumph.

This difference between early migrations, both domestic and international, of Chinese and Europeans is embedded in language. It was not until relatively late that the Chinese settled on a term equivalent to "migration" to describe movements of people unforced by states. The word was *yimin*, which came from an older term describing an official decision to move people (for defence or economic reasons or due to a disaster). Originally denoting enforced movement,[202] its recasting in the new sense was probably a calque on the English word "migration," free of assumptions about the reason for moving. It reached China via Meiji Japan, where it first acquired its modern meaning.[203]

However, older, value-laden terms, with implications absent from the European conceptualisation of migration, have remained enshrined in China's vocabulary of migration. Traditionally, Chinese saw the movement of people differently from Europeans, and the difference persists. *Lü*, "to stay away from home," is used of Chinese residing (even for decades) in another place in China or overseas, whence *lü Mei*, used of Chinese residing in America. Other words include *qiao*, "to sojourn away from one's native place," as in *Huaqiao*, "a Chinese (*Hua*) sojourning overseas," and *liu*, "to stay somewhere for a time," as in *liuxue*, "to study abroad." Even the indentured labourer was known not as a "labour migrant" but by other names. Some, like coolie and piglet, were pejorative, but the favoured term was, again as we have seen, *Huagong*, "Chinese labourer," on the pattern of *Huaqiao* and *Huashang* ("overseas-Chinese merchant"), again implying attachment to China and sojourn rather than settlement.[204]

The special features of Chinese migration captured in the old words were the result of many factors. They included inhibitions imposed on migrants by families and lineages; a Chinese ideology of migration, deeply rooted in Confucian thinking; existing structures of domestic migration

[202] Wang Gungwu 2000, 10 and 48-9.

[203] Daniel Trambaiolo tells me that the entry in *Nihon kokugo daijiten* supports the idea that the word in its modern meaning arose in Meiji Japan and then spread to China. Steven Harrell points out that the old word is a verb-object compound ("move people") whereas the new word is a compound noun ("moved people").

[204] Williams 2018 argues against applying the terms "immigration" and "emigration" to Chinese migrants, preferring instead the word "movement."

(with corridors running from native places to the ports and from the ports to overseas, including hostels and associations in sending ports and receiving places); anti-Chinese prejudice abroad, which reinforced clannishness; and, in the Nanyang, China's proximity, the relative openness to the world of migrants' sending places, and a tradition of temporary migration and long-distance sea travel.

Sociologists paint the engine of Chinese migration as structural forces created by globalisation and treat it as a manifestation of general socioeconomic movement. However, Yong Chen, in his study on the trans-Pacific Chinese community in San Francisco, argues that Chinese migration was driven not by blind panic and hunger but by rational decisions informed by knowledge and experience,[205] for the migrant-sending places had long been open to the sea, remote from Beijing, and among China's oldest commercial markets. China's migrants, including Huagong, who formed the great majority, were enacting a drama that for many was familiar. Trade with California had led to mixing with foreigners and knowledge of the West even among ordinary Chinese. While poverty was its main driver, the migration was rarely blind and more likely than (say) Indian migration to be self-generated rather than simply the result of "Western imperialist disruptions."[206]

For Cantonese and Fujianese, migration was embedded in collective memory and experience. Migration from Europe, not bounded earth but a mental construct, cohering tenuously around its one religion, one language family, shared mythologies, some common history, and a tradition of cultural exchange,[207] lacked the clustering of Chinese migration. Europeans migrated from many places and backgrounds to all continents, whereas most Chinese migrated from a handful of counties in adjacent provinces and stayed in Asia. Europeans entered unfamiliar realms inhabited largely by strangers, whereas Chinese landed in settings where their dealings were with fellow-provincials or, at most, Chinese from other provinces.

Until recently, most history was written along national lines, but today transnational historians of maritime Asia have identified a

[205] Yong 2000, 13-41.

[206] Look Lai 1993, 38.

[207] In other respects, Greek thought, Christianity, the Renaissance, the Enlightenment, nationalism, the industrial revolution, etc., rendered Europe more single than Monsoon Asia with its many religions, several language families, and short common history, especially in the Nanyang, where most Chinese migrants ended up.

Mediterranean-style nexus in Monsoon Asia, centred on the South China Sea. Its commonalities include dense population, rice-culture, a humid climate, and a sameness of geology, topography, flora, and fauna. Admittedly, the Mediterranean analogy has its limits. The South China Sea lacks "staging posts" like Crete or Cyprus and is wide-open to contiguous oceans, unlike the Mediterranean, which is pinched at either end. It had no Roman Empire, no Pope, no Latin. However, for centuries monsoon-governed trade routes linked the Nanyang with Guangzhou and Xiamen. The Nanyang ports were multi-lingual, multi-ethnic, and multi-religious, joined by networks of commerce and migration. Chinese merchants came to dominate trade in the region, and helped connect European markets with China. Seafaring traders congregated in the well-stocked, well-located ports, promoting cultural diversity and hybridity. Merchants linked the ports and hinterlands in a regional chain long before Westerners arrived. Cities in south China became motors of exchange, completing the maritime circle and turning the Nanyang into a Mediterranean of sorts. Despite China's on-off closure in the Ming and Qing, trade and diaspora persisted.

So travelling south from China was a less radical departure than were transoceanic migrations by Europeans. The junks were "floating hells," but the routes were ancient and endurable. Arriving in the Nanyang ended a journey through territory unfamiliar yet not alien, for the migrations grew out of a trade that had plied the Nanyang ports for centuries. Most labour migrants travelled in groups under community brokers who enabled their external interactions. They were received in the docks by compatriots and collared by the remittance shop, whose clerks noted down their addresses at home and abroad. Few Europeans spent their time before embarkation, at sea, and on landing so well cocooned.

Chinatown with its buildings and street scenes heightened the sense of familiarity. The migrants' passage through Treaty Ports had prepared them for the distinctive cityscape. Some embarked promptly in the ports, but many lived for a while in the dockside barracoons that worked as antechambers to migration. They lived among their own, for inland counties ran hostels in the towns. However, many gained a smattering of other dialects or of Pidgin English, as a linguistic preconditioning for Chinatown.

Chinatown was in part the result of a response to exclusion and preserved a world of kin and community. Chinese remained the most enclaved migrants, because of racist segregation and their own collectivism. Where Europeans joined the main economy and remigrated within hostlands,

Chinese joined the ethnic economy, adding a rice-bowl dimension to their enclavement. They conducted their relations with authorities through their leaders, appointed from above or thrown up from below, as in China, where magistrates were the bottom level of a predatory state.

Both Europeans and Chinese exported an ethos, but Chinese did not try to refashion their surroundings by it, bound as they were to China. Chinese migrants conducted their relations with other peoples in a frontier society ethnically diverse and hybridised. Their Nanyang destinations were cultural and commercial meeting places. Chinese responded differently from Europeans to geographic dislocation because of their physical and cultural closeness to home and their exclusion. If they developed political awareness, they focussed it on Chinatown and China. Some "racial" hybridisation did happen, especially in the early decades, but most migrants kept a Chinese identity. Only settled generations engaged in deep inter-ethnic exchange.

Most European migrants intended to settle. Few saw emigration as temporary. Although they began in enclaves, most dispersed, joined the mainstream, and more or less acculturated. Many came from villages threatened by dissolution and the collapse of old communities. Their families depended on them for money and to help others migrate, but the home tie frayed, especially when whole-family migration started. Domestic disharmony, individual discontents, and dislike of family authority drove the departure of many. Some returned—lots of English (mostly briefly) and 5 percent of Germans—but most stayed. From remote Australia, fewer still returned.

Chinese, whose sense of homeland belonging was usually overwhelming, repatriated in droves. Southeast Asia was nearer to China than white settlements to Europe, so getting home was easier—remittance couriers managed several round trips a year. For Europeans, the distance, the scattering, and the cost were greater. In 1850, it took fourteen weeks to sail to America and longer to Australia. Steam shortened sailing times and the sense of distance, but the passage remained daunting. New arrivals marvelled on arrival at black swans or, at a later date, futuristic cities. Chinese returning was well organised and cheap, while few Europeans could afford the fare.

Chinese migrants, including Huagong, lived life mostly in a Chinese key. Chinese emigration coincided with the height of China's crisis of sovereignty—this too focused migrants' attention homewards. Their cultural and geographic closeness to home and their marginal status abroad consolidated the homeland identification. But homeland did not yet necessarily mean nation. The racism of colonial society in Southeast Asia and of white-settler society disposed Chinese to nationalism, but Chinatown long remained a place of mixed allegiances.

These local allegiances have recently returned to prominence in China and even played a role in the rise of *qiaopi* studies, whose emergence can be understood in the context of the regionalisation of historiography as well as of politics and economics. Cantonese and Fujianese historians proud of the special character that centuries of navigation stamped on their provinces argue that venturing abroad made them outward-looking. To express this idea some have borrowed Hegel's idea of an oceanic culture, which Hegel had applied to England and America but not to China. Ocean peoples, said Hegel, are creative and radical, but the Chinese are river-based and suffer despotism. Nations like China that shun navigation do not know freedom and sink into stagnation and superstition, whereas sea peoples are creative, industrious, and without limits, like the ocean, a "free element," brave and transcendent rather than closed and conservative. *Qiaopi* historians reject Hegel's dismissal of China as "the realm of theocratic despotism" and argue that China, especially its sea-facing parts, also had an oceanic culture and must reclaim it. Even so, they insist that China's oceanic tradition was no replica of foreign models. Instead, it had Chinese characteristics, including an urge to preserve the homeland tie. In that regard, China's heroes were quite unlike Robinson Crusoe, the "British ocean hero." They fulfilled humanity's "eternal wish" to conquer nature but remained responsible to ancestors and kin. So the historians implicitly assert the superiority over other parts of China of the southeastern littoral: Fujian, separated from the hinterland until recently by geography; and Guangdong, furthest away from the stagnant culture of the landlocked heartland. Their focus on enterprise and expansion chimes with China's current efforts to establish a "new silk road," but whereas Beijing's emphasis is on the land route through Central Asia, strategists in the southeast talk about the southern "silk road on water," which included the *qiaopi* trade.

Conclusions

The main arguments of this chapter are that Chinese differed from Indian and Javanese indenture in several ways. (a) The state played a relatively small role in handling and sponsoring it, whereas Indian and Javanese labour migration was managed by colonial states representing colonial interests at the point of the migrants' departure and arrival and along the connecting corridors. (b) Slavery was a material and consequential antecedent of Indian and Javanese indenture, but not of Chinese indenture. (c) Huagong were more assertive and combative than Indian and Javanese labour migrants, as reflected in the kongsi and *hui* tradition. (d) Women, and hence families, figured much less in Huagong communities than in Indian and Javanese migrant communities, except transnationally, which in part explains Chinese migrants' greater intractability. (e) Huagong, living largely as bachelors, were more likely to stay fixated on the ancestral home, to which they were bound along stable corridors not only by Confucianism but by institutions such as the *qiaopi* trade—a trade that lacked an equally robust equivalent in the Indian and even more so in the Javanese diaspora. (f) The settled community of Chinese merchants and other urbanites in the Nanyang, though similar in many ways to its Indian counterpart, was more numerous, more deeply entrenched, served by a denser web of institutions, more resourceful, and more self-governing and played a more important role in the labour diaspora, so that Huagong could more easily slip away or plan a post-indenture future for themselves; and it had no similarly organised Javanese equivalent. (g) Huagong were more likely to work in mining, which in Southeast Asia as elsewhere had a reputation for militancy, self-reliance, and independence. (h) The Chinese labour diaspora had a longer history and a wider repertoire of institutions, including remnants of traditional Chinese village practices described by J. J. M. de Groot as "inherently republican." (i) Whereas the British and the Dutch dominated the "coolie trade" within their own empires, many countries had a hand in the Chinese trade.

In the early twentieth century, colonial governments came under pressure from nationalists in the colonies and the source-countries of indentured labour, including from the governments of India and (at a certain point) China, and from labour movements and liberal abolitionists in the imperialist countries to reform the "coolie system." To the extent that the reforms brought benefits, South Asians were the main recipients. The relatively high degree of regulation of South Asian labourers in Southeast Asia made them a test case for new kinds of intervention, especially in Malaya. In the late nineteenth century, Indian immigrants were bonded to the colonial state in Malaya, as their nominal "protector," with which they had little option but to engage. Despite the loss of autonomy, the relationship "opened up new possibilities for their emergence as political subjects—subjects who could make claims." The issue of "Indians overseas" and their suffering as a result of racism and indenture roused the anger of Indian nationalists and reformers, as well as of British campaigners. Their actions put Indian indenture at the top of the agenda of the movement to abolish indenture and helped bring about its end.[208]

There was little comparable interest in Chinese political circles in the conditions endured by Chinese labourers overseas. For most of the nineteenth century, the Qing Dynasty regarded its migrants as dangerous and even treacherous. In the fourth quarter of the nineteenth century, the Qing switched to a policy of protecting Chinese in foreign lands, although the old law prohibiting emigration remained nominally in force until 1893.[209] Chinese nationalist leaders did engage with the emigrant communities, but with a stress on China's domestic troubles. The relative weakness of the unsupported Chinese labour diaspora at the start of the twentieth century is well illustrated by an episode in the Transvaal in 1904, when plans to introduce new Chinese labour into South Africa sparked a major debate. The contractual conditions proposed to China were such that the Indian government would, it was said at the time, have rejected them.[210]

Starting in the 1910s, Chinese governments in Beijing and the provinces and later in Guangzhou and Nanjing tried to address migrant issues. However, China's efforts were thwarted by its leaders' lack of real control within the country and of diplomatic clout abroad. There was little equivalent of the British regulation of South Asia's labour diaspora.

The Chinese labour diaspora in Southeast Asia suffered because of its "foreign" status and lack of domestic backing. The Chinese came to be seen as self-governing rather than disciplined and "protected," like the Indians, and as a difficult people beyond the control of the colonial state. In 1922 a secret British memorandum stressed "the importance to the British Empire of an Indian labour force in British Malaya" to counter the threat formed by the Chinese labourers' transnational connections.[211]

Both Indian and Chinese indenture featured in the international discussion in the 1910s and 1920s on how to reform and abolish bonded labour, especially after the creation of the ILO. Crispin Bates argues that

[208] Amrith 2010, 243.
[209] Yen Ching-hwang 1985.
[210] Harris 2010.
[211] Amrith 2010, 242 and 253.

the reformers looked for inspiration to India, and that "the complex rules and regulations established to manage the system of indentured labour [...] contributed to the evolution of the concepts of workers' and human rights."[212] The Chinese contribution was far smaller. The main exception was the recruitment of hundreds of thousands of Huagong to work for the Entente Powers in the First World War, which helped to a limited extent to change attitudes to indenture.

Javanese migrant labourers occupied a place on the spectrum between the regulated Indians and the less regulated Chinese. Most remained, from start to finish, within the bounds of the empire that ruled them. Like the Indians, they were colonial subjects (though not citizens—a status reserved for Europeans and inhabitants of the much more thinly populated Netherlands West Indies[213]). This gave them advantages over the Huagong. They were more likely to live in families and freer to move around within the Indonesian Archipelago (although they remained subject to penal sanctions until 1931).[214]

In India, the dominant narrative of Pax Britannica is nowadays often challenged[215] and the emphasis has come to fall less on the stability than on the chaos that British rule engendered.[216] Broad swathes of rural society in India were thrown into turmoil in the nineteenth century and the relationship between migrant labourers and their sending places came under the same strain as in China, or even greater strain, at least until the 1930s and the war, when China's *qiaoxiang* collapsed into even greater chaos.[217]

So Huagong experienced indenture in a different way from Indian and Javanese labour migrants. However, the distinct features of Chinese indenture tended in the past to be obscured by approaches that conflated indenture with slavery or reduced it to a simple manifestation of the impact of globalisation on "peripheral" economies, thus neglecting its variety and

[212] Bates 2017, 13.

[213] Jones 2012, 31.

[214] Termorshuizen 2008, 263.

[215] Burton 2015 argues that protest and dissent was its main feature.

[216] Wilson 2016.

[217] By late 1938, an estimated 1,351,655 migrants had returned to Guangdong alone from Southeast Asia, Hong Kong, and Macao (Huang Qinlin 2012, 55-59). For Fujian, see Shen Huifen 2011.

historical specificity. This conflation and reduction has been endorsed, for political reasons, even by a minority of Chinese writers on indenture, who take a crudely ideological stance on the subject.

References

Adas, Michael. 1986. "From Footdragging to Flight: The Evasive History of Peasant Avoidance Protest in South and South-East Asia." *The Journal of Peasant Studies*, vol. 13 no. 2, 64-86.

Allen, Richard B. 2017. "Asian Indentured Labor in the 19th and Early 20th Century Colonial Plantation World." In *Oxford Research Encyclopedia of Asian History* (published online), 1 and 6.

Allen, Richard B. 2022. "Introduction: Slavery, Slave Trading, and Bonded Labor Studies in Asia." In Allen, ed., 2022, 1-32.

Allen, Richard B., ed. 2022. *Slavery and Bonded Labor in Asia, 1250–1900*. Leiden: Brill.

Amrith, Sunil S. 2009. "Tamil Diasporas across the Bay of Bengal." *The American Historical Review*, vol. 114, no. 3, 547-572.

Amrith, Sunil S. 2010. "Indians Overseas? Governing Tamil Migration to Malaya, 1870–1941." *Past & Present*, no. 208, 231–261.

Amrith, Sunil S. 2011. *Migration and Diaspora in Modern Asia*. Cambridge: Cambridge University Press.

Amrith, Sunil S. 2015. "Connecting Diaspora Histories: Indians and Chinese in Colonial Malaya." In Jayati Bhattacharya and Coonoor Kripalani, eds, *Indian and Chinese Immigrant Communities: Comparative Perspectives,* London: Anthem Press, 2015, 13-24.

Baay, Reggie. 2015. *Daar werd wat gruwelijks verricht: Slavernij in Nederlands-Indië*. Amsterdam: Athenaeum-Polak and Van Gennep.

Bates, Crispin. 2000. "Coerced and Migrant Labourers in India: The Colonial Experience." *Edinburgh Papers in South Asian Studies*, no. 13.

Bates, Crispin. 2017. "Some Thoughts on the Representation and Misrepresentation of the Colonial South Asian Labour Diaspora." *South Asian Studies*, vol. 33, no. 1, 7-22.

Bates, Crispin, and Marina Carter. 2012. "Enslaved Lives, Enslaving Labels: A New Approach to the Colonial Indian Labor Diaspora." In Sukanya Banerjee, Aims McGuinness, and Steven C. McKay, eds, *New Routes for Diaspora Studies,* Bloomington IN: Indiana University Press. 2012, 67-92.

Bates, Crispin, and Marina Carter. 2017. "Sirdars as Intermediaries in Nineteenth-century Indian Ocean Indentured Labour Migration." *Modern Asian Studies* vol. 51, no. 2, 462-484.

Behal, Rana. 2014. *One Hundred Years of Servitude: Political Economy of Tea Plantations in Colonial Assam*. New Delhi: Tulika Books.

Belle, Carl Vadivella. 2015. *Tragic Orphans: Indians in Malaysia*, Singapore: ISEAS.

Benton, Gregor. 2007. *Chinese Migrants and Internationalism: Forgotten Histories, 1917-1945*. London: Routledge.

Benton, Gregor. 2010. "China, Cuba, and the Chinese in Cuba: Emigration, International Relations, and How They Interact." In Zheng Yongnian, ed., *China and International Relations: The Chinese View and the Contribution of Wang Gungwu*, London: Routledge, 2010, 158-176.

Benton, Gregor, and Terence Gomez. 2008. *The Chinese in Britain, 1800-Present: Economy, Transnationalism, Identity*. Houndmills: Palgrave Macmillan.

Benton, Gregor, and Hong Liu. 2018. *Dear China: Emigrant Letters and Remittances, 1820–1980*. Oakland, CA: University of California Press.

Blussé, Léonard. 1999. "Chinese Century: The Eighteenth Century in the China Sea Region." *Archipel*, no. 58, 107-129.

Bosma, Ulbe. 2009. "European Colonial Soldiers in the Nineteenth Century: Their Role in White Global Migration and Patterns of Colonial Settlement." *Journal of Global History*, no. 4, 317-336.

Bosma, Ulbe. 2019. *The Making of a Periphery: How Island Southeast Asia Became a Mass Exporter of Labor*. New York: Columbia University Press.

Breman, Jan. 1985. *Of Peasants, Migrants and Paupers: Rural Labour Circulation and Capitalist Production in West India*. New Delhi: Oxford University Press.

Breman, Jan. 1989. *Taming the Coolie Beast: Plantation Society and the Colonial Order in Southeast Asia*. Delhi: Oxford University Press.

Breman, Jan. 1996. "The Village on Java and the Early Colonial State." In Mason C. Hoadley and Christer Gunnarsson, eds, *The Village Concept in the Transformation of Rural Southeast Asia: Studies from Indonesia, Malaysia and Thailand*, Richmond, Surrey: Curzon Press (Nordic Institute for Asian Studies, Studies in Asian Topics, no. 20), 1996, 3-28.

Burton, Antoinette. 2015. *The Trouble with Empire: Challenges to Modern British Imperialism*, Oxford, Oxford University Press.

Chatterjee, Sumita. 1997. Indian Women's Lives and Labor: The Indentureship Experience in Trinidad and Guyana, 1845-1917. PhD, University of Massachusetts Amherst.

Chevaleyre, Claude. 2013. "Acting as Master and Bondservant: Considerations on Status Identities and the Nature of 'Bond-Servitude' in Late Ming China." In Alessandro Stanziani, ed., *Labour, Coercion, and Economic Growth in Eurasia, 17th–20th Centuries*, Leiden: Brill, 2013, 237-272.

Chevaleyre, Claude. 2022. "Human Trafficking in Late Imperial China." In Allen, ed., 2022, 150-177.

Chew, Daniel. 1990. *Chinese Pioneers on the Sarawak Frontier, 1841-1941*. Singapore: Oxford University Press.

Choi, Wai Kit. 2018. "Making Capitalism with Gangsters: Unfree Labor in Shanghai's Cotton Mills, 1927–1937." *International Labor and Working-Class History*, vol. 94, 107-132.

Claver, Alexander. 2014. *Dutch Commerce and Chinese Merchants in Java: Colonial Relationships in Trade and Finance, 1800-1942*. Leiden: Brill.

Cole, G. D. H. 1923. *Labour in the Coal Mining Industry, 1914-21*. Oxford: Clarendon Press.

Darnell, Maxine. 1999. Responses and Reactions to the Importation of Indentured Chinese Labourers. Working Paper Series in Economic History, University of New England School of Economic Studies, no. 99-2, November.

Das, Anjan Kumar. 2019. The Health of Indian Migrant Plantation Workers: Malaya 1870-1939. Taylor's University, School of Medicine, Kuala Lumpur.

Davis, Kingsley. 1951. *The Population of India and Pakistan*. Princeton NJ: Princeton University Press.

De Bruin, A. G. 1918. *De Chineezen ter Oostkust van Sumatra*. Issued by Het Oostkust van Sumatra-Instituut. Leiden: Brill.

De Groot, Cornelis. 1887. *Herinneringen aan Blitong, Historisch, Lithologisch, Mineralogisch, Geographisch, Geologisch en Mijnbouwkundig*. The Hague: H. L. Smits.

De Kat Angelino, A. D. A. 1931. *Colonial Policy*, vol. 2, *The Dutch East Indies*. Translated by G. J. Renier. The Hague: Martinus Nijhoff.

Desai, Ashwin, and Goolam Vahed. 2015. *The South African Gandhi: Stretcher-Bearer of Empire*. Stanford: Stanford University Press.

Douw, Leo. 2012. "Mainland Chinese Migrants in Taiwan, 1895-1945: The Drawbacks of Being Legal." In Barak Kalir and Malini Sur, eds, *Transnational Flows and Permissive Polities: Ethnographies of Human Mobilities in Asia*. Amsterdam: Amsterdam University Press, 2012, 189-206.

Entrikin, J. Nicholas. 1991. *The Betweenness of Place: Towards a Geography of Modernity*. Baltimore MA: Johns Hopkins University Press.

Faruqee, Ashrufa. 1996. "Conceiving the Coolie Woman: Indentured labour, Indian women and Colonial Discourse." *South Asia Research*, vol. 16, no. 1, 61-76.

Fruin, R. 1923. "Immigratie van Java." Supplement to Deli Planters Vereeniging, Mededeling no, 14, *De Arbeidsregeling voor de Buitengewesten van Nederlandsch Indië*, Medan: Köhler, 54-76.

Furnivall, J. S. 1939. *Netherlands India: A Study of Plural Economy*. Cambridge: Cambridge University Press.

García Triana, Mauro, and Pedro Eng Herrera. 2009. *The Chinese in Cuba, 1847-Now*. Edited and translated by Gregor Benton. Lanham: Lexington Books.

Gedenkboek Billiton, 1852-1927. 1927. 2 pts. The Hague: Martinus Nijhoff.

Ginés-Blasi, Mònica. 2021. "Exploiting Chinese Labour Emigration in Treaty Ports: The Role of Spanish Consulates in the 'Coolie Trade.'" *International Review of Social History*, vol. 66, no. 1, 1-24.

Gong Kai. 2016. "Wan Qing Zhongguo nüxing chuyang de lishi kaocha" ("Historical research into female overseas migration in the late Qing"). *Kaifeng jiaoyu xueyuan xuebao*, vol. 36, no. 7, 7-9.

Guilmoto, Christophe Z. 1993. "The Tamil Migration Cycle, 1830-1950." *Economic and Political Weekly*, January 16-23, 111-120.

Hamashita Takeshi. 2015. "Comparison of Home Remittance System between India and Chinese Migrants in Southeast Asia: Nineteenth and Twentieth Centuries." In Jayati Bhattacharya and Coonoor Kripalani, eds, *Indian and Chinese Immigrant Communities: Comparative Perspectives*, London: Anthem Press, 2015, 43-54.

Harris, Karen L 2010. "Sugar and Gold: Indentured Indian and Chinese Labour in South Africa." *Journal of Social Sciences*, vol. 25, nos. 1-3, 147-158.

Heartfield, James. 2017. *The British and Foreign Anti-Slavery Society, 1838–1956: A History*. Oxford: Oxford University Press.

Heidhues, Mary Somers. 1991. "Company Island: A Note on the History of Belitung." *Indonesia*, no. 51, 1-20.

Heidhues, Mary Somers. 1992. *Bangka Tin and Mentok Pepper: Chinese Settlement on an Indonesian Island*. Pasir Panjang : Institute of Southeast Asian Studies.

Heidhues, Mary Somers. 1993."Chinese Organization in West Borneo and Bangka: Kongsi and Hui." In David Ownby and Mary Somers Heidhues, eds. *"Secret Societies" Reconsidered: Perspectives on the Social History of Modern South China and Southeast Asia*. Armonk, NY: M. E. Sharpe, 1993, 68-88.

Heijting, H. G. 1925. *De koelie-wetgeving*. The Hague: Van Stockhum.

Heinoldt, C. 1897. *Emigratie van Chineezen naar Banka*. N. p.: n. p.

Hoefte, Rosemarijn. 1998. "A Passage to Suriname? The Migration of Modes of Resistance by Asian Contract Laborers." *International Labor and Working-Class History*, vol. 54, 19-39.

Hoefte, Rosemarijn. 2012. "Plantations and Labour in the Caribbean in the Long Nineteenth Century." *International Review of Social History*, vol. 57, 257-268.

Hoefte, Rosemarijn. 2017. "Indentured Labor." In Karin Hofmeester and Marcel van der Linden, eds, *Handbook Global History of Work*, Berlin: De Gruyter, 363-376.

Hoi Ying Chen, Katherine. 2016. "The Transnational Journey of an Indonesian Chinese Couple in Hong Kong: The Story of One Family, Three Places, and Multiple Languages." In Li Wei, ed., *Multilingualism in the Chinese Diaspora Worldwide: Transnational Connections and Local Social Realities*, London: Routledge, 237-254.

Houben, Vincent J. H. 1999a. "Introduction: The Coolie System in Colonial Indonesia." In Vincent J. H. Houben and J. Thomas Lindblad, eds, *Coolie Labour in Colonial Indonesia: A Study of Labour Relations in the Outer Islands, c. 1900–1940*, Wiesbaden: Harrassowitz Verlag, 1999, 1-24.

Houben, Vincent J. H. 1999b. "Before Departure: Coolie Labour Recruitment in Java, 1900-1942." In Vincent J. H. Houben and J. Thomas Lindblad, eds, *Coolie Labour in Colonial Indonesia: A Study of Labour Relations in the Outer Islands, c. 1900–1940*, Wiesbaden: Harrassowitz Verlag, 1999, 25-42.

Huang Qinlin 2012. "Guomin zhengfu shiqi Guangdong de liangci nanqiao jiuji huodong" ("Two movements to relieve the suffering of migrants in Guangdong under the Republican Government"). *Wuyi daxue xuebao (shehui kexue ban)*, vol. 14, no. 1, 55-59.

Huff, W. G. 2001. "Entitlements, Destitution, and Emigration in the 1930s Singapore Great Depression." *The Economic History Review*, vol. 54, no. 2, 290-323.

Huzzey, Richard, and Henry Miller. 2022. "Colonial Petitions, Colonial Petitioners, and the Imperial Parliament, c. 1780-1918." *Journal of British Studies* http://dro.dur.ac.uk/34092/

Indrayana, Denny. 2017. "*Pribumi*: Making Sense of a Troubled Term." *Indonesia at Melbourne*, October 24.

Ingleson, John. 1986. *In Search of Justice: Workers and Unions in Colonial Java, 1908-1926*. Singapore: Oxford University Press.

Jayawardena, Kumari, and Rachel Kurian. 2015. *Class, Patriarchy and Ethnicity on Sri Lankan Plantations: Two Centuries of Power and Protest*. Hyderabad: Orient Black Swan.

Jones, Guno. 2012. "Dutch Politicians, the Dutch Nation and the Dynamics of Postcolonial Citizenship." In Ulbe Bosma, ed., *Post-Colonial Immigrants and Identity Formations in the Netherlands,* Amsterdam: Amsterdam University Press, 2012, 27-48.

Karmakar, Krishna G. 2015. "Colonial Rule and Its Effects on India's Rural Economy." *Journal of South Asian Studies*, vol. 3, no. 3, 277-288.

Kartomi, Margaret J. 2012. *Musical Journeys in Sumatra*. Baltimore: University of Illinois Press.

Kaur, Amarjit. 2004. *Wage Labour in Southeast Asia since 1840: Globalisation, the International Division of Labour and Labour Transformations*. Houndsmill: Palgrave Macmillan.

Kaur, Amarjit. 2013. "Indian Migrant Workers in Malaysia." *New Mandala*, 2 pts, February 20-21.

Knight, Roger. 2011. "Indenture, Grand Narratives and Fragmented Histories: The Dutch East Indies, c. 1880-1940." In Marcel van der Linden, ed., *Humanitarian and Changing Labor Relations: The Long-term Consequences of the Abolition of the Slave Trade*, Leiden: Brill, 2011, 419-432.

Kort historisch overzicht van de werving voor de Bankatinwinning buiten Banka, benevens van de maatregeln in verband met die werving getroffen, bijgewerkt tot 1 juli 1928. National Archive, Jakarta, Algemene Secretarie, Grote Bundel, TZG Agenda, file no. 8436, 1-3.

Kumar, Ashutosh. 2015. "Songs of Abolition: Anti Indentured Campaign in Early Twentieth Century India." In Pratap Kumar, ed., *Indian Diaspora: Socio-Cultural and Religious Worlds*, Leiden: Brill, 2015, 38-51.

Kynoch, Gary. 2005. "'Your Petitioners are in Mortal Terror': The Violent World of Chinese Mineworkers in South Africa, 1904–1910," *Journal of Southern African Studies*, vol. 31, no. 3, 531-546.

Lal, Vinay. 2017. "Indian Servitude in the British Empire." In Radha Sarna Hegde and Ajaya Kumar Sahoo, eds, *Routledge Handbook of the Indian Diaspora*, Abingdon: Routledge, 17-27.

Lamb, Nicole. 2014. "A Time of Normalcy: Javanese 'Coolies' Remember the Colonial Estate." *Bijdragen tot de Taal-*, Land- en Volkenkunde, no. 170, 530–556.

Lasker, Bruno. 1950. *Human Bondage in Southeast Asia*. Chapel Hill: University of North Carolina Press.

Le Moli, Ginevra. 2021. "'Parity with All Nations': The 'Coolie' Trade and the Quest for Recognition by China and Japan." *Leiden Journal of International Law*, 1-19. doi:10.1017/S092215652100042X. Published August 19.

Lee Hock Guan. 2013. "Shades of Citizenship: Betwixt the Civic and the Ethnic." In Daljit Singh, ed., *Southeast Asian Affairs 2013*, Singapore: ISEAS, 2013, 168-190.

Lee, Sharon M. 1989. "Female Immigrants and Labor in Colonial Malaya: 1860-1947." *The International Migration Review*, vol. 23, no. 2, 309-331.

Li, Huaiyin. 2005. *Village Governance in North China: Huailu County, 1875-1936*. Stanford CA: Stanford University Press.

Liem, Giok Kiauw Nio, and Patricia Tjiook-Liem. 2009. *De rechtspositie der Chinezen in Nederlands-Indië 1848-1942: Wetgevingsbeleid tussen beginsel en belang*. Leiden: Leiden University Press.

Liu Zhenggang and Wang Liwa. 2008. "Wan Qing Huaren nüxing bei youguai chuyang qianxi" ("Preliminary research on Chinese women abducted overseas in the late Qing"). *Wuyi daxue xuebao (shehui kexue ban)*, vol. 10, no. 4, 11-15.

Lockard, Craig A. 1971. "The Javanese as Emigrant: Observations on the Development of Javanese Settlements Overseas." *Indonesia*, no. 11, 41-62.

Look Lai, Walton. 1993. *Indentured Labor, Caribbean Sugar: Chinese and. Indian Migrants to the British West Indies, 1838-1918*. Introduced by Sidney W. Mintz. Baltimore: The Johns Hopkins University Press.

Look Lai, Walton. 2009. "Asian Diasporas and Tropical Migration in the Age of Empire: A Comparative Overview." *Journal of Chinese Overseas*, no. 5, 28-54.

Lovins, Christopher. 2022. "Korea: A Slave Society." In Allen, ed., 2022, 178-200.

Lu Wendi, Chen Zexian, and Peng Jiali, eds. 1985. *Zhongguo guanwen shu xuanji* (A selection of official Chinese documents). In Chen Hansheng, ed., *Huagong chuguo shiliao huibian* (A compilation of edited historical materials regarding going abroad by Huagong), Beijing: Zhonghua shuju, 12 vols, 1981-1985, vol. 1, pt 1.

Lutz, Jessie G. 2009. "Chinese Emigrants, Indentured Workers, and Christianity in the West Indies, British Guiana and Hawaii." *Caribbean Studies*, vol. 37, no. 2, 133-154.

Mahase, Radica. 2021. *Why Should We Be Called 'Coolies'? The End of Indian Indentured Labour*. Abingdon: Routledge.

Mahmud, Tayyab. 2012. Cheaper than a Slave: Indentured Labor, Colonialism and Capitalism. Seattle University School of Law Legal Paper Series # 12-34.

Manjapra, Kris. 2018. "Asian Plantation Histories at the Frontiers of Nation and Globalization." *Modern Asian Studies*, vol. 52, no. 6.

McKeown, Adam. 2004. "Global Migration, 1846-1940." *Journal of World History*, vol. 15, no. 2, 155-189.

McVey, Ruth T. 1965. *The Rise of Indonesian Communism*. Ithaca: Cornell University Press.

Metcalf, Thomas R. 1979. "Rural Society and British Rule in Nineteenth Century India." *The Journal of Asian Studies*, vol. 39, no. 1, 111–119.

Mishra, Amit Kumar. 2015. "Sardars, Kanganies and Maistries: Intermediaries in the Indian Labour Diaspora During the Colonial Period." In Sigrid Wadauer, Thomas Buchner, and Alexander Mejstrik, eds, *The History of Labour Intermediation: Institutions and Finding Employment in the Nineteenth and Early Twentieth Centuries*, International Studies in Social History, vol. 26, New York: Berghahn, 368-387.

Moll-Murata, Christine. 2016. "Tributary Labour Relations in China During the Ming-Qing Transition (Seventeenth to Eighteenth Centuries)." *International Review of Social History*, 61 (Special Issue S24, *Conquerors, Employers and Arbiters: States and Shifts in Labour Relations, 1500–2000*), 27-48.

Mongia, Radhika. 2018. *Indian Migration and Empire: A Colonial Genealogy of the Modern State*. Durham: Duke University Press.

Moore, Brian L. 1977. "The Retention of Caste Notions among the Indian Immigrants in British Guiana during the Nineteenth Century." *Comparative Studies in Society and History*, vol. 19, no. 1, 96-107.

Oekan Soekotjo Abdoellah. 1987. Transmigration Policies in Indonesia: Government Aims and Popular Response. https://doi.org/10.1111/j.2050-411X.1987.tb00501.x

Om, Prakasch. 1998. "The Trading World of India and Southeast Asia in the Early Modern Period." *Archipel*, vol. 56, *L'horizon nousantarien. Mélanges en hommage à Denys Lombard*, vol. 1, 31-42.

Ownby, David. 1993."Introduction: Secret Societies Reconsidered." In David Ownby and Mary Somers Heidhues, eds, *"Secret Societies" Reconsidered: Perspectives on the Social History of Modern South China and Southeast Asia*, Armonk, NY: M. E. Sharpe, 1993, 3-33.

Pabottingi, Mochtar. 1991. Nationalism and Egalitarianism in Indonesia, 1908-1980. PhD, University of Hawaii.

Palmier, Leslie H. 1960. "The Javanese Nobility under the Dutch." *Comparative Studies in Society and History*, vol. 2, no. 2, 197-227.

Paulus, Jozlas, compiler. 1919. *Encyclopaedie van Nederlandsch-Indië*, second edition, 2 vols. The Hague: Martinus Nijhoff.

Pelzer, Karl J. 1935. *Die Arbeiterwanderungen in Südostasien: Eine wirtschafts- und bevölkerungsgeographische Untersuchung*. Würzburg: Konrad Triltsch.

Pelzer, Karl J. 1957. "The Agrarian Conflict in East Sumatra." *Pacific Affairs*, vol. 30, no. 2, 151-159.

Ransmeier, Johanna S. 2017. *Sold People: Traffickers and Family Life in North China*. Cambridge MA: Harvard University Press.

Rapport betreffende Chineezen-Werving op Billiton. 1905. BrRG-33 = 16072 KIT.

Reddock, Rhoda. 2017. "South Asian Plantation Histories and their Enduring Legacies: Indian and Atlantic Ocean Connections." *Development and Change*, vol. 48, no. 1, 189–200.

Reid, Anthony. 1970. "Early Chinese Immigration into North Sumatra." In Jerome Chen and Nicholas Tarling, eds, *Studies in the Social History of China and South-East Asia: Essays in Memory of Victor Purcell, 1896-1965*, Cambridge: Cambridge University Press, 1970, 289-320.

Reid, Anthony. 1979. *The Blood of the People: Revolution and the End of Traditional Rule in Northern Sumatra*. Kuala Lumpur: Oxford University Press.

Reid, Anthony. 1983. "Introduction: Slavery and Bondage in Southeast Asian History." In Anthony Reid, ed., *Slavery, Bondage and Dependency in Southeast Asia*, St Lucia, Brisbane: University of Queensland Press, 1-43.

Reid, Anthony. 1997. "Introduction." In Anthony Reid, ed., *The Last Stand of Asian Autonomies: Responses to Modernity in the Diverse States of Southeast Asia and Korea, 1750–1900*, New York: St. Martin's, 1997, 1–25.

Rengasamey, Pushpavalli A., and Sivachandralingam Sunda. 2012. "Peranan dan Perkembangan Tabung Imigrasi Tamil di Tanah Melayu, 1907-1938" ("The Role and Development of the Tamil Immigration Fund in Malaya, 1907-1938"). *Sarjana*, vol. 27, no. 2, December, 38-49.

Rengasamey, Pushpavalli A., and Sivachandralingam Sundara Raja. 2020. "A Critique on the South Indian Labour Fund and the Malaysian Indian Plantation Workers." *Kemanusiaan*, vol. 27, no. 1, 115–133.

Richardson, Peter. 1977. "The Recruiting of Chinese Indentured Labour for the South African Gold-Mines, 1903-1908." *Journal of African History*, vol. 18, no. 1, 85-108.

Roopnarine, Lomarsh. 2006. "The Return of East Indian Indentured Servants from the Caribbean to India, 1838-1920." *Journal of Caribbean History*, vol. 40, no. 2, 308-324.

Roopnarine, Lomarsh. 2010. "The Indian Sea Voyage between India and the Caribbean during the Second Half of the Nineteenth Century." *Journal of Caribbean History*, vol. 44, no. 1, 48-74.

Rudner, David West. 1994. *Caste and Capitalism in Colonial India: The Nattukottai Chettiars*. Berkeley: University of California Press.

Sandhu, Kernial Singh. 1993. "The Coming of the Indians to Malaysia." In K. S. Sandhu and A. Mani, eds, *Indian Communities in Southeast Asia*, Singapore: ISEAS, 1993, 151-89.

Sen, Samita. 2004a. "'Without His Consent?': Marriage and Women's Migration in Colonial India." *International Labor and Working Class History*, vol. 65, 77-104.

Sen, Samita. 2004b. *Women and Labour in Late Colonial India: The Bengal Jute Industry*. Cambridge University Press.

Shamsul Bahrin, Tunku. 1967. "The Pattern of Indonesian Migration and Settlement in Malaya." *Asian Studies*, vol. 5, no. 2, 233-257.

Shen Huifen. 2011. "Gudi qiucun: Taiping Yang zhanzheng shiqi Fujian de fanxiang nanqiao" ("Seeking refuge in one's native place: Refugee migrants who returned to the countryside in Fujian during the Pacific War"). *Shijie minzu*, no. 6 (2011), 59-68.

Shen Huifen. 2012. *China's Left -Behind Wives: Families of Migrants from Fujian to Southeast Asia, 1930s–1950s*. Singapore: National University of Singapore Press.

Siddique, Sharon, and Leo Suryadinata. 1981. "Bumiputra and Pribumi: Economic Nationalism (Indiginism) in Malaysia and Indonesia." *Pacific Affairs*, vol. 54, no. 4, 662-687.

Siegel, Jeff. 1988. "Introduction." In Richard Keith Barz and Jeff Siegel, eds. *Language Transplanted: The Development of Overseas Hindi*. Wiesbaden: Otto Harrassowitz, 1-23.

Singh, Sandhu Kernial. 1969. *Indians in Malaya: Some Aspects of Their Immigration and Settlement (1786-1957)*. Cambridge: Cambridge University Press.

Singh, Sherry-Ann. 2019. "Indian Indentured Laborers in the Caribbean." In Steven Ratuva, ed., *The Palgrave Handbook of Ethnicity*, Singapore: Palgrave Macmillan, 1-17.

Southall, Roger. 1988. *Labour and Unions in Asia and Africa: Contemporary Issues*. London: Palgrave Macmillan.

Stibbe, D. G., and C. Spat, with E. M. Uhlenbeck, eds. 1927. *Encyclopaedie van Nederlandsch-Indië*. Second edition. 8 vols. The Hague: Martinus Nijhoff, vol. 5.

Stokes, Eric. 1978. *The Peasant and the Raj: Studies in Agrarian Society and Peasant Rebellion*. Cambridge: Cambridge University Press.

Stoler, Ann Laura. 1985. *Capitalism and Confrontation in Sumatra's Plantation Belt, 1870-1979*. New Haven: Yale University Press.

Suryadinata, Leo. 2015."China's Nationality Laws and the Chinese Overseas." In Jayati Bhattacharya and Coonoor Kripalani, eds, *Indian and Chinese Immigrant Communities: Comparative Perspectives,* London: Anthem Press, 2015, 43-54.

Tan Chee-Beng. 2000 "Socio-cultural Diversities and Identities." In Lee Kam Hong and Tan Chee-Beng, eds, *The Chinese in Malaysia,* Shah Alam: Oxford University Press, 37-70.

Termorshuizen, Thio. 2008. "Indentured Labour in the Dutch Colonial Empire, 1800-1940." In Geert Oostindie, ed., *Dutch Colonialism, Migration and Cultural Heritage: Past and Present,* Leiden: Brill, 2008, 261-314.

Thampi, Madhavi. 2015. "Indian Soldiers and Policemen in China in the Colonial Period." In Jayati Bhattacharya and Coonoor Kripalani, eds, *Indian and Chinese Immigrant Communities: Comparative Perspectives,* London: Anthem Press, 2015, 187-196.

Thompson, Edgar T. 1932. "Mines and Plantations and the Movements of Peoples." *American Journal of Sociology,* vol. 37, no. 4, 603-611.

Tinker, Hugh.1974. *A New System of Slavery: The Export of Indian Labour Overseas 1830-1920.* London and New York: Oxford University Press.

Tirtosudarmo, Riwanto. 2005. The *Orang Melayu* and *Orang Jawa* in the "Lands Below the Winds." CRISE Working Paper, no. 14.

Tjandra, Surya. 2016. Labour Law and Development in Indonesia. Doctoral Thesis, Leiden University.

Trocki, Carl A. 1993. "The Rise and Fall of the Ngee Heng Kongsi in Singapore." In David Ownby and Mary Somers Heidhues, eds. *"Secret Societies" Reconsidered: Perspectives on the Social History of Modern South China and Southeast Asia.* Armonk, NY: M. E. Sharpe, 1993, 89-119.

Tsai Chutung. 1910. "The Chinese Nationality Law, 1909." *The American Journal of International Law,* vol. 4, no. 2, 404-411.

Turnbull, C. M. 1977. *A History of Modern Singapore, 1819-2005.* Singapore: Singapore University Press.

Vahed, Goolam. 1995. The Making of Indian Identity In Durban, 1914-1949. PhD, Indiana University.

Vahed, Goolam, and Ashwin Desai. 2012. "Indian Indenture: Speaking across the Oceans." *Man in India,* vol. 92, no. 2 195-213.

Wang Gungwu. 1970. "Chinese Politics in Malaya." *The China Quarterly,* no. 43, 1-30.

Wang Gungwu. 2000. *The Chinese Overseas: From Earthbound China to the Quest for Autonomy.* Cambridge, MA: Harvard University Press.

Wang Gungwu. 2018. *Nanyang: Essays on Heritage.* Singapore: ISEAS.

Warner, H. William. 2020. "The Kabuliwalas: Afghan Moneylending and the Credit Cosmopolis of British India, c. 1880–1947." *The Indian Economic & Social History Review,* April 2020.

Wertheim, Wim F. 1993. "Conditions on Sugar Estates in Colonial Java: Comparisons with Deli." *Journal of Southeast Asian Studies* vol. 24, no. 2, 268-284.

Wickramasekara, Piyasiri. 2015. "Migration Regimes and their Linkages for Family Unity, Integrity and Development." In Marion Panizzon, Gottfried Zürcher, and Elisa Fornalé, eds, *The Palgrave Handbook of International Labour Migration: Law and Policy Perspectives*, Houndmills: Palgrave Macmillan, 146-180.

Williams, Michael. 2018. *Returning Home with Glory: Chinese Villagers around the Pacific, 1849 to 1949*. Hong Kong: Hong Kong University Press.

Wilson, Jon. 2016. *India Conquered: Britain's Raj and the Chaos of Empire*. London, Simon and Schuster.

Wong Tze-ken, Danny. 2000. "The Chinese in Sabah: An Overview." In Lee Kam Hing and Tan Chee-Beng, eds, *The Chinese in Malaysia*, Shah Alam: Oxford University Press, 2000, 382-405.

Yacob, Shakila. 2007. "The United States Rubber Company in Southeast Asia,1910–1942." *Enterprise and Society*, vol. 8, no. 1, 136-174.

Yang Tongling, Lin Zhang, Li Xinyun, Tan Enli, and Li Ensi. 2004. *Hunqian mengrao de guxiang—Bangjia dao* ("Lost in a reverie about one's native place: Bangka Island"). Beijing: Zhongguo youyi chuban gongsi.

Yen Ching-hwang. 1985. *Coolies and Mandarins: China's Protection of Overseas Chinese During the Late Ch'ing Period (1851-1911)*. Singapore: Singapore University Press.

Yong Chen. 2000. *Chinese San Francisco, 1850-1943: A Trans-Pacific Community*. Stanford: Stanford University Press.

Yun, Lisa. 2008. *The Coolie Speaks: Chinese Indentured Laborers and African Slaves in Cuba*. Philadelphia, PA: Temple University Press.

Zhu Jieqin. 1984. "Shijiu shiji zhongqi zai Yindunixiya de qiyue Huagong" ("Indentured Huagong in Indonesia in the mid nineteenth century"). In Chen Hansheng, ed., *Huagong chuguo shiliao huibian* (A compilation of edited historical materials regarding going abroad by Huagong), Beijing: Zhonghua shuju, 12 vols, 1981-1985, vol. 5, 217-243.

Zurndorfer, Harriet T. 2022. "Economic, Social, and Legal Aspects of Slavery and Indentured Labor in Late Ming China (1550–1645): What the Huizhou Documents Tell Us." In Allen, ed., 2022, 131-149.

CHAPTER 4

The Penal Sanction

The main goal of this chapter is to clarify the long and complicated history of legislation on indentured labour in the East Indies, on the basis of official publications and other literature from the colonial era and with special reference to Chinese indenture. It looks chiefly at regulations issued centrally, in the context of a trend towards standardisation, and only in passing at their variation between islands and sectors.[1]

Why this focus on legislation? Law is the mainstay of indenture and one of two main keys to it (the other being economics), regardless of under which colonial power. Rana Behal, a historian of South Asian plantation labour, asks how such a repressive system could survive in the British Empire at a time when liberal sentiment was high. His answer is that labour laws and reports

> served to legalize certain abuses and to create a carapace of perfunctory oversight under which new forms of abuse and degradation could be innovated by planters. If planters and creditors [...] were the grim reapers of labour power, the colonial judiciary and bureaucracy provided the scythe. [...] [T]he very language of improvement and imperial trusteeship, especially from the 1870s onwards, functionally served to legitimate and shroud the multiple ways in which labour exploitation was rendered *easier* over time.

[1] On differences in regulations and practices, see Houben and Seibert (2013, 178–192).

G. Benton, *Chinese Indentured Labour in the Dutch East Indies, 1880–1942*, Palgrave Macmillan Transnational History Series,
https://doi.org/10.1007/978-3-031-05024-4_4

In wasteland or jungle settings in frontier societies, wherever workers were scarce, a main function of the colonial state was to mobilise labour and direct it, semi-captive and inexpensive, to the estates and mines. European and other capitalists joined with officials to ensure, by means of legal codes or otherwise, an uninterrupted flow of "cheap, obedient, disciplined labour," an alliance in which the government acted as "a support of planters and [...] created legitimacy for the use of extra-legal authority." To justify the laws, the "coolie" was pictured "as intrinsically absconding, unlawful, violent, indolent, or untrustworthy." The key moment in the consolidation of the new system in British India came in 1865 with the insertion, under the new Act VI of the legal code, of a "punitive contract" with which to discipline the unruly worker.[2] Roughly the same happened in the East Indies, with a time lag of some fifteen years. In 1880, the promulgation of the first "coolie ordinance" was the corresponding key moment in the consolidation of the penal sanction.

The chapter takes a longer view than most accounts of indenture, given that indenture survived far later in the East Indies than in most places. Indenture was banned in India in the 1910s and the Forced Labour Convention was adopted by the ILO in June 1930, brought into force in May 1932, and even ratified by the Netherlands in 1933. But despite this ratification, indenture remained on the books in the East Indies until the Japanese invasion.

Not all administrators approved of the penal sanction. In the British Empire, some sought to mitigate the abuses associated with it, and in the early twentieth century their efforts started to bear fruit.[3] This also happened in the East Indies, though again with a time lag. Generally, however, Dutch officials and capitalists approved of the punitive and coercive aspects of legislation. Like the British, they were good at interpreting the law to their own advantage and using its leeway as a screen.[4] Dutch colonial law was easy to get round, given the shortage of officials and policemen. According to Wim Wertheim,

> there was hardly any governmental interference in the activities of the big estates. Though formally penalties for transgressions of coolie contracts by

[2] Behal (2014), as summarised in Manjapra (2018).

[3] Jayawardena and Kurian (2015).

[4] Manjapra (2018, 9 and 18).

the labourers had to be handled by the civil service fulfilling judiciary functions, in practice the estates mostly behaved as though they were the competent authorities.[5]

Early Regulations and Legislation

The call for labour contracts in the East Indies first came in the early nineteenth century, with the growing injection into the economy of a system of paid labour and the need to ensure the employer that the worker fulfilled his contractual obligations and there would be enough workers.[6] As a corollary, workers were supposed to be protected against financial disadvantage as a result of ignorance when signing contracts and to be guaranteed good treatment and the right to repatriation after the expiry of their contracts.[7]

On Sumatra and other Outer Islands, indenture was the main form of employment on the plantations and in the mines. (In Java, which had a village economy, the abundance of labour made importing workers unnecessary and there was no widespread tradition of paid labour until late in the nineteenth century.[8]) An increase in production and a demand for better communications between the plantations and the factories and between the factories and the coast led to a growing reliance on compulsion in Sumatra, using regulations later exported to other islands.

The first steps towards protecting workers but without yet subjecting them to a penal sanction were taken in Java. In January 1819, Stb. no. 10 required any contract with a Javanese to be registered with the official Resident, a high-ranking civil servant who was declared responsible for checking agreements and ensuring that they had been made individually rather than collectively.[9] This regulation concerned all contracts, but labour contracts were in reality widely ignored. In 1838, individual contracts were no longer required, a change from the 1819 law, which had banned collective agreements, and agreements had to specify wages, pro-

[5] Wertheim (1993, 269–270).

[6] Heijting (1925, 16).

[7] De Graaf and Stibbe (1918), Stibbe and Spat (1927, 229).

[8] Some question the extent to which the Dutch in Java continued to use extra-economic coercion after 1830 and suggest that the workforce had already been partly proletarianised and was in that sense free (Knight 1988; Bosma 2011).

[9] The *Staatsblad van het Koninkrijk der Nederlanden*, abbreviated in this study as Stb., is the Dutch Bulletin of Acts and Decrees.

vision of food and housing, the number of days to be worked, etc. The contract was oral and often went unregistered. The then majority view was that it should be withdrawn, and De Kat Angelino, a senior Dutch advisor, later said that it had put the whole apparatus of indigenous laws and customs at the disposal of employers "for exacting the observance of the compact from their workmen." The ordinance was superseded in 1903 by Stb. no. 108, which reverted to the previous ban on agreements supervised by elders and notables.[10]

The first regulation for workers brought in "from elsewhere," i.e., from other islands or countries, required their registration and the fulfilment (by the employer) of contracts, "to prevent [the workers] being turned into slaves" (or, in De Kat Angelino's formulation regarding an act in 1854, "for the gradual limitation and softening of slavery"). This regulation was only really relevant to the Outer Islands, where employers usually had no choice other than to import workers. In nearly all cases, "elsewhere" meant China (taking Javanese to Deli on a large scale did not start until 1885).

The regulation was aimed chiefly at stopping the clandestine import of slaves. The local authorities were required to register workers and ensure that they had arrived freely. The regulation set a limit of eight years on agreements, which could only be renewed through an official. A fine of f100 was, in theory, to be levied on any employer of a worker found to be unregistered. If the permitted period of hire was exceeded, the employer had to pay the worker f10 per month above the contracted wage. Given that workers "from elsewhere" were usually Chinese, the reference in articles 26–31 changed, from workers "from elsewhere" to "Oriental Foreigners" (Chinese and also, in a few cases, Japanese, Arabs, and Hindus).

A new law in 1863 decreed that contracts must be in writing and (again) individual rather than collective, and was seemingly also applicable to labour contracts. However, the regulation was often ignored, except in cases where labourers had received advances. Most contracts were oral, again contrary to the law. The regulation was aimed at prohibiting collective agreements of the sort encouraged by the 1838 ordinance. This ordinance had sought to encourage independent agriculture, but the authorities came to regret that aim, for private farming was in competition with government cultivation. It restored the old system of individual agreements and made contracts freer, potentially depriving employers of

[10] De Graaf and Stibbe (1918), De Kat Angelino (1931, 495–496).

the support of traditional village arrangements that sanctioned labour contracts. In reality, however, contracts often went unregistered.

A draft regulation of the Raad van Indië (Council of the East Indies, an advisory body) in 1862 allowed private agreements provided they did not last longer than a year. A draft coolie ordinance in 1864 and a draft law in 1865 excluded the police from any part in such agreements, a view supported on other occasions between 1869 and 1879 and subsequently, on the grounds that practice in Java showed that registration was a pointless formality. Employers resented the Resident's right to disallow the registration of contacts at his own discretion and to annul them.[11]

The penal sanction was the core element in the Dutch system of indenture, and its adoption preceded the 1880 ordinance by decades.[12] It first appeared in Java in 1829, in the form of a Surabaya police regulation, applicable to servants who breached civil agreements. It was designed to protect employers more than workers. Even where apparently even-handed, its specifications were generally interpreted in a way friendly to the employer. It remained in force for more than one hundred years, and was known to officials as "the whip."[13]

Bruno Lasker, commenting on the 1829 regulation, explained that colonial employers, stung by the awakening Dutch conscience, "sought to devise ways in which they might escape the stigma of slave-owners and yet have the advantage of disposing over labor crews bound to their work and costing little more than their subsistence."[14] For leaving one's job without permission, the regulation set a fine of f25, eight days in prison, or thirty strokes of the cane. The second and third punishments applied only to Indonesians and Chinese (i.e., not to Europeans). The regulation was initially confined to Surabaya, given that in Java the rural population was in collective thrall to the plantations of the colonial state. In 1851, it was extended to the whole of Java and Madura except Batavia and to parts of the Outer Islands and was defended in other decrees starting in 1862.[15]

[11] Heijting (1925, 1); De Kat Angelino (1931, 494–497) and 503–504; De Graaf and Stibbe (1918), *Manual* (n.d., 5).

[12] Indenture and the penal sanction were equated in colonial parlance. In an English gloss to a Dutch text, H. Cohen de Boer, of the Ondernemersraad, identified the penal sanction as "indentured labour" (Cohen de Boer 1930, 4).

[13] Van den Brand (1918, 687–689), quoted in Breman (2020, 472).

[14] Lasker (1950, 218).

[15] De Graaf and Stibbe (1918), Heijting (1925, 2, fn. 1), Furnivall (1939, 181–182), Tjandra (2016, 30, fn 5).

In his account of the penal sanction, defined as the resort to criminal provisions to enforce compliance with a civil-law employment contract, Heijting pointed out that the 1829 Surabaya regulation was one of very few labour laws at the time that specified a penal sanction for the servant (*dienstdoende*) as well as the master (*dienstbruiker*). Other regulations issued for other parts of Java made no reference to the master-servant relationship. Their sole rationale was to protect workers against deception and "aberrations" and for officials to alert workers to their rights. No mention was made of penalties for breaking agreements. The same was broadly true of regulations adopted on the Outer Islands. Not until 1868 were officials instructed to acquaint Oriental Foreigners with the contents of article 1603 of the Civil Code regarding the relationship between master and servant. Not until 1872 did the Dutch colonial authorities generally adopt a system of work contracts that focused on protecting the employer rather than the employee. From then on, however, they looked ever less to protecting workers against deception and coercion and ever more to enforcing workers' obligations and threatening them with jail, on Sumatra's East Coast and in other regions.

Even before 1872, a new path had been struck on the Outer Islands, in Deli and on Bangka, where penal sanctions of a sort had operated for years. However, the Deli arrangement had no legal foundation (*wettiging*), unlike in Surabaya. Under it, planters administered punishments and dealt with minor transgressions by Chinese and Indonesians on the authority of the Sultan, whose despotic legal and policing powers they inherited. Acting on their own initiative, the planters concluded work contracts containing criminal provisions with Chinese and Klings (Indians), as was customary on the Malay Peninsula, and punished infringements. Thus the criminal provision crossed over into Dutch practice through British Malaya. In the early days, Chinese and Indonesians working in Deli had counted as subjects of the Sultan. In 1872, however, they became subjects of the government of the East Indies. Under the new regime, "Straits contracts" became invalid and new legislation was needed.

A solution was found in the replacement of Stb. 1829 no. 8 by art. 2 no. 27 of the General Police Punitive Regulation for Natives (Stb. 1872 no. 111), which introduced fines and unpaid labour on public works for those who "refused to work." In Java, employers wanted workers who had received an advance and failed to repay it to be prosecuted for fraud. This sentiment was reflected in the 1872 article. In exacting penalties for breaches of labour agreements, the article generalised a sanction that had previously existed with full legal recognition only in the 1829 Surabaya regulation and only within a limited geographic area.

The new 1872 regulation generalised the informal Deli arrangement by setting custodial sentences for employees who broke their contracts. Subsequently, the penal sanction was extended and revised. In Deli, planters demanded a more detailed specification of mutual rights and obligations, on the grounds that tobacco growing required a particularly dependable workforce. Further regulations regarding relations between workers and employers came into force (at least nominally) even before the 1880 ordinance and its revisions. On Bangka, where miners had been deemed to be in government service ever since 1832, an 1845 regulation penalised deserters—a provision, as Heidhues pointed out, that antedated the penal sanction proper.[16]

After the 1872 regulation, it turned out that there were too few police and officials to administer it in the event of resistance. This meant that a worker could ignore his contract and simply quit. The planters therefore agreed among themselves that such workers should not be hired by a new employer and, with the approval of the local authority, could be escorted from prison to their old place of work.

Some members of the Dutch Parliament, while accepting the need to regulate the relationship between employers and workers "from elsewhere," thought that article 2 no. 27 went too far, on both "dogmatic-juridical" grounds (a contract in private law should not be protected by a state sanction) and on ethical grounds (it would deliver workers into slavery). Members of different parties criticised the idea that a worker but not an employer could be prosecuted for breach of contract and demanded the withdrawal of the penal sanction, seen as a form of slavery. This marked the start of a political struggle in the Netherlands between proponents and opponents of indenture, which the latter initially lost.

Starting in the mid 1870s, Dutch planters began cooperating more closely, to tighten their grip on the workers, whip their own ranks into line, bring pressure to bear on the colonial government, and combat British criticisms of Dutch actions. This led, in 1879, to the founding by the planter (later Minister of Colonial Affairs) J. Th. Cremer of the Deli Planters Vereeniging (Deli Planters' Association, DPV), which aimed to get the "coolie question" regulated. Cremer and others had already brought a lawyer to Deli to help draft an ordinance decreeing a punitive

[16] Heidhues (1992, 44–45).

regime on the Malayan model. The planters played a key role in creating the "coolie ordinance" in 1880.

The adoption of the 1880 ordinance was preceded by a series of related steps not always consistent with it. Stb. 1875 no. 59 introduced regulations requiring foreigners brought into the region to be registered within eight days and their wages, advances received, etc. checked to ensure that the recruitment had been voluntary and in compliance with article 1603 of the civil code (covering the relationship between master and servant or worker) and by art. 2 no. 27 of the General Police Punitive Regulation for Natives (Stb. 1872 no. 111), penalising refusal to work, etc.

On October 2, 1877, a preliminary draft of the ordinance was published for criticism and comment. The Second Chamber approved it for Deli, where special conditions were seen to obtain, but not for the Outer Islands as a whole. A difference of opinion arose between the Governor General and the Council of the East Indies regarding art. 2 no. 27. The East Indies government thought it should be preserved, to guarantee *arbeidszekerheid* ("security of labour," i.e., ensuring employers' access to and control of labour). However, Dutch politicians continued to oppose it, although only for Indonesians, and prohibited it as such in 1876. The retention for workers "from elsewhere" of the master-servant article (Stb. 1872 article 2 no. 111) was justified before the Chamber on grounds of the special importance of the enterprises for which they were recruited, although it was recognised as a deviation from accepted principles.

A vote in the Second Chamber led, on May 12, 1879, to the withdrawal of art. 2 no. 27, on the eve of the promulgation of the "coolie ordinance," thus exempting native and other workers from punitive sanctions. However, this measure was contravened by a new Article 328a in the Wetboek van Strafrecht voor Inlanders (Criminal Code for Natives) that criminalised anyone who, to "secure an advantage over an employer," took money in the form of an advance for work that he failed to carry out, while articles 1601–1603 of the civil code, again dealing with relations between workers and employers, were declared applicable to Indonesians and those on a par with them throughout the East Indies. Yet it proved hard to demonstrate dishonourable intent at the point of receipt of an advance, so the sanction was rarely applied (De Kat Angelino called it "useless").[17]

[17] De Kat Angelino (1931, 498–499 and 503), Heijting (1925, 2–5), De Graaf and Stibbe (1918), Stibbe and Spat (1927, 230), Breman (1989, 35–38 and 136–143).

The reluctance of Dutch legislators to apply the penal sanction in civil disputes and their desire to separate the civil, penal, and administrative spheres of jurisdiction did not always pass the test of practice and the principle was often breached. The arguments to which the penal sanction gave rise dominated the later political debate on colonial labour law. As Margo Groenewoud observed, the liberal leanings of many legislators meant that "from then on the infliction of penal laws by authorities would be justified only when the general interest was at stake."

The replacement in 1879 of Art. 2 no. 27 of the Criminal Code by Art. 328a was followed in 1880 by the first coolie ordinance, designed to ensure *arbeidszekerheid* by means of the penal sanction. Except for a brief toying with an end to the penal sanction after World War One, the system stayed basically intact until the intervention of external forces (discussed below) more than a decade after the war.

The 1880 ordinance was part of a wider evolution in Dutch colonial labour legislation that began in Surinam (Dutch Guiana) and the Dutch Antilles. After the abolition of slavery in the Netherlands West Indies in 1863, the Dutch acted more or less like their British counterparts in the region after 1834. On the islands, most ex-slaves continued working for their old owners, so emancipation did not greatly boost the demand for labour. In Surinam, however, the plantations experienced a shortage, remedied by bringing in Portuguese, Chinese, and Indians and a roughly equal number of Javanese, under penal sanction. The increased reliance on foreign labour, principally from British colonies, led to the introduction of new laws in 1874 and 1879 (the Strafverordening and its later revision), during the years in which the coolie ordinance for the East Indies was in preparation.[18] These new laws helped pave the way for the ordinance.

In the East Indies, the planters wielded ever greater police powers. In 1876, they told the government that "in Deli we can confidently say that without our help the police would be unable to cope with any crime or transgression within our companies." Unhappy with how things stood, they sent the government a draft regulation on workers' and employers' rights and duties, based on regulations in Surinam and the Straits Settlements.

These legislative adjustments reflected major changes in those years in the economy of the East Indies. Furnivall, a British colonial servant, pointed out that by the 1870s, "the problem of control over labour had

[18] Groenewoud (1995, 72), Kloosterboer (1960, 32–37), Lockard (1978).

assumed a new character," for "the centre of interest had shifted from domestic service to industrial production with imported labour, especially in the tobacco plantations of East Sumatra, where thousands of Chinese coolies were employed."[19] Agriculture, including sugar, previously under government control, was thrown open to Western capital, and Western companies flooded in. The labour issue posed new and urgent questions to which the coolie ordinance was intended as the answer.[20]

The First Coolie Ordinance, 1880

On July 13, 1880, the coolie ordinance for Sumatra's East Coast came into being. The regulations promulgated in the 1870s, together with the decree of 1879, were taken up in the ordinance, a major and historic legislative act. The new regulations were repeatedly supplemented and substantially revised in 1915 and again in 1917, 1921, and 1925.

The need to import workers into thinly peopled regions was the rationale behind the ordinance, but the need for labour discipline was in itself a major goal of the employers, regardless of the population shortage. In Java, the focus had been on protecting workers, but on the Outer Islands the employers' interests were supreme. Capital had to be protected against arbitrary actions by labour, for the workers could use their scarcity to put pressure on the bosses, "before whose gate in the wilderness there was no chance of a throng of people seeking work." The "general" interest, crucial to negate Parliament's underlying hostility to the use of penal law in civil disputes, was declared at stake. The circumstances were, said Furnivall, extraordinary, and in extraordinary circumstances labour could only be controlled by extraordinary laws. This would not be the last time that expediency and the declared need for emergency measures to defend an ill-defined general interest trumped principle in Dutch colonial labour policy.

Furnivall noted that although the declared aim was to protect employers' investment in bringing labourers to work, the effect was "to put [them] at the employer's mercy." Inevitably, this led to abuses, especially on Sumatra's East Coast, where the recruitment of "prime-quality labourers" degenerated into a sort of slave trade.

[19] Furnivall (1939, 181–182).
[20] De Kat Angelino (1931, 498).

De Kat Angelino looked more favourably on the new ordinance, which he saw not just as part of a single thread in the quest for labour security for the employer, starting in 1829, but as a continuation of a second and even longer thread, starting in 1825, "exclusively directed towards the protection of all those who had lost the free disposal of their own labour either for life, or temporarily owing to debt or to a contract," a thread that was "in many respects ultra modern." "All this is lost out of sight," he added, "when one pays attention only to the penal sanction as though it were the one thing contained in these ordinances." The penal sanction was, he concluded, an attempt "to place both parties in a satisfactorily regulated relation, and [...] to compel them to behave as a good master and a good workman."[21]

The ordinance specified the need for written agreements to be registered locally to ensure that recruits had entered them freely. It capped engagements at three years, set a ten-hour working day, and stipulated that workers should receive good treatment, accommodation, and medical care. Workers were permitted to complain to the local administration, but in the company of at most two workmates (evidently, to avoid collective expressions of solidarity). They should follow orders and not absent themselves without written permission; and they could be sacked for incompetence as long as their employer first informed the administration. An official could terminate a contract on a worker's behalf if the employer breached its terms. A worker who deserted or refused to work could be sentenced to three months' forced labour and repeat offenders to up to twelve months'. An employer who terminated a worker's contract would have to pay his ticket home. Agreements made elsewhere in the East Indies or abroad in a place where sufficient control was exercised over emigration also had to meet the requirements of the ordinance. Art. 8 of the new ordinance summarised the penal sanction as follows:

> Every wilful infringement of the labour contract is punished, on the side of the employer with a fine of not more than one hundred guilders, on the side of the labourer with compulsory labour on public works in return only for his keep and without wages for the duration of not more than three months. In case of duly authenticated continual incapacity to perform the work which a labourer undertook by contract, the employer can consider the con-

[21] Furnivall (1939, 183 and 353), De Kat Angelino (1931, 498–510), Heijting (1925, 5), De Graaf and Stibbe (1918, 362).

> tract as terminated after having informed the head of the local administration. The facts by which the labourer is deemed to have wilfully broken his contract are (a) desertion, (b) a continued refusal to work.

The ordinance stipulated that a labourer had to serve out his contract even after release from prison, which struck many observers as counterproductive (and had, by the 1920s, given way in many cases to repatriation). But the compulsion had a point. A period in jail would mean little to a deserter, an unpayable fine even less. However, if allowed to go free after his punishment, he could sign on elsewhere and get a new advance or join one of the bands of "tramps" against which the police were proving powerless.

The Dutch authorities claimed that the ordinance worked well and saw it as a solution to abuses that had earned them a bad name. For the first five years, up until 1885, the ordinance applied almost exclusively to Chinese, who were thought by the Dutch to be unlikely to complain, given that they were used to penal sanctions in the Straits Settlements and Malaya. In reality, the ordinance did little to improve their conditions. Ostensibly even-handed, it operated overwhelmingly in the employers' favour.[22]

The ordinance and the penal sanction, which initially applied only to Sumatra's East Coast, were followed by revised ordinances for other sparsely populated regions, which similarly made recruitment subject to officially registered contracts and penalised breach of contract, indolence, etc. In 1889, a new coolie ordinance replaced that of 1880. It is discussed in greater detail below, in the section on free labour.

The 1880 ordinance was originally applicable only to agriculture and mining. It stipulated that workers from outside the East Indies could only enter into service if the terms of the ordinance were respected. For such workers, written agreements were compulsory, though they were optional for workers from parts of the East Indies other than Sumatra. Punitive and coercive clauses were retained for workers from abroad. However, natives could choose between a contract with a penal clause and one without.

Planters' exercise of police powers continued even after 1880. In 1883, the Government Commissioner suggested that members of staff in enterprises be appointed as police chiefs. The government rejected this

[22] De Kat Angelino (1931, 507–514), Heijting (1925, 7), Stibbe and Spat (1927, 229–230).

proposal, but the employers' police function was institutionalised in 1887 by the introduction on Sumatra's East Coast of a regulation whereby a staff member catching a criminal "red-handed" would count as exercising police powers. The term "red-handed" was interpreted liberally. Employers kept people locked up for days and dissuaded them from complaining.

In 1886, the Resident of Sumatra's East Coast tacitly confirmed the planters' police function when he decreed that no one should be kept locked up for more than 24 hours. This practice continued until 1901, when the Resident withdrew the 1886 circular at the request of company administrators prosecuted for exceeding the detention limit. However, the Resident told the planters that "a habit that had become so deeply rooted could not be undone by a stroke of the pen" and let it be known, by word of mouth, that they could continue the practice.[23]

Powers granted to mine administrators to prosecute Chinese on Belitung were abolished in 1892, when misdemeanours previously handled by mine staff were transferred to the Assistant-Resident. The conflict sparked by this decree shows how difficult it was to operate a policy of "one size fits all" in the complex landscape of labour relations in the East Indies when regulations developed for plantations were translated to the mining sector. Employers on Belitung lamented the gap between official prescription and local circumstance. "Strictly enforced," they said, it meant "grafting tobacco onto tin." Belitung's tin miners were well organised and employers and officials depended heavily on their cooperation and far less so (than, for example, on Bangka) on force, so the managers and the Assistant Resident thought the penal sanction unnecessary. "It was extremely difficult," said Heijting, "to adjust the general coolie ordinance, which had been made specially for tobacco cultivation in Sumatra, to the circumstances of [Belitung]."[24]

In 1896, after the changes decreed in 1892 had come into force, a new ordinance was laid down for Belitung. Though broadly the same as that set out in 1889 for Sumatra's East Coast, it criminalised workers who refused to do overtime in the event of disasters or to carry out water control, a special problem in the tin mines. New to the ordinance was a stipulation that workers who went to court or jail or were sick or on leave and failed to return promptly to their places of work could be forcibly returned by police or by the employer acting as police.

[23] Heijting (1925, 9–14), De Graaf and Stibbe (1918, 362), Van Blommestein (1917, 41).
[24] *Gedenkboek*, pt 1, 50 and 60.

Admirers of the labour regime on Belitung, where the term penal sanction was rendered by the euphemism "actual execution on the person [*reëele executie op den persoon*]," contrasted its laxity with Bangka's punitive approach. They pointed out that in 1920–1921 only 923 transgressions of the Coolie Ordinance and only 360 of the Police Punitive Regulation were registered among Belitung's 20,865-strong workforce. But although the rate of transgression was lower than elsewhere, still one in twenty workers suffered a sanction.[25] Belitung employers claimed to reserve the sanction for "incorrigible elements not open to persuasion." However, the number of Chinese on Belitung "corrected" in 1917–1924 continued rising until the start of the economic malaise in 1923, which put labour on the back foot for a while. The offences related mainly to pass laws. They included "running away and roaming around," disturbing the peace, fighting, laziness, and refusal to work. Those perceived as constantly in trouble were removed, "like bad apples." On Bangka, the state-run mining company Banka Tinwinning was governed by a special ordinance that underwent a number of revisions, culminating in 1920 in a regulation that specified the same punishments regarding contracts as in the general ordinance.[26]

Despite the changes at around the turn of the century, migrants continued to be unfree at the point of their departure from the homeland and remained so at the destination, until they had redeemed their debt.[27] Migrants taken south by shipping interests were held on board "on speculation, [...] at the risk of the ship, [...] until an employer was found who paid to the ship the actual expenses plus a margin of profit." Those recruited in Hong Kong were assembled in hostels by managers, who took them south and found them employers with whom they then signed contracts. In the East Indies, the system of indenture remained intact, cemented by the ordinances.[28]

[25] Breman (1989, 270), Mollema (1922, 173), Heijting (1925, 11).

[26] *Gedenkboek*, pt 2, 68; Stibbe and Spat (1927, 230).

[27] Planters in Malaya reported in 1911 that "[m]any of the so-called 'free' coolies arriving in the Straits are not really free as they arrive here under the obligation to refund the cost of their passage, etc. which is deducted from their pay in the usual manner" (*Malaya Tribune*, July 12, 1922).

[28] Lu Wendi et al. (1984, 47), MacNair (1923).

Free Labour

The history of labour contracts in the East Indies is complicated by their variety, which was not just regional. They included agreements dependent on word of mouth and two forms of "free" labour alongside contract labour. The term "free" was first used in relation to contracts in the East Indies in 1861. An official review in 1872 ended in the adoption of article 2 no. 27 of the Police Penal Regulation, which, as we have seen, extended the penal sanction to the Outer Islands. It was some time before the concept of free labour was more clearly defined.[29]

The coolie ordinance of 1880 made the penal sanction obligatory for workers "from elsewhere," in the years before the start of Javanese transmigration. The Dutch continued to place obstacles in the way of a transition to free labour. In the 1870s and 1880s, casual labour not bound by contract accounted for between 10 and 20 percent of the workforce, but this percentage subsequently shrank. The revised coolie ordinance of 1889 made a concession in respect of free labour, by allowing the employment of local people on a casual basis, but planters continued anyway to bind them contractually and the DPV banned its members from employing casual workers. The proportion of free workers declined to 4–5 percent in the years surrounding the 1889 revision, evidence that the revision had the opposite effect of that seemingly intended. The free labourers included very few Chinese and Javanese and were mostly Bataks and Malays.[30]

Although free labour migration became theoretically possible in 1889, it received little attention until 1911, when a regulation was issued covering labourers "from elsewhere" who wanted to contract on a basis other than that set out in the ordinances. This was described as an attempt to attract "good and respectable elements," unlike the general run of "no good" labour migrants, and thus to encourage indirect agricultural colonisation, the accelerated as opposed to natural formation of settlements of "free" workers and their families, either as direct colonies of labourers and their families, which the planters favoured, or "indirectly" in the form of agricultural colonies, entailing greater independence. Labourers thus recruited were not under penal sanction and no longer needed to appear before the recruiting commissioner in Java.

[29] Stibbe and Spat (1927, 230).

[30] Breman (1989, 136–138).

Circulars issued in October 1912 announced that while contracts affecting non-natives had up to then been bound by the coolie ordinance, contracting parties could now choose whether to include a penal sanction for the labourer. Other requirements were also dropped. No registration was necessary, no model was prescribed for the contract, the contract could be oral, and parties could agree to whatever they liked. But again, the contract entailed obligations and sanctions and was free only in that it entailed no penal sanction. For employers, the penal sanction remained anyway in force—they could be fined for neglecting their obligations. The worker, for his part, was liable for breach of contract under article 1603 of the Civil Code.

Many labourers recruited under a contract without penal sanction were unaware of the difference between their contract and an ordinance-style one. Some employers used the new freedom to their own advantage, to reach agreements of indeterminate duration, effectively freeing themselves from possibly irksome obligations. Probably because of this lack of job security, contracts of this sort, free (for the worker) of penal sanctions, were quite rare. For years, they made up only a small percentage of the overall number—free workers from Java and China on Sumatra's East Coast numbered 841 in 1912 and 9,509 in 1922. The estimates for such workers included an indication of the number of women in this category—2,767 out of 12,126 in (for example) 1920, hardly compatible with colonisation.[31]

The 1889 ordinance had retained punitive and coercive clauses for workers from abroad but had introduced a choice for Indonesians. The 1915 ordinance (discussed below) retained punitive and coercive clauses but again introduced a choice, though this time the other way round—not for natives but for Chinese. However, the choice meant little in practice, for either group, and the employer "again proved, from an economic point of view, infinitely stronger than the worker."

Employers opposed the free labour regulation because it meant that the penal sanction applied only to them and not to the worker, posing a threat to their enterprises that the contract system seemed to guarantee. Planters "constantly and systematically" tried to prevent or undermine a transition to free labour. They demonstrated their muscle by ignoring or manipulating provisions they deemed against their interests. After 1889, they simply insisted on employing natives under a coolie contract, as they had been

[31] Heijting (1925, ch. 5 and 117–122), De Kat Angelino (1931, 535–536).

doing for years, and laid off time-expired workers rather than retain them as free workers or colonists. Every year, thousands left—83,897 between 1906 and 1915.

As for Chinese labourers, the choice offered them by Governor-General Idenburg in the 1915 ordinance—to accept or refuse a coolie contract—was, as Van Blommestein saw, simply an opportunity to act against their own best interests. Even without a coolie contract, employers would still have to provide medical care, housing, etc. Why were punitive and coercive measures necessary in the case of workers who agreed to a coolie contract but not of others? Idenburg failed to say. In fact, there was no good reason for workers to choose a coolie contract, but this was not made clear to them. Contrary to expectations, there was therefore little growth in the number of free contracts. "No use had been made" of the opportunity, said J. S. C. Kasteleyn, former chief administrator of the Amsterdam Deli Company, in 1916.

Ignorance was not the only or even the main explanation for the slow pace of the transition to free labour. Labourers were unequipped to resist nefarious practices by recruiters. Although free labour was as much under the protection of the labour inspectorate as contract labour, labourers felt safer under the sanction—not least because in parts of the East Indies free labourers were subject to local taxes not levied on contract labourers. Workers had much to fear from choosing wrongly, so the new option led neither in 1889 nor in 1915 to a sustained rise in the proportion of free workers. By 1917, free workers had fallen to just 3.5 percent and forced labour "was, and continued to be, the rule."

Idenburg also hoped that changes to the terms of re-engagement under a contract would speed the transition to free labour. Previously, re-engagement had been for three years, but it had now been halved to eighteen months. Van Blommestein was less sanguine, for there was nothing in the ordinance to stop an employer from re-engaging an employee again and again, as had commonly happened in the past (British India's "indenture after indenture").

De Kat Angelino, in 1931, praised the free-labour system and was optimistic about its prospects. But although more and more oil workers were rejecting the sanction, only one tobacco worker in five was free. Even as late as 1927, the 29,579 free labourers on the East Coast were outnumbered eight to one by contract labourers, despite an increase in organised free migration. Even in 1931, contract labourers outnumbered free labourers among Chinese by more than two to one (30,426 to 13,990) and among Javanese by 172,181 to 133,848. By then, however, the total number of contract labourers on the Outer Islands had fallen substantially, to 203,366 (as against 156,267 free labourers)—a significant reduction over 1924, when there were around 175,500 on Sumatra's East Coast and around 97,000 elsewhere.[32]

In some industries, the pattern of Chinese employment in the mid 1920s was becoming more complex. On Belitung, where the mines employed 16,147 men in 1924, 2,514 were described as "working on their own account, e.g., clearing land," 4,736 were employed "privately," and 4,726 were *langkong*, day labourers contracted casually (and including skilled workers such as carpenters and masons).[33] Between 1928 and 1938, the balance of free to indentured in the workforce as a whole swung decisively towards the former. In 1928, 247,799 worked under the penal sanction, compared with 30,000 free labourers under the sanction-free 1911 contract. In 1930, the 63,444 Huagong in the East Indies, mostly under indenture on the Outer Islands, outnumbered free workers by nearly five to one.[34] By 1938, 4,600 were under penal sanction compared with 185,000 "free labourers.[35]

Estimating the number of free labourers is difficult. On Bangka, it was hard to say how many of the "miscellaneous workers" who slightly preponderated in 1919 over those members of the 45,000 workforce categorised as miners were free.[36] Of the 18,323 miners on Bangka in 1930, 15,089 were contract workers (i.e., indentured) and 3,323 were "free." In 1930, recruits were shipped free of charge from China to Mentok in Bangka but were obliged to pay back part of the sum paid by the employer to the recruiter. On Belitung, a far greater proportion were indentured—14,218 out of 14,275.[37]

Other forms of free labour were performed by individuals working independently or in groups.[38] Collectives of this sort, known as "self-

[32] Furnivall (1939, 355–356), Van Blommestein (1917, 41–61), Breman (1989, 265), De Kat Angelino (1931, 536–537), Stibbe and Spat (1927, 233).

[33] *Gedenkboek*, pt 2, 78.

[34] Wang Linqian and Wu Kunxiang (2002, 169), Lu Wendi et al. (1984, 64–68). It is not clear whether they were all under indenture.

[35] Reid (1979, 45). However, the penal sanction had been retained in revised regulations promulgated in 1931 (Wu Fengbin 1988, 154).

[36] Guowuyuan [May] (1920b, 4–5).

[37] Pelzer (1935, 95–97).

[38] Houben (1999, 17).

administered," were not usually covered by the coolie ordinance. For example, employees of enterprises in south and east Borneo were nearly all time-expired contract workers and classified as casual (*los*). According to the coolie ordinance, a worker from outside the East Indies could only be employed by written agreement, but by 1910 it was customary for Chinese to take on fellow-Chinese by oral contract—to build dams, open up new land, etc. Small teams of free Chinese workers moved around offering their services to tobacco, coffee, or rubber estates or to mining companies. They were better paid than workers under contract but less trusted.[39]

Panglongs (sawmills), which also employed free labour, were a category apart, under a panglong regulation. Coolie ordinances were made applicable to jungle clearance and shipbuilding but not to panglongs, where conditions were notoriously bad. Panglongs continued to be treated separately even in later years. Panglong regulations were issued in 1923 and 1924. The panglongs were under the administration of the regions, which exercised police powers to deal with the abuses associated with them. Many Chinese ended up on panglongs after indenture.[40]

Deli's Millions

In 1902, the lawyer Johannes van den Brand published a pamphlet titled *De Millioenen uit Deli* (The Millions from Deli). Written from a militant Christian standpoint, it exposed the exploitation of Chinese and Javanese indentured labour on Sumatra and the enormous profits reaped by the planters. In a sequel, the author pictured its effect on Dutch public opinion:

> Could it be true? [...] After reading my pamphlet, this question must have been on the lips of anyone who, though never having been to Deli, was familiar with it from colonial reports or stock-market listings. Anyone who saw the bringing in of the annual harvest of golden apples could hardly suspect that the magic tree was rooted in a swamp; that the juices that flowed up the trunk and became shiny fruit were mingled with blood and tears. They heard only the merry song of the reapers: the sowers' lament did not

[39] De Graaf and Stibbe (1918), Van Blommestein (1917, 45, fn.), Heijting (1925, 122–123).

[40] Heijting (1925, 11–12), Stibbe and Spat (1927, 238). On panglongs, see Erman (2017) and Pastor (1927) and Chap. 6; and Appendix B.

> reach their ears. Now that a weak echo of it has finally been heard, they are baffled and doubts their ears. Could it be true?[41]

Practices of the sort that Van den Brand exposed had already been brought to the attention of the Dutch parliament, but it took his pamphlet to rouse a wide response. The pamphlet "thrilled with indignation" the public in the Netherlands and the East Indies.[42] Commentators observed that those in charge of supervising the coolie ordinance were overwhelmed by their responsibilities and unable to perform them. Even the conservative De Kat Angelino concluded that labour legislation empowered the employer at the cost of the worker and allowed "a spirit of roughness," personal aggression, and gross ill-treatment, for dependence "is the origin of all abuse of power."[43]

Equally consequential was the international scandal that Van den Brand set going. The pamphlet tarnished the Dutch reputation throughout the world, for the plantocracy was multinational and covered by an international press. A Protestant parliamentarian declared that "the honour of the Dutch nation is at stake."[44]

In 1903, the Dutch government commissioned a legal officer, J. L. T. Rhemrev, the public prosecutor in Batavia and a member of the Justice Council, to investigate.[45] This marked the start of a gradual revision of labour law. Rhemrev's report was a devastating criticism of the contract system and a catalogue of its abuses: beating with sticks in practically all enterprises investigated, deprivation of freedom, with or without physical torture, manslaughter by Europeans, many murders by Indonesians and Foreign Orientals of people "of their own sort," and an atmosphere in which the employer and his underlings saw themselves as lords and masters and the worker was wholly dependent on them.[46] Minister Cremer spoke of "a general collapse of morality."[47] Jan Breman said, in his study on the report, that "for decades it was deliberately kept out of the way of all but a small circle of initiates (officials and planters),"

[41] Van den Brand (1903, 6).

[42] Furnivall (1939, 353).

[43] De Kat Angelino (1931, 521–524).

[44] Groenewoud (1995, 77).

[45] Rhemrev is Vermehr written backwards. Children born to Indonesian women and Dutch fathers were in many cases given the father's surname but written backwards.

[46] Heijting (1925, 15), De Graaf and Stibbe (1918).

[47] Furnivall (1939, 354).

and by the time its political sensitivity had diminished and it had lost its "stamp of secrecy, [...] its presence in the colonial archives went unnoticed due to a lack of interest."[48]

After Rhemrev's investigation, the government in the East Indies seemed on the point of a major change, from controlling labour to protecting it.[49] In reality, however, true reform proved impossible, because of obstruction by vested interests and the administration's lack of commitment. Establishing a Court of Justice at Medan did not result in the thorough-going protection of labour. A series of attempts starting in 1909 to abolish penal sanctions were frustrated by politicians in the East Indies and the Netherlands. Due to "local circumstances," penal clauses were maintained even in state enterprises and even after the passing of yet another ordinance in 1924.[50]

Some changes did ensue, but they were often ineffective, not just because of planters' resistance and government inertia but because of Rhemrev's failure to go to the root of the matter, despite his moral revulsion. To the extent that reforms came about in the four decades leading up the Japanese invasion, it was (as we shall see) more because of natural evolution and external pressures than of Dutch state policy.

Anglo-Dutch Relations and the Penal Sanction

In her study on involuntary labour after slavery,[51] Wilhelmina Kloosterboer argued that while economics helps to explain the ending of unfree labour, its real cause was the abolitionist "spirit of the times" and international disapproval. The three main drivers were British decisions on indenture in the Straits Settlement and India; pressures exerted by the League of Nations and the ILO between the wars; and the US Tariff Act of 1930.

A first clash of interests and ideology between the British and the Dutch came in 1910, when the British pioneered the abolition of indenture in the Straits Settlements. This implied conferring a new free status on Javanese working on rubber plantations in the Straits, where they were prized as industrious and acculturated. The Dutch were unhappy with the implications of the freeing of their colonial subjects in diaspora from

48 Breman (1988, 19).
49 The report was eventually published in Breman (1987).
50 Furnivall (1939, 353–355).
51 Kloosterboer 1960, cited by Groenewoud (1995, 73).

indenture, for fear of setting a precedent for the East Indies and leading to an ever greater outflow of labour migrants. Critics accused Dutch and British rubber interests of creating a "quite unnecessary fuss" about the effects of abolition on the labour market.[52] Given that Sumatra and the Straits were competing for Javanese labour, the Straits government feared that it would lead to a Dutch ban on emigration, so it struck a deal with the Dutch whereby binding labour contracts were signed not in the Straits but before embarkation in the East Indies. On this occasion, the Dutch had the stronger hand, but it was the last such conflict in which the Dutch came out on top.

Margo Groenewoud identifies two further clashes on indenture that the Dutch lost. The first, in 1913, concerned a crowd of British-Guyanese balata-bleeders working in Surinam and subject to the *arbeidsverordening* (labour regulation), which allowed contracts under debt bondage. This was similar in its effects to the penal sanction and as controversial, especially after a Dutch proposal in 1911 to tighten the controls on forestry workers in the colony. The regulation led to a conflict between the British Consul in Paramaribo and Surinam's Governor, in which the Consul denounced Dutch labour law as "the authority on which despotic power was wielded unchecked." The Consul had to resign, but the abuses he identified threatened to become a scandal. In 1914, British officials discreetly forced the Dutch Government to refrain from tightening the *Arbeidsverordening*, a victory attributed to Britain's ability to manipulate the flow of labour into Surinam.

The second conflict followed the British decision in 1916 to end Indian migration to Surinam, at a time when indenture was about to end in India. The first the Dutch knew about the abolition was when their Consul in London read about it in *The Times*. Dutch officials fought to retain their access to Indian labour but failed.[53]

The Labour Inspectorate and the Labour Office

Van den Brand's pamphlet and Rhemrev's report on the plantocracy's terrorising of its workforce were a "black page" in Dutch colonial history.[54] After the scandal, Dutch attitudes towards the penal sanction began to

[52] *North-China Daily News*, June 20, 1913.
[53] Groenewoud (1995, 73–76).
[54] Breman (1989, xi).

change. Members of parliament denounced the sanction and an organisational framework was created for the reform of labour relations. However, the bodies set up to implement the reforms lacked political and financial support. In the early 1920s, during the economic malaise, the drive for labour reform waned and opposition to the penal sanction lost steam. The conviction grew that to abolish the penal sanction would destabilise the colonial economy, so in the end it was retained for the last two decades of Dutch rule.

The three main aims of the planned reforms were to define the rights and duties of worker and employer more precisely, ensure adequate inspection of workers' conditions, and replace contract labour with free labour.[55] To realise them, a Labour Inspectorate was created in 1904 and a Council of Justice was established in Medan. The tasks of the Inspectorate were to supervise recruitment in Java, ensure that the ordinances were observed on the Outer Islands, and improve labour relations.

The steps taken between 1909 and 1911 to phase out the penal sanction and switch to free labour were limited in scope. The penal sanction was by definition incompatible in any form with labour freedom. In 1889, it had been retained for Chinese but Indonesians were given a choice. In 1911, Governor-General Idenburg gave workers from elsewhere (mostly Chinese) the same choice, having in the meantime, in 1909, made a contract compulsory for Javanese. The inconsistency was symptomatic of general confusion and irresolution.

The first head of the Labour Inspectorate, a temporary appointee, was Bernardus Hoetink, who took up office in 1904. Hoetink's appointment did not, to judge by his record and his promise to work closely with the planters, bode well for the new body, and has been described as drawing its "sting." A student of the Sinologist Gustaaf Schlegel, Hoetink had worked for 28 years as an interpreter in the East Indies administration. He went to China in 1889 to study Chinese, but was also charged (together with his better-known fellow Sinologist Johannes de Groot) with recruiting labourers for the Deli planters, whose representative in China he became. Between 1888 and 1890, Hoetink and De Groot recruited 15,000 Chinese and drew praise in Parliament. The Dutch Ambassador in Beijing refused to join in this human trafficking and was therefore unpopular with the planters (unlike the German consuls in Guangzhou and Shantou, decorated by the Dutch for helping out). Hoetink returned to

[55] Furnivall (1939, 354).

China for a second study visit in 1898 and resumed recruiting. In 1900, back in Batavia, he spent three years inspecting mines and plantations. In government eyes, he was well equipped to be Labour Inspector.[56] The part he and De Groot played in recruitment is a shameful episode in Dutch Sinology of which De Groot seemed later "not to have felt so proud."[57]

Among Hoetink's achievements was the drafting of a model contract that corrected departures from the prescribed approach and imposed greater uniformity. Convinced that existing contracts betrayed workers' interests, he set up new ones on the basis of his own draft ordinance and with employers' help. In 1906, the Resident of Sumatra's East Coast agreed that only contracts that met Hoetink's specifications would be registered. The legality of the Hoetink draft was confirmed in 1910.

In general, however, Hoetink was more a friend of the planters than of the workers. According to Breman, he "enjoyed a great deal of credit in entrepreneurial circles, [...] as a valuable defender of industrial interests."[58] His model (revised in 1907) took "tactful" account of existing practices. By 1906, the uniformity he sought had been achieved.[59] However, when he resigned, it was as "a disillusioned man," such were the frustrations of his post.[60]

After Hoetink's retirement, labour inspection improved somewhat. Following a brief period of stagnation, new staff were hired. However, the Inspectorate's remit remained limited to supervising the recruitment of Javanese for work overseas and the treatment of labourers on the Outer Islands. The Inspectorate was criticised as too fragmented to manage labour effectively. Officials complained that it lacked coordination, so that the government was buffetted by conflicting advice from all quarters, including "experts, semi-experts, and non-experts," "irredeemably condemning the central authority to impotence."

[56] Kuiper (2017, 862–890), Blussé and Nie (2018, 29).

[57] Franke (1923, cxx), quoted in Kuiper (2017, 898), fn. 159. Kuiper praises Hoetink for achieving fine results under difficult circumstances, judged by "the standards of the time," but accepts that Dutch China specialists ended up "consolidating the exploitation of coolies rather than warranting their rights" (Kuiper 2017, 891 and 898). One thinks of Luz Mercedes Hincapie's description, in her essay on the Cuban saccharocracy, of Nicolás Tanco Armero as a trader in "the treacherous business of a *letrado*" (Hincapie 2010).

[58] Breman (1989, 255).

[59] Heijting (1925, 19–20).

[60] Breman (1988, 28).

In 1907–1908, a new Labour Inspectorate was set up to replace the temporary one. Its staff comprised a chief of service, two inspectors, and adjunct-inspectors with interpreters. It was put under the Ministry of Justice rather than, as previously, the Department of Civil Service, so that regional administrators were less able to thwart its efforts. After 1908, it extended its operations, and its staff had grown by 1914.

In the 1910s, the Labour Inspectorate became more radical. A report argued that the main fault in the worker-employer relationship lay in the employer's dominance (although it conceded that he "stood, in terms of education and civilisation, at a far higher level than the worker"). It described wages, food, accommodation, and medical care as "generally satisfactory and even very good in some companies" but said that many goals went unachieved. Inspectors were dismayed, on visiting companies, by the staff's unpleasant tone when addressing workers. A worker who asked for information might be derided as "the biggest stinker" and threatened even in the presence of inspectors.

Writing in 1925, Heijting noted some of the Labour Inspectorate's successes. Wages had risen where necessary, measures had been taken to stop overseers syphoning off workers' cash, and housing and medical care had improved. However, the progress was far from universal. The Inspectorate's failures were due in part to a shortage of staff and of Chinese and native interpreters. A more fundamental problem was its conflicting responsibilities: to protect workers but at the same time to support employers, for example in the event of "unreasonable" strikes. It therefore fell between two stools. Employers who had got used to acting with impunity accused it of encouraging workers to complain. The newly formed association of assistants (lower-level Dutch or otherwise white plantation managers) accused it of provoking "ever more shameless behaviour on the part of coolies."

For a while, on the eve of the economic malaise in 1920, lawlessness seemed to be on the rise even among the companies' administrative staff. Police on Sumatra's East Coast reported 39 administrators (*beheerders*) for infringements and charged Europeans with 90 acts of physical violence. Contract workers, though far more numerous, were charged with only 28 attacks, six on non-Europeans, in response to beatings, eight concerning work and five concerning wages.[61]

[61] De Kat Angelino (1931, 499), Stibbe and Spat (1927, 231–234), Heijting (1925, 24–25 and 30–63), De Graaf and Stibbe (1918).

The Inspectorate was sorely tested during the malaise. Workers fell ever deeper into debt. In one company, the collective debt to the Chinese head-tandil totalled f19,500. Wages were slashed and 24,000 workers were sacked. Many became tramps and a threat to social order.

The Inspectorate was not entirely unsuccessful. Observers commented that European staff were trying harder to learn labourers' languages. Officials helped mediate in strikes. Only eight police reports were made regarding administrators after the start of the malaise, while "coolie attacks" fell by two thirds. (The attackers were mostly Javanese.) The number of reported *klapzaken* (beatings by Europeans) fell from 118 in 1921 to 74 in 1922. The Inspectorate tried to set up monthly meetings between planters and workers' representatives, although that plan came to nothing.

However, there is no evidence that the old methods of control, including violence, stopped completely. Speaking of the 1900s, Jan Breman concluded that "[o]nly a very small percentage of the many abuses practised by the planters ever penetrated to the offices of the colonial government on Sumatra's East Coast, let alone to Batavia," that "even when this did occur, the planters were seldom prosecuted," and that "if complaints were ever received, they were usually hushed up."[62] Assistants' dealing out blows to labourers and sexually abusing female labourers and labourers' wives was rife, and put down to their enforced bachelordom.[63] Conditions had improved somewhat by the 1920s, but official attempts to limit the planters' power failed to end the violence. In 1927, one hundred Europeans were convicted of beating workers, and the violence continued even after the start of the Depression. Far more widespread was abuse by Asian mandurs (overseers), who, unlike the Europeans, were present during working hours and were convicted of assault on 846 occasions in 1927 (and 704 in 1929). This represented one conviction for every 400 contract labourers—according to De Kat Angelino, an underestimate.[64]

Labour reform in the East Indies was partly influenced by developments in the ILO, which held its first International Labour Conference in 1919. When the League of Nations passed its Slavery Convention in 1926, the ILO took the chance to raise the issue of indenture. The colonial powers, who had a majority on the ILO's governing body, resisted calls for a

[62] Breman (1989, 143).
[63] Heijting (1925, 24–25).
[64] De Kat Angelino (1931, 539–555).

ban and compromised by urging the ILO instead to study ways of stopping such labour "from developing into conditions analogous to slavery." A "colonial clause" in the ILO's 1919 constitution allowed states to exempt colonies from ratifying "universal" norms, so colonial labour was conveniently classed as "native labour," governed by less stringent norms.[65] These norms required contracting parties "in territories in which compulsory or forced labour for other than public purposes still survives" to end it "as soon as possible," class it as exceptional, and keep the League of Nations informed of any steps to apply the Convention. However, a contracting party could still declare "that its acceptance of the [...] Convention does not bind some or all of the territories placed under its sovereignty, jurisdiction, protection, suzerainty or tutelage in respect of all or any provisions of the Convention."[66]

Dutch officials and colonial business interests used these concessions by the League of Nations and the ILO to defend the penal sanction, arguing that the retention of punitive laws by other colonial powers, particularly in Africa and New Guinea, justified the Dutch approach. They noted that states not yet in a position to comply fully could still be members of the ILO.[67]

In the 1920s, the East Indies government went ahead with some changes in order to qualify for fuller participation in the ILO. A Bureau for Social Affairs was established to extend supervision beyond state enterprises and plans were laid for a Labour Office and Labour Department. The Labour Office was installed in December 1921, to centralise and integrate approaches to the problems created by the rapid development of the East Indies, and in 1923 the Labour Inspectorate came under its control. It had three sections, dealing with labour legislation and statistics, Java and Madura, and trade unionism. Underfunded and understaffed, because of the government's financial difficulties at the time, it made little headway.[68]

In 1923, at the time of its incorporation into the Labour Office, a section of the Labour Inspectorate was added to cover the Outer Islands.

[65] Maul (2007, 478–481).

[66] Slavery Convention, September 25, 1926, Maul (2012, 18).

[67] Heijting (1925, 142–143).

[68] The level of staffing of the Dutch Office of Labour was (even proportionately) far below that of the British labour-related bureaucracy in India, to judge by the *Report of the Royal Commission on Labour in India* [1929], Calcutta: Government of India Central Publication Branch, 1931.

This new body was also at first small and ineffective. By 1930, however, it had expanded and acquired new powers. These included free access to enterprises, access to firms' books and staff, and the right to issue summonses. It was responsible for free labourers as well as contract workers, but only for those recruited under a labour agreement; and for supervising workers at all levels, from the European and foreign or native employees of big enterprises down to panglong workers and small companies run by Chinese, British Indians, and Indonesians. However, up to half a million labourers, including 80,000 Chinese, worked on the Outer Islands, so "despite the expansion of the inspectorate into a bureau, there was little realistic chance that it would make much difference" given its small staff. Its powers were anyway purely preventative—punitive functions were left to the judiciary. It relied on "tact and gentle persuasion, coupled with its moral ascendancy over the administrators."[69] Its restriction on the Outer Islands to workers under the coolie ordinance excluded most free workers from its remit.[70]

However, the Inspectorate's fundamental problem was that its goals were incompatible with indenture. Many of its officials had known this from the start. As early as 1905, Hoetink had admitted that there could be no improvement in the conditions of the plantation workforce as long as the old ordinance remained in force.[71] But he had no doubt that it would be years before a law specifying mutual rights and duties on the basis of a system of free labour came into being.

So the Inspectorate's lack of administrative sanctions and the failure of the colonial state, under pressure from employers, to abandon the penal sanction, together with the Inspectorate's lack of human and material resources, left it hamstrung. While some things improved, others stayed the same or worsened. In 1923, the penal code was revised to outlaw strikes and laws were passed to limit the power of trade unions. Collective bargaining between management and employees was not encouraged, except for Europeans, and for most of the time there was no official machinery for settling labour disputes. Strikes were few, isolated, and often futile.[72]

[69] Stibbe and Spat (1927, 231–236), De Kat Angelino (1931, 501–502 and 583).
[70] Houben (1999, 16).
[71] Breman (1988, 28).
[72] Tjandra (2016, 35–39).

A New Coolie Ordinance, 1905–1915

Before his appointment as Labour Inspector, Hoetink was charged with drafting a new coolie ordinance. His proposals included increasing obligations on the employers and abolishing the penal sanction.[73] The East Indies Government rejected his suggestions, even after they had been watered down to make them palatable to the planters.[74] In 1905, the Minister of Colonies commissioned A. F. van Blommestein, a legal officer in the East Indies on leave in the Netherlands, to carry out a general revision of labour legislation as applicable to Sumatra's East Coast.

Van Blommestein's research was supported by Hoetink, by then back in the Netherlands. He produced a new draft ordinance, completed in 1908 and made public in 1910. Should punitive clauses be retained? Van Blommestein favoured their gradual abolition. He allowed that they could be retained for immigrants on their first engagement and for Chinese hired as field coolies (*veldkoelies*) on tobacco plantations, but for all other categories of workers, including time-expired labourers re-engaging for a further term, breaches of contract should incur no punishment.

De Kat Angelino, a theorist of Dutch colonialism, found Van Blommestein's distinction between "apprentices and old hands" well-founded (although he favoured a gentler transition away from the penal sanction). In retaining punitive powers in the case of field workers and new immigrants, Van Blommestein was reflecting planter opinion: tobacco farming (done mainly by Chinese) depended on the regular availability of labour, and importing immigrants was costly. He added that field workers on a good wage would probably give no cause for punishment. His draft dropped clauses prescribing punishment for resistance, threats to the employer or his personnel, drunkenness, and indolence, arguing that they were general offences.

Van Blommestein mitigated the residual compulsion in his draft by allowing breach of contract where there were compelling reasons; where there were no compelling reasons but the worker paid reparations of f2.50 per month for the duration of the contract; and where the regional administration deemed the worker unsuitable. He also proposed extending a worker's freedom of movement by collecting money for repatriation only from the worker's first employer (to make it easier for him to change jobs),

[73] Kuiper (2017, 893–894).
[74] Breman (1989, 264).

shortening the maximum duration of immigration contracts, and capping advance payments on re-engagement.

Contracts were to be for a maximum of thirty months in the case of immigrants, twelve months plus a few days at the end of the harvest year for field workers other than immigrants, and twelve months for other categories. "Orientals" (so Van Blommestein argued) would not be motivated to emigrate without an advance, but the chance that they might fritter it away made the cap necessary. The regulations on duration of contract, advances, and wage-deductions to repay debts should be such that employers could recover their advances and time-expired workers be free of debt. A contract could be ended only by the worker's death, or as a result of its expiry, or by mutual agreement, or for compelling reasons, including bad behaviour on the worker's or employer's part and the danger of attacks (by bandits, etc.) or epidemics. A contract terminated unilaterally would go before a judge, who would assign fault. An employer who behaved unreasonably would have to pay the worker thirty times the daily wage. A worker who left his job without good reason could be forced either to return to it or to pay off his debts plus f2.50 per month to cover the unfulfilled part of his contract. These clauses would apply only to immigrants and field workers. "All other workers are unconditionally free": they could breach the relationship at any time, as could the employer, even without compelling reasons. However, the worker would lose outstanding wages and contractual benefits.

Where written contracts were not prescribed, agreements with workers "from elsewhere" would no longer need to comply with the ordinance, a first step towards legislating for labour free of penal sanctions. Native labourers or labourers equated with them who were not part of the native population could, if they wished, enter into a written agreement on the basis of and with the consequences set out in the ordinance. However, they would no longer have to do so, a crucial distinction.

All contracts would have to meet requirements set out in the ordinance regarding the conditions of work, wages, advances received and to be received, the duration of the agreement, accommodation, medical treatment, return to place of provenance after completion of a contract, the right of the administration to declare an agreement void, and so on. In the case of Indonesians though not of foreigners, breach of contract would only be punishable in special circumstances.

Most officials and employers believed that to abandon the penal sanction would kill off agricultural industry, so Van Blommestein's draft was fiercely resisted. On some points, as we have seen, he retreated. Planters argued that "the contract worker produces more than the free worker"; and a system of free labour would encourage employers to poach, a point that the Labour Inspectorate accepted. The government at first withheld judgment but later adopted an ordinance that contradicted the draft on key points.

However, the existing 1889 model did not meet local requirements in all respects. Employers began reaching extempore oral agreements that were rarely in the workers' interest. A typical agreement stipulated that contracts should be tied to debt repayment, adding an extra year to the 3-year maximum. The uniformity that Hoetink sought seemed further away than ever, so that central guidelines were increasingly sidelined and the Labour Inspectorate was unable to clean things up. Between 1908 and 1915, several new ordinances were decreed for different regions, adding to the confusion.[75]

Coolie ordinances had been designed to cope with underpopulation on the Outer Islands. In 1913, however, planters in parts of Java also demanded an ordinance, so that workers brought in from elsewhere could be forced to comply with contracts.[76] The government ruled out penal sanctions, but the planters' demand signalled a change in attitude to the penal sanction. In the past they had justified it on the grounds of the labour shortage: now they did so on the grounds of discipline.

In the years leading up to the proclamation of the 1889 coolie ordinance, the treatment meted out to workers in the mines and on the estates had, in Heijting's words, "left much to be desired." He showed through various examples that the new ordinance had not stopped abuses, including torture and woundings.

Finally, on June 22, 1915, a decade after Van Blommestein had first started drafting a new law and a year after his return to the Netherlands, the 1889 ordinance was replaced. However, the new ordinance was quite different from Van Blommestein's draft, and Van Blommestein fiercely attacked it in a pamphlet.

Even before its 1915 revision, the 1889 ordinance had already undergone numerous changes, and Kasteleijn said that the 1915 ordinance

[75] De Kat Angelino (1931, 529–530), Heijting (1925, 15–22), De Graaf and Stibbe (1918), Van Blommestein (1917, 29–30).

[76] A penal sanction for agricultural workers was introduced in Java in 1872 but relinquished in 1879, on the orders of the Dutch Parliament (Bosma 2019, 121).

"cannot actually be called new." The penal sanction remained. "Excessive indolence" no longer figured in it, but the sanction continued to apply to other breaches of the contract by worker or employer—in the worker's case, they included failing to turn up to work on time, deserting, and refusing to work. Also retained was the ruling that recalcitrant workers could be escorted back to work by the employer's staff, exercising police powers.[77] A Bangka Chinese view was that by granting mine chiefs the right to carry out punishments, the new regulation led to an even harsher regime than the one that it replaced.[78]

However, the new ordinance made some concessions to opponents of the penal sanction. It gave the Governor-General the power to shorten the duration of labour agreements, including for all enterprises within a region or part of it, and to annul the penal sanction in the whole region or part of it and for all agreements or some when circumstances allowed. The Director of Justice expressed the hope that a free working population would, if employers cooperated, gradually evolve, at which point ordinances and penal sanctions could fall away.

In 1931, De Kat Angelino listed gains of the 1915 ordinance. He noted that although workers could be employed by written agreement, with the consequences set out in the ordinance, including the penal sanction, such agreements were no longer obligatory. Other changes concerned the length of the working day, days of rest, overtime (which now required the worker's agreement), piece work, holidays, and related issues.

Starting in 1915, immigration contracts were only valid when confirmed in documents (*akten*) delivered in person by the regional administration, except when agreed in Java or in a place where sufficient control was exercised over the contract worker's expatriation, validated by an official and seen by the Labour Inspectorate. In the next few years, most of the Outer Islands acquired their own labour legislations. By January 1, 1924, all eighteen regions had their own ordinance or were covered by other laws.[79]

[77] Heijting (1925, 22–23), Stibbe and Spat (1927, 233–234), Van Blommestein (1917), De Graaf and Stibbe (1918, 364–365).

[78] Yang Tongling et al. (2004, 83).

[79] Heijting (1925, 22 and 27), De Graaf and Stibbe (1918), De Kat Angelino (1931), 537–539. In fact, there were sixteen coolie ordinances.

Van Blommestein's Criticism of the 1915 Coolie Ordinance

After the issuing of the 1915 ordinance, Van Blommestein's rejected draft was discussed in the Second Chamber in March 1917. Plejte, Minister of the Colonies, raised three objections: it was a leap in the dark rather than a measured response to circumstances; it deviated from existing precepts; and it stripped the employer of powers permitted him in European legislation. Also, it assumed that colonisation by free workers would succeed, although officials doubted a surge in Javanese transmigration (De Kat Angelino later called colonisation an idea "thirty or forty years ahead of its time"). Officials also argued that free labourers were more likely to abandon paid work than workers under contract and were less productive. Plejte was therefore not alone in opposing a fundamental revision of the coolie ordinance of the sort Van Blommestein proposed.

In 1917, Van Blommestein published a bombshell pamphlet criticising the revised ordinance. He compared it unfavourably with the situation in British India, which was abolishing contract labour, and criticised the lack of pressure on planters to promote colonisation. Kasteleyn replied that penal and compulsory clauses remained in the 1912 Labour Code for British Malaya and the Straits Settlements and that the Dutch ordinance envisaged a committee of planters to pursue colonisation. Kasteleyn's point was echoed by C. Lulofs, a Dutch researcher, who wrote that although indenture had been replaced in Malaya by oral monthly contracts for Chinese and Indians, penal sanctions had not as such been dropped.[80]

Van Blommestein's main argument was that inclusion in the legislation of the penal sanction and the "strong arm" regulation, whereby companies could force absconders back to work, left things more or less unchanged. The Minister, he said, had argued that the new ordinance would speed up the transition from contract labour to free labour, but the opposite was true. He made two main counter-proposals which would, not immediately but in a matter of years, create the conditions for an end to coercion: an extension of recruitment by time-expired labourers (a point Plejte accepted) and renewed attention to a functioning programme of colonisation.

[80] Heijting (1925, 125–127), De Kat Angelino (1931, 532–534).

To support his argument against the penal sanction, Van Blommestein insisted that it had either been abolished or was about to be in most other countries and that even some Dutch politicians saw it as a negation of the principle of personal freedom. He added that to retain indenture even when re-engaging a seasoned labourer made no sense, and quoted a British committee on indenture in 1871:

> An indenture justifiable to ensure payment by the immigrant for services rendered, that is for his passage out, which payment, it seems, can be insured in no other way. It may also be defended on the ground of his helplessness on arrival in a new country; for, if a man must necessarily be dependent on others for the preservation of his health, there is no harm in recognising the fact by law. It would seem, that immigration as far as the coolies are concerned, has failed to fulfil its purpose, if, after being acclimatised, after learning their work and paying for their passage out, they must still be brought under indenture after indenture.

He also quoted Lord Hardinge's acknowledgement "of the deep and genuine disgust to which the continuance of the indentured system has given rise" in India.

Van Blommestein's core argument was that the penal sanction deviated from the principle, established in May 1879, that a worker could not be punished for non-compliance with a contract, and should therefore be regarded as permissible only under special circumstances or temporarily and only if the overriding goal was to remove those circumstances. The sole reason to include a penal sanction in the first Coolie Ordinance in 1880 had been the absence of an employable native population on Sumatra's East Coast. The new ordinance should stress such circumstances and force employers to end them, and thus to end the deviation from principle.

Van Blommestein noted that the usual justification for the penal sanction was the initial cost of recruitment. However, this argument only applied to a contract entered into by the worker in his place of origin or on arrival overseas and not in the case of subsequent agreements. He also pointed out that although the 1915 ordinance was presented as part of a long-term project to reduce the scope of the penal sanction, in fact it extended it to new sectors. The 1889 ordinance had applied the penal sanction to agriculture and industry. Although it was subsequently cut back to agriculture and mining, in 1915 it was extended to cover both industry and commerce.

Van Blommestein concluded by looking at the Dutch colonial state's plans for ending the need for penal measures and the underpopulation said to account for them. He explained that the changes that he sought could only come about gradually. Although he did not say how long, he was clearly thinking in terms of years, punctuated by transitional reforms.[81]

Colonisation by workers' settlements was, in Van Blommestein's view, a necessary precondition for abolishing the penal sanction, but planters and reactionary officials were hampering its realisation. For them, colonisation would rob employers of their land and give it to colonists; while ending the penal sanction would rob them of their authority. Employers therefore turned against colonisation, and the regulation governing it was withdrawn in 1927.[82] Van Blommestein summarised in a single point the employers' view of colonisation: its goal should be "acquiring colonies of workers and of workers prepared to work" rather than establishing settlements of free settlers from which labourers could be recruited. The true solution to the problem of underpopulation was, he said, for the new legislation to drop its punitive sanctions and safeguard labour relations by law.[83] However, the switch to "free" labour was in reality still decades away.

The Penal Sanction, 1915–1931

In the decade up to 1924, conservatives and reformers waged war over the penal sanction. Its critics included parts of the East Indies government, parts of the Second Chamber, and, after 1918, the Volksraad (an advisory body), as well as the nationalist Sarekat Islam and the Comité Nieuw Indië, a Dutch liberal association agitating for East Indies autonomy. The Government toyed with reform but eventually stuck with the new ordinance. Despite criticisms made by what De Kat Angelino called "some of the best social and political forces," the Government found the 1915 ordinance a big improvement on the old, and pointed to new forms of recruitment and worker colonisation as the way forward. A provisional armistice "more favourable to the sanction" than to free labour ensued, and an eventual short-term victory for the status quo.[84]

[81] Van Blommestein (1917, 5–26, 30–37 and 68–77).

[82] De Kat Angelino (1931, 578–581).

[83] Van Blommestein (1917, 78, 88–101), Planters Comite [*sic*], *Meedeling* no. 8, *Overzicht van Verschillende Adviezen in zake de Afschaffing der Poenale Sanctie*, 1920, 5–6.

[84] De Kat Angelino (1931, 539–541).

Why did the government consider removing the penal sanction? Within the East Indies, it hoped to use the threat of abolition to force the planters to accept the plans for colonisation, a main plank in its strategy. Developments in world politics and Britain's abolition of indenture were an added spur, for the Dutch were reluctant to be seen to resist the political tide. But although the postwar calls for reform in the East Indies chimed with worldwide efforts spearheaded by the ILO, Dutch officials and business interests eventually watered down their commitment to change. Obstructive proposals started to rise on all sides, and the government eventually buckled to the planters' lobby. The retreat was a result both of the failure of Dutch political leadership, which was hesitant and disunited, and planters' intransigence.

The Dutch parliament set up a commission on the penal sanction (and other matters). This commission recommended replacing the sanction with a public-law regulation banning the cessation of labour without the permission of the Labour Inspector, who could set a penal prosecution going, and allowing labourers to be escorted back to work but only by the police, a regulation that would expire after colonisation. A contract could be terminated with sufficient cause or if the worker paid an indemnity—a proposal also made by Van Blommestein.

After 1915, the East Indies government strove to shorten the duration of the labour contract and to remove its penal and compulsory clauses entirely or in part, but (again) depending on the progress of labour colonisation. To pressure employers into speeding up colonisation, in 1918 it announced that the sanction would be abolished in a few years' time and colonisation was the only way forward.

Van Blommestein had argued that workers and their families from Java, organised in self-sustaining settlements of free workers as pools on which employers might draw, was the best way of solving the problem of underpopulation without resort to coercion. However, he accepted that colonisation could not extend to "foreign colonists," i.e., Chinese, for as foreigners they were ineligible for land grants. When, at the turn of the century, the chief administrator of the Deli Maatschappij had suggested letting Chinese settle in large communities near Medan to breed pigs and raise vegetables on land unsuitable for tobacco and thus to "strengthen ties with China and make it easier to get coolies in the future," the Sultan said no, on the grounds that large settlements of imported Chinese labourers would result in "the displacement of the native."[85]

This exclusion did not prevent some Deli planters from experimenting with Chinese colonisation in 1923, when the DPV tried to colonise a group of Chinese workers in Deli. However, the workers and the women imported under the scheme preferred to buy land in China with their savings and their one-off pension payments,[86] so the experiment failed. In their calculation, if they worked for twenty years for a single employer, they would be eligible for a payout of $100, which was probably worth more than the pension of $7 a month they would get in Deli. There were anyway too few Chinese women to form self-reproducing colonies, and those that did arrive in the early twentieth century left to invest the family savings in China.[87] (In the late nineteenth century, up to one third of married miners departed annually.[88])

Colonisation by Javanese had long been under consideration but had generally failed to take off.[89] In 1916, plans for colonisation began to crystallise and planters indicated for a while that they were prepared to cooperate. In 1918, a commission under Lulofs persuaded employers to agree to turn five percent of tobacco workers and three percent of rubber workers into colonists each year for the following five years, whereafter by an additional one percent a year, so that in fourteen years' time 95 and 75 percent of tobacco and rubber labourers would be colonists. Under Lulofs' plan, the further development of the penal sanction would depend on colonisation. The employers were unconvinced, but at the time they could see no alternative. However, the government did not stick to this timetable—regrettably, in De Kat Angelino's opinion—and decided to accelerate the transition by abolishing the sanction before 1925 and by 1922 in the case of re-engagement, regardless of colonisation's success. Planters turned their backs on the scheme when it became clear that it was part of the wider plan to abolish the penal sanction.

Because of its vacillation, the government lost the planters' trust, at a time of gathering economic clouds (portending the malaise) that would

[85] De Bruin (1918, 3 and 52–53).

[86] *Mededeling no. 22 (1932), DPV, Een en ander over Javanenkolonies en arbeidersvestigingen ter Oostkust van Sumatra*, 45

[87] Mededeling no. 22 (1932), Deli Planters Vereeniging, *Een en ander over Javanenkolonies en arbeiders-vestigingingen ter Oostkust van Sumatra*, 45.

[88] Heinoldt (1897, 4).

[89] Heijting (1925, 107–109), De Kat Angelino (1931, 578–579).

undo even the best-laid plans. Having promised to abolish the penal sanction altogether, the East Indies government declared in 1921 that it would abolish it "before 1926," and only in the case of re-engagements.[90] In 1923, at the end of the depression, colonisation began to look ever less realistic, especially in the short term, and the government retreated further still. A new ordinance in 1924 accepted that the basis for labour agreements as set out in the 1915 ordinance would have to be retained, in the interests of the state, for "as long as local circumstances do not make superfluous a sanction stronger than a merely civil one." The Volksraad agreed, as did most of its Indonesian members, although (like most of the Second Chamber) they described the institution as "a necessary evil."

However, the Lulofs commission proposed further revisions concerning colonisation and the ordinances, including an end to prosecution under the penal sanction on the employer's initiative and, most importantly, a revision of the coolie ordinance every five years, starting in 1930, with a view to gradually abolishing the sanction. The parliament, according to De Kat Angelino, "wanted to convey that it had bowed to necessity, but that, like the Parliamentary Commission, it had no wish to admit in principle the continuation of the sanction."

By 1924, the inevitability of abolition of the sanction had been generally accepted, at least in principle, but in the meantime every effort would be made to perfect it in the course of its five-yearly revision. A stipulation, copied from Dutch labour law, allowing the dissolution of a contract at the request of either party, for urgent reasons, was adopted. Other amendments were also introduced.

Defenders of the ordinance continued to argue for the retention of the sanction. They pointed to the claim that 80 percent of labourers re-engaged under a new contract after the expiry of the original contract as proof that the ordinance was widely accepted. However, this argument ignored the role played by monetary inducements and the mandurs' financial stake in pressuring workers to re-engage.[91]

[90] Deli Planters Vereeniging, *Mededeling no. 14, De Arbeidsregeling voor de Buitengewesten van Nederlandsch Indië*, Medan: Köhler & co., 1923, 14.

[91] Heijting (1925, 167–183), De Kat Angelino (1931, 539–555).

The British and the Ending of Indenture

The British coped more successfully than the Dutch with the transition to a freer form of labour in their colonies. For all the advantages of state-regulated indenture from an employer's point of view and the corresponding disadvantages from a worker's, the switch in British colonies came about less as a result of workers' actions than at the wish of the employers, who came to see indenture as contrary to their economic interests, despite having defended it for decades. Indenture and recruitment through official channels had three main drawbacks for the employer. It did not stop recruits deserting, sometimes in droves; the penal sanction was seen by many not just as a result of the labour shortage but as its "most potent cause," by hampering "the natural flow of labour";[92] and it was costly.

In the Straits Settlements and Malaya, indenture became ever dearer because of the control of Indian recruitment by a handful of companies that at every possible opportunity raised their fees, intolerably so during the rubber boom of the early twentieth century, when the need for labour rocketed.[93] Planters and officials set out to explore alternative ways of acquiring workers and settled on one based on ties of kinship, known generally as the kangani system, and discussed in the following chapter. For employers, switching to it had the advantage of seeming to yield to the growing climate of moral indignation surrounding indenture. Encouraged by a colonial commission in 1910, planters in Malaya went over in greater numbers than ever to the new system, supervised by the colonial state, as state-regulated indenture came to an end in 1917.

In British Malaya, the formal abolition of indenture (first for Indians, in 1913, and then for Chinese, in 1914) coincided with the culmination of a decade-long slide in the number of Huagong entering the Malay Federation, from 7,462 in 1900 to just 863 in 1909. This decline affected recruitment in the East Indies, for the two streams were linked. However, Huagong recruitment picked up throughout much of the next two to three decades. In 1930, 110,541 Huagong were employed in Malaya.[94] In North Borneo, an abolition ordinance was not introduced until January 1933.[95]

[92] Mohapatra and Behal (1991).
[93] Gordon (2004).
[94] Lu Wendi et al. (1984, 50–51 and 64–68).
[95] "Indentured Labour," *South China Morning Post*, November 19, 1932, 22.

The British found it hard to convince a sceptical Malayan public that Chinese indenture was no longer practised. In 1934, when Chinese immigration resumed after the Depression, officials were dismayed at the suggestion that new arrivals were "in some way akin to indentured labourers" and denied that re-indenture or anything reminiscent of it had ever happened "over the last twenty years."[96] But the perception that indenture had survived in fact if not in name was hard to overcome.

Under the kangani system, the recruits' passage overseas was financed by a new Indian Immigration Fund, set up (as the Tamil Immigration Fund) in 1910, to which all planters contributed. Since the recruit received no monetary advance, he incurred no debt, at least in that respect. Some observers said that the new system did away with the need for a penal sanction, since the labourer was now debt-free. (Even so, the penal sanction continued to figure in the Labour Code until the mid 1920s.) However, while labourers were legally free to leave their jobs, in practice it was in the kangani's interest to stop them leaving. In that regard, he was aided by his foreman's role, for his recruits were generally allocated to the estate that he himself helped manage. On top of his official wage, he received a commission (called "head [or pence] money") for days worked by the recruits, who were likely to be in debt to him, as their money-lender and shopkeeper. The new system therefore kept some elements of indenture. The idea that it was free was to that extent a fiction.[97]

The Penal Sanction after 1915

Political leaders in both The Hague and the East Indies continued for several years to debate the pros and cons of the penal sanction. In 1917, Sarekat Islam, the first big nationalist party in the East Indies, called for its abolition. The East Indies government rejected it in June 1918 and set 1925 as the year of its abolition. Also in 1918, Volksraad members asked for the penal sanction to be removed for workers who re-engaged or who

[96] *Malaya Tribune*, October 24, 1934.

[97] Gordon (2004), Mishra (2015, 379), Behal (2013, 4 and 18). Behal says that kangani recruits had to pay their own passage through a system of advances. However, according to Pelzer (1938, 70–71), "[t]he Indian Immigration Funds pay the expenses of recruiting, i.e. the train fares […], transportation to the places of employment in Malaya or Ceylon, and recruiting allowances which cover the expenses of the kangany and give him a commission for each labourer."

repaid part of their advance and passage money,[98] and Assistant-Resident J. Tideman called for a labour law that would avoid unjust outcomes and for a transition to free labour. The head of the Labour Inspectorate, E. J. van Lier, also favoured abandoning the penal sanction for re-engagements, but only after four years, to allow for a transition, and after six years for Chinese, since it would take more than four years to replace Chinese with Javanese. The Governor of Sumatra's East Coast wanted to do away with punitive clauses after four years in the case of re-engagements and to reduce first engagements to two years, and then to abolish the penal sanction altogether, perhaps within twelve years.

Most planters were unhappy with these proposals. Agreements under civil sanction were impossible because of the "chasm between the character of Western and Oriental workers," so a penal sanction should be kept until the embedding in the coolie mind of the notion of a contract in civil law and the schooling of a generation in the idea of hard work. In 1919, the DPV rejected a speedy abolition of the penal sanction and proposed a longer transition. In 1921, the planters' leader Fruin again spoke up for the penal sanction and asked what the "political reasons" were for abolishing it in 1925, since the ILO in Washington had accepted its retention by colonies.

Reform-minded officials like Lulofs countered that Chinese and Indian workers in the Straits Settlement of Malacca were on a month-long oral contract that was renewed unless relinquished by either side (against payment of a month's wages). Sanctions were rarely used, given the ease with which workers could leave their jobs. Although the system led to a big turnover of workers, the losses were offset by the Indian Immigration Fund, which insured employers against non-payment of recruitment costs. That workers favoured the high wages and freedom to change employer was evidenced by the few attacks on staff.

Lulofs also pointed to the worldwide rise of the labour movement, making a "collective refusal of service" increasingly likely, in which case "bringing tens of thousands to justice will be impossible." Like others, Lulofs recommended abolishing the penal sanction in the case of re-engaging workers, who did not need to be imported and were presumably satisfied with existing terms. Such was the rate of re-engagement that on many tobacco estates re-engaged and free workers made up 75 percent of

[98] Heijting (1925, 97–99, 127–128, and 157).

the workforce, while new recruits still under penal sanction, already just 25 percent of the workforce, would soon have shrunk to nothing.

However, the Dutch government was, in the end, unwilling to back down from its basic attachment to the penal sanction. When in July 1920 Thajib et al. proposed that the penal sanction should expire for all contract workers in September 1923, and immediately for re-engaged workers, the East Indies government responded that it would drop the sanction "at the appropriate time." Later in the same year, however, having briefly flirted amid the postwar optimism with the idea of annulling the sanction and securing the necessary workforce by colonisation, it argued that abolishing the sanction, even for re-engaging workers, would cost f20 million a year, or 5 percent of total capital, at a time when Sumatra's East Coast contributed around f10 million annually to the treasury. As for colonisation, even in 1923 it was deemed "inconceivable" within the near future, so the sanction "must in the meantime be retained for many years."

Critics of the government noted that in 1919 the planters had considered introducing a contractual notice of just four months, a compromise made in the belief that the penal sanction was on its last legs. However, the government had failed to respond. Now that the government had shown its hand, the planters abandoned their conciliatory stance, especially given the effect on business of the economic malaise. Having implied an end to the penal sanction and habituated planters to the idea, it changed its tune and succumbed to the diehard interest.

In November 1923, the Volksraad resolved to keep the penal sanction, a decision that even Indonesian members approved, either because it now seemed inevitable or because they felt that abolishing it suddenly would create labour problems, that its imperfections were exaggerated, and that a system based on civil-law sanctions would harm agriculture.

How long would a sufficiently dense population take to emerge from colonisation? Officials doubted that Javanese would wish to colonise permanently and noted that even where colonisation had established a core population, in southern Sumatra, it had proved expensive (5,000 families cost fl million) and ineffective. It risked creating an excess population and would require the withdrawal from cultivation of good tobacco land on behalf of settlers "whose laziness and vagabond nature would reappear once they became free."[99]

[99] The quotation is from Dr Broersma, writing in *Algemene Landbouwweekblad*, October 7, 1923, 450.

The Director of Justice summarised the situation as follows: "The Government urgently needs the penal sanction in the coming period, unconditionally and as a major means, now more than ever, to help safeguard the country's prosperity and development. It regards this penal sanction as a strict, exceptional measure, but one justified by the particular circumstances of the Outer Islands, due to their thin population and, given that the penal sanction has developed alongside the Labour Inspectorate, fully justified before the court of practical morality."[100]

The Comité Nieuw Indië raised moral and political objections to the penal sanction. For example, more than 30 percent of contract workers were punished annually and as many as 60–70 percent in the state-run coal mines.[101] The system discriminated against wives and children, who became vulnerable to sexual abuse. Gambling and opium were used to force contract workers to re-engage. The worker was afraid to speak his mind, so beatings went unprosecuted. Moreover, only Indonesians and Chinese were subject to the penal sanction, which was exercised exclusively by Europeans and therefore inherently racist. If the sanction had a pedagogic value, why was it not abandoned when workers re-engaged?

Government spokespeople responded with the usual arguments: without coercion, hygiene would suffer; the penal sanction was a function of the underdeveloped labour market on the Outer Islands and the need to recruit workers at great cost from elsewhere and to bind them to their contracts; and the penal sanction was an extreme measure dictated by adverse circumstance, but the date of its abolition could not be set in advance, as the East Indies government had thought possible in 1918 and as the minority now wanted. Meanwhile, the Labour Inspectorate had brought about improvements. De Kat Angelino attacked the idea that the East Indies was the only place left with a penal sanction—it was "still the general rule," while the East Indies government was "in the van of colonial labour legislation." Abuse was rare—and anyway, it happened not just

[100] Heijting (1925, 128–156).

[101] Mr Marchant, a Dutch politician, said that the Planters' Association estimated that only 1.12 percent of field coolies carrying out "skilled labour" had been punished, as against 5.04 percent of those under their first contract and 3.20 percent under re-engagement contracts (Heijting 1925, 164). According to the Labour Inspection, in 1927, of a total of 240,000 contract labourers, 9,206 were punished once, 1,328 twice, 384 three times, 137 four times, 43 five times, 12 six times, 7 seven times, 1 eight times, and 1 even more frequently. Those punished therefore amounted to 11,000 or 4.5 percent of the total; around 8,000 were newcomers, themselves a minority (De Kat Angelino 1931, 513, fn. 1).

on the Outer Islands but also in Java, where the penal sanction did not apply.

As late as the 1910s, even reform-minded officials like Van Blommestein saw punitive penalties as hard to avoid in the case of a first engagement, for although unjust in principle, they had to be available *in extremis.* Yet no one advocated the penal sanction absolutely. Most saw it as abnormal and wanted it replaced once circumstances allowed. For the Labour Inspectorate, Van Lier called it outdated, although it could not yet be abolished; the Director of Justice said in 1918 that it should expire for re-engaging contracts after four years and otherwise after seven; the Governor of Sumatra's East Coast said twelve years; Schneider on behalf of the rubber planters wanted to reduce it from a primary to a subsidiary means of coercion; the DPV merely wanted a longer transition than seven years; Lulofs advised making it expensive for employers, and thus forcing them to cooperate in the transition to free labour; Vierhout thought it could be dropped within three to seven years; and the Volksraad members Thajib et al. thought it could be dropped in three. In November 1923, Kiès called the penal sanction a necessary evil for the time being. Koesoemo Joedo said keeping it was inevitable in the absence of anything better. Moelia wanted it enforced until enough labour was available. Sujono, Kamil, and Djajadiningrat saw it as a necessary but provisional evil that required adequate safeguards. Wiranata Koesoema did not reject it altogether as an educational device, because of the lack of organisation among employees. Dwidjosewojo rejected it in principle but considered it admissible for a number of years yet to be determined. Soerakoesoemah approved of it, but only for the time being. Kerkkamp had many objections, but indicated ways round them. Other European members wanted to keep it until there was a guarantee of industrial security. The Comité Nieuw Indie wanted to ban it where it had not yet been introduced and to remove it from where it was no longer wanted. In 1924, a majority of the committee investigating Van Blommestein's draft ordinance favoured retaining the penal sanction in a milder form, with a view to its gradual abolition, and the Minister of Colonies called it an extreme remedy for abnormal conditions that would fall away as circumstances changed.

So there was much support for the provisional retention of the penal sanction. In 1923, even the provisionality was dropped. The Second Chamber agreed that the aim was to abolish the sanction "progressively," but an amendment containing the words "desirability of provisional retention" was rejected by the Volksraad at the request of the East Indies government, so that "the proven necessity to preserve the system unchanged" remained. The Director of Justice told the Volksraad on November 23, 1923: "The Government needs the penal sanction urgently, unconditionally and integrally for the coming period, as one of the most important means that, now more than ever, will help safeguard the country's prosperity and pre-development [*voorontwikkeling*]."

Heijting saw the decision as a step in the wrong direction, at a time when "the desirability of a transition to a practical jobs contract shorn of penal provisions was almost universally recognised." He deeply regretted the failure to make provision for a transition in 1918 or 1919—when the East Indies Government had in principle decided to drop the penal sanction within years, when the Director of Justice had proposed 1925 as a deadline, when the Governor of Sumatra's East Coast had argued for a twelve-year transition, and when the planters' associations, under extreme pressure, had made detailed proposals for colonisation and an end to the penal sanction within fourteen years. A compromise with the planters had been within the government's grasp, but there was no consultation and the moment had been missed. The penal sanction was to be retained indefinitely.

What were the government's arguments now in favour of retention? To put an immediate end to the existing system would destroy the prosperity of the Outer Islands; abolishing the sanction, if only for re-engagements, would cut profits and lead to an outflow of capital to neighbouring colonies; regional heads of government were unanimously in favour of keeping the sanction; colonisation had failed to solve the problem of labour supply, given the reluctance of transmigrant Javanese to settle; experiments with free workers in 1907 had failed; large firms opposed relinquishing the penal sanction; and the Amsterdam Trade Association and the Colonial Bank had warned that abolition would lead to an agricultural slowdown.

Other supporters of the penal sanction mounted a more positive defence, arguing that it had changed radically and for the better. De Kat Angelino, for example, said that it was "administered by impartial judges [...] for the general good" and could no longer serve as an instrument in the first instance of the employer.[102]

[102] Heijting (1925, 156–183), De Kat Angelino (1931, 541–542).

The Curtailment of Indenture, 1929–1930

The first real steps in the East Indies towards the abolition of indenture and the penal sanction were taken in response to external rather than domestic developments: the onset of the Great Depression in 1929 and the US Tariff Act of 1930. The latter led to a ban on the importation into the US of goods produced by forced labour, the former to a slashing of the rubber price. Until 1930, less than a quarter of workers on the Outer Islands were free.[103] Between 1929 and 1934, after the changes, the number under indenture collapsed from 87 to just 4 percent. In 1930, the professional recruitment of contract workers for the East Indies was, theoretically, abolished. As Furnivall optimistically noted: "[T]here has been a great development towards making the relations between employer and employee less artificial, and more permanent and social." The Dutch colonial authorities were pushed in this direction by the US ban on tobacco produced by contract labour, which led to a switch to free labour on tobacco plantations in Sumatra.[104] By 1937, more than 90 percent of Javanese farming tobacco in Deli were classed as free.[105]

In the early 1920s, the most vocal opposition to relinquishing the penal sanction in the East Indies was by employers, principally the DPV and the Ondernemersraad (employers' council), backed by their allies in the metropole. Although predominantly Dutch, their membership was to a significant extent international.

The Dutch government's lack of a firm, stable focus played a major role in its failure to navigate a way out of crisis. A comparison with British India helps explain the Dutch failure to stand firm. In British India, a lobby representing the managing agency houses, which controlled three-quarters of India's industrial capital, similarly campaigned to resist the Government's new industrial policy, which entailed an unwelcome degree of state intervention.[106] The agency houses were, like the planters, hostile to nationalist opinion, but their efforts failed, and for several reasons.

The nationalists were well organised in India and eventually trained their sights on indenture, at home and overseas. In the East Indies, mainstream nationalists were readier to compromise—even the Comité Nieuw Indië was prepared to postpone its abolition. Dutch abolitionists were,

[103] Boeke (1942, 142), quoted in Lasker (1950, 222).

[104] Furnivall 355–356. See also Lasker (1950, 223).

[105] "Nu en vroeger," *Soerabaijasch Handelsblad*, February 13, 1937.

[106] Misra (1999, 4–12).

like the French, less vociferous than British reformers, who (acting, admittedly, more on Smithian than on humanitarian grounds) waged a powerful campaign. The East Indies government therefore came under less pressure from both local nationalists and metropolitan abolitionists.[107]

In the East Indies, the planters' taxes bankrolled the government's welfare programme. They objected to colonisation on the grounds that colonists were unlikely to become regular workers and because colonisation would deprive them of access to land, for long-term leases were available only for wild lands and local people opposed re-leasing land to Europeans.[108]

Three other things made the British more likely than the Dutch to yield to nationalist opinion. First, the Dutch stayed neutral in the First World War and were therefore better equipped to counter sedition than the government in wartime India, which lacked the military reserves to deal with large-scale unrest. Second, wage growth in British Indian migrant destinations overseas meant that labour was easier to attract than in the past, making indenture less necessary,[109] and an economic argument for its abolition started to gain ground.[110] In the East Indies, on the other hand, officials and employers continued to support the economic case for its retention.[111] Third, the Dutch establishment's attachment to the East Indies, and its reluctance to destabilise the powerful private sector, can also be explained by the colony's crucial role in protecting the Dutch economy, a point developed in Chap. 6.

Defenders of indenture continued, even in the 1920s, to predict that its abolition would leave the Outer Islands with insufficient labour. Traditionalists argued that "coolies come from the worst of [...] people and can be educated to regular work only by means of the penal sanction," and anyway enjoyed "far greater protection than other native laborers." To abolish the penal sanction immediately would ruin the economy in the Outer Islands and damage government finances. The planters were a powerful lobby and had the government by the throat, for their taxes financed its welfare programme at a time when the price of tropical products was at rock bottom.

[107] Emmer (2011, 273).

[108] Vandenbosch (1931).

[109] Northrup (1995, 147–148).

[110] Bates et al. (2017, 2–4). This was not everywhere the case. In some British West Indian colonies, planters in need of labour petitioned the Government of India after 1917 for a scheme to replace indenture, in order to overcome labour shortages (Mahase 2021, 12).

[111] Heijting (1925, 156–159).

In 1929, the struggle against forced labour received a big boost when the ILO put it on the agenda of its Twelfth Conference in Geneva. Apologists for the penal sanction denounced the ILO's "socialist" view of labour and its "tendentious and distorted view" of the East Indies. However, when the Dutch and East Indies governments eventually agreed to start abolishing indenture, it was partly as a direct and indirect result of this conference. One Dutch observer noted that getting rid of the penal sanction would be at "considerable cost to the government, for the large plantation owners on the East Coast of Sumatra have fought and are still fighting every inch of the ground." But the tide had turned against indenture almost everywhere, and the East Indies was unable to withstand it.

Indentured labour was not originally on the agenda of the ILO conference in 1929, but it was raised as an urgent issue by E. Kupers, a Dutch labour representative, who said that penal sanctions were a form of forced labour that left the labourer "bound hand and foot."[112] Kupers' speech set in motion a process that ended in a major Dutch retreat.

Undiplomatic comments opposing the penal sanction made in Batavia by the ILO Director Albert Thomas in January 1929, shortly before the Geneva conference, greatly offended members of the Ondernemersraad, who called him rude and aggressive. However, it did not escape the British Consul in Batavia at the time that the employers' leader, Professor Treub, was ready to give up on the issue. Treub continued to argue that penal sanctions were necessary in colonial enterprises, but he conceded that the power of decision in the matter lay with the Dutch government. The Consul concluded: "Even our capitalist 'die-hards' had begun to realise that the 'Penal Sanction' is doomed, quite apart from the merits of the case and if only because international public opinion is turning steadily against it. The present endeavours of the 'die-hards' are thus in the direction of delaying the disappearance of the system for as long as possible, and securing some working substitutes in place of it when at last it goes."[113]

At around the same time as the ILO meeting, a protectionist tariff bill, the Smoot-Hawley Act, began its passage through the US House of Representatives. The Act would, in theory, have prohibited the importation into the US of Sumatra's rubber, tobacco, palm oil, and tea. In the event, this did not happen, as a result of the "consumptive demand exception"—products "not mined, produced, or manufactured in such

[112] Vandenbosch (1931, 318–324), Cohen de Boer (1930, 3 and 6).
[113] Cited in Groenewoud (1995, 81–82).

quantities in the United States as to meet [its] consumptive demands" were excluded. However, an amendment narrowed its focus to tobacco farmed under the penal sanction.[114]

As a result of the conference, the Dutch were held up to shame by their competitors, including the British, who flaunted their own supposed virtues and deflected attention away from their own practices. The *North-China Herald*, a mouthpiece for British interests, contrasted India and Malaya with the Netherlands East Indies. It urged the US to look not at Malaya in its search for abuses but "at other countries where rubber is produced, [...] not under the supervision of governments skilled in handling that special type of employee."[115]

The threat of sanctions drove the Dutch to a concession, although it turned out to be less radical than expected: to abolish the penal sanction within ten years, during which time employers would increase the proportion of free labourers annually by a specified percentage, and to go ahead with colonising the Outer Islands with free Javanese immigrants. In 1931, the penal sanction was removed from tobacco farming. In any case, by that time the labour market had tilted massively in the employers' favour and led to a collapse in wages of up to 75 percent, lessening the need for non-market coercion. In 1931, even the planters resolved "emphatically and irrevocably" to abandon the penal sanction.[116]

According to the new timetable, indenture would pass step by step into oblivion. Enterprises formed before 1921 would not be allowed to use indentured labour after 1940; those set up between 1922 and 1927, after 1946, for 90 percent of their workforce; and those between 1928 and 1930, the same, but for 100 percent of their workforce; while half of the workers in enterprises formed between 1931 and 1941 would be free by 1942.[117] So indenture was not abolished but progressively mitigated, as Chinese officials noted in 1939.[118] According to another timetable, proclaimed in 1930 by the Volksraad, at least 25 of any one hundred workers

[114] *The North-China Herald and Supreme Court & Consular Gazette*, April 29, 1930, Vandenbosch, (1931, 318–319), Groenewoud (1995, 81–83).

[115] "Indentured Labour," *North-China Herald*, June 2, 1931, 293. The *North-China Daily News*, May 27, 1931, written in identical terms.

[116] Groenewoud (1995, 81).

[117] Zhu Jieqin (1984, 242–243).

[118] *Huaqiao nianjian* (Overseas Chinese Yearbook), ch. 5, "Nanyang zhi Huagong" (Huagong in the Nanyang), published in 1939 by Singapore's Overseas-Chinese Commercial Publishers (Huaqiao shang baoshe), 60–76, reprinted in Lu Wendi et al. (1984, 43–68) at 51.

would have to be "free" by January 1932, and the rest would be under contract. This ratio would progress to 40:60 by January 1934 and 50:50 by January 1936. However, no final date was given for the complete abolition of indenture.[119]

In the event, the proportion of workers under penal sanction fell more rapidly than planned. In 1935, the government gained the planters' assent to abolish the penal sanction by 1946. In 1939, the ILO's Penal Sanctions Convention brought new pressure to bear on the Dutch, who in November 1941 decided to repeal the Coolie Ordinance altogether, while letting current contracts run their course. In 1942, just before the Japanese invasion, the Volksraad passed a law regulating migrant labour that was interpreted in part as a response to the Convention.[120] By 1939, penal sanctions were no longer enforced in any Dutch colony.

The Dutch pledge to curtail the penal sanction did not happen out of high idealism. It was consistent with the interests of the colonial state and the employers, who had been panicked by the threat of sanctions and influenced in the 1930s by trends on the labour market that made the penal sanction increasingly redundant. Ten years after the government pledge to remove it, the final nails were hammered into the coffin-lid of Dutch indenture.

After 1939, world attention regarding colonial labour abuse switched to the British, long-time critics of the Dutch. British colonial labour policy had always complied more with the international consensus, which the British had played a big part in shaping. In the 1920s, British colonial administration became more centralised and better funded, a development that chimed with the founding of the ILO. The same went, in 1929, for Britain's adoption of the Colonial Development Act and its establishment, a year later, of the Colonial Labour Committee. The penal sanction had not been used in British colonies in Asia since 1932.[121] In the East Indies, in contrast, Dutch business interests had managed to outmanoeuvre the compromised Dutch state and stave off a similar evolution.

However, the British claim to virtue, bolstered by references to Britain's role in the abolition of slavery, was tarnished by its failure to ratify the 1939 convention. At the start of the Second World War, Major Granville Orde Browne, the newly appointed Labour Adviser to the British Colonial

[119] Pelzer (1935, 108).
[120] Lasker (1950, 223–224).
[121] Groenewoud (1995, 83–86).

office, rejected the idea of abolishing the penal sanction on grounds of principle, arguing that sanctions had "a genuine use as an educative measure in primitive conditions."[122] In 1942, Ernest Bevin, Minister of Labour in Britain's wartime coalition government, said a decision to ratify the 1939 Convention had been put off.[123] During the war, penal sanctions were even re-introduced in some British colonies. In 1955, at the time of the second convention on penal sanctions, and throughout the 1950s, sanctions continued to operate in British colonies in Africa.[124]

Indenture and Capitalism

What does the life-cycle of indenture in the East Indies tell us about the relationship between capitalism and extra-economic coercion? In a study on prewar Shanghai, Wai Kit Choi criticised the neoclassical (and Marxist) theory that unfree labour is incompatible with capitalism, except as a functional solution to labour scarcity in a pre-mechanised economy; and that, being inefficient and unprofitable, it will fall away once capitalism matures.

According to Choi, however, the use of coercion does not necessarily contradict the "normal" course of capitalism. Choi tested his proposition against labour recruitment in Shanghai's mechanised cotton mills between 1927 and 1937. Under the *baoshengong* system, labourers were indentured to contractors working for the mills: while under the newer *yangchenggong* system, they were hired directly and not subject to indenture.

Workers indentured under the *baoshengong* system suffered violence and super-exploitation and were less productive than *yangchenggong* workers, who dealt with managers rather than contractors. Why then was the less productive system kept? Choi identifies the cause in "the complex power relations between different social institutions in Shanghai." The contractors associated with the mills were affiliates of the Green Gang, a criminal organisation that dominated Shanghai and supported Chiang Kai-shek's Kuomintang state, on which the cotton capitalists depended. Their *baoshengong* system of indentured labour was rooted in pre-capitalist institutions that "mediated the capitalists' exercise of power over

[122] Cited in Groenewoud (1995, 85).

[123] Hansard, February 19, 1942, vol. 377.

[124] Banton (2004, 302), Groenewoud (1995, 86).

workers."[125] Its roots in society were so deep that it took Mao Zedong's revolution to remove them.

In many respects, indenture in the East Indies resembled domestic indenture in Shanghai. Overseas indenture was directly colonial, but domestic indenture was also associated with foreign companies, both Japanese and British. The two systems followed similar patterns. The main differences were that in China the indentured workers were women whereas in the East Indies they were men; and modern indenture in the East Indies was no longer directly embedded in premodern social structures, whereas in China traditional powerholders controlled much urban labour.

The original argument for indenture in the tropics was the lack of workers and the need to create supply lines to labour-exporting places, whereas in labour-rich China indenture was prized instead as a means of control. Starting in the 1920s, however, production in the East Indies was becoming increasingly mechanised and Javanese labour had already flooded into the Outer Islands, lessening the shortage and further destroying the rationale for coercion. But planters continued to press for its retention—to prevent chaos and preserve discipline, as in China.

Domestic indenture survived in China for as long as capitalism. Indenture in the East Indies was also long-lived, although it might have conformed more closely to economic theory in time, for by the early 1930s its days were numbered. Interested parties were, however reluctantly, giving up on it. Even so, it hung on. In the end, the death blow came not from below, in the form of labourers' resistance, but from outside and above. Reformist officials and politicians built a moral case for its abolition, supported by the ILO. Capitalist interests in the US denounced it as unfair competition and threatened retaliation. But it can hardly be said to have withered due to the internal logic of capitalism.

References

Banton, M. K. 2004. "The Colonial Office, 1820–1955: Constantly the Subject of Small Struggles." In Douglas Hay and Paul Craven, eds, *Masters, Servants, and Magistrates in Britain and the Empire, 1562–1955*, Chapel Hill: University of North Carolina Press, 251–302.

[125] Choi (2018).

Bates, Crispin, Marina Carter, and Vishwanaden Govinden. 2017. The Abolition of Indian Indentured Migration to Mauritius. Unpublished paper.

Behal, Rana. 2013. *Coolies, Recruiters and Planters: Migration of Indian Labour to the Southeast Asian and Assam Plantations during Colonial Rule*. Crossroads Asia, Working Paper series no. 9.

Behal, Rana. 2014. *One Hundred Years of Servitude: Political Economy of Tea Plantations in Colonial Assam*. New Delhi: Tulika Books.

Blussé, Leonard, and Nie Dening. 2018. *The Chinese Annals of Batavia, The Kai Ba Lidai Shiji and Other Stories (1610-1795)*. Leiden: Brill.

Boeke, Julius Herman. 1942. *The Structure of Netherlands Indian Economy*, New York: Institute of Pacific Relations.

Bosma, Ulbe. 2011. "The Discourse on Free Labor and the Forced Cultivation System: The Contradictory Consequences of the Abolition of the Slave Trade in Colonial Java, 1811–1870." In Marcel van der Linden, ed., *Humanitarian and Changing Labor Relations: The Long-term Consequences of the Abolition of the Slave Trade*, Leiden: Brill, 2011, 387–418.

Bosma, Ulbe. 2019. *The Making of a Periphery: How Island Southeast Asia Became a Mass Exporter of Labor*. New York: Columbia University Press.

Breman, Jan. 1987. *Koelies, Planters en Koloniale Politiek: Het arbeidsregime op de grootlandbouwondernemingen aan Sumatra's oostkust in het begin van de twintigste eeuw*. Dordrecht: Foris Publications.

Breman, Jan. 1988. "Het beest aan banden? De koloniale geest aan het begin van de twintigste eeuw." *Bijdragen tot de Taal-, Land- en Volkenkunde*, vol. 144, no. 1, 19–43.

Breman, Jan. 1989. *Taming the Coolie Beast: Plantation Society and the Colonial Order in Southeast Asia*. Delhi: Oxford University Press.

Breman, Jan. 2020. "Colonialism and Its Racial Imprint." *Sojourn: Journal of Social Issues in Southeast Asia*, vol. 35, no. 3, 463–92.

Choi, Wai Kit. 2018. "Making Capitalism with Gangsters: Unfree Labor in Shanghai's Cotton Mills, 1927–1937." *International Labor and Working-Class History*, vol. 94, 107–132.

Cohen de Boer, H. 1930. *Het Koelie-contract te Genève*. The Hague: D. A. Daamen's Uitgevers-Maatschappij.

De Bruin, A. G. 1918. *De Chineezen ter Oostkust van Sumatra*. Issued by Het Oostkust van Sumatra-Instituut. Leiden: Brill.

De Graaf, S., and D. G. Stibbe, with W. C. B. Wintgens, eds. 1918. *Encyclopaedie van Nederlandsch-Indië*, second edition. 2 vols. The Hague: Martinus Nijhoff.

De Kat Angelino, A. D. A. 1931. *Colonial Policy*, vol. 2, *The Dutch East Indies*. Translated by G. J. Renier. The Hague: Martinus Nijhoff.

Emmer, Pieter C. 2011. "'As Always, the Trouble is with the French.' Britain, France, the Netherlands and the Colonial Labor Market in the 19th Century." In Marcel van der Linden, ed., *Humanitarian and Changing Labor Relations:*

The Long-term Consequences of the Abolition of the Slave Trade, Leiden: Brill, 2011, 263–283.

Erman, Erwiza. 2017. "Chinese Taukeh, Labourer, and State Control: Case Study of Panglong in Eastern Region of Sumatra (1890-1930)." *Wacana*, vol. 18, no. 2, 514-539.

Franke, Otto. 1923. "Gedächtnisrede des Hrn. Franke auf J. J. M. de Groot." In *Sitzungsberichte der Preussischen Akademie der Wissenschaften*, 1923, cxvii-cxxvi.

Furnivall, J. S. 1939. *Netherlands India: A Study of Plural Economy*, Cambridge: Cambridge University Press.

Gedenkboek Billiton, 1852–1927. 1927. 2 pts. The Hague: Martinus Nijhoff.

Gordon, Alec. 2004. "Dynamics of Labour Transformation: Natural Rubber in Southeast Asia." *Journal of Contemporary Asia*, no. 34, 523–546.

Groenewoud, Margo. 1995. "Towards the Abolition of Penal Sanctions in Dutch Colonial Labour Legislation: An International Perspective." *Itinerario*, vol. 19 no. 2, 72–90.

Guowuyuan qiaogong shiwu ju, eds. [May] 1920b. *Nanyang He shu Wangjia dao Huagong qingxing diaocha shu* (An Investigation into the Situation of Huagong on Dutch-ruled Bangka Island in the Nanyang). Beijing: Guowuyuan qiaogong shiwu ju.

Heidhues, Mary F. Somers. 1992. *Bangka Tin and Mentok Pepper: Chinese Settlement on an Indonesian Island.* Pasir Panjang: Institute of Southeast Asian Studies.

Heijting, H. G. 1925. *De koelie-wetgeving.* The Hague: Van Stockhum.

Heinoldt, C. 1897. *Emigratie van Chineezen naar Banka.* N. p.: n. p.

Hincapie, Luz Mercedes. 2010. "Pacific Transactions: Nicolás Tanco Armero and the Chinese Coolie Trade to Cuba." *Journal of Iberian and Latin American Research*, vol. 16, no. 1, 27-41.

Houben, Vincent J. H. 1999. "Introduction: The Coolie System in Colonial Indonesia." In Vincent J. H. Houben and J. Thomas Lindblad, eds, *Coolie Labour in Colonial Indonesia: A Study of Labour Relations in the Outer Islands, c. 1900–1940*, Wiesbaden: Harrassowitz Verlag, 1999, 1–24.

Houben, Vincent, and Julia Seibert. 2013. "(Un)freedom: Colonial Labor Relations in Belgian Congo and the Netherlands East Indies Compared." In Ewout Frankema and Frans Buelens, eds, *Colonial Exploitation and Economic Development: The Belgian Congo and the Netherlands East Indies Compared*, Abingdon: Routledge, 2013, 178–192.

Jayawardena, Kumari, and Rachel Kurian. 2015. *Class, Patriarchy and Ethnicity on Sri Lankan Plantations: Two Centuries of Power and Protest.* Hyderabad: Orient Black Swan.

Kloosterboer, Willemina. 1960. *Involuntary Labour since the Abolition of Slavery A Survey of Compulsory Labour Throughout the World.* Leiden: Brill.

Knight, Roger.1988. "Peasant Labour and Capitalist Production in Late Colonial Indonesia: The 'Campaign' at a North Java Sugar Factory, 1840–70." *Journal of Southeast Asian Studies*, vol. 19, no. 2, 245–265.

Kuiper, Koos. 2017. *The Early Dutch Sinologists (1854–1900): Training in Holland and China, Functions in the Netherlands East Indies.* 2 vols. Leiden: Brill.

Lasker, Bruno. 1950. *Human Bondage in Southeast Asia.* Chapel Hill: University of North Carolina Press.

Lockard, Craig A. 1978. "Repatriation Movements among the Javanese in Suriname: A Comparative Analysis." *Caribbean Studies*, vol. 18, nos. 1–2, 85–113.

Lu Wendi, Peng Jiali, and Chen Zexian, eds. 1984. *Guanyu Dongnan Ya Huagong de siren zhuzuo* (Private individuals' writings about Huagong in Southeast Asia). In Chen Hansheng, ed., *Huagong chuguo shiliao huibian* (A compilation of edited historical materials regarding going abroad by Huagong), Beijing: Zhonghua shuju, 12 vols, 1981–1985, vol. 5.

MacNair, H. F. 1923. "The Chinese as Contract Laborers." *The Weekly Review*, June 2.

Mahase, Radica. 2021. *Why Should We Be Called 'Coolies'? The End of Indian Indentured Labour.* Abingdon: Routledge.

Manjapra, Kris. 2018. "Asian Plantation Histories at the Frontiers of Nation and Globalization." *Modern Asian Studies*, vol. 52, no. 6, 2137–2158.

Manual of Netherlands India (Dutch East Indies). n.d. Compiled by the Geographical Section of the Naval Intelligence Division, Naval Staff, Admiralty. London: His Majesty's Stationery Office.

Maul, Daniel Roger. 2007. "The International Labor Organization and the Struggle against Forced Labor from 1919 to the Present." *Labor History*, vol. 48, no. 4, 477–500.

Maul, Daniel Roger. 2012. "Prologue: Separate Worlds—The ILO and 'Native Labour,' 1919–39." In *Human Rights, Development and Decolonization: The International Labour Organization, 1940-70.* London: Palgrave Macmillan, 17-27.

Mishra, Amit Kumar. 2015. "Sardars, Kanganies and Maistries: Intermediaries in the Indian Labour Diaspora During the Colonial Period." In Sigrid Wadauer, Thomas Buchner, and Alexander Mejstrik, eds, *The History of Labour Intermediation: Institutions and Finding Employment in the Nineteenth and Early Twentieth Centuries*, International Studies in Social History, vol. 26, New York: Berghahn, 368–387.

Misra, Maria. 1999. *Business, Race, and Politics in British India, c. 1850–1960.* New York: Clarendon Press.

Mohapatra, Prabhu, and Rana Behal. 1991."'Tea and Money versus Human Life': The Rise and Fall of the Indenture System in the Assam Tea Plantations, 1840–1908." *Journal of Peasant Studies*, vol. 19, nos. 3–4, 142–172.

Mollema, J. C.. 1922. *De ontwikkeling van het eiland Billiton en van de Billiton-Maatschappij*. The Hague: Nijhoff.

Northrup, David. 1995. *Indentured Labor in the Age of Imperialism, 1834–1922*. New York: Cambridge University Press.

Pastor, G. 1927. *De panglongs*. Weltevreden: Landsdrukkerij.

Pelzer, Karl J. 1935. *Die Arbeiterwanderungen in Südostasien: Eine wirtschafts- und bevölkerungsgeographische Untersuchung*. Würzburg: Konrad Triltsch.

Pelzer, Karl J. 1938. "Present Day Labour Migration in India." In *International Geographical Union, eds. Comptes rendus du Congrès international de géographie*. Leiden: Brill, 65-75.

Reid, Anthony. 1979. *The Blood of the People: Revolution and the End of Traditional Rule in Northern Sumatra*, Kuala Lumpur: Oxford University Press.

Stibbe, D. G., and C. Spat, with E. M. Uhlenbeck, eds. 1927. *Encyclopaedie van Nederlandsch-Indië*. Second edition. 8 vols. The Hague: Martinus Nijhoff, vol. 5.

Tjandra, Surya. 2016. Labour Law and Development in Indonesia. Doctoral Thesis, Leiden University.

Van Blommestein, A. F. 1917. *De Nieuwe Koelie-Ordonnantie voor de Oostkust van Sumatra*. Amsterdam: Scheltema and Holkema.

Van den Brand, Johannes. 1903. *Nog Eens: De Millioenen uit Deli*. Amsterdam: Höveker and Wormser.

Van den Brand, Johannes. 1918. "Arbeidswetgeving." *Vrijzinning Weekblad*, no. 1, 687–689.

Vandenbosch, Amry. 1931. "Colonial Labor Problems: The Labor Contract With Penal Sanction in the Dutch East Indies." *Pacific Affairs*, vol. 4, no. 4, 318–324.

Wang Linqian and Wu Kunxiang, eds. 2002. *Zaoqi Huaqiao yu qiyue Huagong (mai zhuzai) ziliao* (Early materials relating to overseas Chinese and indentured Huagong [piglet trade]). Chaoshan: Chaoshan lishi wenhua yanjiu zhongxin, Shantou shi wenhua ju, Shantou shi tushu guan.

Wertheim, Wim F. 1993. "Conditions on Sugar Estates in Colonial Java: Comparisons with Deli." *Journal of Southeast Asian Studies* vol. 24, no. 2, 268–284.

Wu Fengbin. 1988. *Qiyue Huagong shi* (History of indentured Chinese labour). Nanchang: Jiangxi renmin chuban she.

Yang Tongling, Lin Zhang, Li Xinyun, Tan Enli, and Li Ensi. 2004. *Hunqian mengrao de guxiang—Bangjia dao* ("Lost in a reverie about one's native place: Bangka Island"). Beijing: Zhongguo youyi chuban gongsi.

Zhu Jieqin. 1984. "Shijiu shiji zhongqi zai Yindunixiya de qiyue Huagong" ("Indentured Huagong in Indonesia in the mid nineteenth century"). In Chen Hansheng, ed., *Huagong chuguo shiliao huibian* (A compilation of edited historical materials regarding going abroad by Huagong), Beijing: Zhonghua shuju, 12 vols, vol. 5, 217–243.

CHAPTER 5

Recruitment

The recruitment of indentured labour in south China went through several stages over time, ranging from the kongsi system and the "coolie trade" years to professional, courier, and clan recruitment. The stages were roughly consecutive, but they were also discontinuous and even retrogressive, as old methods disappeared and then resurfaced. In some cases, the labour exodus was geographically random, in others it was region-bound. In the case of random recruitment, recruiters took labour from where they found it, with the collusion of crimps and boarding-house owners in Hong Kong and other southern ports or by way of Singapore and Penang. Serial recruitment along established corridors yielded relatively homogeneous ethnic and sub-ethnic communities at the receiving end.[1]

The manner of Chinese recruitment to the East Indies was influenced by other migration streams, especially that of Javanese to Sumatra, as Dutch laws spread across the islands, and of Indians to Malaya. Javanese and Indian labourers were sometimes described by terms drawn from a Huagong lexicon, and this shaping also worked the other way round. Chinese words such as *xinke* and *laoke* (laukeh), "new guest" and "old guest," referring to new recruits and old hands, were applied to labourers

[1] The term sub-ethnic refers to regional, linguistic, and ethnic divisions among Hans (Honig 1992).

G. Benton, *Chinese Indentured Labour in the Dutch East Indies, 1880–1942*, Palgrave Macmillan Transnational History Series, https://doi.org/10.1007/978-3-031-05024-4_5

of other ethnicities, in whose languages they became embedded, in confirmation of the mutual shaping of different methods of recruitment across different labour diasporas. However, the recruitment of Huagong to the East Indies after the fall of the VOC was more complicated and less standardised than in the case of inter-island recruitment, given the greater distance and the need for border-crossings, and of recruitment from India, where the colonial state acted as an organising and supervising centre.

The recruitment and exploitation of Chinese labour was managed by a hierarchy of whites and Chinese, administrators and police chiefs, and Chinese brokers. The exploitation started at the point of recruitment, when the recruiter might illegally retain part or even all of the fee due to the recruits. The hierarchy was, for more enterprising Chinese, a ladder out of poverty.

Until the 1920s, indenture was the norm, but Chinese were recruited under other systems too. Some started and finished their lives as free labourers, although "freedom" was sometimes worse than bondage. Others became free after paying off their debts. In the jungle, Chinese loggers, sawyers, and charcoal-burners, including time-expired indentures and others who had never been under contract, toiled out of sight under Chinese bosses and were nominally free, but their lives were even more miserable than those of formally bonded workers. Still others formed independent gangs that were relatively free to negotiate their own conditions.

Chinese Labour Migration to the Nanyang

In dynastic times, domestic migration was used by the imperial state to people frontier regions or places overwhelmed by natural or military catastrophes. Alongside state-driven migration, people moved around along corridors of kinship, native place, and other solidarities, leaving Chinese cities ethnically shaped by pockets of regional identity.[2] Chinese migrants aimed to remain sojourners rather than settle—single males retained ties to their sending villages and used them to survive and make a living. The same ties played a major part in the transition from domestic to overseas migration.[3]

[2] Goodman (1995, 3–4); Kuhn (2008, 43–46).
[3] Pan (1998, 46–48).

Chinese migration to the Nanyang began centuries before the start of modern-style indenture. Although illegal under the *haijin* ("sea ban") during most of the Ming Dynasty (1368–1644) and for much of the Qing (1644–1911), prohibition was not easily enforced, especially when dynasties declined.

An early wave of Chinese refugees turned up on Bangka after the defeat of the rebel army under Huang Chao (875–884) by the Tang.[4] A bigger wave reached the Nanyang after the founding of the Song (960–1279), when Chinese merchants settled in Southeast Asian ports. Chinese settlement of Belitung is said to have started in 1292, after the fall of the Song, when members of the vanquished Hakka resistance to the Yuan Dynasty fled abroad and laid grounds for the Hakka diaspora.[5] After the Ming (1368–1644), Chinese settlement spread still further across the Nanyang and with it labour migration, aided by Malay potentates. In 1620, 1400 labour migrants left Xiamen for the Indonesian Archipelago.

The isolationist Qing tried to stop foreigners recruiting villagers for employment overseas, but the foreigners defeated the ban by bribes or force of arms. In 1785, the British East India Company recruited Chinese to work in Malaya.[6] The Dutch VOC, led by Jan Pieterszoon Coen, Governor-General of the East Indies in the early seventeenth century, seized Chinese junks at sea, confiscated their cargos, murdered their crews, and enslaved the survivors. In 1921, a Chinese diplomat recalled Coen's atrocities in a note to the British Colonial Office:

> From the sixteenth to the nineteenth century, Chinese labourers were in great demand in countries newly colonised. The capture of Chinese labourers was resorted to when amicable means to purchase them failed. Mr Coen, the first governor of the Netherlands Indies, in the official "Advice" he left for his successor in 1623, said that Chinese slaves were "of better service" to the Dutch than any others, that "in Batavia, Amboina, and Banda we require a multitude of as many labourers as possible," and that if there was to be a war with China (as seemed likely) we "should gather together as big a force as we can [...], raid various places along the Chinese coast, capture as many men, women and children as possible, [...] and use them to people Batavia, Amboina, and Banda."[7]

[4] Yang Tongling et al. (2004, 101–102).

[5] Deng Rui (2004, 57).

[6] Li Minghuan (2012, 207–228).

[7] Letter to the British Colonial Office from the Chinese Foreign Ministry, April 2, 1920, held in the archive of the Academia Sinica. For the source that the official quoted, see Colenbrander 1920–1922, vol. 3, 293 and 306 (thanks to Michel Hockx for this Dutch source).

The transportation of Chinese to Southeast Asia took off after Britain's abolition of slavery in 1833, China's defeats in the Opium Wars (1839–1842 and 1856–1860), the incorporation of China's southern ports into the world economy, and China's easing of its emigration ban. In 1858, the Tianjin Treaty gave Western powers the right to recruit labourers in China. Agents set up businesses in Hong Kong and other ports, served by Chinese crimps and brokers. The Treaty was renewed by the 1904 Emigration Convention regarding "the Employment of Chinese Labour in British Colonies and Protectorates."

Most early migration in or before the colonial period was conducted by Chinese themselves, organised in kongsis operating directly out of China or through Nanyang entrepôts. Kongsis also played a major role in running the mines and plantations that employed the migrants overseas.

We saw earlier that the kongsis pioneered indenture in the Nanyang, for new arrivals had to work off their passage before they could make the transition from labourer to shareholder and access kongsi privileges. Long before the arrival of the Dutch, and their expansion out of Java, kongsis established settlements across the archipelago, with the encouragement of local sultans. They cooperated closely with the Dutch after the formation of the VOC, but they also waged a long and bloody resistance to Dutch rule in the nineteenth century.[8]

Sources date the opening of the tin mines on Bangka to 1710, under the patronage of the Sultan of Palembang and kongsi management, although the mines were probably older.[9] Between 1806 and 1811, when parts of the East Indies were under French rule, Chinese started coming in ever greater numbers to found mines and pepper plantations on Bangka, while others made a living as fishermen.[10] In 1816, Lin Baji, a third-generation Bangka Chinese, bought groups of labourers in Hong Kong and Singapore for f40 and sold them in Bangka for f80.[11] The kongsis organised the provision of labour from the Hakka counties. They also organised secondary migration of Chinese across the Strait of Gandar to Belitung, where the Dutch found rich tin deposits in 1852. These secondary migrants included both Peranakans and Totoks, who imported Chinese methods of organisation and mining technologies. At first, the kongsis

[8] Phoa Liong Gie (1936 [1992], 6–7 and 16–17).

[9] Wazar (1956, 209–11); Yang Tongling et al. (2004, 209).

[10] Lu Wendi et al. (1985a, 391).

[11] Yang Tongling et al. (2004, 79).

had police powers, like the indigenous kampong chiefs.[12] In time, as we saw in an earlier chapter, they evolved through the Dutch connection from groups based on geosanguinous ties and practising relative equality into what Heidhues described as "cooperative alliances of complete strangers, many of them pressed into service in the back alleys of Singapore," no longer in any real sense egalitarian.[13]

Recruitment in China by foreigners peaked in the late nineteenth century, when labourers were persuaded, tricked, or forced into going overseas by *baotou* (labour contractors) working for European and Chinese employers in Southeast Asia. Alongside this "professional" recruitment, funded by Western investors and often assisted by consuls, Chinese communities in Guangdong and Fujian were scoured for recruits by local agents known as *shuike* and *ketou*, sons of the communities. This style of recruitment was associated with the remittance trade conducted across the South China Sea. Later, employers unhappy with the cost of professional recruitment and the tensions that accompanied it experimented with *laoke* or clan recruitment, first in India and then in the East Indies. However, clan recruitment was not necessarily less rapacious than professional recruitment and there was never a strict line between the two.

Recruitment by *ketou* was originally associated with mining on the two tin islands. Dutch interests on Belitung in the 1860s were unhappy with existing methods of professional recruitment, which delivered poor-quality recruits who died early in unacceptably high numbers. In 1866, two local Chinese employers began organising teams of *ketou* that delivered *xinke* in such volume that the costs of recruitment sank to next to nothing. The quality and quantity of recruits improved, and costs remained stable until the First World War.[14]

The route from China to the Nanyang was navigated before the late-colonial period by ocean-going junks or wangkangs, carried south by the winter northwesterlies.[15] Later, Huagong arrived by steamship, but junks continued to operate right through until the 1930s—in secret, if necessary, to avoid colonial bans.[16]

[12] *Gedenkboek* (1927, pt 1, 9–11, and pt 2, 68–69).

[13] Heidhues (1991, 4–7, 1992, 44).

[14] Mollema (1922, 165–166).

[15] Heinoldt (1897, 2).

[16] *Nanyang shangbao*, September 25, 1929.

Indenture is usually analysed functionally, as a concomitant of capitalism in colonial settings.[17] Where recruitment for indenture is studied comparatively, the axis of comparison is usually international, which risks leaving its domestic progenitors out of the picture. However, analysing Huagong recruitment in the light of its domestic origins yields a more complex picture. This is especially true in the Chinese case, where foreign control and influence was weaker than in direct colonies.

The tie between Chinese practices domestically and internationally is clear at every stage of the development of the Chinese labour diaspora. Historically, kongsi domestic recruitment preceded the kongsi role overseas. When in the early twentieth century Chinese and foreign firms began recruiting domestic Huagong directly from the villages, *shuike* and *ketou* played a major role, and had many features in common with the letter couriers and *minxinju* that traditionally transmitted messages, things, and people within China, using networks of post boats and river steamers.[18]

Contract labour and indenture were commonplace in Chinese domestic industry until 1949, two decades after the start of its final demise in the East Indies. In Shantou, labourers were organised into twenty "houses" or hongs serving the different regions from which they were recruited. They were then sent out for employment in cotton mills and on the railways. The contractor paid the recruits in arrears so that they were forced to borrow from him, resulting in a classic form of bondage. Contractors retained much of the recruits' wages—"wharf coolies" on $2.58 a day received only $0.60. The contractor, in his turn, was exploited by the employer, who saddled him with paying the employee's family a monthly sum and held him to account when workers went missing.[19] Contractors were natives of the same districts as the recruits, like the *laoke* in Southeast Asia,[20] underlining the strong connection and resemblance between domestic and international labour recruitment.

[17] Choi (2018).

[18] Benton and Liu (2018, 34–35 and 43).

[19] Pelzer 1935, 92; "Chinese Contract Labour: A System Where the Middle-Man Takes the Greater Profit," *The North-China Herald and Supreme Court and Consular Gazette*, September 29, 1933. On the contract system in the Hong Kong dockyards and the Shantou system, see the files in the Hong Kong Public Records Office, HKRS 41, D. & S. No. 1/425(2)-1/1441 and 1/5180-1/5197.

[20] Honig (1983, 424).

Ebbs and Flows in Modern Recruitment

The recruitment of Huagong ebbed and flowed violently over the years. The changes were rarely expected and created difficulties for would-be migrants and new opportunities for the forces preying on them. The migrants were especially vulnerable during the crises of 1921–1922 and 1929–1933, but dangers along the route were omnipresent.

Demand rather than supply was the main factor in the fluctuations. In 1929, 264,591 Huagong went to Malaya, compared with just 218,868 in 1930, while the number leaving for China in the same two years rose from 164,826 to 199,800.[21] According to other figures, more than 100,000 unemployed Huagong had returned to Hong Kong, Xiamen, and Chaozhou from Malaya and Singapore by late 1930, and a further 200,000 were deported from Singapore in the following two years.[22] The fall in Huagong numbers in the East Indies coincided with a collapse of tin and rubber prices and the arrival of news of the collapse in the Chinese ports, as well as a fourfold rise in ticket prices. Migrant-receiving countries took urgent measures to reduce the inflow. Siam banned foreigners, and the East Indies raised the head tax on free migrants from fl00 to fl50 and on indentured Huagong to f75.[23] Between January 1930 and March 1934, 210,000 Huagong were said to have been "lost" to the Malayan economy. Chinese immigration picked up a little in 1933 and 1934, when the number of Chinese miners in Malaya grew by more than 20 percent to 50,000. However, the new arrivals were less likely to follow old forms of employment. Only 5.7 percent headed for the rubber estates, and only 0.06 percent for the mines.[24]

Sometimes the receiving ports in the Nanyang banned new migrants altogether. On May 8, 1931, the Singapore authorities forbade males aged fourteen or above to enter the port from August to the end of October. On May 14, citing the low price of rubber and tin, they sent unemployed Huagong back to China for an indefinite period.[25] At around the same time, the British tightened curbs on Huagong immigration to Malaya.[26]

[21] Lu Wendi et al. (1984a, 52–53).

[22] *Kung Sheung Evening News*, November 27, 1930; *The China Press*, May 26, 1933.

[23] *Shen bao*, September 14, 1930.

[24] *Malaya Tribune*, October 24, 1934.

[25] *Xianggang gongshang ribao*, May 8 and 14, 1931.

[26] *Xianggang Huazi ribao*, May 12, 1931.

In Sumatra in 1931, huge numbers of Javanese and Chinese contract labourers were sacked and left destitute, often in remote areas where no land was available for them to cultivate, pushing them into "vagabondage, pauperism, criminality, and unrest." In February, 700 Chinese "vagabonds" were identified as having been involved in fights, usually among themselves. The planters were contractually obliged to repatriate former employees, but they often failed to do so. Time-expired workers were allowed to settle, especially if they could fend for themselves. Hundreds of Huagong were repatriated from the East Indies at the expense of the authorities, rising to more than one thousand in 1929–1931, costing up to f50,000 a year. Regulations concerning Huagong changed frequently. Far fewer Chinese were repatriated by the employers than were Javanese, by a factor of ten or fifteen to one—in 1930, 1444 Chinese went at a cost of f50,042, compared with 26,114 Javanese and an unspecified number of dependants, sent much more cheaply given the shorter distance.[27]

The fluctuations were reflected in the boarding-house industry in Hong Kong, where the number of functioning hostels rose and fell repeatedly. In 1918, during a slump, only 13 of the 22 Class IV boarding-houses survived at end of year. In 1924, when emigration boomed, 618 licences were issued for Class V boarding-houses as against 396 in 1923; in 1925, 479 were issued; in 1926, 332. In later years, numbers continued to rise and fall.[28] The volume of labour immigration (in the form of quotas) was turned up and down and even off.

Fluctuations in the trade cycle were also reflected in the rate of rejection of recruits during the pre-departure vetting in the sending ports. The imposing and lifting of immigration quotas led to an apparent manipulation by officials in Hong Kong and overseas of the number of "decrepits," elderly and infirm labourers. Sometimes their numbers swelled, as the economy dipped. At other times, they contracted, when more recruits than usual were deemed fit to work. In 1922, when emigration out of Hong Kong dropped by between one half and one third and stopped altogether to Belitung, the number of decrepits sent back to Hong Kong from Southeast Asia shot up, to 417 from North Borneo and 1013 from

[27] Arsip Nasional R. Ind. Department van Binnenlandsch Bestuur, Afdeeling AB, AD, AE, AI, C, CD, and D, 1924–1942, archive no. 405, May 26, 1931.

[28] The statistics can be found in the Administrative Reports issued annually by the Hong Kong Government.

Penang.[29] In 1923, when emigration to Bangka and Deli grew by between 50 and 100 percent, the percentage of decrepits slumped.[30] In 1925 and 1926, the on-off tap was further loosened and far fewer assisted migrants were rejected on arrival than in previous years. Between 1929 and 1933, however, at the height of the Depression, those mines employing Huagong that did not close shed their old and infirm workers and increased the work-load of those retained.[31] In 1930, when many observers expected an imminent rebound from the recession, most assisted emigrants (8316 out of 8413) in Hong Kong were passed as fit for work. In 1931, after it had become clear that the economic crisis would be exceptionally severe, the vetting intensified and a far smaller proportion (3317 out of 4397) was accepted. The percentage rejected in 1931 was ten times greater than in 1930.[32]

The purging of potential recruits along the way, by company agents, doctors, and colonial officials in Hong Kong and overseas, meant that on average only around two-thirds of those recruited in Hong Kong ended up in jobs. (Recruits absconding played a minor role in the loss.) It is difficult to identify the exact causes of the fluctuation, since many different factors and decision-makers played a role. However, it is unlikely to have been just a coincidence that 1916, when 117,653 emigrants left Hong Kong compared with 63,275 in 1915 and the smallest percentage of recruits was rejected by the Belitung employers, was a year of acute labour shortages (see Table 5.1).[33]

The imposition of quotas could could take immigrants by surprise. In 1928, large batches of Huagong were laid off in Malaya and sent back to China. At the same time, however, new migrants flowed in the opposite direction, unaware of the lay-offs.[34] In 1935, when the rubber price shot up, Singapore raised its quota of Huagong from 1000 to 4000 a month, in addition to several thousand extra-quota labourers brought in by specially licensed recruiters.[35] The rush led to an epidemic of cheating of incoming Huagong and their dependants, by hostel owners and their

[29] [Hong Kong] Administrative Reports for the Year 1922.
[30] [Hong Kong] Administrative Reports for the Year 1923.
[31] Wu Fengbin (1988, 161).
[32] [Hong Kong] Administrative Reports for the Year 1931.
[33] [Hong Kong] Administrative Reports for the Year 1916.
[34] *Xianggang Huazi ribao*, August 11, 1928.
[35] [Hong Kong] Administrative Reports for the Year 1934.

Table 5.1 Rate of rejection of and average cost of recruiting a *xinke*, 1912–1925

Year	*Number in Hong Kong*	*Number sent to Belitung*	*Rejected in Belitung*	*% hired*	*Cost per sinkeh*
1912	3461	1700	85	48	f101
1913	4238	1958	48	45	f70
1914	3467	2149	69	62	f68
1916	3508	2775	14	79	f48
1917	3549	2584	9	73	f76
1918	3017	1984	3	66	f178
1919	8604	5443	31	63	f179
1920	5974	3280	5	55	f176
1921	3531	1998	12	57	f113
1923	3068	2140	15	70	f96
1925	3724	2624	16	70	F92

Source: Wu Fengbin (1988, 183–184)

criminal associates.[36] In March 1937, the quota again rose, to 6000, as the economy continued to recover.[37] The change was accompanied by new restrictions, notably the levying on arrivals of an entry fee of $50. Despite supposedly ameliorative measures, there was a further leap in profiteering by the shipping lines.[38] The adjustments continued right up to and beyond the start of the Second World War. In late September 1939, for example, the British started to make it easier for Huagong to go south, to deal with a shortage of tin workers in Malaya.[39]

During the depressions, tens of thousands of Huagong who were not repatriated were loosed onto the streets of towns and cities throughout the Nanyang. In 1923, tens of thousands roamed the countryside.[40] In the early 1930s, Dutch companies in Sumatra dismissed workers whose contracts had expired and reneged on their obligation to send them home. To deal with jobless migrants, in January 1938 the East Indies government proclaimed a series of exceptional measures aimed mainly at Huagong,

[36] *Shen bao*, April 8, 1936.
[37] *Tianguang bao*, March 21, 1937.
[38] *Xianggang gongshang ribao*, March 21, 1937.
[39] *Dagong bao*, September 30, 1939.
[40] *Xianggang gongshang ribao*, June 10, 1933.

who formed the greatest number of foreign workers and were hit by a long list of restrictions and punishments.[41]

The changing attitude on the part of colonial authorities to the demography of labour migration resulted in big swings in the gender composition of the migrant inflow. As we have seen, colonial planners envisaged replacing immigration by on-the-spot reproduction by family units and even by "colonies" in the shape of permanent self-sustaining settlements, in order to secure an adequate supply of labour. The strategy was aimed chiefly at Indians and Javanese in the Nanyang, for planters agreed that Huagong would not be interested.[42] However, a colonisation strategy was implicit in the growth of Chinese female immigration, both to Malaya and to the East Indies. Moves to correct the gender imbalance in Indian and Chinese migration led to a transition from a community of immigrants to a settled one and to a partial feminisation of the Huagong workforce. In 1926, 29,636 women and children migrated from Hong Kong, almost twice as many as the 15,082 who left in 1925, an increase seen by officials as "remarkable." Of the 19,500 female adults (aged 16 and over), the majority (13,000) were going to join relatives or husbands, while 5200 sought work as maidservants.[43] In 1927, the number of women and children increased by a further 60 percent on 1926, 66 percent of them to join relatives and 25 percent to work as maidservants.[44] By 1930, as a result of efforts by officials in Malaya to equalise the sexes, the male-female ratio among new arrivals had narrowed to 3:2.[45] During the worst years of the Depression, the number of arriving females and minors fell, but far less precipitously than that of assisted males—in 1929, by 4.2 percent, compared with a 51 percent drop in male migration.[46] In 1934, the number of male assisted migrants, mostly to the East Indies, rose slightly, by 1505, confirming that the worst of the Depression was over, but again the number of women and children shot up, to 33,467, compared with 12,190 in 1930.[47] In 1937, when the number of male assisted emigrants rose only slightly, to 7564, the number of women and children almost doubled over

[41] Lu Wendi et al. (1984a, 66–68 and 294).

[42] Deli Planters Vereeniging, *Mededeling uitgegeven door de Deli Planters Vereeniging*, jaargang 1, no. 2b, July 1918, 9.

[43] [Hong Kong] Administrative Reports for the Year 1926.

[44] [Hong Kong] Administrative Reports for the Year 1927.

[45] *Shen bao*, September 14, 1930.

[46] [Hong Kong] Administrative Reports for the Year 1930.

[47] [Hong Kong] Administrative Reports for the Year 1934.

the previous year, to 85,530.[48] The Japanese invasion of China slowed the flow and the Pacific War stopped it, but at first the drop was less than might have been expected—from 42,753 in 1938 (compared with 1466 male assisted emigrants) to 28,574 in 1939, despite the war.[49]

This feminisation transformed the nature of Chinese society in British Malaya, as we saw in an earlier chapter. In 1921, there were nearly three men for every one Chinese woman in Malaya. By 1930, however, the Chinese birth rate had risen from 1.71 per thousand in 1921 to 4.09, and by 1947 the male-female ratio had fallen to 1228 to 1000.[50]

The collapse of recruitment through Hong Kong at the start of the 1930s was repeated in other Huagong-exporting ports. In Shantou, a major link to the East Indies, the number of recruits going overseas more than halved. The monthly inflow of Huagong into Singapore shrank between August 1930, when Singapore introduced restrictions, and October 1931 from 2321 to 1160. In the East Indies, the landing fee levied on migrants went up from f25 in 1921 to f50 in 1929 and to f100 in April 1931 and then to f150, to be paid at the port. Siam and Vietnam also raised their fees. Remittances fell by 20 percent, an index of Huagong impoverishment.[51] In 1930, 115,791 Chinese left Shantou for the Nanyang and only 3767 returned, whereas in 1931 the 58,138 leavers were outnumbered (for the first time) by the 65,866 returners.[52]

Dutch officials in the East Indies feared that alongside labour recruits dangerous radicals might slip into the East Indies, so they did their best to weed out "intellectuals posing as Huagong." By 1930, "alien Orientals" had to pay a fee and to be vouched for by a tax-paying resident. Labourers needed no papers, but intellectuals had to show a passport and were interrogated about their schooling and politics. However, it was easy for intellectuals to infiltrate the crowds of arrivals, who spoke a profusion of dialects that baffled official interpreters and were aided by their "secret script which is so hard to decipher and their spirit of solidarity." If intellectuals were admitted, it was on temporary visas of three to six months followed by other extensions culminating, after ten years, in permanent residence, though this was no guarantee against expulsion. Reports of

[48] [Hong Kong] Administrative Reports for the Year 1937.
[49] [Hong Kong] Administrative Reports for the Year 1938 and 1939.
[50] Lin Shuihao et al., eds, (1998, vol. 1, 208).
[51] The f100 and f150 figures applied to free migrants—indentured Huagong paid f75.
[52] *Shen bao*, January 25, 1932.

alleged Communist plots against the social order were backed up by allegations of the secret depositing of Communists by proas sailing into remote creeks on the Outer Islands.[53]

Hostels

Hostels associated with migrants' dialects and sending places were primary links in the chain of Chinese labour recruitment and numbered in their thousands, especially in the southern ports of exit. Their ancestry can be traced to the *hang* or lodges that accommodated merchants and artisans and served as trade or journeymen's associations, and to the *huiguan* or guilds that served as liaison places for men from the same county or province. Common-origin organisations like the *hang* and *huiguan* acted as common-interest groups and had common-occupation equivalents, rougher versions of which served unskilled labourers temporarily on the move, as hostels, eating places, meeting places, and centres of information for job-seekers.[54] The *hang* were also known as *kezhan*, among other names. These inns or lodges kept features of the older institutions, especially a native-place tie.

Known as boarding-houses in English, such hostels were found in Chinatowns worldwide, in the Treaty Ports and leased territories, and in Hong Kong. After the Revolution of 1911, when public opinion in China swung against the Huagong trade, the authorities in Shantou, a centre of Dutch recruitment, were forced to regulate the "piglet hostels." Much of the trade switched to Hong Kong. Shantou and Haikou remained centres of emigration to the East Indies, especially of "free" migration (i.e., financially unassisted), but their role diminished.[55]

In Hong Kong, boarding-houses were brought under administrative control and divided into seven classes by an ordinance in 1917. Class I Chinese boarding-houses, or hotels, of which Hong Kong had four in 1918, were run on European lines for elite travellers; Class II, of which there were 16, were large boarding-houses used principally by independent emigrants, and could accommodate 2475 people; Class III, of which

[53] "Chineesche communisten: Kan de immigratiedienst verantwoordelijk gesteld worden?—De samenwerking met de Straits" (Chinese Communists: Can the immigration service be blamed?—The cooperation with the Straits), *Bataviaasch nieuwsblad*, April 2, 1930.

[54] Moll-Murata (2008).

[55] Wang Linqian and Wu Kunxiang (2002, 48–49).

there were 29, were small boarding-houses for independent emigrants, capable of accommodating a total of 1431 people. At the lower end, Class IV boarding-houses were for assisted emigrants, i.e., any male who intended "to labour for hire in some place beyond the limits of the [Hong Kong] colony and has received assistance in the way of the payment of passage money, subsistence or otherwise." Assisted emigrants were forbidden to lodge in any other place. In 1918, only 13 such hostels survived, because of a wartime decline in assisted emigration. Class V, "lodging houses for coolies," for which 476 licences were issued in 1918, were unsanitary and were frequently closed down.[56]

Kezhan interacted where necessary with local authorities and in Hong Kong and Singapore were licensed (like many of the older guilds). Also like trade and native-place associations, they had ties to secret societies or *bang* and to China's underground counterculture. The boarding-master, like the *shuike* and the *ketou*, was an essential link in the internal structure of dockside recruitment and of indenture. Many *kezhan* were set up and operated by *ketou*.

The hostels played a major part in recruiting Huagong, an encounter that led in many cases to the de facto indenturing of Huagong even after the banning of contracts in Hong Kong and Malaya. In the early twentieth century, many of the Huagong passing through Hong Kong were classed as free, for in theory they paid their own fare, with loans from kinsmen or fellow-villagers who had already migrated, and sought work only after arriving in the Nanyang. In many cases, however, their stay in the port and the cost of the ticket was cushioned by the hostels on condition that debts incurred were paid back from wages earned at the destination. Most such arrangements were informal, but they were based on a village or county tie and there was little question of the debtor defaulting. The interest mounted rapidly and the terms were severe, so the arrangement easily resulted in debt and indenture.[57]

Where they could get away with it, hostels cheated the companies whose recruits they accommodated by false accounting or by failing to weed out unsuitable recruits. But the main victims were the recruits themselves, for in the world of labour recruitment deception was usual. From the recruit's point of view, the sole mitigation was the role played by native-place ties, but these same ties kept him in the boarding-master's grip.

[56] Hong Kong Administrative Reports.
[57] Lu Wendi et al. (1984a, 51–52).

Belitung-bound *xinke* awaiting passage in 1920 were treated under an arrangement that illustrates the general pattern. Their dispatch was executed by two main actors in the traffic: a bank, the Nederlandsch-Indische Handelsbank, arranged their vetting and accommodation and the Java China Japan Line shipped them south.[58] They were fed, accommodated, and given f8 a day, on top of which the recruiter received commission, in violation of Hong Kong law at the time. Their expenses in Hong Kong were to cover a stay limited to 14 days, after which the agent or *xinke* paid. In fact the ship was frequently delayed beyond a fortnight, and if a *xinke* fell ill, his time in Hong Kong was prolonged even further, again at his own cost. If the departure was postponed for long enough, the *xinke* might be hired to do dock work, but the pay due to him ended up in the agents' and the hostel owners' pockets, a practice that Chinese officials denounced but almost always in vain. The labour contract subsequently issued on Belitung was less equitable than that endorsed in Hong Kong and was said to have been difficult to understand. The duration of the contract would suddenly lengthen, from four months to 360 days, and illegal deductions were made from wages for board and lodging in the port. In some cases, what was originally a one-year contract would become a three-year contract.[59]

Over time, hostels tended to become associated not just with places of provenance but with destinations and even firms. In 1906, for example, 20 "piglet hostels" in Singapore and 23 in Hong Kong served Bangka's tin mines and plantations. In such cases, the companies ran the crimping and accommodation.[60]

Alongside the licensed houses in Hong Kong were others set up by criminals, often on the outskirts, where the authorities were less in evidence and footsore job-seekers were sitting ducks. One press report described how hostel-owners seized their "guests," gagged and bound them, put them in sacks, and loaded them onto ships bound for the Nanyang, with the connivance of the local police, and sold them to Western or Chinese companies on arrival.[61] Recruits were abused in all the

[58] Mollema (1922, 155).
[59] Guowuyuan [January] (1920a, 13–22), [May] (1920b, 8).
[60] Yang Tongling et al. (2004, 80).
[61] *Shen bao*, April 30, 1929.

ports. In 1925, for example, *Nanyang shangbao* described how "piglets were cheated and abducted by treacherous merchants in China, [...] imprisoned in a dark room, and fed nothing but gruel. Few escaped."[62] The deception and abuse continued even after the Pacific War. In 1946, for example, China's Foreign Ministry remonstrated with the Hong Kong authorities about the "tricking" of more than 700 "piglets" and the Qiaowu Committee demanded to know whether China had laws to forbid foreign recruitment after 897 Huagong were tricked into indenture.[63]

Professional Recruitment

In the late eighteenth and early nineteenth centuries, especially after the demise of the kongsis as autonomous collectives, professional agents employed by foreigners and Chinese in the Indonesian Archipelago became main organisers of the "piglet traffic." This trade started even before the increase in the number of Treaty Ports after the Second Opium War. Between 1782 and 1868, 1.5 million people from Chaozhou alone migrated under such arrangements.[64] The professionalisation of labour export became easier as the old rural elite, which had traditionally brokered state demands on the peasants and protected them from predators began losing control over the villages. The driving out of these old-style gentry patrons began during the chaos of the late Qing and climaxed in the early twentieth century.[65]

Traders recruited either directly from China or from labour markets in British-ruled Penang and Singapore. Recruits crimped in the villages or who had made their own way to the ports were gathered together by agents who arranged their onward journey. This happened in all China's foreign-controlled ports. Further points of transit grew up overseas. In the mid nineteenth century, Singapore was already a massive market-place for buying Chinese labour, attended by recruiters from all over Southeast Asia.

In the British case, the authorities played a far bigger role, setting up recruitment agencies in Hong Kong, Guangzhou, Xiamen, and Shantou staffed by paid officials who cooperated with the Chinese authorities and

[62] *Nanyang shangbao*, June 30, 1925.

[63] Foreign Ministry file 020000001585A, June 1946-December 1948, Academia Sinica, July 10 and August 20, 1946. On the continuing export of Huagong to the East Indies in 1946, see Lu Wendi et al. (1981, 636ff).

[64] Liu Jin (2009, 8).

[65] Benton (1999, 177).

did their best to suppress illegal crimping. They also claimed to have improved the conditions of recruitment by drawing in China-based missionaries.[66]

These efforts did not stamp out abuse, which continued to run rampant, but they set the British on a collision course with Dutch traders and officials, who took a more casual approach to recruitment and relied more heavily than the British on private agencies. When the Chinese and British authorities insisted on greater protection, Dutch officials switched where possible to channelling recruits through a bureau in Shantou, which issued contracts of dubious legality.

Recruits brought in through Singapore or Penang by agents working for the Dutch were under the supervision while in transit of the Chinese Protectorate, formed by the British in 1877 and headed by the Protector of Chinese, also known as the Secretary of Chinese Affairs.[67] The Protectors' job was to ensure that regulations were observed. This arrangement inevitably sparked conflict between British and Dutch. Despite protective measures, recruitment "long remained a dirty business" in Singapore and Hong Kong and the recruits were handled "as if in prison."[68]

After the establishment of the Protectorate, Dutch planters tried to switch to a direct system of labour recruitment. In 1888, the Chinese began allowing direct emigration to Deli. Workers were recruited in China but signed their contracts only after reaching Deli and were styled "free" because of the absence of a contract signed in China. This was an improvement from the angle of both the employer and, in some ways, the recruit, for there was a fall in the recruitment bonus paid by the employer and the recruits were apparently less likely than in the Straits Settlements to have been cheated. After 1890, the DPV gave up recruiting in the Straits altogether, although large numbers of other Chinese bound for the East Indies continued to pass through them.[69]

From the Dutch point of view, recruitment through Singapore had several drawbacks apart from British interference. The city was a favoured destination, and many Chinese recruited by agents working for the Dutch

[66] Look Lai (1989, 124–125).

[67] De Graaf and Stibbe (1918, 363). On the Protectorate, see Sai (2021).

[68] *Gedenkboek* (1927, vol. 2, 59).

[69] *Xianggang gongshang ribao*, November 26, 1921; Pelzer (1935, 75 and 91–92). In 1925, 80,492 Chinese entered the East Indies through the Straits; in 1928, 97,027 did.

deserted on arrival, sometimes aided by their *ketou* escorts. In 1882, a Dutch steamship company opened a direct line from Hong Kong to Batavia that temporarily put an end to the absconding, but the line closed in 1884. Finally, in 1908, the Java-China line was born and a direct link from Hong Kong to the East Indies was restored.[70] With it, Dutch recruitment through Singapore and the associated troubles became less common for a while.

Hong Kong, as a British colony, also had a Protectorate of Chinese, which preceded that in Singapore by a couple of decades. It too interfered in labour recruitment and made increasing demands on recruiters. These included a medical examination of recruits, photographs, and personal records and a period of at least two days in a "licensed boarding house," subject to inspection to test for infections. These requirements cost the Dutch and their agents time and money, for many recruits were declared unfit and had to be repatriated. Moreover, boarding houses secretly reinstated men declared unfit, causing further trouble for the company. Consequently, the Belitung mining company switched to using just one boarding house in Hong Kong. However, because of the company's greater role, emigration to Belitung was classed as "assisted," which added to the company's administrative costs. In an attempt to stop this happening, advances previously paid to recruits were turned into bonuses available only after arrival on Belitung.

The medical examinations in Hong Kong bore heavily on the price of a recruit. In 1912–1925, more than one third of *xinke* were rejected on medical grounds, at great cost to the recruiter. In 1916, for example, when 593 of 3508 *xinke* were rejected in Hong Kong, the cost per *xinke* was f48, whereas in 1919, when the number rejected rose to 2446 out of 8604, it quadrupled to f179.

On arrival in the reception camps in the East Indies, newcomers were given a couple of days to rest and get over the injections and sea-sickness. They were fed great quantities of rice to beef them up and inducted into the habit of regular showering. In some places, open-air cinemas were set up to entertain them. The initiation was gradual and the pace of work was initially slow. A main cause of contention during these early days was the labourers' assignment to a work-gang. This required tactful handling, for

[70] Wu Fengbin (1988, 182).

the recruits wanted to stay with people they knew and tended otherwise to become obstructive.[71]

Some companies in the East Indies organised professional recruitment in villages in counties with a tradition of labour migration and ran the entire operation, using steamships belonging to shipping lines with which they regularly associated. Chinese employers, usually descendants of immigrants, kept ties to their ancestral communities and made new ties overseas, which made made recruitment easier. Dutch officials sometimes played a role, though their intervention was technically illegal.

Much of the recruitment in nineteenth-century China was done by *baotou* contractors, also called *zhuzaitou* ("piglet bosses"), working under contract for Chinese and foreign-owned enterprises. Andrew Liu, writing about tea-growing, explains that domestic *baotou* acted both as recruiters and managers of the labourers and learned the language (a Minnan dialect) of the tea masters and the tea-shop and tea-factory owners they served, although they and their workers were from Jiangxi. This relationship mirrors that of the *baotou* who worked for foreign employers in China and abroad, as multilingual compradors and agents. The *baotou* were efficient managers of labour and exercised both "overt enforcement powers" and "a repertoire of mythologies and customs" to keep their charges hard at work.[72]

The labourers recruited under indenture by *baotou* in China were known as *baoshengong* (contract labourers), a system used in the 1920s and 1930s in Chinese and foreign-owned cotton mills.[73] In the Yangtze delta, contractors worked in tandem with gangers in the mills to recruit women and girls from villages in Subei, the poverty-stricken part of Jiangsu north of the Yangtze, in much the same way as male labourers were exported to the Nanyang. The recruits could be fined or beaten and were not allowed to leave their dormitories. They received their wages indirectly, through the ganger, who creamed off a share and stinted on board and lodging.[74] Wai Kit Choi argues that the violence and extreme exploitation they experienced was a product of class, gender, and familial relations

[71] *Gedenkboek* (1927, vol. 2, 62–67).

[72] Liu (2015, 158–164).

[73] On nomenclature and categories, see Honig (1983).

[74] Choi (2009). See also Honig (1986).

in the villages rather than a way of maximising the mill-owners' profits.[75] Choi's findings translate easily to Huagong recruitment.

Chinese recruited in Penang and Singapore by professional Chinese brokers to work in the East Indies were subject to numerous deceptions. They were not made aware of their eventual destination. Even the Chinese Protectorate in Singapore was not always able to prevent last-minute substitutions of unfit for fit workers at the point of embarkation, to circumvent controls.[76] Recruits promised light work ended up doing heavy work. An accountant who had been promised office work ended up harvesting tobacco. A demobilised soldier thought that he was joining the Dutch army.[77]

Latin American Recruitment of Chinese Labourers

In the nineteenth century, Cuba and in Peru were the two main Huagong destinations. In Cuba, where slavery was not abolished until 1886, Huagong worked side by side with black slaves on plantations, after their importation by Chinese agents known as *corredores* ("runners"). The importation began in 1846, to resolve a crisis in the sugar industry caused in part by British harassment of the slave trade. The labourers arrived under contract, mainly through the Portuguese colony of Macao, in the years before the Chinese, Americans, and British forced the Portuguese to crack down on the trade. The famous *Report of China's Cuba Commission* (1877) found that nearly all the labourers had been kidnapped or "decoyed abroad," that the provisions of a previous Sino-Spanish treaty had been violated, and that more than one in ten of those enlisted (some say as many as 16 percent) had died during the Middle Passage.[78] In Peru, where the slave trade ended in 1810 and slavery in 1854, Huagong worked on the plantations and mined guano. Chinese brokers exploited recruits by providing loans and selling goods at high prices from their shops on the plantations and embezzling wages, and later joined Peru's emerging petty bourgeoisie and merchant and landowning class.[79] The absence from Latin America of *shuike* and *ketou*, who retained their ties to communities in

[75] Choi (2018).

[76] *Xianggang gongshang ribao*, November 26, 1921.

[77] "De werving van Chineezen," *De Sumatra Post*, April 20, 1929.

[78] Mauro García Triana and Pedro Eng Herrera (2009, 141–142), Hu-Dehart (1994, 45), Narvaez (2010, 101–102).

[79] Gonzales (1989).

China and therefore had to act with greater constraint, can be explained by its distance from China. Not until late in the century did chains begin to form across oceans to link migrants in Latin America to their home communities.

The Latin American variant of Chinese indenture created a template that spread to Africa, where through British intermediacy it was adopted on the Spanish-controlled island of Fernando Po. However, few Chinese labourers ended up in the colony, although Spanish on the island tried to recruit Huagong (by way of Cuba and later directly from China, in 1928). Recruiting missions by Spanish officials in China, Southeast Asia, South America, and the Caribbean seem to have been abortive—most of the recruits were African.[80]

The methods of the Creole planters and their Chinese contractors in Latin America were for a while copied in China, where crimps working directly for foreigners gained a reputation for cruelty and deception. These practices continued even after the banning of the Macao "coolie" trade in 1873, as a result of British pressure (designed to rein in Britain's Spanish competitors) and political developments in Portugal. The Western planters and mine owners, as well as some Japanese, ran offices in the ports that were linked to Chinese contractors. The recruiters included not just employees of colonial companies but diplomats, adventurers, and even (as we have seen) freelancing Dutch Sinologists.

Shuike and *Ketou*

Some Chinese agents collected and delivered labourers for employment in the Nanyang and elsewhere in Southeast Asia independently of the foreign and overseas-Chinese companies. They went under a bewildering variety of names, depending on period, dialect, and place. This study generally refers to them as *shuike* ("water-guests," i.e., couriers) and *ketou* ("guest chiefs," translated as crimps or "coolie brokers"), except where necessary to make local distinctions.[81]

Shuike started out as informal couriers whose main job was "selling" Huagong to entrepreneurs in Southeast Asia. This function came to include not just escorting the labourers themselves but helping the wives

[80] Martino (2016, 39 and 182).

[81] Ma Chujian (2008, 21–32), Jiang Bowei and Cai Mingsong (2008, 267), Benton and Liu (2018, 35).

and dependants of the small minority of married Huagong to join them overseas, taking the Huagong home in old age or on expiry of their contract, escorting them back to China to marry, and "repatriating" children born to Huagong overseas.[82]

Would-be migrants without contacts overseas were particularly in need of the protection of someone familiar with the route and tied to networks in the ports of exit and entrance. The best *shuike* had charisma as well as managerial skills and a sound knowledge of languages, geography, and foreign ways as well as an unblemished reputation. He paid the costs along the route and charged a fee of several tens of dollars, at times, several hundred. Migrants paid the fee and the expenses from their wages, at a high rate of interest.[83] Once the trade became regular, junk-owners and shipping companies favoured the *shuike* with special terms.[84]

This trade in migrants was centuries old, but it peaked in the late Qing and continued into the 1930s. Even in 1932, 5000 households in Zhaoan (a coastal city in Fujian) lived off it. Once established, the trade acquired a second focus, the remittance to China of migrants' earnings overseas, which is thought to have started in the early nineteenth century.[85] Others see the transition from courier to broker the other way round, as a result of remittance couriers providing new arrivals with bridging loans, which broadened into a regular trade in the supply of labour.[86] Whatever the case, *shuike* and *ketou* became ever harder to differentiate and each acquired multiple functions, including not just the homeward transmission of money and the to-and-fro transmission of messages and Huagong but the importing of Nanyang produce to China and of Chinese goods to the Nanyang. Many *ketou* made an even greater profit on trading in Chinese goods than on the migrant trade.[87] In the Nanyang, *shuike* and *ketou* combed the mines and plantations for customers wanting to remit. The object of their trade was *renxincaiwu*, "people, letters, money, and goods."[88] Only after the shutting down of routes from China in the 1930s

[82] Liu Jin (2009, 16).
[83] Huang Jiaxiang (2010, 502–503).
[84] Yang Qunxi, ed., (2004, 59).
[85] Chen Lie (2008, 228–229). On Zhaoan: Huang Jiaxiang (2010, 503–504).
[86] Lin Sha (2008, 354–357, at 355).
[87] *Gedenkboek* (1927, vol. 2, 61).
[88] Yang Qunxi, ed. (2004, 77).

did the *ketou* function (taking people south) come to an end, although the remitting and repatriating continued.[89]

Shuike and *ketou* took labour migrants' remittances back to their families in China even before the institutionalisation of remittance and couriering. The *shuike* trade is said by some Chinese historians to have started in Southeast Asia in the seventeenth century, while others think it predated even the Ming. It peaked in the Qing's Guangxu reign (1875–1908), when more than twelve hundred couriers operated in Xiamen alone and another eight hundred in Shantou, and when several thousand big and small remittance houses linked the *qiaoxiang* to migrant centres in Asia, Australia, and the Pacific. A second peak came in 1927, when 223,033 migrants left through Shantou, often under *ketou* escort. Between 1904 and 1935, 2.96 million migrants left China by way of Shantou and 1.46 million returned, nearly all of them Huagong going to or coming from the Nanyang.[90]

Over the decades, the couriers helped knit the migrants and the economy of their places of provenance into a single transnational entity. The *shuike* and *ketou* were particularly active in Hakka regions, although the relative neglect in scholarship of Hakka regions has helped hide the Hakka ascendancy.[91] Indonesia alone had more than 360 Meizhou Hakka *shuike* even as late as 1948, on the eve of the Chinese Revolution. Couriers bought land and property in China on behalf of migrants, paid visits to their clients' relatives in the *qiaoxiang*, supervised the state of their fields, and paid respects on their behalf at ancestral graves. But despite the poor communications between Hakka counties and the coast, a far smaller proportion of Hakka women went to the East Indies than other women. Chaozhou or Guangfu women were more likely to migrate than Hakka women.[92] The Hakka connection frayed physically—some wives saw their husbands just once every few years or every decade, or even never.

The remittances went under different names in different places but are commonly called *qiaopi*, a compound of *qiao*, "to sojourn overseas," and *pi*, letter, remittance, or batch (of remittances). Tens of millions of *qiaopi* and a smaller but nonetheless massive number of replies (*huipi*) passed

[89] Jiao Jianhua and Xu Cuihong (2004, 166–167), Xiao Wenping (2004, 259).
[90] Chen Xunxian (2010, 185).
[91] Xiao Wenping (2004, 253).
[92] Xia Yuanming (2008, 388) and Xia Shuiping and Fang Xuejia (2004, 184).

across the Nanyang in the 150 or so years of the trade.[93] In some places, a distinction was made between *chidanshui* ("freshwater eaters"), couriers at the domestic end, and the *liucushui* ("saltwater skaters") who connected China and the Nanyang. In Guangdong's Guangfu region, domestic couriers were called *xunchengma* ("town-patrolling horses") or, if they specialised in goods, *zoudanbang* ("lone travellers"). *Xunchengma* sometimes escorted Huagong abroad.[94]

Most *shuike* and *ketou* were first-generation emigrants with vibrant links to sending places and to migrants and remitters. A pristine reputation and people to vouch for them were advantageous. The couriers had many features in common with the letter couriers[95] who had transmitted messages and things within China before the birth of a modern postal culture. *Shuike* operated in all the main migrant destinations, including Southeast Asia, the Americas, and Oceania, although in time they died out almost everywhere except in Southeast Asia.[96] They were in many cases *huixiangke* (returned villagers), bottom-up recruiters drawn from the grass roots.[97]

The migrants they shepherded to the coast were peasants with little or no schooling or experience of travel, and generally poor. The escorts not only guided them along the way but found them work on arrival and loans to tide them over until pay-day. Although they charged for their expertise, their relationship to the *xinke* was usually based not just on profit but on social ties.[98]

In some regions, the great majority of Huagong were taken abroad by *shuike*, *ketou*, or kinsmen returned from overseas and with an amateur knowledge of the trade. This practice was particularly prevalent in Hakka areas. There, as we have seen, poor communications and difficult terrain made travel difficult, and more than 80 percent of migrants were escorted by *shuike* or relatives. Meizhou is less than one hundred miles from Shantou, but the journey took three days in the years before migrant investors, in 1906, funded a railway. Up until 1940, 90 percent of towns

[93] On the number of qiaopi and huipi, see Deng Rui (2010, 103–104).

[94] On terms, see Mo Zhen, ed. (2013, 29), Yang Qunxi, ed. (2004, 57) and Benton and Liu (2018, 14–18). On *xunchengma*, see Liu Jin (2009, 61–62).

[95] *Xìnke*, not to be confused with *xīnke*, "new guest." See Benton and Liu (2018, 34–35) for the similarities.

[96] Forms of couriering have revived everywhere in the new labour diaspora, including in the Americas, Europe, and Australasia.

[97] Chen Jianbo (2004, 148–50).

[98] Wu Hongli (2008, 366).

and villages around Chaoshan were not linked to postal and modern financial networks.[99] The Hakka chains could be interminable. One Hakka in the East Indies took 400 relatives abroad; another, one thousand.[100]

In regions geographically less challenging, some migrants maintained their own home ties, made their own way abroad, and took remittances home rather than send them. In such places, *shuike* were fewer. For example, migrants from the island of Hainan, then part of Guangdong, could return home far more easily from Vietnam, less than 250 miles away, than migrants from Singapore to Guangdong and Fujian, nearly 2000 miles away. Even so, many were escorted by *shuike* to work on the Annan farms, leaving in June and returning in September.[101] The remittances of Hainan's Huagong totalled at least $1 trillion between 1927 and 1938 and transformed the island's economy.[102]

At first, *shuike* and *ketou* operated as part of the floating migrant population and rarely from fixed premises. However, they often stayed together in hostels in the sending and receiving ports, for safety and convenience. Parts of Shantou became a home from home for Meizhou Hakkas, who could speak Hakka in the dockside hostels. In time, escorts became associated with shops and businesses, which gave them credence, the appearance of stability, and a place in which to stay, meet remitters, and accommodate clients.[103] The shops and businesses ranged from grocery stores and restaurants to medical shops and goldsmiths.[104] Some couriers lived in *hangguan* ("trade buildings") or *piguan* ("*pi* buildings"), which they clubbed together to finance. The hostels or barracoons the migrants lodged in were, as we have seen, associated with particular regions or dialects.[105] At the destinations, *shuike* toured the hostels and fanned out from the ports to the mines and plantations to collect remittances and market intelligence. As the trade in *qiaopi* and labourers became more settled, some shops and hostels frequented by *shuike* and *ketou* made the transition to remittance offices, usually as a sideline. Like many migrant businesses, they were multifunctional—only 10 percent of remittance shops in Chaozhou in the 1930s dealt exclusively in remittances. Such businesses

[99] Xia Yuanming (2008, 388), Lin Tengyun (411–416) and Wu Kuixin (2004, 200–207).
[100] Xia Shuiping and Fang Xuejia (2004, 184).
[101] Yang Qunxi, ed. (2004, 66–67).
[102] Zhang Shuoren (2013, 204–213).
[103] Lin Tengyun (2008); Benton and Liu (2018, 35).
[104] Huang Zijian (2013, 133).
[105] Yang Qunxi, ed. (2004, 483).

traded information as well as conveying remittances and escorting and accommodating migrants, handled the migrants' boat tickets and onward accommodation, helped them with paperwork, and lent them money, at a high rate of interest. The capital they used to finance labour trafficking came from the profits of the remittance trade and vice versa.[106]

Some couriers expanded their recruiting and remitting into substantial businesses, even banks, with offices in the *qiaoxiang*, the ports, and overseas. The trade in Huagong and *qiaopi* were aspects of a single system, and the *shuike* and *ketou* were both generalists in the management of migration and actors in the world of low-level (and very occasionally high-level) transnational finance. Collectively, they knitted these institutions into an ever-denser network in which all of the aspects of migrant economy and society merged, bringing unprecedented prosperity to the migrant-sending areas. A few, however, made little profit and led hard lives, not much removed from those of the migrants they served and lived among.[107] *Ketou* escorted free as well as assisted or indentured labourers. Free labourers either worked for a relative or acquaintance or found a job after arriving.[108]

There was no strict division between professional company recruiters and independent couriers, people-traffickers, and labour brokers. Where it was profitable to do so, *ketou* played a crucial role in delivering recruits to company agents. The Dutch Twelve Companies, formed by mining and planting interests in Sumatra, maintained a headquarters in Hong Kong. The Hong Kong-based Holland China Handels Maatschappij, with branches in several ports, also handled recruitment. The recruitment centre in Hong Kong used by the Belitung mining company was capitalised by Chinese and made hundreds of thousands of yuan a year. Its main shareholder, Guo Zailin, was born on Belitung. The company had ties to individual *ketou*, to *ketou* gangs, and to hostels.[109] *Ketou* charged companies f35 for each Bangka-bound *xinke*, while the *xinke* himself received HK$7, comprising HK$3 while in the hostel and HK$4 on shipboard. The onward ticket was supplied by the Hong Kong headquarters. If the

[106] Benton and Liu (2018, 14–18 and 40–41). On multifunctionality, see Chen Liyuan (2008). On the kezhan, see Jiao Jianhua and Xu Cuihong (2004, 167) and Lin Qingxi (2010, 213). On the multifunctionality of the *piju* and associated institutions, see Yang Qunxi, ed. (2004).

[107] Mo Zhen, ed. (2013, 44 and 55). On the prosperity, see Li Xiaoyuan (2008).

[108] Wang Linqian and Wu Kunxiang (2002, 49).

[109] Lu Wendi et al. (1985a, 434).

xinke passed the medical, he received HK$80, which included travel costs and was not, at least in theory, deductible from later wages. Those failing the medical for miners were supposed to be sent home free of charge, but some were secretly sold on to plantation owners for a lesser price (f20–25), to grow pepper, gambier, coffee, and other crops. Strict selection was said to be essential because of the demanding nature of mine-work—according to the Dutch Resident in 1897, 6000 recruits were expected annually, of whom 3500 were selected. The recruitment happened indirectly, without the agreement of the Chinese authorities, and anonymously—the companies involved did not reveal their recruits' names and villages of origin. Investigations in Sumatra by Chinese officials belonging to the Qiaogong Committee uncovered cases in which recruits from Shantou and elsewhere in Guangdong were tricked by *ketou* and sold on to Hong Kong hostels. The investigators remonstrated with the Dutch in Bangka, though it is unlikely that much happened.[110]

The remitting role of *shuike* and *ketou* solidified a financial tie between migrant and sending place, while their role as back-and-forth couriers maintained a physical tie. Escorts and remittance agents usually worked cooperatively or were one and the same. In 1938, when war reached Fujian, Xiamen's hostels moved in their entirety to the nearby island of Gulangyu, which remained under foreign protection until the outbreak of the Pacific War in late 1941.[111] After 1949, under the Communists, the Qiaolian (Returned Overseas-Chinese Federation) wrote thousands of letters on behalf of migrants' dependants in the villages and tracked down hundreds of missing Huagong.[112]

Wartime Couriering

Remitting and escorting continued even during the war against Japan. In 1941, when Japanese military strength in China was at its peak, between three and four hundred *shuike* went back and forth several times a year to Meixian, carrying $2 million in remittances.[113] Two major routes opened into the *qiaoxiang*, each carrying migrants and remittances. These routes

[110] Heinoldt (1897, 2–3) and Guowuyuan [May] (1920b, 5–7).

[111] Hou Weixiong (2009, 136–141).

[112] Zou Qiudong and Su Tonghai (2009).

[113] Xia Yuanming (2008, 375–376) and Wu Hongli (2008, 366).

formed after the Japanese closed Hong Kong, which had played a role in earlier wartime contacts.

The first route was through Guangzhouwan (Kwangchowan), an anomalously French enclave on Guangdong's Leizhou Peninsula. Guangzhouwan's economy was controlled by merchants from Chaoshan, a centre of couriering. Traffickers exported hundreds of workers to Africa between 1916 and 1929 from Guangzhouwan. In 1941, thousands of passengers left aboard steamers bound for Hong Kong, as part of a massive smuggling operation carried out by fake "French" smugglers in collusion with Japanese,[114] thus resuming earlier efforts that Chinese authorities had intervened to stop.[115] The French continued until 1941 to export labourers to Madagascar, which received 3637 Fujianese recruits[116] before the Guangzhouwan route was closed down.

The second and far bigger wartime route into the *qiaoxiang*, a land route for a trade traditionally done on water, was through Dongxing, a border crossroads between China and Vietnam. The establishment of the Dongxing route in 1942 led to a wartime boom in the region and a flow of remittances and refugees that continued until the Japanese capture of Nanning in 1944 and revived briefly after the Japanese surrender. It alleviated the devastation wreaked by the war on Chaoshan, by injecting $10 million a month into the economy during a famine in 1943. Teahouses, restaurants, and hostels mushroomed in the town to serve the migrants who crowded in from the east, the scores of *guiqiao*, and thousands of refugees from Vietnam. The route, through bandit-infested mountains, was far from secure, and Shantou merchants employed several dozen well-armed men to protect it. Up to 90 percent of those who used it were said to have died.[117]

[114] Guangzhouwan lunchuan chu Bakou diaocha biao (List yielded by investigation of Guangzhouwan steamers leaving Bakou), doc. no. 4/26877, November 1942, and doc. 4/23722, June/July 1941, both in the Second Nanjing Historical Archive.

[115] Wu Fengbin (1988, 445–456).

[116] Guowuyuan qiaoban, eds. (2005, 218).

[117] Benton and Liu (2018, 115–118), Liu Jin (2009, 35–36), Yang Qunxi, ed. (2004, 103 and 118).

LAOKE RECRUITMENT

This form of recruitment was in many ways a top-down copying by employers of the *shuike/ketou* system of recruitment, except that most of the recruiters were time-expired workers, veterans (*laoke*) re-engaged by their overseas employers. This switch happened in many migrant-sending areas, where professional brokers had alienated would-be recruits by their ruthless methods. The *laoke* were more acceptable both to the employer, on cost grounds, and to the worker, to whom they were to some extent accountable through the moral economy to which both belonged. The switch away from recruiting through Singapore to using *laoke* was welcomed by Huagong miners, who saw Singapore as a centre of the "piglet" trade.[118] Even *laoke* recruiters who profited excessively were usually seen as value for money by those they trafficked.[119]

In the East Indies, *laoke* recruitment is sometimes said to have started in the early decades of the twentieth century and to have been copied from British India, where recruiters were known as RERs (returned-emigrant recruiters), a term coined in the 1830s.[120] In fact, it began even before the twentieth century. The habit of attracting fresh labour by allowing existing labourers to return to China to spread the news seems to have been as old as the Dutch presence in the archipelago. In 1619, 300 of the 800 Chinese, mainly taken by force to work as "people of the land" (agricultural labourers), were sent back from Batavia in the apparent certainty that five times as many (1500) would turn up to replace them.[121] According to De Groot, clan recruiting (another name for the practice) started in the 1860s. In the early 1850s, John Francis Loudon (who set up the Billiton mining company in 1851) sent his assistant S. W. Van Haeften to bring workers over directly from China, by way of Hong Kong and Whampoa (Huangpu). The recruits, accompanied by free Chinese migrants, arrived of their own accord.[122] In 1866, time-expired labourers were given leave to return to China to bring back fellow villagers. Disciplining was left to the recruiters and the clan migrants "soon saw Belitung as a piece of China."[123]

[118] Rapport (1905, 13).

[119] Li Minghuan (2012, 212–213).

[120] Bates (1992, 239–240). By mid-century, RERs were recruiting one fifth of Indian arrivals in Mauritius.

[121] Groeneveldt (1898, 68–70).

[122] Hess and Hess (1912, 34), for Mangar and other Belitung tin mines.

[123] *Gedenkboek* (1927, vol. 2, 59–60).

When planters started farming tobacco in Sumatra in 1869, they initially used labour delivered by brokers in the Straits Settlements, but the brokers' methods earned the planters a bad name and frightened off new recruits. Deli in particular became the object of "a perfect hatred" on the Chinese labour market, and recruits became "perfectly mad if the word 'Deli' be heard on board."[124] At this point, a change in tactics was considered necessary. Mollema's history of tin-mining on Belitung dates the start of *laoke* recruiting to 1873–1874, when the *ketou* who had previously monopolised much of the trade were supplemented by *laoke* sent home on leave.[125] In 1875, another group followed, to recruit from the villages and advertise for Deli. At first the scheme floundered, because of the lack of a direct sea-link to the East Indies, sabotage by Chinese officials, and British objections. In 1888, however, it was revived by Dutch officials in league with the planters' body, whose agents in China oversaw the operation. The planters combined recruitment with the provision of a remittance service for recruits, again illustrating the close tie between acquiring workers and returning money and letters to their dependants. By the end of the century, up to 1200 recruiters headed to China annually at their employers' expense in advance of the northwesterlies, to gather *xinke* and wait for the December and January winds to blow them back south.[126]

The *laoke* scheme came into its own in the 1910s, when rubber cultivation took off in Sumatra. By that time it was mainly used, still under its Chinese name, to recruit Javanese—in 1910, a full 5 percent of Javanese contract-workers were sent back to Java as *laoke* recruiters.[127] It also boomed for a while in south China and was encouraged by Hong Kong's Secretary for Chinese Affairs, who said in 1911 that Hong Kong wanted to encourage employers and labour contractors "to recruit free labour for their own estates though the medium of recruiters sent back by them to China for that purpose."[128]

Recruitment of kin or fellow villagers by the Chinese *kepala* ("head coolie") on a visit to China was a long-standing and logical arrangement in Malaya too, where *kepala* played the role of *laoke*. In 1912, after the passage of a new labour code, the system was officially recognised. This

[124] Breman (1989, 132).
[125] Mollema (1922, 166).
[126] Heinoldt (1897, 3–4).
[127] *Mededelingen uitgegeven door de Deli Planters Vereeniging*, October 1919, vol. 2, no. 7, 5–7.
[128] *Malaya Tribune*, July 12, 1922.

go-ahead for a *laoke*-style system was linked to the plans for the abolition of indenture in 1913 and 1914, clarified in 1915 by additional laws that forbade Chinese to enter into written labour contracts (which would have implied indenture).[129]

Like *shuike*, the *laoke* was a member of the same lineage, village, or dialect group as his recruits. Dutch officials and employers argued that the system righted wrongs inherent in professional recruitment, for the recruiters were not profit-driven and therefore had no incentive to recruit indiscriminately. Where a choice was available between a *laoke* and a *shuike/ketou*, however, migrants seem to have preferred the latter, who were seen as better at taking people (including the wives of established migrants) over long distances.[130]

According to some Dutch accounts, each *laoke* recruited on average no more than a couple of Huagong. This was presented as an advance on the old system of mass recruitment by strangers. In reality, however, most *laoke* in 1905 delivered between ten and twenty *xinke*, for each of which they received a payment of f20 in Hong Kong and a further f80 on arrival overseas, and were paid only if they delivered more than three recruits. Otherwise, they received only travel and accommodation costs.[131]

Under the recruitment ordinance, each recruit received a mat to lie on, a tray, a mug, and three meals a day and, on the journey, 50 cents a day in the case of adults and 25 cents in that of children, plus an advance. In theory, recruiters who failed to provide the advance (which evened out at around f30) could incur a fine of f500 or three months in jail,[132] but most recruits only received it after signing their contract on arrival in Sumatra. The contract was not necessarily kept to and was acknowledged to be an administrative formality. Because of the advance, recruits were indebted to their employer from the start, the debt being the basis for their indenture. The bounty paid the *laoke* per recruit in 1905 equalled four months' pay (4 × f5) for a labourer in his first year and more than two months (2 × f9) for an old hand. If the *laoke* brought back twenty recruits, he could potentially receive a sum equivalent to the wage paid over four years to an

[129] *Malaya Tribune*, October 24, 1934.

[130] Xiao Wenping (2004, 258).

[131] Lu Wendi et al. (1985a, 433–434) and Guowuyuan [January] (1920a, 12).

[132] Heinoldt (1897, 3) and Heijting (1925, 81).

experienced worker. Clearly the *laoke* had every reason to recruit as widely as possible and the so-called cap seems to have been a fiction.[133]

The widespread change to *laoke* recruitment came about primarily because the cost of professional recruitment was constantly rising. The price of an indenture in the Nanyang could be ten to twenty times that paid by the crimp in China.[134] Relatively few clan recruits were classed as "bad elements," which reduced the overall price still further by excluding trouble-makers and potential absconders. The recruits were more tractable in the hands of fellow-villagers, which again made the system more profitable and efficient.

Employers also hoped that the change would help to counter the charge of enslavement levelled at them by Dutch liberals and trade unionists.[135] To demonstrate the morality of *laoke* recruitment, they falsely claimed that the recruiter did not benefit materially from it, save for a fixed daily payment. The Labour Inspectorate was not entirely happy with *laoke* recruitment, precisely on those grounds. The employers countered that the ratio of *laoke* to recruits was only 1: 1.06, which would rule out a financial incentive. In reality, however, the ratio could be much higher. *Laoke* recruitment reduced the cost of recruitment but not necessarily the scale, or not by as much as claimed.[136] Moreover, agents continued to give cash advances that were subsequently deducted from labourers' wages to reimburse the recruiter and the employer.

Laoke methods paralleled changes in the recruitment of labour for factories in Chinese cities in the same period.[137] As we saw earlier, a similar system was used in the 1920s by mill managers to recruit workers directly, with the help of village heads, thus cutting out the contractor's role. The recruits, known as *yangchenggong* (apprentices), were not indentured or beaten and were supposed to receive formal training and professional supervision. The "new workers' villages" built to accommodate them call to mind the plans for workers' colonies in Sumatra. Professional recruiters

[133] Rapport (1905, 3–4).

[134] Li Minghuan, 210.

[135] Jakarta National Archive, Algemene Secretarie, Grote Bundel, TZG Agenda file no. 8436.

[136] Heijting (1925, 81–91 and 140–141), De Kat Angelino (1931, 570–571) and Heinoldt (1897, 3).

[137] Honig (1983, 441).

played no role, and the recruit required a recommendation from an established worker, a sort of *laoke*.[138]

Laoke working for the Dutch received detailed instructions on how to carry out recruitment. The assignment was not risk-free. The *laoke* had to make clear to families the nature of the arrangement and to ensure that recruits were able-bodied, aged twenty to forty, in good health, disease-free, and new to the Nanyang—and not to have been in the Communist Party or served in the army, for ex-soldiers sometimes spelled trouble and were recruited only for special purposes. The *laoke* bore the costs incurred if a recruit failed to meet requirements. Each *xinke* received $5 to cover his transfer to Hong Kong, while the *laoke* received $10. The *laoke* had to keep the *xinke* safe while awaiting shipment and was forbidden to transfer "possession" of a *xinke* to another, and had to report transgressions by the hostel to the company's representative.

Dutch claims that the *laoke* method had replaced professional recruitment by the late 1920s were only partly true. In 1932, most mines in Bangka recruited "new guests" through old ones, but the process was guided and administered by the Twelve Companies in Hong Kong, which represented employers. There was no high wall between the two methods. In Deli-Medan, the plantations continued to use professional recruiters deployed through the Twelve Companies. Even the mining companies on Bangka and Belitung sent their *laoke* into China through agencies administered by the Twelve Companies, which gave them ID and accommodation.[139]

In 1930, C. Lankamp of Banka Tinwinning agreed that clan recruitment was superior to professional recruitment, "with all its dark practices," but added that it was no "absolute guarantee [...] of good coolies." It should therefore supplement rather than replace professional recruitment, which should be "maintained without any revision," on economic grounds. The Deli Planters' Association in Hong Kong also used both methods simultaneously, with former professional recruiters managing clan recruitment. Squeeze by Chinese officials played a role in both cases, and Dutch diplomats had a hand in clan recruitment. Some powerful

[138] Choi (2018).

[139] Lu Wendi et al. (1984a, 294–296), extracted from the Guomindang's *Waijiao bu gongbao* (Diplomatic bulletin), 1932, vol. 3, no. 4, 58–87; Wu Fengbin (1988, 151).

voices complained that clan recruitment was harder to control and privileged quantity over quality.[140]

British and Dutch planting and mining interests in Malaya tried to reform Huagong recruitment, given the abuses and the opposition to it in China, where recruiters were increasingly prosecuted for kidnapping.[141] In 1910, the planters proposed setting up a recruitment office to kill off the agencies. However, they rejected the idea of a Chinese Immigration Panel on the lines of the Tamil Immigration Fund, on the grounds of cost and to keep recruitment in private hands. In 1920, machinery for the systematic recruitment of Chinese was "as far off as ever." Despite its supposed "morality," *laoke* recruitment did not necessarily deliver a tractable recruit. Even under the *laoke* system, passengers to the Nanyang sometimes seized control of the vessel and forced it to change course and recruits bound for Bangka "repeatedly" threw the captain and crew overboard and sailed to Singapore.[142]

Labour Recruitment in the First World War

The recruitment of Huagong underwent reform in the early twentieth century as a result of two experimental schemes. In 1904, 60,000 Huagong were recruited to work in the Witwatersrand gold mines in South Africa, under new British regulations.[143] These regulations, partly based on those drafted by the Qing after China's defeat in the Second Opium War, set a five-year limit on indenture and guaranteed a free return.[144] The new rules influenced the wider evolution of British policy on Chinese labour recruitment. It was no accident that an official of the Malay Government was appointed as the Transvaal Emigration Agent in Hong Kong.[145] In May 1916, an even bigger scheme was launched by the warlord Beiyang Government (1912–1928) in Beijing. Under it, Britain, France, and Russia were allowed to recruit a Chinese Labour Corps, whose quarter of a million ancillaries performed non-military tasks at and behind the front

[140] Jakarta National Archive, Algemene Secretarie, Grote Bundel, TZG Agenda file no. 8436.

[141] *Malaya Tribune*, July 12, 1922.

[142] Heinoldt 1897, 4. The Chinese habit of seizing control of vessels taking them south was practically as old as the Dutch occupation of the East Indies (Groeneveldt 1898, 237–238).

[143] Ngai (2017, 59–78) and Richardson (1982).

[144] Bailey (2011a, 38).

[145] *Malaya Tribune*, July 12, 1922.

in the First World War. Unlike the half million Indian labourers recruited to support British operations in the war, the Huagong spent the war in Europe rather than in the colonies.[146]

The agreements regarding Huagong led to a flurry of new Chinese regulations. Some Chinese hoped that they would tighten China's grip on labour recruitment and promote a more general reform.[147] The Beiyang Government's main aim in offering the Allies labourers was to get their support for the return to Chinese sovereignty of Germany's Chinese concessions and to win equal rights for China more broadly.

However, China's Republican negotiators were novices on the world stage, falsely buoyed by Woodrow Wilson's seeming commitment to self-determination for oppressed peoples. Their expectations were comprehensively dashed. Instead of restoring Chinese sovereignty, the postwar Versailles Peace Treaty in 1919 recognised Japanese claims to German rights in Shandong. The Allies' concessions to Chinese nationalism were withdrawn and the "coolie traffic" revived. It was during this wartime experiment that Chinese officials replaced the term Huagong with Qiaogong ("sojourner workers"), to signal the temporary nature of the migration and to underline the government's commitment to its citizens abroad. However, the conditions set by Beijing for the recruitment were flouted.

In negotiating the arrangement, Chinese officials tried to set a new tone. Foreigners were expected to act transparently, by stating in advance the duration of the contract (nominally five years, but terminable after three), wage rates, and working hours, as well as providing free medical treatment and agreeing to the inspection of embarkation in China and the welfare of labourers abroad. As in India under the Immigration Fund Ordinance, recruits received free passage and were in theory free of debt. However, the penal sanction was retained and fines, wage deductions, imprisonment, hard labour, and deportation could be applied.[148] The Chinese recruiters were expected to maintain a formal register of names and adhere to enlistment regulations rather than operate a free-for-all,[149] but a free-for-all is what often ensued.[150] Labourers continued to be

[146] Singha (2020).

[147] For Chinese law and indenture in this period, see Ma Huiyue (2015).

[148] Chen Sanjing (1975, 98–99) and Ma Huiyue (2015, 123).

[149] Lu Wendi et al. (1985b, 1813–1823).

[150] Ma Huiyue (2015, 122 and 127).

cheated at the point of recruitment and endured dangerous conditions and racist discrimination in Europe,[151] leading to strikes and demonstrations in which Chinese were shot dead. The unreformed British attitude was evident from a private report that boasted that the wartime contract "gave us power over [the Chinese labourers] for a long period of time with the option of getting rid of them in a moderately short time."[152] The pay and conditions in Russian contracts were even worse: it is not surprising that huge numbers of Huagong joined the October Revolution in 1917.[153]

But although many of the innovations in Chinese legislation on recruitment were honoured more in the breach than in the observance, they created a model that some reform-minded officials could try to emulate. Even before the war, in March 1912, the provisional government set up in Nanjing by Sun Yat-sen banned the "piglet trade," though Sun resigned before the ban could become law. Many opposed the Beiyang Government's contribution to the Allied effort, and in 1914 critics demanded an end to recruitment in Xiamen and Shantou. However, local governments went their own way, and Beijing was under pressure not just from the Allies but also from Germany, which weakened its hand still further.

In 1916, overseas-Chinese interests represented in the Beiyang Government expressed their concerns about the pact with the Allies, particularly regarding abuses committed by Chinese agents of the Russians, and called for China to stay neutral. Critics said the Russians were transgressing the agreed area of recruitment and China's Ambassador in Russia, Liu Jingren, originally opposed recruitment altogether. In 1917, the Beiyang Government set up Qiaogong Affairs Bureaus to improve the supervision of recruitment and took new steps to avoid indebtedness and indenture and the use violence. However, its efforts were only partly effective. Some officials sabotaged recruitment regulations, others enriched themselves by taking bribes. Overseas, the new contracts had a greater impact. In France, diplomats and overseas Chinese formed ties to Huagong and called on Beijing to protect them. Beijing responded by sending special envoys to France, Britain, and Russia, to mediate conflicts and negotiate better terms for the postwar demobilisation.

[151] On the Huagong in France and Britain, see Benton (2007, 65–66).

[152] Xu Guoqi (2011, 39). Other studies on China's wartime labourers in Europe include Bailey (2011a, 35–52) and Alexeeva (2021).

[153] Benton (2007, ch. 2).

After the Chinese Labour Corps' return to China in 1919, officials in Beijing instructed provincial authorities to put its members' experience in the war to use in China's industrial modernisation. However, little or nothing came of this campaign. In Guangzhou, Sun Yat-sen's southern government announced a programme for overseas Chinese and Huagong in 1921 and a member of the Guangdong parliament raised the issue of "peasants from Hailufeng being exploited on Sumatra's tobacco plantations."[154] However, Sun's main preoccupation at the time was with staving off financial bankruptcy and maintaining his fragile hold on power.

In Europe, a hoped-for crucible of Chinese labour emancipation, several hundred left-behind Labour Corps recruits joined the modern proletariat in car factories and mines around Paris and Lyons. A handful joined the French Communist Party and went to Spain to fight Franco when the Huagong were elbowed out of the factories, ostensibly under a first-in first-out rule. Most Chinese in Britain and France between the wars worked in laundries and restaurants, under conditions not much short of full indenture. Such was the extent of their immiseration that in 1935 an urgent call went out for their repatriation.[155] Even Chinese seafarers remained bonded to their employers until a further wave of war-induced agitation in 1939, spearheaded by Communist organisers.[156] So the progress made in protecting China's labour migrants during the war in Europe was not translated into a new deal for Huagong in Europe or at sea, let alone in Southeast Asia.

The Chinese Labour Corps after the Armistice

The old colonial view of Huagong survived the war, as shown by events during their repatriation from France. In June 1918, a Chinese power-broker in Vancouver wrote to the Canadian Minister of Immigration proposing their employment in Canada as indentures, to cultivate land "under military discipline and military pay, with the understanding that they would be returned to their country after the war." Nothing came of the proposal, which was opposed by Canadian soldiers' organisations.[157]

[154] *Dagong bao (Tianjin ban)*, March 13, 1921.

[155] *Shen bao*, August 29, 1935.

[156] Benton and Gomez (2008).

[157] "Canada Considers Coolie Question, Import of Chinese Labour," *The Shanghai Times*, June 25, 1918.

However, in November 1919, during the transhipment across Canada of demobilised Labour Corps units, the Chinese Consul in Vancouver revived the idea, suggesting "the retention there, under indenture, of the thousands of coolies now *en route* to China from France, [...] with a view to reducing the cost of living in and of developing British Columbia." Building companies and fruit growers also called for the importation of "indentured Oriental labor" "under well-defined regulations." When the scheme failed, some demobilised repatriands broke loose from their guards and vanished into Chinatown.[158] Mutinies of this sort had long been a favoured way of evading anti-Chinese exclusion laws in North America, a practice that turned rampant during the Second World War, when one in four Chinese seafarers in New York jumped ship.[159] British planters also tried to divert demobilised labourers from France to Malaya, to work on the rubber plantations, but the British Government rejected the proposal as a breach of faith.[160]

China's postwar disillusionment with the Labour Corps experiment and the labourers' rebelliousness put an end to the prospect of transporting Chinese labour overseas under the supervision of the Chinese state and receiving states. The refusal of many Huagong to go quietly in 1919 foreshadowed the wartime rebellions by Chinese seafarers on European ships in the Second World War. However, reformers' hopes that state-sponsored recruitment would lead to a reshaping of China's handling of labour issues were dashed. China's fragility minimised the impact of reforms, although some officials tried to keep them alive. After the war, repatriated workers denounced their treatment in Europe as a betrayal and some were radicalised. This had first happened in South Africa in 1906, when workers broke loose from the compounds and preferred to roam the streets and starve rather than submit to men "lower in scale of civilization."[161] In France, links formed between some Huagong and Chinese Communist students, and in Russia the radicalisation went much further and deeper.[162]

Why did the Chinese negotiators' hopes for a postwar reform of recruitment fail? The main flow of Chinese labour was towards Southeast Asia,

158 Lu Wendi et al. 1984b, vol. 7, 353; Reuters, November 29, 1919.

159 Benton (2007, 58–59).

160 *Malaya Tribune*, July 12, 1922.

161 *The North-China Herald and Supreme Court and Consular Gazette*, April 12, 1906.

162 Benton (2007).

which was untouched by fighting and where Huagong were employed by private companies rather than by states. In any case, the Allies' agreement with Beijing was cynical and and no basis for permanent reform. Another stumbling block to change was Japan's occupation of Manchuria, in 1904, which consolidated a massive wave of migration from north China that overwhelmed the Chinese authorities, providing rich pickings for officials and normalising indenture. Finally, the main source of overseas migration was in China's far south, where the Beijing-based government had no authority and where the newly formed Nationalist Government, first in Guangzhou and later in Nanjing, was constrained by foreign interests and warlord cliques.

A systematic focus on supporting China's migrant labourers was therefore impossible and the wartime reform gained no momentum. Not all the measures adopted in South Africa and Europe were forgotten. Here and there, the Chinese inspection teams that occasionally turned up in the Nanyang continued to insist on transparency in contracts and tried to ban monetary advances that would trap recruits into indenture. However, they were no match for the colonial officials and employers, especially in the East Indies, where an enlightened approach to labour issues was far from the norm even in the 1930s.

Labour Recruitment Linked to Foreign States in China in the Inter-war Years

One outcome of the Labour Corps experiment was to excite the attention of labour-trafficking states lower down the international hierarchy, which concluded that Chinese labour was up for sale and tried to recruit it. However, their efforts rarely succeeded, partly because of protests on the streets and because it was easier for the Chinese authorities to reject recruiters from weak states than from big powers. Officials in the provinces had a venal interest in selling access to the local labour market, but central interests stood in the way of deals. In 1916, the Beiyang warlords hoped not only to make money but to improve their international standing. After the war, however, none of the supplicant states could offer anything in return, apart from kickbacks. Chinese public opinion had seen the previous arrangement come apart in 1919 and rejected ones that seemed to lack even a shred of advantage.

The two European states that tried hardest to interest China in a state-to-state scheme in the interwar years were Spain and Italy. The Spanish approach was reminiscent of the worst days of the "coolie traffic" to South America, where it had survived into the early twentieth century in Mexico and Panama,[163] countries used chiefly as illegal gateways into the United States by traffickers.[164] In 1921, more than 400 Huagong were smuggled into Mexico despite efforts by Beijing to stop them,[165] and in 1922 a Spanish ship took 1500 Chinese labourers there but was prevented them from landing and seems to have vanished from the record.[166]

In 1928, a Spanish envoy tried to recruit Huagong to work on Fernando Po, an African island colony known as a dumping ground for dissidents and with a reputation for extreme abuse. The Spanish legation in Peiping (Beijing) enlisted the support of the Mayor of Qingdao, Zhao Qi, who—"for the good of both the nation and the people, and not for myself"—said the scheme would lessen unemployment and starvation. In the new climate of reform, even Zhao Qi (later a quisling under the Japanese) expressed at least a semblance of concern for the recruits' welfare,[167] while the Spanish, posing as enlightened internationalists, offered a deal mimicking the wartime reforms and presented as an economic and diplomatic opportunity for Nanjing. Huagong in south China had had their chance, said Spain's negotiator—now it was north China's turn. The Africans were "too stupid," whereas "the workers of your honourable country are the best in the world." China and Spain could develop Fernando Po in the interests of both, in an international alliance. The Huagong would contribute even more to the nation than the students who went to Paris in 1919 under the famous work-study scheme. This offer was no Spanish anomaly. It was phrased in similar terms to one made shortly afterwards by the British Governor of Borneo, who said that "the natives were too stupid" to build roads and develop agriculture.[168] With Zhao Qi's support, two thousand recruits were brought together to await shipment, but the

[163] Wang Linqian and Wu Kunxiang (2002, 207).
[164] Mei Weiqiang and Zhang Guoxiong, eds. (2001, 240) and Wu Fengbin (1988, 358).
[165] Academia Sinica archive, Beiyang Foreign Ministry 03-31-001-04-002, July 1921.
[166] *Shen bao*, October 25, 1922.
[167] *Shen bao*, December 26, 1928.
[168] *Shen bao*, November 14, 1929.

Nanjing Government banned it, pressured by protestors, and communicated the prohibition to Hong Kong, Macao, and other Chinese ports.[169]

After the ban, provincial authorities were instructed to take further measures against "unscrupulous recruiting agents"[170] and in 1929 the Commissioner of Reconstruction, Ma Chiu Taoon, went to Geneva to propose resolutions to the ILO regarding Chinese labour overseas.[171] On and off, officials continued into the early 1930s to seek reform, and in 1933 Chinese representatives in the East Indies called on Nanjing to get the Dutch to end the "vicious exploitation of coolie laborers" in the mines.[172] However, Nanjing lacked the machinery for such a campaign, and was in any case deflected from such concerns by the military threat posed by Communists in the south and the Japanese in the northeast.

Italy also tried to recruit Huagong. Again, corrupt Chinese diplomats rose to the bait. In 1935, Italy asked for 7000 Huagong to serve in Italian Somaliland, in support of Mussolini's Second Italo-Ethiopian War, but was thwarted by a protest movement.[173] In 1936, however, a shipload of 200 Huagong passed through Singapore on their way to Ethiopia to build roads for the Italian Government and transport ammunition. The Chinese ambassador in Italy denied having arranged permission for the contracts with Nanjing's approval, but rumours of Italian agents recruiting labourers remained rife.[174] Chinese officials confirmed that "in Shantou traitors

[169] Wu Fengbin (1988, 448) and Li Anshan (2000, 262). The episode was chronicled in *The China Weekly Review*: "Spanish Colonial Administration Recruits Chinese Laborers at Tsingtao," December 8; "Tsingtao Governor Defends Spanish Coolie Trade," December 22, 1928; and "Coolies for Spanish Colonies Detained at Tsingtao," December 29, 1928. Official documentation on this incident is in the archive of the Academia Sinica in Taipei (Guomin zhengfu xingzheng yuanqiaowu weiyuan hui, eds, *Xibanya shangren sizhao Huagong fu Feizhou Fannengdubo dao kaiken yi an xubian*, January 1929), together with an extensive English-language summary apparently taken from *The China Sphere*, a short-lived publication from Qingdao edited by William M. Cornwell; and Guomin zhengfu qiaowu weiyuan hui, *Ben hui duiyu Xibanya daibiao zai Hua zhaogong fu Feizhou Fannengdubo dao kaiken yi an zhi jingguo* (Our Committee's view of the case of Spanish representatives in China recruiting labour to go to Fernandopo Island in Africa to reclaim wasteland), November 1928.

[170] *China Overland Trade Report*, January 21, 1929.

[171] *China Overland Trade Report*, May 3, 1929.

[172] "Vicious Exploitation of Coolie Laborers Charged in Mines of the Dutch East Indies," *The China Press*, June 5, 1933.

[173] Li Anshan (2000, 264–265).

[174] "Coolies For Africa?: Chinese Pass through on Italian Liner," *South China Morning Post*, April 13, 1936.

have set up a coolie-recruiting organ to trick bankrupt peasants into going to East Africa."[175]

By the 1930s, state-sponsored contracting in China had largely come to an end, except in places under Japanese influence or control, like parts of Fujian and Manchuria and Taiwan. Nanjing greatly extended its direct rule in the 1930s, from four provinces to eleven, and its victory over the Communists in 1934 gave it greater control in south China, so that it was able to stabilise its authority. Moreover, nationalist feeling was growing on the streets, and its targets included not just the Japanese and the Western concessions but the contractors trafficking Huagong overseas and to Manchuria.

The resistance was transnational. Chinese associations overseas fed intelligence to the authorities in China, often along Huagong networks. Community leaders rallied support for Chinese and Huagong interests and against abuse and exploitation. In Cuba, for example, Chinatown leaders alerted their contacts in Hong Kong of the high rate of unemployment and vagabondage among Huagong in Cuba and urged a stop to recruitment.[176] Chinese Communists, who became more influential in Chinatown and maritime labour in the 1930s, also played a role. China's labour diaspora was potentially formidable, and Communist leaders began to look more closely at its problems and how to harness its power.

In the Second World War, there was no repeat of the Labour Corps. In January 1940, a Chinese diplomat went to Europe to discuss a British plan to recruit 100,000 Huagong to go to France,[177] but nothing came of it. In 1939, the Japanese newspaper *Asahi Shimbun* reported that the British and French had requested three million Huagong and that the Nationalists (by then in Chongqing) had agreed, to obtain foreign currency. But China's Foreign Office called the story a fabrication, although it did mention providing "reserve manpower."[178] In 1940, the British Consul-General in Shanghai denied a similar rumour.[179]

[175] Yan Xishan shiliao 116-010108-0325-100, March 13, 1936 (Academia Sinica archive); *Kung Sheung Evening News*, September 14, 1935.

[176] *Xianggang Huazi ribao*, April 20 and September 16, 1921.

[177] Academia Sinica archive, Foreign Ministry 020-990500-0042, January 12, 1940.

[178] *South China Morning Post*, November 14, 1939. Other reports mentioned the figure of 300,000 (Guomin zhengfu, November 15, 1939, file 001000005388A, Academia Sinica archive).

[179] "No Coolies Shipped to Europe," *The North-China Herald and Supreme Court & Consular Gazette*, June 5, 1940.

By the late summer of 1941, shortly before the start of the Pacific War, the Chinese Government had overcome its reservations about exporting labour to the Anglo-American bloc. A year earlier, Chiang Kai-shek had not decided whether to strike a deal with the Japanese. In 1936, he was apparently even prepared to let Germany recruit a few score Huagong as part of its war preparations.[180] Now, however, alarmed by Japan's treaty with Wang Jingwei's puppet regime in Nanjing and encouraged by British and US loans and Soviet material aid, he was more firmly set on an anti-Japanese course. Cities in the United States requested 3000 Huagong to dig air-raid shelters, to which Chongqing agreed. (No labourers were actually sent.)[181]

It is easy to see why the Nationalists in the late 1930s might agree to resume exporting labour. China was in a struggle for national survival. However, even if Chiang Kai-shek had wanted to send Huagong, he could hardly have done so from his base in the relatively remote Chinese hinterland. In 1916, Beijing had seen the export of Huagong non-combatants as a means to getting a seat at the top table. Now, however, China was a combatant. The Allies needed its military support, and even the Japanese were eager for a time to parley with Chiang. The Nationalists had no need for the Huagong as a bargaining chip. They could have sold Huagong for pounds and dollars, but loans and aid from the Allies helped fill their coffers. In any case, China's experience with the Labour Corps had been negative, while the ILO's denunciation of indenture had made it harder for any self-respecting government to sell its workers.

Japanese Labour Recruitment in the Interwar Years

The Japanese too recruited Huagong to work in Japanese-ruled Manchuria. Leaving for Manchuria, an exonym for China's three northeastern provinces, was known as *chuguan* ("leaving the pass [into Manchuria"]), as opposed to *chuguo*, ("leaving the country"), one land-based, the other sea-based. *Chuguan* recruitment in north China created an even bigger movement of population than in the south. The distinction between

[180] Newspaper clipping from May 16, 1936, in Foreign Ministry file 11-35-09-00-029, 193012-194711, Academia Sinica archive.

[181] Academia Sinica archive, Foreign Ministry 11-33-02-09-044, 193901-195004; *Xinxin xinwen*, September 8, 1941, and *Dagong bao*, August 29, 1941. On Chiang Kai-shek's eventual decision to get off the fence in 1940, see Benton (1999, 765–818).

chuguan and *chuguo* became less material in 1931, when the Japanese annexed Manchuria as an informal colony, paraded as the independent nation-state of "Manchukuo." The Japanese also recruited labour to work across the sea in the Japanese metropole[182] and to Japanese-ruled Taiwan, ceded to Japan by the Qing in 1895, where the number of Huagong at one point surpassed 60,000. The Japanese controlled this migration in large part through systems of labour procurement set up before 1931 and institutionalised in advance of Japan's invasion of China.

In Taiwan, a single company (Nanguo) under a Japanese director had a monopoly licence over Huagong recruitment between 1904 and 1940. After an initial ban on importing Huagong into Taiwan, the number of migrants more than doubled, to 39,050 in 1930.[183] Taiwan was not only in the Sinophone but the forms of Chinese spoken on the island were close to speech-forms of Fujian and Guangdong, across the Taiwan Strait, the places of provenance of most Huagong, to whom some Taiwanese had ties of blood. Huagong migration to Taiwan was more circular than settled, because of the proximity of its origin. These linguistic, family, and geographic ties lessened the foreigner status that Japan tried to impose on Huagong. The jobs done by them were not so different from those done by Taiwan natives. Japan's colonisation of Taiwan made even more open the enmity between it and China, so that China was less able to protect its nationals in Taiwan even than in Southeast Asia. The enmity deepened after Japan's annexation of Manchuria in 1931 and the full invasion of China in 1937.[184]

Millions of labourers left North China for Manchuria as seasonal and long-term migrant labourers or settlers to escape widespread famine. Recruits migrated along networks or were transported by recruiting offices that subcontracted to Chinese or foreign agents.[185] Twenty-five million Han Chinese migrated to Manchuria between the 1890s and 1945, peaking in 1927 and 1939, and 16 million returned.[186] Nanjing had little jurisdiction over this migration even before the annexation and the war. Much Chinese labour in Manchuria was forced, swelled by captured troops and conscripted peasants.[187]

[182] For scholarship on the Huagong in Japan, see i. a. He Tianyi, ed. (1995).
[183] Zheng He (1933).
[184] Douw (2012, 189–202).
[185] Gottschang and Lary (2000, 59–60).
[186] Stewart (1940, 214–215).
[187] Tucker (2005, 25–26).

Plans to recruit Huagong to work in Japan were announced in 1917, presumably inspired by the Chinese Labour Corps (Japan was an ally of the Entente Powers). The intention was to recruit a few dozen Chinese on a three-year contract (as in the European scheme).[188] Chinese press reports denounced the treatment of Huagong in Japan in the early 1920s as abusive. New arrivals complained of being robbed and cheated at the dockside,[189] but worse was to come. In 1923, in the wake of the Kantō earthquake, 700 Huagong (and 6000 Koreans) were massacred by police and vigilantes after the government falsely accused them of planning terrorism and robbery.[190] The massacre did not stop the flow of Huagong into Japan, both legal and illegal.[191]

During the war, 38,000 Chinese contract workers and conscripts worked in Japan, rising to a far greater number in the last year of the war. The conditions approached slavery, and 6830 died.[192] Other Huagong were enslaved in Japanese-occupied Southeast Asia.[193]

Japanese labour recruitment was unusual in that most recruits stayed on the Chinese mainland, in Manchuria. Even recruits in Taiwan remained within the Sinophone. Only recruits exported to Japan left the Chinese-speaking world. Unlike most other Chinese labour diasporas, however, these latter worked in the metropole rather than in a colony. This migration perpetuated labour bondage in its most extreme form, as slave labour. In north China, it consolidated the old view of Huagong, strengthening the impression of Chinese state impotence and official corruption.

Like the British and the Dutch, the Japanese adjusted the recruitment tap according to their needs. Restrictions were sometimes imposed to protect Japanese, Korean, and Taiwanese workers' interests. In 1934, 700 Huagong were sent back to Shanghai from Japan,[194] not long after 20,000 Huagong had been transported to Rehe (Jehol), a buffer province between

[188] "Labour Supply in Japan: Demand for Our Workmen," *Peking Daily News*, September 12, 1917.

[189] *Shen bao*, August 19, 1923.

[190] For the response of the Beiyang Foreign Ministry, see the Academia Sinica Archive, 03-31-006-01-0045, November 20, 1923, and 03-31-008-03-042, September 1, 1924.

[191] "Chinese Stowaways for Japan," *The North-China Herald and Supreme Court and Consular Gazette*, January 30, 1926.

[192] Rice (1990, 40–41). The Japanese also exported Huagong to Southeast Asia during the war. In 1941 and 1942, for example, they sent several thousand to Saigon (Foreign Ministry file 11-29-10-07-011, October-November 1941 and 11-4-2056 1942).

[193] Heidhues (1992, 183).

[194] *Tianguang bao*, September 4, 1934.

China proper and Manchukuo.[195] In 1935, the Japanese banned Huagong from crossing into Manchuria, to prevent them from competing for jobs with Japanese and Korean migrants.[196] In 1936, they restricted Huagong recruitment for the Taiwan mines, to slow the growth of Taiwanese unemployment.[197] In 1936, the restrictions on migration into Manchuria were relaxed and one million labourers flooded in. By 1941, the flow had become a trickle, in an unorganised protest against the Japanese treatment of Chinese. To overcome the boycott, Japanese agents in north China vaunted "the glories of Manchukuo," but recruits remained hard to entrap.[198] The final chapter came in the winter of 1945, when the Chinese army repatriated five thousand labourers.[199]

Japanese recruitment differed from the norm of Huagong recruitment. Much of the movement into Manchuria was permanent from the outset, rather than temporary. In Taiwan, too, the migration became increasingly permanent. As for the Chinese labour diaspora in prewar Japan, where Huagong were a tiny and despised minority, it was treated with exceptional cruelty, an extreme realisation of the view of Chinese as migrants without rights.

Criminality and Recruitment

A connection between criminality and labour recruitment was often the norm, in China and among Chinese abroad. "Secret societies" (a term used by Westerners for the brotherhoods, sects, and gangs that controlled Huagong migration) were led by local powerholders, who ran a shadow system of control. Huagong were vulnerable to these organisations during the breakdown of the Chinese state in peripheral regions, even after China's reunification in 1928, and overseas, where the Chinese state could do little to protect its citizens.

[195] *Shen bao*, March 29, 1934.

[196] *Kung Sheung Evening News*, March 21, 1935.

[197] *Shen bao*, July 24, 1936.

[198] "Increased Coolie Immigration from Shantung to Manchuria," *The China Weekly Review*, November 21, 1936; "Coolie Migration to Manchukuo Ending," *The China Weekly Review*, June 14, 1941.

[199] Minguo shiqi Xinjiapo diqu dang'an xuan bian (Selected edited documents from the Singapore region in the Republican period), doc. no. 4/12138, Junshi weiyuan hui dianqing anzhi you Ri qianhui Huagong an (Document regarding request by the Military Commission to organise the return from Japan of Huagong), November-December 1945.

In the 1930s, when depression hit the Southeast Asian economy and Southeast Asian governments imposed immigration quotas, the Chinese press carried daily reports on criminal trafficking. The restrictions were supposed to bring order to the southward flight, but often they had the opposite effect. Crackdowns led to a spate of secret transports of Huagong to Singapore, organised by gangs in Hong Kong.[200] In 1939, nearly two years after the Japanese invasion of China, large numbers of migrants sailed south to escape the war, despite the imposition in Singapore of a monthly quota of just 500 men and women and despite the tricks played by brokers, shipowners, and boarding-masters, who took advantage of the migrants' panic and desperation by charging record prices for tickets and for accommodation on arrival.[201] Both the Qing and China's two successive Republican governments tried to suppress the criminal gangs. In 1921, the State Council in Beijing instructed Gu Weijun (Wellington Koo) to get the League of Nations to ban recruitment from places like Hong Kong and Macao, because of reports of a spate of abductions.[202] Chinese merchant organisations overseas tried to keep provincial authorities in China informed of the abductions,[203] and the police added their voice. In 1930, the police in Guangzhou denounced the agents of a mining company for "enticing Chinese scum to recruit Huagong to work abroad as coolies, for 70 cents a day and in desperate living circumstances."[204] However, such efforts had little effect. In 1936, 600 new arrivals from Shantou and Chaozhou were arrested in Bangkok, accused of infiltrating the border, sentenced to one hundred days of hard labour, and deported. In Singapore, where the quota of immigrants rose from one thousand to four thousand a month after a rise in the rubber price, Huagong were charged by traffickers for non-existent hostel places in Singapore. Hundreds of migrants were hidden around the decks of Singapore-bound steamships and exploited by a network of traffickers, agents, hostels, *ketou*, and crew.[205] Young women and children not subject to quotas were trafficked out of Shantou in batches of fifty by older women posing as their relatives, to end as "piglets" in Bangkok, Singapore, and elsewhere.[206]

[200] *Xianggang Huazi ribao*, June 9, 1936.
[201] *Shen bao*, March 18, 1939.
[202] *Xianggang Huazi ribao*, April 9, 1921.
[203] *Xianggang Huazi ribao*, April 10, 1922.
[204] *Xianggang Huazi ribao*, April 8, 1930.
[205] *Shen bao*, April 8, 1936.
[206] *Shen bao*, May 15, 1939.

Some of the recruits remained in touch with their families through remittance houses but others disappeared forever, apart from a few who turned up again after war. Many in Southeast Asia ended up in the claws of the worst exploiters, their European bosses and their gangers, who abused them impunity. What better way to render them invisible and untraceable than to unname them? The records maintained by employers commonly omitted employees' given names. Given chain-migration, many labourers inevitably belonged to the same lineage, so it was not unusual to have the likes of Big Liu and No. 2 Huang on the pay-roll.[207]

Corruption and the Switch from Chinese to Javanese Recruitment

Over the years, Dutch recruitment of Chinese labour gradually came under stricter control, although corruption remained rampant. Ostensibly, Dutch officials stayed aloof from labour recruitment and expected businesses to acquire their own workers, but in reality they often intervened, including to their own advantage.[208] Dutch diplomats and agents engaged in deceptions to which the Hong Kong Secretary of Chinese Affairs was at times party. For example, when monetary advances were outlawed in 1915, under Hong Kong's Asiatic Emigration Ordinance, the Secretary told the Dutch Consul to advise recruiters to withhold paying them until after arrival in the East Indies and not to mention them in contracts.[209] Other colonial administrators were also accomplices to fraud. When an official of Banka Tinwinning visited Hong Kong to reorganise labour recruitment endangered by reforms and supposedly "hanging by a thread," the Consul General and officials of Dutch banks and companies as well as planters' agents reassured him that the flow of recruits outstripped demand, despite the publicly announced constraints.[210]

In China itself bans on recruiting workers for overseas existed for the most part on paper only and officials invariably found ways to profit from

[207] Yang Tongling et al. (2004, 80).

[208] Deli Planters Vereeniging, *Mededeling no. 14, De Arbeidsregeling voor de Buitengewesten van Nederlandsch Indië*, Medan: Köhler & co., 1923, 5.

[209] *Gedenkboek* (1927, vol. 2, 61).

[210] Jakarta National Archive, Algemene Secretarie, Grote Bundel, TZG Agenda file no. 8436.

the trade. Difficulties usually arose only when Chinese officials rejected the share of squeeze on offer. In 1922, *The Straits Times* explained that

> even after the Chinese Government has fully assented to emigration the palms of a good many understrappers may have to be oiled profusely before the would-be emigrant dare leave his home. He might slip away easily if the matter were one that concerned himself alone, but in China they have a way of holding a whole family answerable [...], and many a man stays at home because he cannot square the headman and dare not expose his relatives.[211]

British officials in Malaya and the Straits Settlements responded more accommodatingly and inventively than those in the East Indies to Chinese officials' desire to cash in on the Huagong trade, perhaps because of their greater familiarity with Chinese political culture at the time and their greater experience of dealing with Chinese in Hong Kong, Shanghai, and elsewhere. They reminded the Chinese that the remittance system showed that exporting labour benefitted China more than keeping it at home, and even suggested providing passages to the Nanyang at a nominal rate, paying the Chinese government a dollar or two for each emigrant permit in order to "create goodwill" and facilitating remittances from Huagong wages. They based their thinking on the calculation that officialdom in China was "more paternal [than in British India], and we must bow to their views on all such matters."[212] It is not clear whether the dollar premium was ever paid, but cheap passages and the facilitation of remittance became the norm in some circumstances, not just in Southeast Asia. (Remittances were sent on behalf of members of the wartime Labour Corps and, after the war, by the Blue Funnel line in Europe, to give just one example.[213])

Resistance by Chinese labour bodies and patriotic officials occasionally interrupted the Huagong traffic, but such resistance was usually futile and even dangerous. Chinese Communists who denounced the recruitment in articles in the Chinese press risked their lives, and a few hundred dollars was usually enough to get the articles spiked and their authors denounced and blacklisted.

[211] *The Straits Times*, October 7, 1922.

[212] Jakarta National Archive, Algemene Secretarie, Grote Bundel, TZG Agenda file no. 8436.

[213] Benton and Gomez (2008, 208).

Hong Kong was not the only port from which illegal shipments of labourers left for the Nanyang. Dutch employers found willing accomplices in official circles in many places and could shop around more widely if difficulties arose as a result of political opposition or official interference. The Consul General in Hong Kong and the agent of N. I. Handelsbank told the Banka Tinwinning official that the Dutch "had experienced no difficulties in recruitment in Amoy [Xiamen]."[214]

In time, however, the flow of labour into the East Indies became increasingly unreliable, particularly to Bangka. There were several reasons for this change. It was in part because of obstruction in Hong Kong, Singapore, and China but also because of Bangka's bad reputation. A short history of Banka Tinwinning's efforts at recruiting a Chinese workforce illustrates the obstruction that it faced at every turn. The switch after 1885 from Chinese to Javanese recruitment in Sumatra was driven by financial and political considerations—the recruits were cheaper and the Dutch controlled the general setting. However, given the difficulties and frustrations of recruiting Chinese labour, it is easy to see why the disadvantages were judged to outweigh the advantages and Javanese transmigration became a more attractive alternative.

Up until around 1869, the company recruited Chinese labourers through the kongsis, but recruitment then became the domain of professionals regulated to some extent by the East Indies government, which set quotas and capped the advances paid to recruits. In 1886, Bangka's Dutch Resident suggested that the Government send a Tinwinning official to Hong Kong to supervise recruitment, but the proposal was rejected. Also in 1886, J. J. M. de Groot tried to hire several hundred Chinese with the help of a German company in Xiamen but got nowhere. In 1901, the first delivery of recruits took place by steamship, and deliveries now happened several times a year rather than once or twice a year, as in the junk age.[215] In 1903, however, an entire second shipment of recruits refused to sign their contracts, and many others were declared unfit. In 1905, the East Indies government sent the Officer for Chinese Affairs in Mentok, A. van de Stadt, to Singapore and China to improve procedures, but his efforts failed in China, again because of official obstruction. Recruitment through Singapore also faltered initially, although it later took off.

[214] Jakarta National Archive, Algemene Secretarie, Grote Bundel, TZG Agenda file no. 8436.

[215] On the frequency of deliveries, see Yang Qunxi, ed. (2004, 68).

In July 1907, the Hong Kong government started allowing free emigration to Bangka and Belitung under an "assisted emigration" scheme. The contracts had to be vetted in Hong Kong and on a par with those for emigrants to Singapore, and were arranged by Van de Stadt through the Holland China Handels Compagnie (HCHC). The HCHC recruited mainly from boarding houses, where poor nutrition was found to damage recruits' health. HCHC was judged to have performed poorly, but efforts between 1911 and 1923 to hire Chinese professional recruiters in the French enclave of Guangzhouwan and in Singapore, Macau, and Hainan also failed. In 1923, the arrangement with HCHC ended, but a rival recruiter charged with delivering one hundred workers delivered only 21. In 1922, the East Indies government sent Van de Stadt to organise *laoke* recruitment through Singapore and Hong Kong for Banka Tinwinning, but this too failed, and Van de Stadt instead proposed a gradual transition to mechanisation, the promotion of re-engagement, and the recruitment of Javanese, to which the government agreed in 1926. So in the case of Banka Tinwinning, the tactic of *laoke* and clan recruitment largely failed in the 1920s. The government provided credit of f30,000 to fund a scheme of *laoke* recruitment but the only *laoke* to turn up vanished without trace after pocketing an advance of f70.

The transition from Chinese to Javanese recruitment began in the 1880s and quickly gathered pace in succeeding decades. By the 1920s, Huagong recruitment had become marginal and was largely confined to niches such as tobacco and mining, which Huagong had traditionally dominated in the East Indies and for which they supposedly had a "racial" aptitude. Beyond that, Chinese were dearer and seen as less docile and incompatible with Dutch colonisation schemes.[216] The obstructions increasingly encountered by Dutch recruiters in Hong Kong, Singapore, and China speeded the transition to Javanese recruitment. In 1925, the Dutch colonial government refused Banka Tinwinning permission to set up a recruitment office in Hong Kong and ordered it to recruit Javanese instead. In addition, the East Indies authorities feared importing a Communist virus from China along with the recruits.[217] By 1931, when recruitment in China was once again viable, the Depression was in full

[216]The average cost of importing a labourer from China was fl20 in 1912–1913 and fl42 in 1927–1928, having peaked in 1919–1920 at f235. In 1937, the cost was fl50 ("Nu en vroeger," *Soerabaijasch Handelsblad*, February 13, 1937).

[217]Kort historisch overzicht (1928).

swing, while advances in mechanisation and the switch to Javanese labour meant that Chinese were no longer in demand.[218] On December 31, 1931, the DPV ceased all recruitment in China.[219]

Seafarers

Chinese seafarers first enlisted on ships of Britain's East India Company in the late eighteenth century and later spread across the world along the "arteries of Empire" created by steam. Like landside Huagong, they were recruited by dialect and place of provenance and controlled by gangers, known as Number Ones. In the First World War, thousands were hired to replace white seafarers redeployed into the Royal Navy. They were recruited in much the same way as land-based Huagong and similarly subject to labour bondage, and the two groups were hired often from a common labour pool. In 1927, during the political turmoil in China, leftists in Shanghai protested against Dutch shootings of Huagong in the East Indies and called on Chinese sailing Dutch ships to go on strike.[220] Calls were raised to extend the reforms won by Huagong at sea, for example the ban on beatings, to Huagong on land, especially in the East Indies.[221]

In Europe and the Americas, the dockland streets in which Huagong gathered between sailings were known as *Huabu*, Chinaports, the nautical equivalent of Chinatown. Seafarers were a major force in the global Chinatown and more integrated into the Chinese revolutionary movement and the local labour movement than other Chinatowners. They fought trade-union battles both on a general front and against the class of predatory contractors.[222] The three worlds of Huagong on land, at sea, and in the docks were closely intertwined and some Huagong moved agilely between them, deserting, absconding, and switching jobs in search of higher pay or to escape abuse.

[218] National Archive, Jakarta, Algemene Secretarie, Grote Bundel, TZG Agenda, file no. 8436.

[219] Pelzer (1935, 93).

[220] *Shen bao*, June 9, 1927.

[221] Ma Huiyue (2015, 114).

[222] For the United States, see Kwong (2001, 116–118). The tie between Chinatown and the American left broke down after the revival of anti-Chinese sentiment in the 1950s.

The Chinaport was dominated by the shipping-master (or crimp), who supervised the seafarers' signing-on and discharge, and the boarding-master, who put them up between sailings. Crimping had been abolished in the nineteenth century in Europe, as a form of bondage or indenture, but it was retained, exceptionally, for seafarers from China. European shipping lines were in no hurry to dispense with the intermediaries that managed Chinese crews. The relationship between shipping-master and boarding-master mirrored that between crimp and hostel owner in the recruitment of Huagong for Southeast Asia. Huagong were sold into indenture not just in the Nanyang but in Britain and continental Europe, to work in restaurants and laundries. All but a handful of Chinese seafarers were recruited in deals that guaranteed the shipping-masters and Number Ones commissions and a hefty cut from wages. Shipping-master and boarding-master were in some cases one and the same person (whence the term crimping-house for the seafarers' lodgings).[223] The role played by boarding-houses in the seafaring economy was officially recognised in Hong Kong, where "residential clubs for seamen" were listed alongside boarding-houses "for employees of firms."[224]

In the late 1930s, seafarers were one of the last great reservoirs of Chinese labour employed by Western capital. Together with Indians, they comprised 27 percent of seafarers on foreign-going vessels, and during the war the Chinese Seamen's Union claimed 10,000 members in Liverpool, its worldwide centre. Thousands of other Chinese seafarers were stranded in Australia after the fall of Singapore. Chinese seafarers in the first half of the century were pictured by as cheap and biddable and received a small fraction of the white wage, but their wartime militancy changed the perception of them.[225]

On land, the shipping-masters and boarding-masters kept the seafarers in a form of indenture based on debts accumulated in the crimping-houses, including through the sale of opium and organised gambling, while on shipboard the Number One charged for favours. Seafarers' unions, led by Communists, campaigned to improve wages and conditions, especially

[223] Benton (2007, 48–52).

[224] Administrative Reports issued annually by the Hong Kong Government.

[225] On the transformation of the "seafaring coolie" into a "maritime worker," see Balachandran (2011).

during the Second World War, when seafarers achieved a reputation for rebelliousness. Commentators noted their "emergent nationhood," and white Communists encouraged solidarity. Their abscondings into Chinatowns while at anchor showed their growing assertiveness, fuelled by racism in the shipping industry. Sadly, the internationalism was hard to sustain, but shipboard unionisation made a return to the old system difficult.[226]

Chinese Bonded Labour in Australia and the South Pacific

In British-ruled parts of the South Pacific and in Australia and New Zealand, the Chinese labour diaspora was tiny, marginal, and often transitory, and remained so until well after the relaxation of restrictions on Chinese immigration starting in the 1950s. Labour bondage played a part in it in Australia and New Zealand, especially in early colonial Australia and even more so on smaller islands. Geographically, Australasia and the Western Pacific fall outside the purview of this study, but they are relevant as comparands of indenture in the Nanyang, which they matched in character and in some places outdid in longevity.

In the 1830s and the 1840s, several thousand Chinese labourers went to Australia to work under indenture and to make up for the decline in convict labour. However, this indenture gave way to a credit-ticket (*shedan*) system. Under it, Chinese were technically free but actually in thrall to the individual, firm, or Chinatown association that paid for their ticket. The bond was not legally enforceable, unlike formal indenture, but it was informally enforced by native-place ties.[227] Large-scale trafficking of Chinese labourers into Australia continued throughout the interwar years, for employment in market gardens, laundries, or restaurants.[228] The bondage was consolidated in 1901 by the Immigration Restrictions Act, which put Chinese recruits at the mercy of their sponsors,[229] for the act prevented labourers from entering the wider labour market and allowed their repatriation.

[226] Benton (2007, ch. 5).

[227] Fitzgerald (2007, 64–65).

[228] *Overland China Mail*, July 14, 1937.

[229] Williams (1999, 30).

Huagong in the South Pacific were recruited under indenture in a stricter sense.[230] This indenture lasted even longer than in the East Indies, an anomaly that Dutch apologists for the penal sanction were not shy of trumpeting.[231] Twenty thousand Chinese went to the South Pacific as indentured labourers between 1865 and 1941.[232] As late as 1935, the British recruited 24 Huagong to work on a five-year contract on Fanning Island, a barren atoll.[233] Indenture in the British Western Pacific saw many of the same abuses as its Dutch, Spanish, French, and other equivalents, which the British hypocritically denounced. The excesses and the role played in them by officials in Hong Kong drew harsh comments from opposition members of the British Parliament and from the League of Nations' Mandates Commission.

Samoa was not untypical, and can serve as an example. Companies in Samoa and New Guinea recruited thousands of Huagong while under German control, before the First World War, and continued to do so when the islands become League of Nations mandates administered by New Zealand and Australia.[234] The Germans were notoriously cruel and the target of complaints from both the Guangdong-Guangxi and the Beijing

[230] For Samoa, see Noa Siaosi (2010); the files of *The Anti-Slavery Reporter and Aborigines' Friend*, 1920–1925; *Shen bao*, August 17, 1929; Lu Wendi et al. (1984c, 71–72); *The Straits Times*, February 7, 1923; *South China Morning Post*, August 4, 1936; *Shen bao*, October 9 and 13, 1936; and Chinese Foreign Ministry files, October 1945-May 1947, Academia Sinica. For Fiji, see Gounder (2011, 1); Lu Wendi et al. (1984c, 55–56); and Lu Wendi et al. (1981, 127). For Nauru, see Lu Wendi et al. (1981, 127, 1984c, 59–64, 401–403); *Hong Kong Daily Press*, November 23, 1932; *North-China Daily News*, March 6, 1924; and Rankine (1995, 152–158). For New Guinea, see Lu Wendi et al. (1984c, 59–64 and 401–403). Huagong on Christmas Island *Christmas* were tattooed with the characters *mai chee chai*, "bought as a piglet" and described living on the island as a form of slavery. See National Library of Australia, TRC 2047/11, Christmas Island Project; Neale (1988, 22 and 37–86); and Waters, 4 and 93. For the French Pacific, see Lu Wendi et al. (1984c, 51–53 and 389), and Nanjing Second Historical Archive, Doc. 6-1512, July 17, 1929. Reports to Nanjing noted that thousands of Huagong were shipped through Guangzhouwan and other French-controlled ports to plantations in New Caledonia and other places. In Tahiti, the French and the British started recruiting Chinese miners in 1910 and continued doing so until 1966.

[231] Figures for Chinese migration to these places through Hong Kong can be found in Hong Kong's annual Administrative Reports.

[232] Willmott (1998). For the 1910s and early 1920s, see Guowuyuan qiaoban, eds. (2005, 205).

[233] *Tianguang bao*, August 29, 1935.

[234] Yuan Li and Chen Dazhang (1991, 479–487).

governments, which in 1907 sent an inspector whose report led to promises to reform that the Germans barely kept. The British maintained existing indentures while denouncing indenture in principle and declined to "submit a question forbidding Chinese indentured labour in the mandated areas to the Council of the League of Nations."[235] The Mandate authorities first sought to recruit Huagong through Shantou, without Chinese permission, and later got the British to allow their importation through Hong Kong. The labourers were liable to corporal punishment for infringing labour discipline. In theory, they were supervised by a Chinese consul,[236] but a journalist described them as shut up in compounds "with never a hope of liberty."[237] New Zealand's Methodist Church investigated the conditions of indentured labour "throughout the South Seas" and strongly supported the institution, for "indigenous free labour is impracticable in the present generation."[238]

Colonial Office files on Samoa reveal the criminality and casual racism of the colonial rulers, including Hong Kong's Governor Sir Reginald Edward Stubbs, who ignored China's southern government in Guangzhou and connived instead with the warlords in Beijing to get indentures. His response to a suggestion that Javanese might be hired instead, due to political unrest in China, was that "I always understood the Javanese were a lazy lot." Stubbs preferred to recruit in Hong Kong, where the government "would ensure that the business is properly conducted." According to another message, the source was switched from Guangzhou to Xiamen to evade a ban imposed by Guangzhou.[239]

Under pressure in parliament from Labour Party opponents of indenture in its extreme interpretation, as a form of slavery designed "to make money for white owners," from trade unions, from New Zealanders who "do not like colored labor," and from Samoans opposed to importing labour, the New Zealand Government promised in 1923 to abolish indenture in Samoa and replace it with free labour, "subject to certain

[235] *The Canton Times*, March 31, April 19, and June 8, 1920.

[236] Lu Wendi et al. (1984c, 65–70).

[237] *Hong Kong Daily Press*, January 8, 1923, citing an article by John H. Harris in the *Manchester Guardian*.

[238] *The Straits Times*, March 12, 1923; *The North-China Herald and Supreme Court & Consular Gazette*, March 24, 1923.

[239] British Colonial Office, April 1920 (file held in the Academia Sinica archive). CO. See also Letters to Chinese Foreign Ministry, March 19 and April 2, 1920 (same place).

safeguards," and to repatriate time-expired labourers.[240] In 1924, however, British abolitionists reported that "the old system goes on practically unchanged, for the old contracts continue."[241] The conditions under which the Huagong were held provoked violent resistance on land and riots on the sea journey from Samoa to Hong Kong. In 1929, 250 Huagong strikers wrecked the Chinese Labour Office and the police opened fire, killing four. In 1936, 503 indentured Chinese remained on Samoa, with more than 400 at the outbreak of the Pacific War. In August 1936, the New Zealand Government promised to repatriate all indentured labourers from Samoa, but the planters protested and the government relented.[242]

The indenturing of Chinese on Oceania's continental islands and in Melanesia, Micronesia, and Polynesia confirms the wider findings of this study—that indenture continued even after its supposed demise after the First World War and lasted in some cases right through until and even after the Second World War. Indenture survived not only in the Dutch East and West Indies and in French, Spanish, and Italian colonies but in the British Empire's southernmost colonies and dominions. This British-sponsored indenture was not an aberration but a policy of the British colonial establishment, whose officials channelled Huagong through Hong Kong when the Chinese authorities refused to cooperate. Naturally, the Dutch used it to counter the British charge that Dutch colonialism was uniquely immoral.[243]

A Comparison of Indian, Javanese, and Chinese Recruitment

In pre-colonial India, long-distance domestic labour migration proceeded in a steady stream under the sultanate, which used it to recruit soldiers and workers. A similar system continued under the East India Company and

[240] *The Canton Times*, March 31 and April 19, 1920; *Hong Kong Daily Press*, August 1, 1923.

[241] "Chinese Labour in Samoa," *The Anti-Slavery Reporter and Aborigines' Friend*, April 1924, vol. 14, no. 1, 28; "Western Samoa," *The Anti-Slavery Reporter and Aborigines' Friend*, January 1925, vol. 14, no. 4, 144.

[242] *South China Morning Post*, August 4, 1936; *Shen bao*, October 9 and 13, 1936.

[243] Tweede Kamer, Handelingen der Staten-Generaal, 84ste Vergadering, June 12, 1924.

survived into the British Raj.[244] Indian capitalism established an early trade diaspora that led to permanent settlements, but they were smaller than those formed by Chinese in the Nanyang.[245] In pre-colonial days, labour migration does not seem to have happened in South Asia on the same scale as that run in China by the kongsis, which continued into modern times and helped shape the Chinese labour diaspora. In colonial days, most Indian migration was controlled by the British, in India and abroad. They licensed and monitored the recruitment and set up recruitment offices throughout northern India. Before migrating, the migrants worked under conditions of virtual servitude. Magistrates oversaw migration to plantations in British colonies. There was some illegal or "free" migration under the control of merchants,[246] but less than in the Chinese case.

The recruitment of Indian and Chinese labourers took many forms, from place to place and over time. In his study on the British West Indies in 1859–1866, Walton Look Lai lists their commonalities and differences. In both China and India the British state played a role in regulating recruitment for the West Indies. It excluded privately sponsored recruitment and lessened abuse of the sort practised in the Latin America labour trade. In the West Indies, the British subsidised the cost of both Chinese and Indian immigration, although planters bore two thirds of it. The labourers, under five-year contracts, were immobilised by pass-laws and penal sanctions. However, Chinese indenture had special features, due mainly to international competition for Chinese labour and China's nominally sovereign status. There was no provision for a return passage after the expiry of indenture, wages were less standardised than in Indian contracts, the workday was shorter, Chinese received financial inducements to take their family, Chinese were more likely than Indians to get food rations and a vegetable garden, and Chinese women were admitted only under contracts of residence, binding them to a plantation but not a job.[247]

The funding of Chinese labour migration to the West Indies was supervised by the authorities, but in the Nanyang Huagong recruitment was

[244] Kumar (2017, 20–27). Haynes and Roy (1999) discusses the long-distance migration of Indian weavers long before colonial times. According to Chakraborty n.d., 6, the volume of migration is uncertain in the pre-census era, when there were no systematic records of people who crossed the national border or moved between regions.

[245] Jain (1989, 155–156).

[246] Mishra (2015, 373).

[247] Look Lai (1998). For Look Lai's comparison of Chinese and Indian migration, see Chap. 3.

rarely under the same scrutiny. China was neither a colony nor in complete control of its own ports and borders, so its migrants were in some senses freer to make their own decisions and to choose their own destinations than Indians and Javanese, who migrated along routes set by the authorities, and to invent creative strategies to bypass bans on Chinese entry. Their principal method was the credit-ticket system, widely used to finance the recruitment of Chinese labour in North America and Australia and often described as an alternative to indenture, but the two methods had elements in common. If a broker or lineage mate, perhaps himself a veteran migrant, bought the migrant's ticket, the migrant remained bonded to him until the loan had been paid off.

In the United States and Australia, most early Chinese migrants arrived under the credit-ticket system, which was sometimes organised illegally and experienced as a form of slavery.[248] The system was connected to Chinese "clan stores," which also handled remittances.[249] In the United States, the Chinese community was "vertical from the indentured laborer to the importer-padrone," cemented by racism into a transclass bloc.[250] In Australia in the 1850s, goldseekers were part of an "organised system of emigration which by the 1870s included working gangs moving from country to country seeking contracts."[251] Migrants recruited by kin or crimps resented the bondage system, which prevented them from choosing their employers. As a result, the Chinese community in Australia was sharply divided by social class. However, many took advantage of poor communications to abscond.[252]

In colonial times, Indian—and, later, Javanese—indentures were for years recruited by formally appointed and licensed contractors. Professional recruitment also happened in China but under less or no regulation, because of wars and warlordism. Local officials and strongmen took advantage of the chaos, so recruitment was generally more corrupt and dearer. In both India and China, recruitment by professional outsiders gave way in time to recruitment by insiders, defined by Samita Sen as "non-market agents recruiting within the closed world of kin, caste and village relations."[253] The change to insider recruitment was welcomed by

[248] Liu Jin (2009, 11).
[249] Chang Zengshu (2008, 455–460) and Walden (1995, 183).
[250] Benton and Gomez (2008, 297).
[251] Williams (1999).
[252] Benton (2007, 90).
[253] Sen (2010, 3).

officials anxious to avoid blame for the abuses associated with professional recruitment.

The recruiters that took over from the professional agencies went under many names, each with its own connotations, the best-known being sardars, kanganis, and maistris.[254] The names were not ethnically specific. Chinese versions of Indian terms were used and vice versa. Sardars, kanganis, and maistris were associated with different parts of India but recruited in broadly the same way and played a similar role in plantation life, as traditional-style authorities. Such was the overlap that reports often applied the term kangani generically, to all labour agents.[255]

Employers in the East Indies were aware of these changes and took steps in the same direction. Officials in favour of abolishing the penal sanction pointed out that recruitment costs were kept low in Malaya by means of the Immigration Fund and that workers hired for fourteen days, with no deprivation of freedom or fine, still stayed in their jobs.[256]

However, Dutch employers lacked some of the advantages of their British counterparts. They had less grip on recruitment in China than the British, who controlled Hong Kong and Singapore and had a stronger presence in the Treaty Ports.[257] The Dutch recruitment ordinance of 1909,[258] roughly equivalent to the Immigration Fund run by Britain to finance debt-free labour migration, was comparatively ineffectual. In Sumatra and Bangka-Belitung, the Dutch found it harder to attract labour than the British in Malaya, who safeguarded migrant interests more forcefully than the Dutch, so they had more reason to preserve the penal sanction and lagged behind the British efforts to abolish it.

China's unregulated *laoke*, *shuike*, *baotou*, and *ketou* recruiters had much in common with their Indian counterparts. In India, there was no strict division in labour brokerage between professional recruiters and informal brokers. Samita Sen has pointed to the close connection and

[254] Kangani, or sirdar, is just one of several names under which the recruiters were known (Bates and Carter 2017, 462–463).

[255] Mishra (2015, 373–384) and Sen (2010, 3–4).

[256] Heijting (1925, 160) and Pekelharing (1924, 17).

[257] The Dutch stationed a Consul in Xiamen in 1890, mainly to arrange emigration of labourers to the East Indies, but he soon left and was not replaced. Apart from him, there were no Dutch Consuls—all the Netherlands Consuls were foreign merchants who, according to the Sinologist De Groot, "were not eager to exert themselves [...] and were not respected by the Mandarins" (Kuiper 2017, 456 and 884).

[258] Ind. Stb. no. 123, February 10, 1909.

cooperation between the two groups, despite the state's and capitalists' efforts to keep them apart and distinct.[259] In China, too, the distinction between professional outsider and informal insider was blurred. Many *laoke* and *ketou* had both outsider and insider characteristics and connections to a professional structure run by Westerners.

But for all the commonalities, there were differences that link to wider issues in the comparative study of indenture. The kanganis were "men of clout and relatively high social standing in their localities" and often of good caste.[260] The sardars were supposed to recruit from within their own community and remain accountable to it. However, this assumption was based on a colonial stereotype of a closed and static "traditional" rural society, whereas sardar recruitment extended beyond the sardars' place of origin and to "tribal" groups particularly vulnerable to abuse. Like the kanganis and maistris, sardars exercised hegemony because of their social and cultural status, formalised by laws enacted in the 1870s. Their links to professional recruiters further removed them from the local circles they were supposed to represent but from which they became increasingly alienated.[261]

China's *laoke*, *shuike*, and *ketou* lacked their Indian counterparts' legal identity and caste advantage. Like Indian and Javanese villages, Chinese villages were hierarchically organised, but the hierarchy was relatively open. Chinese recruiters lacked formal status and had no traditional role in village governance, except insofar as they depended on institutions such as *huiguan* and *tongxianghui* for support.[262]

In Indonesia, the Dutch authorities took measures to control labour migration between Java and the Outer Islands, having initially superimposed their own recruitment system on networks left over from precolonial times. The manner of recruitment of Javanese was worse than that of Indians, because of abuse and malpractice by recruiters "on the ground," but better than that of Chinese, according to Thio Termorshuizen, who likens it to the slave trade.[263]

Some measures taken in the East Indies were not unlike those in British India, but the Dutch approach was less systematic.[264] The recruitment was

[259] Sen (2010).
[260] Mishra (2015, 376–377).
[261] Sen (2010) and Mishra (2015).
[262] Benton and Liu (2018).
[263] Termorshuizen (2008, 279 and 303).
[264] De Graaf and Stibbe (1918), Heijting (1925) and De Kat Angelino (1931, 567–569).

from Java and Madura, early labour exporters under colonialism and the transmigration programme, designed to move labour from densely to thinly populated places. The protection accorded incomers was less extensive than that accorded Indians in Malaya. The recruitment was led not by state bodies but by two commercial firms.[265] The recruiters, or *wevak*, were thoroughly hated because of the ruthless methods, deceit, connivance with village headmen, and abductions for which they were notorious.[266]

When Dutch methods of recruitment began to converge with those used in India, the commercial agencies were in many cases replaced by personal recruiters much like kanganis and *laoke*. Again as in India (and British-ruled Hong Hong), the recruitment was supervised at the point of embarkation and disembarkation. Safeguards were introduced and ordinances centralised procedures.[267]

Tobacco planters on Sumatra's East Coast initially employed Bataks and Malays, but given the reluctance of local Malays to join the workforce, Chinese recruitment at first became the norm.[268] Chinese continued to dominate mining in the East Indies right up until the Japanese invasion, but their numbers in proportion to the general workforce kept falling while that of Javanese kept rising.[269]

Two main principles governed British and Dutch labour recruitment. The colonial authorities encouraged recruitment of their "own" workers in their respective empires. According to the British and Dutch governments, these measures were necessary because wrongs met abroad were hard to redress, although economic calculation was a more likely reason. Like the British, the Dutch reserved the right to send inspectors overseas and to "perpetuate" the link to Dutch nationality among labourers abroad (though this link was not equivalent to British Indians' imperial status).[270]

So British and Dutch recruitment of Indian and Javanese labourers and British, Dutch, and other nations' recruitment of Huagong differed crucially regarding destinations. The British and the Dutch rarely allowed other countries to recruit their imperial subjects and tried to keep an eye on their "nationals" working under another flag. China was the only one

[265] Kaur (2004, 44 and 86–90).
[266] Lockard (1971) and Bosma (2014).
[267] Kaur (2004, 90).
[268] Stibbe and Spat (1927, 229).
[269] Furnivall (1939, 355).
[270] De Graaf and Stibbe (1918, 363) and De Kat Angelino (1931, 565).

of the three main sources of indentured labour that was not a colony or colonial power. Huagong ended up by definition in countries beyond Chinese jurisdiction. Chinese authorities sometimes tried to protect their citizens overseas but rarely succeeded.

The same was true at the point of embarkation. The British in India and the Dutch in Java controlled their own ports, whereas most Chinese labourers left through ports under foreign control. In principle, however, British officials in Hong Kong and the Straits Settlements were supposed to protect Chinese from maltreatment by recruiters acting for other countries (including the Netherlands) and their colonies. For example, in 1886 the authorities in Hong Kong forbade recruitment for Bangka, citing abuses.[271]

In the 1880s, the recruitment of Javanese became more common, after professional recruiters set up recruitment offices in Javanese ports. The Dutch authorities initially played little role in this recruitment. Then, in 1887, they forbade the export of labourers to foreign countries (save in special cases), a prohibition repeated in January 1918. General recruitment remained chaotic, because of competition among recruiters, recruits' fear of recruiters, and the recruits' credulousness. Eventually, in 1896, deception of recruits by crimps became so overwhelming that officials decided to keep a closer eye on the traffic. This had little effect and a more systematic approach was adopted, in the form of recruitment ordinances.

The Dutch recruitment ordinances, extending into the 1920s, were intended to protect "natives" from exploitation. They gradually extended to all aspects of recruitment, including (in 1921) recruitment outside the scope of the recruitment ordinance. The changes meant less for Chinese recruits than for Javanese, for whom they were largely intended. In any case, legalities mattered less in China, where Dutch agents and even diplomats had no qualms about skirting rules and usually did so with impunity.

By the 1910s, Javanese preponderated on the Sumatran plantations and it was thought urgently necessary to increase the regulation of Javanese recruitment. The measures taken had implications, direct and indirect, for the Chinese. The existing coolie ordinance was complemented in 1909 and 1911 by an ordinance regulating recruitment and relations between workers and employers. More extensive regulations were adopted in 1914 and 1915. These regulations, applicable to Indonesians and those "on a par" with them, were repeatedly revised and supplemented. Recruitment was still left

[271] Heidhues (1992, 57).

to professionals, but the new system led the planters to appoint their own labour agents. These agents needed a licence from a regional authority to work through ports selected by the government. However, the controls on recruitment were lax: too few checks were done, and recruits continued to be cheated. As a result, professional recruitment was unpopular with recruits, so that employers ended up recruiting "the worst elements of society."

Employers frustrated by the shortcomings of professional recruitment and its high cost switched increasingly to *laoke* recruitment. According to Furnivall, the *laoke* method created a tie between plantations and the villages that fed them labourers and made "relations between employer and employee less artificial, and more permanent and social." This "living connection" lessened the possibility of misrepresentation, for recruiter and recruit were linked and deceit by the former could lead the latter's family to seek redress or revenge. This change away from professional recruitment also affected Chinese, partly as a result of pressures from Chinese and colonial authorities. Professional recruiting was said by De Kat Angelino to have disappeared by 1930.[272]

However, *laoke* recruitment of both Javanese and Chinese had only meagre results and did not, as envisaged, in itself lead to a weakening of the penal sanction. The Javanese emigrants escorted by *laoke* to Sumatra were supposedly free. But the main reason they were not confronted with the contents of a contract before leaving Java was because its terms would have put them off, and they invariably signed a contract on arrival in Sumatra.[273]

In 1916, the Deli Planters' Association set up an office in Samarang in Java using *laoke*, who received a payment of fl0 for each recruit delivered, and ran agents in China. *Laoke* recruitment was, at least in theory, compatible with the government's plans for colonisation by free workers and their families. Colonisation was to represent the final stage of labour recruitment in the East Indies. Designed to attract free migrant workers to settle permanently in families in self-sustaining communities in the ambit of the colonial estates, it was mostly restricted to Javanese, who were citizens of the colonial state and had civic rights (such as they were). However, in 1934 the scheme was shelved, though not the emphasis on the recruitment of married couples.[274]

[272] De Graaf and Stibbe (1918), Heijting (1925, 83–84), De Kat Angelino (1931, 567–569), and Furnivall (1939, 355–356).

[273] Van Blommestein (1917, 79–83).

[274] Stoler (1985, 44).

Colonisation was not appropriate in the case of the overwhelming majority of Chinese in the East Indies, who were bachelors (or lived as such) and foreign nationals. Some employers did try to apply the strategy to Chinese workers,[275] but the schemes seem invariably to have failed, as we have seen. Planters were under no illusion that Chinese *xinke* would want or would be allowed to form workers' settlements in Sumatra and drew the obvious conclusion: that such a scheme would require the replacement of Chinese by "natives."[276] For Chinese, the main relevance of colonisation was that it accelerated the winding down of Chinese recruitment.

This comparison of Chinese recruitment and its Indian and Javanese counterparts points up some of the special features of Chinese indenture. Historically, large-scale overseas labour migration started later in India and Java than in China, where merchants and labour-brokers defied the Ming-Qing bans and vigorously pursued maritime trade relations, while organisations such as the kongsis exported labour under a sort of indenture. As a result, Chinese labourers in the Nanyang had a longer tradition on which to draw and could sometimes look for support to settled diasporic communities. Chinese were recruited to perform indentured labour inside and outside China, across several jurisdictions, whereas Indian and Javanese indenture was practised mainly within India or Java or in other British or Dutch colonial territories. The state's role in Chinese recruitment differed from that in India and Java, given the weakness of the Chinese state in the south and the role foreigners played in undermining it, through their concessions, colonies, and spheres of influence. Because Indians and Javanese rarely moved outside their "own" colonial empires, the colonial state played a far greater role in managing their recruitment than did the Chinese state in supervising its labour diaspora, which resided in places beyond Chinese control and had a reputation for independence. Indian and Javanese migrants sometimes organised their own recruitment independently of the colonial authorities, but they had nothing to match the *shuike/ketou* system that played such a key role in south China's migrant economy. In Java, labour recruitment was largely commercial and executed by professionals. Javanese recruiters lacked established corridors linking villages to plantations and were less embedded in the patron-client relationships and migration networks that characterised Huagong

[275] Heijting (1925, 86–87).

[276] *Mededelingen uitgegeven door de Deli Planters Vereeniging*, July 1918, vol. 1, no. 2B, 9.

recruitment.[277] Recruitment proceeded more effectively in India and Java, where it was protected by the authorities, than in China, where attempts by foreign employers to recruit were resented by many as an intrusion. The frequent failure of these attempts was crucial in the switch in the Indonesian Archipelago from Chinese to Javanese recruitment.

The export of Chinese labour in the form of Huagong and the import of remittances were moments in a single process. Without the Huagong, there would have been no massive *qiaopi* inflow. Huagong created *qiaopi*, but *qiaopiju*

also created Huagong, by strengthening the economic ties between labour diaspora and family, lineage, or sending community and financing new migration. At times, the *qiaopi* element was ascendant, as economic depressions and bans on immigration took hold and particularly after the Japanese invasion of China and the Pacific War and the decades-long pause in the export of Chinese labour after Mao Zedong's victory in 1949 and the rise of nationalist movements in the Nanyang.

The two points of reference of the Chinese labour diaspora, overseas and in the *qiaoxiang*, were a transnational totality, criss-crossed by interlinking corridors. The export of Chinese labour helped transform Southeast Asia and sustain the domestic economies of the colonial powers. However, the fruits of Huagong labour, remitted in the form of *qiaopi*, also helped transform China. The *qiaopi* trade was an indispensable contribution to China's economic modernisation and perhaps even to its survival as an independent nation-state, although until recently this contribution has often gone unremarked. Labour export and the import of the labourers' earnings was one of China's earliest excursions into the modern world economy and matured into a stable industry, leading to the birth of an original financial system, transnational and domestic, and to city-building in coastal regions near the geographically peripheral *qiao xiang* and in Shanghai and Hong Kong, whose economies were massively indebted to the *qiaopi* trade. The invisible import it represented saved China from bankruptcy in the 1930s by hugely compensating for China's trade deficit—the ratio of total remittances to total trade deficits was 168 percent in 1903 and 108 percent in 1928, its two peak years. Even after 1949, remittances continued to play a crucial role, especially during the economic embargoes imposed on China.

Such was the role of remittance import and labour export in south China's economic burgeoning that historians in Fujian and Guangdong link it, as we have seen, to Hegel's "oceanic" culture, a term they borrow

[277] Bosma (2019, 124 and 183).

to express the idea that sea-borne, sea-facing peoples are a "free element," creative, industrious, and adventurous. Because of this sea culture and seaward gaze, southern entrepreneurs excelled at mobilising cultural and business capital in a special Chinese form of capitalism, cosmopolitan and modern yet built on familism, "traditional" social networks, and associated values, with its roots deep in centuries of Chinese enterprise.[278]

Regarding the effect of remittance import and labour export on the economic transformation of India and Java, I have found no systematic studies to match those on China, but I will try to pull together one or two potential elements of a comparison. Although Tamil migration was the largest regional component of Indian migration within the British Empire, the contribution of overseas Tamil labour to the prosperity of Tamil Nadu was less important than to that in the colonies where Tamils settled.[279] Like most Huagong, the early Tamils were indentured labourers and confined to the plantations. Non-Tamils were more likely than Tamils to settle in Southeast Asia as traders or professionals, but their numbers were relatively small. Tamil remittance to Tamil Nadu was not invested in productive sectors of the economy and was far smaller than (say) Malayalee investment in Kerala, which has the highest literacy rate in India.[280] A study on remittance-based migrations in India in the twentieth century concludes that although the welfare of the residents of source regions of migration was enhanced by money inflows from destination regions, the relationship did not lead to substantial industrialisation.[281] The impact of migration and remittance on the Chinese economy was therefore much greater. One might speculate on possible causes of such a difference, including the stronger Chinese focus on the home community.

Conclusions

The recruitment of Chinese peasants and rural workers for employment overseas had much in common in the late-colonial years with the recruitment of domestic labour for employment in the Chinese towns and cities, by both foreigners and Chinese. Up until 1949, pre-capitalist mechanisms

[278] Chen Xunxian (2004, 187–92), Luo Zeyang (2004, 208–14). This issue is discussed in Benton and Liu 2018, especially ch. 3.

[279] Guilmoto (1993, 117).

[280] Personal communication, Terence Gomez.

[281] Tumbe (2012, 87–112).

shaped the domestic allocation of Chinese labour, despite the emergence of a modern industrial sector in the Treaty Ports. In urban areas, unskilled workers and peasants were often as likely as in the countryside to work alongside people of the same provenance or clan, and they were far less likely to join the labour movement than skilled and semi-skilled urban workers. Many had only a temporary attachment to the city, and most retained their native-place ties.[282] Such people trusted gangs and associations based on village, dialect, and lineage above trade unions and got their jobs through *baotou*, who escorted them from their homes, accommodated them in dormitories, and supervised their labour, wielding ties of clan or native place to whip them into line.

Most labourers working under indenture in the Nanyang and elsewhere overseas were similarly recruited, by brokers who could claim a prior primordial tie to them. But some overseas and domestic workers were recruited outside normal channels, by brokers to whom they had no prior tie, or were kidnapped or cheated into leaving home, in some periods and places more than in others. Given that recruitment for a job abroad was a relative novelty and the physical rupture was far greater, it was a more likely site for deception by labour brokers than the domestic labour market. Most at risk were migrants cutting the knot and leaving to put a greater distance between themselves and impossible debts or unwanted family burdens.[283]

For decades, Nanyang recruitment had been dominated by kongsi-style organisations whose leaders were known to the lineages of the villagers they recruited and acted in expected ways. Kongsis bestowed advantages on the migrant, but in the late nineteenth century they were reduced in the Nanyang to little more than an employers' tool. Perhaps as a result of this weakening of the kongsi, traditional sources of migration may have started to dry up. It would seem, for example, that the percentage of Hakkas among recruits fell in many places, despite the persistence of Hakka strongholds like that on Belitung, where in 1922 half the workers were still from Meixian and most of the rest were from neighbouring counties with a Hakka presence.[284]

[282] Perry (1993).

[283] See Appendix A.

[284] Heidhues (1991, 9). Hakkas stopped going to Bangka in the 1920s and 1930s (Heidhues 1992, 113).

Colonial officials and employers regretted the demise of community-based recruitment, which was cheaper and more profitable, and took steps to restore it. In the early twentieth century, employers throughout the Nanyang started returning time-expired Huagong to their villages to bring back clansmen, a method first consolidated in India. Even so, Huagong seem increasingly to have found themselves in labour-gangs with no familiar faces and where different Chinese languages were spoken.

In another respect, overseas recruitment was subjected, at least in theory, to ever more rigorous official supervision and control. A whole apparatus grew up in Hong Kong and the Treaty Ports and in the Straits Settlements, where in the late nineteenth century Protectors of Chinese had been appointed to prevent abuses. However, the officials were often bested by the traffickers and the vetting was less thorough when the demand for labour rose and less intensive in the Dutch than in the British case. There was little equivalent in domestic recruitment of this revamping. Some foreign companies in China did try to professionalise it, but they were unable to make much headway against the entrenched power of local gangs.

References

Alexeeva, Olga V. 2021. "Between Scylla and Charybdis: Chinese Laborers under the French-American Supervision in France during World War I." In Robert B. McCormick, Araceli Hernández-Laroche, and Catherine G. Canino, eds, *An International Rediscovery of World War One: Distant Fronts*, Abingdon: Routledge, 139–158.

Bailey, Paul. 2011a. "'An Army of Workers': Chinese Indentured Labour in First World War France." In Santanu Das, ed., *Race, Empire and First World War Writing*, Cambridge: Cambridge University Press, 35–52.

Bailey, Paul. 2011b. "The Sino-French Connection and World War One." *Journal of the British Association for Chinese Studies*, vol. 1, 1–19.

Balachandran, G. 2011. "Making Coolies, (Un)making Workers: 'Globalizing' Labour in the Late-19th and Early-20th Centuries." *Journal of Historical Sociology*, vol. 24, no. 3, 266–296.

Bates, Crispin. 1992. "Tribal Migration In India and Beyond." In Gyan Prakash, ed., *The World of the Rural Labourer in Colonial India*, Delhi: Oxford University Press, 1992, 205–245.

Bates, Crispin, and Marina Carter. 2017. "Sirdars as Intermediaries in Nineteenth-century Indian Ocean Indentured Labour Migration." *Modern Asian Studies* vol. 51, no. 2, 462–484.

Benton, Gregor. 1999. *New Fourth Army: Communist Resistance Along the Yangtze and the Huai, 1938–1941*. Berkeley CA: University of California Press.

Benton, Gregor. 2007. *Chinese Migrants and Internationalism: Forgotten Histories, 1917–1945.* London: Routledge.
Benton, Gregor, and Terence Gomez. 2008. *The Chinese in Britain, 1800–Present: Economy, Transnationalism, Identity.* Houndmills: Palgrave Macmillan.
Benton, Gregor, and Hong Liu. 2018. *Dear China: Emigrant Letters and Remittances, 1820–1980.* Oakland, CA: University of California Press.
Bosma, Ulbe. 2014. "Migration and Colonial Enterprise in Nineteenth Century Java." In Jan Lucassen and Leo Lucassen, eds, *Globalising Migration History: The Eurasian Experience (16th–21st Centuries)*, Leiden: Brill, 2014, 151–179.
Bosma, Ulbe. 2019. *The Making of a Periphery: How Island Southeast Asia Became a Mass Exporter of Labor.* New York: Columbia University Press.
Breman, Jan. 1989. *Taming the Coolie Beast: Plantation Society and the Colonial Order in Southeast Asia.* Delhi: Oxford University Press.
Chakraborty, Subhas Ranjan. n.d. "Colonialism, Resource Crisis and (Forced) Migration."
Chang Zengshu. 2008. "Aozhou taojin Huagong de 'yinxin' " ("The Australian Gold-miners' 'Silver Letters'"). In Wang Weizhong, ed., *Di erjie qiaopi wenhua yantao hui lunwen xuan* ("Selection of Papers from the Second Qiaopi Culture Symposium"), N. p.: Gongyuan chuban youxian gongsi, 2008, 455–460.
Chen Jianbo. 2004. "Dui dangqian qiaopi wenhua yanjiu de sikao" (Some Thoughts on Contemporary Research into Qiaopi Culture). In Wang Weizhong, ed., *Shou jie qiaopi wenhua yanjiu hui lunwen ji* (Papers from the First Qiaopi Cultural Symposium), Shantou: N. p., 2004, 148–150.
Chen Lie. 2008. "Guanyu Chaoshan qiaopi wenhua ruogan wentide qiantan" ("Some Observations on Some Questions Concerning Chaoshan Qiaopi Culture"). In Wang Weizhong, ed., *Di erjie qiaopi wenhua yantao hui lunwen xuan* ("Selection of Papers from the Second Qiaopi Culture Symposium"), N. p.: Gongyuan chuban youxian gongsi, 2008, 225–236.
Chen Liyuan. 2008. "Qiaopi jingying wangluo de zuzhi xingtai yanjiu" ("Research into the Organizational Form of the Management of the Qiaopi Network"). In Wang Weizhong, ed., *Di erjie qiaopi wenhua yantao hui lunwen xuan* ("Selection of Papers from the Second Qiaopi Culture Symposium"), N. p.: Gongyuan chuban youxian gongsi, 2008, 185–194.
Chen Sanjing. 1975. *Huagong yu Ouzhan* (Huagong and the European War). Taipei: Zhongyang yanjiu yuan jindai shi yanjiu suo.
Chen Xunxian. 2004. "Shilun Qing dai Chao bang qiaopi ye dui wo guo yuanshi jinrong shichang de cujin yu gongxian" ("On the Chao Gang's Acceleration of and Contribution to Our Country's Primitive Financial Market in the Qing Dynasty"). In Wang Weizhong, ed., *Shou jie qiaopi wenhua yanjiu hui lunwen ji* (Papers from the First Qiaopi Cultural Symposium), Shantou: N. p., 2004, 187–192.
Chen Xunxian. 2010. "Lun 'yinxin hefeng' " ("On 'Silver and Letter in one Envelope'"). In Wang Weizhong, ed., *Di san jie qiaopi wenhua yantao hui lun-*

wen xuan ("Third Symposium on Research into Qiaopi Culture"), Hong Kong: Tianma chuban youxian gongsi, 2010, 181–189.

Choi, Wai Kit. 2009. "Revolutionary Shanghai: Rethinking Class and the Politics of Difference through Chinese Communism." *Science & Society*, vol. 73, no. 2, 242–260.

Choi, Wai Kit. 2018. "Making Capitalism with Gangsters: Unfree Labor in Shanghai's Cotton Mills, 1927–1937." *International Labor and Working-Class History*, vol. 94, 107–132.

Colenbrander, H. T., compiler. 1920–1922. *Jan Pietersz. Coen, Bescheiden omtrent Zijn Bedrijf in Indië*. 4 vols. The Hague: Martinus Nijhoff.

De Graaf, S., and D. G. Stibbe, with W. C. B. Wintgens, eds. 1918. *Encyclopaedie van Nederlandsch-Indië*, second edition. 2 vols. The Hague: Martinus Nijhoff.

De Kat Angelino, A. D. A. 1931. *Colonial Policy*, vol. 2, *The Dutch East Indies*. Translated by G. J. Renier. The Hague: Martinus Nijhoff.

Deng Rui. 2004. "Cong Meizhou shi qiaohui de fazhan guocheng kan qiaopi ju xingshuai" ("Looking at the Rise and Fall of Qiaopi Offices from the Point of View of the Development of Overseas Remittances in Meizhou"). In Wang Weizhong, ed., *Shou jie qiaopi wenhua yanjiu hui lunwen ji* (Papers from the First Qiaopi Cultural Symposium), Shantou: N. p., 2004, 57–64.

Deng Rui. 2010. "Qiantan qiaopi de zhongyao zuoyong ji kaifa liyong" ("On the Important Role and Uses of Qiaopi"). In Wang Weizhong, ed., *Di san jie qiaopi wenhua yantao hui lunwen xuan* ("Third Symposium on Research into Qiaopi Culture"), Hong Kong: Tianma chuban youxian gongsi, 2010, 103–117.

Douw, Leo. 2012. "Mainland Chinese Migrants in Taiwan, 1895–1945: The Drawbacks of Being Legal." In Barak Kalir and Malini Sur, eds, *Transnational Flows and Permissive Polities: Ethnographies of Human Mobilities in Asia*. Amsterdam: Amsterdam University Press, 2012, 189–206.

Fitzgerald, John. 2007. *Big White Lie: Chinese Australians in White Australia*. Sydney: UNSW Press.

Furnivall, J. S. 1939. *Netherlands India: A Study of Plural Economy*. Cambridge: Cambridge University Press.

García Triana, Mauro, and Pedro Eng Herrera. 2009. *The Chinese in Cuba, 1847–Now*. Edited and translated by Gregor Benton. Lanham: Lexington Books.

Gedenkboek Billiton, 1852–1927. 1927. 2 pts. The Hague: Martinus Nijhoff.

Gonzales, Michael J. 1989. "Chinese Plantation Workers and Social Conflict in Peru in the Late Nineteenth Century." *Journal of Latin American Studies*, vol. 21, no. 3, 385–424.

Goodman, Bryna. 1995. *Native Place, City, and Nation. Regional Networks and Identities in Shanghai, 1853–1937*. Berkeley: University of California Press.

Gottschang, Thomas R., and Diana Lary. 2000. *Swallows and Settlers: The Great Migration from North China to Manchuria*. Ann Arbor: Center for Chinese Studies, University of Michigan.

Gounder, Farzana. 2011. *Indentured Identities: Resistance and Accommodation in Plantation-Era Fiji*. Amsterdam: John Benjamins.

Groeneveldt, Willem Pieter, 1898. *De Nederlanders in China*. The Hague: Nijhoff.

Guilmoto, Christophe Z. 1993. "The Tamil Migration Cycle, 1830–1950." *Economic and Political Weekly*, January 16–23, 111–120.

Guowuyuan qiaoban qiaowu ganbu xuexiao, eds. 2005. *Huaqiao Huaren gaishu* (General situation of overseas and ethic Chinese). Beijing: Jizhou chuban she.

Guowuyuan qiaogong shiwu ju, eds. [January] 1920a. *Nanyang He shu Wanlitong dao Huagong qingxing diaocha shu* (An Investigation into the Situation of Huagong on Dutch-ruled Belitung Island in the Nanyang). Beijing: Guowuyuan qiaogong shiwu ju.

Guowuyuan qiaogong shiwu ju, eds. [May] 1920b. *Nanyang He shu Wangjia dao Huagong qingxing diaocha shu* (An Investigation into the Situation of Huagong on Dutch-ruled Bangka Island in the Nanyang). Beijing: Guowuyuan qiaogong shiwu ju.

Haynes, Douglas E., and Tirthanka Roy. 1999. "Conceiving Mobility: Weavers' Migrations in Pre-Colonial and Colonial India." *The Indian Economic & Social History Review*, vol. 36, no. 1, 35–67.

He Tianyi, ed. 1995. *Zhongguo laogong zai Riben* ("Chinese labour in Japan"). Beijing: Xinhua chuban she.

Heidhues, Mary F. Somers. 1991. "Company Island: A Note on the History of Belitung." *Indonesia*, no. 51, 1–20.

Heidhues, Mary F. Somers. 1992. *Bangka Tin and Mentok Pepper: Chinese Settlement on an Indonesian Island*. Pasir Panjang : Institute of Southeast Asian Studies.

Heijting, H. G. 1925. *De koelie-wetgeving*. The Hague: Van Stockhum.

Heinoldt, C. 1897. *Emigratie van Chineezen naar Banka*. N. p.: n. p.

Hess, Frank L., and Eva Hess. 1912. *Bibliography of the Geology and Mineralogy of Tin*. Smithsonian Miscellaneous Collections, vol. 58, no. 2, City of Washington: The Smithsonian Institution.

Honig, Emily. 1983. "The Contract Labor System and Women Workers: Pre-Liberation Cotton Mills of Shanghai." *Modern China*, vol. 9, no. 4, 421–454.

Honig, Emily. 1986. *Sisters and Strangers: Women in the Shanghai Cotton Mills, 1919–1949*. Stanford: Stanford University Press.

Honig, Emily. 1992. *Creating Chinese Ethnicity: Subei People in Shanghai, 1850–1980*. New Haven, CT: Yale University Press.

Hou Weixiong. 2009. "Gulangyu yu Minnan qiaopi ye yizhi" ("Gulangyu and the Site of the Minnan Qiaopi Trade"). In Chen Xiaogang, ed., *Huiwang Minnan qiaopi: Shoujie Minnan qiaopi yantao hui lunwen ji* (Looking Back on Minnan Qiaopi: Collection of Papers of the First Minnan Qiaopi Conference), Quanzhou: Huayi chuban she, 2009, 136–141.

Hu-Dehart, Evelyn. 1994. "Chinese Coolie Labor in Cuba in the Nineteenth Century: Free Labor of Neoslavery." *Contributions in Black Studies*, vol. 12, 38–54.

Huang Jiaxiang. 2010. "Zhaoan qiaopi ye liubian" ("Flow and Change in the Zhaoan Qiaopi Trade"). In Wang Weizhong, ed., *Di san jie qiaopi wenhua yantao hui lunwen xuan* ("Third Symposium on Research into Qiaopi Culture"), Hong Kong: Tianma chuban youxian gongsi, 2010, 502–510.

Huang Zijian. 2013. "Malaixiya qiaopi: Shehui shi ji qiaohui shi shiliao" ("Malaysian qiaopi: Historical materials for social history and remittance history"), in Zhongguo qiaopi shijie jiyi gongcheng guoji yantao hui zuwei hui, eds, *Lunwen ji* (Conference Papers Collection), Beijing: n.p., 131–141.

Jain, Prakash C. 1989. "Emigration and Settlement of Indians Abroad." *Sociological Bulletin*, vol. 38, no. 1, 155–168.

Jiang Bowei and Cai Mingsong. 2008. "Jinmen minxinju (piju) jingying moshi zhi tantao" ("Discussion of the Operational Model of the Jinmen Remittance Shop"). In Wang Weizhong, ed., *Di erjie qiaopi wenhua yantao hui lunwen xuan* ("Selection of Papers from the Second Qiaopi Culture Symposium"), N. p.: Gongyuan chuban youxian gongsi, 2008, 264–278.

Jiao Jianhua and Xu Cuihong. 2004. "Jindai pixin ju tese tanyuan" ("Origins of the Special Features of Modern Remittance Offices"). In Wang Weizhong, ed., *Shou jie qiaopi wenhua yanjiu hui lunwen ji* (Papers from the First Qiaopi Cultural Symposium), Shantou: N. p., 2004, 164–173.

Kaur, Amarjit. 2004. *Wage Labour in Southeast Asia since 1840: Globalisation, the International Division of Labour and Labour Transformations.* Houndsmill: Palgrave Macmillan.

Kort historisch overzicht van de werving voor de Bankatinwinning buiten Banka, benevens van de maatregeln in verband met die werving getroffen, bijgewerkt tot 1 juli. 1928. Arsip Nasional, Jakarta, Algemene Secretarie, Grote Bundel, TZG Agenda, file no. 8436, 1–3.

Kuhn, Philip A. 2008. *Chinese among Others: Emigration in Modern Times.* Lanham: Rowman and Littlefield.

Kuiper, Koos. 2017. *The Early Dutch Sinologists (1854–1900): Training in Holland and China, Functions in the Netherlands East Indies.* 2 vols. Leiden: Brill.

Kumar, Ashutosh. 2017. *Coolies of the Empire: Indentured Indians in the Sugar Colonies, 1830–1920.* Cambridge, Cambridge University Press.

Kwong, Peter. 2001. *Chinatown, New York: Labor and Politics, 1930–1950.* Revised with a new introduction. New York: The New Press.

Li Anshan. 2000. *Feizhou Huaren Huaqiao shi* (History of overseas and ethnic Chinese in Africa). Beijing: Zhongguo Huaqiao chuban she.

Li Minghuan. 2012. "'Playing Edge Ball': Transnational Migration Brokerage in China." In Barak Kalir and Malini Sur, eds, *Transnational Flows and Permissive Polities Ethnographies of Human Mobilities in Asia,* Amsterdam: Amsterdam University Press, 2012, 207–228.

Li Xiaoyuan. 2008. "Qiaopi yu Chao Mei qiaoxiang diqu renmin shenghuo fangshi de bianqian" ("Qiaopi and Changes in Life-style of the People in the Chao and Mei Areas"). In Wang Weizhong, ed., *Di erjie qiaopi wenhua yantao hui lunwen xuan* ("Selection of Papers from the Second Qiaopi Culture Symposium"), N. p.: Gongyuan chuban youxian gongsi, 2008, 287–295.

Lin Qingxi. 2010. "Chaoshan qiaopi zai renshi" ("Once Again Recognizing Chaoshan Qiaopi"). In Wang Weizhong, ed., *Di san jie qiaopi wenhua yantao hui lunwen xuan* ("Third Symposium on Research into Qiaopi Culture"), Hong Kong: Tianma chuban youxian gongsi, 2010, 207–117.

Lin Sha. 2008. "Xiamen qiaopi ye de chansheng he fazhan" ("The Origins and Development of the Xiamen Qiaopi Trade"). In Wang Weizhong, ed., *Di erjie qiaopi wenhua yantao hui lunwen xuan* ("Selection of Papers from the Second Qiaopi Culture Symposium"), N. p.: Gongyuan chuban youxian gongsi, 2008, 354–357.

Lin Tengyun. 2008. "Cong qiaopi he piju shouju tan Meizhou Huaqiao yu Shantou bang de guanxi" ("Talking about the Relationship between the Meizhou Overseas Chinese and Shantou on the Basis of Qiaopi and Piju Receipts"). In Wang Weizhong, ed., *Di erjie qiaopi wenhua yantao hui lunwen xuan* ("Selection of Papers from the Second Qiaopi Culture Symposium"), N. p.: Gongyuan chuban youxian gongsi, 2008, 411–416.

Liu Jin. 2009. *Wuyi yinxin* ("Wuyi silver and letters"). Guangzhou: Guangdong renmin chuban she.

Liu, Andrew B. 2015. The Two Tea Countries: Competition, Labor, and Economic Thought in Coastal China and Eastern India, 1834–1942. PhD, Columbia University.

Lockard, Craig A. 1971. "The Javanese as Emigrant: Observations on the Development of Javanese Settlements Overseas." *Indonesia*, no. 11, 41–62.

Look Lai, Walton. 1989. "Chinese Indentured Labor: Migrations to the British West Indies in the Nineteenth Century." *Amerasia* vol. 15, no. 2, 117–138.

Look Lai, Walton. 1998. Imperialism, Indenture and Diaspora: The Origins of the West Indian Chinese Community. Paper for the UK Society for Caribbean Studies, Warwick University.

Lu Wendi, Chen Zexian, and Peng Jiali, eds. 1981. *Guanyu Huagong chuguo de Zhongwai zonghexing zhuzuo* (Comprehensive writings from China and abroad concerning Huagong migration). In Chen Hansheng, ed., *Huagong chuguo shiliao huibian* (A compilation of edited historical materials regarding going abroad by Huagong), Beijing: Zhonghua shuju, 12 vols, 1981–1985, vol. 4.

Lu Wendi, Chen Zexian, and Peng Jiali, eds. 1985a. *Zhongguo guanwen shu xuanji* (A selection of official Chinese documents). In Chen Hansheng, ed., *Huagong chuguo shiliao huibian* (A compilation of edited historical materials regarding going abroad by Huagong), Beijing: Zhonghua shuju, 12 vols, 1981–1985, vol. 1, pt 1.

Lu Wendi, Chen Zexian, and Peng Jiali, eds, 1985b. *Zhongguo guanwen shu xuanji* (A selection of official Chinese documents). In Chen Hansheng, ed., *Huagong chuguo shiliao huibian* (A compilation of edited historical materials regarding going abroad by Huagong), Beijing: Zhonghua shuju, 12 vols, 1981–1985, vol. 1, pt 4.

Lu Wendi, Peng Jiali, and Chen Zexian, eds. 1984a. *Guanyu Dongnan Ya Huagong de siren zhuzuo* (Private individuals' writings about Huagong in Southeast Asia). In Chen Hansheng, ed., *Huagong chuguo shiliao huibian* (A compilation of edited historical materials regarding going abroad by Huagong), Beijing: Zhonghua shuju, 12 vols, 1981–1985, vol. 5.

Lu Wendi, Peng Jiali, and Chen Zexian, eds. 1984b. *Meiguo yu Jianada Huagong* (Huagong in America and Canada). In Chen Hansheng, ed., *Huagong chuguo shiliao huibian* (A compilation of edited historical materials regarding going abroad by Huagong), Beijing: Zhonghua shuju, 12 vols, 1981–1985, vol. 7.

Lu Wendi, Peng Jiali, and Chen Zexian, eds. 1984c. *Da Yangzhou Huagong* (Huagong in the Pacific). In Chen Hansheng, ed., *Huagong chuguo shiliao huibian* (A compilation of edited historical materials regarding going abroad by Huagong), Beijing: Zhonghua shuju, 12 vols, 1981–1985, vols. 8–10.

Luo Zeyang. 2004. "Qiaopi wenhua yu haiyang wenhua" ("Qiaopi culture and oceanic culture"). In Wang Weizhong, ed., *Shou jie qiaopi wenhua yanjiu hui lunwen ji* (Papers from the First Qiaopi Cultural Symposium), Shantou: N. p., 2004, 208–214.

Ma Chujian. 2008. "Chao bang pixin ju yu qiaohui liutong zhi fazhan chutan" ("Preliminary Research into the circulation of remittances by the Chao Gang remittance Ooffice"). In Wang Weizhong, ed., *Di erjie qiaopi wenhua yantao hui lunwen xuan* ("Selection of Papers from the Second Qiaopi Culture Symposium"), N. p.: Gongyuan chuban youxian gongsi, 2008, 21–32.

Ma Huiyue. 2015. *Jindai qiyue Huagong falü* (Laws on modern Chinese indentured labour), Beijing: Falü chuban she.

Martino, Enrique. 2016. Touts and Despots: Recruiting Assemblages of Contract Labour in Fernando Pó and the Gulf of Guinea, 1858–1979. PhD, Humboldt Universität.

Mei Weiqiang and Zhang Guoxiong, eds. 2001. *Wuyi Huaqiao Huaren shi* ("A history of Wuyi's overseas and ethnic Chinese"). Guangzhou: Guangdong gaodeng jiaoyu chuban she.

Mishra, Amit Kumar. 2015. "Sardars, Kanganies and Maistries: Intermediaries in the Indian Labour Diaspora During the Colonial Period." In Sigrid Wadauer, Thomas Buchner, and Alexander Mejstrik, eds, *The History of Labour Intermediation: Institutions and Finding Employment in the Nineteenth and Early Twentieth Centuries*, International Studies in Social History, vol. 26, New York: Berghahn, 368–387.

Mo Zhen, ed. 2013. *Haibang chengfu: Guangdong qiaopi dang'an* (Fragrance from Abroad: Guangdong's Qiaopi Archive). Guangzhou: Lingnan meishu chuban she.

Moll-Murata, Christine. 2008. "Chinese Guilds from the Seventeenth to the Twentieth Centuries: An Overview." *International Review of Social History*, no. 53, 213–247.

Mollema, J. C.. 1922. *De ontwikkeling van het eiland Billiton en van de Billiton-Maatschappij.* The Hague: Nijhoff.

Narvaez, Benjamin Nicolas. 2010. Chinese Coolies in Cuba and Peru: Race, Labor, and Immigration, 1839–1886. PhD, The University of Texas at Austin.

Neale, Margaret. 1988. *We Were the Christmas Islanders: Reminiscences and Recollections of the People of an Isolated Island—the Australian Territory of Christmas Island, Indian Ocean, 1906–1980.* Chapman, ACT: N. p.

Ngai, Mae. 2017. "Trouble on the Rand: The Chinese Question in South Africa and the Apogee of White Settlerism." *International Labor and Working-Class History,* vol. 91, 59–78.

Noa Siaosi, A. S. 2010. Catching the Dragon's Tail: The Impact of the Chinese in Samoa. MA thesis, University of Canterbury.

Pan, Lynn, ed. 1998. *The Encylopedia of the Chinese Overseas.* Singapore: Archipelago Press.

Pekelharing, N. R. 1924. *De groote cultures in Ned.-Indië en eenige naburige Koloniën* (The great cultures in the Neth. East Indies and neighbouring colonies). Weltevreden: Landsdruk, 1924.

Pelzer, Karl J. 1935. *Die Arbeiterwanderungen in Südostasien: Eine wirtschafts- und bevölkerungsgeographische Untersuchung.* Würzburg: Konrad Triltsch.

Perry, Elizabeth J. 1993. *Shanghai on Strike: The Politics of Chinese Labor.* Stanford: Stanford University Press.

Phoa Liong Gie. 1936 [1992]. "The Changing Economic Position of the Chinese in Netherlands India." In M. R. Fernando and D. Bulbeck, eds, *Chinese Economic Activity in Netherlands India: Selected Translations from the Dutch,* Singapore: Institute of Southeast Asian Studies, 5–18.

Rankine, Wendy. 1995. "From Nauru to Nowhere: Pacific Island Chinese Evacuee Workers in Central Australian Wolfram Mines, 1942–43." In Paul Macgregor, ed., *Histories of the Chinese in Australasia and the South Pacific,* Melbourne: Museum of Chinese Australian History, 1995, 152–158.

Rapport betreffende Chineezen-Werving op Billiton. 1905. BrRG-33 = 16072 KIT.

Rice, Richard. 1990. "Japanese Labor in World War II." *International Labor and Working-Class History,* no. 38, 29–45.

Richardson, Peter. 1982. *Chinese Mine Labour in the Transvaal,* London: Macmillan.

Sai, Siew-min. 2021. "Benevolent Technocracy: The Chinese Protectorate, Migration Control and Racialised Governmentality in Colonised Malaya." *Journal of Southeast Asian Studies,* 1–23. https://doi.org/10.1017/S002246342100059X

Sen, Samita. 2010. "Commercial Recruiting and Informal Intermediation: Debate over the Sardari System in Assam Tea Plantations, 1860–1900." *Modern Asian Studies,* vol. 44, no. 1, 3–28.

Singha, Radhika. 2020. *The Coolie's Great War: Indian Labour in a Global Conflict, 1914–1921*. London: Hurst.

Stewart, John R. 1940. "Chinese Migration to Manchuria Setting New Records." *Far Eastern Survey*, vol. 9, no. 18.

Stibbe, D. G., and C. Spat, with E. M. Uhlenbeck, eds. 1927. *Encyclopaedie van Nederlandsch-Indië*. Second edition. 8 vols. The Hague: Martinus Nijhoff, vol. 5.

Stoler, Ann Laura. 1985. *Capitalism and Confrontation in Sumatra's Plantation Belt, 1870–1979*. New Haven: Yale University Press.

Termorshuizen, Thio. 2008. "Indentured Labour in the Dutch Colonial Empire, 1800–1940." In Geert Oostindie, ed., *Dutch Colonialism, Migration and Cultural Heritage: Past and Present*, Leiden: Brill, 2008, 261–314.

Tucker, David. 2005. "Labour Policy and the Construction Industry in Manchukuo: System of Recruitment, Management, and Control." In Paul H. Kratoska, ed., *Asian Labour in the Wartime Japanese Empire: Unknown Histories*. New York: Routledge, 25–60.

Tumbe, Chinmay. 2012. "Migration Persistence across Twentieth Century India." *Migration and Development*, vol. 1, no. 1, 87–112.

Van Blommestein, A. F. 1917. *De Nieuwe Koelie-Ordonnantie voor de Oostkust van Sumatra*. Amsterdam: Scheltema and Holkema.

Walden, Sue. 1995. "The Tin Fields of Northeast Tasmania: A Regional Variation?" In Paul Macgregor, ed., *Histories of the Chinese in Australasia and the South Pacific*, Melbourne: Museum of Chinese Australian History, 1995, 177–190.

Wang Linqian and Wu Kunxiang, eds. 2002. *Zaoqi Huaqiao yu qiyue Huagong (mai zhuzai) ziliao* (Early materials relating to overseas Chinese and indentured Huagong [piglet trade]). Chaoshan: Chaoshan lishi wenhua yanjiu zhongxin, Shantou shi wenhua ju, Shantou shi tushu guan.

Waters, Les. 1983. *The Union of Christmas Island Workers*. Sydney: George Allen and Unwin.

Wazar, R. M. 2004 [1956]. "Tinnen Munten van Bangka." *Erts: Maandblad der Billitonbedrijven*, October 1956, no. 10. Reprinted in Yang Tongling, Lin Zhang, Li Xinyun, Tan Enli, and Li Ensi, *Hunqian mengrao de guxiang—Bangjia dao* ("Lost in a reverie about one's native place: Bangka Island"), Beijing: Zhongguo youyi chuban gongsi, 2004, 209–211.

Williams, Michael. 1999. *Chinese Settlement in NSW: A Thematic History*. A Report for the NSW Heritage Office.

Willmott, W. E.1998. "The South Pacific." In Lynn Pan, ed., *The Encylopedia of the Chinese Overseas*, Singapore: Archipelago Press, 1998, 292–296.

Wu Fengbin. 1988. *Qiyue Huagong shi* (History of indentured Chinese labour). Nanchang: Jiangxi renmin chuban she.

Wu Hongli. 2008. "Chuxi Minnan qiaopi wenhua" ("Preliminary investigation into Southern Fujian's qiaopi culture"). In Wang Weizhong, ed., *Di erjie qiaopi wenhua yantao hui lunwen xuan* ("Selection of Papers from the Second Qiaopi Culture Symposium"), N. p.: Gongyuan chuban youxian gongsi, 2008, 358–369.

Wu Kuixin. 2004. "Qiaopi chuandi guandao de gengzu yu shutong" ("The blocking and dredging of the channels through which qiaopi were delivered"). In Wang Weizhong, ed., *Shou jie qiaopi wenhua yanjiu hui lunwen ji* (Papers from the First Qiaopi Cultural Symposium), Shantou: N. p., 2004, 208–214.

Xia Shuiping and Fang Xuejia. 2004. "Meizhou keshu diqude shuike ye shulüe" ("Discussion of the shuike trade in the Meizhou Hakka region"). In Wang Weizhong, ed., *Shou jie qiaopi wenhua yanjiu hui lunwen ji* (Papers from the First Qiaopi Cultural Symposium), Shantou: N. p., 2004, 179–186.

Xia Yuanming. 2008. "Meizhou keshu diqu de shuike yu qiaopi ye shulüe" ("Short Account of the Shuike in the Meizhou Hakka Region"). In Wang Weizhong, ed., *Di erjie qiaopi wenhua yantao hui lunwen xuan* ("Selection of Papers from the Second Qiaopi Culture Symposium"), N. p.: Gongyuan chuban youxian gongsi, 2008, 370–390.

Xiao Wenping. 2004."Kejia shancun de shuike, qiaopi, yu qiaoxiang shehui" ("Shuike, qiaopi, and qiaoxiang society in the Hakka mountain villages"). In Wang Weizhong, ed., *Shou jie qiaopi wenhua yanjiu hui lunwen ji* (Papers from the First Qiaopi Cultural Symposium), Shantou: N. p., 2004, 253–263.

Xu Guoqi. 2011. *Strangers on the Western Front: Chinese Workers in the Great War.* Cambridge MA: Harvard University Press.

Yang Qunxi, ed. 2004. *Chaoshan diqu qiaopi ye ziliao* (Materials Concerning the Qiaopi Trade in the Chaoshan Region). Shantou: Shantou shi tushu guan.

Yang, Tongling, Lin Zhang, Li Xinyun, Tan Enli, and Li Ensi. 2004. *Hunqian mengrao de guxiang—Bangjia dao* ("Lost in a reverie about one's native place: Bangka Island"). Beijing: Zhongguo youyi chuban gongsi.

Yuan Li and Chen Dazhang. 1991. Haiwai Huaren ji qi juzhu *di gaikuang*. (Survey of overseas Chinese and their settlements). Beijing: Zhongguo Huaqiao chuban gongsi.

Zhang Shuoren. 2013. "Minguo shiqi Hainan qiaohui wenti shulun" ("On Some Questions Regarding Hainan Overseas Remittances in the Republican Period"). In *Hainan yimin lunwenji* (Collection of Essays on Hainan Emigration), edited by Hainan wenhua yanjiu zhongxin, Singapore: Xinjiapo Hainan wenhua zhongxin, 2013, 204–221.

Zheng He. 1933. "Taiwan Huagong gaikuang" (The general situation of Huagong in Taiwan). *Laogong yuekan*, vol. 1, no. 6, 107–110.

Zou Qiudong and Su Tonghai. 2009. "Shuo 'huipi'" ("About 'huipi'"). In Chen Xiaogang, ed., *Huiwang Minnan qiaopi: Shoujie Minnan qiaopi yantao hui lunwen ji* (Looking Back on Minnan Qiaopi: Collection of Papers of the First Minnan Qiaopi Conference), Quanzhou: Huayi chuban she, 2009, 70–74.

CHAPTER 6

Huagong Life and Labour Under the "Coolie System"

This chapter looks at Huagong labour and indenture, mainly in the Dutch East Indies, from start to finish—its gradations, procedures, and institutions and the everyday experience of living and working under it. Indenture had the same core definition everywhere, but it was realised in different ways in different places. It comprised a series of transitions, from initiation to habituation to exit and departure, that not everyone successfully negotiated or even finished. Some Huagong handled the opportunities indenture offered skilfully and achieved their goal of a return to China in triumph, or a rise to power in the lower indenture hierarchy overseas. Others—probably the great majority, the percentage is unquantifiable—died forgotten and in poverty. Indenture is usually associated with plantations, but on the Outer Islands it happened in two other main areas, mining and logging, each of which was organised differently. State-owned enterprises were run on different lines from private ones, a difference exemplified by the contrast between the two tin islands. The sites on which Huagong worked in the East Indies differed in nature from tropical enterprises employing indentured labourers in other parts of the world, because of their genesis and social context. Chinese employers on the Outer Islands behaved differently from, and not necessarily better than, Europeans. "Free" Huagong played a big part in planting, mining, and logging, especially in the final years of the penal sanction. However, their working lives, and the attendant abuses, were no less harsh, and perhaps in some respects harsher, than those endured by formally indentured Huagong.

G. Benton, *Chinese Indentured Labour in the Dutch East Indies, 1880–1942*, Palgrave Macmillan Transnational History Series,
https://doi.org/10.1007/978-3-031-05024-4_6

The Recruitment Procedure before Departure

For the first few decades, labour recruitment in the East Indies was largely in Chinese hands, as it had been before the Dutch arrival. The procedure was rough and ready, as we have seen. Contracts were drawn up with little regard for accuracy or truth, the main purpose being to trap workers into conditions that fell far short of those promised.

In the late nineteenth and early twentieth centuries, Dutch colonial officials and employers instituted a system of controls aimed at ensuring a more regular flow of labour, improving the quality and lowering the cost of recruits, cutting out the middleman, and warding off criticisms by homeland critics and by Chinese officials and British competitors. However, the monitoring was often ineffective and suffered from laxness and indifference on the part of the monitors and sabotage by recruiters.

Dutch recruitment through British colonies was subject to British regulations. Protectors of Chinese were expected to board ships transporting labourers, inspect the depots in which they were held before embarkation, witness the contracts, and ensure that the labourers had understood them.[1] Inter-colonial rivalries played a role in this. However, collusion between British and Dutch officials and corruption by them and their Chinese agents often undermined the process.

On the Outer Islands, recruitment and employment was governed after 1880 by the coolie ordinance (*tiaolie*), the labour contract (*hetong*), and the labour agreement (*tiaoyue*). The first set out the basic legal principles of employment and stipulated the need for a written contract or agreement. The latter two documents, which set out the terms of employment, were similar in character.[2] Although agreements were often perfunctory, they gradually became more explicit.[3]

The agreements imposed obligations on both worker and employer. The worker had to work for as long as his contract required and to comply with his other contractual obligations, except when given written

[1] MacNair (1923).

[2] Contracts for Bangka and Belitung are in Lu Wendi et al. (1985, 395–405 and 434–439).

[3] For an agreement applicable to all regions in 1925 and 1927, see De Kat Angelino (1931, 607–610). Earlier versions were harsher (Heijting 1925). Such agreements were intended primarily for Javanese, but the 1880 Ordinance said they should also apply to "workmen arriving from elsewhere," mainly China. Such agreements did not necessarily apply to small enterprises, including those run by Chinese. Special regulations were devised in 1923 to cover panglongs (De Kat Angelino 1931, 505, 577, and 583).

permission to deviate. The employer had to ensure that the worker knew what he was signing up for, treat him well, pay him regularly, protect him against financial loss, provide him with free accommodation and medical treatment, allow him access to official labour inspectors, help his family if he fell ill or died, and if necessary repatriate him at the end of his contract. In theory, the penal sanction applied to both worker and employer. Agreements were individual rather than collective and, starting in 1863, written rather than oral, but corners were cut.[4]

On the Outer Islands, the main beneficiary of the Coolie Ordinance governing contracts and agreements was the employer. The *Encyclopaedie van Nederlandsch-Indië* left no doubt: "If on Java one was always aware of the need to champion the interests of the employees, here [on Sumatra's East Coast] it was above all a matter of protecting the employers. They needed supporting in their efforts to secure sufficient workers from elsewhere and to be protected against arbitrariness on the part of the latter. Last and not least, one had in mind the need to take to heart the general interest, with regard to the steady development of agriculture." As for the penal sanction, regarding "the subjection of workers and employers to the provisions of the ordinance,... a number of punitive provisions were listed of which those opposing *any arbitrary infraction of the contract on the part of the worker* and excessive indolence are the most important."[5]

The Core Element of Indenture

Indebtedness is the core feature of indenture, secured in the East Indies by the penal sanction. The biggest debt was the labourer's passage overseas and the expenses incurred on the way to and in the port of departure and at sea and on arrival. The transport cost was nearly always borne by the worker. In the East Indies, debt bondage survived in some cases up to 1942, although by that time it was exercised less nakedly.

The indenture and the date of its maturation was registered in the contract—written or oral—into which employer and employee entered,

[4] This information on contracts and agreed draws on Deli Planters Vereeniging, *Mededeling no. 14, De Arbeidsregeling voor de Buitengewesten van Nederlandsch-Indië*, Medan: Köhler & co., 1923, 7–10; De Graaf and Stibbe 1918, 360; and Arsip Nasional, TZG Agenda, file 6725, January 24, 1924, 6.

[5] De Graaf and Stibbe (1918, 362–363). Italics in the original.

usually at the port from which the migrant left. In the case of recruits for the East Indies, however, this did not always happen. Where the journey started in Hong Kong or passed through Singapore, especially after the abolition of indenture in British India and Malaya, the contract was often agreed (or dictated) only after reaching the East Indies, to skirt Chinese or British prohibitions on indenture. The terms of indenture contracts were often found on arrival to have changed, to the advantage of the crimp or employer. In some cases, the indenture was handled by the captain or a member of the crew of the ship taking the worker south and similarly manipulated.

Many Huagong who migrated to Southeast Asia in the early twentieth century were listed as "assisted migrants." This designation was also applied to Indian labour migrants, but with a different meaning. Starting in the early twentieth century, most South Asian labour migrants received an "assisted" passage financed by the colonial state and sailed debt-free. Chinese labour migrants in Southeast Asia, in contrast, were usually "assisted" by employers or their agents or by community or family sponsors and incurred a debt recoverable as a condition of indenture or a variant on it.[6]

The ticket south was not the sole source of the initial debt. Even Indians recruited under the free-passage scheme might accumulate debts in the course of their recruitment and transportation, so that an element of debt-bondage remained. Once deposited on a plantation, remote from sources of support, they were vulnerable to the same dependency and exploitation as an out-and-out indenture. Whether "free" or indentured, they remained bound by contracts with penal provisions until the early 1920s.[7] However, the plight of Chinese assisted migrants bound for the East Indies was worse, for they carried not just debts acquired along the way but the major debt of transportation—and they were subject, unlike South Asians after the abolition of indenture, to the penal sanction.

Generally on recruitment, a Huagong received a sum of money to cover the cost of his accommodation and the purchase of tools and clothing and of food in the dockside hostel and on shipboard, plus a small amount to be remitted by the recruiter to the recruit's family to signal his safe arrival at the coast. This initial payment was, for the recruit, part of the

[6] Some Chinese migration to the Caribbean was sponsored by the British colonial state, as in India (Look Lai 1993, 45).

[7] Kaur (2006, 453).

attraction of indenture—money to spend on himself and his family. However, he did not always receive the entire sum. Many recruiters held back all or part of it. To aid the deception, they told the recipient that the payment was a special favour and he should keep quiet about it. In other cases, recipients were told that the board and lodgings provided in the port would not be deducted from their future pay, although it usually was.[8]

Remittances to the recruit's family were another chance for the recruiter to swindle the recruit, especially where they were not known to one another and the recruiter could not easily be held to account. Even where the remittance was delivered, it often fell short of the amount promised, and what was said to be a payment later turned out to be a loan, repayable with interest.

New arrivals in the Nanyang were quickly circled by predators. Their treatment reflected the official view of them, as possible trouble-makers. They were ferried ashore in the early 1920s on small boats and herded together in barracoons behind barbed wire, with Javanese soldiers to stop them escaping, "like prisoners-of-war." Along the perimeter, hawkers sold fruit and cakes, which the recruits bought through the wire. The recruits mocked the drills done outside the wire by local guards, said to be sufficiently well trained to take the mockery in their stride.[9] The sport with the new recruits was never-ending. In 1937, a Chinese reporter described the arrival in Deli of dozens of "new piglets" under armed escort, eager to be get rich and mobbed by denizens who quizzed them about China and tried to cheat them.[10] A visiting Chinese official noted that "the more astute among the recruits realised they had been rooked, while only the foolish retained their illusions."[11] The recruits were roped together and marched off through the town to their place of work, to the amusement of crowds who laughed and clapped while trying to spy out acquaintances.

The recruits likened the barracoons to prisons, while the Dutch called them "pigsties." The *xinke* were stripped, disinfected, and vaccinated against smallpox, typhoid, and cholera. Their distinguishing physical features were noted down in case they later tried to escape, and their thumbprints were taken. After an official had read out their rights and duties, they signed the contract and received their identity cards. They were then

[8] Guowuyuan ([January] 1920a, 14).
[9] *Gedenkboek* (1927, vol. 2, 66).
[10] *Shen bao*, February 2, 1937.
[11] Guowuyuan ([January] 1920a, 22–23), Lu Wendi et al. (1984a, 458–459).

escorted on foot or in vehicles to their new home, for months or years or forever.

Most recruits wanted to work alongside people who spoke the same dialect or were fellow villagers. Such an arrangement was also in the company's interest, for it put recruits at ease and helped teach them the ropes.[12] However, the arrangement became less commonplace in the twentieth century as the sources of labour in China diversified.

Among those jostling for the recruits' attention were staff of the remittance-shops, intent on signing up remitters. Their lure was to offer to send a token remittance or *qiaopi* to the recruit's family in China, with payment deferred until pay-day. Thus the agent gained both the remitter's trust and his workplace and family addresses. This relationship was essential for the remitter, who had no other way of sending money, and good for the shop, which could hope to retain the remitter's custom for as long as he stayed abroad. A member of a clan association would often help sign up the recruit on the shop's behalf, thus initiating him into a protective network. The introductory *qiaopi*, designed to let his family know that he had arrived safely, was the "safe-and-sound *qiaopi*."[13]

The Huagong's biggest debt was the cost of his ticket and other expenses met by the recruiter. This debt hamstrung and immobilised the Huagong, who had to keep working until it was repaid. This arrangement, which survived into the 1930s, was a continuation in new form of the method employed by kongsis in the nineteenth century and earlier.

Migrants who borrowed the fare from a fellow-villager could repay it privately or through a clan association.[14] In theory, such an arrangement was better than indenture, but not always so, for private credit could lack transparency and was more easily manipulated. Those who had obtained their ticket abroad through an agent were bound by their contract to repay it. In the case of professional recruitment, the debt might be directly to the employer. Where the recruitment happened through an intermediary, the recruit might be bound to the intermediary. However, the

[12] Lu Wendi et al. (1984b, 282–284), Wu Fengbin (1988, 182), Mollema (1922, 155–157).

[13] Yang Qunxi, ed. (2004, 53).

[14] Debts accrued by purchase of paper identity for entry into the United States in the 1930s under the illegal "paper sons" scheme show the extent of exploitation. Papers cost around $100 for each year of the "son's" age—a 33-year-old could expect to pay $3,600 out of his future wages or with the help of his family. Most immigrants earned $25–50 a week, so the repayment could take up to five years (Hsu 1997, 57).

outcome was much the same, for the debt was often purchased by the employer on delivery of the recruit and inserted into the labour contract. This contract specified the amount and frequency of the monthly payment from the worker's wage, to clear his debt. The calculation offered yet another opportunity for the employer to cheat the recruit, by inflating the debt.

Ju-k'ang T'ien has described the different forms of unfreedom embodied in the credit system that financed Chinese migration to Sarawak, which had its counterpart in the East Indies. Newcomers arrived under the guardianship of an established clan-mate for whom they had to work, in return for food, pocket money, and "instruction in tropical life." This apprenticeship was supposed to last for six months, after which the new arrival could set up independently. However, if he arrived with empty pockets (most did), he acquired a debt that bound him for years. To acquire land, he had to take out a further loan from a shop tied into the clan system, the only available source of credit for him. Rural shops, in turn, were short of capital and had to borrow from outsiders, so the loan passed through different hands, each of which took interest of a few percent. To plant pepper or padi, further long-term credit was needed, at an interest rate of around 30 percent. Burdened by ever mounting debt, the debtor might try to flee, but clanship was a strong lock. The system of patronage and credit pervaded all levels of society, in town and village.[15]

Dutch colonial officials were aware of the opprobrium attached to indenture and often denied practising it. Kat Angelino, one of the system's best-known apologists, repudiated any tie between "contract labour in the Indies and the obligation to work as a result of debts incurred," for although "[a]dvances may be given to workmen [...], debts bear no relation to the contract" and labourers in the East Indies were "protected against debt." However, the Coolie Ordinance issued in 1915 and modified in 1928 specified that labour agreements should mention "[t]he amount and the way of settlement of advances made." This was a clear reference to contractual debt, even though the new ordinance no longer allowed recruiters to make labourers repay "business expenditure" and said that advances should be regulated.[16] Earlier practices had been more nakedly founded in coercive debt, incurred by the receipt of earnest

[15] T'ien (1953, 63–70 and 107–118).

[16] De Kat Angelino (1931, 504, fn. 1, 567, and 596).

money[17] and the production of enforceable agreements, oral or written. Chinese recruits commonly agreed to such contracts without understanding them or under duress. Even so, any breach of the contract, even one committed out of ignorance, constituted a criminal act liable to a penal sanction.[18]

In the East Indies in the 1920s, contracts for immigrants, usually Chinese, were in theory for a maximum of thirty months and accompanied by a personal advance and funds to cover job-related costs. Contracts for non-aliens, mainly Javanese, were for a maximum of twelve months, with no advance. The official explanation for the advance was that "Orientals [i.e., Chinese] cannot be moved to emigrate" without one. The labourer was contractually obliged to work for the company that had recruited him or to which the broker had delivered him. That obligation continued until the labourer had cleared his debt, at which point he could change jobs. As long as the contract remained in force, part of his wage was docked monthly, at a rate adjusted step-wise across the number of years set by the contract, so that "after the expiry of the contract the employee is deemed debt-free." The labourer promised in the contract to pay off the debt by working the specified number of years, days, and hours, at an appropriately calibrated rate. The labourer could not abandon his employer before fulfilling his contract, except for "pressing reasons" (usually to do with family matters in China) or if his employer took pity on him, and only after paying off his debts and compensating the employer for unworked months, at the rate of f2.50 a month.[19] (Some companies allowed Huagong who found it difficult to take to life in the East Indies to leave ahead of schedule.[20]) Where a debt had not been cleared through monthly deductions, it could in theory be paid off at the end of the contract, but usually the worker was declared insolvent and forced to re-indenture.

The system of advances was, according to Bruno Lasker, "the core of the evil" of the indenture system:

> [T]he professional moneylender impoverishes the people but rarely enslaves them. The employer who makes a regular practice of giving wage advances,

[17] Breman (1989, 28).
[18] Kaur (2004, 39).
[19] Heijting (1925, 17–18 and 116).
[20] Mollema (1922, 154).

> on the other hand, often does so deliberately with the intention of sapping the independence of those who work for him, of transforming the independent worker into a cringing retainer who will do what he is told at almost any wage and under any kind of working conditions as long as he is not left to starve.

The system was discussed under the topic of debt bondage at international labour conventions throughout the 1920s and 1930s, but it was not until the late 1940s that governments began preparing practicable measures to restrict it.[21]

The rate at which a worker completed his contract depended on his physical strength and health. On average, one-year contracts were completed within eighteen months, but weaker men took two years and men who fell ill might remain under contract for up to three years.[22]

The Phasing of Indenture

The crucial difference between indenture and slavery is that whereas the slave was property, bonded for life, the indenture was bonded for a set term. Some slaves gained their freedom and some indentures remained indentured for life, as a result of their inability to pay off their debts, and indentures were often treated no less and often more brutally than slaves. However, the key distinction was that the indenture was under contract, implying legal personhood, and the date of his exit was set, though not necessarily ever reached.

In the East Indies as elsewhere, the way to exit was along a series of steps. The transition from *xinke* to *laoke* mirrored the transition under the old kongsi system from recruit to shareholder, achieved by working off one's debts.[23] Where companies boasted that their workers were debt-free, this was untrue of the *xinke*, who remained in debt until his elevation to *laoke*.[24]

[21] Lasker (1950, 126 and 165–167).

[22] "Vicious Exploitation of Coolie Laborers Charged in Mines of East Indies," *The China Press*, June 5, 1933.

[23] Heidhues (1993, 76).

[24] Heidhues (1991, 9).

During his first year, the *xinke* remained on the lowest rung of the pay-scale, a practice justified on the grounds that he was least profitable during the first months of his contract, when he was inexperienced, unacclimatised, and still to be work-hardened. The demands made on new recruits were supposedly less exacting than on old hands.[25] However, repatriated labourers interviewed in the 1960s called the first few months the worst.

The employer was keen to recoup his investment in the recruit as quickly as possible. Keeping wages low at the start of the contract, when the recruit was least equipped to stand up for himself, made sense. The hope was that the memory of the initial squeeze would fade in years two and three, when wages rose, so that the now experienced worker could be persuaded to re-engage.[26]

In the 1920s and the 1930s, the cost of recruiting and transporting a recruit from China to the East Indies was around sixty dollars, or approximately f120.[27] In the years 1918–1920, employers capped the monthly wage of "first-winter guests," i.e., *xinke* who had not completed their first 360 working days, at f5–7.5, as against f9 a month for "second-winter guests" and up to f21 for "third-winter guests," who had already worked for 8–900 days. Even assuming that a *xinke* was only half as profitable as a worker in his third year, the profit created by his underpayment in year one usually matched and even exceeded his recruitment costs. Not all employers recouped the cost of recruitment in one earmarked payment. For example, the relatively liberal and paternalistic Billiton [Belitung] Company exacted a repayment of f30, which was less than the actual cost of recruitment, put at f70–80 between 1870 and the 1910s and rising as high as f176 in 1920.[28] However, the company made up much of the shortfall by paying *xinke* just f5 a month.

Xinke were subject to special restrictions. They could not be rehired or move to a new job in their first year. Companies formed by time-expired *laoke* were forbidden to employ *xinke* "straight off the boat" or to send agents back to China to make recruits, to prevent them from freeloading on schemes set up by their Dutch competitors.

After signing off at the end of their first year, labourers were in theory free to choose a new workplace, unless still immobilised by debt. This

[25] *Gedenkboek* (1927, pt 2, 67).

[26] Vandenbosch (1931, 320).

[27] According to Heidhues (1992, 74–75), at the turn of the century the price was around $15, or f30.

[28] Mollema (1922, 154 and 165).

moment of transition, known in pre-mechanisation days as the *wandel-periode* (walking period), required extensive paperwork by the company head office. It was a moment of inspection and weeding out. On Belitung, Dutch officials spent several weeks in August visiting mines and checking miners' credentials and work-sheets and signing them on or off, as the case required. During the checking, deserters who had vanished from the records resurfaced among the *transiganten* (workers who failed to register officially) and were handed over to the police, to be employed without pay on public works.[29]

In the late 1910s, second-winter guests became eligible after working 400–500 days for a card that qualified them for a small pay rise (to f9 a month). Known as a grey card, it bore the bearer's photo and was evidence of the expiry of his contract. The bearer could use it to go back to China or to get work with another company within the same region—for example, a Bangka Huagong could work for another company on Bangka, though not yet as a free worker. Chinese employers mostly recruited only such second-winter guests.

The grey card issued to a second-winter guest was the first in a set of colour cards that governed the migrant's terms of residence. In 1917, the Dutch brought in a regulation that permitted a time-expired labourer, say a miner, who had worked for 800–900 days or three continuous years, to switch to an industry other than mining. To do so, he had to apply for a green card, which cost f2, and to register with the mining bureau. A third-winter guest could earn up to f15 a month, or—if working for a Chinese company—up to f21. But even a green card did not make the holder altogether free. For a Bangka Huagong to move to a place other than Bangka in the East Indies, he had to go one colour further. After working for five years or more, he became eligible for a yellow card, with which he could work or settle throughout the East Indies and in Singapore.[30] He could also apply to the Dutch authorities for land, and become a pepper grower, a fisherman, or a shopkeeper. But few achieved this step.[31]

[29] *Gedenkboek* (1927, pt 2, p. 74). On *transiganten*, see Mollema (1922, 172).

[30] Lu Wendi et al. (1985, 440–441), Guowuyuan ([January] 1920a, 22–24), Wu Fengbin (1988, 171–172).

[31] Yang Tongling et al. (2004, 88).

Release from Indenture

According to Dutch indenture regulations in the early 1920s, an indenture was due for release after 360 days. In reality, however, most indentures served a 2- to 3-year and in some cases a 5-year term. Some recruits were deliberately misinformed and what started out as a one-year contract turned out to be longer. Others were told, in Hong Kong, that they would become free after working for four months but ended up having to work for 360 days.[32] The 360-day rule made it hard and even impossible to complete the term of an indenture within a year, for it was incompatible with the stipulated 26-day month with the right to holidays and days off (and thus uncounted) due to illness.

The contract was tilted heavily in the employer's favour, and release from indenture was difficult to secure without fulfilling every clause of it. Workers with addictions were at the greatest disadvantage, given their ever-mounting debt. Some employers released unwilling workers,[33] and workers sometimes ran away to Chinatown. But escape was difficult, given the system of passes.

By 1931, the world economic crisis had changed the picture greatly, making an extension to the limit on indenture unnecessary from the employers' point of view. For much of the 1930s, labourers struggled to keep their jobs rather than fled them.[34] Also in 1931, the Dutch ruled that contracts (and liability to the penal sanction) should expire exactly two years after their starting dates. Again, this ruling was difficult to reconcile with other regulations, but it was compatible with the economic climate, which favoured shedding rather than retaining labour.[35]

Time-expired Huagong were free to join the teams of workers that contracted to work on small-scale projects for big companies, for example clearing jungle; to become independent farmers or fishermen; or (in the 1930s) to work in towns and cities, which were by then rapidly

[32] Guowuyuan ([January] 1920a, 14 and 21).

[33] *Gedenkboek* (1927, pt 2, 61), Mollema (1922, 154).

[34] Tian Yu (1929).

[35] Wu Fengbin (1988, 169–171), Lu Wendi et al. (1984b, 47). This is ch. 5 of *Huaqiao nianjian* (Overseas Chinese Yearbook), titled "Nanyang zhi Huagong" (Huagong in Nanyang), published in 1939 by Singapore's Huaqiao shang baoshe, 60–76, republished here with some excisions.

industrialising.[36] "Considerable numbers" went on to work as vegetable planters, sawyers, blacksmiths, shop-keepers or assistants, fish-hawkers, sampan-men, and so on.[37] The cumulative effect over several decades of their release transformed local demography. Between 1920 and 1931, 65,178 Huagong (including a small number of dependants) were freed from indenture and allowed to remain in the colony.[38]

Reindenture

A debt-free Huagong could either re-engage with his original employer, leave to work for another company in the same place, or return to China. Re-engagement was the most popular choice, especially in the early years. In 1881, between 80 and 90 percent of "good coolies" re-engaged "without any force or inducement" at the end of their first year.[39] Release from one contract therefore usually led to another, the main change being a wage rise. The worker was selling himself back into indenture, for which inducements were available. "New guests" generally looked forward to the end of their indenture, but employers put a premium on the experience and profitability of "old guests," so they tried to retain them for as long as possible by extending their contracts year by year, and in some cases for four or five years.

Reindenture led in many cases to an improvement in status and elevation, as *laoke*, to the role of senior worker or even overseer. However, Huagong who re-engaged because of continuing debt, often caused by addiction, confronted a worse fate, including the prospect of interminable labour. This was the fate of reindentured Chinese labourers on all continents.[40]

Where a Huagong had failed to meet the 360-day rule or repay his debts, the advantage lay with the employer at the time of the annual reckoning, the "big pay-day." He could be refused release and made to re-engage on less favourable terms than a debt-free worker. Such refusals led to protests and litigation. In the ten years up to 1922, more than 500

[36] Zhu Jieqin (1984, 242–243), "'Qiyue Huagong' huidao zuguo" ("'Indentured labourers' return to the motherland"), *Renmin ribao* (People's Daily), July 3, 1960.

[37] *The Deli Coolie Question* 1881–1882.

[38] Lu Wendi et al. (1984b, 248–249).

[39] *The Deli Coolie Question* 1881–1882.

[40] On reindentured labourers (*recontratados*) in Spain in the 1860s, see Balboa Navarro (2021).

workers appealed on grounds of "illegal detention" at the point of expiry of their indenture.[41]

"Head-coolies" used tricks, threats, and inducements to trap labourers into re-engagement. "It is reported," claimed one reporter, with an element of rhetorical exaggeration, "that not one in a hundred has been able to settle his debt with his employer from the first term to the day of his death."[42]

There were several ways in which the employer could ensure reengagement. The main debt comprised costs associated with the Huagong's induction and passage abroad, owed either to the company or to an intermediary acting on its behalf. This debt was substantial, but if things went to schedule, it was cleared by the wages system, which factored in its recoupment along an annually adjusted sliding scale. However, this loan or advance was not the sole source of a labourer's indebtedness. There were other ways in which administrators could add to it with incidental and optional debts, including small sums handed over in a traditional gift-bearing red envelope called a *godspenning* (earnest penny or God's silver, given to bind a contract), wrapping the intent in a veneer of piety.[43] Ponniah Arudsothy, writing about the role of the kangani as shopkeeper and moneylender in the British system, described the labourer's indebtedness to the kangani as a "variant of the indenture system," since "the debt-bondage relationship between servant and master still remained, although indirectly."[44] The same was true of Huagong debts under the Dutch. In the East Indies, however, this "indirect" indenture came on top of that incurred at the point of recruitment, i.e., of indenture in its technical sense of direct servant-master indebtedness registered in the initial contract.

Repatriates and Remigrants

Huagong who had paid off old debts and avoided new ones and saved to buy land or property in China were free to "return home in glory after becoming rich" (*ronggui guli*) and realise a central goal of Chinese native-place ideology.[45] Between 1900 and 1924, usually more Huagong

[41] Wu Fengbin (1988, 171–172), Yang Tongling et al. (2004, 88).

[42] "Vicious Exploitation of Coolie Laborers Charged in Mines of the Dutch East Indies," *The China Press*, June 5, 1933.

[43] *Gedenkboek* (1927, pt 2, 68–70).

[44] Arudsothy (1986, 75), quoted in Kaur (2004, 68).

[45] On migration and native-place sentiment, see Qin (2016).

returned to China than left. (In 1924, 129,859 returned, average for the time.)[46] In the 1930s, however, a far smaller proportion returned.[47]

From Belitung, the first group went back in 1869–1870, after which hundreds returned each year in good times—around 1,500, until the crises of the early Republic brought the number back to 974 in 1921. In 1907, the Billiton Company started up a steamer-service that took repatriates back to Hong Kong and Shantou, accompanied by European staff who helped them cash their savings. (In 1921, f386,388 was cashed, nearly f400 per employee.) The passage to China, timed to follow the annual pay-day, was advertised at "a moderate cost," though indenture agreements implied that the repatriation would be funded by the employer.[48] According to a company almanac, "veterans" returned at company cost while "volunteers" paid their own way. Other sources say that most indentures financed their own return.[49]

That some companies subsidised repatriations was presented by the companies as responsible management, but it was also self-interested. When the economy was thriving and competition for labour was fierce, the spectacle of prosperous repatriates and supportive employers was a way of encouraging others to follow suit. Employers even claimed to allow a disgruntled minority to return to China without completing their contracts, on the grounds that they were "tropics-weary."[50]

Some repatriates, having gone home and settled their affairs, perhaps by marrying and investing the wealth acquired abroad, later returned to the East Indies, bringing new recruits. These returners, known to planters as "volunteers" (*vrijwilligers*),[51] were prized acquisitions, not just because of the recruits they brought in tow but because they knew the ropes and were more useful than men at the start of their indenture. By successfully completing their contract and paying off their debt, they had shown their mettle. They were also less easy to manipulate. But even a time-expired and debt-free labourer might land up back in indenture, for he would get

[46] Lu Wendi et al. (1981, 543).
[47] Lu Wendi et al. (1984b, 303).
[48] Mollema (1922, 156–157).
[49] Lu Wendi et al. (1984b, 292), *Gedenkboek* (1927, pt 2, 84).
[50] *Gedenkboek* (1927, pt 2, 84).
[51] Mollema (1922, 154–155).

an advance of $10 plus smaller advances at Chinese New Year and on festival days and to cover his expenses.[52]

Some unemployed contract workers were returned to China against their will. In Hong Kong, charitable institutions like the Tongwah Hospital intervened where possible to receive them and transfer them to the countryside. Others stayed in the ports, where they remained destitute or joined Huagong gangs.[53]

The fate of Chinese deported from Bangka and Belitung is often a mystery. Two instances from 1940 suggest that the Dutch were indifferent to what might happen to those sent back through the Japanese naval blockade of China, apparently as part of an experiment designed to test the blockade. Some landed in Hong Kong, others went on to Xiamen and nothing more was heard of them. Some deported on board a ship sunk by a Japanese patrol escaped with nothing but their lives and received a severe beating from their captors.[54]

Sources of Debt

Labourers accumulated debts by buying food and provisions, first in the dockland shops while awaiting embarkation and later in on-site stores at the destination; and by smoking opium, drinking alcohol, and gambling. Other sources of debt included remittance (organised by the company or remittance shops) and prostitution.

Shops and canteens run by Chinese associations in the ports sold new recruits tropical clothing and work equipment, at inflated prices. The owners were vendors of labour as well as provisioners, so the customer was also the commodity. Shop-owners fed and accommodated Huagong at a cost that they recouped by selling them to employers. Many siphoned off the advance due to the worker, who could leave with a debt of fl0 and even fl00 "without having seen a cent of it." Because of this, the shop-owners were known as people sellers.[55] The Dutch claimed that recruitment in China had been reformed and was subject to "sharp controls, so

[52] *The Deli Coolie Question* 1881–1882, paragraphs 21–27 of the Report of the Chinese Protectorate, Singapore and Penang, for 1881, signed by W. A. Pickering, Esq., Protector of Chinese, S. S., with Statement of Labour Contracts in Singapore, appended.

[53] [HK] Administrative Reports for the Year 1931.

[54] Alg. Secretarie etc. File 10396, 1939–1940.

[55] "De panglongs," *Bataviaasch nieuwsblad*, November 1, 1927.

that the newcomers on their journey hither thrive and are not cheated by boarding-masters and wharf sharks."[56] The evidence suggests differently.

At the destination, shops run by the company or its Chinese manager and his family (typically his wife) sold practically everything a labourer might require, on credit. In 1905, pork (to supplement the products of the company kitchen) and clothes were 30–50 percent dearer than in the towns. The rate of interest on debts in 1905 was as high as 50 percent. By the mid 1930s, however, it was nine cents for every f2.50 owed, while money deposited by Huagong earned interest of 3 percent a month.[57] For obvious reasons, Huagong were most vulnerable in remote locations. Shopowners' accomplices in the company made unwarranted deductions from the wages of labourers who refused to frequent the shops and charged them for food whether or not they ate it.[58]

The same system was practised in the Netherlands, where it was known as *gedwongen winkelnering* (forced shopping), a variant on the truck system used in Britain in the early years of the Industrial Revolution. It was unpopular and led to rolling strikes before its abolition in 1909, but it survived, together with its name, in the East Indies.[59]

Opium was a major part of Huagong life. The Netherlands ran a highly profitable opium monopoly (the *opiumregie*) on the importation, production, and sale of opiates[60] in the East Indies and resisted the efforts of prohibitionist countries like China and the United States to restrict opium consumption. The Dutch in the East Indies introduced their monopoly in 1894 and by 1921 had extended it across the colony. Ostensibly aimed at cutting consumption, a goal consonant with the purpose of the International Opium Commission (founded in 1909), the *opiumregie* was in fact a welcome windfall.[61] It even became a department of the colony's Ministry of Finance. Proportionate to their numbers, Chinese were the biggest consumers—in 1927, 83,242 of the 177,122 known addicts were Chinese. Between 1900 and the Japanese invasion, the Dutch earned fl–1.5 billion (at current value) from the trade.[62]

[56] Mollema (1922, 166).

[57] Rapport (1905, 10), "Vicious Exploitation of Coolie Laborers Charged in Mines of East Indies," *The China Press*, June 5, 1933.

[58] Yang Tongling et al. (2004, 88).

[59] Baay (2015, 237).

[60] Van Luijk and Van Ours (1993).

[61] Chandra (2000).

[62] Derks (2012, 319–341).

On Belitung, the Dutch claimed to have worked hard to eradicate opium use and an almanac published in 1927 asserted that opium "had no disastrous consequences for Billiton's Chinese miners" and that 99 percent of "regular workers" did not use it.[63] In reality, the Billiton Company, like the colonial state, earned royally from the drug, as holder of the opium lease, and Chinese addicts were described by the French doctor Georges Thibout (writing in 1912) as slaves to labour and opium.[64]

On Bangka in 1923, at least 10 percent of *laoke* were users. Users were not recruited after 1919, on government orders, but veteran miners included 1,800 addicts, retained as an indispensable part of the experienced workforce, despite a pledge to restrict opium use whatever the cost.[65]

The scholar Ta Chen (Chen Da), one of China's first sociologists, visited Bangka in the 1930s and described a group of elderly men:

> They had lived here for ten to thirty years. Most of them were over fifty-five years old. From a conversation with 31 of them, it appeared that of this number two had visited China twice since they first left it, seven once, and the other twenty-two not at all. They seemed to assent to the explanation given by one of them: "We have no money. Our wages are small; and gambling and opium smoking have taken the little we could save from these small earnings."[66]

Worldwide efforts after the founding of the League of Nations to ban opium did not prevent it continuing to be sold officially in the East Indies, where 30 percent of Chinese miners smoked it after 1904 and the average Huagong spent one third of his income on it, accruing debts to his employers that grew at 5 percent a month. Addiction was hard to avoid in the closed Huagong communities, where smoking opium (like drinking alcohol, gambling, and using prostitutes) was often *de rigueur*.[67]

Dutch commentators explained opium use as a necessary incentive for "Orientals" in the absence of supposedly more typical spurs to industry—primarily, the family. Only opium, it was said, could drive the Chinese to

[63] *Gedenkboek* (1927, pt 2, 56). The source conceded, however, that in 1915–1916, 36.4 percent of langkongs were users. Mollema (1922, 168), made a similar claim.

[64] Derks (2012, 303–305).

[65] Alg. Sec, Grote bundel, TZG Agenda 7577, Dienst der Opiumregie, November 3, 1923.

[66] Chen (1940, 189–190).

[67] Wu Fengbin (1988, 173–174), Lasker (1950, 129).

work long hard hours.[68] However, poverty and exclusion were a more obvious explanation for addiction, which was most acute among *xinke* and the "free" workers employed by Chinese bosses. Both groups lived in greater insecurity than *laoke*.[69] In 1918, the Opium Directorate reported the receipt of f9.4 million from opium sales on the East Coast of Sumatra, almost exclusively to Chinese, a rise of 8.8 percent on 1917. An ethnic Chinese on the Volksraad calculated that the entire income of Chinese, except for that used to buy bare necessities or remitted, went on opium and ended up in the treasury.[70] Many Chinese miners and plantation workers were "in the end unable to work without the goad of opium, or even with it, [...] and likely to die by the roadside."[71]

Huagong with addictions could earn a higher than average monthly wage (up to f30) and received special inducements. Chinese officials inspecting Bangka and Belitung in 1922 were puzzled by this, given the debilitating effect of opium, and concluded that lower-level managers saw addicts as easier to push around. Addicts were also more vulnerable to petty exploitation, for while the profits that derived directly from production were the company's, profits from addictions often went to on-site managers or their wives.[72]

So the interests of the big companies did not always coincide with those of their underlings, at a time when reformers were keen to clean up the colonies. For many years, the Billiton Company tried to reduce the power of the opium monopolists and moneylenders who were behind the credit system that had many Huagong in its grip. It finally managed to introduce its own *opiumregie* in 1907, but in 1922 it had still not managed to stop the sale.[73]

Some companies embraced the power of opium to subdue the workforce. Edward Alexander Powell, a one-time American consular official, explained that employers chained labourers to the plantations by providing advances that were spent on food, medical attendance, and above all

[68] *Het Nieuws van den Dag voor Nederlandsch-Indië*, September 13, 1922.

[69] Heidhues (1991, 9).

[70] "Het Chineesche koelievraagstuk in Deli," *De Sumatra Post*, December 4, 1919.

[71] "De opum-kwestie ter Oostkust van Sumatra," *Het Nieuws van den Dag voor Nederlandsch-Indië*, March 17, 1920. But the author argued against a ban, to avoid loss to the treasury and unrest among users.

[72] Lu Wendi et al. (1985, 440–441), Wu Fengbin (1988, 171–172), Guowuyuan [January] (1920a, 24), Lu Wendi et al. (1984b, 289).

[73] Mollema (1922, 166–168).

opium at the plantation store. He quoted a letter from the former Assistant Protector of Labour of British North Borneo:

> One sees a large number of healthy, able-bodied Chinese coming into the country as laborers and, at the end of a year or two, instead of going back to their homes with money in their pockets and healthy with outdoor work, they go back as broken beggars, pitifully saturated with disease or confirmed drug fiends. It is really sad to see some of them return home after a struggle of four or five years to save money—a struggle not only against themselves and their acquired opium habit, but against the numerous parasites which always fatten on laborers.[74]

Gambling was the other main source of indebtedness. The colonial administration tried to curtail gambling, but it was thwarted not just by the gamblers but by the interests that profited from their addiction. These included the government itself, for which gambling was a major revenue source.[75] On the plantations, gambling was particularly rife during the barn period, before re-engagement, when labourers treated the crop in the fermentation barns. Chinese supervisors bought the right to the gambling premises and took a 10 percent cut of stakes, while lending to the gamblers. Some employers also gave out loans to get borrowers to re-engage. Gambling was, said Ta Chen, "a device often deliberately used to prevent the wage-earners from leaving their employment to improve their lot."

Reforming gambling was difficult if not impossible. In 1918, one company sacked its supervisor and distributed gambling profits among the gamblers, but it was unable to control the workforce without the supervisor and had to re-engage him.[76] Other efforts to confine gambling to licensed sheds simply drove it underground.[77] According to Ta Chen, gambling on Bangka "carried on freely during the intermission between shifts, in other off hours, and on holidays."[78] The head tandils were among Medan's most inveterate gamblers, waging stakes of up to f3–4,000.[79]

[74] Powell (1921, 63–65).

[75] The same was true of British Malaya and the Straits Settlements, where Chinese gaming houses survived for more than a century despite attempts as early as 1805 to suppress them (Lasker 1950, 148–149).

[76] Heijting (1925, 100–101).

[77] Mededeling no. 20, Deli Planters (1929, 10).

[78] Chen (1940, 189–190).

[79] De Bruin (1918, 88).

Gambling remained a major industry among Huagong and happened even on working days, despite bans. It even spread to Sumatrans and Javanese, to the frustration of kampung heads.[80]

Huagong at Work

Huagong worked in many fields, ranging from large-scale industrial enterprises in urban areas and rural plantations to handicrafts and market gardening. However, they were best known, until the 1930s, as miners, "field coolies," and jungle loggers. The different ways in which Huagong labour was organised on the estates and in the mines and panglongs are described in Appendices A and B. The following account of Huagong labour on Sumatra (including Bangka and Belitung) draws on reports by Dutch and Chinese officials, supplemented by secondary studies.

Huagong pay varied from place to place, job to job, and year to year and according to seniority and length of service. In 1881, according to tobacco planters, labourers were credited on average with $78 for the 18,000 trees they planted during their 8 to 9 months in the field, plus one cent per ten bundles of leaves removed to the fermentation shed and 0.4 cents per bundle of sorted leaves, yielding an average yearly wage of $100 to $110. However, this sum fell after the deduction of advances, to between $7 and $17 for a *xinke* and from $22 to $32 for a *laoke*, though balances of $50 to $60 were possible.[81] In 1905, a *xinke* on Belitung in his first year carried an average debt of f51.20, including advances, cost of passage (f30.60), a f2 registration fee, a holiday advance, and barbers' fees. Few were in a position to pay off their debts at the end of the first year from their annual wage of f60 (12 × f5). If for whatever reason they had worked fewer than 26 days a month, they could expect extra charges for food on days not worked, at the rate of 15 or 25 cents a day, pushing repayment even further into the future.

"Volunteers," time-expired *laoke* recruited on the spot at no extra cost rather than imported, were contracted to work for a year at f7 a month plus board. As "casual" labourers (langkoengs), they could become

[80] Alg. Sec, Grote bundel, TZG Agenda 7077, report of Adjunct-Inspecteur van den Arbeid A. H. N. Kruisboom, June 23, 1918.

[81] *The Deli Coolie Question* 1881–1882.

shareholders in a numpang, which gained them privileges. Especially capable and reputable langkoengs could earn f15 a month.[82]

On Belitung, mining numpangs began recruiting in May, under leaders chosen in consultation with senior mine managers. Their activities were regulated by the foreman. Each miner received an advance of f10 at the start of the numpang year, of which f5 were sent back to China while the rest was used to meet numpang costs, including accommodation and the interest paid to kongsi shareholders (at a rate of 4–8 percent of yield). Where output was low because of poor terrain, shareholders were compensated with a "gratification" payment of f25. Other payments went to the team leader, the team clerk (in charge of accounts), the cook, the pig rearer, the vegetable farmer, etc.

The administration and organisation of labour in mining, planting, and logging had much in common, but each industry had unique features. Chinese mining communities were more solidary and compact, with a tradition of self-organisation the collective memory of which persisted even into the 1920s. On the plantations, life was shaped by the rhythm of the harvest. The panglongs, even more remote from society than the mines and estates and therefore invisible, were especially vulnerable to abuse.

The mining communities had a longer history than the plantation workers and were ethnically more uniform and less likely to employ Javanese. On the plantations, Javanese women often worked together with Chinese men. The miners were generally fitter and stronger than the plantation labourers, who in some cases had been rejected as miners during the selection process in the East Indies.

In the 1930s, the demographic balance between Chinese and Javanese shifted even more completely than in the past towards the latter, especially on the plantations. This trend was speeded by the imposition on new Chinese recruits of a landing fee of f150. By 1937, the Deli plantations employed just 12,000 Huagong, as against 200,000 Javanese.[83]

This section ends with a fragmentary statistical overview of the Huagong presence in mining and planting in Sumatra and on Bangka and Belitung in the early twentieth century, in particular after the abolition of indenture elsewhere.

[82] Rapport (1905, 1–2). For numpang, see Chap. 2.
[83] "Het ronselen," *Soerabaijasch Handelsblad*, February 13, 1937.

Table 6.1 Chinese miners on Bangka, 1910–1918

1911	21,292
1912	22,296
1913	21,436
1914	21,406
1915	19,050
1916	19,628
1917	18,910
1918	18,658

Source: Wu Fengbin (1988, 147–148)

Table 6.2 Chinese miners on Bangka, 1929–1932

	Total indentured	*Died*	*Unfit for work*	*Deserted*	*Deported or expelled*	*Automatically completed contract*	*Persecuted*	*Percentage persecuted*
1929	15,782	87	124	303	91	106	1,693	10.73
1930	15,089	87	154	220	385	161	1,922	12.74
1931	11,023	75	135	110	238	192	1,641	14.88
1932	5,537	36	63	67	117	1,004	1,856	33.34

Source: Wu Fengbin (1988, 166)

Table 6.1 shows the number of Chinese miners on Bangka in the 1910s. They were distributed across an average of 350 mining sites, indicating an average of around 60 miners per site. Table 6.2 gives the number of miners on Bangka in the Depression, with statistics regarding their mortality, fitness, and treatment, including abuse. Wu Fengbin notes that the Dutch had various tactics to apply where necessary against dissidents: declare them unfit, expel them, "persecute" them, etc. He also points out that the charge of "desertion" often covered up abuse, and that "completion of contract" could be a way of expelling undesirables or supernumeraries—which would explain why "completions" rocketed in 1932, during the economic crisis, when nearly one in five Huagong "automatically completed" his contract and one in three claimed to have been "persecuted." Table 6.3 shows changes in the Chinese workforce on Belitung between 1914 and 1925.

Table 6.3 Chinese miners on Belitung, 1914–1925

	Average strength	*Went private*	*Evacuated to Hong Kong*	*Removed to Singapore*	*Repatriated*	*Died in the mines*	*Died in hospital*
1914	16,139	51	243	53	1773	73	112
1915	14,212	400	253	71	1299	69	66
1916	15,828	123	153	121	1513	34	79
1917	16,103	361	179	150	1963	37	86
1918	16.075	179	126	147	1305	76	118
1919	19,548	254	352	148	1859	51	178
1920	20,865	237	300	113	2355	74	135
1921	20,375	702	351	235	1522	46	90
1922	17,541	585	432	236	1385	37	59
1923	17,370	283	165	142	1576	38	46
1924/1925	16,146	266	268	131	1133	37	58

Source: *Gedenkboek* (1927, pt 2, 86)

Table 6.4 shows the number of contract workers and "day coolies" on the plantations on Sumatra's East Coast between 1892 and 1922. It reveals the switch from a majority-Chinese to an overwhelmingly Javanese workforce. The total number of Chinese on the East Coast far exceeded that in the categories listed in these tables. In 1916, for example, they were said to number 160,000. [84]

Few Huagong worked in Deli before the rise of tobacco farming in the late nineteenth century, which brought in hundreds of thousands of labourers including tens of thousands of Chinese, "frugal, physically strong, and able to see beyond tomorrow" and for whom "tobacco is the culture par excellence," in one Dutch opinion. In 1915, 37,608 Huagong worked on the Deli plantations. Thousands more worked in trade and crafts and 4,000 in the Deli sawmills and the charcoal furnaces and as fishermen. By 1918, 99,236 Chinese were employed on the East Coast of Sumatra, nearly all of them men.[85] In 1932, 170,000 Chinese worked in Deli (cf. more than 300,000 Javanese), almost all of them indentured.[86]

[84] *Deli Courant,* April 5, 1916, cited in De Bruin (1918, 91).
[85] De Bruin (1918, 1–3).
[86] Deli Planters (1929, 6–7).

Table 6.4 Contract workers and "day coolies" on Sumatra's East Coast, 1892–1922

	Chinese	*Javanese*
1892	39,963	9,708
1893	41,051	10,467
1894	42,876	10,467
1895	48,204	15,168
1896	48,548	17,081
1897	49,827	18,729
1898	50,846	22,256
1899	55,762	26,487
1900	59,038	29,802
1901	54,482	28,863
1902	56,287	33,823
1903	58,066	34,572
1904	54,281	33,490
1905	49,664	27,452
1906	63,105	27,917
1907	51,418	41.065
1908	54,902	57,230
1909	51,458	46,189
1912	50,975	58,529
1913	57,842	60,633
1914	28,168	86,652
1915	26,946	84,084
1916	42,518	114,952
1917	38,784	134,453
1919	13,338	74,118
1921	28,714	177,722
1922	27,400	113,640

Source: Heijting (1925, 106)

Payment

When tin-mining first started on a large scale on Bangka in the early eighteenth century, under the kongsi and the Sultan of Palembang, the tin was purchased (at $6 a picul) and the miners were paid by tekos, a local rendering of the Chinese *taikong*,[87] intermediaries or brokers. The tekos financed the entire process, from clearing the land to acquiring tools and building the smelt ovens. Two thirds of the payment came as food and provisions and the remaining third as tin coins, called pitis, which each teko produced for his own district, beyond which they had no validity. For the miner, this was a way of saving for remittance to China. For the teko,

[87] Also rendered taykong, tauke, etc.

who set the rates of exchange, always to the workers' disadvantage, it represented an interest-free loan. Inscriptions on the coins were linked to the secret societies imported from China, which dominated miners' social life. Many of the shops used such privately minted estate- or shop-money and gave change in it. In 1907, after the birth of the Inspectorate, there were calls for the system to be banned, but it took years to eradicate.[88]

By the start of the 1920s, the mining industry on Bangka and Belitung was in full swing and on the point of mechanisation, which transformed the relationship between capital and labour. The payment system worked differently on each island, as did methods of remuneration.

On Bangka, payment was according to performance. A Chinese foreman in charge of four hundred miners received f300 a month, his deputy f150, and his secretary, accountant, and general-affairs clerk f60, with other grades receiving f30. Labourers were paid directly by the Dutch management, under a day-work system.[89] A *xinke* received f6.24 a month for the first six months of his employment and f9.36 for the second. The book-keeper and the secretary received f30–60 a month, the ganger f150, and the big boss f300 guilders. To put this income into perspective, at the time one pound of pork cost f0.6–0.8, one pound [*sic*] of alcohol f0.12–0.18, and a set of clothes f3–5. By this reckoning, a worker in 1919 received too little in the first six months and just enough in the second.[90]

On Belitung, miners and company were initially, in the nineteenth century, independent of one another. The miners worked on their own account, with technical help from the European management where necessary, and built their own accommodation, water systems, gardens, etc. This system evolved between 1885 and the turn of the century, after a number of lean years, into a more recognisably capitalist enterprise, though it retained vestiges of the old system.[91]

Miners in their first year on Belitung received f5 a month, but in their second they became shareholders of a numpang, on a collectively agreed income adjusted through a system of debits and credits to the days each member worked. The numpang took its decisions at a general assembly. Only the mine head and his clerk were paid by the kongsi (in effect, the company). They too were registered as miners and given the same pay and advances but with perks of between f150 and f250 a year.[92] The assembly

[88] Heijting (1925, 79–94). On the coins, see Wazar (1956, 209–11).
[89] Lu Wendi et al. (1985, 405–409).
[90] Lu Wendi et al. (1985, 392), Guowuyuan [May], eds, 58–61; Wu Fengbin (1988, 168).
[91] Mollema (1922, 159–162).
[92] For an idealised Dutch description of the *numpak*, see *Gedenkboek* (1927, pt 2, 68–70).

set the conditions under which administrative staff were employed. The latter included the team head, clerk, cook, vegetable grower, and pig-keeper. The numpang sold tin to the company at f20 per picul—unlike the Bangka miners, who sold their labour power. Payment happened according a quantum (i.e., piecework) system, whereby a team received a profit-share if its output rose above a quota set on the basis of the estimated yield. When the quantum was not met, a wage was paid according to a default agreement, as a fall-back. The quantum system was known as *maobaogong*.[93] A subsidy was available for sites poorer in tin, to make mining it worthwhile. The scheme was said to be generous—even the least productive miner received a bonus. As we have seen, the numpang also paid a percentage of its yield to non-working or retired shareholders. The numpang could impose fines on members who undermined group discipline.[94]

The mines were administered at lower levels by experienced miners. When problems arose that could not be resolved independently, European managers were drawn in. The Chinese supervisors contracted wage levels with the labourers, on condition that the wage did not drop below the company minimum. They paid out the monthly, occasional, and festive advances specified by the contract, handled local recruitment, and provided food and gear.

In the early 1920s, numpangs employed more than half the workforce on Belitung—7,971 out of a total of 11,821 workers. The rest worked on their own account and were paid monthly. Numpang members received a share of the balance left over in the annual account, paid out at the end of the working year in late May. Officials, workshop employees, and other categories were also paid monthly, while day-workers (langkoengs) were paid by the job (unless it lasted longer than a month). A plethora of minor teams were paid by the year and settled accounts among themselves. The annual payment system formed the basis for a complex mapping of Belitung into districts and sub-districts, each with its own Malay and Chinese name and a number and separated from the rest by a watershed or artificial line.[95]

The Labour Inspectorate favoured the Belitung system, which paid and treated its miners better than on Bangka. The miners' housing on Belitung was said to be superior to that even of the *veldpolitie* (field police).

[93] I could not find the word *maobao* in any dictionary or source. Could it be a transliteration of Dutch *mijnbouw*, "mining"?

[94] Lu Wendi et al. (1985, 433–434), Rapport (1905, 7–9).

[95] Mollema (1922, 157–159).

Recruitment for Belitung in China benefited from Belitung's good name, while Bangka's suffered.[96]

The switch to a quantum system diminished the power of the Chinese mine-heads and increased that of the Dutch management. It began in 1904, when falling profits and the effects of the depreciation of the dollar on the Chinese domestic economy necessitated an intervention by managers in the system of remuneration and a rise in miners' pay. This led in 1910–1911 to a more complete introduction of the quantum calculation and the "dawning of the age of technology," which reduced the mine heads' independence and began to put an end to the old way of working. Younger and stronger miners welcomed the change. The proportion of shifts that failed to achieve the quantum was usually small.[97]

But the piecework system was disastrous for many. Reports by Chinese envoys described the sufferings of weaker men working in the mines alongside hardened veterans. A Jiangxi scholar tricked into indenture drowned himself in a river. A Hunan teacher wrote four valedictory poems before hanging himself. A disillusioned recruit fled into the jungle but was captured and died from a beating.[98]

In 1922, miners on Bangka received 50 percent less than on Belitung for the same work. To make up the shortfall, Banka Tinwinning announced a quantum scheme of its own, presented as a first step towards the abolition (thought at the time to be in the offing) of the penal sanction. However, the Bangka quantum scheme failed, for reasons not entirely clear—perhaps because it applied only to *laoke* who went to Bangka on their own account and not to those brought in by the company.[99] The imminence of mechanisation, which happened to the detriment of the numpangs, played a role, as we shall see.

Mining

Each of the mines that comprised a company was divided into executive, administrative, and mechanical sections, all of which came under the direction of the mine head and the supervision of company officials. The mine head was assisted by a deputy.

[96] "In de Billitonsche Mijnen. I. Arbeidsvoorwaarden.—Singkeh en Laukeh," *Bataviaasch Nieuwsblad*, Batavia, September 26, 1928.

[97] Mollema (1922, 163).

[98] Yang Tongling et al. (2004, 85).

[99] "Tweede Blad. Het winst-aandeel-systeem," *Het Nieuws van den Dag voor Nederlandsch-Indië*, Batavia, September 13, 1922.

The first layer centred on a "big foreman" assisted by staff designated as number two, three, four, etc., who had direct charge of the workers. The secretary was in charge of book-keeping. The general-affairs administrator was in charge of brewing alcohol, collecting firewood, making baskets (for removing earth), pig-rearing, and vegetable-growing.

The second layer supervised the workforce (mainly *xinke*) at pit level, according to a piecework or day-work system. *Laoke* foremen organised the extraction and separation of the ore and its transportation and stacking, as well as building and maintaining water systems and timber supports, clearing grass and reeds from the mine pools, preventing illegal encroachments, and entering the jungle to gather fuel for the pit railway.

The third layer (mainly *laoke*) handled pit machinery, as we have seen.[100]

At the start of the twentieth century, a ten-hour day was standard, with reveille at 5 am and a 6 am start and 6 pm finish, interrupted by meal and rest breaks when the labourers dozed in hammocks. In the early 1920s, the working day was shortened by an hour. Labourers got two days a month off but on different days from one another, so the mine was never still. Each year there were fifteen festivals when work stopped. Workers who missed a day or half a day had to register their absence on a board, to avoid a fine.[101]

Until the 1930s, when they shifted in large numbers to factory work, Huagong in the East Indies were associated mainly with mining and field labour. In time, plantation labourers came to predominate, but historically Huagong were associated more with mining, which they virtually monopolised on the tin islands, although mining was also an indigenous industry in the archipelago. As we have seen, mining was the first and for a long time practically the only job that Huagong did in the East Indies, starting at the latest in the eighteenth century, when they imported Chinese technologies to Borneo and Sumatra. They continued to play a role in it right through until the end of Dutch rule and beyond. Mining had of course been going on for centuries in China, unlike industrial planting, and was more lucrative than planting.

The Chinese imported not just technologies but the kongsi, territorial partnerships in the form of self-governing armed corporations that originated in frontier regions of south China, described in Chap. 3. These corporations, based on pooled capital, shared profits among men of common geographic provenance and were associated by Dutch observers with

[100] The charts on which this section is based can be found in Lu Wendi et al. (1985, 406–408).

[101] Rapport (1905, 7–8), Mollema (1922, 179).

the idea of primitive democracy, although they were dominated by local Chinese strongmen. In Kalimantan in Borneo in the eighteenth century, strings of kongsi banded together in mutual defence in confederations up to 20,000-strong.[102] The kongsi institution spread to Belitung, where Europeans set up tin mines in 1860. However, the kongsis on the tin islands never achieved the same power and scale as in Kalimantan. Each came in time to be associated with a single boss, known to non-Chinese as the Congsee.

The decline and demise of the kongsi started in the late nineteenth century. On Belitung, its last stronghold in the East Indies, there were already five times as many kiauwkoengs (day labourers) as sinhoens (kongsi shareholders) in one mine in 1875.[103]

However, associations with kongsi features continued to operate well into the twentieth century, with the toleration of the Dutch. On Bangka up until the mid-nineteenth century, the kongsi served as a collective unit through which mining was organised by Chinese (with Europeans providing capital and markets), although it lost its territorial authority during the brief period of British rule (1811–1815), after which European administrators replaced the kongsi heads. Under the Dutch, large-scale mining on Bangka was organised as a state enterprise. The kongsis were co-opted into the administration and polarised into a collaborating elite and the mass of members. Heidhues wrote that even before the end of the nineteenth century kongsis

> had little in common with the ideal of cooperative endeavour and democratic control. Instead, it was a means to control labour and to bring the greatest profits for the mine owners and for the tin company—in this case [on Bangka,] the colonial government.[104]

Even more extreme was the degeneration of the kongsi in Sumatra's timber industry, which gained a particularly shocking reputation for abuse and where kongsis survived in name only and exhibited none of their once-prized spirit. Only the *hui* (secret societies), also described in Chap. 3, preserved some of the collectivist tradition.

[102] Kuhn (2008, 46 and 84–85).
[103] *Gedenkboek* (1927, pt 2, 86–87).
[104] Heidhues (1992, 18–54 and 76).

On Belitung, mining was in private rather than state hands. Dutch private companies developed mining on government contracts of 25–35 years, with three eighths of the profit going to the state. The mines were highly profitable. Annual tin production, estimated at more than 80,000 *dan* a year, yielded an annual income of fl6 million, which after the subtraction of fl0 million costs left a profit of f6 million.[105] Although elements of Chinese self-organisation were successfully adapted to the Dutch system on Belitung, the kongsi remained, essentially, an "expedient" of the Billiton Company, run by a tiny minority of shareholders and used to "organize, discipline, and pay the workers and to handle dealings with the Company." However, the idea of common risk and cooperation survived in the numpang team, a constituent of the broader kongsi, which assigned it to a designated site in the mining concession and provisioned it. The numpang divided profits among working shareholders and attended to workers' welfare, and was "Belitung's version of a kongsi." In 1905, all miners on Belitung except newcomers and casual labourers were shareholders in a numpang and received a share of takings. Towards the end of the colonial period, some features of the Belitung model were transplanted onto Bangka.[106]

Observers distinguished between Huagong in Deli and Bangka and those on Belitung.[107] The Huagong on Belitung were less "crude" than in Deli and more peaceable than on Bangka. The Belitung mine chiefs congratulated themselves on recruiting amenable peasants rather than the "scum of the cities." "The characteristic frankness of the Chinese and the benevolence of the European staff have," claimed the company, "created a pleasing relationship."[108] Employers in Deli and Bangka were urged to copy Belitung, particularly its recruitment, which usually happened through *laoke*. The other big difference was that whereas on Bangka the miner was a wage worker, on Belitung he was a numpang shareholder, so

[105] Lu Wendi et al. (1985, 428).

[106] Heidhues (1991, 4–5, and 1992, 79 and 105), Rapport (1905, 7).

[107] For an even more dramatic contrast, see Erwiza Erman's study on the Ombilin coalmines (which included a few Chinese miners) in West Sumatra, characterised by an insecurity "attributable to the culture of violence embedded in and internalized among the forced labourers, most of them political prisoners and criminals" (Erman 2017, 516–517, drawing on Erman 1999).

[108] Mollema (1922, 152).

the employer was more attentive to his grievances.[109] Many Dutch, however, despised the miners as "uncivilized."[110]

In the 1920s, the numpangs on Belitung were still component parts of a kongsi. Mine heads and numpang heads were responsible for running mines and had police powers across the entire district of their placement, like a kampung (village) head. Most were Peranakans,[111] found by the Dutch to be "more civilised."[112] At lower levels, the numpang ran the mine administration, headed by men "chosen for their excellent qualities." Numpang heads received shares from the company and supervised team accounts.

The terms used to describe mine administrators and employees on Bangka and Belitung were carried over into the twentieth centuries from the earlier period in which kongsis had run their own affairs. Although power relations within the kongsi changed after the consolidation of the Dutch administration, names remained much the same as those described by Cornelis de Groot in 1887.

The early kongsi chose the mine head at a general assembly, to serve for a year—although in later times the assembly lost its power and the mine head answered to the higher administration. The cashier or book-keeper, also initially responsible to the assembly, kept the books, oversaw provisions, and had clerks (*mijnschrijvers*) render the Chinese record into Malay, so that senior administrators could read it. Clerks recorded expenditure and advances in their numpang books and the cashier recorded the information in the company issuance book. The cashier also kept books relating to local traders, for although the company delivered the major items, smaller items (clothes, shoes, tea, spices, etc.) were bought locally, on credit. Together, these two men led the mine, in consultation with shareholders. The authorities on Bangka and Belitung left kongsis to their own devices in many regards, except for financial accounting. The kongsi appointed a vegetable farmer, a swineherd, a cook, a brewer, and a basket maker, to victual and equip the mine, also on an annual basis. Foremen were appointed where the kongsi was sufficiently big, also for a year. In small mines, the vegetable farmer, cook, and swineherd were the same

[109] Rapport (1905, 13).

[110] Paulus (1919, 161).

[111] Rapport (1905, 11).

[112] Heidhues (1992, 119), says that in 1915 nearly all mine-heads were local born Peranakans.

person. In big mines, the cashier was exempt from labour, while the mine head and other officials were exempt where possible.[113]

The shareholders of an old-style kongsi had either themselves been miners or had hired a labourer to work on their own behalf. It was generally thought that it was best for shareholders to work, to prevent the degeneration of the kongsi, but kongsis often gave in to pressure from local Chinese traders, officials, opium sellers, etc. who wanted to be non-labouring shareholders. These new shareholders provisioned the mine and became its creditors, so that free miners were wary of becoming shareholders and inheriting the debt.[114]

Even after the demise of the kongsi as an independent institution, the administration remained much the same, in Deli and on the tin islands, with similar staff similarly named. On Bangka, the Tinwinning corporation had offices in several towns, each staffed by an *opziender* (inspector) and a mandur. At first, the offices were run by Europeans, but in later years there were too few Europeans to do the work so many of the mandurs were Peranakans.[115] Each handled two to three mines.[116] Each office had several hundred armed police on call, to crack down on the Huagong if the need arose. Mines were divided by the value of their output into big, small, tiny, and partnership-operated. By the end of the nineteenth century, each mine had acquired a number.

In later times, mine leaders were experienced workers selected and paid by the Dutch, and supported by a Number One and sometimes a Number Two, several section leaders, and a mechanic to look after the machines. A section leader was in charge of 30 to 40 workers and responsible for checking output and quotas. The cashier delivered accounts to the Peranakan administrators, with whom he was in regular touch.

Breman describes these people as an "intermediate class, made up of Chinese from Penang who had been educated, and of a combination of various races. […] Although downgraded and slighted, they were indispensable in the day-to-day running of the [enterprise]."[117] Dutch officials and employers worked hard to turn the clerks and overseers, especially those drawn from the "second generation" (immigrants' descendants),

[113] Yang Tongling et al. (2004, 82).

[114] De Groot (1887, 336–339).

[115] Rapport (1905, 10).

[116] For Malay mining terms and their Chinese transliteration, see Yang Tongling et al. (2004), 339.

[117] Breman (1989, 88).

into "solid Chinese," and advised that they be paid well, to prevent them from developing "conflicts of interest," i.e., siding with the workers.[118] Chinese were generally excluded from the highest ranks, because Dutch administrators knew that their white staff would resist such appointments.[119]

The numpangs kept a "big book" listing the rights and duties of its leader and workers and recording matters such as the amount of tobacco and matches each received, the value of the day tasks performed by workers and the cook, the wage for barbers and porters, and even the number of times a year the barber shaved a workers' head. (The cutting of the queue after 1911 led to adoption of a "native" style, the so-called coconut-tree crest.) The big book included a current account that each miner could consult and copy into his pocketbook. At the end of the working year, the worker received his annual wage minus small debts and advances given at festivals and New Year. The wage on the tin islands itself was not governed by the Coolie Ordinance, although the contract wage (which was lower) could be applied as a punishment.[120]

The Chinese foremen were an "indispensable link" between the European managers and employers and the miners, appointed on account of their seniority, authority, and competence. They played a bigger role in the enterprise than the European assistants who formed the bottom layer of the white administration and were for the most part unqualified, except by being white.[121] The Chinese supervisors were usually called tandils (from a Malay word borrowed from Tamil or Klingalese), or head tandils in the case of senior overseers, whereas Malays of the same rank were called mandur, rendered on Belitung and elsewhere as taikong. On Belitung, the taikong worked alongside the labourers.[122] Most overseers were seen by the workers as potential enemies and tools of the Dutch, who "used Chinese to control Chinese," although they sometimes shielded workers against the assistants.[123] According to the Sinologist De Bruin, the Chinese head tandil "has spies among the workers and knows what

[118] Arsip Nasional, TZG Agenda, file 6725, January 24, 1924, 6.

[119] TZG Agenda, file 6725, January 24, 1924.

[120] *Gedenkboek* (1927, pt 2, 69–70).

[121] Letter, *De Sumatra Post*, Medan, June 28, 1920. On the social background of the European staff, see Stoler (1985, 29).

[122] Melbourn (1894), Rapport (1905, 3).

[123] Wu Fengbin (1988, 162).

everyone is up to. He will speak the majority language of the Chinese and know all the coolies inside out."[124]

When large-scale mining first started on Bangka in the nineteenth century, operations were by hand and shovel. The mines were enclosed by trees so massive that it took several men to link arms around them. Snakes and crocodiles infested the creeks and jungle, to the miners' terror. Some of the tin ore could be easily extracted, from under a few feet of soil, but the deepest mines had to be shored up with timber to prevent them from collapsing and were accessed down a series of steps supported by planks. The miners worked at speed, under the foreman's whip. When it rained, the pits filled with water and a Chinese-style wheel was used to remove it. Accidents and broken bones were not unusual.[125]

Planting

Plantations as a form of agricultural mass production are associated in early capitalism with slavery and colonialism. They were most successful in the tropics, where harvests are not seasonally restricted and can be continuous. After the abolition of slavery, indentured labour took over as the main workforce in the plantation economy.

Up until the arrival of the Dutch on Sumatra, agriculture was by shifting cultivation, which Chinese (echoing a Dutch stereotype) dismissed as "potatoes and dry rice" and evidence of "native indolence."[126] The plantation economy in the East Indies began much later than mining and (unlike mining) had no precedents in China's migrant-sending regions.[127] However, it was not long before plantation Huagong outnumbered Huagong miners.

During the first decade of planting, the Dutch had to import labourers from China, for local people were unwilling to do such work and the British in India discouraged emigration unless a British official could supervise it. In 1888, Edward Harper Parker, an English barrister, author, and Sinologist, paid a visit to Deli and wrote a damning account:

[124] De Bruin (1918, 92–93).

[125] Wu Fengbin (1988, 157–158).

[126] Lu Wendi et al. (1985, 428).

[127] There was perhaps a marginal connection between tea plantations in China and labour networks overseas, but in the nineteenth century there was no real unfree or overseas labour even in Huizhou, known in the Ming for bonded labour. In India, however, networks of contract labour did overlap with migrant networks (Andrew Liu, p. c., via Arunabh Ghosh).

> Very few Englishmen owned tobacco-interests; the most energetic, and the least tender to the Chinese, seemed to be the Germans. I found the rules made by the authorities fairly good on paper; but on visiting the tobacco-fields, and closely enquiring from the coolies themselves, I was convinced that the majority of them were in a position little removed from virtual slavery. In the first place, they had to sign bonds to serve for a minimum time (three to five years) at fixed wages; then they had to guarantee repayment of their passage-money and outfit; every encouragement was given to them to "extend their term" and to spend as much of their money as possible in "tuck-shops," brothels, and other places provided for their recreation; the food they bought and the opium they smoked brought profit at their expense to either the administration or "the owner"; loans were offered freely; penalties for breach of discipline were heavy; and the "laws of evidence" were such that practically the white man was able to "work the case" in his own interest. Every possible obstacle which the law allowed was directly or indirectly put in the coolies' way to prevent their leaving for China with their earnings; but they were invited to send savings and to coax their relatives to come too. The influence of "smart" Chinese was used to compel the unwilling. Nearly all the coolies I saw said, on their own behalf and on that of their friends, that they would be only too glad to escape with their possessions, if they could. Of course the Dutch and German planters put a very different colour upon the story. They said (which was true) that the accommodation was good; the medical attendance adequate; food sufficient, and not excessively dear; hours reasonable; amusements and pleasures to be got for the paying; but that order and discipline had to be preserved with a strong hand. Yet, the coolies were infinitely worse off than the same Chinamen in English and French colonies. In a surreptitious way the planters hoodwinked the officials, who perhaps made little effort to be undeceived, and the whole system appeared to me [...] to be negative if not positive slavery; but still a mild slavery.[128]

By 1900, when Parker's sketch was published, conditions had improved, especially on Bangka and Belitung, where mining and planting coexisted and the plantations were smaller and more likely to be run by Chinese. Recruits rejected by the mines were sold on to planters and time-expired miners could invest in a small garden, to grow cash crops. In the early twentieth century, Bangka was a centre of the spice industry, principally white pepper, which Chinese began growing in the late nineteenth

[128] Parker (1902), excerpted in De Bruin (1918, 81–82).

century.[129] It employed 7,648 Chinese workers in 1930, when Bangka pepper was world-famous. Employees were known as Huanong, "Hua farmers," to distinguish them from Huagong. Sites worked by Huanong increased between 1910 and 1933 from 587 to 8,234 and accounted for 4,289 tons of white and 480 tons of black pepper exports in 1926, after Huanong investors started raising two harvests a years and doubled the plants per hectare.[130] Pepper became increasingly important in the 1930s, when ever greater numbers switched to planting after the collapse of tin production. By the late 1930s, Bangka had more than 5,000 unemployed Huagong. Tin production on Belitung had come almost to a standstill,[131] and Chinese mine owners on Bangka were earning more from pepper than from tin, having fended off the colonial state's attempts to appropriate its cultivation.[132] Others switched to fishing, hunting, gathering, and pig-rearing, while on Belitung some ran brickyards and lime-kilns.[133]

Bangka remained overwhelmingly undeveloped for decades. Pepper covered less than one percent of the surface in 1920. Even so, it played a major part in the economy. East Indies pepper accounted for 92 percent of world output in 1936. Plantations were opened on unowned jungle land, mostly by Chinese and natives, licensed and taxed by the Dutch. Big plantations managed tens of thousands of bushes, smaller ones thousands. Each bush was worth fl.8 a year and each worker tended a thousand bushes. The 7,000 Huanong therefore raised more than 7 million bushes costing fl2.6 million.

Half the Huagong worked as miners and half on plantations in 1920. Employment contracts were simple and limited to 360 working days. Labourers could borrow fl0 at the start of the contract and more at up to 30 percent interest. They received food and two sets of shirts and pants of coarse cloth and lived in primitive accommodation. Most plantations were within easy reach of commercial centres, along roads. The pace of work was slow, except in the high season. Wages were settled on an individual basis. Most labourers received f25 a month, never less than fl5, paid at the year's end. Special contracts applied to *laoke*, who could borrow up to f50 interest-free, and bonuses were paid to more productive workers. The

[129] Lu Wendi et al. (1985, 391)
[130] Yang Tongling et al. (2004, 93–94).
[131] Lu Wendi et al. (1984b, 259).
[132] Bosma (2019, 106).
[133] Paulus (1919, 161 and 305).

regime on the plantations was said by Chinese observers to be less harsh than in the mines. Workers were less resentful than the miners and could leave at will. The owners could, if necessary, call in troops or prosecute workers, but rarely did so.[134]

On the Deli plantations to the west, Huagong endured a stricter regime, under Western bosses. Wages were set by the planters' associations: f0.35 a day and f0.38–0.40 on a second engagement for Javanese, and f0.33–0.35 for Chinese. The Labour Inspectorate tried to restrict the planters' power, but to little effect.[135]

Tobacco farming on Sumatra started in 1869, with the founding of the Deli Company on a concession awarded by the Deli Sultanate. Javanese labour was said to be unsuitable, for the crop required careful growing of which "local people were incapable." Chinese were imported to do the work, and soon accounted for 90 percent of the tobacco workforce.[136] Only in the late 1920s did tobacco companies start employing Javanese (for the first time in sixty years) on a relatively large scale as "field coolies" in East Sumatra—in 1930, there were 5,141 Javanese compared with 21,158 Chinese; in 1931, 6,209 Javanese compared with 18,990 Chinese.[137]

Sumatran tobacco entered its heyday between 1920 and 1924. Production doubled to 18,163,714 kilos and it became a major export prized throughout the world.[138] Sumatran planters practically monopolised the import of wrapper leaf into the US, a monopoly that worked to their disadvantage during the 1930 dispute on tariffs.

Huagong tobacco-farmers were organised in groups of 30–40 under a tandil and divided into "field coolies," who were *laoke*, and "assistant coolies," *xinke* who had not yet worked off their contracts. The "field coolies" remained "at the embankment" for months on end, unlike Javanese, who returned daily to their quarters. Other Huagong known as company workers chopped down jungle and reclaimed the fields in an eight-year rotation. Experienced workers could grow 20,000 plants a year and newcomers between 5,000 and 8,000.[139] A Chinese view was that the Dutch made

[134] Guowuyuan [May] (1920b, 3–6 and 59–61), Lu Wendi et al. (1985, 392 and 425–426).
[135] "De arbeidsverhoudingen ter Oostkust," *De Sumatra Post*, Medan, July 24, 1919.
[136] MacNair (1924), *Nanyang shangbao*, February 4, 1924.
[137] Pelzer (1935, 95).
[138] Wang Linqian and Wu Kunxiang (2002, 167–168).
[139] Pelzer (1935, 94–95), *Nanyang shangbao*, February 6, 1924.

better use of Huagong labour than the British in Malaya, because of stricter labour regulations and better methods of cultivation.[140]

In Malaya, too, Huagong played a central role in the mines and on the plantations, many of them under Chinese ownership. One observer denounced the Malays as lazy and the Indians as plodding and praised the Chinese as "hard-working, enterprising, independent, economical, and resourceful," with "a perseverance and doggedness of purpose." On Sumatra, however, Huagong labour on the rubber plantations was rapidly eclipsed by cheaper Javanese, who outnumbered Huagong by 12,000 to 9,000 in 1910 and by 130,000 to 11,000 in 1919.[141]

The plantation is often pictured as uniform, centralised, and governed by a strict division of labour, an undiversified product of global capitalism lacking the variety of mining, with its deeper roots. However, specialists in it distinguish between different products and technologies and reject the lumping together of, say, tobacco plantations in the East Indies and coffee plantations in Brazil.[142]

Studies of the plantation system in the East Indies demonstrate its importation of cultural features from China. The production system on the tobacco plantations of North Sumatra was based on individual rather than on group effort and had much in common with traditional Chinese agriculture, more like gardening than farming. This horticulturist style was characteristic of Huagong tobacco farming in Deli-Medan, as the interviews in Appendix A confirm. Each "field coolie" was given responsibility at the start of the growing season for seven-tenths of a hectare that he planted, tended, and harvested. He then delivered the harvest to the fermentation barn and was paid according to the quantity and quality of his leaves.[143] Dutch planters' response to criticism of their employment system by William Pickering, the Protector of Chinese in Singapore, supports the case for a discriminating view. Pickering thought that the Dutch system encouraged abuse and recommended that it switch to a fixed monthly wage, to make relations equal and predictable. But the tobacco planters believed that a fixed wage and the "gang system" would never make a good leaf, which required the "extreme delicacy, care, attention, [and] strict

[140] *Nanyang shangbao*, March 12, 1924.

[141] Lu Wendi et al. (1984b, 256), *Tianguang bao*, April 11, 1936, Nair (1931). The Chinese Protectorate in Malaya was introduced in part because of the abuse of Huagong by Chinese employers (Lasker 1950, 148).

[142] Jackson (1969).

[143] Pelzer (1935, 95).

accuracy" only a labourer tending "the crop of tobacco grown on the ground given to him for the purpose" could deliver.[144]

Tobacco-planting in Deli and elsewhere in the East Indies grew out of an earlier putting-out system, which helps to explain the continuing downward delegation of responsibilities. The special characteristics of tobacco growing on the plantations have led some scholars to class it as a form of sharecropping or even smallholding,[145] but this analysis is wrong. Sharecropping is a legal arrangement between a landowner and a tenant whereby the tenant retains a share of the crop. However, Huagong on the tobacco estates received not a crop-share but a wage based on the number of leaves delivered, a form not of sharecropping but of piece-work, and were subject to strict labour discipline, including by the state, and part of an industrialised system.[146]

In the East Indies and the Malay Peninsula, gambier and pepper, like tobacco, were grown under a system of shifting cultivation not generally associated with plantations and not much known in China outside Xishuangbanna. In Southeast Asia, however, it was widely practised, and Chinese swiddeners copied their swiddening from local people.[147] The production, pioneered by kongsis, was labour-intensive. Chinese planters shared social ties with the workers and the returns to both were related to output and market prices. Groups of semi-dependent planters worked together under an entrepreneur or syndicate to clear land, moving on once the site was depleted. Control was exerted

> through a hierarchy extending from the financiers to these field labourers in which, however, the ties were not simply economic; rather, the relationships between individuals in this hierarchy represented one segment of the intricate web of alliance within the entire, largely self-sufficient, Chinese community and were founded on specifically Chinese socio-cultural criteria, including speech-group, kinship, village-of origin and secret society affiliations.

[144] *The Deli Coolie Question* 1881–1882.

[145] Bosma (2019, 106). Pelzer (1935, 94–95), a source Bosma quotes, does not bear out the sharecropping theory.

[146] On the organisation of tobacco-planting, the piece-work system, and the regime of rewards and punishments, see Appendix A.

[147] Fox et al. (2009).

European officials identified these enterprises as classic examples of plantations, noting their extent, centralised management, specialised production, and processing facilities. However they failed to remark the plantations' "affiliations with Chinese culture and the adoption of a shifting system of cultivation."[148] Chinese-run enterprises of this sort persisted into the twentieth century. Although the plantations set up in North Sumatra after 1870 were mainly under the control of Dutch and multinational corporate capital, they retained features of their Chinese origins. In that respect, they mirrored Belitung mining, which also preserved kongsi features.[149]

Panglongs

The timber- and firewood-producing panglongs were essential to the industrial development of British and Dutch colonies in Southeast Asia.[150] They operated mainly for export. The name panglong was a Chinese loanword of Minnan origin meaning lumber mill, to which it was usually taken to refer (although others say it denoted the sledway along which timber exited the jungle).[151] Industrial exploitation of the forest in the East Indies was first subjected to colonial law in 1865, in Java. In the 1880s, panglongs sprang up in jungles and on secluded islands along the East Coast of Sumatra, whence they supplied Singapore and other places with timber, charcoal, and firewood. In the early twentieth century, De Bruin counted more than one hundred Chinese wood-cutting firms along the Deli coast, served by one hundred sampan boatmen (probably an underestimate). By 1930, 476 panglongs each covering up to 500 hectares employed 3,500 people.[152]

The sled-borne timber was rolled to the coast, by teams of pole-wielding and chanting Huagong, along sledways leading gently downwards in the direction of the drag. Cribwork structures up to 15 feet high and between 5 and (on curves) 25 feet wide stretched for miles into the jungle, bridging swamps and dips. The sledways, greased to roll the logs, were a source of

[148] Jackson (1969, 38–39).

[149] Trocki (2011, 86–87), describes the origins and organisation of the pepper, gambier, and tin trade.

[150] For an extended description of the panglong system, see Appendix B.

[151] Arnot (1929, 233–237).

[152] On the origins of forest exploitation in the East Indies, see Ivan Ruzicka, "Forest Exploitation in Indonesia: Past and Present," *Indonesia Circle*, vol. 6, no. 16, 3–15, at 3–4.

great danger to the panglong workers, a large number of whom collected chest and leg wounds. Left untreated, they caused suffering and death in the tropical conditions.[153] Where the sledway ended at an unnavigable waterway, the timber was rafted downstream to a tongkang mooring.[154]

Unlike some other sectors of the colonial economy, panglongs were not only manned but owned and managed by Chinese, most of whom lived in Singapore. New arrivals received 40 cents and old hands 60–80 cents a day, including food as part of the rate of hire, while mandurs received up to one Singapore dollar a day.[155] Some panglong workers formed kongsis that settled accounts annually with contractors.[156] The non-resident owners played little or no role in day-to-day management and were often even unaware of their panglongs' whereabouts. Instead, they left on-site mandurs to deal with the panglongs and monitored them remotely with the help of the tongkang skippers who ferried in labourers and provisions and brought back time-expired or sick labourers and the timber and firewood. The panglongs were for decades generally untouched by labour regulations and renowned for their cruelty, scandalous even by Dutch colonial standards. In 1902, colonial ordinances were extended to all jungle exploitation with the exception of panglongs. In the 1910s, the panglongs and charcoal kilns that employed thousands of Huagong in the East Indies began to come under supervision, resulting in some modest changes, but the Labour Inspectorate was not made responsible for their supervision until 1924, and logistical problems continued to hamper panglong inspection.[157] The panglongs' exclusion from supervision was due in part to the ethnicity of their owners, who were left to their own devices, but more so to their invisibility. Their isolation made them even more prone than mines and plantations to abuse and for a long time deprived their workers of even minimal protection. According to De Kat Angelino,

> [i]n the Chinese panglongs, or wood-cuttings, in the distant territories of Bengkalis, and in the Riouw Archipelago, situations have been discovered in 1918 such as the East Coast of Sumatra has not known at its worst period.

[153] "De panglongs," *Bataviaasch Nieuwsblad,* November 1, 1927; De Bruin (1918, 51).
[154] Tongkang: a large boat or junk in the East Indies.
[155] Arnot (1929, 236).
[156] Mollema (1922, 157).
[157] *Staatsblad* 1924, no. 175, De Bruin (1918, 50). See also Heijting (1925, 12, 29, and 82) and Stibbe and Spat (1927, 229–238).

> Yet in this case also there was no contract, no sanction and the Chinese workmen were in the service of Chinese employers.[158]

Erwiza Erman's study on panglongs between 1890 and 1930 shows that panglongs were organised in much the same way as the tin and gold mines worked by Chinese. The labourers built their own kongsi houses in the jungle, for themselves and the panglong head and his mandurs. Each house had a small temple, a kitchen, and a long dormitory for the labourers, and might in time come to form the focus for a small jungle community, growing its own vegetables but otherwise dependent on supplies from Singapore.

Dutch efforts to reform the panglongs began in 1893, after the Chinese Protectorate in Singapore denounced them as a form of slavery, but lack of funds, personnel, and suitable naval vessels and poor planning stood in the way of change. The investigators found that panglong workers were massively indebted to their bosses, mainly because of their opium habit and dependence on company shops. The owners in Singapore used the jungle to keep the workers incommunicado. Labourers were forbidden to board visiting tongkangs and would-be escapers through the jungle were nearly all were captured by local people and returned to the panglong, where they were beaten and forfeited any wages due to them. Absconders who managed to reach another panglong were usually allowed to stay, but initially without pay.

The Dutch were in no hurry to dismantle the panglong system, from which they took fees and taxes amounting in 1932 to fl1,000,000. The self-governing Malay sultanate of Riau-Lingga also benefited massively from it.[159]

Newspapers in China and the East Indies tried to expose the panglong scandal and force the authorities to act. Reports focused on the high number of deaths and the constant threat not just from supervisors but from the climate and wild animals and from opium addiction.[160] The labourers' best hope of escape, according to one report, was to hijack a tongkang and flee by water, but this was a dangerous and potentially fatal option.[161]

[158] De Kat Angelino (1931, 523).
[159] Erman (2017), De Bruin (1918, 50–51).
[160] *Bataviaasch Nieuwsblad,* November 1, 1927; *Shen bao,* June 3, 1934.
[161] De Bruin (1918, 51).

The relationship in Southeast Asia between forest-felling and tigers has been described in a study on colonial Singapore whose findings probably also apply to Sumatra.[162] Encounters with tigers claimed the lives of perhaps thousands of Chinese, in a setting dominated by "uncaring administrators [and] profit-driven investors." Crocodiles and snakes, along with local gangs that robbed the panglong dwellers, were a deterrent to flight.[163]

Mechanisation

Mining became more mechanised in the Nanyang in the 1920s, when new pumping and drilling systems and the modern dredge were introduced, resulting in a reduction in the demand for labour. The plantations, on the other hand, became mechanised only at the level of processing, by a permanent force of wage labourers, while contract labour continued to plant and harvest. This bifurcation continued into the Depression, which made hand labour even cheaper.[164] Mechanisation in the fields and sheds was rare in the East Indies even in the late-colonial period. Tobacco growing, as we have seen, followed "a predatory form of cultivation in which a large part of the acreage lay fallow for several years while a comparatively small area was very worked."[165] Labour-replacing measures were not introduced to the same extent as in mining or in transportation, done partly by locomotives.[166] So mechanisation mainly affected the mining sector.

Although mechanisation did not become standard on Bangka and Belitung until the 1920s, Chinese mechanics played an essential role in production even before then. In Mangar, mechanisation was completed in 1914, when mechanised dredging became the rule.[167] Mechanics from Guangzhou and Hong Kong worked in the East Indies as government employees in the docks or in private factories and engineering works.[168] In mining areas, most mechanical work was done by *laoke*, who tended pithead railways, waterwheels, evaporators, lathes, concrete mixers, bailing buckets, sand-removers, troughs, and pump dredgers.[169] Initially,

[162] Powell (2016).
[163] Erman (2017, 531).
[164] Kaur (2004, 50 and 114).
[165] Breman (1989, 99).
[166] Wiseman (2001, 222 and 431–432).
[167] *Gedenkboek* (1927, pt 1, 61), Kamp (1960), cited in Van den Berg (1999, 218).
[168] MacNair (1924).
[169] Guowuyuan [May] (1920b, 31).

mechanisation took a simple form, using basic equipment. *Laoke* managed water pipes that spurted the mineral-rich mud from the mines and washed away the sand, work often performed along the seashore and known as tin-lake work. The process required little labour.[170]

While beneficial in terms of productivity and quality, mechanisation is often incompatible with workers' health and safety, especially where (as in the East Indies) workers' safety is anyway generally neglected. When badly administered, it can lead to an increase in accidents. That the introduction of the quantum system roughly coincided with mechanisation lessened still further the attention to safety.

On Bangka, one of the first steps towards mechanising mining led to a disaster that initially undermined miners' trust in the new machines. In 1910, a powerful but unstable water pump brought about a collapse on the first day of its operation, killing seven Huagong. Others were killed by collapses in a neighbouring pit. For a while, the men switched back to working with their bare hands, pickaxes, shoulder poles, and winnowing baskets.[171]

On Bangka, mechanisation was practically the final blow to the kongsi's managerial role. Bangka's reputation in China was so bad at the time that the tin authorities decided that mechanisation was the best remedy for the labour shortage. The complement of engineers was increased between 1896 and 1926 from three to eighteen, led by a newly appointed chief engineer, with a parallel increase in supervisors. Working with mechanised pumps was hard and dangerous at first, and for a while miners experienced life under the new labour regime as grim. In time, however, mechanisation led to improved conditions. It also led to a leap in profits, from f400 million in the ninety years up to 1910 to f350 million in the fifteen years from 1911 to 1925. The Huagong themselves profited less or not at all. They became increasingly superfluous and were replaced by Javanese. On Belitung, mechanisation led after 1922 to the demise of the numpang, an increase in the European role in management, and a switch to hourly wages.[172]

The mining companies explained mechanisation as a response to a drop in tin-richness rather than to "labour troubles" and the miners' "backward

[170] Guowuyuan [January] (1920a, 38).
[171] Yang Tongling et al. (2004, 85).
[172] Heidhues (1991, 9, and 1992, 71, 117, and 127–130).

mentality."[173] The drive for "scientific" production generally undermined collective decision-making. Previously, workers had chosen their free days collectively and spent their evenings together. After mechanisation, all this changed. Production became continuous, organised in three shifts that operated day and night.[174] Each shift lived apart and members of different shifts were less likely to know one another.

Mechanisation led to changes in the accounting system. In the past, reporting on the labour performed by teams and individuals over the year on Belitung and calculating wages had been a leisurely affair, a brief moment of recreation in a calendar of relentless toil. During the *wandelperiode* or "walking period," Huagong were free to roam around the island for a few days, on foot or by *piepkar* (a roofed wheelbarrow), to visit friends and relatives, pay back or call in debts, and buy gifts to send to China. The *wandelperiode* lasted until the company report was sent off to the Netherlands, after which quotas for the following year were set and work resumed. The *wandelperiode* was finally finished of by mechanisation, when the reporting period shortened.[175]

In the 1920s and the 1930s, when mechanisation gathered pace, the mines tripled in productivity because of the introduction of new pumping machines. Where mining was done by hand, it was easy to judge a worker's productivity, but mechanisation undermined the old system of accounting. A company almanac remarked that "now the company is becoming part of the lofoeng [shareholding] system, it's a co-shareholder." Mechanisation had been promoted ever since the 1880s, in an attempt to reduce reliance on Chinese labour, both in Malaya and on Bangka.[176] In wholly mechanised sectors, labourers and their team leaders no longer directly controlled production and management passed into European hands. The old system whereby self-administering teams paid wages annually gave way to monthly payments. The numpang system could no longer be preserved, except among marginal groups like day labourers and charcoal burners.Elements of the system still applied where ore was privately delivered to the company or where "coolie societies" operated (among

[173] *Gedenkboek* (1927, pt 2, 51).
[174] Wu Fengbin (1988, 158).
[175] *Gedenkboek* (1927, pt 2, 71, 74, and 82).
[176] Bosma (2019, 111).

groups like charcoal burners), but it became more common for day labourers to be paid by the day or by the job.[177]

In the 1930s, mechanisation also reduced the Huagong workforce in urban settings. In Singapore, an automatic coaling system using mechanical grabs replaced manual labour by Huagong.[178] Mechanisation coincided with layoffs throughout the economy at the start of the Depression, which disguised its impact. Mines closed and old and infirm employees lost their jobs.[179]

Food

The provision of food for Huagong on their way to the East Indies was perfunctory, and employers complained of the effect on recruits' health. Victualling while awaiting shipment could be costly and, for many, a first step into debt. On the steamships, food counters offered basic fare on which the migrants could spend their meagre allowances. On the junks, conditions were worse and people died. Not until 1909, when labour recruitment for the Outer Islands came under regulation, did the food provided in the recruiting depots have to satisfy minimum standards.[180]

On the Outer Islands, most of the mines and plantations were far from markets, and feeding workers fell to the employer. The Coolie Ordinances did not specifically require employers to provide food, but some authorities made provision part of the contract. At first, rice was exchanged for tin.[181] Regional ordinances and offices of the Labour Inspectorate called for the insertion into model contracts of clauses regarding the delivery of food, which was subsequently either provided routinely or sold in company shops, using cash or coupons. Some administrations kept the price of rice below the market price plus transport costs. On Bangka, the quality and quantity of food was contractually regulated, although miners complained that it was often insect-infested.[182] Employers at first used a primitive and unreliable measure to dispense rice, but in 1911 the Labour Inspectorate imposed a litre measure.

[177] Gedenkboek (1927, pt 2, 87–93).
[178] *The China Press,* October 16, 1935.
[179] Wu Fengbin (1988, 161).
[180] De Kat Angelino (1931, 565–566).
[181] Mollema (1922, 83).
[182] Heidhues (1992, 114 and 121).

Different systems of victualling applied in different circumstances. Javanese received coconut oil, Chinese lard; some workers received all their food, others just rice.[183] On Belitung in the early 1880s, miners received a picul of rice a month,[184] which was more than enough, and used the excess to hire local people to do odd jobs. To end the practice, the company switched to monthly payments of f2.5, raised to f3.5–4 after protests.[185] Most labourers ate three times a day—rice-gruel at 7 am and 5 pm and a main meal of fish, rice, and vegetables at 11 am—and supper if they were on night shift. The diet consisted of the same three staples: coarse food grain, salted fish, and soybeans, accompanied by half a bowl of arrack. The mandur usually syphoned off part of the ration, but what remained was in theory enough to fill a stomach. In later years, workers due a food ration as part of their salary received 35 pounds of unpolished rice a month. However, in the mines five pounds of this was held back by the mandur to feed the pigs and chickens raised on site, so each labourer received on average a pound of company rice a day. This was too little for three meals, so the labourer had to supplement it with purchases from the mandur's shop, at inflated prices. The diet led to bloating, diarrhoea, and worse. On Belitung, the food was better than in other places, but miners complained of its monotony.[186] "Non-essential" items (including tea and tobacco) had to be bought in the company shop.[187]

On-site cultivation and "forced shopping" did a better job than company provision to keep the workers fed. On Bangka and Belitung, mining communities ran vegetable gardens and a pigsty and henhouse near their accommodation. In well-kept vegetable gardens of the sort run by diasporic Chinese throughout the world, permanent husbandmen, experienced in farming and livestock rearing, met the demand for Chinese food. What could not be grown was procured by the company shop in dried or salted form. So successful was the husbandry that pork-imports from China and Java had ceased by the 1910s.

Some employers provided farming tools at reasonable prices, the so-called adat price, to promote nutrition and good health, and lent employees f2.50 a month to buy spices, preserves, and above all tea, to prevent

[183] Heijting (1925, 92–94).
[184] Defined variously, but set in Hong Kong at 133.3 pounds.
[185] *Gedenkboek* (1927, pt 2, 71 and 82).
[186] Lu Wendi et al. (1985, 418–419).
[187] Heidhues (1991, 9).

water-borne infections.[188] The inspection of food and the provision of drinking water and tea played a big part in disease prevention, alongside vaccinations against smallpox and typhus, good latrines, and the removal of refuse.[189]

By 1928, however, the companies' commodification of the food supply and the trend away from collective provisioning and self-reliance had led to the disappearance of most vegetable gardens. Instead, administrators bought supplies on the market and charged for them.[190]

Pensions

After the establishment of the Labour Inspectorate in 1904, the authorities paid greater attention to welfare issues such as retirement pensions. Pensions on the Deli plantations, if paid at all, were designed to tie workers to their jobs. The pension took effect after a given period of service, uninterrupted and under just one employer. Heijting put it at half the worker's average wage—f7.50 a month in 1921 and more for tandils and mandurs, but in other places it comprised around one fifth of the final wage, with f3.60 a month for workers with 15 years' service and f4.80 for those with 25.[191] Workers were expected to supplement their pensions from savings, though many had none. Some "loyal" retirees were allocated a house and yard and access to medical care. Javanese received their pension by post, whereas Chinese could choose between periodic payments and a one-off payment (a "gift") of $100, which many preferred and subsequently invested in land or property in China.[192] A pension could be terminated if the pensioner "behaved badly" or the company went bankrupt.[193]

On Belitung, the focus of pension reform was initially on Europeans, for whom the right to paid leave after ten years' service was recognised in 1871. In 1895, an account was set up to subsidise a pension fund, which came into being between 1899 and 1905. In 1921, the pension system was revised and improved. Chinese and "native" officials in the administration and the police were included in a new fund along lines similar to

[188] Mollema (1922, 178–179).

[189] De Kat Angelino (1931, 554, fn. 2).

[190] Heidhues (1992, 114–115). The soil no longer supported cultivation.

[191] Heijting (1925, 97–99).

[192] *Mededelingen uitgegeven door de Deli Planters Vereeniging*, no. 10, May 1921, 8–11. By 1925, the one-off payment had risen to f150 (Heijting 1925, 98–99).

[193] 8e Verslag der Arbeidsinspectie, 25–26, cited in Heijting (1925, 99).

that for Europeans. In 1924, the issue of Chinese mine heads and numpak heads due for retirement became more pressing during the drive for standardisation of production, and their previous records of service were increasingly ignored. Officials provided retired Chinese supervisors with handouts of cash and rice, described as charity, but these were later replaced by a pension based, "in time-honoured style," on the number of piculs of tin whose production a supervisor had overseen during his career, recompensed at the rate of f0.25 a picul.[194] On Bangka, miners in 1922 received a rudimentary pension of 40 catties of rice a month and a bed in a home for the elderly.[195]

Housing

Accommodation featured in "coolie contracts" in the East Indies from the start, and in 1838 became a contractual obligation on the employer. Together with advances, accommodation was a major argument in the eyes of employers for retaining the penal sanction, as part of a supposedly reciprocal and equal exchange, as important as the debt acquired on account of the passage overseas.

Opponents of the penal sanction pointed out that employers were bound under contract to provide accommodation that was "decent" or "satisfactory," or pay a fine of fl00. However, even in 1920 up to 80 percent of housing fell below or well below a standard qualified by Chinese inspectors on a visit to the tin islands as "acceptable."

Critics also questioned the argument that housing was part of an indenture quid pro quo. Van Blommestein pointed out that all the land was in the hands of concessionaries, so it was impossible for an immigrant "to get a patch of land, however small, to build a house on and provide for his own needs. But those needs *had* to be met, so that the employer *had* to do what was necessary." In any case, the penal sanction was hardly relevant, for in 1911 the colonial legislator had required employers to provide suitable accommodation not just for contract-workers but for all workers.[196]

In housing as in all other respects, "coolies from elsewhere" were treated far worse than Europeans and local staff, including ethnic (as

[194] *Gedenkboek* (1927, pt 2, 134 and 147–148).

[195] Heidhues (1992, 155), "Tweede Blad: Het winst-aandeel-systeem," *Het Nieuws van den Dag voor Nederlandsch-Indië,* September 13, 1922.

[196] Van Blommestein (1917, 38–48). On "free" workers, see De Kat Angelino (1931, 535).

opposed to migrant) Chinese. Huagong were also treated differently from Javanese, who were likely to bring their families and receive private accommodation and who qualified for settlement under colonisation schemes that allocated land and houses to married workers.[197]

The houses of the whites were "large, spacious, carefully constructed, equipped with a great deal of luxury items, and surrounded by a veranda, and rested in many cases on low stone pillars." Accommodation for the labourers, known as "coolie lines," on the other hand, was primitive, although by the 1930s some companies were providing favoured workers with small yards and houses of their own.[198]

Chinese inspectors in Sumatra in 1920 identified three classes of "dormitory huts." Category A, raised a foot above the ground, comprised brick white-washed structures under red-tiled roofs 60 metres long and 2 metres wide and divided into 30 one-man cells. Each cell had a door at one end and a window at the other, covered with wire gauze. The buildings were surrounded by vegetation and flowers. Each cell had a bed and a small table holding an oil-lamp. Dormitories of this sort, built in the late 1910s, made up 20–30 percent of Huagong accommodation. The inspectors found it "passable." Category B comprised wooden buildings raised two feet above the ground with wooden roofs poorly shielded against the elements, classed as "not altogether unacceptable." Category C, the worst sort, comprised brick-and-tile barrack-style structures 30 metres by 6 and 6 metres high with two storeys and 10 one-man cells on the ground floor, each with a lamp and table. The upper storey was cramped, windowless, and poorly ventilated, with two or three occupants to a room, sleeping on mats.[199] The rooms measured 2.5–3.5 or 3.5–4 metres, with kitchens and henhouses at the rear. Some had running water—otherwise tea was available. At harvest-time, occupants might sleep in field huts.[200]

On Bangka in the early nineteenth century, single miners lived communally, in a kongsi house, while their married workmates lived in separate huts. In the twentieth century, most Bangka miners lived eight to a room in long wooden sheds with cement rather than earthen floors and an allotted sleeping space of four square metres.[201]

[197] On this scheme, see Stoler (1985, 38–41).
[198] Pelzer (1935, 109–110).
[199] Lu Wendi et al. (1985, 419–420).
[200] Stibbe and Spat (1927, 231–234), Heijting (1925, 30–63).
[201] Heidhues (1992, 114–115).

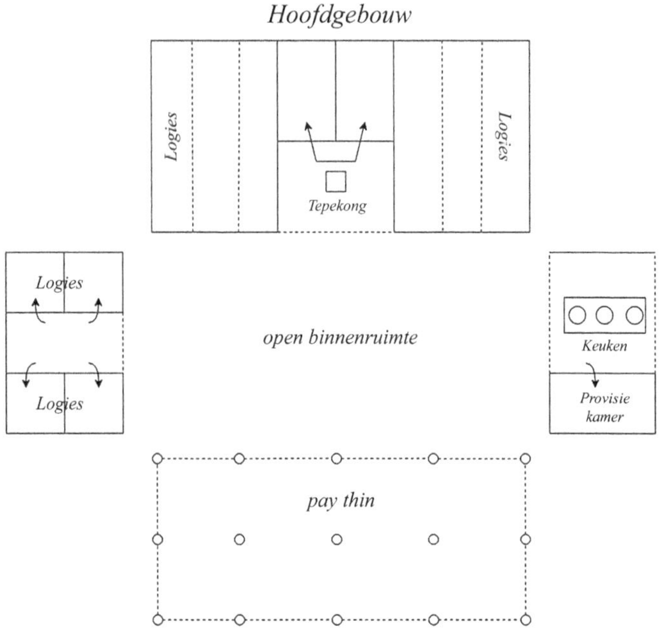

Fig. 6.1 Numpang housing on Belitung in the 1910s. Key to sketch: *hoofdgebouw* = main building, *logies* = quarters, *open binnenruimte* = open interior, *keuken* = kitchen, *provisie kamer* = provision room, tepekong = altar, *pay thin* = worship hall (Mollema 1922, 174)

On Belitung, numpang housing in 1905 was described as "extremely primitive."[202] By the 1920s it had improved somewhat and acquired elements of a Chinese style, as illustrated by Mollema in his sketch of a typical cluster (see Fig. 6.1). The buildings were permanent structures made of wood. A main building housed senior workers along corridors either side of a vestibule housing the altar. Opposite the altar was the paithin ("worship hall"), for dining and recreation. Between the main building and the paithin was a square flanked by workers' quarters and a kitchen and provisions room, together with a small arrack still. The workers slept four to a

[202] Rapport (1905, 10).

room on mats behind mosquito nets.[203] The lay-out of the complex was practically identical with that described forty years earlier by a Dutch visitor to Bangka.[204]

Each labourers' settlement had a shop, run by a Chinese, and huts for leisure activities, including film shows. Some had football fields and some bigger ones had clinics and even schools and temples. Other buildings served the planting or mining economy: sheds for tools and machinery, smithies, stables to house draft animals, drying barns, fermentation barns, sorting barns, the occasional factory, an administrative centre, and a power plant. Most plantations were connected to a road network along which the product was carried to the factories or the railway.[205]

Workers' Health

Medicine and public health in the colonial world were said by critics to function as "tools of Empire"—to protect colonial garrisons, colonial administrators, and European traders and settlers.[206] Ecological degradation, including climate changes and alterations in the insect fauna as a result of changes in land use, combined with workers' overcrowding to create a new order of diseases and challenges to public health in colonies everywhere.[207] In the East Indies, health campaigning was eventually extended to cover the basic needs of contract-workers, but its main role was to protect the colonial state and profits.[208]

The ill health of the colonised raised greatest alarm when it threatened the colonial economy or the elite. It was treated by technical interventions such as mass vaccination rather than by social and economic measures. The Dutch opposed what they saw as a "naive" faith in hygiene education and promoted a mixture of "native" customs and a techno-scientific and top-down approach imposed where necessary by force (and characterised by the public health chief in West Java as *laissez-mourir*).[209]

[203] Mollema (1922, 174–178).
[204] Heidhues (1992, 61–63).
[205] Pelzer (1935, 109–111).
[206] Brown (2004, 309).
[207] Das (2019).
[208] Pols (2018) focuses on the role played by colonial medicine in disillusioning Indies medical practitioners with colonialism and thus speeding decolonisation.
[209] Quoted in Gouda (2009, 2–3).

In the early colonial period, little or no provision was made for Huagong health in the Sumatran jungles. On Bangka in the 1810s and 1820s, "Bangka fever" (probably cholera) killed hundreds. On Belitung, one third of miners died annually in the 1850s. In 1865, 34.21 percent of 2,078 Chinese miners on the island died, and 10.41 percent in 1866. In 1870, the mortality rate fell to 1.78 percent, mainly because of a decline in the incidence of beriberi and dysentery. However, the number of Chinese with leg ulcers—associated with jungle clearance—grew from 15 to 39 percent.[210] In the 1860s and again in the 1890s, outbreaks of beriberi killed hundreds. On Bangka and Belitung, 50–60 percent of new arrivals died in 1861–1862, and later 5 percent of 12,000 workers died on Bangka.[211] In 1902, half of a group of 48 *xinke* died within a month of arriving on Bangka of a disease known in Chinese as *huoshaoxin*, for which doctors could find no remedy.[212]

In 1901, the health inspector described plantation hospitals as filthy and the treatment of inmates as cruel and revolting. The mortality reports were underestimates, for planters "were wont to cast aside terminally ill or dying coolies in the bush outside the estate."[213] An official report on Belitung admitted that the percentage of deaths was higher than announced because the Billiton Company "did not compel [sick miners] to go to hospital."[214]

The Dutch declared public health a matter for attention in 1820, when the Regents administering Java were instructed to keep an eye on it. For most of the nineteenth century, however, they did little to conceal their lack of concern for workers' as opposed to soldiers' health. The health of contract workers first become an issue in British colonial regulations, whence the idea spread to the East Indies. In Britain, indenture was defended precisely on health grounds, as we have seen,[215] and it was even claimed that medicine "justified imperialism."[216] In the East Indies, too,

[210] De Groot (1887, 345 and 353–354).

[211] Heidhues (1991, 3, and 1992, 36 and 61–64), Mollema (1922, 183–184).

[212] Yang Tongling et al. (2004, 87). *Huoshaobing* is sometimes rendered as pyrosis or cardialgia, but this seems unlikely.

[213] Breman (2020, 465–466).

[214] Rapport (1905, 12).

[215] Quoted in Van Blommestein (1917, 19).

[216] Brown (2004, 9).

the colonial interest argued in the 1920s that penal sanctions were essential for maintaining health and hygiene.[217]

In the early years, basic hospitals run by Chinese or Malay healers and visited weekly or fortnightly by a physician were set up on plantations. Chinese hospitals opened on the Outer Islands on Riau in 1828 and on Bangka in 1849, and became leprosaria. In the second half of the nineteenth century, most leprosaria closed, but in 1890 an international congress declared the disease contagious and thereby caused the authorities to take notice. Wealthy Chinese founded several leprosy facilities on Sumatra. In the 1890s, civilian hospitals were created with the support of enterprises, missionaries, and the government, as part of the worldwide rise of a modern hospital movement. Expenditure on health services doubled and measures to deal with popular health and hygiene began to take effect. Medical care on Sumatra's East Coast was, by the early twentieth century, for the most part good. By 1910, 22 "central" plantation hospitals, with 23 doctors, served 170,000 workers. In 1916, their number had risen to 35. Mortality more than halved over 1913, from 22.2/1,000 to 10.18/1,000. The bigger hospitals had X-ray machines and laboratories.[218] By 1918, Deli was at the forefront of medical progress in the East Indies. Twenty-two European doctors worked in 17 hospitals. "Estate hospitals" (or clinics) and a pathological laboratory and quarantine station were maintained, at an annual cost of f960,000. This investment equalled more than a quarter of the civilian medical budget for the whole of the East Indies and more than half of the army's medical budget—proportionately, according to De Bruin, sixty times as much as the sum spent by the state on maintaining the health of the general civilian population. It was also an enormous advance on expenditure at the start of the century. In 1901–1902, for example, just f24,629 had been spent on medical care on Belitung.[219] Because of the new investment, Huagong mortality fell by three quarters in twelve years, from 60 per thousand in 1897 to 15 in 1909. Between 1910 and 1930, under the Ethical Policy (designed to improve the welfare of colonial subjects) and the new civil medical service, private and public hospitals sprang up around the mines and plantations,

[217] Heijting (1925, 156–160).
[218] Stibbe and Spat (1927, 231–234), Heijting (1925, 30–63).
[219] Rapport (1905, 12).

with a rise from 32 to 301 in the number of company hospitals. By the late 1920s, the government employed 600 doctors, 1,100 nurses, and 400 vaccinators and ran more than 400 policlinics and 200 nursing homes—still too few to deal with the incidence of "popular diseases,"[220] but a great improvement.[221] The improvement continued until the retrenchment of hospital development in the Depression.[222]

Health provision for the colonial masses in the East Indies came to feature in official regulations and indenture contracts in the late nineteenth century, alongside housing. Triggers of the reform included the effect of high mortality not just on profits but on the reputation of the colony, which depended greatly on China and Singapore for recruits. Fear of discredit and adverse reports contributed to a change in the Dutch treatment of sick Huagong. Having first dumped them on the kongsis, they now funded separate premises to hold them. For the same reason, planters opposed the Bangka authorities' plan to discard sick and dying miners in Shantou. In the end, the miners were sent to the mountains south of Jakarta, to recuperate before returning to China.[223] Humanitarian concern among nationalists, Christians, socialists, and others in the East Indies and the Netherlands roused by criticism in the League of Nations and the ILO also played a role. However, even humanitarian work was viewed in the context of preparation for war and the chance of risings against colonial rule.[224]

The idea that health measures in the East Indies had a racist rationale is contested by colonial apologists but borne out by a comparison of the treatment of leprosy in the East Indies and in Surinam. In Surinam, from 1790 through until 1950, leprosy sufferers were compulsorily segregated, whereas in the East Indies segregation was usual only in Batavia and, to a lesser extent, Deli. This, according to researchers, was because in Surinam the Dutch colonisers were in everyday contact with slaves and indentured labourers, as they were in Batavia, a rare place in the East Indies where Europeans lived alongside Asians. As for Deli, the plantations were at first worked mainly by Chinese, seen as a prime vector for leprosy. Elsewhere

[220] De Kat Angelino (1931, 37, 86–87, 327, and 331). "Popular diseases" were malaria, hookworm disease, plague, smallpox, abdominal diseases, framboesia, tuberculosis, venereal diseases, leprosy, beriberi, goitre, and contagious opthalmia.

[221] De Bruin (1918, 83–84).

[222] Zondervan (2016, 17–18, 72–73, 116–117, 120–121, and 186).

[223] Heidhues (1992, 64).

[224] Van Bergen (2019).

in the East Indies, contact between Europeans and leprosy sufferers was too limited to necessitate strict segregation. Even in Deli, the Chinese influx led only to minor restrictions (for example, a ban on leprous children attending schools) rather than to compulsory segregation, on the grounds of cost. When, in 1890, the Deli planters opened a small asylum for leprosy sufferers, most of them Chinese, to protect the workforce and themselves from infection, they had to build it privately, since the government continued to reject compulsory segregation.[225]

The planters' view of Chinese lepers as both an ignominy and a menace cries out from De Bruin's account of the Dutch response to the establishment by Christians of a leper institute on Si Tjanang Island, with the Deli planters' support: "This put an end to the annoying wanderings of these unfortunate people," whose "hideous appearance, not to mention the danger of contagion, had given quite a few passers-by a fright" in the years before the lepers' confinement.[226]

The growth in hospital provision on the Outer Islands contrasted starkly with its neglect on Java and Madura. In 1940, Java and Madura's population was roughly twice that of the Outer Islands but with half as many hospitals. In the plantation belt, one hospital served 35,300 people compared with (say) 91,700 in Jogjakarta.[227]

The discrepancy is even greater when demography is factored in. Workers on Sumatra were mostly males in the prime of their lives eating subsidised rice, whereas Java's population was malnourished and normal in terms of age and gender, far more "burdened" by old people and children.[228] On Java and elsewhere, labour was plentiful and therefore less precious and deemed less in need of support.

The underfunding emerges most clearly in cross-colonial perspective. In the East Indies, the ratio of physicians to population in 1940 was 0.22 per 10,000, compared with 1.4 in the Straits Settlements and the Malay States in 1939 and 1.17 in British India in 1940.[229]

Even so, De Kat Angelino boasted that "the level of hygiene in the enterprises on the East Coast of Sumatra is almost unique and is rewarded with mortality figures which belong to the best in the world"—in 1929,

[225] Snelders et al. (2019).
[226] De Bruin (1918, 52 and 113–114).
[227] Zondervan (2016, 218–222).
[228] Stoler (1985, 34–35).
[229] Zondervan (2016, 207).

the death rate for all enterprises was 7.93 and on the East Coast 7.28 per 1000. Nor could he resist seeing this achievement as an endorsement of indenture, arguing that it would have been impossible but for "the security of enterprise guaranteed by contract labour" (while noting, in contradiction of his own logic, that "in future [the relevant clause will] apply also to labourers without contract").[230]

Chinese officials visiting Bangka and Belitung had a more critical view. They identified three types of hospital—new, middling, and old—ranging from brick-and-tile structures equipped with up-to-date medicines, treatments, and facilities to wooden huts dependent for supplies on other hospitals. The inspectors noted a preponderance of Javanese and local doctors and a lack of nurses. Patients had to do much of the work, with the less ill serving the more ill. But because the less ill were quickly discharged, the system often broke down. The nurses that did appear could rarely understand their patients. Medicine was in short supply and hospital food was poor in quality and quantity. A minority of patients slept on steel beds, the rest on plank beds or straw mats. Patients had to do manual jobs around the hospital and to take corpses to the morgue or the dissecting room, and were flogged if they refused.

The inspectors visited hospitals on Bangka and Belitung housing hundreds of Chinese with mental illnesses or leprosy. The two facilities were more or less one and the same, although mental patients outnumbered lepers by around two to one. The inspectors visited prisons with four prisoners to a cell, sometimes with just two beds between them, under a warden who kept them behind bars for months on end even after they had served their sentences. But the jails were relatively empty, since the Dutch preferred hard labour to incarceration.[231]

Reports and memoirs mention the cruel treatment of sick and incapacitated Huagong. Contract workers on Bangka had to work every day except Sunday and festivities and were reportedly forbidden to take consecutive days off, even when sick. Many continued working while carrying contagious diseases. Doctors rarely gave them enough time to recover properly, and recovering patients were beaten if they slacked. Some committed suicide. The Billiton Company confirmed that some miners with typhoid worked on for weeks, because they would otherwise have to pay to feed their replacements. Workers' descendants listed the ailments caused

[230] De Kat Angelino (1931, 554).
[231] Lu Wendi et al. (1985, 421–424).

by hard work, poor food, and poor treatment: not just infectious diseases and their aftermath but scars, stomach ulcers, ulcerated legs, pneumonia, dropsy, colour blindness, and the lasting effects of recurring heatstroke.[232]

Mollema's book on Belitung gives a fairly complete account of Chinese miners' health in the early 1920s. Noting that "large corporations have increasingly recognised that good care for the health of one's workers is not only a matter of humanity but of the financial interest that accrues on money spent, since a sickly coolie is more prone to all kinds of infections and endangers his surroundings," Mollema described the measures taken to deal with beriberi and tropical malaria, which "left the sufferer unsuitable for the job in the long run" and cost money. In 1920, 1,236 miners were treated for malaria with quinine and spent 17,861 days off work. Mollema added that malaria also affected Europeans. Leg wounds and ulcers led in 1920 to 83,835 lost working days and required weeks and even months of care. Treated on the spot, however, they were no longer deadly.

Mollema sketched the history of hospital building on Belitung, starting in 1865, and the effect on miners' health of continuing to work while ill—the miner "preferred to drag himself to work rather than forfeit a day's pay." In 1865, a regulation had come into being that forbade miners from remaining at work with their teams for more than three days (later extended to four) while sick. As a result of the prohibition, and of strictly enforced inspections, the ratio of mortality in hospitals to that in mines (i.e., at work) rose from 1: 4 in 1865 to 1: 0.21 in 1920 (excluding fatal accidents). The cost to the Billiton Company of medical provision (including for Europeans) in 1920 was f316,350.[233]

Labourers' Spare Time

At the end of a day in the fields or in the mines, Huagong had little access to entertainment in the camps, which were usually remote from society. Accounts mention music performances on the erhu and singing after supper.[234] Kongsi houses and the attached paithin were sites of communal activity. Gambling and opium-smoking was commonplace, although officials and employers tried to stop it. Chinese merchants, abetted by

[232] Yang Tongling et al. (2004, 83–87), *Gedenkboek* (1927, pt 2, 71).
[233] Mollema (1922, 183–196).
[234] *Gedenkboek* (1927, pt 2, 82).

supervisors, set up gambling dens and opium dens near places of work. Where there were no brothels, the supervisors privately procured women for the workers.[235] Opium smoking was particularly rife among older Huagong, and Chinese inspectors described gambling as the labourers' "greatest tragedy."[236]

Where not forced by the authorities to crack down on gambling, employers pandered to their workers' obsession with it. However much the authorities tried to stamp it out, the habit was too ingrained to go away, and lower-level managers and even the companies had a material interest in preserving it—it kept the workers happy while trapping them into debt and making it impossible for them to leave. The companies provided various sorts of entertainment for their Javanese employees, including gamelan (music), wayang kulit (puppet-shadow plays), film shows, and even football and (given that the Javanese communities were more likely to include women) dancing. For the Chinese, however, gambling was the main pastime.[237]

Gambling was the subject of the longest section of the Chinese inspectors' report on daily life in the Belinyu mining district, where an astonishing number of people—put by Chinese inspectors at several hundred, including professionals—lived off gambling. Miners gambled with ready cash and on credit, the gamblers' greatest bane and most open to abuse. Different sorts of gambling were associated with Chinese of different provenances. Gambling was so institutionalised that it had its calendar: November was for "gambling for New Year money," March and April for staking one's wages, and June for wagering one's savings. Gamblers fell ever deeper into debt with the gambling bosses, who charged 30 percent interest on gambling loans. The gambling reached fever pitch on official holidays, when dens were overrun.

The communal buildings were used not just for relaxation but for other gatherings, to which workers were summoned by a temple block or wooden bell, also sounded to mark shifts and prayers.[238] Where kongsi houses were built around a shrine or altar, as was often the case, religious activities were a feature of communal life.[239] By the 1920s, however, many

[235] Appendix A; Wu Fengbin (1988, 173).

[236] Lu Wendi et al. (1984b, 288).

[237] Heijting (1925, 100–102).

[238] Lu Wendi et al. (1984b, 286–289).

[239] Pinyin: Dabagong, or Bagong, said to be Tudigong, a tutelary god of the soil. Scholars disagree about its provenance. Some think it was a Chinese import, others that it originated in Southeast Asia (Hui 2011, 193). The ba character is normally read as bo. Heidhues (1992, 44).

of the altars had fallen into disrepair in the wake of the Revolution of 1911, when political activity and reading grew more popular. Kuomintang supporters conducted political education on the tin islands and set up reading rooms.[240] But most mines and plantations were too remote and most labourers were either illiterate or too exhausted by hard work to join in.

There was generally a temple wherever Chinese settled, including temples in or around the bigger towns that were the focus of processions, festivals, and funerals.[241] Temples were the main sites of communal and public speech-group activity in the nineteenth century, and although less so in the secular twentieth century, they continued to play a role in welfare, socialising, and entertainment. They were also important for maintaining homeland and intra-diasporic ties, with mother temples in China or Nanyang cities linking lesser shrines.[242] Temples also participated, as we have seen, in trafficking labourers.[243]

Chinese gods and temples overseas were usually linked to clans and native places. However, Huagong temples were not just overseas extensions of cultural traditions in the sending communities. A temple established by early Chinese miners in Taiping in Malaya was part of a strategy to integrate Cantonese immigrants into a single community after an intra-communal war.[244] In the East Indies, too, temples integrated different speech-groups. On Bangka, as we have seen, Chinese "municipalities" (*gemeenten*) emerged in the island's poly-dialectal environment to represent all Chinese rather than this or that speech group, and the municipalities supported Chinese schools, temples, cemeteries, and public feasts, and—where the Malay element was strong—wayang and bangsawan theatrical performances.[245]

Secular entertainment was available, mainly in the form of local operas. Huagong sometimes walked great distances to enjoy an opera performance in an urban centre. When a troupe performed in Deli, some walked

[240] Heidhues (1992, 160–161).

[241] Guowuyuan [January] (1920a, 48).

[242] Frost (2005, 29–66).

[243] "Slave Traffic Investigated by Police in Nantao Temple," *The China Press*, March 7, 1935.

[244] Xiao Jingliao (2018).

[245] Heidhues (1992, 155–156).

for three hours each way and stayed until late into the night,—and then got up at five the following morning to return to work. Some performances lasted across three or four evenings.[246]

In 1928 and 1929, a Chinese Song and Dance Troupe toured the Nanyang with the aim of transforming its "cultural desert" and instilling Huagong and other Chinese with an anti-colonial consciousness and an awareness of the national language. This was a pioneering effort—previously, the only modern professional musical performances in the region had been by Europeans. However, the troupe's elitist approach and the high ticket price, as well as the dialect barrier, meant that it had a greater impact on the Dutch than on the Huagong.[247]

Where sites of diasporic labour were in easy reach of urban centres of Chinese culture, the way was open for labourers to attend leisure and cultural activities. However, this was not always allowed. Many sites were cut off not only by distance but by employers, who prevented labourers from leaving or only let them out on Sundays or if they acquired a permit.[248] In this respect, the indenture contracts fell far short of those negotiated during the First World War, which specified that Huagong should get the same leave as the French, in addition to during Chinese festivals.[249]

Abuse

Huagong, like most Indians and Javanese, rarely confronted the colonial establishment or campaigned even for moderate reform. Unrest occasionally broke out, but did not become widespread until the late 1940s and the imminent collapse of Dutch rule. The labourers' plight usually attracted attention only when protests were made on their behalf by international bodies or in parliaments. Huagong in the East Indies were particularly powerless, as we have seen, because they lacked the backing of a nation state or nationalist movement focused on diaspora concerns. They were also hampered by sub-ethnic divisions that impeded solidarity and many were demoralised by opium and gambling. Now and then, they rose up against particular injustices, but such rebellions were put down.

[246] De Bruin (1918, 27).
[247] Zhang Beiyu (2020). Kevin Yang sent me this source.
[248] Yang Tongling et al. (2004, 87), Lu Wendi et al. (1985, 448–449).
[249] Ma Huiyue (2015, 104 and 124).

Observers in China knew of the atrocities that Huagong endured in the East Indies, exposed by officials in reports and by the Chinese and international press. The abuse started at the point of recruitment and continued overseas. The maltreatment of new recruits in the Chinese ports happened before an international audience and was visible and notorious. Less known was the overseas abuse. The labour regime was the subject of press reports, parliamentary reports, and publications, like Van den Brand's pamphlet. However, as Van den Brand later admitted, "once the indignation had cooled somewhat, people appeared inclined to listen to excuses, all the more eagerly when they realised the huge financial interests that were at stake."[250] In response, the Dutch government commissioned a report by the Public Prosecutor, J. L. T. Rhemrev. Rhemrev confirmed Van den Berg's findings about abuse and revealed its systematic concealment. As we have seen, however, the Minister for the Colonies refused to submit Rhemrev's scandalous report to parliament and filed it away to gather dust.[251] Even less known, until the publication of reports by the Labour Inspectorate, were the atrocities committed in the panglongs, on remote islands or deep in the Sumatran jungle.

Despite the suppression of Rhemrev's report, Van den Berg's revelations helped shame the authorities into announcing measures. His pamphlet was reported in the English-language colonial press, which concluded that little had changed since Pickering's censure of the Dutch more than twenty years earlier. The scandal threw doubt on the Ethical Policy proclaimed in 1901, and led to a spirited debate in parliament. Although politicians in the Netherlands and the East Indies defended the planters and attacked Van den Brand, the reforms implemented in following years confirmed his criticisms, although he thought they did not go far enough.[252] The first big step to improving the conditions of the workforce was the establishment of the Labour Inspectorate. Some enlightened employers saw that reducing discontent was in their own interests. Even so, the reforms were limited in scope, and the Inspectorate was understaffed, underfunded, and sabotaged by diehards.

The abuse had an international dimension. One example: 210 Huagong from Dalian imported in 1909 by Japanese planters and promised re-engagement on generous terms or free repatriation were instead beaten

[250] Van den Brand (1903, 5).
[251] Rhemrev (1903 [1987]).
[252] Breman (1992).

and starved and received minimal wages subject to numerous deductions. One in ten had fallen ill by the end of the first year. In 1914, the Japanese marched the 183 survivors off at bayonet point and sold them to a Dutch merchant vessel. A Chinese official reported the incident to Singapore, where the Huagong were rescued and repatriated.[253]

After the start of labour inspection, the maltreatment abated in more visible settings and better-run companies, but nowhere was free from it. The following two cases, based on colonial archives, concern two criminals in the mining industry in the East Indies in the second decade of reform, one of them Chinese, on Bangka,[254] the other a white assistant-resident administering a remote mine in Central Kalimantan.[255]

The Bangka file concerns Bong Kong Hian, a Kapitan Cina (a rank in the colonial administration) whose criminal activities and sexual predations led to a "severe reprimand." However, as a "loyal, dutiful officer" and a forceful personality, able to keep order among the miners, he was spared punishment. During China's 1911 Revolution, he had developed political ambitions. He fought with other Chinese for control of the mines on Bangka and used his office to promote his financial interests. His thugs smashed up gambling dens run by his rivals. Bong and the Dutch cooperated in a criminal conspiracy, even after the colony's "ethical" turn, on the colony's showcase tin island.

The Jangkang Baru file, based on reports by the Labour Inspectorate between 1917 and 1919, tells how an Australian, Forbes, terrorised Huagong while running a Japanese mining company. The owners had got officials to exempt their mine from the clauses on accommodation and medical care in the Colonial Ordinance. They failed to register workers, manipulated their wages, sold them rice at inflated prices, housed them poorly, and deprived them of clean drinking water. Forbes was charged by labour inspectors with beating a Chinese labourer senseless, strapping him to a raft, and floating him down a crocodile-infested river—a common way in "wild" regions of disposing of malcontents. The labourer was rescued by a local kampong head. Forbes' house was burned down, presumably in revenge. The arsonists escaped prosecution, but Forbes tied them up and goaded an ape into abusing them. Charged with attempted murder, he was allowed by local officials to flee to Singapore.

[253] Wu Fengbin (1988, 137).

[254] Alg. Sec, Grote bundel, TZG Agenda, no. 6782 (1915).

[255] Alg. Sec, Grote bundel, TZG Agenda, no. 7077 (1919).

Apart from rare accounts of atrocities emanating from within the colonial system, the voices of the Huagong themselves were rarely heard, because they were isolated, illiterate, and politically unorganised. Three known exceptions are the reports made in 1920 made by Chinese inspectors after visiting Bangka and Belitung; the interviews taken from retired repatriates in Guangdong in 1963 (Appendix A); and recollections by the descendants of Bangka miners, published in Beijing in 2004.[256]

Banka Tinwinning, founded in 1816, was a state-owned rather than a private company. Commentators have sometimes assumed that private enterprises were more to blame than state enterprises for the abuse associated with indenture. Given Banka Tinwinning's longevity, size, visibility, bureaucracy, political connections, and leading role, one might expect it to have been compliant with the regulations applied to mining in 1891. In fact, it used punishment and compulsion extensively, and its reputation was worse than that of private companies on Belitung.[257]

When Chinese officials visited Bangka in 1920, the Labour Inspectorate had already been in existence for sixteen years. However, abuse of Huagong by mine supervisors continued practically daily according to the officials, who gave numerous examples (with names of victims and perpetrators, dates, locations of the crimes, and the victims' ages) of workers beaten or secretly murdered, buried in the jungle, and listed as absconders. Victims showed the inspectors their wounds and scars.The officials reported cases of labourers tortured to death in such a way that the wounds were invisible and of victims clamped in bamboo frames of the sort used to constrain pigs and then drowned. The part of the report on cruelty and killings, said to be "innumerable," was the second longest of 27 sections. The Chinese officials calculated the rate of killings on the basis of the size of the workforce (50,000), the number returning annually to China (fewer than 500), and the number recruited annually (more than 3,000)—not a scientific approach, but an indication of the officials' view of the Dutch. They accused the colonial state of covering up crimes against Huagong and showing little interest in investigating complaints, and urged China to send a permanent representative to the island to protect the miners.[258]

[256] In 1906 or 1907, the Qing official Qian Xun was sent to the Nanyang on a fact-finding mission. He received numerous complaints from Mentok alleging torture leading to suicide (Yang Tongling et al. 2004, 83).

[257] De Kat Angelino (1931, 160 and 551).

[258] Lu Wendi et al. (1985, 411–418).

Miners' descendants repeated the inspectors' findings: "The foremen were good at covering things up, the Dutch government was insufficiently concerned to follow up cases thoroughly, and our country had no official stationed here long-term." The descendants accused the Dutch of whipping and killing workers. A feature of the abuse, according to reports from the time and later recollections, was the use of martial arts to discipline and kill workers, said to have happened "daily."[259] Reports in the Dutch and Chinese press suggest that employers were generally unhappy with recruiting ex-soldiers, who were often hostile to authority, but some hired Huagong willing to do "military service" as henchmen and paid them a 30 percent premium.[260] Kick boxers staged exhibition fights to intimidate the workforce:

> Father [said the son of one Huagong] told us that the Dutch government and the mine bosses were consumed with great hatred [for Chinese]. The mine boss was the Dutch government's representative in the mine. He was their accessory to murder. The mine boss secretly nurtured a ferocious gang of slaughterers. These goons conspired to kill innocent workers at any time or in any place. Father said that one weak and frail labourer, who had been ill for days and unable to work, had been cursed and berated by the overseer. The labourer said a few words in his own defence. The overseer set about him without a word, fists flying, and killed him on the spot. His corpse was buried like a dog in the sandy waste. Father told us that the mine boss had brought over a group of strong and vigorous toughs who were good at martial arts. He used them to beat people up and keep order. They even used to kill each other. One worker called Liu Hui, a giant of a man, more than six feet tall, was a strong and skilful fighter. He challenged an overseer called Zhong Yongjin to a fight, Cantonese-style. They fought each other to a bloody standstill. Father said that the cruellest punishment was beheading. From time to time they used to behead rebellious miners. Here's how they did it. They ordered a rebellious worker to go into the hills to cut down shrubs and bushes to stiffen the dyke around the mine pond and stop the tin lake from overflowing when it rained. [...] While the worker was chopping down the undergrowth, a goon cut off his head from behind, with a big sword, and the head rolled across the ground. The corpse was devoured by wild pigs or giant lizards. His housemates realised that he was never going to return and reckoned that he had become a headless ghost. To dazzle the

[259] Yang Tongling et al. (2004, 83–85).
[260] *Tianguang bao*, April 29, 1934.

workers, the supervisors performed tricks disguised as "miracles" of superhuman strength. [...] The miners were too ignorant to realise.[261]

Such stories are not irrefutable testimony. The reports from 1920 rely on allegations and hearsay and the inspectors were biased. However, their listing of names, times, and places lends them credibility. As for the 1963 interviews, they were edited to a political end. Evidence to corroborate or contradict them has not survived, and the memories of many of the elderly interviewees were fading. However, if they are the only means left to construct a story of indenture from below, we should allow them. Taken separately, these three accounts amount to little, but as a body of evidence gathered from dozens of informants from different backgrounds and with different experiences, they cannot be discounted.

Resistance

Political or ethnic repression, racism, economic exploitation, immiseration, and class antagonisms are essential to theories of revolt, and Huagong in the East Indies experienced them all. Class and racial friction created a constant undercurrent of unrest and occasional outbursts of mass violence. However, the penal sanction was an effective means of keeping the lid on the resentment caused by exploitation and racism and a main explanation of why the Chinese record of rebellion in the East Indies was thin, even though China's rural classes had played a major role in the hundreds of major and tens of thousands of minor armed risings that punctuated two thousand years of Chinese history and eventually supported Mao's revolution. But there are other reasons too for the failure of China's labour diaspora to live up to its reputation for ungovernability.

Miners in China were often at the forefront of revolutionary activism,[262] and in the mid eighteenth century miners' kongsis in West Borneo waged a war of resistance against Dutch rule. In later decades, however, as we have seen, the kongsis lost their territorial function and were incorporated into the colonial economy.[263] Sub-ethnic Chinese labour settlements gave way to a mixed workforce in which different speech-groups worked alongside one another and even alongside Javanese. They also lacked external support of

[261] Chen Yingqiu (2004).
[262] Perry (2008, 1147–1164).
[263] Fernando and Bulbeck, eds, (1992, 92–120).

the sort Indian and Javanese labour migrants received from political movements. Except for in Cuba, where (as we have seen) anti-colonial forces solidarised with runaway Chinese and embraced them as part of the "raceless nation,"[264] indentured Chinese generally remained isolated.

Chinese plantation workers in Sumatra were even less likely than miners to organise in their own defence.[265] Unlike mining, industrial agriculture was not generally practised in south China, and Chinese peasants recruited to the plantations had no experience of industrial-style labour collectives.

In the twentieth century, other developments further weakened Huagong resistance. Reforms and an increase in inspection led to an improvement in conditions, while the 1930s slump led to the collapse of workers' communities. Thousands returned to China or left for the towns, where they eked out a living in Chinatown.

Even so, every decade of the first half of the twentieth century saw Huagong protests and small risings, starting with the "Liu Yi war" in 1900, the best-known Chinese rebellion in the East Indies. In it, the eponymous leader, a Hakka miner, rebelled against the Dutch on Bangka and killed officials, for which he was put to death. Liu Yi's rebellion entered the collective memory of Bangka Hakkas and inspired miners to declare a second Liu Yi war in 1924, followed by a wave of strikes and riots in the late 1920s.[266]

When Sun Yat-sen's 1911 Revolution broke out in China, twenty thousand Huagong on Bangka rioted and some died, and Bangka Chinese sent money to support him. In 1914, in Mampawa in Western Borneo, Huagong rebels won local Dayaks to their side by promising to exempt them from taxation if they helped incorporate the region into the Great Chinese Republic as a new state. The "leader" of the movement was named as Soen Kap Sen, described as a member of the Young Chinese Party, probably a reference to Sun Yat-sen, whose name must have been borrowed to give the rebellion credibility.[267]

[264] Benton (2009, xii–xiii).

[265] The best-known act of resistance in Deli was the killing by five Chinese plantation workers, apotheosised as the Five Ancestors, of a Dutch assistant in 1892. They became a local legend and "inspired numerous adaptations in Sinophone fiction and on stage, sometimes conflating more than one historical event. These adaptations have, in turn, filtered back into historical writing" (Stenberg and Minasny 2022).

[266] Hong Sisi (1985, 280), Yang Tongling et al. (2004, 113). On the labour unrest on Bangka in the 1920s and 1930s, see also Heidhues (1992, 161).

[267] De Bruin (1918, 107–111). The party usually referred to as the Chinese Youth Party was not founded until 1923 (Hirayama 2013, 227), so De Bruin must be referring to another group.

Up to the second Liu Yi war, Huagong in the plantation belt retained their reputation for belligerence, measured by attacks on the European assistants who bullied them. In 1925–1927, 65 attacks were recorded, 16 of them by Chinese and the rest by Javanese. Chinese by that time made up only around one-eighth of the workforce.[268]

Throughout the 1920s, and especially in 1928 and 1929, strikes and desertions were reported on the tin islands and in the plantations. Despite Belitung's relatively good name, it too was the site of disturbances and strike threats by *xinke*. That *laoke* steered clear of the unrest was taken as proof that it was the result not of labour conditions but of agitation by outsiders: "The differences in nature and conditions of sinkehs [*xinke*] and laukehs [*laoke*] have sharpened in recent times. The civil war in China has brought to the boil all sorts of clamorous, rebellious, and easily inflamed spirits, and the Billiton Company has had more than its fair share of these psychically infected people."[269] In October 1929, "coolies on various plantations were found plotting to kill Dutch planters on neighbouring plantations. Sixteen coolies were identified as part of the plot. Troops were sent in and restored calm."[270]

The slump dampened the miners' militancy, although resistance was reported on Bangka in 1930 and 1934. In the late 1930s, however, miners on Bangka and Belitung again became militant.[271] Socialist ideas had taken hold among them, under the influence of the revolution in China, and an increase in disputes and clashes caused employers to switch even more to employing Javanese. When the world economy revived in 1936, Huagong in Malaya and Indonesia staged a wave of strikes that peaked in 1937, spreading from the plantations to other sectors.[272]

So like Asian plantation workers almost everywhere except in the Caribbean, Huagong in Southeast Asia played little role in the anti-colonial struggle history or in its social and national imaginaries, as we saw in a previous chapter. At most, they practised small deceptions on their crimps, boarding-masters, and employers. Such acts were endemic, so I will mention just a couple. In 1917, colonial officials were puzzled by a sudden leap

[268] *De Planter: Orgaan der Vakvereeniging voor Assistenten in Deli*, year 18, no. 359 (January 2, 1926), 5643, year 19, no number (January 17, 1928), 6337, and year 20, no. 404 (January 4, 1928), Lindblad (1999, 72).

[269] "In de Billitonsche Mijnen. I. Arbeidsvoorwaarden.—Singkeh en Laukeh," *Bataviaasch Nieuwsblad*, Batavia, September 26, 1928.

[270] *Nanyang shangbao*, October 22, 1929.

[271] Wu Fengbin (1988, 175–178).

[272] Lu Wendi et al. (1984b, 59–68 and 259).

in the percentage of recruits refusing to go abroad after the medical exam—3.03 percent, compared with 0.8 percent in 1916. An investigation showed that it was due "to indiscriminate recruitment of loafers from Canton [Guangzhou] gambling houses, who by refusing got sent back free of charge."[273] In 1937, a Dutch employer who poached a worker from another company was generally obliged to pay a proportion of the old employer's crimping costs. However, the obligation did not apply to companies with fewer than twenty employees, so Chinese employers in Sumatra took advantage of the exemption (and saved themselves the cost of importing workers) by registering no more than twenty staff and listing supernumeraries as the boss's "uncle, brother, or [business] partner."[274]

Profits

The extreme exploitation of the East Indies began in the seventeenth century under the Dutch East India Company. By 1887, Bangka's Resident calculated that "each worker in the government mines brings the country an annual net profit of ca. f400."[275] In the 1920s and the 1930s, despite half-hearted reforms, debt-bondage continued to put the wage-earner at an extreme disadvantage and cushioned the employers against the worst shocks. During the Depression, when the price of plantation products fell by 75 percent and the value of exports dropped from a notional 100 in 1925 to 18.5,[276] the capital invested earned a dividend similar to that in Europe before the Depression. Bruno Lasker, a champion of reform, attributed this to the "the extremely low cost of labor and [...] the fact that, with the employment of contract labor and with short-term planting contracts with local farmers, the consequences of reduced markets could to a large extent be devolved upon the helpless producers." Practices such as the penal sanction immunised enterprises against risks that brought down sectors not similarly protected.[277] External profits gained on the world market were matched in miniature in the mines and plantations by internal profits, taken from the labourers by bosses, supervisors, gangers, criminals, brothel owners, and opium or gambling-den owners.

[273] [Hong Kong] Administrative Reports for the Year 1917.
[274] "Het ronselen," *Soerabaijasch Handelsblad*, February 13, 1937.
[275] Heidhues (1992, 75).
[276] Landheer (1941, 195).
[277] Lasker (1950, 208–209).

The surplus extracted by capitalism and the state was a massive boon to the Dutch economy, "a stream of invigorating wealth, [for] the Indies have a European as well as an Asiatic function and the life blood of the Netherlands comes from here."[278] The drain was, proportionately, around ten times greater than the British drain on India, measured by the addition made to the domestic product by the remitted part of colonial wealth. The East Indies contributed 13–14 percent of Dutch national income, not counting the income of the colony's Dutch expatriates,[279] proportionately much bigger than the British (and French) gain from empire and the loss of which would, at the time, have devastated the Dutch economy. Tax revenues from Sumatra were a mainstay of the colonial exchequer. The return to foreign direct investment in the East Indies between 1919 and 1938 was 2.5 times higher than that to investment in the Dutch domestic economy. The Dutch presence in the East Indies was far denser than the British presence in India, particularly in civil administration, mining, and plantations: proportionately, eight times bigger.[280] This is the background to the reluctance of officials in the East Indies to end indenture in the short term and, in 1923, to their determination to retain the penal sanction, at least for the time being, to avoid instability.

In 1931, Chinese writing from Dutch sources about the profit produced in the East Indies by Huagong and Javanese in 1927, identified sugar as the most profitable crop—2.39 million tons were exported, worth f365,322,000. Rubber exports were 130,000 tons, equal to 32 percent of world output and worth f332,000,000. Tobacco exports, produced mainly by Huagong, totalled 36,300 tons, worth f119,599,000. Tin exports, in which Huagong also predominated, yielded f70,000,000.[281]

The annual rate of return on investments in the East Indies was very high in 1919–1928, at 14.3 percent, but fell in 1929–1938, during the Depression and its aftermath, by 2.8 percent.[282] It collapsed even further in 1939–1948, by 22.6 percent. However, the Billiton Company was still able in 1938 to dip into its reserves (estimated at f11,450,000) to pay a

[278] Gunter (1939, 359).

[279] Baudet and Fennema (1983), quoted in Bosma (2014a, 162). See also Brandon (2019).

[280] Maddison (1989, 646–647 and 656), Buelens and Frankema (2016).

[281] *Dagong bao Tianjin ban,* April 7, 1931. Wang Linqian and Wu Kunxiang (2002, 172), estimate the profits in hundreds of millions of guilders for the years 1920–1926.

[282] Buelens and Frankema (2016, 213–214).

dividend of 50 percent (while pledging just fl,000 to the Committee for Relief of the Civilian Population in China).[283]

The 1920 Chinese report on Bangka calculated the annual contribution of the island's 22,365 Huagong to tin profits at 40 million silver dollars, assuming a per capita output of 9 *dan* a year, at f250 per *dan*. Wu Fengbin made a similar calculation for 1925–1926, by which time per capita output had doubled, to 18.74 *dan*, presumably because of mechanisation. The Dutch marketed 323,230 *dan* of tin, valued at f60,718,000, leaving a profit of f43,197,000 after deducting net costs of fl7,521,000. If the net cost of one *dan* of tin was f54.20 and its value was fl87.84, yielding a profit of fl33.64 per *dan*, then each worker produced tin to the value of f3,520.12 against costs of f374.8, i.e., the profit was 9.39 times greater than the cost. As for Bangka's spice plantations, which occupied less than one percent of the surface in 1920, their 7,000 workers, each tending one thousand bushes, produced an output valued at fl2.6 million a year.[284]

The Dutch authorities stipulated a gradual rise in the daily wage year on year and from the first half of the year to the second. However, rates differed from place to place and between categories, as we have seen. Wu Fengbin shows that between 1929 and 1933, wages rose from c. fl22 to fl56 a year but the cost of a labourer fell from f447 to f336, mainly due to a big fall in recruitment and only a slight rise in repatriation costs (see Table 6.5).[285] (The number of Huagong in East Sumatra between 1929 and 1933 fell from 26,819 to 12,803.[286]) Consumer prices also fell in those years, by 23.7 percent in the Netherlands and even more steeply in the East Indies, from an index of 147.9 in 1929 to 59.5 in 1933 (although the price of manufactured imports remained stable).[287] However, food was usually provided by employers, so the employee would not necessarily have benefited commensurately from the fall in the rice price (from 16.4 to 6.6 cents per kilo[288]).

[283] Alg. Sec., Grote bundel, TZG Agenda, file no. 10370, June 26, 1939.

[284] I have corrected the arithmetic.

[285] According to the Labour Inspectorate, the base rate of "coolie" wages in East Sumatra fell between 1929 and 1933 from 42 to 32 and the average payment to Chinese field coolies per thousand plants fell from fl1.98 to fl0.72 (Lindblad 1999, 74; Leenarts 1999, 153).

[286] Lindblad (1999, 72).

[287] Landheer (1941, 195), Statistics Netherlands' database.

[288] Leenarts (1999, 152).

Table 6.5 Daily Huagong labour costs in guilders, 1929–1933

	1929	*1930*	*1932*	*1933*
Wage	0.349	0.374	0.441	0.445
Bonus	0.030	0.032	0.032	0.034
Food	0.481	0.477	0.306	0.258
Accommodation	0.040	0.049	0.011	0.005
Medicine, etc.	0.094	0.099	0.053	0.074
Recruitment cost	0.195	0.157	0.069	0.016
Repatriation cost	0.032	0.034	0.138	0.090
Total cost	1.225	1.220	1.020	0.922
Total annual cost	447	445	372	336

Source: Wu Fengbin (1988, 167–168)

Huagong Society in Perspective and Transition

In the final decades of Dutch rule, many Huagong negotiated the transition to new fields of activity, at a much faster rate than the official switch to free labour. The strengthening of the urban sector of Chinese labour in the East Indies and throughout the Nanyang in the interwar years was an outcome of powerful new economic and demographic trends. An additional explanation for the speed at and the extent to which Huagong society diversified and its obvious versatility lay in its relationship to Chinatown and the ethnic-Chinese economy.

Theoretical discussions of the "plantation complex" have been criticised for reducing it to a European imposition, for seeing it as the outcome of a uniform and predetermined process, largely undifferentiated and unchanging, and for eliding its specificities.[289] The "plantation model" was originally built on findings and perceptions drawn from the Atlantic prototype and taken to apply universally. But special historical circumstances, both in its antecedents and the local setting, crucially shaped the plantation economy and its transitions.[290]

The plantation economy in the East Indies had much in common with its counterparts in the Caribbean and elsewhere in tropical Asia. Like them, it was marked, as a mode of production, by a rigid racial hierarchy,

[289] Bieber, ed., (2018, xii–xxxvi). Bieber's book, like the term "plantation complex," mainly concerns pre-nineteenth-century plantations, but some of his arguments also apply to later times.

[290] Curtin (1998).

profound inequality, production organised along military-industrial lines for the world market, strong linkages to the colonial state, and a coerced and highly exploited workforce with few rights. However, Asian indenture as a whole and Chinese indenture in particular differed in crucial respects from the Atlantic version, although the latter became the textbook model.

The first obvious difference is that Asian indenture had an antecedent in but rarely sprang directly from slavery.[291] The same goes even more for the Chinese labour diaspora, as I mentioned earlier. This shaped the way in which the Asian plantation complex started and evolved, especially in the case of Huagong, who were more self-reliant, resilient, resourceful, and better organised than the relatively atomistic plantation society of the Caribbean (although even there the stasis is exaggerated).[292]

James C. Jackson defined the standard model as follows:

> [P]lantation agriculture is usually described as an essentially tropical phenomenon and an institution of Western capitalism. The plantation is presented as a large-scale agricultural unit depending on heavy, typically foreign investment, extensive land holdings, a massive supply of labour, usually non-European, alien and cheap, a sharp division of labour with a highly centralized management, a high degree of specialization, frequently amounting to monoculture, the production for export of a narrow range of crops, mostly perennials, and the possession of industrial plant for processing its products.

But he added that "listing these supposedly diagnostic criteria provides no adequate basis for understanding the nature and mechanisms of this complex and widespread agricultural system," since many plantations did not conform to them or did so only partly. He pointed to the lack of a generally accepted definition of plantation agriculture, which had a semi-millennial history and could not be reduced to a single type.

Features that distinguish Nanyang plantations can be summarised as follows. (1) Many were pioneered not by Western capitalists but by Chinese corporations and funded by Chinese financiers in the Straits Settlements, in partnerships that often gave participants, including labourers, a financial stake. (2) Relationships were usually based on Chinese speech-groups, kinship, and places of provenance. (3) Chinese "secret societies" (kongsis and *hui*) and numpangs cemented the alliances. (4) The land concessions obtained by Chinese were typically cultivated by ten

[291] Behal (2014, 3).
[292] Dupuy (1983).

to fifteen planters (in contrast to the more massive European-owned plantations). (5) Chinese planters ran a form of management that was centralised but partly incorporated Chinese social relations.[293]

Another major difference concerns the role played by mining and plantations in the Caribbean and the Nanyang. In support of his criticism of what he sees as the homogenisation of peripheries by world-systems scholarship, Ulbe Bosma argues that in island Southeast Asia "corporate plantations and mining enterprises did not emerge as the dominant forces [...] but still left ample room for smallholders to produce for the global market." In 1930, for example, smallholders on the Outer Islands added more than twice as much of the value of export crops as plantations.[294] In the Caribbean, on the other hand, plantation agriculture dominated most economies.[295]

Finally, the relationship between the plantation economy and urbanisation was different in the two regions. The Atlantic plantation economy is typically portrayed as antithetical to towns. According to Wolf, "[i]f there is a town in the vicinity of the plantation, it is usually small and stunted in growth, for the real center of power and wealth lies on the plantation."[296] In fact, port towns played a more vibrant role in plantation systems in the Caribbean than Wolf allows, even for slaves.[297] However, Wolf's thesis holds in principle. In the Nanyang, on the other hand, towns and cities played a major role in regional economies. The link between Huagong and the towns was particularly strong, mainly due to the power of Chinatown and the ethnic-Chinese economy. It is true that in 1930 only 2.8 per cent of the population of the Outer Islands was urban, compared with 6.7 percent in Java. However, in regions populated by Huagong the urban economy and society were buoyant and disproportionately Chinese. On the tin islands, urban Chinese equalled or exceeded Huagong in numbers. In Medan, the seat of the Deli Sultanate, they numbered 10,997 out of a total population of 26,980 in 1915 and 35,600 out of 76,584 (a plurality) in 1931.[298] Within easy reach of Deli and the tin islands and a

[293] Jackson (1969, 36–39).

[294] Bosma (2019, 11 and 181). On Java, however, 80 per cent of the added value came from plantations.

[295] Pantin (1980, 17).

[296] Wolf (2001, 217).

[297] Burnard (2017).

[298] Damanik (2020, 42). Medan continued to grow at an annual rate of 6 percent between 1930 and 1961, reaching a population of 111,000 in 1940 (Leinbach 1987; Colombijn 2010, 413–416).

magnet for Chinese were the Straits Settlements, island Southeast Asia's most urbanised territories in 1911. Singapore, a primate city, and Penang had populations of 311,303 and 271,376 respectively, of whom 72 and 40.6 per cent were Chinese.[299]

In the Caribbean, the planter class inhabited another world from the slaves and their descendants. Urbanisation was for many years far weaker and intermediate classes and labour markets were far smaller. The Caribbean city "typically started out as a seaport [...] and a nest of pirates, filibusters and corsairs." It served the imperial powers as a military base and support station and aided their monopolisation of resources. Isolated from rural settlements and unable to absorb their migrants, it took time to become ethnically diverse. Merchants and local representatives of the metropole were generally of the same nationality. Late into the twentieth century, it continued "to be the presence of the Western World in the region."[300]

Properties of cultural life special or attributed to the Atlantic plantations have been falsely generalised to define the plantation complex as a whole. The anthropologist Eric Wolf, remarking on the part played by class oppression in homogenising culture in the plantation economy, creating communities that embody the class chain of command to the exclusion of other factors, and reducing social diversification, argued that "[w]herever the plantation has arisen, or wherever it was imported from the outside, it always destroyed antecedent cultural norms and imposed its own dictates, sometimes by persuasion, sometimes by compulsion, yet always in conflict with the cultural definitions of the affected population."[301] This argument ignores the creolist understanding of creole culture, even in its Atlantic form, as an assertion of the creative genius of the human spirit rather than an external imposition and that linguistic creolisation, a product of the pidginisation and hybridisation of languages created by the extreme mixing of ethnic groups and encapsulating the plantation effect, preserves elements of languages and cultures that survived the Middle Passage.[302] In any case, the destruction of cultures, supposedly inescapable in the plantation environment, was far less a feature of the Nanyang plantations. The workforce was less diverse and not, on the whole, violently

[299] Dodge (1980, 438), Bosma (2019, 151–153).
[300] Casimir (1992, 82–86).
[301] Wolf (2001, 217).
[302] Alleyne (1988).

extracted from many places and thrown together in one—unlike the African diaspora, a product of "the transplantation of isolated individuals" rather than of "tribal units that can count on a minimum of institutionalized relations."[303] Ethnic-Chinese communities had existed for centuries in the Nanyang ports. Chinese led the early development of mining in the Nanyang and founded many of the mines and plantations and most or all of the panglongs. They also played a central role in Huagong recruitment. Chinatown was constantly washed by new waves of migrants, ensuring the persistence of Chinese language alongside mildly or radically creolising forms of it. Creolisation happened mainly among the earliest settlers, where Chinese creoles came to form communities of their own, separate from surrounding Malay and other Chinese cultures. But even many creolised Chinese retained their ancestral language and some later revived their Chineseness, a process recognised as resinification.[304]

Whereas workers in the Caribbean and the Pacific spoke dozens of languages and communicated first through pidgins and then creoles, most Huagong lived in settlements where Chinese remained the main language. The mixing of Chinese speech groups led to linguistic change and Chinese on the Nanyang plantations borrowed words from one another and from Malay, English, and Dutch. However, the mixing was in no way as extreme as on Caribbean (and Australian) plantations. Although Chinese language and culture evolved, it was retained by most Huagong, until and beyond the collapse of the colonial state.

Huagong in the East Indies were not subject to "colonisation," the transformation of migrant communities into self-reproducing settlements, unlike other workers. Until the 1920s and the 1930s, theirs was a male society, oriented transnationally towards place of origin. Small Chinese-owned enterprises operated alongside big European ones and depended on the same shifting workforce, in a relationship that was symbiotic: the small companies employed the big companies' surplus workforce and cooperated with them economically, sometimes in stable partnerships.

Labourers' geographic mobility—with consent or, as flight, without it—has a long history in the annals of forced labour. It was endemic in colonial enterprises, which were policed to stop it. However,

[303] Casimir (1992, 156).

[304] On the "assimilation" of Chinese in Indonesia, see Zhou Nanjing et al. (1996).

"uncontrollable running" continued, throwing up maroon communities around the Caribbean.[305]

Huagong in the Nanyang were especially mobile, despite efforts to stop them. Chinatowns served cast-out or fleeing Huagong as bolt-holes, offering work and refuge in an economy managed by diasporic associations and "secret societies" to which a deserter might gain admission, by virtue of dialect, provenance, or ancestry. Huagong could move from a European company to a smaller Chinese one, or vice versa, or between a mine and a plantation. Cities in the East Indies in the colonial period, far from being "small and stunted," were major population centres in which Chinese played a central role, with ten times more urban than indentured Chinese in the 1930s.[306]

Indians in British Malaya faced a more difficult transition from rural to urban living. Amarjit Kaur sees the difference as a result of Indians' greater dependence on the colonial system and the plantation, which "infantilised" them by providing housing, crèches, and vegetable and livestock plots. As a consequence, they found it far harder than the Chinese to move from the plantations to the towns.[307]

For some Huagong in the East Indies, the proximity of Chinese-speaking urban communities provided cultural and educational opportunities, access to associations, and, for the children of the minority of Huagong in families overseas, the possibility of a Confucian or modern education. Bangka had a dozen Chinese private teachers in 1879. By 1899, Bangka and Belitung together had sixty-three Chinese schools with scores of pupils.[308] Other labourers invested in the Chinatown economy rather than repatriate their savings or undergo reindenture.[309]

Transitions tend to be wanting in the "plantation model," which neglects its internal dynamic and capacity for change. Many have argued that the legacy of pure plantation economy "militates in the direction of

[305] Rediker et al. (2019).

[306] However, precolonial port cities in the region were less magnificent than sometimes portrayed (Bosma 2019, 23).

[307] Kaur (2013, pt 2).

[308] Heidhues (1992, 162–163).

[309] In Cuba, too, Chinese managed the transition from indenture thanks to their role in Cuba's independence wars, their entrepreneurial spirit, and the immigration of Chinese merchants from California and from China, which led to the emergence of a more developed and complex Chinatown with a greater range of classes, economic types, and opportunities for former indentures and their offspring (López 2013).

stability [...] and continuity," even after slavery,[310] and inhibits the development of new sectors.[311] However, there are many pathways along which the indenture complex evolves, especially in the Chinese case.

On slave plantations, slave status was inherited from an enslaved mother. Plantations hiring indentures, in contrast, had no claim on their workers' offspring. Promoting labour settlements (of Javanese) shows that handing down jobs was seen as a possible solution to the problem of ensuring a supply of labour,[312] but colonisation was never an option for Huagong and there was little intergenerational transmission of Huagong status (save when China-born migrants joined their elders overseas). Rather, the generational progression for Indies-born descendants of Huagong was upward or outward—up into management or out into society, where they could deploy their linguistic and other skills and the contacts they maintained both *in situ* and in China.

For Huagong children, school was the avenue out of manual labour and into clerkdom or petty trade, or into Chinatown. In the late 1910s, 800 Chinese attended a dozen "modern" Chinese schools in Bangka's ten ports, not counting those enrolled in smaller old-style private schools in the villages. The Dutch, intent on assimilating Chinese children, were accused by visiting Chinese officials of trying to force parents to send them to Dutch schools and of withholding support from Chinese schools,[313] which they saw as a vector for radical ideas, especially in *xinke*-dominated places.[314]

The entry of ever more urban Chinese into modern sectors of the economy created yet more pathways out of indenture. These sectors were in part tied to the mines and plantations, whose raw materials they processed and whose needs they served. They also manufactured consumer goods, sometimes using modern technologies.[315]

In Malaya, where indenture ended first, this led to a rise in Huagong factory employment in the mid 1930s, when the plantations were stagnating. Table 6.6 shows the changing distribution of the Huagong workforce between 1934 and 1937. Factory work was conducive to improved labour

[310] Pantin (1980).

[311] Mandle (1972, 61).

[312] Stoler (1985, 38–41 and 44), Maassen (1937).

[313] Lu Wendi et al. (1985, 420–421), Guowuyuan [May] (1920b, 50)-53.

[314] Alg. Sec, Grote bundel, TZG Agenda 7702, Departement van Onderwijs en Eeredienst, January 26, 1924.

[315] Kaur (2004, 129–130).

Table 6.6 Chinese employment in British Malaya, 1934–1937

	Plantations	*Mines*	*Factories*
1934	72,688	27,573	27,223
1936	60,842	47,187	38,065
1937	75,589	51,906	44,585

Lu Wendi et al. (1984, 53–58)

relations, especially where the factory was big, managed by modern methods, and located in urban centres and therefore open to inspection.[316] By 1931, many mines and plantations in Malaya were "worked by Chinese labor under the ownership of the Chinese," who ran a number of big rubber factories. In the Outer Islands, rubber was a smallholder rather than a plantation crop, farmed by Javanese and Chinese linked by Chinese traders to the Singapore market. According to a leader of the British government, "[i]t is to the individual enterprise, industry, and thrift of the Chinese merchant and petty trader, the Chinese craftsman, the Chinese coolie, and, above all, the small Chinese contractor with his 'kongsi' or guild, that the great wealth and development of British Malaya are mainly due."[317]

Industrialisation proceeded even more quickly in the East Indies than in Malaya and faster on Sumatra than on Java. The Outer Islands had half Java's population in 1930,[318] but the number of boilers used in factories—an index of industrialisation—grew between 1900 and 1930 at nearly twice Java's rate, from 387 to 2,410, and was only 345 short of Java's total. Even in the 1920s, between two and 2.5 times as many consumption goods were imported into Sumatra per capita than into Java.[319] Most factory employees were probably Chinese, given Chinese capitalists' domination of small-scale industry, their prominence in sugar, oil, and soap manufacture and rice milling, the close-knittedness of the Chinese community, and the decline in indenture.[320] Ex-Huagong played an important role in industrialising Deli, Bangka, and Belitung, as well as other cities.[321]

[316] Houben (1999, 118).

[317] Nair (1931), Bosma (2019, 11 and 107).

[318] *Volkstelling* (1930, 70 and 77), cited in Van der Eng (2002, 490).

[319] Bosma (2019, 102).

[320] Furnivall (1939, 334, 409, and 434). Employment in manufacturing in the East Indies grew from 4–5 per cent of the employable population in 1930 to 7.1 percent in 1939, when 300,000 of the 2.8 million in manufacturing were in larger industrial manufacturing (Bosma 2019, 146, 150, and 231, fn. 82).

[321] Zhu Jieqin (1984, 242–243).

In the 1930s, the Chinese population in the East Indies and elsewhere in Southeast Asia became more permanent, despite repatriations during the Depression, and came to look at least in some respects quite like the European community, in that it comprised (permanent) *blijvers* and (temporary) *trekkers*, including more and more *trekkers* who worked outside the mines and estates and were "taking root." This happened especially after the end of the Pass System, the recognition of Dutch-Chinese schools, and the improvement in Chinese legal status. Although one in three Chinese remained in commerce, nearly one in five worked in industry in 1930, while others were professionals, craftsmen, or clerks in European firms, particularly on the Outer Islands.[322] The growth in the 1920s of Chinese political organisations and the arrival of Chinese representatives after the establishment of China's new government in 1928 consolidated the community and strengthened its institutions, especially its schools,[323] and was underlined in 1935 by the election of Ko Kwat Tiong to the Volksraad, described as "the first step" towards proper Chinese representation.[324]

On the tin islands, the urban Chinese workforce grew rapidly in the early 1920s, when the already substantial Chinese urban population came to outnumber the miners, while in Deli it greatly outnumbered the rural Huagong. On Belitung in 1920, one thousand "miscellaneous workers" ran their own Chinese domestic economy unregulated by the Dutch. Chinese metal workers manufactured Chinese and Malay head ornaments for women and children and sold them from small shops. Ironworkers specialised in manufacturing tools, iron bedframes, iron-wire, iron rods, etc. Carpenters from Guangzhou, seen as "the crown jewel of Chinese enterprise" on Belitung, built houses in modern European and Asian styles and ran workshops and factories that earned them tens of millions of guilders, using Western tools to produce work considered equal in quality to Western manufacture. Chinese builders, plasterers, and bricklayers also built houses on the island. Local non-Chinese began entering the trade, in the footsteps of the Chinese, but big projects were still done by Chinese, some of whom switched to work connected with the mining industry. More than one hundred tailors and needleworkers from Meixian or of Hakka ancestry dominated the clothing industry. Cane and rattan workers made use of materials available in the nearby jungle and requiring little

[322] Furnivall (1939, 409–413).
[323] Heidhues (1992, 161–162).
[324] *Mata Hari* (Semarang), February 26, 1935.

capital. More than one hundred Hakka barbers earned up to fl0,000 a year each, and never less than fl000. Cantonese shoemakers and scores of laundry workers thronged the streets. Chinese funerary objects and Guan Yin statues were in great demand, given the large number of temples on Belitung (one for every dozen Chinese families), and were a rich source of employment. Dentistry, previously a European and Japanese monopoly, became a Chinese domain, mainly in the hands of Tianmenese from Hubei.[325] Professional photographers took photographs to be sent back to China. At the bottom of the Chinese social pile, five to six hundred handymen did odd jobs around the shops and kitchens and were hired mainly by dialect.[326]

Broader changes in the colonial economy in Southeast Asia and in Huagong demography in the 1920s and the 1930s, foreshadowed in previous chapters, accelerated the growth of a settled working class within the broader Chinese diaspora in the region, situated (as Kah Seng Loh points out) between Huagong and Huashang (the Chinese merchant). This change started before the Depression but quickened and intensified as a result of it. The steep rise in female Chinese immigration in the second quarter of the century, coinciding with ever greater numbers of Huagong leaving their traditional areas of employment (as a result of lay-offs) during the Slump and taking up employment in the factories, led to a proliferation of Chinese nuclear families and an unprecedentedly large natural increase in the Chinese diasporic population, starting in the 1920s.[327] Thus a range of factors combined to undermine the institution of indenture and pave the way to its dissolution even before its formal abolition in its last stronghold in the East Indies.

Conclusion

Indenture as practised in Dutch colonies was a variant of a world method of coercion from which, as a legal system, it differed little. Its legal component, the penal sanction, was a generic term in international law for

[325] For Tianmen migration, see Benton and Gomez (2008, 204–205).

[326] Guowuyuan [January] (1920a, 46–51) Lu Wendi et al. (1985, 451–453).

[327] Loh (2022, 148–157). However, the emergence of a populous Chinese urban working class led not to class-style solidarity but to its opposite: "working-class networks became ambivalent and even oppressive" during the crisis years of the 1930s. Loh is talking about Singapore, a "city of nuclear families," but his comment also applies to other parts of the Nanyang.

punishment by the state for breaching contracts, but the term was not widely adopted in that context and was particularly associated with Dutch colonialism.

In the nineteenth century, most European powers with tropical colonies practised indenture. The Dutch treated their indentures brutally, but probably no more so than the British before they abolished indenture and less so than the French, Spanish, and Italians. Nor did the Dutch top the league of indenturers. Far more labour migrants (put by some at many millions[328]) left British India between 1834 and 1917 than the one million that left Java for other parts of the Dutch empire,[329] while millions more migrated under indenture within India. However, the British population in 1900 was eight times the Dutch. Proportionately, the Dutch therefore came a good second.

The main way in which Dutch indenture stood out is that it lasted longer, up to the start of the Pacific War. Here, the Dutch ran true to form, having been the last Europeans to abolish slavery in the West Indies. Within the British system, passage money generally ceased to be a source of indebtment in the 1910s, paralleling the Allies' eschewing of debt bondage for the Huagong sent to Europe in the First World War.[330]

Even in the East Indies, indenture did not necessarily entail a penal element, in the sense of a punishment inflicted by the state. In the mid nineteenth century, the sanction in Dutch colonial legislation applied for a while to the employer rather than the employee. In 1909, in response to developments in India and Malaya and to domestic criticism, Dutch officials introduced measures weakening the penal clause, and in 1911 provision was made for "free" contracts without the penal sanction (although the "freedom" had its limits).[331] In Surinam, the colonial Government left provision for a penal sanction out of legislation at one point, since Javanese migrants "would be too far from home to run away."[332] For a long time, however, the penal sanction was the defining and abiding feature of Dutch indenture, a core term in its vocabulary and practically synonymous with it.

[328] Rana Behal (2014, 3), estimates that more than 30 million migrants, nearly all of them labourers, left India for overseas British colonies between 1834 and 1937. See also Northrup (1995, 64).

[329] Hoefte (2017, 367).

[330] Xu Guoqi (2011, 39).

[331] Tjandra (2016, 32).

[332] Lockard (1971, 51).

Dutch indentured labour also differed in its provenance. Initially, the Dutch acquired much of it from China, like the Spanish, whereas most British indentures were Indian. Indentured labour was in many places diverse in geographic origin, but less so in the Dutch case—not until the start of the twentieth century did Javanese outnumber Chinese in Sumatra. The Huagong recruited by the Dutch lacked the colonial tie of Indians to the Raj. Huagong were more likely than Indian or Javanese migrants to act independently and be assertive; and they were aliens and treated as such. The Chinese labour diaspora in the East Indies preceded the consolidation of Dutch rule by decades if not centuries and the diaspora was for a long time in major respects self-governing, which left an indelible mark on Huagong even after the Dutch had tightened their grip on the East Indies. Both in the Indonesian Archipelago and the Malay Peninsula, Chinese pioneered mining and planting in precolonial times and continued in some respects as rivals and partners of the colonial administrators.[333]

Retaining the penal sanction after the British had generally relinquished it left the Dutch exposed to criticism. British criticism, which started at the time of the first colonial ordinance in 1880 and continued right through to the 1930s, was unrelenting and deserved, but it was also hypocritical and self-serving. In 1881, William Pickering, Protector of Chinese in Singapore, citing "the general impression amongst respectable Chinese" in Penang, accused Dutch planters of treating their recruits in a cruel and predatory way, but the planters responded, not without justification, that their critics' main concern was to induce the recruits "to enter their own service"[334] and pointed in later years to the retention of indenture in tiny and remote British colonies even after its supposed abolition. In 1931, fifty years after Pickering's censure, the United States House of Representatives denounced the Dutch penal sanction as a form of forced labour. However, the focus of American criticism quickly switched from the products of indenture *in toto* to tobacco, the sole product whose import would threaten US interests, again illustrating the self-serving character of much of the revilement.

At the start of this book, I noted the findings of some recent studies on diaspora that correct the monochrome view of indentured labour in tropical colonies. I also noted the particular usefulness of Kuhn's importation

[333] Bosma (2019, 109–110).

[334] *The Deli Coolie Question* 1881–1882.

into Chinese studies of the elegantly simple metaphor of a busy two-way migration corridor, a channel of "cultural, social, and economic" transactions (to which one can add political). North-south corridors from the age of sail and new ones in the age of steam were used as passageways by travellers of all sorts, including traders and emissaries of the Chinese state and above all labour migrants and their traffickers and escorts. Many of the corridors crossed the territory of two or more political regimes before reaching their end-point. Even in China, warlords and colonial powers vied with local and national authorities to control the domestic gateways to them. In Hong Kong and the Treaty Ports and in the Nanyang entrepôts and places of transit and arrival, British and Dutch colonial officials competed to impose their different policies, purging the "decrepits" and sending back those suspected of intending to engage in political activity. British and Dutch worked hard to weaken each others' hand and standing. The Dutch resented the British role as keepers of the main corridors to the Nanyang and the British accusations of Dutch abuse, which they hurled back. Both British and Dutch resented the attempts of Chinese brokers and merchant networks to control the traffic. Dutch planters and mine-owners tried to wrest it from British and Chinese hands by bypassing the British-ruled Straits Settlements and establishing new corridors that directly linked migrant-sending regions to ports in the East Indies and were supported and licensed by the Qing authorities. Dutch planters and mine operators opened their own routes south, using *laoke* networks as their recruiters.[335] Generally the *laoke* acted as agents of their employers, but some took the money and ran to Chinatown, or delivered their charges to better-paying destinations.

As two-way conduits, the corridors were used not just by repatriands but by by remitters of wealth accumulated in the south, including Huagong. The remittances that flowed north helped rescue and transform the economy of south China. Chinese capitalism flourished along the corridors, and overseas-Chinese capital and labourers' remittances poured back up them from the Nanyang into the cities of southeastern China and Shanghai, where (as we have seen) they played a unique and often overlooked role in helping to modernise China's national economy and even contributed massively to its survival in the first half of the twentieth

[335] Gregory Jany makes these and other incisive observations about the history and politics of the corridor in his *Imperial Crossings*.

century.[336] The remittances attracted the attention of employers in the East Indies, who tried to control them for their own purposes. However, they usually failed.

Corridors linked migrant-sending to migrant-receiving places everywhere after slavery, but they differed greatly in nature. Comparative studies of indenture in the Caribbean and the Nanyang are few in number, as are comparative studies of labour diasporas in general. Even rarer are comparisons of the different national components of labour diasporas in a single region or country.[337] In that respect, this book offers an original perspective on the study of labour diaspora, not just by noting incidental differences between its Atlantic and Southeast Asian variants but by considering in depth those between the Chinese, Indian, and Javanese labour diasporas in the Indonesian Archipelago and the Malay Peninsula. The corridor concept is ideally suited to such an approach, in that it views migrations as a totality of cultural, social, and historical factors and can therefore best capture their specificity.

Chinese migration corridors were better endowed institutionally and more variegated than those of other migrants, because of their greater age and diversity and their roots in China's rich tradition of domestic migration, which they extended beyond the high seas. Indian corridors in late-colonial times were more closely monitored, by the British, and the corridors along which Javanese crossed to Sumatra were comparatively undeveloped. Unlike their Indian and Javanese equivalents, the Huagong corridors started in places that were under a regime nominally sovereign and independent, though with semi-colonial features. On the way south, the corridors were likely to pass through Hong Kong or a Treaty Port and long-established Chinese-majority settlements like Singapore and Penang, which served, in the now conventional metaphor, as the interdependent nodes and links of migrant networks and as primitive decompression chambers. Whereas Javanese were initially recruited to the plantations not freely or spontaneously but by professional agencies and under the surveillance of specialised state institutions and licensing agencies that penetrated deep into society,[338] the recruitment of Chinese labour was less likely to be subject to official controls and more likely to be organised by village-based Chinese recruiters. As a result of the variety of ways in which Chinese

[336] Kuhn (2008, 185), and Benton and Liu (2018, 105–109 and 180–181).
[337] A notable exception is Bhattacharya and Kripalani (2015).
[338] Lindquist and Xiang (2019, 42–43).

labour was recruited, Chinese corridors were relatively chaotic. Until the 1930s, fewer women travelled along them, independently or in families, which made them rowdier still. Army deserters migrating south along them caused trouble for colonial planters and officials, or ended up acting as their henchmen. Sometimes, mutinous Huagong and rogue labour escorts captured exits from the corridors, by commandeering the vessels carrying them south, throwing the crews overboard, and changing course.

Chinese migrants not only imported Chinese institutions down the corridors but copied practices learned along them. An obvious example is swiddening, a feature of farming throughout Southeast Asia but not of China's sending regions. Swiddening was also rare in plantation systems, and in Southeast Asian its introduction can be seen in part as a Chinese innovation.

The corridors were a conduit not just for labour but for ideas about how to recruit, organise, and employ it. The gang system used on plantations in the Americas had little in common with the farming of tobacco and other crops by Huagong on plantations in Sumatra, which was horticulturalist in character, as in China. Even colonial indenture had antecedents in China, in the *baoshengong* and kongsi systems of recruitment—the kongsis practised a China-born form of indenture long before the adoption of indenture by Western companies. (It is not known whether traditional Chinese indenture was connected, other than in its kongsi form, to colonial indenture.)

A nominally independent power, the Chinese state (in its various emanations) tried to assert itself along the corridors by diplomatic and other means, to set up consulates, keep a protective watch on migrant affairs, raise money, create political bases, and forearm against a feared invasion from the south.[339] Generally speaking, however, Chinese politicians in the colonial era had no choice other than to put most effort into solving China's domestic crisis of sovereignty and winning its national and civil wars. To the extent that Chinese politicians mobilised the diaspora behind a political goal, it was to raise funds for political movements in China rather than to stir up the diaspora, whereas Indians and Javanese were more successful in exporting political movements. As for consulates, Chinese consular representation in the East Indies remained weak and ineffective.

[339] Jany (2021, 43–47).

The focus in early writing on labour migration in the colonial setting on the role played by the colonial apparatus in creating misery and ill-health was a proper response to the evils of forced labour and the denial of human dignity, but such writing risks losing sight of the role of migrant networks in contesting and resisting colonial exploitation. By concentrating on the actions of colonial states, it makes the "colonial subject" less visible. By reducing migrant labour to a homogenous object in a dependent and shackled periphery, it ignores the differences between its various streams, homogenises them, and neglects their historicity. It looks mostly at the destination and less at the route and the point of origin and return.

It also risks missing major sub-cultures of indenture, which had their roots both in institutions like the kongsis, exported along the corridors from sending places, and in differences in power relations as a result of different labour environments and traditions. Hence colonial administrators complained of attempts to "graft tobacco onto tin" and to apply a labour policy of "one size fits all" that threatened to sabotage their delicate relationship with the tin miners on Belitung, who remained ethnically united at a time when mining on the neighbouring island of Bangka was losing its Hakka identification and on whose cooperation employers and officials heavily depended.

The new studies I have mentioned offer theoretical and pragmatic arguments for redressing this one-sidedness and open perspectives that I have explored in this book. In particular, I have drawn attention to the differences in the political culture of the three big labour diasporas in the Nanyang, to the ability of the Chinese to stand up for themselves better than the two other in many ways apparently less vulnerable groups, and to the social, cultural, and historical roots of these differences.

But although a networks approach to colonial history lays bare inadequacies of the centre-periphery model and shows the need for a more complex geography of connections, one should not forget that exchanges along migration corridors happened against the background of staggering inequalities of wealth and power. The balance might occasionally and exceptionally tip a little towards migrants, sending places, or indigenous polities, but it generally stayed firmly tilted in the direction of the colonial state and the capitalist economic order that it served. Migrants went south under insuperable constraints, their flow turned on and off by border authorities to produce massive fluctuations up or down, depending on economic needs. Some slipped south independently, evading the controls, but by the twentieth century most egresses were tightly sealed. Chinese migration brokers did their best to manipulate the flow and thus the price of labour, but rarely to much effect, except during economic booms. For most of the 1920s and the 1930s, Chinese migrant solidarities were in rapid decline. Huagong continued to lack access to representative institutions abroad and to suffer the consequences of state, racial, and national oppression, and they rarely enjoyed the support of a sympathetic metropolitan or homeland lobby. China's steepening descent into chaos after the Revolution of 1911 and in the 1920s disrupted labour migration and weakened the grounds for solidarity and cohesion still further. Dialect ties frayed. The number of migrants from regions without a tradition of migration and the incidence of the predatory trafficking of destitute and desperate Huagong grew. The corridors became less familiar and safe. The advantage was increasingly with the traffickers and the employers in the south who paid them. So the mutuality between colonial governments and planters, the policing of the corridors, the penal sanctions and other one-sided legal powers in the hands of colonial employers, and the resort to coercion and fraud in the recruitment of non-white labour ruled out systematic reform and an end to abuses in the interwar East Indies.

References

Alleyne, Mervyn. 1988. *Roots of Jamaican Culture*. London: Pluto Press.

Arnot, D. B. 1929. "Timber Extraction in Johore." *Empire Forestry Journal*, vol. 8, no. 2, 233–237.

Arudsothy, Ponniah. 1986. The Labour Force in a Dual Economy. PhD, Glasgow University.

Balboa Navarro, Imilcy. 2021. "Las Recontratas de Coolies: A Medio Camino entre la Esclavitud y la Libertad Formal (Cuba, Década de 1860)." *Tzintzun. Revista de Estudios Históricos*, no. 74, 127–160.

Baudet, Henri, and Meindert Fennema. 1983. *Het Nederlands belang bij Indië: Analyse van de politieke en economische gevolgen van de dekolonisatie van Indonesië. Hoe stelden overheid en bedrijfsleven zich op en wat was hun onderlinge relatie?* Utrecht-Antwerpen: Het Spectrum.

Baay, Reggie. 2015. *Daar werd wat gruwelijks verricht: Slavernij in Nederlands-Indië*. Amsterdam: Athenaeum-Polak and Van Gennep.

Behal, Rana. 2014. *One Hundred Years of Servitude: Political Economy of Tea Plantations in Colonial Assam*. New Delhi: Tulika Books.

Benton, Gregor. 2009. "Editor's Introduction." In Mauro García Triana and Pedro Eng Herrera, *The Chinese in Cuba, 1847-Now,* edited and translated by Gregor Benton, Lanham: Lexington Books, 2009, xi–xxxii.

Benton, Gregor, and Terence Gomez. 2008. *The Chinese in Britain, 1800-Present: Economy, Transnationalism, Identity.* Houndmills: Palgrave Macmillan.

Benton, Gregor, and Hong Liu. 2018. *Dear China: Emigrant Letters and Remittances, 1820–1980.* Oakland, CA: University of California Press.

Bhattacharya, Jayati, and Coonoor Kripalani, eds. 2015. *Indian and Chinese Immigrant Communities: Comparative Perspectives.* London: Anthem Press.

Bieber, Judy, ed., 2018. *Plantation Societies in the Era of European Expansion.* Abingdon: Routledge.

Bosma, Ulbe. 2019. *The Making of a Periphery: How Island Southeast Asia Became a Mass Exporter of Labor.* New York: Columbia University Press.

Bosma, Ulbe. 2014a. "The Economic Historiography of the Dutch Colonial Empire." *The Low Countries Journal of Social and Economic History*, vol. 11, no. 2, 153–174.

Brandon, Pepijn. 2019. "Dutch Capitalism and Slavery." *Historical Materialism*, September.

Breman, Jan. 1989. *Taming the Coolie Beast: Plantation Society and the Colonial Order in Southeast Asia.* Delhi: Oxford University Press.

Breman, Jan. 1992. "Een advocaat van kwade zaken: Het koloniale milieu aan Sumatra's oostkust in de eerste decennia van deze eeuw." *De Gids*, no. 155, 476–492.

Breman, Jan. 2020. "Colonialism and Its Racial Imprint." *Sojourn: Journal of Social Issues in Southeast Asia*, vol. 35, no. 3, 463–92.

Brown, Spencer H. 2004. "A Tool of Empire: The British Medical Establishment in Lagos, 1861–1905." *The International Journal of African Historical Studies*, vol. 37, no. 2, 309–343.

Buelens, Frans, and Ewout Frankema. 2016. "Colonial Adventures in Tropical Agriculture: New Estimates of Returns to Investment in the Netherlands Indies, 1919–1938." *Cliometrica*, no. 10, 197–224.

Burnard, Trevor. 2017. "Towns in Plantation Societies in Eighteenth-Century British America." *Early American Studies*, vol. 15, no. 4, 835–859.

Casimir, Jean. 1992. *The Caribbean: One and Divisible.* Santiago, Chile: Economic Commission for Latin America and the Caribbean.

Chandra, Siddharth. 2000. "What the Numbers Really Tell Us about the Decline of the Opium Regie." *Indonesia*, no. 70, 101–123.

Chen, Ta. 1940. *Emigrant Communities in South China.* New York: Secretariat, Institute of Pacific Relations.

Chen Yingqiu. 2004. "Huiyi baba sushuo de Huagong xuelei [blood and tears] shi" ("Recalling father's account of the Huagong history of blood and tears"). In Yang Tongling, Lin Zhang, Li Xinyun, Tan Enli, and Li Ensi, *Hunqian mengrao de guxiang–Bangjia dao* ("Lost in a reverie about one's native place: Bangka Island"), Beijing: Zhongguo youyi chuban gongsi, 2004, 592–593.

Colombijn, Freek. 2010. *Under Construction: The Politics of Urban Space and Housing during the Decolonization of Indonesia, 1930–1960.* Leiden: Brill.

Curtin, Philip. 1998. *The Rise and Fall of the Plantation Complex: Essays in Atlantic History.* Cambridge: Cambridge University Press.

Damanik, Erond Litno. 2020. "Ethnicity Situation and Intolerant Attitudes in Multicultural Societies in the Medan City." *Humaniora*, vol. 32, no. 1, 39–50.

Das, Anjan Kumar. 2019. *The Health of Indian Migrant Plantation Workers: Malaya 1870–1939.* Taylor's University, School of Medicine, Kuala Lumpur.

De Bruin, A. G. 1918. *De Chineezen ter Oostkust van Sumatra.* Issued by Het Oostkust van Sumatra-Instituut. Leiden: Brill.

De Graaf, S., and D. G. Stibbe, with W. C. B. Wintgens, eds. 1918. *Encyclopaedie van Nederlandsch-Indië*, second edition. 2 vols. The Hague: Martinus Nijhoff.

De Groot, Cornelis. 1887. *Herinneringen aan Blitong, Historisch, Lithologisch, Mineralogisch, Geographisch, Geologisch en Mijnbouwkundig.* The Hague: H. L. Smits.

De Kat Angelino, A. D. A. 1931. *Colonial Policy*, vol. 2, *The Dutch East Indies.* Translated by G. J. Renier. The Hague: Martinus Nijhoff.

Deli Planters Vereeniging. 1929. *Regeling en Wenken.* Second revised edition.

Derks, Hans. 2012. *History of the Opium Problem: The Assault on the East, Ca. 1600–1950.* Leiden: Brill.

Dodge, Nicholas N. 1980. "Population Estimates for the Malay Peninsula in the Nineteenth Century, with Special Reference to the East Coast States." *Population Studies*, vol. 34, no. 3, 437–475.

Dupuy, Alex. 1983. "Slavery and Underdevelopment in the Caribbean: A Critique of the 'Plantation Economy' Perspective." *Dialectical Anthropology*, vol. 7, no. 3, 237–251.

Erman, Erwiza. 1999. Miners, Managers and the State: A Socio-Political History of the Ombilin Coal-Mines, West Sumatra, 1892–1996. PhD thesis, University of Amsterdam.

Erman, Erwiza. 2017. "Chinese *Taukeh*, Labourer, and State Control: Case Study of *Panglong* in Eastern Region of Sumatra (1890–1930)." *Wacana*, vol. 18, no. 2, 514–539.

Fernando, M. R., and D. Bulbeck, eds. 1992. *Chinese Economic Activity in Netherlands India: Selected Translations from the Dutch.* Singapore: Institute of Southeast Asian Studies.

Fox, Jefferson, et al. 2009. "Policies, Political-Economy, and Swidden in Southeast Asia." *Human Ecology: An Interdisciplinary Journal*, vol. 37, no. 3, 305–322.

Frost, Mark Ravinder. 2005. "*Emporium in Imperio*: Nanyang Networks and the Straits Chinese in Singapore, 1819–1914." *Journal of Southeast Asian Studies*, vol. 36, no. 1, 29–66.

Furnivall, J. S. 1939. *Netherlands India: A Study of Plural Economy.* Cambridge: Cambridge University Press.

Gedenkboek Billiton, 1852–1927. 1927. 2 pts. The Hague: Martinus Nijhoff.

Gouda, Frances. 2009. Discipline versus Gentle Persuasion in Colonial Public Health: The Rockefeller Foundation's Intensive Rural Hygiene Work in the Netherlands East Indies, 1925–1940. Rockefeller Archive Center Research Report.

Gunter, John.1939. *Inside Asia*. London: Hamish Hamilton.

Guowuyuan qiaogong shiwu ju, eds. [January] 1920a. *Nanyang He shu Wanlitong dao Huagong qingxing diaocha shu* (An Investigation into the Situation of Huagong on Dutch-ruled Belitung Island in the Nanyang). Beijing: Guowuyuan qiaogong shiwu ju.

Guowuyuan qiaogong shiwu ju, eds. [May] 1920b. *Nanyang He shu Wangjia dao Huagong qingxing diaocha shu* (An Investigation into the Situation of Huagong on Dutch-ruled Bangka Island in the Nanyang). Beijing: Guowuyuan qiaogong shiwu ju.

Heidhues, Mary F. Somers. 1991. "Company Island: A Note on the History of Belitung." *Indonesia*, no. 51, 1–20.

Heidhues, Mary F. Somers. 1992. *Bangka Tin and Mentok Pepper: Chinese Settlement on an Indonesian Island*. Pasir Panjang: Institute of Southeast Asian Studies.

Heidhues, Mary F. Somers. 1993."Chinese Organization in West Borneo and Bangka: Kongsi and Hui." In David Ownby and Mary Somers Heidhues, eds, *"Secret Societies" Reconsidered: Perspectives on the Social History of Modern South China and Southeast Asia*, Armonk, NY: M. E. Sharpe, 1993, 68–88.

Heijting, H. G. 1925. *De koelie-wetgeving*. The Hague: Van Stockhum.

Hirayama, Nagatomi. 2013. "Partifying Sichuan: The Chinese Youth Party in Sichuan, 1926–1937." *Frontiers of History in China*, vol. 8, no.2, 223–258.

Hoefte, Rosemarijn. 2017. "Indentured Labor." In Karin Hofmeester and Marcel van der Linden, eds, *Handbook Global History of Work*, Berlin: De Gruyter, 363–376.

Hong Sisi. 1985. *Yindunixiya Huaqiao shi* (History of overseas Chinese in Indonesia). Beijing: Haiyang chuban she.

Houben, Vincent J. H. 1999. "The Quality of Coolie Life." In Vincent J. H. Houben and J. Thomas Lindblad, eds, *Coolie Labour in Colonial Indonesia: A Study of Labour Relations in the Outer Islands, c. 1900–1940*, Wiesbaden: Harrassowitz Verlag, 1999, 109–130.

Hsu, Madeline. 1997. "Gold Mountain Dreams and Paper Son Schemes: Chinese Immigration under Exclusion." In Chinese Historical Society of America, eds. *Chinese America: History and Perspectives, 1997*, San Francisco: San Francisco State University, 46–60.

Hui, Yew-Foong. 2011. *Strangers at Home: History and Subjectivity among the Chinese Communities of of West Kalimantan, Indonesia*. Leiden: Brill.

Jackson, James C. 1969. "Towards an Understanding of Plantation Agriculture." *Area*, vol. 1, no. 4, 36–41.

Jany, Gregory. 2021. *Imperial Crossings: Chinese Indentured Migration to Sumatra's East Coast, 1865–1911*. Council on East Asian Studies, Yale University.

Kamp, A. F. 1960. *De standvastige tinnen soldaat, 1860–1960: N. V. Billiton Maatschappij*. The Hague: Billiton Maatschappij.

Kaur, Amarjit. 2004. *Wage Labour in Southeast Asia since 1840: Globalisation, the International Division of Labour and Labour Transformations*. Houndsmill: Palgrave Macmillan.

Kaur, Amarjit. 2006. "Indian Labour, Labour Standards, and Workers' Health in Burma and Malaya, 1900–1940." *Modern Asian Studies*, vol. 40, no. 2, 425–475.

Kaur, Amarjit. 2013. "Indian Migrant Workers in Malaysia." *New Mandala*, 2 pts, February 20–21.

Kuhn, Philip A. 2008. *Chinese among Others: Emigration in Modern Times*. Lanham: Rowman and Littlefield.

Landheer, Bartholomew. 1941. "Financial Policy of the Dutch East Indies." *Far Eastern Survey*, vol. 10, no. 17, 195–200.

Lasker, Bruno. 1950. *Human Bondage in Southeast Asia*. Chapel Hill: University of North Carolina Press.

Leenarts, Ellen. 1999. "Coolie Wages in Western Enterprises in the Outer Islands, 1919–1938." In Vincent J. H. Houben and J. Thomas Lindblad, eds, *Coolie Labour in Colonial Indonesia: A Study of Labour Relations in the Outer Islands, c. 1900–1940*, Wiesbaden: Harrassowitz Verlag, 1999, 131–155.

Leinbach, Thomas R. 1987. "Economic Growth, Development Planning and Policy Alternatives in Medan, Indonesia." *Journal of Southeast Asian Studies*, vol. 18, no. 1, 118–140.

Lindblad, J. Thomas. 1999. "Coolies in Deli: Labour Conditions in Western Enterprises in East Sumatra, 1910–1938." In Vincent J. H. Houben and J. Thomas Lindblad, eds, *Coolie Labour in Colonial Indonesia: A Study of Labour Relations in the Outer Islands, c. 1900–1940*, Wiesbaden: Harrassowitz Verlag, 1999, 43–78.

Lindquist, Johan, and Biao Xiang. 2019. "Space of Mediation: Labour Migration, Intermediaries and the State in Indonesia and China since the Nineteenth Century." *Revue Européenne des Migrations Internationales*, vol. 35, nos 1–2, 39–62

Lockard, Craig A. 1971. "The Javanese as Emigrant: Observations on the Development of Javanese Settlements Overseas." *Indonesia*, no. 11, 41–62.

Loh, Kah Seng. 2022. "Coolies and Crisis in Singapore: The Great Depression in the 1930s and the Chinese Working Class." In Chi-cheung Choi, Tomoko Shiroyama, and Venus Viana, eds, *Strenuous Decades: Global Challenges and Transformation of Chinese Societies in Modern Asia*, Berlin: De Gruyter, 142–166.

Look Lai, Walton. 1993. *Indentured Labor, Caribbean Sugar: Chinese and. Indian Migrants to the British West Indies, 1838–1918*. Introduced by Sidney W. Mintz. Baltimore: The Johns Hopkins University Press.

López, Kathleen. 2013. *Chinese Cubans: A Transnational History*. Chapel Hill: University of North Carolina Press.

Lu Wendi, Chen Zexian, and Peng Jiali, eds. 1981. *Guanyu Huagong chuguo de Zhongwai zonghexing zhuzuo* (Comprehensive writings from China and abroad concerning Huagong migration). In Chen Hansheng, ed., *Huagong chuguo shiliao huibian* (A compilation of edited historical materials regarding going abroad by Huagong), Beijing: Zhonghua shuju, 12 vols, 1981–1985, vol. 4.

Lu Wendi, Chen Zexian, and Peng Jiali, eds. 1984a. *Guanyu Huagong chuguo de Zhongwai zonghexing zhuzuo* (Comprehensive writings from China and abroad concerning Huagong migration). In Chen Hansheng, ed., *Huagong chuguo shiliao huibian* (A compilation of edited historical materials regarding going abroad by Huagong), Beijing: Zhonghua shuju, 12 vols, 1981–1985, vol. 4.

Lu Wendi, Chen Zexian, and Peng Jiali, eds. 1985. *Zhongguo guanwen shu xuanji* (A selection of official Chinese documents). In Chen Hansheng, ed., *Huagong chuguo shiliao huibian* (A compilation of edited historical materials regarding going abroad by Huagong), Beijing: Zhonghua shuju, 12 vols, 1981–1985, vol. 1, pt 1.

Lu Wendi, Peng Jiali, and Chen Zexian, eds. 1984b. *Guanyu Dongnan Ya Huagong de siren zhuzuo* (Private individuals' writings about Huagong in Southeast Asia). In Chen Hansheng, ed., *Huagong chuguo shiliao huibian* (A compilation of edited historical materials regarding going abroad by Huagong), Beijing: Zhonghua shuju, 12 vols, 1981–1985, vol. 5.

Ma Huiyue. 2015. *Jindai qiyue Huagong falü* (Laws on modern Chinese indentured labour). Beijing: Falü chuban she.

Maassen, C. C. J. 1937. *De Javaansche landbouwkolonisatie in de Buitengewesten*. Batavia: Landsdrukkerij.

MacNair, H. F. 1923. "The Chinese as Contract Laborers." *The Weekly Review*, June 2.

MacNair, H. F. 1924. "The Chinese in the Dutch East Indies." *The China Weekly Review*, September 20.

Maddison, Angus. 1989. "Dutch Income in and from Indonesia, 1700–1938." *Modern Asian Studies*, vol. 23, no. 4, 645–670.

Mandle, Jay R. 1972. "The Plantation Economy: An Essay in Definition." *Science & Society*, vol. 36, no. 1, 49–62.

Melbourn, G. Fraser. 1894. *The Planter's Manual: An English, Dutch, Malay and Keh Chinese Vocabulary*. Deli-Sumatra: n. p.

Mollema, J. C. 1922. *De ontwikkeling van het eiland Billiton en van de Billiton-Maatschappij*. The Hague: Nijhoff.

Nair, A. R. 1931. "British Malaya Owes Debt to Chinese Settlers." *The China Press*, September 26.

Northrup, David. 1995. *Indentured Labor in the Age of Imperialism, 1834–1922.* New York: Cambridge University Press.

Pantin, Dennis. 1980. "The Plantation Economy Model and the Caribbean." *Bulletin*, vol. 12, no. 1, Institute of Development Studies, Sussex, 17–23.

Parker, Edward Harper. 1902. *John Chinaman and a Few Others.* London: John Murray.

Paulus, Jozlas, compiler. 1919. *Encyclopaedie van Nederlandsch-Indië*, second edition, 2 vols. The Hague: Martinus Nijhoff.

Pelzer, Karl J. 1935. *Die Arbeiterwanderungen in Südostasien: Eine wirtschafts- und bevölkerungsgeographische Untersuchung.* Würzburg: Konrad Triltsch.

Perry, Elizabeth J. 2008. "Reclaiming the Chinese Revolution." *The Journal of Asian Studies*, vol. 67, no. 4, 1147–1164.

Pols, Hans. 2018. *Nurturing Indonesia: Medicine and Decolonisation in the Dutch East Indies.* Cambridge: Cambridge University Press.

Powell, Miles Alexander. 2016. "People in Peril, Environments at Risk: Coolies, Tigers, and Colonial Singapore's Ecology of Poverty." *Environment and History,* no. 22, 455–482.

Powell, Edward Alexander. 1921. *Where the Strange Trails Go Down: Sulu, Borneo, Celebes, Bali, Java, Sumatra, Straits Settlements, Malay States, Siam, Cambodia, Annam, Cochin-China.* New York: Charles Scribner's Sons.

Qin, Yucheng. 2016. *The Cultural Clash: Chinese Traditional Native-Place Sentiment and the Anti-Chinese Movement.* Lanham: University Press of America.

Rapport betreffende Chineezen-Werving op Billiton. 1905. BrRG-33 = 16072 KIT.

Rediker, Marcus, Titas Chakraborty, and Matthias van Rossum, eds. 2019. *A Global History of Runaways: Workers, Mobility, and Capitalism, 1600–1850.* Oakland: University of California Press.

Rhemrev, J. L. T. 1903 [1987]. Rapport van de resultaten van het mij bij Gouvernements Besluit van 24 Mei 1903 No. 19 opgedragen onderzoek. In Jan Breman, *Koelies, Planters en Koloniale Politiek: Het arbeidsregime op de grootlandbouwondernemingen aan Sumatra's oostkust in het begin van de twintigste eeuw,* Dordrecht: Foris Publications, 1987, 315–408.

Ruzicka, Ivan. n.d. "Forest Exploitation in Indonesia: Past and Present." *Indonesia Circle*, vol. 6, no. 16, 3–15.

Snelders, Stephen, Leo van Bergen, and Frank Huisman. 2019. "Leprosy and the Colonial Gaze: Comparing the Dutch West and East Indies, 1750–1950." *Social History of Medicine*, vol. 34, no. 2, 611–631.

Stenberg, Josh, and Minasny Budiman. 2022. "Coolie Legend on the Deli Plantation: Tale, Text, and Temple of the Five Ancestors." *Bijdragen tot de taal-, land- en volkenkunde*, vol. 178, nos. 2–3, 159–191.

Stibbe, D. G., and C. Spat, with E. M. Uhlenbeck, eds. 1927. *Encyclopaedie van Nederlandsch-Indië*. Second edition. 8 vols. The Hague: Martinus Nijhoff, vol. 5.

Stoler, Ann Laura. 1985. *Capitalism and Confrontation in Sumatra's Plantation Belt, 1870–1979*. New Haven: Yale University Press.

Tien, Ju-K'ang. 1953. *The Chinese of Sarawak: A Study of Social Structure*. London: Department of Anthropology, London School of Economics and Political Science.

The Deli Coolie Question [1881–1882]. KIT BrRN—40 KIT = 1953.

Tian Yu. 1929. "Wulidong Huagong jinkuang" ("Recent situation of Huagong in Belitung). *Nanyang yanjiu,* published by Jinan University's Nanyang Culture Department, vol. 2, no. 4, 282–293.

Tjandra, Surya. 2016. Labour Law and Development in Indonesia. Doctoral Thesis, Leiden University.

Trocki, Carl A. 2011. "Opium as a Commodity in the Chinese Nanyang Trade." In Eric Tagliacozzo and Wen-Chin Chang, eds, *Chinese Circulations: Capital, Commodities, and Networks in Southeast Asia*, Durham: Duke University, 2011, 84–106.

Van Bergen, Leo. 2019. *The Dutch East Indies Red Cross, 1870–1950: On Humanitarianism and Colonialism*. Lanham MA: Rowman and Littlefield.

Van Blommestein, A. F. 1917. *De Nieuwe Koelie-Ordonnantie voor de Oostkust van Sumatra*. Amsterdam: Scheltema and Holkema.

Van den Berg, Jurrien. 1999. "Tin Island: Labour Conditions in the Billiton Mines in the Nineteenth and Early Twentieth Centuries." In Vincent J. H. Houben and J. Thomas Lindblad, eds, *Coolie Labour in Colonial Indonesia: A Study of Labour Relations in the Outer Islands, c. 1900–1940*, Wiesbaden: Harrassowitz Verlag, 1999, 209–230.

Van den Brand, Johannes. 1903. *Nog Eens: De Millioenen uit Deli*. Amsterdam: Höveker and Wormser.

Van der Eng, Pierre. 2002. "Bridging a Gap: A Reconstruction of Population Patterns in Indonesia, 1930–61." *Asian Studies Review*, vol. 26, no. 4, 487–509.

Vandenbosch, Amry. 1931. "Colonial Labor Problems: The Labor Contract with Penal Sanction in the Dutch East Indies." *Pacific Affairs*, vol. 4, no. 4, 318–324.

Van Luijk, Eric W., and Jan C. van Ours. 1993. How to Control Drugs: The Lessons of the Opiumregie in the Dutch East Indies (1894–1940). Research Memorandum 1993–30, Vrije Universiteit Amsterdam.

Wang Linqian and Wu Kunxiang, eds. 2002. *Zaoqi Huaqiao yu qiyue Huagong (mai zhuzai) ziliao* (Early materials relating to overseas Chinese and indentured Huagong [piglet trade]). Chaoshan: Chaoshan lishi wenhua yanjiu zhongxin, Shantou shi wenhua ju, Shantou shi tushu guan.

Wazar, R. M. 2004 [1956]. "Tinnen Munten van Bangka." *Erts: Maandblad der Billitonbedrijven*, October 1956, no. 10. Reprinted in Yang Tongling, Lin Zhang, Li Xinyun, Tan Enli, and Li Ensi, *Hunqian mengrao de guxiang—Bangjia dao* ("Lost in a reverie about one's native place: Bangka Island"), Beijing: Zhongguo youyi chuban gongsi, 2004, 209–211.

Wiseman, Roger. 2001. Three Crises: Management in the Colonial Java Sugar Industry, 1880s–1930s. PhD, University of Adelaide.

Wolf, Eric R., with Sydel Silverman. 2001. *Pathways of Power: Building an Anthropology of the Modern World*. Berkeley: University of California Press.

Wu Fengbin. 1988. *Qiyue Huagong shi* (History of indentured Chinese labour). Nanchang: Jiangxi renmin chuban she.

Xiao Jingliao. 2018. "Xianju gumiao zhen manbang: Lalü zhanzheng yu He Xiangu xinyang zai Yingshu Malaiya de kaizhan" ("Pacifying the wildland": The Larut Wars and the beginning of the He Xiangu cult in British Malaya"). *Zhongyang yanjiu yuan jindai shi yanjiu suo jikan*, no. 100, 47–84.

Xu Guoqi. 2011. *Strangers on the Western Front: Chinese Workers in the Great War.* Cambridge MA: Harvard University Press.

Yang Qunxi, ed. 2004. *Chaoshan diqu qiaopi ye ziliao* (Materials Concerning the Qiaopi Trade in the Chaoshan Region). Shantou: Shantou shi tushu guan.

Yang Tongling, Lin Zhang, Li Xinyun, Tan Enli, and Li Ensi. 2004. *Hunqian mengrao de guxiang—Bangjia dao* ("Lost in a reverie about one's native place: Bangka Island"). Beijing: Zhongguo youyi chuban gongsi.

Zhang Beiyu. 2020. "A Bright Moon Roaming in Nanyang: Li Jinhui and the Chinese Song and Dance Troupe." *Paan*, no. 1, 134–150.

Zhou Nanjing, Chen Wenxian, Lin Liushun, and Zheng Min, eds. 1996. *Yindunixiya Huaren tonghua wenti ziliao huibian* (Materials on the assimilation of Indonesian Chinese). Beijing: Beijing daxue Yatai yanjiu zhongxin.

Zhu Jieqin. 1984. "Shijiu shiji zhongqi zai Yindunixiya de qiyue Huagong" ("Indentured Huagong in Indonesia in the mid nineteenth century"). In Chen Hansheng, ed., *Huagong chuguo shiliao huibian* (A compilation of edited historical materials regarding going abroad by Huagong), Beijing: Zhonghua shuju, 12 vols, 1981–1985, vol. 5, 217–243.

Zondervan, Sjoerd. 2016. Patients of the Colonial State: The Rise of a Hospital System in the Netherlands Indies, 1890–1940. PhD, University of Maastricht.

Appendix A

Liu Yuzun, Huang Zhongyan, Gui Guanghua, and Wu Fengbin, eds, *"Zhuzai" Huagong fangwen lu* ("Transcripts of interviews with Chinese 'piglet' labourers"), Guangzhou: Guangdong renmin chuban she, 2016 [1963, 1978].

The Heart-Rending Story of Indentured Chinese Labour: Report on an Investigation of Forty-four Coolies Who Worked on Plantations on Former East Sumatra and in Tin Mines on Bangka

This is a slightly condensed translation of a set of interviews taken in 1963 by a team of social scientists from Xiamen University. Where unable to ascertain the Indonesian names of places and plantations, I have retained the Chinese form.

Huang Zhongyan, Liu Yuzun, Wu Fengbin, and Gui Guanghua, "Preface"

In May 1963, we went to the Jize Farm in Yinjiang in Guangdong to carry out an investigation. The object of the investigation was forty-four veteran labourers who, having sold themselves into indenture, returned to China from Indonesia. They had been trafficked between 1900 and 1940 to plantations and tin mines. We wanted to know how they had been trafficked; how they had laboured, lived, and struggled; and how they had eventually escaped their indenture.

G. Benton, *Chinese Indentured Labour in the Dutch East Indies, 1880–1942*, Palgrave Macmillan Transnational History Series,
https://doi.org/10.1007/978-3-031-05024-4

We came to realise the following.

- Economic and political oppression by imperialism, bureaucratic capitalism, and the landlord class was the main reason for the trafficking.
- Under the Western colonialists' cruel system of indenture slavery, Chinese "piglets" lived miserable lives and many died as a result of their exploitation.
- However cruelly the colonialists oppressed them and however strictly they controlled them, the colonialists were unable to stop the coolies' resistance and desire for liberation.
- The great majority of the Overseas Chinese "piglets" actively built the economy in the country where they lived and were oppressed. People who unreasonably and absurdly slander Overseas Chinese as exploiters and a Fifth Column confound black and white and have a hidden agenda and calumnious intent.

1. Overview

The forty-four "piglets" comprised twenty tobacco-plantation workers, five rubber-plantation workers, and nineteen tin miners. They came from three provinces (Guangdong, Guangxi, and Hubei) and twenty-six counties and cities. Before emigrating, almost all were young and vigorous peasants of a low cultural level—almost all were illiterate or semi-literate.

As for the immediate causes of their emigration, they were as follows. Some left because land rent and taxes were too heavy, and they were unable to cope with frequent natural disasters; some because warlord depredations and rampant banditry made life in the villages difficult; some because of the white terror carried out by the Kuomintang reactionaries, who press-ganged young men into the army and made it impossible for them to stay at home; together with various other causes. But the basic reason was the cruel system of imperialist, bureaucratic capitalist, and feudal oppression, which drove people to the wall and forced some to sell themselves into indenture overseas.

Expressed in terms of percentages: onerous land rent and lack of livelihood at home (68.2 percent); escaping white terror and press-ganging (9 percent); natural disasters (4.5 percent); swindling and abduction (4.5 percent); and other causes (13.8).

The coolies emigrated at different times. Before 1919, the great majority were trafficked to work on plantations, and most sailed from Shantou. Those trafficked to work in tin mines mostly left starting in 1923. Most were from Chaozhou, Hakka villages, and counties in Guangdong and southeastern Guangxi, and most left through Hong Kong.

After they had been trafficked abroad, they lived the miserable lives of slaves under the colonial system of indenture. The period of indenture varied, usually from two to five years. Because the colonialists implemented a cruel regime of servitude and applied despicable measures to corrupt indentured labourers (such as tempting them with prostitutes, gambling, drinking alcohol, and smoking opium), they were able to extend the date of their release from indenture, so that very many were forced to renew their indenture time and again, thus practically becoming slaves for life. Like Zhou Yazhao and Chen Yaxing, one of whom spent thirty years and the other thirty-one years as an indentured slave on a Dutch plantation.

The tragedy of a life enslaved left terrible scars on these veteran workers' bodies. Many became old before their time. Even men in the prime of their lives were bent at the back or contracted asthma and various other occupational diseases. They were victims of the Western colonial system of indentured servitude, and testimony to it.

2. The causes of the trafficking

Even before they were trafficked overseas as "piglets," the forty-four labourers had experienced a sad and bitter life. Most were peasants, and the majority (36 people, or 86.4 percent) were poor and lower-middle peasants. At the time of their trafficking, all were young and able-bodied, and the great majority were their families' main source of labour power. Forty (90.9 percent) were between the ages of seventeen and thirty. Some had drifted into the cities as temporary labourers who, eventually, were unable to escape the fate of being trafficked.

What led these young able-bodied men to abandon their families and to turn their backs on their ancestral places in exchange for a life of slavery? According to the labourers themselves, the main reason was the cruel exploitation and oppression they suffered in old China at the hands of the landlords and the reactionary bureaucrats.

In old China, agriculture's main productive asset—land—was overwhelmingly in the hands of the reactionary bureaucrats and landlords. According to Zeng Jiu, who was trafficked in 1912, "the entire village [of Chentouchong in Lian County in Guangdong] belonged almost exclusively to the big landlord Luo Wuhe. He had so much land it was hard to calculate clearly. Apart from Lian County, he owned a lot of property in Lianshan and Yangshan. In our village, just a handful of families had a tiny bit of land, all the rest were Luo Wuhe's tenant farmers." Huang Chengzhao, who was trafficked in 1910, said: "[In Shikengwei Village in Longchuan County in Guangdong], the moneybags Huang Bingyi ranked among the biggest landlords. He had land capable of producing more than one thousand dan, all the poor people in the village's four lineages rented land from him." Since the bureaucrats and landlords owned almost all the land, they were able to treat the landless poor peasants cruelly and rapaciously.

The main form that landlord exploitation of the peasants took was rent paid in kind. The proportion was usually fifty-fifty between tenant and landlord, the so-called half-and-half system. But there was also the sixty-forty system in favour of the landlord, and even more unequal ones. According to Yang Jincuan, a labourer trafficked in 1911, "[in Shiqiaotou Township in Guangdong's Puning County], land rent was calculated on the basis of the fact that there were two crops a year, divided into big winter and small winter (indicating the volume of output). The big-winter harvest was the rent, the small-winter harvest went to the tenant." This division favoured the landlord by even more than sixty-forty.

Under the rent-in-kind system, the greater part of the product of the landless peasants' hard labour was given to the landlord. Many people engaged in subsidiary work, did odd jobs, chopped and sold firewood or cut hay, and toiled away like beasts of burden, but even so they were unable to give their families the lowest level of subsistence and were always hungry. Zeng Jiu's family rented three mu from the landlord and harvested fifteen dan of paddy a year. The rent was nine dan, and nine dou were kept back for planting, which meant that each year they retained a harvest of a little over five dan. The family comprised five people, and even though adults and children all did extra jobs, it was still hard to sustain a livelihood. Landless peasants with no extra labour power fared even worse. The family of Zhou Yazhao, who was trafficked in 1900, comprised three people, but the father and mother were already old, and although they sought short-term work in the village, it got harder and harder to find such work the older they got, so they constantly starved. Zhou Yazhao himself was forced starting at the age of twelve to take work towing merchants' boats [along rivers or canals] at a semi-starvation wage.

These lower-middle peasants without enough land to feed them lived hard lives. The best land, the wooded hills, and the ponds all belonged to the landlords and the despotic gentry. The lower-middle peasants usually only had scattered plots of inferior land or dry hill fields and low-lying water-logged land. When it rained too heavily or didn't rain at all, not a single grain was reaped; if they irrigated it, again they had to deal with the landlords' extortion and racketeering. Even if they slaved away all year, life was still hard. There were five people in the family of Liu Yaping, who was trafficked in 1910: "We planted low-lying water-logged land that yielded four to five dou. We could only sow one crop of paddy and one of sweet potatoes a year, but there were constant floods, so the harvest was meagre. We couldn't even manage a bowl of cooked rice, we lived off rice water with a few sweet potatoes mixed in." Chen Yaxing, who was trafficked in the same year, had a family of six: "Our family had two mu of hillside land. But the crop was poor, and all the brothers starved."

Apart from the predations of the landlord, the reactionary government's exorbitant taxes and levies were another cause of the peasant' suffering and bankruptcy. The taxes and levies went under many names. The heaviest was the land tax. Then there was Boxer reparations, military expenses, and miscellaneous expenses. These taxes were borne almost exclusively by the poor, lower-middle, and middle peasants. The landlords and despotic gentry colluded with government officials to offload these taxes and levies onto the backs of the peasants, even in their own name. They even privately apportioned various taxes and levies to line their own pockets.

Under the oppression of the landlords, evil gentry, and feudal-bureaucratic officials, the poor peasants were constantly netted up by usurers charging high rates of interest. According to veteran labourers, the usurers were usually the landlords themselves, riding on their backs. They loaned money out at usurious rates, while at the same time running pawn shops. The landlord Luo Wuhe in Lian County "was the biggest usurer. He gave loans himself, and loaned to smaller creditors who loaned on to tenants." The landlord Huang Bingyi in Longchuan County "ran more than a dozen shops [in Shikengwei] and controlled the rice market in the region. He also ran two pawn shops where you could pawn farm tools (ploughs, harrows, hoes, sickles, etc.). The monthly interest was 2.5 percent. Whenever there were crop failures, poor people used to pawn whatever they could." But taking high-interest loans was like quenching your thirst with poisoned wine, it could get you into even deeper trouble.

Usury was an important means by which landlords acquired land owned by lower-middle and some middle peasants. Due to hardship, Liu Yaping "used his meagre holdings as collateral for a loan from a rich man. A few years later, the land was taken over completely by the landlord."

The veteran labourers had a limited understanding, and did not fully realise that they were forced out of their villages by imperialist invasion and oppression. But imperialist aggression was precisely the cause of the transformation of China into a semi-colony, as Mao Zedong pointed out. Imperialism violently wrested political and economic privileges from China, captured Chinese markets with manufactured commodities, seized Chinese raw materials, undermined China's natural economy, and destroyed Chinese handicrafts, so that the Chinese peasantry was bankrupted. So imperialism was also a major cause of the expulsion of Chinese labourers from the villages and their trafficking overseas.

Politics too played a role. After the 1911 Revolution, the imperialists colluded with China's feudal bureaucrats and landlords to throttle that revolution and to step up their aggression against and their nibbling away at China. They manipulated wars for territory among Chinese warlords so that China's civil wars multiplied, its politics became ever more confused, and its national crisis deepened. No few of the veterans we interviewed left their villages during the period of political confusion and were trafficked as a result. For example, Zhong Yasheng, who lived a life of semi-starvation, left home in 1915, afraid of the military turmoil in Guangdong, and was trafficked in the same year. Xu Yaer also fled his village, in 1924, after Chen Jiongming's armed rebellion in the Dongjiang region, when Xu's elder brother was press-ganged into the army. Xu Yaer himself escaped to Hong Kong, whence he was trafficked overseas.

In 1927, Chiang Kai-shek launched his counter-revolutionary coup against the Chinese Communist Party, and ruled the worker and peasant masses by sanguinary means. He seized able-bodied men everywhere to fight his civil war and subjected the country to white terror—that was one of the political causes of the forced departure of the veteran labourers from their villages. Zhu Fuzhong took part in the Northern Expedition and later in the [Communist-led] Guangzhou Uprising in 1927, but after the defeat of the uprising he was forced by Chiang Kai-shek's white terror to flee to Hong Kong, where he was jobless and was trafficked overseas. Li Gui's family, which comprised thirteen people, of whom six brothers were able-bodied labourers, was unable to keep going because of cruel landlord exploitation and the hardships of life, as well as Chiang Kai-shek's practice of press-ganging—in Li Gui's village, one able-bodied man in three was taken, and even two in five. Li Gui's two younger brother were forced to join the army. He thought the same would happen to him, so he fled the village and ended up being trafficked.

Feudal forces in the villages ran wild. Feudal landlords, despotic hegemons, evil tyrants, local bandits, and reactionary armed forces colluded everywhere to rob and harm the people. That was another reason that some veteran labourers left home and became destitute and separated from their kin. He De was bullied and humiliated by an evil tyrant and robbed in broad daylight—he had no choice other than to leave home and seek a livelihood elsewhere. Yan Gui had no choice because of bandits rampaging through his village other than to leave. Qian Zhen's father was killed by the reactionary army after false accusations that he was a local bandit, and his home was burned to the ground and looted. Afterwards, the landlord evicted Qian's family from the land he had leased to them, and Qian had no way out other than to be trafficked overseas.

Cruel oppression and exploitation by imperialists, officials, and feudal forces made it hard for poor and lower-middle peasants to survive, and they lost the ability to resist natural disasters. When natural disasters came, the peasants collapsed into out-and-out bankruptcy, starvation, and extinction. Peng Jingchu's village suffered a flood and most of the land his family rented turned into a sandbar, so in despair he left home. Hong Shuigui's village was hit by a typhoon and all the salt pans along the coast were destroyed. Peng Jingchu's older brother and sister-in-law moved to another village to work as hired labourers and he himself went to seek work in Hong Kong. Jiang Yali and Zhang Panliang were both middle peasants. Jiang lost his paddy field as a result of a huge windstorm and an inundation; Zhuang suffered a drought and was forced to leave his village.

So large numbers of Chinese labourers were trafficked directly from the villages as "piglets" as a result of imperialist, bureaucratic capitalist, and feudal oppression and the threat of starvation. Others first left the villages and drifted to the towns and cities, but there national industry, handicrafts, and commerce was on the verge of collapse as a result of the destruction wreaked by these three forces. They were unable to find a way out and ended up in the hands of "piglet" traffickers.

In the course of the interviews, some veterans, like Liu Tai and Deng San, said they were trafficked as a result of gambling debts. They came from labouring families of people who earned their own living and depended on hard graft to eke out a minimal existence. They too suffered at the hands of the three forces. They were too poor to gamble, so they staked their bodies instead, in the illusory hope of winning enough to free themselves from their misfortune. As a result, they were netted up by the traffickers and became slaves.

Xu Shiwu and Huang Yada were abducted into indenture. The "piglet" traders were a product of the old Chinese social system. It was precisely because the reactionary ruling class turned a blind eye to their evil actions that they were able to indulge in their savage habit of selling people into slavery.

Obviously, these veteran labourers were forced into servitude and did not go "of their own accord."

3. The experience of trafficking

Being trafficked was a humiliating experience. The traffickers sold them on to the colonialists like animals. According to the veteran labourers, before 1919 the Dutch colonialists had for a long time run "piglet"-purchasing black shops in Shantou. These black shops either operated under the signboard of a "foreign firm" or as an "office," the main point of which was to traffic labour. They didn't themselves go into the villages to buy "piglets" but instead used an extensive network of Chinese "piglet" traders in the villages and cities, who carried out abductions. After abduction, the "piglet" would be exported by the black shop. These black shops were closely tied to the Twelve Companies set up by the Dutch planters in Deli. The Yuanxing Foreign Firm in Shantou, one of the biggest black shops, was a labour-trafficking body that came directly under the Twelve Companies. It practically monopolised the "piglet" trade in Shantou. The Twelve Companies didn't have a special "piglet"-carrying steamer at Shantou. They first transported the "piglets" to Deli and from there to various plantations. Not until 1919 did they close their black shop in Shantou and transfer it to Hong Kong, where they continued their evil work of trafficking people into servitude.

Whether in Shantou or Hong Kong, large numbers of inns or hostels were set up specially as part of "piglet" trafficking, by local tyrants and gang masters. The veterans called them *undefined* ("guest firm"). There the "piglets" would be gathered together. They were closely supervised and kept under strict discipline. After the "piglets" had been gathered together in such a place, it was practically impossible to escape. Chen Yazhou recalled how, in 1912, there were 22 *kehang*. He and others could recall their names.

The labourers were called "piglets" and the traffickers were called *ketou*, literally "guest-head," i.e., gangers. These scum were in some cases landlords and local tyrants from the villages, but most were local ruffians and hoodlums. Some were *laoke* ("old guests") who had returned to China from overseas. They were bodyguards of top Chinese overseers in the Dutch plantations or of gang leaders in the Bangka tin mines. Their job was to return to China and to abduct and sell workers.

The tricks and deceptions that the gangers used to abduct "piglets" were sinister and crafty. They can be summed up as follows: pretend to sympathise with poor people's predicament; tell lies about life in the Nanyang, and paint it as prosperous, for example, say that work is easy to find there and wages are high; tell them they won't need to buy a ticket for the boat, and the ganger will pay for their passage to Shantou or Hong Kong and for their accommodation, and that they will even get an allowance for settling in. Seduced by such honeyed words, many veteran labourers fell straight into the trap and were sold into servitude. Liu Ying's case is a prime example. The ganger told him: "Life is good in the Nanyang, everyone has his own kitchen and wears silk shirts and silk trousers." The ganger was believed, and the labourer was trafficked.

After the "piglet" had been abducted into the *kehang*, he usually had to go to the Dutch foreign firm to undergo the trafficking procedure and sign a contract of indenture. This involved four steps: oral interview, physical examination, signing of the contract, and taking of a photograph.

When the ganger took the "piglet" to the foreign firm, a Dutch labour contractor usually requested an oral deposition. Questions included the following: "Are you entering voluntarily into indenture?" "Do your parents agree?" The person selling himself into indenture, whether tricked or abducted, can only say yes, once having ended up in this prisoner's cage. Sometimes, to save time and trouble, labourers were asked to answer the questions collectively, by raising their hands. The colonialists' hypocritical intent was to record in a document the labourers' declaration and thus to cover up the crime of selling them into servitude.

After the interrogation came the physical examination. According to regulations, the person being examined had to strip off and walk in a circle. Sometimes a "doctor" would pinch his upper arm or his buttocks to see how strong he was. If everything seemed in order, the examination was over. The physical examination in the foreign firm in Shantou was relatively basic, while that in Hong Kong was a lot stricter. The colonialists in Hong Kong were mainly recruiting indentured labour to work in the mines, so they needed strong men. As well as making the "piglets" strip off, they made them lift large loads of stone or wood, tested their reflexes, and got them to jump over a wooden bench. Both in Shantou and in Hong Kong, any special physical features (e.g., scars) were put on file.

That was probably so that "piglets" could be identified if they escaped and were re-caught.

After the physical examination came the signing of the indenture. The contract was in written form. (Some veterans said it was oral, but they were probably wrong, for many were illiterate and the gangers handled the contract on their behalf.) The contract stipulated that the indenture was purely voluntary. It specified the length of the indenture and stipulated that during the period of its validity the indentured person must under all circumstances obey all the buyer's assignments and should under no circumstances dissent from them. The indentured labourer put a fingerprint to the contract and added a signature,[1] after which the contract was given a serial number and a photo was taken of the labourer with a wooden placard round his neck with his name and number on it. At this point, the transaction had been completed.

The "piglet" traders often changed the indentured person's name. We noticed during our research that many of the names were written with simple strokes and included numbers. It turned out that these names were not the bearers' original names. Why the changes? On the one hand, to simplify them and make them easier to call out and to distribute assignments, but even more importantly to preserve their anonymity so that their families would be unable to track them down. For example, after Huang Yada was abducted, his family sought him for three years to no effect. The fact that names could be changed at will is a measure of the moral depravity of the "piglet" trade.

The methods used by the trade were akin to practices in livestock markets. After the transaction had been completed, the buyer gave his purchase some "sale silver," dressed up as a "family allowance." According to veterans, in Shantou before 1919 a "piglet"'s sale silver was nominally 30–50 silver dollars, and at most 70. This money was not given directly to the indentured person but to the ganger or the *kehang*. After deductions for travel to Shantou and subsistence and accommodation, procedural costs, etc., there was little left. The amount left over was either gambled away by the "piglet" trader or vanished into the trader's pocket, on the pretext of remitting it to the indentured labourer's family. But none of the "piglets'" families ever received "consolation money." In Hong Kong the "piglet"'s "sale silver" was even smaller, and sometimes amounted to next

[1] If the labourer was illiterate, the ganger would sign on his behalf. After the signing, the buyer would "reward" him with a few dollars.

to nothing. After the completion of formalities and the signing of the contract, the "piglet" received between 5–7 dollars' "signing silver," as well as clothes, a crude mat, and some articles for daily use from the *kehang* the night before embarkation.

The sale silver was actually payment in advance. According to the veteran labourers, the plantations in East Sumatra stipulated that *xinke* ("new guests"), on joining the plantation, would have to complete three years as unskilled labourers (later changed to two) before becoming eligible for release from indenture, and the entire amount of recruitment expenses would not be recovered; if, however, he had been promoted midway to a tobacco job, and thus been paid as an old guest, he would have to pay back the entire recruitment costs, to the point where the entire amount of the wages received offset the recruitment expenses, and only then could he be released. The veteran labourers also mentioned that unskilled work was paid at a lowly rate of fl0 a month, whereas growing tobacco brought in at the very least f200 a year (calculated on the basis of 15,000 plants a year at a rate of fl0 per thousand plants and three months' picking on a wage of f50), i.e., f80 more a year than an unskilled labourer or f240 over a three-year period. This discrepancy uncovers the secret of the colonialists' stipulation that new guests did not need to pay back their entire recruitment costs after working for three years. The new guests did unskilled work for three years on a low wage and received f240 less over that period than a tobacco worker, which sum was sufficient to offset recruitment costs. The Bangka tin mines had a similar provision: new guests earning f0.24 a day had to work for two years before becoming eligible for release. These new guests were also on a low wage—compared with "free tin miners," who earned f0.51 a day, a difference of f0.27. Over the course of two years, this difference added up to more than fl60. The new guests' relative shortfall was again sufficient to offset recruitment costs. The traffickers' bragging about "a free ticket back to China" and a "family consolation allowance" was nothing but a hoax.

The veteran labourers provided a lot of material about the "piglet" boats and life on the boats. The Dutch colonialists in Shantou and Hong Kong had special boats on which to transport "piglets." Some regular steamers transported "piglets" as well as goods and ordinary passengers. Very few of the steamers out of Shantou stopped along the route to Medan in East Sumatra. In contrast, nearly all the steamers out of Hong Kong stopped in Singapore for a day or two to unload passengers and goods before sailing on to Mentok in Bangka or to Medan. From Hong Kong to

Bangka four ships specially transported "piglets" to the mines; while three on the Hong Kong-Medan line transported "piglets" to the plantations.

On shipboard, the "piglets" were kept in the hold—sometimes more than one thousand at a time. The hold was crowded and stifling hot, and food and hygiene were very basic. Seasickness and illnesses were rife. These "piglet" boats were a re-enactment in the twentieth century of the "floating hells" on which Western colonialists transported black slaves to the Americas in the seventeenth century. The sea journey took five to seven days to Mentok or Medan. On arrival, the "piglets" were immediately taken to the tin mines or plantations to begin their indenture.

4. The system of indentured servitude on the plantations of East Sumatra and the "piglets'" life and labour
   (a) The Deli tobacco plantations

Deli, on the east coast of Sumatra, had already started growing tobacco before the nineteenth century, but not on a big scale. Its tobacco is considered mellow, and it is used to make cigars. In the twentieth century, Sumatra had more than sixty tobacco plantations. All the veteran tobacco workers we interviewed had worked in Deli. All the score of plantations on which they worked were Dutch-owned apart from one that was British-owned. The Dutch plantations were dominated by the Twelve Companies.

The tobacco plantations practised crop rotation and generally speaking rotated once every eight years. The field had to be left fallow for eight year, or in some cases for five or seven years, depending on size. So the extent of the plantations was far greater than that of the actually planted area.

The plantation workers were mainly Chinese "piglets" and Javanese, together with a small number of Indians. Most plantations had around four hundred Chinese. The Twelve Companies' Songgoushifo Plantation had more than 800 Chinese workers in 1912, and the smaller Eluolingjie plantation had more than 200 in 1905.[2] Javanese exceeded Chinese in all cases, by a factor of between two and even three or four. Zeng Jiu, who worked on the Songgoushifo plantation between 1912 and 1914, described as the Twelve Companies' biggest plantation, said: "It had 3–4000 workers, and more than 800 Chinese, including more than 600 tobacco workers and more than 100 unskilled workers. There were more

[2] Here and elsewhere, the translation uses the Chinese name, since the translator was unable to ascertain the Malay name.

than 2000 Javanese, of both sexes in equal measure." Zhou Yazhao said of the Eluolingjie Plantation in 1905: "It was smaller in extent, with just over 200 Chinese and nearly 1000 Javanese."

Workers of different nationalities on the plantations worked and lived separately, did different sorts of work, and were treated differently. Zeng Jiu recalls: "Tobacco growing was done by Chinese, not by Javanese. Javanese men built dykes, repaired roads, did weeding, cleared ditches, and did other heavy labour; Javanese women did weeding, removed insects, etc. The Javanese were known as 'company workers.' They did the heavy jobs, but they were paid less that the Chinese who tended the tobacco plants."

The Chinese were all contract workers under indenture. The great majority came from Huizhou, Puning, Lufeng, and Chaozhou in Guangdong. A few were from Leizhou in Guangdong and Fujian. Because Chaozhounese preponderated, Chaozhou dialect became the main language.

In 1929, the Deli tobacco planters stopped buying "piglets" from China. Between 1929 and 1933, under the influence of the world economic crisis, starting in 1931, the Deli tobacco plantations were unable to recover and collapsed. Many stopped producing tobacco either partly or wholly, and closed down. By 1939, only a handful remained. By the eve of the Pacific War, almost all had closed.

Many tobacco plantations switched to rubber. If that was difficult, they were sold off to private owners to be put to other uses. The switch to rubber had already started in the early twentieth century. Usually simultaneous efforts were exerted on two crops—they continued to plant tobacco, while at the same time using the plantation labour force to plant rubber saplings on land that had lain fallow for a given time. After a while, the switch was complete and tobacco was no longer planted.

(b) The administration and control of the Deli tobacco plantations

The Deli tobacco plantations used mainly Chinese and Javanese indentured labour. These indentured labourers were the objects of the colonialists' exploitation and the source of their super-profits. As a result, they paid close attention to the methods by which they controlled the indentured labourers and ran a strict administration.

The veteran labourers provided us with detailed accounts of the administration on the Deli tobacco plantations. Zeng Jiu, talking about the Songgoushifo Plantation, said:

The tobacco plantations were production units directly subordinate to the big Dutch companies. Their top officials and administrators were the "big bosses" [i.e., managers]. [...] Under the big boss was the "big treasury" [the director of accounts], who took care of the accounts; then there were between eight and ten "number-two bosses" [technical officers], each of whom directly managed between six and ten overseers, arranged technical measures, and took direct charge of production. They were also subject to a division of labour—half managed the Chinese, half the Javanese. The big bosses, the big treasury, and the number-two bosses were all Dutch. The Chinese labourers called them "white monkeys."

Big Chinese overseers managed the Chinese labourers on behalf of the big bosses, while Javanese "big *wanlü*"[3] managed the Javanese. The big overseers and the big *wanlü* took their orders from the big bosses, arranged production tasks, assigned quotas, and calculated and distributed wages. They controlled labourers with the help of small overseers and small *wanlü*. A small overseer usually controlled between 34 and 40 workers. The Songgoushifo Tobacco Plantation had 20 small overseers. [...]

None of the big bosses, big treasuries, number-two bosses, big overseers, or small overseers took part in production. They merely supervised and controlled the workers' labour. The number-two bosses, the big overseers, and the small overseers carried a club or stick that they used both to strike people and to test the quality of produce. They used the stick to prod the soil in the fields or the ditches and if they thought that it didn't meet specifications they would penalise the labourers and make them carry out repairs. The fiercest were the number-two bosses. If the labourers slacked even slightly, they got to taste the number-two boss's club.

The small overseers were usually selected from among Chinese labourers who had served their indenture or redeemed it. Those selected had to know about planting, be "loyal," be "docile," have the support of the big overseer, and be appointed by the big boss. Many small overseers were fellow-villagers or bodyguards of the big overseers. Their wages were roughly twice as big as those of ordinary labourers—around f30 a month.

Most of the big overseers were promoted from among the ranks of the small overseers. Their wage was roughly f40–50 a month [other accounts say f100]. But that wasn't the principal source of their income. Their extra earnings far exceeded their wages. These extra earnings came from holding gambling parties, peddling opium, lending money at high rates of interest, running grocery stores, and buying cheap and selling dear. The Dutch tacitly condoned the big overseers' outrages, who gave the big bosses big annual bribes and still retained a sizeable income for themselves. People who

[3] *Wanlü* was a Chinese word for mantri.

> had been big overseers for several years were able to build big houses and take wives and concubines.
>
> The big overseers were the plantation overlords. They commanded a body of men directly under them and serving them. They hired an "accountant" (a recorder or note-taker) to help them keep records, make calculations, settle accounts, and help run the financial side. They employed three people, one to make and receive payments and purchase goods, one to administer purchases and keep accounts, and one to do odd jobs, such as running errands. Their pig-sties employed four people to raise pigs. Their vegetable gardens employed five to six people to raise vegetables. They also employed three or four pastry cooks and other cooks, and kept three or four concubines. [...] These employees were not part of the Dutch company, whose wages were paid entirely by the big overseer.
>
> There was no standing military guard on the plantation, but there was a Dutch-Indonesian militia in the nearby port. If fights broke out on the plantation, or if something even worse happened, the militia would immediately clamp down. [...] Generally there were three "bodyguards" on each plantation, armed with guns—one to escort and protect the big boss, one to escort the big overseer, and one to be stationed at the plantation mound (the general office). Apart from protecting and escorting high-ups and intimidating the labourers, their main job was to arrest runaways still under indenture. [...]

Yang Jincuan provided the following material regarding the Lianwu Plantation in Eastern Padang:

> There were altogether 400 Chinese on this hill plantation. It was divided into many "companies," each of which had at least 30 labourers, and usually more than 40. Each hill plantation had a Chinese big overseer and each company had a small overseer. The big overseer controlled the treasury and the bodyguards, who helped him with his tasks. The small overseers controlled production and did not themselves take part in labour. Apart from Chinese there were Javanese labourers (male and female) and a small number of Klings[4] and Bengalis. There were more Javanese than Chinese. The Javanese were overseen by big *wanlü* and small *wanlü*. The Bengalis specialised in driving the ox-carts to transport the tobacco leaves.

[4] A word used in parts of Southeast Asia to denote someone of South Asian origin, also spelt Keling.

The system practised in the Deli plantations, the so-called "two-track administration," was an embodiment of the colonialists' divide-and-rule policy and of "using Chinese to control Chinese" and "using Javanese to control Javanese."

They strictly segregated Chinese and Javanese—ostensibly out of respect for national customs and sensibilities, but in reality to set each against the other. They used only Chinese to grow the tobacco, and paid them slightly more than they did the Javanese. They stipulated that Javanese could only do unskilled work such as building dykes and repairing roads and paid them less. They deliberately propagated the absurd idea that Javanese were "stupid" and didn't understand the techniques of growing tobacco, in order to deepen the segregation and fire up national contradictions, so that the two groups would be unable to unite against the Dutch oppressors. Why did they not allow Javanese to grow tobacco? In order to prevent them from gaining the necessary technical skills and propagating them among their fellow-Javanese, so that the Dutch could continue to monopolise production—naturally they kept their strategy a secret. Moreover, keeping Javanese wages low was a way of maintaining the Indonesia-wide policy of suppressing Javanese.

The Dutch strategy of nurturing a body of Chinese overseers and Javanese *wanlü* to control the workers had an ulterior and evil purpose. On the one hand it made the workers easier to exploit, and on the other hand it deflected the workers' resistance onto their own nationals. Whenever the system of indenture provoked resistance, the colonialists put all the blame on the overseers, sacked and replaced them, cheated the labourers by sacrificing the "running dogs," and thus covered up their own crimes.

The Deli plantations ran a system of "rewards and punishments." According to veterans, the rewards and punishments were not clearly set out, and were made known to the labourers by word of mouth, by the overseers and *wanlü*. As a result, rewards were not guaranteed and punishments could be applied arbitrarily.

There were two main forms of reward: the old-age pension and "sharing out extra profits" in the form of bonuses. Any labourer that worked on a plantation for 25 (or in some cases 30) years could, in theory, retire on a pension. But according to veteran labourers, this system was never realised. This was because a labourer was never likely to live for 25 years under such a regime. He either died of hard work or managed, by hook or by crook, to redeem himself midway through his indenture and leave the plantation. Some people worked for 30 years but were then told by the Dutch that they had not worked continuously on just one plantation, so they were ineligible for a pension. Zhou Yazhao grew tobacco for 30 years and Chen Yaxing for 31 years, but neither got a pension. Obviously the system was hot air, and the only ones to get pensions were the big and small overseers. The bonus system was also a scam. It stipulated that if everyone worked well, the company would reward them financially, with a share of the profits. In reality, however, no one ever got a bonus, apart from a small number of overseers.

If the reward was an illusion, the punishment was only too palpable, even if a mistake committed was minimal. Sometimes labourers felt the big or small overseers' whip even when they had done nothing wrong whatsoever. Apart from physical punishment, the Dutch colonialists were fond of putting people into solitary confinement. Solitary confinement suggests imprisonment, but it was not. Anyone accuse of slacking by a number-two boss or an overseer or of "sabotaging production" was put into solitary confinement, i.e., unpaid hard labour. This could go on for a week, a fortnight, and even a month. During this period, unskilled labourers had their wages deducted, while tobacco-growers had to pay the entire wages of those assigned to replace them. These tricks were applied endlessly. Sometimes labourers who finished their work on time were maliciously accused of loafing on the job, while labourers who unintentionally damaged a tobacco plant were accused of sabotage and punished by solitary confinement. Zhou Yazhao told us:

> While I was working on the Eluolingjia Plantation picking tobacco leaves on the embankment, I carelessly damaged a leaf and made a small hole in it. As a result, I was given 13 days' solitary confinement. During that period, I had to do hard labour every day, for example, carrying buckets of mud, carting excrement, and repairing roads. I got poor-quality food and not a cent in pay.

This so-called hot-and-cold treatment was applied in order to guarantee the capitalists' rule over their labourers and the system of exploitation. The rewards went only to the overseers, the punishments only to the labourers, so that the overseers would assiduously serve the capitalists' interests and the workers would be intimidated into submission.

(c) The system of exploitation on the Deli tobacco plantations and "piglet" labour and livelihood

The "piglets" on the Deli tobacco plantations were oppressed both by the owners and by the big and small Chinese overseers. The owners exploited the surplus value created by the labourers. After wages and other expenses had been deducted, the value created by the tobacco-growers and the unskilled labourers added up to an amazingly high level of profit for the plantation owners.

According to veteran labourers, a tobacco-worker might grow between 15,000 and 20,000 plants in a season, each yielding 25–30 leaves. One hundred dried leaves weighed roughly one English pound, and the leaves of 10,000 plants weighed more than 100 kilos. So in one season a tobacco-worker would produce 15–20 quintals of dried tobacco. In the twentieth century, a quintal of Deli dried tobacco was worth around f200, so each worker's output was worth f3–4000. The tobacco-workers were concerned only with growing tobacco, while building dykes, repairing roads, etc., was done by unskilled labour, so each tobacco-worker's output was worth that of roughly three unskilled labourers. In other words, one tobacco worker and three unskilled labourers created f3–4000 worth of wealth in the course of one growing season. Their wages, on the other hand, were paltry. A tobacco worker received f10–12 for 1000 plants, i.e., f150–240 for 15,000 to 20,000 plants. Even if one takes into account four months of plucking leaves and stringing them together, and selecting from them (at f0.75 a day, i.e., f100 in all at most), the sum total still remains below f300. An unskilled labourer received f120 a year, so the wages of three unskilled labourers did not exceed f400. The four men together only received f700 a year. In that way, the Dutch planter made an annual profit on the four of f2,500–3000. An average plantation employed 400 people, which would mean an annual profit of not less than fl million. Even after deductions to cover management expenses, the profit was at least several hundred thousand guilders of pure profit. According to Liu Yaping, when he was working at Taiyuan Plantation in Deli, a Dutch number-two boss told him complacently: "All you have to do is pick four leaves from each plant, that's the production cost, all the rest is pure profit." Four leaves represented between one fifth and one sixth of a plant, so the planter took from the labourer's hands between four fifths and five sixths of his effort. What a confession by this Dutch exploiter!

The big overseer normally used the methods of a feudal labour contractor to exploit the Chinese labourers. For example, he forced them to buy produce—vegetables, pork, cakes, pastries, and other daily goods—from his own shop at high prices, or sold expensive opium, and he fleeced them by loaning money at usurious rates. Otherwise, he would take his revenge in a hundred different ways, or beat them up and curse them for no reason; or they would be given smaller plots, or the payment rate would be fiddled to their disadvantage.

The tobacco workers' income was paltry, but their work was backbreaking. Their main job was to grow tobacco. They spent nine or ten months in the field each year, also called "climbing the dyke." After the land was distributed, they had to "turn over the dyke," do the weeding, clear away branches, break up stones, and clear them away. Then they had to loosen the soil, plant the seeds, put up an awning, spread manure, and nurture the sprouts. After that came "dividing up the tobacco hill," i.e., splitting the turned and loosened soil into rows of tobacco 20 feet long and 1.5 feet wide, with two feet in between. Then holes were dug, each containing a plant, 1.5 feet away from the next plant. Each row comprised two sub-rows. After applying a fertiliser base, the saplings were transplanted. If the plants withered, they had to be replaced immediately. Otherwise, you were fined one guilder, deducted from your wages. The plants needed a lot of watering, and you had to carry water constantly. From first thing in the morning to late at night, the water bucket was never off your shoulder. You could only rest when the watering was over. When the leaves were almost ripe for picking, insects became particularly active, and you had to catch them. The Dutch planters didn't use chemical fertiliser, and the only way to deal with insects was to catch them by hand. By the time the plants were man-sized, the picking began. The picking followed strict procedures. Usually you picked no more than two leaves at a time. The leaves were placed on a rack and the rack was placed inside a small shack. The shack was made of grass and put either on the dyke or alongside the small path. It was up to 13 metres high and divided into 13 layers. After the leaves had been put in the shack, 40 or so were strung together and hung on a bamboo pole and replaced on the rack. After around three weeks, the leaves were dry and could be taken down from the rack. Each lot of 40 leaves was tied into a bundle, fermented, and sent to the warehouse, where the bundles were classified according to quality.

From preparing the land to harvesting took around 8 months. During that time, the tobacco workers worked 10 hours a day, from 6 in the morning to 11 and from one o'clock in the afternoon to 11 at night. The work was done entirely in the open. At picking time an extra shift was added at night for stringing—if you put it off until the next morning, the overseer was likely to send someone over to string it for you, and then you'd lose some income.

Working conditions were atrocious. The tobacco workers divided the leaves according to quality. Leaves were either yellow, red, green, black, broken, or dead, and the first four categories were subdivided into top, middle, and lower quality. They were then bundled up according to class and carted off for export.

The production process was now over. Now came the accounting stage, the payment of wages. The tobacco worker and the unskilled labourer were paid differently. The latter was paid by the day, at a rate of between f0.32 and f0.35, though there was an adjustment after 1925—when Zheng Yaqing and Zhuang Panliang did unskilled labour, they received between f0.45 and f0.47 a day. On the fifteenth day of every month there was a "small grain" distribution, worth f3.70. At the end of the month, on the thirtieth, the remainder was paid, in the form of "big grain." The next day was a holiday, but unpaid.

The tobacco worker's wages were calculated according to a rather complicated system. A contract-work system was applied during the planting and growing, but this changed to a piece-work system during the period of picking and selecting. During the planting period, payment was calculated according to the number of plants and labour costs were assessed on the basis of the quality and volume of the tobacco. A new guest might earn f9–10 per 1000 plants, whereas an old guest could earn f10–12. During the picking period, each lot of 40 leaves was strung together in what was called a rod. The payment for 100 rods was f0.70, yielding an income of f20–30. During the period of selection, the standard 40 leaves were gathered together in a bunch. Every 100 bunches were worth f0.70, and it was possible in one day to select 120–140 bunches, thus earning roughly one guilder. In the period before the "big accounting," each tobacco worker only received an advance amount of grain, 35 pounds of rice a fortnight and f2–3 in cash, which were deducted during the big accounting. At the big accounting, each tobacco worker received a wage of f250–300. The new guests had to deduct f150 indenture money (the so-called recruitment money), f5–6 for tools, f70 to pay back the grain advance; f1.40 for accommodation (in a dormitory); medical fees (f2), etc. Then there were the big overseer's deductions. In general, the new guest had little to show for a year of back-breaking labour—probably less than f20. The old guests earned more, for they did not have to deduct "indenture silver," just f14 signing-on money, but most were in debt to the big overseer, so in many cases they too had little left after the big accounting. As a result, in general neither old nor new guests were able to save. They didn't dare leave the plantation and had no option other than to sign a new contract and carry on growing tobacco.

The indentured labourer's life was hard. After a day of toil, they were invariably tired out, but they had to get up the next morning at four or five o'clock. First they washed the rice in preparation for breakfast, and even more importantly they took a cold shower. The new guests had to shower five times a day, or they would be unable to bear the heat while working in the fields and would have been in danger of dying of heat-stroke. If a new guest died, it constituted a loss to the Dutch planter, so every morning at four the small overseers would kick them out of bed and force them to take a cold shower. After a cold shower, there was no way of getting back to sleep—all you could do was sit and wait for daybreak. All the tobacco workers suffered from sleep deprivation, and there was no guarantee of the necessary period of rest.

When "climbing the dyke," the tobacco workers slept in reed huts. Workers belonging to the same company lived together in the same place, where they were amenable to control by the small overseer.

The labourers did their own cooking. Rice was provided by the plantation owner or the big overseer, supplemented merely by salted fish and salted vegetables. If you wanted fresh vegetables or meat, you had to buy it at exorbitant prices from the big overseer.

Generally speaking, the Chinese labourers went unclothed. During the day and at night, all they wore was a pair of shorts, and they were otherwise naked from the waist up. Many had nothing other than a set of clothes, which they wore at New Year or at gatherings. Such a set cost more than f2, and many could not afford one. Few had mosquito nets, and most simply submitted to the bites, leading to frequent cases of malaria.

Not every plantation had a clinic. Usually four or five plantations had one hospital, or *rumah sakit*, between them. These hospitals were very primitive and could only cure common ailments. If you fell seriously ill, the only thing was to resign yourself to your fate. It was said that labourers could get free medical treatment, but the plantation owners deducted f2 in medical charges annually from the wages of every worker.

The workers had no political rights. Trade unions were strictly forbidden. There was absolutely no freedom of association. During the day they were forced to engage in arduous toil, and at night they were so tired that they fell asleep immediately. It was a life no different from that of an animal.

(d) The East Sumatra rubber plantations

These rubber plantations were founded in 1905. Five of our 44 interviewees were sold directly to the East Sumatra rubber plantations under indenture. They arrived around 1910, and their comments apply only to the early period of the rubber plantations. The plantations on which they worked were clustered in the Ashahan-Qishalan area. The Qishalan plantations were all Dutch-owned apart from one that was owned by Americans. Many rubber plantations were originally tobacco plantations.

The labourers, of whom there were some 1000, were Chinese and Javanese, with Javanese forming the great majority. Most of the Javanese were women. Unlike on the tobacco plantations, technical operations, like planting the young rubber trees and rubber tapping, were done by Javanese rather than by Chinese, who merely did unskilled work such as tending the dykes, digging the soil, levelling the land, weeding, replacing big trees, and tending the roots. This swapping of roles has two possible explanations: rubber techniques were relatively straightforward, and lowly paid Javanese women could replace the relatively highly paid Chinese; and rubber planting was a relatively recent technology and the plantation owners didn't want the Chinese to get control of it and propagate it more widely.

The organisational structure, administrative structure, and methods of rule on the rubber plantations and Chinese living and working conditions were not unlike those on the tobacco plantations. This was perhaps because the rubber plantations arose from the tobacco plantations. They belonged to the same monopolistic organisation and followed the same beaten track.

Because Chinese on the rubber plantations only did unskilled labour, their working hours were long, the work was heavy, and the wages were low, so many Chinese abandoned the rubber plantations at the end of their indenture. There were fewer and fewer Chinese and Chinese were gradually replaced by Javanese.

5. The system of indenture in the Bangka tin mines and Chinese "piglet" labour

(a) The Bangka tin mines

Bangka is one of Indonesia's three big tin islands (the other two are Belitung and Sinkep). It has been mining tin longer than the other two, and is the biggest tin-producing island. Tin mining is concentrated in the foothills and river valleys in the east and north of the island.

Dutch tin mining first started in Mentok, where the Dutch set up their general mining bureau. In the early twentieth century, the bureau moved elsewhere, and bureau offices were set up to supervise mining.

The Bangka tin mines were entirely managed and financed by the Dutch, whatever their size. If a private individual mined tin ore or found it in discarded mud, usually he had to hand it over to the company, or he would be prosecuted for breaking the company's monopoly.

The big mines had hundreds and even as many as 1000 workers. They held copious deposits of the mineral and were amenable to large-scale production, for which they had the necessary equipment. A small mine would have just over 100 miners or even just a few dozen, and they were relatively ill-equipped. This disparity was not inalterable. When the big mines were on the verge of exhaustion, most miners left and so, gradually, did the machines, so the big mines became small mines. Conversely, when big deposits were confirmed in the small mines, they became big mines.

Apart from the Dutch-financed big and small mines, some private individuals set up mining organisations but on a very small scale, with a dozen or so miners each. These mines were run by fathers and sons or by second-generation Chinese who knew about mining. First they had to request permission from the Dutch mining companies to set up a mine, and when they did so, they started hiring miners. They were not allowed to work in the Dutch mining areas and had to do their own surveying and open their own pits. These small mines and the big companies entered into contracts with one another. The companies supplied the miners with food and sometimes loans and even rented them clapped out machines, while the small mines sold their tin to the companies. The contracts stipulated that if tin was not supplied according to a given schedule, the contract became null and void and the food and loans would have to be repaid. The mine owners permitted the establishment of tiny mines in the hope of acquiring more tin, but as soon as the tiny mines struck rich veins of ore, the big owners annexed them. The miners' gangs and confederations assumed full responsibility for their own profits and losses, but they were minuscule in scale. They were formed by miners who had come to the end of their indentures and run by one individual chosen by general acclamation. This individual requested permission from the company. Profits were shared.

This sort of organisation was highly unstable—it often broke up, whereupon the partnership and capital was disbanded or transferred elsewhere, or invested in a new mine.

Nearly all the Bangka tin miners were Chinese, mainly from Guangdong and Guangxi, and Hakkas predominated. Hakka became the main language of the Bangka mines. Before and after 1925, the mine owners started hiring Javanese, but in limited numbers.

Mining in the Bangka region depended mainly on human labour power. It was not until the 1920s that machines began to be used, but only in a rudimentary way—mainly to extract water and mud, and fuelled by firewood or charcoal. In the 1920s, the practice of hosing down mud to get tin ore was not yet widespread, and only began to be used more widely in the 1930s, though never on a great scale. The machines were only part of the working procedure. The main component was human labour. Right up to the eve of the Pacific War, the colonialists continued uninterruptedly to import "piglets" via Hong Kong, and the system of indenture was all along preserved.

(b)The administrative system and methods of rule in the Bangka mines

The supreme ruling body of the Bangka tin mines was the Bingang General Mining Bureau. Offices under this bureau administered mining in the various sub-regions. The bureau had a General Administrator known to the Chinese as "King Tin." The sub-regions had administrators known to the Chinese as "Taigeweixi." All these people were Dutch.[5]

Each mine had a boss, appointed by the Taigeweixi from among the big overseers. Most of them were second-generation Chinese, or Chinese promoted from among the ranks of men whose indentures had expired. The necessary qualifications were a knowledge of mining and loyalty and obedience to the mine owners. Many mine bosses took their own grown-up offspring into the mines so that they could learn how to control the miners. Should they be spotted by the Taigeweixi, they ran a chance of being appointed as the bosses of newly opened mines, or of continuing in their father's or elder brother's footsteps and becoming bosses in their turn.

[5] It is not clear what *taigeweixi* and (two paragraphs down) *yaxinle* mean. The last three syllables of *taigeweixi* might represent the Dutch word *gewest*, "district," with *tai* meaning "highest." *Yaxinle* might be a Cantonese transliteration of the Dutch word *opziener* (supervisor).

Naturally, they included in their ranks men who had become bosses though bribery. Dynasties easily arose, with a feudal taste.

The Taigeweixi did not control the mines directly. There were supervisors who visited the mines and inspected them. They were Dutch, and were known as "Yaxinle." Their status was higher than that of a mine boss. Each supervised two or three mines, and the mine bosses had to report to them on the quality of the tin and the situation in the area. The Yaxinle, in his turn, reported to the Taigeweixi, and the Taigeweixi to King Tin. In some regions Chinese served as Yaxinle, but they were known as "manle." Most Taigeweixi inspected each mine once every two to three months. At year's end, the mine bosses congregated in the offices of the bureau to receive instructions from King Tin by way of the Taigeweixi, and set tasks for the coming year.

The mine boss looked after production, etc. Under him was a big ganger and a small ganger who took care of output and assigned jobs. They were the mine boss's main technical assistants. There was also an accountant who helped the mine boss calculate output, calculated time worked, and handed out wages. There was also a bodyguard who looked after food and general affairs. In direct charge of actual mining was the work leader (*daigong*), whose main job was to supervise production. Each work leader controlled 30–40 miners, whom he could beat and abuse at will. Each mine had a small clinic and a medical orderly. Another man, known as "general stores," looked after meals. Mechanised mines had technical officers who maintained and repaired the machines. They were also allocated labourers to do basic tasks. All the above belonged to the Dutch companies' staffing structure. The mine bosses also hired vegetable growers, pig rearers, and alcohol fermenters whose wages they themselves paid.

The mine boss's position was similar to that of the big overseers in the plantations of East Sumatra. They were powerful, and rode rough-shod over the miners. They ran gambling parties, sold opium, opened shops, bought cheap and sold dear, exploited the workers, practised usury, and cheated and extorted money from the miners. The mine owners tolerated this behaviour.

The mine owners controlled the Chinese labourers by means of Chinese mine bosses, just as in East Sumatra. The only difference was that they weren't able to use divide-and-rule tactics, since nearly all the miners were Chinese.

The Bangka mines had a system of rewards and punishment. They too promised the labourers pensions and profit-sharing bonuses, but in reality the only recipients of bonuses were a small handful of gangers who acted as the capitalists' running dogs, while pensions went only to work leaders and above.

The mining companies practised a system of so-called "bonuses on completion of a job" and incentives for those who worked on holidays. Any miner who worked 26 days in any given months (or 27 days in the longer months) received a bonus of one guilder at the end of the month, and any who worked on Sunday got double time, and triple time for New Year, Autumn Festival, etc. This was a scam, but many fell for it.

Days off on Sundays and at festivals were the fruit of a long-term struggle on the miners' part. Since mining was burdensome and there was no appropriate time to rest, it was difficult for miners to continue working year after year. As a result of a struggle by the miners and pressure from public opinion, the owners grudgingly agreed to allow the miners to rest on Sundays and at festivals, but they also believed that if at such times the mines were not kept going and maintained (e.g., by drawing off the water from the accumulating pools), production on the following day might suffer. They therefore devised this system of incentives to persuade worker to forego their days off. In fact, the value of a worker's labour far exceeded that of a day's pay plus incentive.

The system of rewards and punishments in the Bangka mines was much stricter and more fiercely enforced than on the plantations of East Sumatra. The veteran labourer Lin Bao retains to this day the "release document," which has columns headed "illness," "crime," "absconding," "slacking," etc., with special attention to whether or not a labourer had "committed a crime." Anyone accused of committing a crime, even falsely, was severely punished.

Sick labourers got a note from the doctor, but pay stopped during illness, and you had to buy your own food. If you didn't get a doctor's note, then after three days' absence from work you were marked down as a "slacker" and put in solitary confinement, even if you were really ill. A slacker was also someone unable to meet his quota—in minor cases, you were cursed and beaten, in major cases you were put in solitary confinement. If you absconded and were caught and brought back, you received a severe beating plus solitary confinement. "Committing a crime" was a very elastic concept that included disobedience, defying the work leader, damaging equipment, and anything else the labourer could be accused of, and the punishment was solitary confinement. The latter meant two to three weeks' hard labour, loss of pay, the obligation to make up lost time at the point of expiry of indenture, and an extension to the period of indenture.

All the mining areas practised a day-wage system, but there was a daily quota for excavating and removing earth. The mine bosses and the work leaders urged the miners to exceed the quota to get bigger bonuses, and if anything was not to their liking they would start kicking and hitting people, or would beat them up using shoulder poles or "iron fists" ("three-star mallets"). They even set up their own torture chamber in which they tortured labourers who consistently missed the quota or resisted orders. Even the "doctor" took part in this criminal abuse, and, on the pretext of giving treatment, colluded with the mine bosses and the work leaders to give electric shocks to labourers who had been beaten up or had come seeking medical attention. Most of the gangers were strong and ruthless, and were chosen by the mine owners precisely for those attributes. No few labourers died as a result. Others unable to stand the abuse and humiliation hanged themselves or walked out into the sea and drowned.

The Dutch mine owners supported and engineered this system, and the mine bosses and work leaders were their tools. Yan Gui heard with his own ears how a mine owner told a mine boss and a ganger: "If you kill one, ten will turn up for his job, if you kill a hundred, a thousand will turn up." But the owners hid behind the scenes and let the mine bosses and the gangers do their dirty work.

(c) The "piglets'" living and working conditions in the Bangka tin mines

In the 1920s, the Bangka mines, to a greater or lesser extent, used machines, but only to draw off water or excavate mud. The machines were out of date and frequently broke down. They were only good for certain tasks, and most of the mining was done by hand and shoulder.

After a mine had been projected, the surface soil would be removed by human excavation, and then the mining would begin. While removing the surface soil, wooden supports would be driven in on all four sides, to prevent the earth collapsing. The pit would be excavated to a depth of five metres, and the ore-bearing soil would be excavated and washed. The only tools used in this process were hoes, manure baskets, and carrying poles. When the soil and ore was being carried away, the manure baskets had to be full to the brim—a weight of up to 100 pounds or more—and the miners proceeded in a file and were not allowed to stop midway, or they would get a whipping. There was a gangplank without any protection on either side, and sometimes the miners slipped from exhaustion and fell into the pit, breaking their hand or leg and even dying. During collapses, there were instances when miners were buried alive.

By the 1930s, some mines had switched to wheelbarrows and hoses and had electrified some procedures, but human power continued to predominate. There was little relief for the miners, who continued their dangerous and backbreaking work. Mechanisation by no means ensured their safety. Some workers were injured or maimed by the machines, and some died of electrocution. The mine owners and the mine bosses didn't want to know about injuries and deaths, and never took the necessary measures.

The working day in the mines was around 10 hours, from 6 in the morning to 6 at night (including breaks). The miners were also subject to daily quotas. If the quota was not met, the working time was extended. According to Xu Shiwu, who was tricked into going overseas at the age of 17 (the *ketou* said he was 21), the daily quota in his mine was 6 cubic metres, but because he was young and weak he was unable to meet it and had to work until nightfall (at 7). Although according to regulations you could knock off early once you had fulfilled your quota, most miners didn't dare do so and preferred to spin it out until 6 o'clock. Otherwise, the mine bosses would use the opportunity to up the quotas.

By the 1930s, after mechanisation, the Dutch mine owners, in order to increase production and speed up the return on their investment, changed to a team system. The working day changed to 8 hours, but the machines worked without interruption, forcing the miners to follow suit. Although the working hours had been shortened, the labour regime was intensified and quotas shot up. In the past, half-hour breaks had been permitted, but now they were phased out. Work became even more stressful and onerous.

In 1929–1933, during the world economic crisis, the mine owners ceaselessly forced the miners to work extra shifts and hours, in order to shift the burden of the crisis onto them. At the time, Luo Jie had originally only worked during the day, but now he had to do night shifts, from 7 to 11, but at the same pay.

According to the regulations, each miner had to excavate 3.3 cubic metres a day. But the mine hierarchy did not perform physical labour, so their quota was transferred onto the backs of the labourers, which meant that the general quota increased to 4–5 cubic metres. Every cubic metre required between 28 and 30 trips to the surface, and every load weighed between 100 and 110 pounds, so each miner carried 12,000–15,000 pounds of soil a day. Many mine bosses upped the quota to serve their own interests, on some pretext or other, so that in some cases the quota grew to 7–10 cubic metres.

This arduous labour was performed under the scorching sun. In the the tropics, there was no way of escaping the cruel heat. The miners wore bamboo hats and black shorts made of rough cloth. Otherwise, they went naked, climbing up and down with their full loads, even in rain storms. Any slacking resulted in blows and abuse.

Although the labour was herculean, the pay was astonishingly little. The Bangka mines operated on a daily rate of pay. *Xinke* received the least, though they worked as hard as the *laoke*. For the first six months, got f0.24 a day, which then rose to f0.36 and remained so for the two years up to the end of indenture. A few mines started paying f0.41 in the third year (i.e., the first year after indenture, when they signed up as free miners), rising to f0.46 in year four and f0.51 in year five. However, most mines stuck to f0.36 in year three, increasing by small amounts in each subsequent years, up to f0.51 in year six. After that, there were no further rises.

Despite the downward pressure on miners' wages, the mine owners extorted ever more surplus value to increase their profits. According to veteran labourers' depositions, the daily quota in each mine was in excess of 4 cubic metres. There were 300 days in a working year (deducting rest days and holidays), so the annual quota exceeded 1200 cubic metres. At the time, 300 cubic metres yielded 5.03 piculs of ore, so a miner's average annual output was around 20 piculs. A picul of tin was worth f187, so one mine produced f3,700 worth of tin in a year. But the miners were paid between f70 and f150 a year, as well as receiving provisions worth f160–240, i.e., 7 percent of the total value of tin. Even given a mine's running costs and the costs of its equipment, the Dutch owners profited enormously. It is estimated that in 1925–1926 the Dutch tin mines made a pure profit of more than f40 million.

The Chinese labourers were subject to fleecing and extortion by the mine bosses. Part of their tiny income was stolen from them by the mine bosses' practice of buying cheap and selling dear, and by their high-interest loans.

Exploited and oppressed by the mine owners and the mine bosses, the Chinese labourers' life was hard. Their food was provided by the Dutch General Mining Bureau, but the rice was crude and unpalatable, adulterated with sand, and difficult to swallow. There was little else other than stinking salted fish, rotten vegetable leaves, and acerbic green-bean soup. The labourers were often forced to supplement their diet with expensive food items purchased from the mine bosses. If they ate too little, they were unable to carry heavy loads, so many spent their wages on extra food.

The miners could not afford clothes or even mosquito nets in many cases, so malaria was rife. They lived in cramped quarters, sometimes under zinc-plate roofs. The quarters were crowded and unbearably muggy, like a food steamer. Many miners fell ill, with heat-stroke, malaria, beriberi, intestinal ailments, notalopia, etc. Sick miners were supposed to go to the clinic, but it was short of medicine and the *wanlü* were poorly skilled and often beat and abused patients. If they had only a minor illness, they preferred to seek a herbal remedy. Many miners broke down from overwork. Small ailments became big ones, and even turned fatal.

If a miner was injured at work, he didn't get paid during his absence. Miners kicked out of the mine because of illness or incapacity ended up on the streets and had to beg from other Chinese or seek out a Chinese welfare organisation. Those who died were buried hastily, and no financial support was given to their relatives. As a result of miners' struggles, the mining authorities later agreed to take responsibility for dead miners' children until they reached adulthood, but that was mainly hot air, for few miners had children or families in the neighbourhood.

The miners had no political or trade-union rights. They were forced year in year out to work like slaves. They had no personal freedom, they could be whipped at will, and their existence was not guaranteed. Such was the life of a "piglet."

6. The "piglets'" resistance

The Chinese "piglets" received inhuman treatment on the plantations and in the mines, but they waged an uninterrupted struggle and resistance. Beating the ganger was commonplace, and some were even beaten to death. The resistance was usually in response to a ganger's illegal use of physical punishment, covert deductions from miners' wages, and other forms of violent treatment.

According to Liu Ying, in 1911 one ganger was particularly violent and often beat people with a whip and club. One day, several *xinke* took him by surprise and beat him to death. Huang Si had a similar story: in 1926, in mine 43, the big overseer Cao Yunlong was famous for beating people up. A group of miners who had been his victims got together and took revenge. When Cao turned up at the mine to carry out an inspection, miners who were clearing out the mud with hoes took advantage of the situation to turn their hoes on him and hacked him to death.

In some plantations and mines, because Chinese labourers were prone to resist, the Chinese gangers had no choice but to rein in their fiendish behaviour. Huang Chengzhao recounted how he personally participated in the struggle: "One day, at knocking-off time, the ganger refused to let us go and wanted us to continue working. A dozen of us (all Chinese) were furious, and gave him a beating, so he ran away." Huang Yada recalled how one time in 1927 a plantation ganger had insisted that the new guests had not turned the soil in the prescribed way, and ordered them to do it again. A dozen resisted. They beat him up, and he fled helter-skelter.

Go-slows were another form of resistance. You Yasheng, a labourer in mine 5 in Mentok, worked as a driller. At the time, all the drilling was done by human power. Eight workers organised into two teams revolved the drill by hand, like a millstone. "Whenever the ganger was away, we deliberately slowed down until he returned, and then we told him that the soil was too firm and the drill wouldn't work. What could he do?" On the tobacco plantations, the Chinese labourers often turned up for work but didn't actually do anything. They merely went through the motions, or skimped on the job and the materials.

There were cases of passive resistance, where "piglets" fled into hiding or committed suicide. Many new guests could not stand the animal-like existence and the ganger's violence, so they absconded or hanged or drowned themselves. Yan Gui, who was sold into indenture in 1924, said the new guests found the work very hard at first and often absconded. Thirteen new guests travelled together with him to mine 24. Five absconded, but they were recaptured by the local authorities and sentenced to a year's hard labour. Huang Xiang, who was indentured in 1925, and Li Gui (1933) said abscondings from the mines were frequent. Liu Yaping, who worked on a plantation in Deli in 1910–1912, Xu Shiwu, who worked in a mine in 1926–1929, Luo Jie, who worked in a mine in 1928–1934, and Lin Bao and others, who worked in a mine in 1931–1933, all either saw with their own eyes or heard about new guests on the plantations and in the mines hanging or drowning themselves. This was a passive form of resistance, but it was at the same time an attack on the capitalists, who did not have time to profit from the new guests and had to write off their investment.

Worthy of special note is the "piglets'" resort starting in the twentieth century to strikes, of which there were a series. Some examples follow.

(1) According to Huang Si and Liu Tai, who knew about it from personal experience, in April–May 1924 more than 1000 *xinke* (or around 700, according to Liu Tai) went on strike at various mines in Belinyu. In 1923, when a group of new guests was sold to one of the mines and were about to sign their contracts, the labour contractor said in a speech that they would be released from indenture after 360 working days. However, after 360 days had been worked, the capitalists refused to hold to the agreement, kept the indenture papers, and demanded that they work another 360 days. This aroused their righteous indignation. More than 1000 new guests in three mines went on strike and staged protests at the mining companies' offices. They smashed the windows and demanded that the Dutch stick to the agreement. The colonialists brought in several hundred military police to quell the unrest and arrested more than 100 workers (according to Liu Tai, more than 30). The struggle continued unabated. The workers demanded that they all be imprisoned, and the authorities were forced to release those arrested. Only then did the struggle come to an end.

(2) According to Yan Gui, in 1934 the mine boss Chen Weiying in mine 41made unreasonable deductions from workers' wages, and the entire workforce demanded their restitution. Chen said several days later that he hadn't yet heard back from the company. The workers were furious, and immediately went on strike. Chen paid back the wages the following day, and the strike was called off.

(3) According to Chen Shanfu, in the first lunar month of 1938 a resistance struggle broke out in Mine 3 in the Belinyu area, after some Dutch beat up some Chinese workers for no reason. At around the start of the month, a Dutch father-and-son team of officials went to inspect the mine, and their arrival coincided with the changing of shifts. The bell had already sounded, but the Dutch refused to allow the first shift to leave. The workers tried to argue their case, and pointed out that the second shift had already arrived, but they received blows. The workers were roused to anger. On the evening of the fourteenth, a large group of workers detained the two Dutchmen to argue with them, but the Dutch responded arrogantly, which made the workers even angrier. The workers smashed the windows of the Dutchmen's car and chased them off. The following day, the authorities brought in a couple of dozen military police and prepared to make arrests. The workers stood firm, and many stood up to insist that the Dutch had struck the first blow, for no good reason, and that if the authorities sided with the Dutch, then they would have to arrest the entire

workforce. The authorities were forced to transfer the Dutchmen elsewhere, and fined them fl100. Only then did the unrest abate.

(4) According to He De, in 1941 at the Shaheng mine 3, the colonialists forced the workers to work a night-shift to speed up production, but they failed to provide them with food. The workers went on strike. The mine owners brought in military police, but to no avail. The company then agreed to provide food, and the workers returned to work.

The "piglets'" struggle aimed basically at ensuring workers' safety and improving their living conditions. The actions were spontaneous and disorganised. They failed to transcend the economic level. However, compared with the struggles of the nineteenth-century "piglets," they displayed novel characteristics: the resistance was more widespread, the arena of struggle was broader, and the struggle was more intense, especially in the miners' strikes.

The "piglets'" struggle was highly significant. It was a direct assault on the Dutch imperialist system. It exposed the system's evil and corruption. To a certain extent, it led to improvements in the workers' conditions. At the same time, the struggle showed that the broad masses of Chinese labourers overseas not only made a contribution to the economic development of the countries in which they lived but were a motive force in the struggle against colonialism and imperialism and for national independence.

7. The question of release from indenture and the Dutch colonialists' criminal efforts to thwart it

The colonialists didn't dare brazenly and openly brag about a system of lifelong slavery under indenture, so when buying "piglets," they used various tricks. These included setting limits to indenture and promising "free employment" at the point of completion of indenture, so that those selling themselves into indenture would fall into their trap.

According to veteran Chinese labourers, the so-called year-limit on indenture was different in the plantations of East Sumatra and the Bangka tin mines. The former was for three years, the latter for two. According to regulations, anyone who fulfilled his or her indenture on time and had not been "disciplined" was due for release from contract, free of payment. Moreover, after deduction of the cost of tools, advance provision of food or payment of money, and other items, what remained could be disbursed and release could be brought forward to an earlier date.

The "piglets" wanted above all to see an end to the cruel system of indenture, which naturally put them on a collision course with the colonialists. After the end of the indenture period, the labourers were keen to quit the mines and the plantations and go their own way. Thus the colonialists would lose a skilled workforce that knew the ropes and their profits would suffer.

In that situation, the colonialists used all sorts of tricks—compulsion, blackmail, and deception—to extend the period of indenture. On East Sumatra, they withheld the labourers' "release permit" to force them to stay a few more years. In the Bangka tin mines, there were three kinds of release document: a grey document issued to miners who had completed two years of indenture, and whose possessors were free to return to China or switch to another mine in Bangka, but they were not allowed to be freely employed; a green document issued to miners who had completed three years of indenture, and whose possessors could be freely employed in Bangka but not elsewhere in Indonesia—these documents required the handing over of f3 in procedural fees; and a yellow document issued to miners who had completed five years—this document carried the colonial government's "octagonal stamp" and allowed the bearer to be freely employed anywhere in Indonesia or to move to Singapore. So they were really crafty and came up with all sorts of manoeuvres to prevent Chinese labourers from obtaining their release at the end of two years of indenture. The labourers had no savings—the idea that they could go back to China was nonsense. In fact most "piglets" had to slave away for five years before they got the chance to be a free worker.

The Dutch colonialists used rewards in the form of "signing-on silver" to entice labourers into re-indenture. Miners or plantation workers who had completed their indenture had to sign a new contract if they wanted to stay in their old jobs and to make a cross on the new contract, called signing on. Those who signed on were usually bound for one year. Their wages were somewhat higher than those of new guests and controls were looser, but conditions were otherwise identical—everyone forfeited his freedoms.

Signing on on the tobacco or rubber plantations and in the tin mines did not mean the same thing. According to veteran labourers, the plantation workers received f35 on contract (or in some cases f42 and f49), f14 of which was an advance deducted during the settling of accounts at the end of the new planting season; the labourers on the rubber plantations got f30, including an unspecified advance sum; the miners got f50 (and even as much as f80–100), including an advance of f20. Signing on was a crafty bait to draw the labourers into a trap. The number the colonialists wanted to sign on was determined by their labour needs at the time.

The colonialists used all sort of tricks to prevent release from indenture. They used prostitutes, gambling, drinking, and smoking opium to corrupt the labourers, so that their wages seeped away in all directions and they became so indebted that they had no choice but to sign up for new indentures and the same inhuman existence. The veteran labourers provided much evidence of such practices.

Zeng Jiu recalled: "After a tobacco worker had picked a leaf and put it in the barn, and the big overseers did his calculation—that was the point at which the worker had most money. But then came the overseer's offensive. During the day they made the labourers pick leaves, but at night there were performances, gambling, opium parties, visits by prostitutes, lots of eating and drinking, so that in the twinkling of an eye he was poor again. At the end of the picking season, the overseer immediately started 'receiving coolies' and offering new indentures to the labourers, who were flat-broke by then. In that way, many signed on again and again year after year."

Liu Ying, who had worked on a rubber plantation, said: "They opened three gambling dens near my plantation and five opium dens. There wasn't an official brothel, but the overseer often brought women onto the plantation on a private basis to corrupt the labourers."

The ex-miner Huang Xiang recalled: "The mine owners used all sorts of tricks to keep the workers poor, and conspired to turn them into lifelong 'piglets.' A Dutchman openly declared: 'Don't come to my mine if you're not interested in whoring and gambling.' The gambling was extreme, it went on everywhere, day and night, indoors and out of doors. There were even professional gamblers who would entice labourers who had money to gamble, and told them that if they won they could go home and build a big house. Some labourers lost their money as soon as it came into their hands. [...] The Dutch knew that opium was toxic, but they got their bodyguards to sell opium. Some men who started out as strong as small tigers ended up skin and bones."

The colonialists used these vile tricks to corrupt the labourers. Their despicable aim was to entice the workers into ever greater debt so that they had no choice but to sign on under a new indenture. At the same time, the labourers lost their youthful spirit and vigour, came to hate and blame themselves, and did not dare stand up to capitalist rule, they were indentured slaves for life.

8. "Piglets'" employment after release from indenture

However many vile tricks and fancy moves the colonialists employed, they could not quench the "piglets'" thirst for freedom. Many labourers, after innumerable tribulations, finally shook off the fetter of indentured servitude and escaped the fiery pit of hell.

After their release, the "piglets" faced problems finding work in Indonesia. Some imperialist hack writers and politicians introduce distortions and slander into the debate, and, having an ulterior motive, fan up the provocative notion that these Chinese later became "exploiters." This is a fabrication. The experience of the 39 "piglets" we interviewed explodes this myth.

During the Japanese fascist occupation of Indonesia 39 of our 44 "piglets" were released and then stayed on in the country. From the day on which they left the mines and plantations, they were unemployed and entered the cut-price end of the urban labour market. The great majority continued to live off their labour power, and only a few became petty producers.

Of the 39 labourers released, most became casual labourers, unskilled labourers, petty traders, market-gardeners, etc. Seventeen became casual or unskilled labourers, which was the biggest category, representing 43.6 percent of the total.

Casual labour includes temporary work and farm labour. To do casual labour, you first need to find a gang boss—a *kapala*. The *kapala* would often be contracted by the colonial government to repair roads, dig ditches, and build bridges and other forms of urban construction, or to clear land for new plantations, chop down trees, and repair irrigation works. There were big differences in the price of such labour, depending on place and type of work. An able-bodied labourer could earn one guilder a day. Casual labour was not always available, and after a contract had been fulfilled, the labourers usually had to await new employment. They were often unemployed for longer than they were employed. During the 1929–1933 world capitalist economic crisis, casual labourers were laid off on all sides. According to Hong Shuigui, a former "piglet" who worked as a casual labourer, many mines and plantations closed down, government projects in the cities came to a stop, and released contract workers flooded the labour market. Practically no one could find work, and even if you were lucky enough to do so, the wages were paltry—no more then f0.40 a day. Casual labour became an even more precarious occupation.

Unskilled labour was temporary, and depended on finding an employer. The period of employment was short, and you were often out of work and seeking work. There were many types of casual labour. Sometimes there was casual work available on fishing boats, or as handymen in shops, or as labourers on small farms.

Seven of the released Chinese labourers were carpenters, representing 17.9 percent of the total. Most worked as sawyers in factories. The sawmills practised a piece-work system. According to Liu Ying, when he was working in a sawmill in East Sumatra in 1912–1919, you got f0.13 for sawing a piece of wood more than 3 metres long and 0.5 x 7.5 inches thick (the price included chopping down the tree, getting it to the sawmill, and sawing it up). A strong worker could earn around f30 a month, or f50 in the case of an experienced sawyer. It was basically a form of handicraft—everything was done by hand, using no more than a saw and an axe, it was highly labour-intensive. Working conditions were very poor. Most of the sawmills were in the jungle where humans would normally rarely tread. The atmosphere was unpleasant and oppressive and sawyers caught infectious disorders or died of snake bites. The sawmill owners took advantage of the sawmills' remoteness and isolation to set up small shops where they encouraged workers to get drunk, smoke opium, and gamble, and then took the money out of the workers' wages, so that the workers became indebted and were unable to leave. Four of our seven Chinese sawyers worked their entire lives in a sawmill, starting from their release from indenture right through until 1960, when they returned to China. One worked in a sawmill for 48 years, and the shortest period of employment was 40 years. When they eventually returned to China, what did they have to show for all those years? A stooped back and a broken body.

Seven ran small businesses. These represented 17.9 percent of the total. Some hawked vegetables, fresh fish, or salted fish along the roads, others ran roadside stalls selling groceries, tea, etc. They only just about managed to make ends meet, and when business lagged, they had to eat into their capital. After his release in 1938, Lin Bao invested his seven-year savings of more than f100 in a small business selling fresh fish, but he lost all his capital in two years and had to go back to being a tin miner.

Five ran market gardens, representing 12.5 percent of the total. They used their savings (ranging from fewer than f100 to nearly f200) to buy tools, seed, and saplings and opened up 3–4 mu of uncultivated land, on which they began small-scale production. But under imperialist and feudal oppression, they barely managed to make ends meet, and they lived under the constant threat of bankruptcy.

Only one labourer stayed on in the mine as a free man. Although free miners were not under indenture, their work was unstable and they were the first to be laid off, for example during the 1929–1933 world crisis. Wages were low, roughly f20–30 a month.

One man went to work in a restaurant after his release and earned f30 a month. But such people could be laid off at any time.

One of those released was promoted by the mining company to be work leader.

Such was the situation of our 39 "piglets" before March 1943, when the Japanese invaded. They were all labourers who lived off their labour. Almost all lived hard lives.

During the three years of the Japanese occupation, the casual and unskilled labourers, the hawkers, and the miner were all jobless and forced to roam the villages and the jungle or stay near the deserted mines, grow vegetables on wild land and pick wild fruit, and gradually starve. During that period, Lin Bao contracted oedema. His wife left him for another man, and he gave away his own son for adoption.

After the Japanese surrender, despite the political change, no fundamental change had come about in the ex-"piglets'" job situation or social status. They continued to sell their own labour or to live off it.

The "piglets'" experience shows that although they had fortunately cast off the shackles of indenture under Dutch colonialism, the great majority were still unable to cast off the fate of servitude and exploitation. They could only survive by selling their labour cheaply or following some other manual line of work. The freedom they received after release was merely the freedom to be unemployed, to suffer exploitation, and to endure servitude.

Naturally, after their release a small number of "piglets" rose to become property-owners or became accomplices of the colonial oppression and exploitation of working people, but that happened on a very limited scale. Some people with ulterior motives have sought to generalise the actions of a tiny number of people to the Chinese "piglets" as a whole, but by doing so they confound black and white and sow dissension, so they will surely fail!

Original manuscript, July 1963
Revised in March 1978

Interview with Zhou Yazhao, Chinese labourer on a tobacco plantation in East Sumatra

Interview by Liu Yuzun, May 1963, Zhize Farm, Yinjiang County

Zhou Yazhao, from Shuizhai in Wuhua County in Guangdong, was born in 1880 and is now 83. He is illiterate. In 1900, he went as a "piglet" to Indonesia, where he worked on a Dutch tobacco plantation for 30 years. He was released in 1930. After that, he worked as a peddler in the Guale region, until his return to China in August 1960. He is now frail and deaf, and it is not easy to talk with him. Here are some fragments of our interview.

1. Being sold

My home is in Shuizhai in Wuhua County. Out family was poor, and we had no land. When I was small, father left home to do manual work in Indonesia, but we never heard back from him. There were three of us in the family: my paternal uncle, in his sixties; my mother, who was approaching sixty; and me. My uncle and my mother lived by selling labour in the village, but they were old, so they were rarely hired. We often went hungry.

To find a livelihood, I left home at the age of 12 and went to the Zhenping area to get work towing boats. It was hard and dangerous employment, but I stuck it out for quite a few years. In 1900, at the age of 20, I met a "piglet" trader in Zhenping county town (I forget his name). He cheated me into going abroad [to the Nanyang], where he said it was easy to earn money, and it was less hard work than towing boats. I was seduced by his honeyed words and went with him to Meixian, where I got the boat to Shantou and started preparing to go abroad.

After the "piglet" trader had delivered me to a hostel in Shantou, he disappeared. I stayed there for a few days, and the day before I was due to depart, the hostel boss took me to the Twelve Companies office in Shantou for a physical examination and an interview. The next day I boarded a Twelve Companies steamer bound for Indonesia, and seven days later we docked at Wulaowankao. All I know of what went on is that the Twelve Companies took care of my travel expenses. At the time, I didn't yet know that I'd been sold as a "piglet." I didn't get a cent for selling myself—no doubt the fee was gobbled up by the hostel boss and the "piglet" trader.

2. Thirty years as a "piglet"

After reaching Wulaowankao, we went immediately to the Twelve Companies for another physical examination, and pending the decision I was allocated to a company. On April 14, I was assigned to the Songgoushifo Tobacco Plantation, where I first did a couple of weeks of unskilled labour and then started growing tobacco. The plantation was huge and had more than 600 Chinese labourers and nearly 2000 Indonesians. In the first year, I grew 16,000 plants, but when it came to putting them in the storage barn I only got a small amount of pay (less than f10). The next year, I had to perform the same hard labour. I had to borrow f35 for food and sundry expenses. The following year, at the big accounting, that money was deducted by the big overseer.

I worked there for four years, and in year five I switched to Eluolingji Tobacco Plantation, where I worked for a total of seven years. It was quite a small plantation, with just 200 Chinese and nearly 1000 Indonesians. In 1912, I moved to Xigulanda Plantation to grow tobacco, alongside 4–500 Chinese and more than 1000 Indonesians. I worked there for 17 years, until 1930, when I got my release.

Every year I grew 16,000–20,000 plants, at f8–10 per 1000 plants. The money provided each month for food and the amount distributed at the great reckoning often vanished in just a few days. The big overseer organised gambling everywhere, and swindled us out of our hard-earned cash.

The plantation subjected the "piglets" to cruel oppression. When I was at the Eluolingji Plantation, while taking some leaves out of storage, I inadvertently punctured one of the leaves, and the company put me in solitary confinement for thirteen days. I had to do hard labour during that time, day after day, like carrying mud away in baskets, carrying night-soil buckets on a shoulder pole, and repairing roads. I was given very little to eat, and not a cent in pay.

3. The influence of the 1911 Revolution

When I first arrived at the plantation, all the Chinese still wore pigtails, but when news of the destruction of the Qing Dynasty reached us, we vied to shear them off. Everyone admired Sun Yat-sen enormously.

4. Relations with the ancestral homeland

After arriving in Indonesia, for the first 2 years I wrote letters home, but when I never received an answer, I stopped writing and the link broke.

5. Working after my release

In 1930, after my indenture came to an end, I left the plantation with fewer than f20, but I was still happy to go and to seek another way in the outside world. That's when I came to Legua. I bought a pair of square-bottomed bamboo baskets and things to eat, and peddled them around the streets. Since I had no capital, my profit was minute, and I often starved. Sometimes I put down my baskets and did some casual unskilled work, but at other times that was impossible. I led a vagrant life right down until August 1960, when I returned to China.

Interview with Lin Yajin, a "piglet" on a Deli tobacco plantation

Interview by Gui Guanghua, May 1963, Zhize Farm, Yinjiang County

Lin Yajin, born in Shangpuxiang in Huizhou in Guangdong in 1890, was sold to a Deli tobacco plantation in 1910, aged 20. Two years later, in 1912, he left the plantation to become a casual labourer. In 1939, he became a waste collector. In 1940, after the Japanese surrender, he grew vegetables in the suburbs of Qishalan and also sold poultry. He did this until his return to China in 1960.

Before 1910, more than 500 people lived in my village. We mainly lived off hill farming. Because land was scarce, a long-term hired hand could only earn 10 silver dollars a year, and some not even that much, so many villagers sold themselves into indenture as tobacco workers in Deli. There were thirteen of us in my family, of all ages, with four principal providers. We had land that we sowed with 4–5 dou of grain, and each dou yielded three piculs of unhusked rice. We also rented nine dou from other people and paid back half the yield—a system known as half-and-half.

Our household economy counted as middle, but it was not easy to maintain a living. Later, I heard "piglet" traders claiming you could get rich in the Nanyang, so in 1910 I left home with a "piglet" courier and we took the boat to Shantou, with 14 others bound for indenture. In Shantou, we were taken to a hostel and given 10 dollars each. We paid our own expenses in Shantou. After a few days, we boarded the ship together with a couple of thousand other *xinke*.

After docking in Wulaowan, we took the train to one of the Twelve Companies' plantations in Medan, where our names were taken. The following day, we were taken by bodyguards to the Ganbangbaru Plantation, which was under the Twelve Companies. It had more than 400 Chinese divided into two "companies," and a Chinese big overseer. Each company had a Chinese little overseer.

We were sent to the plantation to grow tobacco. Every fortnight the Dutch company distributed grain. Everyone got f4.10, leaving f2.5 after deductions for rice. Frugal people would spend just over f3 a fortnight, so you could save around 50 cents. Grain was distributed ten times a year. After the leaves had been picked, wages were assessed. We were paid f0.7 per 1000 leaves, bunched together in groups of 40, tied up with string and hung on a bamboo pole. A tobacco worker's monthly income was at most f30 and could be as little as 20. After all the leaves had been picked, the labourers had to move them from the ridges to the earthen storeroom and carry out a selection, according to quality, re-bundle them in groups of 40, and tie them up. Each 100 bundles earned f0.7.

During the growing season, we got one day off every fifteen days. Then we could go to the port and buy food, we didn't need permission. Sometimes new guests ran away, but they didn't know the roads and there was no one to help them, so it was hard to escape. Those who were fetched back ended up in solitary confinement. After the first winter planting, at the big reckoning, indenture silver was deducted. So were the 10 grain distributions, cash distributions, tool money, and so on. You were therefore left with no more than f50–60, so you had to continue growing tobacco. When the big overseer "took on coolies," he got f35 "signing-on silver." The second winter, at the reckoning, there was more money left over after deductions, more than fl00. In 1912, it was announced that the plantation was going over to a labour-gang system. For that sort of work, all you needed was to find a *kapala*, and then you'd get work. The main work was digging fresh embankments in the rubber plantation. First you had to chop down the jungle with an axe, select out the wood, and burn the rest. Then you had to plant new roots. You had to be clean and tidy, or the trees might get termites. After building the embankment, you had to dig ditches for the water. In the case of labour gangs, there was no *guandela* (contract or agreement), everything was contracted, you got more than fl0 for each 100 *yan* (one *yan* was 2 square metres). Sometimes you could earn as much as 7.5 a day, though that sometimes dropped to fl–2. There were no *guandela* restrictions on labour gangs, you could come and go at will, so I went all over the place, from Qishalan to Yaqi, I've been almost everywhere.

In 1930–1931, some of the tobacco plantation in the Deli area had already stopped producing. In the three years before the Japanese southward thrust (in around 1939), there was very little opportunity to do gang work, so I switched to buying waste.

In 1945, after the Japanese surrender, I opened up some land in the suburbs of Qishalan and grew vegetables and raised pigs on it. I farmed about 4800 *yan* of land. I hired a long-term labourer, and sometimes I took on short-term labourers. I myself used to go to the nearby Ganbang area to buy poultry and duck and chicken eggs, and then I would slaughter them and sell them in Qishalan. The business continued until 1960, when I returned to China.

I left for overseas at the age of 20 and lived for more than 50 years in Indonesia. But I never formally married and started a career, so when I came back I was still a bachelor.

Interview with Liu Yaping, a "piglet" on a Deli tobacco plantation
Interview by Liu Yuzun, May 1963, Zhize Farm, Yinjiang County

Liu Yaping, born in 1889 in Ma'an in Huizhou in Guangdong, is now 74. He is illiterate. In 1910 he was sold into indenture in Indonesia where he grew tobacco for two years. He later became a sawyer and remained at the sawmill until his return to China in August 1960.

1. Family situation and indenture

I was born into a poor family. There were my parents, who were in their fifties, two younger brothers (still boys), and me. (A third brother had died aged 4.) We farmed 4–5 dou of low-water land, which yielded only one harvest of paddy a year and one of sweet potatoes, but it flooded year after year, practically every year, so it yielded little. None of us ever got to eat rice and we mainly ate rice water mixed with sweet potatoes.

A local moneybags in the village had land but wouldn't rent it out, instead he got long-term labourers to help him farm it. My parents were too old to do such work, so to keep the family going they had no choice but to mortgage their few dou of land and to borrow money from the moneybags. But how could we clear the debt? After a few years, all the land became his.

There was no way I could earn a living in the village. At the age of 17, I went to Hong Kong to work as an unskilled labourer, but when I got work I only earned a little over one yuan, and otherwise I starved. I stayed in Hong Kong until I was 21, doing odd jobs and part-time jobs (mainly carting soil), and then I returned to the village. Not long after my return, I met Chen Yajing, in a neighbouring village, who had returned from Indonesia to recruit workers. (He had worked on a tobacco plantation in Deli. The big overseer had sent him back to find recruits.) He said it was easy to find work in the Nanyang, you could earn good money, and you didn't have to pay your own ship-fare. Moreover, you got family-assurance money when taking an indenture. I thought, there's no way out for me at home and I can't find work in Hong Kong either, so why not got to the Nanyang and try my luck? So I and three others from other villages went with Chen Yajing to Hong Kong via Guangzhou. Chen told us he was recruiting people on behalf of the Twelve Companies and that the Twelve Companies didn't have a ship sailing directly from Hong Kong to Indonesia, so the five of us would first go to Shantou and then get a ship from Shantou to Deli.

In Shantou, we stayed in a hostel, and then went to the Twelve Companies to have our names taken, and for a physical examination and an interview. The physical examination was mainly to check that we were strong and healthy and capable of working. Among my four new-guest companions was a man called Lin who had a crooked back. The doctor declared him incapable of carrying things, and sent him home. The interview was basically to ask whether we ourselves and our families "agreed" to our going to Indonesia, and whether we had ever worked. If the interview and the physical examination were OK, the company got us to sign and gave us a reward of 4 yuan.

I heard that after leaving our names at the Twelve Companies office in Shantou, the companies gave the hostel owner 70 yuan, from which he was to deduct 30 yuan hostel costs and for the fare to Indonesia, plus 12 yuan for our family assurance, to be sent back by the hostel owner, and the rest was for those entering into indenture. But apart from 3–4 yuan to spend buying this and that, we got not a cent, and the rest was gobbled up by Chen Yajing and the hostel owner. Moreover, the 12 yuan family-assurance money that the hostel owner was supposed to send back to my family was never sent.

2. "Piglets'" labour, wages, and living

The four of us (Lin had already returned to the village) sailed on the Twelve Companies ship to Indonesia. The journey took seven days to Wulaowan. There were nearly 1000 new guests on board, all recruited by the Twelve Companies. In Wulaowan, they dispersed, and I and Chen Yajing went together to the Shawan Delitai Plantation. It was at that point that I realised that Chen was an opium addict. The money he got month after month was too little to support his addiction. He worked for a long time on the plantation and eventually died there, alone and far from home.

After we reached Wulaowan, the Twelve Companies gave each new guest f4. Some people said it was a reward and wouldn't be deducted from future pay, others that it was an advance, so that the new guests could buy a mosquito net, a straw mat, and other things.

I was immediately told to start growing tobacco. According to regulations, a tobacco worker could be released from indenture after a year, but a "company worker" (an unskilled labourer) could only be released after three years. After release, you could go back to China if you liked and the company would pay your fare, but if you wanted to stay on in Indonesia and look for work, you could take your company identity card to the Dutch royal authorities and ask for papers. However, in that case the company would no longer take responsibility for your repatriation.

In the first year, I grew 14,000 plants. In the eleventh lunar month, I started planting the seedlings (each man took care of his own tobacco). Roughly a month later, the saplings had grown, so I transplanted 2000–3000, in batches. My 14,000 plants had to be split into five or six batches before they could be transplanted (this was so they could be well tended and easily picked). After the transplanting, they required roughly three months' tending (fertilising, weeding, loosening of the soil, irrigating), until March of the following year, and then you could start selectively picking them. Some leaves ripened quickly, others didn't. The picking period lasted 2–3 months. By June, the picking was over, and the leaves were stored for selection and bunching. By October and November, the growing season had started up again.

We were paid a piece-rate wage. For every 1000 plants you received about f10 (f12 if they grew particularly well, but otherwise as low as f7–8), from planting right through to picking and storing. Selection and bundling was also piece-work. Every ten bundles (each of forty leaves) earned four cents. I could produce around 200 bundles a day. During the growing season, grain money was distributed twice a month, in the form of an advance on wages, and during storing the great reckoning took place. At the end of the first year, all that remained was a little over f10, because that was then they deducted new-guest money.

The second year I signed on again as a coolie and received f35, but there were still deductions. I actually earned f67.

When I first joined the plantation as a new guest, life was indescribably hard. I started work at 5 in the morning, and worked until 11; in the afternoon, I worked until 5.30. If you arrived even a minute late or left early, you were insulted and abused, and beaten. The company ordered new guests at the start of their employment to work naked except for a towel around the waste, both as a loincloth and for towelling yourself after cold showers. The weather in Indonesia is boiling hot, and people often faint under the fierce tropical sun. Our skin was burned black, and we lost layer after layer of it.

To equip us to deal with the Nanyang climate, the company ordered the overseers to force us to take two cold showers a day, come rain or storm. Between 3.30 and 4 am, the small overseers got us out of bed and escorted us to the showers like prisoners. At 8 or 9 pm, the same happened. At the time, we had long pigtails that took a long time to dry, so it was often past 11 before we got to sleep, and then we had to have another shower at 3 am and sit around until 5 waiting to go to work. The new guests had to work themselves half to death during the day, and they couldn't rest in the evening and got very little sleep, so they were constantly exhausted, day in day out. Some couldn't stand it and quite a few hanged themselves or threw themselves into the river and drowned. The overseers supervised the new guests' showers so they had to put up with it, at least for four months, after which things calmed down.

Everyone in the plantation knew that the white men liked making profit. According to what the white men (the plantation owners) themselves said, the first four leaves of each plant alone took care of production costs (including workers' wages, fertiliser, seeds, and other expenses) and all the rest was pure profit (on average each plant yielded more than 20 leaves).

The white men corrupted us with drugs and alcohol and exploited us to keep us on their plantations forever. They set up gambling houses and opium dens. Two pieces of opium cost f6, later rising to as much as f25. Lots of labourers became addicts and found it difficult to break free from the plantation. They spent the rest of their lives there, doing hard labour.

3. The impact of the 1911Revolution

When we first arrived on the plantation in Deli, we all wore long pigtails [as prescribed by the Qing authorities]. When we heard Sun Yat-sen had overthrown the Qing, we all got very excited and vied with one another to shear them off. Some people didn't want to for the time being, but in many such cases we did it anyway. We would secretly attach a string of firecrackers to their pigtails and light it, creating a sorry plight for the wearers. The Overseas Chinese in Shawan Port all celebrated the victory in China. We plantation labourers went to town and joined in and watched the festivities. The Chinese shops in town had stocked up on firecrackers in preparation for the Lunar New Year, and the shopkeepers took out all the firecrackers and allowed the Overseas Chinese to set them off for free, to celebrate the glorious restoration of Chinese rule [and the end of "alien" Manchu rule], the only condition being that we set them off in front of their shops. The entire town was full of exploding fireworks and the streets were deep in scraps of firework paper. The smell of sulphur was everywhere. The Dutch didn't dare do anything to stop us. Even some of the big white overseers were decent enough to let us go to town to watch the fun.

4. Working after release

After working for two years on the plantation, I was released and sought a different livelihood. Not long after my release, I became a sawyer in a sawmill near Shawan. The job was a bit freer than working on the plantation and the pay was a bit better. I sawed roughly four tons of wood a month, and got more than f50. I stayed at the mill until August 1960, when I returned to China.

My life was always hard. I lived from hand to mouth. I spent decades in that way. I couldn't get a wife.

Interview with Chen Yaxing, a "piglet" on a plantation in Sumatra
Interview by Liu Yuzun, May 1963, Zhize Farm, Yinjiang County

Chen Yaxing, born in Donghai in Lufeng County in Guangdong in 1886, is now 77. He is illiterate. He left China in 1910, and worked on a tobacco plantation for 31 years. After the Japanese southward push, he lived off his own small farm near Shabah, where he grew vegetables and planted paddy. He returned to China in August 1960.

1. Family background and leaving China

In our part of Donghai, all the villagers were poor. We lived off a mixture of farming and fishing. My parents had died a long time before, leaving behind six brothers, of which I was the fifth. Sadly, my sixth brother died young, before I went abroad. We had some hill land yielding 2 dan of grain, but that was too little. I and my brothers were often on the verge of starvation. To keep body and soul together, we regularly caught and sold fish and prawns.

Because life was so hard, at the age of 17 I left home and went abroad in search of work. I looked everywhere, but could find no fixed employment. I got a few days' work here and there, but otherwise I starved.

In 1910, I met an old "overseas guest" from a nearby village. He had come back from Indonesia to recruit labour. He said life was good in the Nanyang, earnings were good, and he could take me. I was convinced by then that there was no chance of work in China, so I decided to go with him. He took me and three other new guests to a hostel in Shantou, where I was sold as a "piglet." When the ship sailed, we were all aboard. Each of us got 52 yuan indenture money, after the old guest had deducted 18 yuan from the original 70 yuan.

It was a Twelve Companies ship, and we sailed directly to Wulaowan. After giving our name to the Twelve Companies, we got f7 more, together with a mosquito net, a rug, and a mat, the money for which would be deducted at the year's-end reckoning.

2. Life on the plantation

Once we reached Indonesia, I was sent to the Balaxilaling Plantation to grow tobacco. The plantation belonged to the Twelve Companies. It had 700–800 Chinese labourers and more than 1000 Indonesians. In the first year, I grew 14,000 plants, and at checking I received a little over f40.

After all the deductions, there was very soon hardly a cent left, so when I signed up year after year for 31 years at the same plantation, every time all I got was f35, and I was never sure whether there would be deductions or not. Usually, I grew 18,000 plants at that plantation.

According to Dutch regulations, after working for 25 years on their plantations, you were eligible for "peace and security" grain, at f7.5 a month. However, even though I'd worked for 31 years, they wouldn't let me have the payment. They said I was still in good health and still wanted to work and the big boss and the overseer said that if I wasn't going to get the money, then that was it, so after that I didn't even dare ask again.

In 1931, I went to the Twelve Companies' Wumao Plantation, where I worked for 6 years. There were more than 600 Chinese. In 1937, I switched to the Ruilijin Plantation, where there more than 400 Chinese.

I worked for 31 years on those three plantations. I did backbreaking labour year after year. I stored the leaves and the days passed by year after year. In 1942, after the Japanese southward invasion, the three plantations closed down and we were jobless, so I cleared some land nearby and grew some early rice and other crops. I carried on doing that until August 1960, living off my own labour, right through until August 1960, when I returned to China.

In 1940, I married a Javanese woman. We didn't have any children. I didn't have any marriage papers, so when I came back in 1960, the old woman was not allowed to come back with me.

Interview with Yang Jincuan, a "piglet" on a plantation in Deli

Interview by Gui Guanghua, May 1963, Zhize Farm, Yinjiang County

Yang Jincuan, born in Shiqiaotou Village in Puning County in Guangdong and now 74, sold himself into indenture in Deli at the age of 22, in 1911. He worked on a tobacco plantation for around 7 years, until 1918. After leaving the plantation, he went to the Medan area to work as an unskilled labourer. He grew vegetables and raised pigs. Before his return to China, he worked hawking vegetables.

Before I left China, my family consisted of my father, his wife (originally taken into the family as a child bride, they hadn't yet got married, that happened later), and three brothers and sisters. We had 4–5 fen of land and a building comprising two houses and a hall. We lived mainly off renting in land and doing odd jobs. In 1911, father was already 50, my younger brother was 19, and my younger sister was 14. The wife was the same age as my brother. The main labour power in the family was me and my brother.

The rent system was as follows: each year there were two harvests, a big winter harvest and a small winter one (thus called because of the size of the harvest). The big winter harvest represented the land rent and the small one accrued to us. Because the yield from the small one was not enough to feed us, we used to do occasional work in the agricultural idle season, for example, a day's work for a family without much labour power—carting manure, weeding, etc. Apart from a couple of meals, that brought in a wage of 20 cents, with which in those days you could buy half a pound of pork or a pound of rice.

Because the family was so poor, when I heard that wages were good in Deli and if you entered into indenture, you not only got a payment but a free ship ticket, I thought I should go too, so I went with five other young villagers to Shantou.

In 1911, the Dutch in Shantou (the Chinese labourers called them "white skins") had a "new guests company" and lots of hostels for labour recruits. First there was a physical examination and then they took a photo and registered you, but they said nothing about how long the labour would last. You got 35 silver dollars from the broker (I heard that the brokers got 7 yuan for each recruit). This sum was paid to my father. We stayed in Shantou for 3–4 days before boarding the ship and going off to Deli.

There were more than 1000 new guests on board. After reaching Medan, we were taken by bodyguards to Badonglianwu Plantation. There were 400 Chinese labourers on the plantation, divided into lots of companies, each employing between 30 and 40 men or more. Each section of the plantation had a Chinese big overseer and each company had a small overseer. Under the big overseer was an accountant and some bodyguards to help him out. The small overseer directed production but didn't actually do any work himself. Apart from Chinese labourers there were Javanese (both male and female) and a very small number of Klings [Indians] and Bengalis. There were more Javanese than Chinese, and there were Javanese big *wanlü* and small *wanlü* to control them. The Klings were in charge of the ox carts and transported the tobacco leaves.

There were two types of division of labour on the plantation: tobacco workers and unskilled workers—the former were all Chinese; and unskilled labourers, where the great majority were Javanese.

Shortly after arriving at the plantation, we were allocated to our sections. The tools—hoes, water buckets, manure baskets, rope—was provided by the Dutch company, but the cost was later deducted from our wages (at the time of the general reckoning; you could return tools to the company, but they would deduct a certain sum for usage).

The first year, I grew 16,000 plants. Working hours were clearly specified—6 to 11 every morning, 1 to 6 every afternoon, a total of 10 hours a day. After 15 days you got one day off, and 3 days off at Lunar New Year.

Everyone arranged their own food. Every fortnight the Dutch gave you f3 living expenses. The living units were based on companies, you lived with labourers from the same company. The walls were made of wood and the roofs of grass. You slept four to a room. You were allowed to leave the plantation on days off, but you had to get permission from the overseer. At work, there were the small overseers and the supervisors to keep an eye on you, but the big overseer would also turn up to carry out inspections, and the Dutch small accountant directed the production technology.

The wages for unskilled labour were 33 cents a day. Working the embankments, planting the seedlings, doing the transplanting, and right through until the picking, all you got was f3 a month. With picking and storing, you went over to a piecework rate. Each plant yielded at least 40 leaves, and even up to 60. You had not only to pick them but to bundle them up with string, and hang them in sets of forty on a bamboo rod before putting them in the shack to dry. After they'd dried, you had to unbundle them and bundle them again into bunches of forty leaves. You got 70 cents for every hundred rods (i.e., 4000 leaves). If all you did was OK, you got 28 cents for every 4000 leaves. When selecting, you had to follow Dutch instructions and split the leaves into five categories, red, yellow, green, black, and broken, with the first four sub-divided into good, bad, and inferior. After that, they had to be bundled up in 40s, and you got 70 cents for 100 bundles. Each bundle weighed 4–5 liang on Chinese scales.

After the leaves had been selected and put into storage, wages were settled at the end of each month, with deductions for food allowances that had been provided during the month and other sums. By October, all the leaves had been gathered in and the selection had been made. Then a general reckoning of the number of plants each worker had grown and the quality of the tobacco was made. New guests got, at lowest, f8 for every 1000 plants, and at most f10, while old guests got f9–13. After that, deductions were made for advances, indenture costs, and tools, and what remained was paid out.

Apart from wages, the labourers had no income. "Consideration money" (i.e., bonuses) was only paid to the big overseers, even the small overseers didn't get any.

The Chinese who went under indenture to Deli could buy themselves free after a year and become old guests. If they didn't want to carry on growing tobacco, they could get papers provided by the Dutch capitalists and leave the plantation and earn a living elsewhere in the Dutch East Indies.

On the plantations, with the support of the plantation owners, the big overseers ran gambling dens and opium dens to press us even harder. During gambling sessions, the big overseer sold opium from his shop. He bought it at 6 cents a piece and sold it at 65 cents, and if it passed through the ganger's hands, the price rose to 70 cents. The big and small overseer also sold snacks on the plantations, at a higher price than in town.

At the big settlement, the storage area buzzed with excitement. The big overseers hired an opera troupe to perform. There gambling for big stakes, and if you lost you could ask the overseer for a loan. People ran up big debts, and as soon as they couldn't pay back, they had to go to the big overseer and ask to sign on for another year and stay on the plantation. Having signed back on, you could get f28, and once the coolie agreed, he could get a further f11.20 for adding his mark (the equivalent of a signature), as a sort of "red envelope" [a bonus]. Some labourers who led a clean and honest life refused to join in the gambling, but when the overseers noticed, they used all sorts of base tricks to threaten and entice them, so that in the end they would agree to carry on at the plantation for another year, in spite of themselves, and in the hope that the following year they would be able to get their release papers. So only a minority finished their indentures on time and got their papers, probably in a ratio of 3 to 10 at the most. On my plantation, of more than 400 Chinese labourers, only 40-odd got their papers in 1912 and were able to leave the plantation.

On the plantation, the big overseers treated the old guests who stayed on somewhat more generously than the new guests when it came to distributing land areas and calculating the price of labour. For example, new guests were contracted to grow 15,000–16,000 plants, and at most 18,000, compared with old guests' 18,000–24,000. The price of labour also differed—f8–10 per 1000 plants for new guests, fl0–12 for old guests.

I worked on the plantation for 7 years, and at the first annual reckoning, f70 were left over, but gambling losses accounted for that. It went on like that for year after, until the seventh year, when I received more than fl00, and—showing great resolution—took my papers and left.

After leaving the plantation in 1918, I joined other Chinese labourers who'd left the plantation to work in a gang as casual labourers around Deli. I got a maximum of f3 a day. That was better than on the plantation, and we were freer. Many of us ended up as sawyers, but some ran vegetable gardens. For a while I was out of work, and returned to the plantation. My income as a returner was quite high, ranging from f60 to fl00. Every year people took their papers, and if those doing so were particularly numerous, the plantation would be in need of labourers. In such cases, the big overseer would go down to the café to recruit people, and offer high rates to those signing on.

I worked for a full 20 years from 1918 to 1938, all in the Deli area, building roads, opening ports, digging ditches, and carting soil, and at most I got just over f3 a day, and sometimes as little as one guilder. I started growing vegetables in 1938. After the Japanese surrender, I made a living hawking vegetables, right through until 1960, when I returned to China.

Interview with Chen Yazhou, a "piglet" on a Deli tobacco plantation

Interview by Gui Guanghua, May 1963, Zhize Farm, Yinjiang County

Chen Yazhou, born in a village in Puning County in Guangdong in 1890, left China in 1912, at the age of 22, for Deli, where he worked on a tobacco plantation for 7 years. From 1920 until his return to China in 1960, he grew and hawked vegetables and raised pigs.

Before 1912, there were nearly 1000 people in our village. It was in a mountainous area with little land. There were already people from the village selling themselves into indenture in Deli before 1900. The big overseer gave a broker papers to return home and recruit labourers, and to take new guests to offices the Dutch plantations ran in Shantou, for a physical examination, a photo, and registration, after which you got free passage on the ship. It was said that brokers could get more than 200 yuan for each new guest. A broker had to get at least three new guests to justify his own fare back.

Before I left China, there was my father and my younger brother, we had a bit of land and a water buffalo, I can't remember how much land, but I know that its produce was only enough to feed the three of us for nine months. So we had to work as temporary labourers, shoulder loads, and chop firewood to make up the shortfall. In those days, a casual labourer got 20 cents a day, but he also got two meals (rice was 40 cents a dou and pork 20 cents a pound). For chopping firewood in the mountains, you needed two days to get there and back, and the wage was more or less the same.

Because the family was in such dire economic straits and regular work was unavailable, our income was limited, so after getting father's agreement, I left home and went to Shantou to become an indentured labourer on a Deli plantation.

In 1912, Shantou was said to have 22 "guest firms" that specialised in recruiting new guests for the Deli plantations. The Dutch Twelve Companies also had an office in Shantou, called the Yuanxing Foreign Firm. The brokers lived in hostels. After reaching Shantou, we went straight to a hostel, where we were met at the door by the hostel manager who knew we'd come to sign on to go overseas. He introduced us to the broker, who took us to the foreign firm. First they asked whether we going to Deli to work of our own free will, and then they took our names and gave us 45 silver dollars each. We had to pay the hostel owner out of it. Before we left, the hostel owner treated us to a meal, and each new guest had to pay the hostel 2 yuan in courtesy money.

Before boarding the ship, we had to undergo a physical examination. We had to strip and jog up and down. They felt our muscles and tested our courage. Those who didn't pass were left behind on shore.

The ship was called "New Assurance," and another was called "Friendly Assurance," they were steamers specially leased by the Twelve Companies to transport new guests. There were several hundred new guests aboard. When we embarked, we each had to get a straw mat. We could roam the ship at will. Food was free—just bad vegetables and salted fish. You could get better food if you wanted, it was known as "eating from a window tray," and cost 9 yuan for 3 people, i.e., 3 yuan each—not many took it.

The steamer docked in Wulaowan. After disembarking, we took a train to the Twelve Companies general office in Medan, where we registered, had our photos taken, and were conducted by a bodyguard to the plantation. The plantation was called Jiningnanma. It had 500–600 Chinese labourers, distributed across 15 companies. There were also more than 1000 Javanese labourers. Around a dozen new guests from my boat went with me to the plantation.

At the plantation, the big overseer assigned us to various tasks, and around three weeks later, we transferred to the plantation. The first year I grew 19,000 tobacco plants.

During the first three weeks, we were paid by the day, at a rate of 35 cents, later raised to 40 cents. Days off were not paid. The Javanese were all unskilled labourers. They were very poorly paid—a mere f8–9 a month.

After our transfer to the plantation, we worked from 6 to 11 in the morning and 1 to 6 in the afternoon. Every fortnight we had a day off. The wages were f4.5 each fortnight, paid 10 times. By the tenth payment, selection of leaves had started, and we were paid on the basis of 70 cents per 4000 leaves (including stringing and hanging). After the picking, we had to transport them into storage and classify them according to quality, at a rate of 42 cents for a hundred bundles of leaves selected and bound together. Often two of us would operate a division of labour, with one selecting and the other binding, and subsequently sharing out the takings.

During the selection, the big overseer sent 5 yuan a month to the labourer's family, and at the end of each month this sum was deducted from the labourer's wages. We none of us knew whether the money was really remitted and that we were not being cheated.

After the storing had been done, the company moved to the big reckoning. The first winter, we got a little more than f9 for 1000 tobacco plants. If the workers had made *salah* (mistakes), he only got f8.

New guests suffered the following deductions:(1) indenture money; (2) tools—1 rake (f1.50), 1 sickle (f0.70), 1 harrow (f0.70), and 1 water bucket (f2.50); (3) 10 advances of grain money in the period leading up to picking; (4) accommodation and bedding (fl.40); medicine (fl.40); (5) string for threading leaves (f0.70); and (6) haircuts (fl.40).

In the case of old guests, the indenture would have been paid off in the first year, but other deductions included the signing-on money at the time of re-recruitment as a coolie.

After all the deductions (which the Chinese labourers on the plantation called the "salt-fish account"), all that remained was f20–30, so I wasn't able to leave the plantation and had to go back to the big overseer and sign on again, for which I got f24, only 14 of which would be deducted the following winter.

By the following winter, I had again managed to grow 19,000 plants, and at the reckoning the payments to old guests were relatively high—f10 per thousand plants (or f9 for *salah* labourers), and even as much as f11 for labourers considered by the big overseer to be "good coolies." After deductions for signing-on money and other items, more than f80 remained. Not everyone received the same, since some worked harder than others, and some received more than f90 and even in excess of f100.

The Dutch company stipulated that labourers who worked for long periods on the plantation, initially 25 years but later brought back to 20 years, would get a pension. Under the scheme, each labourer would get f7 a month, but I heard of very few cases in which it was actually paid.

One plant was capable of yielding 20–30 leaves. During operations, the Dutch small accountant used to turn up constantly to supervise what was going on, and he was very strict towards the labourers. For example, during the selection period, if you inadvertently damaged a leaf and he noticed, you would get at least a week's solitary confinement.

I stuck it out for seven winters on the plantation. After the big reckoning in 1919 (my seventh winter), I decided to get my papers and leave the plantation, and to grow vegetables on wasteland.

All you needed was the agreement of the Indonesian village head, and then you could reclaim some land. I farmed 2500 yan (one yan was the equivalent of two square metres) of land, and grew mainly vegetables and beans. The annual income was more or less the same as on the plantation, but the pace of work was much more leisurely and I was my own master.

Before the Japanese southward invasion, I switched to rearing pigs, but I mismanaged things and lost my capital. As a result, I had to go to Qishalanbacha to grow and sell vegetables, which I did until 1960, when I returned to China.

Interview with Zeng Jiu, a "piglet" on a tobacco plantation in Sumatra

Interview by Huang Zhongyan, May 1963, Zhize Farm, Yinjiang County

Zeng Jiu, born in a village in Lianxian in Guangdong in 1886 and now 77, sold himself into indenture in August 1912 and went via Shantou to the eastern part of Medan in East Sumatra, where he worked for the Dutch Twelve Companies on the Songgoushifo Plantation as an unskilled labourer and a tobacco grower. He left the plantation in July 1914, and did casual gang labour for three years on the Shuanggoubacha Tobacco Plantation, until 1917. Afterwards he worked as a ganger in a sawmill, a recorder, and a shop worker. He returned to China in 1960.

I was born in a poor village in Lianxian in Guangdong. Nearly all the land in the village belonged to the big landlord Luo Wuhe. He had so much land it was beyond counting. Apart from Lianxian, he had land in Lianshan and Yangshan. In our village there were just a handful of families that owned a small amount of land, everyone else rented from Luo Wuhe. He was also the biggest money-lender. He lent money himself, and lent money to small money-lenders. Under the system of feudal oppression and usury, the tenants' lives were very hard. After the harvest, they usually had little left and had to depend on subsidiary employment, e.g., burning limestone, making charcoal, digging coal, chopping firewood, and producing handmade paper.

We were Luo Wuhe's tenants. We rented 3 mu of land, and each year we harvested 15 dan of paddy. Payment was on the basis of six parts to the landlord and four to the tenant, so after paying 9 dan to the landlord and keeping 9 dou for seedstock, we had little more than 5 dan left. There were 7 of us (father, mother, elder sister, younger brother, younger sister, and me) and we had too little to eat, so in the slack season we had to do handicrafts to keep the household going. Father was a hardworking man, and he used to weave bamboo, for example bamboo baskets, night-soil baskets, etc., to earn money, and every August he went up into the mountains to burn limestone and make a tiny profit for the family. The women and children helped father cut bamboo, and mother and elder sister went into the mountains whenever they had time to cut grass, which they first dried in the sun and then carried to town, where they sold it. Between them, they could cut 140 pounds of grass a day (weighed when dry), and every dan was worth between 15 and 25 cents, which added up to 3–5 yuan a month. Even so, our income from the land and from subsidiary employment was not enough to make ends meet, and in the eleventh lunar month each year, after the paddy had been cut, we had to borrow about

30 yuan at a high rate of interest (we borrowed from the small money-lenders). Otherwise, we would have been unable to survive. The interest was 30 percent a month, to be repaid after the early harvest. Otherwise, the interest was stepped up.

Although we were very poor at home, my parents were still keen for me to study for a few years. From the age of 9 to 12, I enrolled in the village private school. After that, we were unable to keep it up, so I dropped out of school and returned home, where I helped father in the fields and cutting bamboo.

In 1901, when I was 15, I was invited by an uncle to leave home and seek a livelihood, as a cook and an apprentice in a shop in Lianzhou City. After working there for 3 years, I left Lianzhou for Hong Kong, where, with the help of a relative, I moved to Beijiang in Guangdong and got a job at the Dacheng Company, where I worked for three years as an odd-jobs man. At first I earned 5 yuan a month, but later it rose in stages to 10 and then 15 yuan, of which I used 6–7 yuan a month for my own needs. The rest I mailed home to my family. In 1907, 3 years after I had joined the company, it went bankrupt because of competition from Japanese coal and closed down. I didn't get another job—instead, I returned home to farm.

Because farming was backbreaking and we still couldn't make ends meet, in 1912—at the age of 26—I privately decided (seduced by the honeyed words of a broker from my village) to try my luck overseas. The broker said he had someone who would pay the boat ticket and meet the travel costs, that wages in the Nanyang were high, that work was readily available, and that I could get rich in a couple of years.

I kept my plans from my father, and simply told him I was leaving the village to find work. The broker specialised in selling "piglets." I got 35 yuan indenture money, but I contracted an eye disease, so I stayed in the hostel in Shantou for more than a month. In Shantou, I had to buy clothes, food for the ship, and various other requisites, so by the time I embarked, I had just over two yuan left. After arriving in Medan, I changed it into Dutch guilders (at the rate of f2.2 to a yuan). When I went into indenture, there was no written contract, only an oral one, that I would work for three years and be released.

On the way out, all the new guests were put in the hold. Food was provided, but it was not good. It was necessary to supplement it with food from the canteen. There were more than 1000 of us, mainly new-guest "piglets."

The ship docked in Medan. On disembarking, we were put in a concentration camp, where we were photographed, given a physical examination, and registered. We were there for three days, after which we were assigned to work in the Dutch Twelve Companies' Songguoshifo Tobacco Plantation. The forms were transferred to the plantation. A photo was attached and people's physical features were noted. I had a scar on my leg that was put on file. The aim was probably to make it hard for us to run away, so they could identify us easily.

While I was in Medan, I wrote a letter home explaining that I'd gone overseas under indenture, that I'd arrived safe and sound, and that as soon as I got rich I would go home. When I reached the plantation, I received a reply, sent by my mother-in-law. At the age of 16, I had become engaged, on the instructions of my parents. My wife's name was Zhang. I paid 35 yuan, but because we were poor the marriage was never finalised. She told me to hurry up and to come back soon, so we could get married. Later, because I was roaming about overseas and couldn't go home, she married someone else. Because I wasn't making big money, I didn't feel like writing home, so I finally lost contact with my family.

The Songguoshifo Plantation was the Twelve Companies' biggest. It was more than 100 kilometres from Medan, near Bandu Port. It occupied around 40 square kilometres of land. It employed 3000–4000 labourers including more than 800 Chinese, of whom more than 600 grew tobacco and more than 100 did unskilled work. There were more than 2000 Javanese (i.e., Indonesians), including both men and women in equal numbers. The Javanese were also under contract, and many of them came as couples, or got together after arriving on the plantation. Most of the Chinese were able-bodied men aged 20–40. There were practically no teenagers, mainly because the company didn't want them and the brokers didn't dare bring them out from China. Even so, a few teenagers claimed to be older than they actually were and managed to insinuate themselves into the plantation. The oldest were over 50. The Chinese and the Javanese were supervised by big overseers or *wanlü*. There was very little contact between the two races, and they were quite deeply segregated. The growing was all done by Chinese, the Javanese couldn't grow. The Javanese males were used for opening up land, repairing roads, hoeing and weeding, digging ditches, and other heavy work; the women weeded, dug out soil round the roots, covered the soil, and removed insects. This Javanese labour was called "company work." When the Chinese first arrived, as new guests, before we knew how to grow tobacco, or when the tobacco season was already over, we all had to do company work. These Chinese new guests and the Javanese company workers were all discriminated against, and people on the plantation used to say they were useless, they were good for nothing. Generally speaking, only a small minority of Chinese had family with them.

The Chinese usually married women of mixed Chinese and Indonesian blood. Because Chinese labourers earned more than the Javanese, it often happened that Javanese women workers or women who had already got divorced went with Chinese. These cohabiting arrangements were not formally recognised as marriage, and if people didn't get on, they could go their separate ways without going through the formality of a divorce. If there were children in such cases, the boys usually stayed with the father and the girls with the mother. This sort of cohabiting sometimes led to clashes between Chinese and Javanese labourers.

The internal administration of the plantation was more or less as follows. The plantation was a unit of production directly subordinate to the big Dutch company. The top man and top administrator was the "big boss" (manager), who took charge of management and administration and reported directly to the general company. Under him was a "big accountant" (chief accountant), who looked after accounts; and 8–10 "bosses number two," who were actually engineers or technicians, each in charge of 6–10 small overseers, and who took technical measures and directly controlled production—half of them controlled the Chinese, half the Javanese. The big boss, the big accountant, and the bosses number two were all Dutch white men (the Chinese labourers called them "white monkeys").

The Chinese labourers were administered on behalf of the big boss by Chinese big overseers (or big *wanlü* in the Javanese case), all single individuals. They received their instructions from the big boss regarding production tasks and allocation of work quotas, and they calculated and disbursed wages. They controlled the labourers through the Chinese small overseers or the Javanese small *wanlü* and made arrangements for production. A small overseer controlled 35–40 labourers, and the Songguoshifo Plantation had some 20 small Chinese overseers. I don't know about the Javanese.

The high-ups, starting with the small overseers, did not take part in production, they merely supervised and inspected the labour of others. The number-two bosses and the big and small overseers carried a club or a stick that they used to beat people and to test the quality of the work.

They would use it to prod the soil or the irrigation ditches and if there was something not to their liking, they would punish the labourers by making them do it again. The number-two bosses were the worst—if the labourers were in the slightest bit negligent, they risked getting a taste of the club.

Most of the small overseers were selected from among contract workers who had finished their indenture. "Loyal" and "docile," they were nominated by the big overseers and appointed by the big bosses. Many of the small overseers were fellow-villagers or bodyguards of the big overseers—through them, the big overseers dominated the labourers. The small overseers' wages were twice those of an ordinary labourer—about f30 a month.

Most of the big overseers were promoted from among the small overseers. They got f40–50 a month. However, their wages were not their main source of income. They acquired extra income by organising gambling and opium sessions, lending money at usurious rates, opening grocery stores, and buying cheap and selling dear. Their outrageous conduct was tacitly tolerated by the Dutch whites. Each year they handed over big bribes to the big bosses, but even so their income was considerable. Many of those who worked as big overseers for a number of years were able to build big houses and get wives and concubines.

You could call the big overseers the plantations' local emperors. They had an organisation that was directly under them and served their interests. They themselves hired an "accountant" (a recorder) to help them keep records, make calculations, and manage money matters. Their shops had a financial administrator who looked after the receipt and payment of bills and also did the buying, someone in charge of sales and accounts, and an odd-jobs man. They raised pigs and employed 4 swineherds. They also ran vegetable gardens with 5–6 workers. Apart from that, they had 3–4 pastry workers. Their meat etc. was more expensive than in the shops in town, and they often forced labourers to buy them. All the profit went to them. These employees were not part of the Dutch system, and the big overseer paid their wages. Their wages were somewhat higher than those of the plantation labourers. They were mostly labourers who had completed their indenture, and they could move around relatively freely.

A Dutch colonial military police force was stationed in the port. Sometimes they came to patrol the plantation. Normally, there were 3–4 bodyguards on the plantation armed with guns. The Songguoshifo Plantation had 3 bodyguards, one to escort and protect the big boss, one to escort the big overseer, and one stationed at the plantation office. Apart from protecting the high-ups and bullying the labourers, their main task was to capture runaways who had not yet completed their indenture. Almost all of them were chosen from among released workers who were known to be strong and brave. Their wages were somewhat higher than those of ordinary workers, and they were exempt from production duties.

I reached Songguoshifo Plantation in September 1912. Because I had no experience of growing tobacco at home and didn't know the techniques, at first I worked as a company labourer, like the Javanese, building embankments and digging ditches. The company worker's day was rather long—from 5–11 in the morning, after which you returned to your quarters to eat, and from 1–5 in the afternoon. The heat was most intense in the afternoon, but the overseers were on the look-out, so you couldn't take it easy or knock off early—that was out of the question. You would get fined, or if you bumped into a white man you ran the risk of solitary confinement, which meant 1–2 weeks' hard labour and deductions from your wages.

After working for 9 months as a company worker, I switched to growing tobacco. Not every company worker made the transition, you had to be diligent and conscientious and to avoid mistakes. Only when the overseer considered that you were a "good coolie" were you transferred to tobacco growing. Some who were the overseer's fellow-villagers, or his good friends, or who behaved submissively towards him and tried to gain his favours, could be transferred ahead of others. The wages for growing tobacco were higher than for company work, and if you were hardworking, had no addictions or bad habits, and managed to save a bit of money, you could buy yourself free earlier, you didn't have work the full three years. But a company worker had to work the full three years before release.

The company worker was on a flat rate of f7.5 a month. On the 15th day of each month, he received a small prepayment of f3.7, to be repaid at the end of the month. The first and 16th day of each month was a holiday—you could go to town and buy things you needed for the month. The Javanese labourers' wages were more or less the same as the Chinese company workers', but the Javanese women earned even less.

The tobacco growers were treated differently from the company workers. Their wage was calculated differently. They were paid not by the month but according to the volume and quality of their tobacco. According to regulations, growing 1000 plants was worth f9–10, which could rise to f14 in the case of high-quality tobacco. In a season, a labourer could grow 15,000–24,000 plants. I only grew tobacco for one year, and I managed

18,000 plants, at a rate of fl0 per thousand. After the harvest, the technical stage began. You had to bake the leaves, string them, divide them into categories, and package them. The growing stage included planting the seedlings, hoeing, irrigating, building up the soil, and picking the leaves, after which they were put into storage. After they had fermented for a while, the leaves were selected, strung, and bound together. This was paid separately, by piece-work. I got 35 cents per 100 bundles, each of 40 leaves. A worker could process 120–140 bundles in a day, separated by quality. If you made mistakes in the selection, or damaged the leaves as a result of clumsiness, you were fined. The wages could be paid in advance, but the big reckoning was made only when the leaves went into storage, at which point, after deductions for food and advances, the wage was paid.

The amount of tobacco produced by a labourer was decided by the big or small overseer. In the case of people they knew, they often added a bit to the calculation to increase the labourer's income, or added a couple of guilders to the calculation for each thousand plants, so everyone was keen to be in their good books and to buy their good will even if it cost them to do so. The big overseer's wife made dumplings and pastries on 11 or 12 days every month and distributed them among the labourers. She charged 10 cents, but they only cost 4 cents to make. Regardless of whether you actually wanted any or not, they were deducted from your pay. We had to put up with that sort of daylight robbery, and to swallow our resentment, or we would land in trouble.

Life as a plantation worker was a tale of woe. The plantation was not yet mechanised, and everything required back-breaking physical labour. Our tools were restricted to hoes, sickles, and manure baskets. Apart from planting, we had to irrigate using recycled kerosene cans, using nothing but our bare hands and shoulders. The company workers were rarely without a rake in their hands, and the tobacco growers rarely without a water bucket. Not until the picking season did our shoulders get a rest. During the picking season it was cooler in the store-room than in the open, and the work was rather more relaxed. So the tobacco workers had a saying "half a year of hard toil, half a year of leisure." Leisure was a relative concept in this instance for picking and selecting leaves also required focus, and was relatively stressful.

The company workers lived in collective quarters that consisted of little more than a room divided up by old planks. The water was drawn from a well. During the growing season, the tobacco workers lived in grass shacks temporarily erected in the fields, and it was very muggy. Not until the selection did they move to the collective quarters near the storage barns, where conditions were a bit better.

Most tobacco workers cooked for themselves. Rice was provided by the Dutch company, but the cost of it was deducted. You could eat as much rice as you wanted, but you had to provide your own vegetables, mostly purchased in town on one's day off. If you wanted fresh vegetables, you had to buy them from the big overseer, who sometimes brought them round the doors. You were practically forced to buy, and the price was higher than in town. At New Year or on festivals, or when wages were paid out, the big overseer slaughtered a pig, but obviously it was not cheap. Most workers lived frugally—they ate three times a day, mostly salted fish and salted vegetables.

The workers went practically naked at all times of the day and night, whether at work or at play, except for a pair of leather shorts. Some even dispensed of the shorts while working, and wore nothing but a loincloth. Many had only one set of clothes, which they wore at gatherings at New Year or during festivals. The cloth used to make these clothes was Shantou *dawu* cloth, the clothes cost a couple of guilders. People with cash to spare could go to the port to buy some, others had to buy them from the big overseer's shop, which charged f3.6. If you lost at gambling or had an emergency, you could sell your shirt to the big overseer, but even if your clothes were completely new and unused, you could only get a guilder for them. Many people couldn't afford mosquito nets, and got bitten all year round.

Many people signed on again and again at the plantation, and lived a never-ending animal existence. According to Dutch company regulations, workers and big and small overseers who lost their jobs due to old age would get an allowance, a pension worth f60 a month in the case of big overseers and f35 in the case of labourers who had worked on the plantation for 15–20 years. However, that was just a paper promise. In reality, very few big overseers managed to work for 10 years, and those that did had, by that time, struck it rich by fair means or foul and soon switched their occupation, so they had no need to run after a paltry pension. But only a tiny number of labourers got a pension even after working for 15 years. Many had saved some money and left the plantation, they spread their wings and flew, while the unlucky ones who stayed on long-term were eventually considered unemployable by the Dutch, and were thrown out at the earliest opportunity. Their actual fate after reaching old age was to roam the streets and hope to be taken in by a Chinese charity or an old persons' home.

There was no hospital at the plantation. If the labourers fell ill, they sought out local remedies for small ailments, but if they fell seriously ill they were taken to a far-away plantation hospital. Usually, several plantations clubbed together to run a single hospital. It had around 4 white medics. While you were at the hospital you didn't have to pay for medicine or treatment, but you had to pay for own food. If you were a company worker, it was deducted from your wages; if you were a tobacco worker, you had to pay someone to replace you on the plantation during your illness. It was deducted from your eventual settlement.

There were no unions—unions were forbidden. There weren't any churches or missionaries either—religious activities were not allowed. However, there were secret associations. There were two sorts, one called Hexing (joint prosperity) and the other Yixing (righteous prosperity). Each organisation was divided into groups and gangs that tried to squeeze each other out. Sometimes there were fights. They were not organisations that led and united the workers in struggle—they were simply in the interests of small gangs of people chasing after power. There were also fellow-provincials' and fellow-villagers' organisations that were purely for welfare, if you fell sick or died, the organisation would deal with it.

The tobacco workers only grew the tobacco, if they wanted a smoke they had to go to the port or the overseer's shop to buy cigarettes, they were not allowed to use their own tobacco. A single plant usually yielded 20–30 leaves, at most 40. When you picked them, you couldn't use the bottom three leaves, and you couldn't use the tender leaves at the top either, and it was absolutely forbidden to keep any for yourself. Mostly the [unused] leaves were burned and their ash was used for fertiliser. If you were caught stealing leaves, you got solitary confinement and hard labour.

To supervise the labourers, the big and small overseers used intimidation, beatings, and the various punishments I've already described. One way they controlled the labourers was by using gangs of their own fellow villagers and promoting company workers to tobacco workers.

Many labourers were anxious to throw off their "piglet" status and, after three years' hard grind, to buy an early release and become a free labourer. While Long Jiguang was Governor of Guangdong, Chen Jiongming resigned and returned to Huizhou. Around 100 of the troops formerly under Chen's command sold themselves into indenture and came to the Songgoushifo Plantation. They feared nothing, and rose up to cause trouble and to beat the overseers. Later, the Dutch expelled them from the plantation and refused to recruit anyone who had been a soldier.

After working on the Songgoushifo Plantation as a company worker for 9 months, I became a tobacco worker, but after a year (a year and 9 months in all) I still hadn't worked off my three years' indenture, which would have meant my release into the ranks of free workers. It was not easy to buy your release early. The conditions for release were that you had to pay off your initial indenture money, including the money paid to the broker, and all loans, as well as the boat fare and all the food consumed since arriving at the plantation (mainly rice). Then there were the tools you had used—their cost also had to be deducted, 40 cents for water and fire-prevention buckets, 50 cents for a rake, 30 cents for a sickle, and 20 cents for a manure basket, a total of fl.40\. If you had all along remained a company worker, you definitely had to complete your three years' indenture. The sole deductions were for rice and advances—indenture costs and travel expenses (including the ship ticket) were not deducted. Their wages were much lower than the tobacco workers', just f7.5 a month. Their low pay was enough to compensate the Dutch for indenture and travel costs.

After the labourers had put the leaves into storage, the big overseers calculated their income. Some had enough left after deductions to buy themselves free. Old guests no longer had to pay off their indenture money, so they were somewhat better off. They had money to spend. However, now came the big overseer's offensive. During the day, the labourers selected leaves, and in the evening there were opera performances, gambling sessions, and opium dens to fleece the labourers out of their earnings. Many workers were penniless in a trice. After the end of the picking season, the big overseers started "recruiting coolies," i.e., tobacco workers, and many who had gambled and lost had to accept the overseer's conditions for reemployment. The overseer gave each labourer f35 as a signing-on fee, which they used to pay their gambling debts and buy provisions for the coming year. This fee was actually an advance that would be deducted at the next big reckoning. Recruiting coolies was restricted to "piglets" who had purchased their release. In that way, many men signed on again year after year. These are the methods that the big overseer used to meet the plantation's labour needs and to guarantee a supply of seasoned workers.

In June 1914, I left the plantation and went to Medan, where a friend introduced me to a gang of labourers working on the Shuanggoubasha Tobacco Plantation near the port of Bagan (more than 70 kilometres from

Medan). We mainly repaired roads. Later I became a sawyer, which was less taxing, and paid around f20 a month. After another three years, I switched to a rubber plantation at the port of Dumujian, where I worked as a sawyer producing planks, and not long afterwards I was promoted to sawyers' small overseer, on a monthly wage of just over f30. I stayed there until 1930. In 1930–1931, I worked as recorder in a sawmill near the port of Sanbandou. The sawmill specialised in producing match-sticks. Between 1935 and 1942, I worked as a shop assistant in a shop in the port of Jialaban. The shop sold cloth and imported goods, metal ware, etc. After the outbreak of the Anti-Japanese War, I earned f2 a month carrying out anti-Japanese and patriotic activities. The shop closed in 1942, after which I was unemployed for a while. Later, a friend got me a job as recorder in another sawmill near the port of Zhandabinye, where I stayed until my repatriation in 1960.

Interview with Zheng Yalai, a "piglet" on a tobacco plantation in Deli
Interview by Liu Yuzun, May 1963, Zhize Farm, Yinjiang County

Zheng Yalai, born in a village in Lufeng County in Guangdong in 1892 and now 70, studied for several years and is quite literate. He sold himself into indenture for two years in 1912 and went to work on a tobacco plantation in Deli. Later, he joined a labouring gang and then became a hawker. He returned to China in August 1960.

1. Family circumstances and leaving China

Most of the families in our village combined farming and fishing. My family comprised our parents and four brothers, of which I was the youngest. We had a lot of labour power but no fields to use it on. We had just one dan of hill land. Every year we fell short by two months, and had to survive by fishing to supplement our income.

In 1912, I set out for Shantou, a two days' journey, in the hope of finding work there. I met a fellow-villager called Ma Cheng who said I should go to the Nanyang. He took me to a hostel and gave me 40 yuan. That's how I ended up under indenture in Indonesia. Before departing, my eldest brother hurried over from the village and insisted I return home, but I thought that going back would not solve my problem, so I gave him the 40 yuan and sold myself into indenture in Indonesia.

2. Life as a "piglet" on a tobacco plantation

In April, I sailed directly from Shantou to Deli. On disembarking, I received f7. I was then sent to Poluozu Tobacco Plantation in Medan. Most of the tobacco workers were from Lufeng, together with a few Hakkas. More than 400 Chinese worked on the plantation. After my arrival, I first worked for a couple of months as a company worker. In June, I transferred to the tobacco storage barn, where I received 42 cents per 100 bundles of leaves. I could manage about 120 bundles a day. Four months later, in October, I was transferred to the fields, to grow tobacco.

In the first year, I grew 15,000 plants. The tobacco grew really well, yielding around 40 leaves per plant. At the big reckoning, the rate was f12 per thousand plants. After deductions for advances, tools, etc., I had f60 left. Before the big reckoning, we received fortnightly food allowances that cost f3.7–4.5, depending on size.

The following year, I again worked as a coolie, and received f42. I increased the number of plants to 19,000, and at the big reckoning I received fl12.

3. Life as a gang labourer after release

After working for two years on the plantation, I obtained my release, and I got a ship ticket from the big boss to return to China and see my family. I didn't stay long before returning to Indonesia, where I joined a labouring gang. I did that for nearly 30 years, right through until the Japanese invasion. Our gang worked everywhere, wherever there was work to be had, but mainly in Qishalan. During that time, I was *kapala* (head man). I led my own coolie gang and did contract work for the Dutch. Sometimes, if we exceeded the quota, we received more than f200 as a reward. After the Japanese invasion, there was no more work, so I switched to selling salted fish.

Interview with Li Yaji, a "piglet" on a tobacco plantation in Deli
Interview by Liu Yuzun, May 1963, Zhize Farm, Yinjiang County

Li Yaji, born in Mimen Village in Xuwen County in Guangdong in 1889 and now 74, is illiterate. He sold himself into indenture overseas in 1912 and worked for four years on a British tobacco plantation in Deli. Later, he became a sawyer in the Menaidang Sawmill, where he worked until his return to China in August 1960.

1. Family circumstances and leaving China

I was born in Mimen Village in Xuwen County. It was a very poor area. My parents died while I was still young (either of illness or hunger, I don't know). I was looked after by my big sister, who had already got married. Starting at the age of just over 10, I went to Haikou, where I produced rice-flour for the owner of a small rice-flour shop.

One day in Haikou, I bumped into Chen Shouxin, from a neighbouring village. He was dressed up like an Overseas Chinese. He said you could earn good money in the Nanyang, and that he could take me if I wanted to go. At the time I was working for someone else and it was very hard, so I agreed to go with him.

Chen Shouxin took me by ship from Haikou to Hong Kong, where he put me in a hostel. I'd heard that "piglets" could earn good money in the Nanyang. I asked Chen for money, but he cheated me—he said I could only get indenture money once I had arrived in the Nanyang, and I believed him. After he had brought me to the hostel, he said something had come up and he needed to return to Haikou, and he asked me if there was anything he could do for me. I gave him four pieces of clothing for him to take back to my elder sister. But when I next heard from her, after having arrived in the Nanyang, I realised he had cheated me. He hadn't returned to Haikou at all, heaven knows where he'd disappeared to.

I stayed for two days in the hostel and was then taken to a foreign firm for a physical examination. We all had to strip off. The medic knocked at our bodies, our legs, and our backs with a small rubber hammer and then took a photo. You could only go to the Nanyang if you passed the fitness test.

A steamer sailed from Hong Kong to Mentok in Indonesia, but there was no direct sailing to Deli. Quite a few of us new guests were bound for Deli, so we first sailed from Hong Kong to Shantou, where we got a ship to Deli. While we were waiting for the ship, apart from being given a small cane basket, there was nothing, we didn't get a cent. Only when we arrived in Deli did we receive a f7 bonus.

2. Life as a "piglet" on a British tobacco plantation

After a sea journey of 7 days, a dozen of us were sent to the red-hair (British) people's plantation as coolies. Near our plantation there were five other British plantations. Our plantation was called Jialawa.

The red-hair plantations and the white people's (Dutch) plantations were basically the same. Every plantation had a red-hair boss under whom a big overseer and several small overseers controlled the Chinese labourers (each small overseer was responsible for 30–40 Chinese). Apart from the big boss and the accountant, the big overseer also had an accountant and two bodyguards (who looked after the food). The big overseer received more than f100 a month, the small ones more than f30. Apart from that, they got a reward from the big boss at the end of the year, and had all sorts of ways of making extra income (from gambling, pig-rearing, distilling alcohol, etc.).

We worked according to a contract system. In my first year, I grew 20,000 plants. From planting the seedlings to picking the leaves (a period of roughly 5 months), I got f10–12 for every 1000 plants. Before the big reckoning, we got an advance of f14 a month (in two monthly instalments), and when I put the leaves into storage, I got more than f80. The subsequent selection and bundling of leaves was also piece-work. I managed 2000 bundles a month, for which I got around f2000.[6]

At the end of the year, I could in principle have bought my release, but I had nowhere to go, so I signed on again as a coolie. I did this three times. I only bought my release in the fourth year. When you signed on again, you got f35, plus f14 for adding your mark, but the latter was deducted (I can't remember whether the f35 was also deducted or not). In years 2 to 4, I grew 20,000 plants. My tobacco was all excellent, and each year I earned f100–120.

The red-hair plantations were huge. Land could not be used two years in succession, and often had to be left fallow for 6 years. I heard that the fertiliser was guano imported from Hainan. If someone's tobacco seedlings died, cash was deducted in proportion to the loss, and if it all died, the labourer concerned had to repay all his advances. The regulations were

[6] This is obviously a mistake.

very severe, if you made the slightest mistake while bundling up the leaves, and made a hole in an otherwise good leaf, you got dragged off into solitary confinement for a week or two.

On the red-hair plantations, nearly all the labourers were Cantonese. They used to say that only Cantonese knew how to grow tobacco, so they never recruited Fujianese.

3. Work and life after release

In 1917, I left the plantation and went to Mingli to work as a sawyer. Sawing was hard work, but you could earn almost fl00 a month, and you were relatively free. When you had enough money in your pocket, you didn't need to work if you didn't feel like it. I was a sawyer for more than 40 years, right up to the time of my repatriation in August 1960.

Interview with Jiang Yali, a "piglet" on a tobacco plantation in Deli

Interview by Gui Guanghua, May 1963, Zhize Farm, Yinjiang County

Jiang Yali, born in Gupu Village in Puning County in Guangdong in 1896 and now 67, sold himself into indenture at the age of 17 in 1913 and went to work on a tobacco plantation in Deli. After 3 years, in 1916, he left the plantation and did gang labour for 17 years in the Deli-Qishalan area. From 1932 to 1960, he hawked fish in Qishalan.

Before 1913, there were more than 3000 people in our village. The great majority lived from farming. Before I left China, we had 4 mu of land, and every year we harvested almost 12 dan of paddy. The family comprised my parents and my younger brother, four of us in all. Economically, we could get by.

In 1913, a big typhoon hit the village and there was severe flooding. Our fields were inundated, and we were plunged into difficulties. So I joined up with a fellow-villager (who had previously worked as an indentured labourer on a tobacco plantation in Deli, and had now come back to Shantou as a broker). Four of us from the village went with him, and we received 45 yuan on entering into indenture.

In Shantou, we were taken to a hostel, and then the broker took us to the Dutch Twelve Companies' Yuanxing Foreign Firm for a physical examination. After passing the test, we got 5 yuan each. The broker escorted us to the steamer, which the Twelve Companies had specially charted for the new guests, and after 7 days at sea we reached Wulaowan. The next day, a bodyguard took us to the plantation.

The plantation was called Badongshilayan. There were more than 300 Chinese divided into 10 companies (afterwards increased to 11). There were more than 600 Javanese and some Klings who looked after the ox-carts.

After reaching the plantation, we found that the Chinese had already started work in the fields, so at first we did unskilled labour. Very soon, however, the plantation required new workers, so we were sent to help grow tobacco. Before the selection of leaves, we received provisions every fortnight—32 pounds of rice (for which f1.6 was later deducted) and f2.5 in cash, a total of f4.10. When the picking started, we switched to piece-rate: for every 100 rods (including the strung leaves) we received f0.70; after the leaves had been put into storage, selection began, for which we received f0.70 per hundred bunches (including threading).

The first year, I managed to grow 16,000 plants, but after deductions at the big reckoning there was little left, so I had little choice but to stay on. When the big overseer "recruited coolies," you got f35 for signing on, which was deducted at the next big reckoning, but not in its entirety. The following year rather more earnings remained, getting on for f70.

The Chinese labourers made their own food, and apart from the land on which the tobacco was grown, each labourer had his own small vegetable plot, which he could use to grow his own day-to-day food. You had a day off every fortnight, when you could go to the little town nearby to buy meat or salted fish. The big overseer ran a small shop that sold basic needs, including chicken slices. On the plantation, relaxation consisted mainly of gambling, which the big overseer controlled and profited from. Grain was distributed, and for gambling and drinking you could borrow money from your more abstemious Chinese workmates, who lent money out at 15 percent monthly interest.

After my third winter on the plantation, I asked for my papers, and left to do casual work as part of a gang. In 1916, most such workers were Chinese who had abandoned the plantations. They earned more than on the plantations and it was not hard to find work.

The work was mainly road building and railroad building, which meant digging holes and carting away dirt. The work was piece-rate, 30 cents for every basket of earth (equivalent to 1 cubic metre). In a day, you could manage 7–8 baskets. The white men (the Dutch colonialists) contracted the work to Chinese *kapala* (headmen). If they needed workers, they would go to the café and seek out the *kapala*. Someone told me that under the contract, the *kapala* got 10 cents for every basket of earth.

Besides repairing roads and railroads, we dug ditches and opened up new land on the rubber plantations. Rubber was on the rise at the time, and some plantations were switching to rubber, so there was no problem finding work.

But things soon took a turn for the worse. In 1932, many plantations closed down (including some rubber plantations), and many Chinese labourers were sacked. It was even hard to find casual work. So I switched to hawking fish.

I bought the fish from Indonesian fishermen (including some Chinese). Early each morning, I cycled down to the area around Qishalan and loaded up with fish. Later, a bus route started up, and things became easier, so I could fetch three times as many fish as previously. At first, I was mobile, selling in small amounts from place to place, but later I set up a stall, and if I had enough fresh fish, I would sell them in bulk to petty hawkers. I ran that business for 28 years.

Interview with Cai Yahua, a "piglet" on a tobacco plantation in Deli

Interview by Gui Guanghua, May 1963, Zhize Farm, Yinjiang County

Cai Yahua, from Nanling Village in Puning County in Guangdong, is now 72. In 1913, he became a "piglet" on a tobacco plantation in Deli. Three years later, in 1916, he left the plantation to work as an unskilled labourer. Before his return to China in 1960, he opened a vegetable garden.

Before I left China, our family comprised our parents, three brothers, two younger sisters, and myself, the eldest son. In 1913, when father was more than 50, we had more than 3 mu of land and depended on the labour of my father, myself, and my two brothers. However, the yield was not enough to sustain the entire family, so we also had to do occasional temporary work for others, in order to boost our income. Casual short-term labour was paid by the day. Apart from two free meals a day, you got 20 cents. However, such work was hard to come by.

Before 1913, people had already been leaving Nanling for Singapore, and others had gone to Deli to work as "piglets" on the tobacco plantations. Because things were hard for our family, I decided to sell myself into indenture in Deli. In 1913, I went to Shantou, where there many new guest firms. Through one of these, I sought out a broker. After a physical examination at the white new guests' firm and a photograph, I received 50 yuan from the broker. Apart from a few yuan I spent on accommodation, the rest I mailed home. A few days later, in May 1913, I set sail out of Shantou (I forget the name of the ship).

On shipboard, the new guests had to provide their own sleeping mats. There were nearly 1000 other new guests on board. Apart from those under indenture, there were the brokers. The whites provided free food, but if you wanted something better, you could order it from a serving window.

We were seven days at sea before reaching Wulaowan. After we had disembarked, we spent one night in the Dutch companies' new-guest firm. The next day, bodyguards took us to the Mingyahongshuzai Plantation. There were more than 20 of us new guests.

There were more than 400 Chinese on the plantation, divided into companies. Because the companies had different amounts of land, the labourers were unevenly distributed. Small companies had more than 30, big ones more than 50. The Chinese big overseer was called Wu Yaci.

When we reached the plantation, the leaves had already been picked and moved to the storage barn. The big overseer allocated me to the selection process. I had to check the leaves for colour and grade them. For every 4000 leaves selected and bundled in 100 batches of 40 I received f0.42. In the storage barn, rice was provided, at a cost of f0.10 a day for new guests and 0.08 for old guests. Each provided his own vegetables. At the time, one guilder was worth around 0.80 silver dollars.

By August, the selection was over, and we went back to the fields. During the allocation of tasks, the big overseer noticed that I knew how to wield a hoe, so he assigned me to growing tobacco. On the plantation, some Chinese labourers had already been assigned to tobacco growing, but if the big overseer saw that they were not adept at raking, they could be sent back to doing general labour and replaced by others.

The first year, I grew 16,000 plants. New guests were contracted to grow 15,000–16,000 plants, but they were paid less than the old guests, no more than a little over f8.

During the planting and the picking period, the Dutch company only gave out f4.20, including f1.20 for rice and f3 in cash. The actual work was assigned by the small overseer, whose job was merely to supervise our labour.

When it came to picking, wages were paid on the basis of the number of leaves strung. There was a small distribution of provisions in mid-month and a large one at the end of the month. Wages were calculated on the basis of f0.42 per 100 rods of strung leaves (a total of 4000 leaves); once the leaves had been strung, they had to be placed in a hut to dry and afterwards bundled together 40 at a time. One hundred bundles were worth one guilder.

Tools included a rake (f1), an axe (less than one guilder), and a big sickle (also less than one guilder), as well as a zinc-lined water bucket. These were provided by the Dutch company, but the cost was deducted at the big reckoning.

The working hours were every day 6–11 and every afternoon 1–6, with one day off every fortnight.

Everyone prepared his own food, and during breaks everyone went to the nearby small town to buy pork and salted fish. Normally, there were people hawking fresh vegetables around the fields, but they mainly hawked salted fish. The workers were allowed to leave the plantation during breaks, they didn't need permission.

The first year, after putting the leaves into storage, at the big reckoning, the big overseer set the price of labour on the basis of the quality of the leaves and the volume of production. On average, each plant produced one bundle (40 leaves) or a bit more. If you grew 19,000 plants, you could get around 17,000 bundles,[7] or 15–17 dan (1 dan was equal to 100 kilos). Therefore, if the yield was average or above average, the official price was rather high, but otherwise it sank. I was told that the Dutch companies made a "gratitude payment" to the big overseer depending on the general volume of output. The first year the price I got was just over f8 per thousand plants. Then there the deductions: the 50 yuan I had received on indenture, tool money, the f4.20 I had received in the form of fortnightly advances, and other sums, after which there was just over f10 left. According to regulations, at the time of a tobacco worker's first big reckoning, as long as he didn't have any responsibilities he could get your papers and leave the plantation and get another job, but new guests had too little left over, so even if you wanted to get your papers, the big overseer would say that the company (the Dutch) are giving out very few papers this years, it's difficult. So when the big overseer started recruiting coolies again, you had no choice other than to put your mark on the contract and continue growing tobacco. I stayed too. When signing on, you got f35, and you were told that when it came to the next big reckoning, only f14 would be deducted.

If Chinese in Deli were assigned to general labour, there wage was only f0.40 a day, and there was the fortnightly grain issuance. You had to work for 3 years and 4 months. Such a worker would pay back his indenture over 3 years, deducted from his wage, which became f0.33 rather than f0.42 in the case of new guests. So unskilled labourers were not released after 1 year but only after 40 months. (Interviewer's note: Cai's evidence is worth studying regarding unskilled labourers' wages: [a] he received f0.33 a day; [b] he received f7.50 a month; [c] at an Overseas Chinese farm in Hainan, a man returned from Indonesia said that he received f0.42 a day. These three figures are different. According to Cai's material, the rice each new guest received fortnightly was deducted at the rate of f1.22, i.e., f2.40 a month, plus f7.50, making a total of f9.90, which is compatible with f0.33 a day. According to Cai, the wage for unskilled labour was f0.42, but the indenture payment was deducted over 3 years. If the wage was f0.42 a day, f0.09 a day was deducted, leaving only f0.33, that means the indenture would already have been paid off. Perhaps some of the big overseers didn't explain the situation clearly, so some labourers thought the original rate was f0.33. The f0.09 deducted each day from an unskilled labourer's wages added up in the course of a year [300 days] to f27, or f81

[7] The figure doesn't seem to add up.

over 3 years, more or less the equivalent of the cost of indenture. This raises the following points: [a] at what rate was the indenture deducted from unskilled labourers' wages; [b] an unskilled labourer's wages were low and his income was meagre, far less than that of a tobacco worker, so deductions were only made on a daily basis, and release took longer than in the case of a tobacco worker; [c] Cai Yahua's situation shows that at the time of indenture, the money received from the broker was actually only part of the advance paid to the Chinese labourer, due for deduction at a later point; and even the money labourers received while signing on at the plantation as coolies was still deductible, except that the deduction was reduced a bit, as a bait for the labourers.)

Later, it seemed to me that tobacco growing was hard and paid poorly. Even if you wanted a smoke you had to fork out for it yourself. So I decided to quit, and joined a gang of labourers. I got my papers in 1916.

Starting in 1916, I worked for 6 years in the Deli region, in a gang. I dug holes and ditches, and earned on average a little more than one guilder a day, but at least a guilder. That was much better than on the plantation. In 1922, I went to Singapore. In 1928, I returned to Deli to do casual labour. After the Japanese southward invasion, I opened up some wasteland and grew paddy, and after the Japanese surrender I turned it into a market garden, and set up a stall selling vegetables.

Interview with Lin Azai, a "piglet" on a tobacco plantation in Deli

Interview by Gui Guanghua, May 1963, Zhize Farm, Yinjiang County

Lin Azai, born in a village in Chaoyang County in Guangdong and now 70, sold himself into indenture in Deli in 1914 at the age of 21. In 1939, he left the plantation and became a shop worker, right through until 1957. In 1957, his sight declined and he entered a reception centre for Overseas Chinese run by the Overseas Chinese General Association in Xianda. He returned to China in 1960.

Before 1914, there were more than 1000 people in my village, and more than 150 households. There was not much land and life was not easy. Many people had no option other than to emigrate, to Annan [Vietnam] or Siam.

Before my leaving home, our family comprised our parents, 6 brothers, my elder brother's wife, a nephew, and 6 nieces, 14 people in all. I was brother number 5. In 1914, my eldest brother was already more than 40. We had lots of labour power but not much land—just 3 mu. It wasn't enough to feed a family of 14, so we had to rent 5 mu from another villager, with whom we shared the harvest from it.

In 1914, I lost around more than 10 yuan gambling, and I thought I'd get told off by my elder brother, so I decided to go overseas. There was a broker in a nearby village who was recruiting labourers for Deli—he was a small overseer on a tobacco plantation. I went to seek him out, and I was recruited together with another 10 of us. The broker took us to Shantou, where we stayed in a hostel, and we were then taken to the Yuanxing Foreign Firm set up by the Dutch in Shantou. They took our names, and we each got 50 yuan. I kept 5 and sent the rest home.

We stayed in Shantou for three days, and on the 19th day of the fifth lunar month, we sailed from Shantou on a Twelve Companies steamer. There were more than 400 new guests on board. The rice was nothing special, it was provided free of charge by the company (the Dutch plantation). If you had money, you could eat from the service window, it cost 4 yuan from Shantou to Deli.

I was told that the Twelve Companies hired two steamers called New Peace and Friendly Peace, which plied between Shantou and Deli, and specialised in transporting new guests. Not long afterwards, Chen Jiongming seized the brokers in Shantou and said he would bore holes in the two steamers and sink them near Shantou, but the Yuanxing Foreign Firm took no notice and hired two more steamers to transport new guests.

The interrogation of the new guests was more or less standard: name, address of village, whether or voluntary, and a declaration that the period of indenture was different for tobacco workers and unskilled labourers. The physical examination was mainly restricted to a few young and relatively feeble types.

After we disembarked at Wulaowan, the broker took us to the Twelve Companies' headquarters in Medan, where our names were taken and some bodyguards took us to the Twelve Companies' Fuluopu Plantation. Ten of us were assigned to this plantation, which had more than 500 Chinese labourers divided into 12 companies. There were also a larger number of Javanese who were segregated from the Chinese. They had different overseers, too. On the plantation, the Chinese were under the control of a Chinese big overseer and some small oversees, while the Javanese were under a Javanese big *wanlü*, who had small *wanlü* under him.

Shortly after our arrival at the plantation, we were assigned to the storage barn, where we selected leaves. Not long afterwards, we were transferred to the tobacco fields.

During the first winter, I managed 16,000 plants. Grain was issued fortnightly—35 pounds at an estimated price of f2, plus f2 in cash, making f4 in all. Old guests got one guilder more.

The working day was 6–11 am and 1–6 pm, with a day off every fortnight. Grain was issued the day before the break, so the following day the labourers all rushed to the small nearby port to buy things to eat, mainly salted fish and pork, and each time they would buy in enough for the following fortnight. On the plantation, all the Chinese had a small vegetable plot, so it was possible to be self-sufficient in vegetables.

The fortnightly grain ration was issued 10 times in all. By the tenth time, the leaves were ready for picking, so payment switched to a piece-rate system. According to Dutch regulations, every 4000 leaves had to be divided into bundles and hung on a bamboo rod, 100 of which held 4000 leaves, paid at a rate of f0.70. In a day, you could on average manage 300–500 rods (not including stringing). After the leaves had been in storage, they were pricked and strung together in bundles of 40, 1000 of which were worth fl.50.

The three or four bottom leaves on any plant were known as dead leaves. Those apart, counting upward, leaves 7–24 were "medium leaves," while the leaves further up were small and of inferior quality. In short, a plant could yield in excess of 30 leaves.

The labourers used rakes (f0.40), harrows (f0.30), axes (one guilder), sickles (f0.40), and water buckets (f3.60). These implements were provided by the Dutch, but after the harvest, at the big reckoning, they were deducted from the workers' wages. If you transferred to storage and no longer needed them, you could sell them back to the company, but at a discount.

At the first big reckoning, the price for 1000 plants was f11, but after deductions only f60-odd remained. Because I had lost money gambling, when the big overseer began recruiting coolies, I stayed on, and received f35 on signing up. But f14 of that were deducted at the next big reckoning. By the second winter, my output had risen to 19,000 plants, at f11.5 per 1000, and more than f100 remained.

I worked on the plantation for 25 winters, transferring to another plantation in 1929, and I didn't quit until 1939.

Some of the Deli plantations had switched to rubber, starting in 1929, and the land under tobacco went into decline. On the eve of the Japanese occupation of Indonesia, very few labourers remained on the plantations.

In 1939, I asked the big overseer for my papers, and after leaving the plantation I joined a Chaozhounese family in Xianda as a restaurant worker. Every month, I got f30–40. By 1957, my eyesight had begun rapidly to decline, and the Xianda Overseas Chinese General Association admitted me to its Poor Overseas Chinese Centre. In 1960, the motherland sent a steamer to Indonesia and I came back to China with other people from the centre.

Interview with Huang Yagai, a "piglet" on a tobacco plantation in East Sumatra

Interview by Wu Fengbin, May 1963, Zhize Farm, Yinjiang County

Huang Yagai, now 80, was born in Lufeng County in Guangdong. He sold himself into indenture in 1915. He first worked for a year on the Laowei Plantation growing tobacco, and after his release he did unskilled labour in the vicinity of the plantation for four years, from 1916 to 1920. After that, he ran a vegetable garden for 40 years (from 1921 to 1960). He returned to China in 1960.

Before I went abroad, there were 4 of us in my family, my elder brother, two young nephews, and me. The nephews were 15 and 9. My sister-in-law had already died, and I myself was not married. We were farmers, but we farmed other people's land. Even so, we had enough to eat.

Why did I go abroad? Because I as unable to repay a debt. So I stole away without telling anyone. Two others left with me. One was Ma Hui, the other was Deng Niubo. We all sold ourselves into indenture in Indonesia.

We walked all the way to Shantou—it took three days. After entering the hostel, we weren't allowed to go out. Before we got the boat, we had a physical examination, but there was no interrogation or photo. Each of us got 40 yuan.

The ship went directly to Wulaowan. After we had disembarked, we went to work on a Dutch plantation called Dilaowei.

The Dilaowei Plantation had a labour force of 1500. The big overseer was called Yahui. He was very fierce. He often used to beat and curse the labourers. The working day was 6–11 am and 1–5 pm. We worked Sundays. We had two days off every month (the 1st and the 16th). Growing tobacco, the first 4 months were the hardest.

When I first arrived, we each got f4–5 a month for food. I grew 17,000 plants, but I only got f31 for the entire year.

Interview with Zhong Yasheng, a "piglet" on a plantation in Sumatra

Interview by Wu Fengbin, May 1963, Zhize Farm, Yinjiang County

Zhong Yasheng, born in Sanjiaolingxin Village in Lufeng County in Guangdong and now 72, sold himself into indenture in 1915. He worked for a year growing tobacco on Ruilijinxin Plantation. After his release, he worked as a carpenter from 1917 to 1956 in the Madashan-Qishlan area in North Sumatra. He returned to China in 1960.

1. Indenture and departure

I lived in a small village of just 10 households and 48 people. Four households (23 people) had the name Zhong, and 5 (20 people) the name Zhang. There was 1 household of 6 people called Wei. We were all farmers, but most of the fields were rented. You couldn't live solely off farming, so lots of people carried firewood or did odd jobs for extra income. Three people went abroad—one Zhong, one Zhang, and one Wei.

There were originally 10 people in our family—mother, elder brother, sister-in-law, 3 nephews, 1 niece, and me and my wife and daughter. We farmed 5 dou of land, handed down to us by our forebears. However, we had a big family, and our income was insufficient to feed us all. We earned a few cents carrying firewood, to help meet living costs. A dan of firewood was worth 20–30 cents. We had to carry it 30 Chinese *li* from the village to the market, and 1 *sheng* of rice cost more than 10 cents. In the village there was no one to borrow money from. We just had to make do the best we could.

In 1915, the family broke up, and 3 months later I went overseas. Why? (1) we didn't have any money, and (2) the village was in turmoil—local warlords were on the rampage. All the villagers joined sects (Elder Brothers, Triads, Red Gang, I forget). Fearing trouble, I thought it best to leave for the Nanyang.

Lots of people from the village had gone to the Nanyang, so when I told mother, she agreed. At first my wife was against me going, but I talked her round.

I left for Shantou by myself, and on the way I bumped into Ma Gui, from Tantou, and two others from Mashan, one called Zhong Yali and the other called Yahe. We were all poor peasants bound for overseas.

The four of us went together to Shantou. Along the way, each paid for himself. Hostels cost just 15 cents, food included. In Shantou, we found the Tianji Hostel, which sold "piglets." We stayed on the second floor, where there were already 3–4 others. It was 10 cents a night, and you could come and go at will. After meeting the hostel owner, he asked me whether my parents knew I was going to the Nanyang and whether any relatives were going with me. He also asked whether I wanted to go. After that, he explained about going to the Nanyang (to Medan) to grow tobacco. When we asked about indenture, he first asked: "How much would you do it for?" I said 50 yuan, and he agreed, and said: "The money can be mailed home, but keep some to spend on things you need." I sent back 40 yuan and kept 10. The other 3 also accepted 50 yuan, but later we learned that some people were getting 60 or 70.

After signing the contract, there was no photo or fingerprinting. Only when we boarded the ship were our names taken and we were given a body search. They felt our buttocks. When we disembarked they didn't give us anything—no mat, rug, suitcase, or food, we had to buy it all with our own money. After disembarking, I only had 4–5 yuan left, which I changed into foreign money.

The boat didn't go via Hong Kong—it went straight to Wulaowan in Medan. The "piglets" all stayed in the hold. There was nothing good to eat on board, just a big pot and some vegetable soup.

The day after our arrival in Wulaowan, we took the long-distance bus to Ganlaling, and then walked for 2 hours to the Ruilijinxin Plantation. There were around a dozen of us.

2. Two years living as a "piglet"

Ruilijinxin was Dutch-owned. The big overseer, Li Yalong, was Chinese. He ran two plantations: Ruilijinxin and Chimao. Each was divided into 6 companies that went by numbers. Every company employed 30–40 people, led by an overseer. The workforce was divided equally between Chinese and Indonesians, and in some cases the latter slightly preponderated. Most of the Chinese were Cantonese, Hakkas, and Chaozhounese, together with a minority of Fujianese.

The workers were all single men,[8] there were no female labourers. Later, at the time of the Kuomintang suppression of peasant associations in the Chaozhou and Shantou region, women as well as men fled abroad, and some women accompanied their men to the plantation, but they didn't grow tobacco. They simply helped out during the picking and

[8] Not true of Zhong Yasheng himself

stringing season. When I first arrived, there were Indonesian women as well as men, they helped clear the jungle, repair roads, etc. The tobacco was grown by Chinese labourers.

When I first arrived, I didn't initially grow tobacco. A dozen of us did unskilled work, like raking the undergrowth, repairing roads, etc. We had to line up at the crack of dawn, at 5 am, for a roll-call, and then start work, right though until 11 am. In the afternoon, we worked from 1 to 5. We did hoeing, raking, and mowing, dug holes, and cut down trees and bushes using big sickles.

At first, we new guests were not accustomed to the work. We had to get up at 3 in the morning to cook food and take a shower. The shower wasn't something pleasant, you were washed down with dozens of buckets of water, from your head to your feet. You had to towel yourself vigorously to get warm again. If you didn't take a shower, or took just a small shower, then when the sun came out your skin would split open, as if with a knife. A Chaozhounese called Ma, one of our group, feared the cold and never took showers, and his skin wrinkled and split in the sun. He might have died had he not been given treatment. You had to shower five times a day, once first thing in the morning, once after knocking off at 11 am, once at 1 pm before returning to work, once at 5 pm after knocking off, and once at 8 or 9 pm before going to bed. The first and the last lasted longest, it was really exhausting.

Unskilled labourers earned f10 a month, and received grain once a fortnight. The grain was provided by the company (as with the tobacco growers), but you had to buy your own vegetables, which cost about f3 a month.

When the tobacco workers started planting, they received a loan of f10 a month, which was deducted at the final reckoning after the harvest.

The planting started in December and continued until mid July, by which time all the harvest had been taken in.

Each person was responsible for 20,000 or fewer plants, I managed 18,000 plants. Planting and readying the soil was not particularly onerous, the most onerous was picking the leaves and stringing them. You couldn't even sleep. You couldn't leave stringing the leaves you'd picked today until the next day, because the next day you'd have to start picking again, or the leaves would turn yellow. Stringing was a real pain, you couldn't just string them any old how, you had to divide them into old, tender, coarse, fine, yellow, green, etc., and you had to string the leaves back to back and front to front, and you had to count them one by one, so that 40 made a bundle. The work went on by day and by night, often beyond midnight, and sometimes even until daybreak. If you had to get someone to help, you had to split the pay 40–60, with you getting just 60.

I only grew tobacco for 1 year, and after deductions all that remained was f65. That year I bought no new clothes, I didn't do any gambling, I didn't borrow any money, and I didn't borrow any money to send home. I only managed to send f5 home when I was doing unskilled labour.

We lived in shacks with wooden walls and grass roofs. Dozens of us lived in the same place. There were hordes of mosquitoes and bedbugs. The latrines were just holes in the ground, covered by planks. It was completely unhygienic. It was a breeding ground for flies and mosquitos. Lots of labourers got malaria.

The tobacco workers were allowed to leave after a year. An unskilled labourer who switched to growing tobacco had to work a year before becoming eligible for release, i.e., 2 years in all. That was what happened to me too.

After my release, I was penniless and didn't dare return home. But I didn't feel free on the plantation, so I left. After that, I went to North Sumatra to be a carpenter in the jungle region, a sawyer. Every month I received f40–50, and sometimes as much as f100. Food cost f20–30, and life was much better than on the plantation. However, I still managed to spend it all, so that after 45 years in the Nanyang I was unable to return home.

When Japan attacked Shanghai [in 1932], [Nationalist General] Cai Tingkai fought well, and we labourers in the Nanyang raised money to support national salvation. Some donated just a few guilders, others tens of guilders, every month someone came round collecting.

After entering into indenture and going overseas, I stayed abroad for 45 years, and at the end I was still a bachelor, weak and infirm. In 1960, I returned to China and was lucky enough to get government support and a place in an old people's home on a state farm.

Interview with Zhuang Yafo, a "piglet" on a tobacco plantation in Deli

Interview by Gui Guanghua, May 1963, Zhize Farm, Yinjiang County

Zhuang Yafo, born in a village in Lufeng County in Guangdong in 1899 and now 64, sold himself into indenture at the age of 20 in 1919 and went to work on a tobacco plantation in Deli. Ten years later, in 1929, he left the plantation and ran a vegetable garden. From 1934 to 1945, he grew rice and plantains. In 1945, after the Japanese surrender, he worked as part of a gang. In 1960, he returned to China.

Before 1919, there were more than 1000 people in our village. There was a lot of land, but most of it was sandy. Because of the poor quality of the soil, it was hard to wrest a living from farming alone, so we had to supplement our income by fishing. Because of the poverty, lots of villagers sold themselves into indenture in Deli. Before I too did so, my family comprised my mother, my younger sister, and me—I was the main earner. We had some sandy fields (I forget how many), but the harvest was poor and we depended mainly on fishing.

Because life was hard all year round and it was hard to make ends meet, I decided to sell myself into indenture and go abroad. In 1919, after I had gone to the new-guest firm in Shantou and the hostel, I was introduced to a broker. We agreed that he would give me 49 yuan (or 50, I forget), and then I would be taken from Shantou to Hong Kong. There were a dozen of us on board. The broker had himself previously worked under indenture in Deli.

In Hong Kong, we went to a "white" hostel where we had our names taken and received a physical examination, by Chinese. The examination consisted basically of lifting a 40-pound load, and walking up and down with it for a few metres. If you weren't strong enough, or you wobbled from side to side, or you couldn't stand straight, then you didn't pass the test and the hostel gave you the fare home. There was also an interview where they asked whether you had come of your own accord. After arriving in Deli, those growing tobacco could get their release after 1 year, whereas unskilled labourers took 23 months. After the procedures were over, the broker gave each of us 5 Hong Kong dollars.

We stayed in Hong Kong for about a fortnight, mainly to await the ship. When the ship docked, we got aboard and left Hong Kong. There were lots of people on board, I cant remember the exact circumstances. We were at sea for 7 days. We disembarked at Wulaowan, and then took the train to the Twelve Companies' headquarters in Medan, where our names were taken and we were escorted to the Duanmanghuo Plantation by bodyguards.

There were more than 300 Chinese on the plantation, divided into twelve companies. There were more than 500 Javanese workers, half of them women. They mainly worked in storage.

I reached the plantation in August or September 1919. I was first assigned to unskilled labour, at a rate of 32 cents a day. There was a small grain distribution every month on the fifteenth, when you got rice and f3, and then at the end of the month there was a big distribution, when you were paid according to your performance that month, with deductions for the small distribution. You got f5–6 on average.

After I'd been working there for several months, the big overseer transferred me to tobacco growing. The first year I grew 16,000 plants. The working day was 6–11 am and 1–6 pm, with a grain distribution every fortnight after which you got a day off. You cooked for yourself, so everyone used the day off to go the nearby port to buy food.

Apart from one day off every fortnight, Chinese holidays were observed. How much time you got off depended on the importance of the festival. You got 3 days for New Year, 1 day for Qingming, half a day for the Dragon Boat Festival, 1 day for the middle of the seventh month, half a day for mid-autumn, and half a day for the winter solstice, in the eleventh month. After the winter solstice, the tobacco workers went into the fields to make their preparations. They bowed before the hill gods and the spirits (someone told me that it was mainly out of respect for those workers who in the past had died in the fields).

On the plantation, apart from picking and selecting, which was piecework, the rest was contract labour. For example, in the first year I was contracted to grow 16,000 plants. In the months from planting to picking, every fortnight we got our distribution, 10 times in all, up until the harvest. The big overseer fixed the payment on the basis of the quality and quantity of the leaves, calculated in units of 1000. As long as the big overseer was satisfied, the price was relatively high, otherwise it was low. Afterwards, the earlier ten distributions were deducted during the big reckoning. The new guests had to pay back their indenture fee, so they received little.

The period from picking to storing was paid as follows.

Picking: the leaves had to meet prescribed quality standards and be strung in bundles of 40 on a bamboo rod. If the rod was long enough, two bundles could be hung from it (i.e., 80 leaves), that was called a big rod. Every 4000 leaves were strung, hung on rods, and put into storage. One hundred rods were worth 70 cents. If you had more leaves than you could manage, you could ask a Javanese woman to help with the stringing, and you would usually give her half the pay, or in some cases 30–40 cents.

Selecting: After taking the leaves into storage, you had to divide those that had already dried into classes: red, yellow, green, black, and broken. The colours were sub-divided into good, average, and inferior. The wage was calculated on the basis of 70 cents per 100 bundles, each of 40 leaves.

In the course of this work, some labourers did not stick to prescribed norms. For example, they created bundles of less than 40 leaves. The Dutch finance man often carried out inspections, and if he came across a bundle of 38 he would issue a warning, and anything less than 38 counted as a *salah* (mistake), in which case you were not only not paid but you had to do the work again.

After the annual big reckoning, I had less than f10 left. When the big overseer started recruiting coolies for the following year, I signed on and received f30. That year I received more money, but I'd developed a gambling addiction and I rarely won, so I stayed on the plantation as a labourer for 10 years growing tobacco. When the tenth year came, some tobacco plantations in the Deli area switched to growing rubber, coffee, and tea, so I got my papers and left the plantation.

After leaving, I opened some land near Deli and grew vegetables, earning more than I had on the plantation. I did this for more than 4 years, and I also grew paddy on more than 2000 yan of reclaimed land. I practised crop rotation, but there was no need to leave it fallow, since the land was highly productive. Each time, using just half the surface area, I harvested more than a dozen bao (1 bao was equal to 100 kilos) of paddy, most of which I sold to the rice-mill. I also reared pigs, chickens, and ducks, and if it got too much for me, I employed 3–4 men to help out.

After the Japanese surrender in 1945, I went back to gang labour, and dug ditches and cleared land for people, right through until 1960, when I returned to China.

Interview with Hong Shuigui, a "piglet" on a tobacco plantation in East Sumatra

Interview by Liu Yuzun, May 1963, Zhize Farm, Yinjiang County

Hong Shuigui, born in 1903 in Dongshui in Lufeng County in Guangdong, is now 60. In 1922, aged 19, he sold himself into indenture in Indonesia, where he worked on a tobacco plantation for three years. Later, he did unskilled labour as part of a gang, and was a hawker. He returned to China in August 1960.

1. Family circumstances and emigration

My mother died when I was 3. Not long after that, my father, because of hardship, went with others to Medan in Indonesia to hawk vegetables. However, he never sent any money back (he kept in touch merely by letter), and the three of us left behind—my elder brother, my sister-in-law, and me—had no land at all and had to earn our living by drying salt along the sea. In a day you could dry roughly 300 pounds of salt. We had to sell it to the government according to a list price. One day's labour was enough to pay for a day's food, but if the weather was bad and we couldn't dry the salt, we went hungry.

In July or August, when I was 16, a big typhoon struck the village and destroyed all the fields along the coast. We could no longer dry salt. My brother and his wife decided that if they stayed in the village they would starve to death, so they moved elsewhere to farm for someone. I was left by myself, and even less able to scratch a living together, so I went to Shantou and took the boat to Hong Kong in search of work. I worked for four months carrying soil. But the work was hard and the pay was poor, just 30–40 cents a day. One day, a broker happened to look me up. He said it would be a good idea to sell myself into indenture in the Nanyang, the pay was good and the work was not too onerous. I believed him, and went with him to a hostel. The next day, the hostel owner took me to the Twelve Companies office in Hong Kong for a physical examination and an interview. They asked me if I was going of my own free will and I said yes, so they signed me up and gave me 7 Hong Kong dollars. I got another 30 dollars on returning to the hostel. I sent all the money back to my brother and his wife.

2. Labour and wages

In September, I sailed directly to Wulaowan. On arrival, I was taken to the Five Companies (not the Twelve Companies) for another physical examination and to sign on again, and I got f7. I was then sent to the Dingwuxingda Plantation to plant tobacco. There were more than 300 Chinese and more than 500 Javanese. The Chinese labourers and the small overseers were all from Lufeng. The small overseers got f35–40 a month, the big overseer f100.

The first year, I grew 17,000 plants and received f18 at the big reckoning. The second and third years I signed up again as a coolie and each time I received f35 coolie money (which was deducted at the end of the year). The big overseer said I worked well, and gave me a bonus of f10 (I don't know whether it was deducted or not). The second year I grew 20,000 plants and got f125 and the third year I grew 23,000 and got f120.

3. Work after my release

After working on the plantation for 3 years, I decided to leave (I found the work hard and the overseer was very strict, we were not at all free). After leaving the plantation, I worked for more than 10 years as part of a labour gang. Mainly we repaired roads for the Dutch authorities, repaired the irrigation system, and repaired small bridges, etc. We worked according to a contract system, the harder you worked, the more you earned. If things went well, you could earn f7–8 a day, and if you had money in your pocket, you could afford to take a few days off if you liked, and go down to the port and take it easy. But if the contract didn't work out well, you earned a pittance. That was especially the case in 1931–1933, when many plantations closed and the authorities suspended many public works. There were labour gangs everywhere, so labour was cheap and you could often earn no more than 30–40 cents a day.

In 1942, after the Japanese southward invasion, I went to Qishalan and spent more than f200 on 3 mu of land. I developed it as a small vegetable garden. I grew vegetables on it for 12 years, and earned tens of thousands of guilders. In 1954 I opened a small shop. I did business worth 15,000 a month, and could just about make a living. In early 1960, I could no longer continue, and I had to sell the shop to an Indonesian. In August 1960, I returned to China.

Interview with Zheng Yaqing, a "piglet" on a tobacco plantation in Deli

Interview by Gui Guanghua, May 1963, Zhize Farm, Yinjiang County

Zheng Yaqing, from Guangtou Village in Chaoyang County in Guangdong, born in 1902, is now 61. In 1927, he left plantation and started working in a shop. After the Japanese marched south, he ran a small plot of land. After the conclusion of the Pacific War, he went bankrupt amid the chaos, and then became a hawker until his return to China in 1960.

Before 1925, there were some 5000–6000 people in our village. There was quite a lot of farmland, but almost all of it was in the hands of landlords in Chaoyang county town. So in the village there were only two sorts of people: those with a tiny bit of land, but who also needed to rent; and those with no land at all, who depended entirely on renting. Many, because of the pressures of life, either went elsewhere to find work where they could or left the village and went abroad. Most went to Siam and Vietnam. A few went to Singapore and Malaya, and more than 30 sold themselves into indenture in Deli.

Before I emigrated, my family comprised my father, my elder brother and his wife, a niece, and me. In 1925, father was already more than 60. He was old and frail, and could only do light work. The main labour power was my elder brother (who was nearly 40) and me. We had no land, and we rented 2 mu of paddy from a landlord, as well as 4 mu of dry land. The paddy yielded 4 dan of grain per mu, of which 2 dan was rent, paid in the first half of the year; in the second half, we planted sweet potatoes and assorted crops, which we sold, using 2 dan of the proceeds to pay the rent for the second half of the year (1 dan was worth 3–4 yuan). On the dry land we grew sweet potatoes, peanuts, and beans.

The rent was expensive, so even though there were 5 of us and we could rent 6 mu of land, we had little left over after paying it, and we often had to hire out our labour. For example, we would carry things to market for people, for 30–40 cents a day. Or we would go to Shantou to work on the docks, where the pay was based on piece-work and you could earn 60–70 cents. Each year I spent 3 months outside the village doing temporary and casual work. It was exhausting. Even so, we could never get enough to eat, so I got father to agree to let me sell myself into indenture in the Nanyang, and went to Shantou.

In Shantou, I met a broker along the way. He had already recruited 4 or 5 men. When he saw me he asked: "Do you want to go overseas to work?" I said, "Yes." I asked him, "What's the price for indenture?" The broker said, “Forty yuan. But you can’t send it home until you have reached Deli, so for the time being you’ll get 5 yuan, for incidental expenses.” When we’d agreed the price, the broker took us all to Hong Kong by steamer. In Hong Kong, he took us to the white-skin hostel, but all the interviewing was done by Chinese. They asked us our names, place of birth, village, address, whether there were others in our family, and whether we had come of our own free will. They also explained that in Deli we could get released after a year if we grew tobacco and otherwise after 23 months. After that, they gave us another 5 Hong Kong dollars.

In the fifth lunar month, we set sail. On shipboard, we needed our own mat. There were more than 300 new guests on board. We docked in Singapore and then continued to Wulaowan—a journey of 7 days in all.

In Wulaowan, we were weighed and measured, our names were taken, our ages were recorded, and note was made of any special physical characteristics. Our photos were taken. Finally, bodyguards escorted us to the plantation. I was assigned to the Hongshuzai Plantation, along with more than a dozen other new guests from the ship. There were more than 600 Chinese on the plantation, divided into 12 companies.

At first, I did 2 months’ unskilled labour, for which I was paid 45 cents a day. After that, I was assigned to growing tobacco. In the first year I grew 18,000 plants. The working day was 6–11 am and 1–6 pm. One hundred rods of (4000) picked leaves brought in fl0.7. If a Javanese woman helped, she got fl0.42 per 100 rods for stringing and fl0.28 for picking. Advances in grain and cash had to be repaid eventually. When the leaves were retrieved from storage, they had to be sorted according to quality, which yielded fl0.7 per hundred bundles. If two people worked together, one to sort and the other to string, the income was divided equally.

Chinese working for the same company lived together, two to a room. Everyone did their own cooking. During the fortnightly breaks, you could leave and go to the nearby port for shopping.

After the second winter, at the big reckoning, the price per 1000 plants was fl11. After deductions, I had more than 90 left. I felt life on the plantation as too restrictive, working non-stop throughout the year, and for relatively small reward. I told the big overseer I wanted to quit and go elsewhere to find work. When I asked for my papers, he said that this year the company (the Dutch General Company) was issuing no papers. So I had no option but to sign on again as a coolie. I got 35, and a declaration that only 4 would be deducted at the next general reckoning.

In the second winter in1926 I grew 1000 more plants than the previous year, 19,000 in all, and at the big reckoning the price remained the same, 11, which meant I was left with more than f100. After settling up, I asked the big overseer for my papers so I could leave the plantation, and I got a job working in a little shop that a friend of mine had opened at a rubber plantation near Mingping. I got f15 a month, later rising to f25. I stayed there until the Japanese southward offensive, when the shop closed.

During the 4–5 years I spent working in the shop, some of the Deli plantations closed completely while others shed a number of their Chinese labourers.

After the Japanese surrender in 1945, the Dutch army fought its way back into Indonesia. One day, when I was returning from the port to the countryside, I discovered the Dutch had declared martial law and I was unable to pass. When martial law was lifted, I discovered that all my grain and peanuts had vanished and that my 40 pigs were all gone. My wife and two children had also disappeared. Later, I discovered that bandits had stolen all my things and abducted my wife. I also learned at around the same time that my father, brother, sister-in-law, and niece had all starved to death during the Anti-Japanese War. Afterwards, I had no choice but to peddle fresh fish from a bicycle, which I did until my repatriation in 1960.

Interview with Zheng Liangzhe, a "piglet" on a tobacco plantation in Deli

Interview by Gui Guanghua, May 1963, Zhize Farm, Yinjiang County

Zheng Liangzhe, from Jiangdong Village in Chaoyang County in Guangdong, born in 1899, is now 64. In 1927, aged 28, he sold himself into indenture on a tobacco plantation in Deli, where he grew tobacco for 6 years. In 1933, he left the plantation and went to work for a labouring gang. On the eve of the Japanese southward advance, he started running a market garden in Qishlan. After Indonesian independence, right through until his return to China in 1960, he remained a labourer.

Before 1927, there were more than 2000 people in my village, and more than 300 households. Because it was between the mountains and the sea, there was very little land and no paddy, just dry land on which to grow sugarcane, peanuts, sweet potatoes, etc. The village's main source of livelihood was the sea: drying salt and fishing. Relatively few dried salt, a little more than 100, but 200–300 fished for a living. Because the village had no paddy, rice had to be imported from outside.

My parents had died even before I went overseas. I had 2 elder brothers and sister-in-law and 8 nieces—twelve people in all, besides me. We had our own salt field, a water buffalo, 2 pigs, and 2–3 mu of rented land (common land). Most of the work—drying the salt, farming the land, and fishing—was done by us three brothers, whereas the wives looked after the pigs and household tasks.

The salt field yielded a little more than 100 pounds a day, which brought in just over 1 yuan, and at most 3 yuan. But you had to give the salt-tax people 24 cents. Apart from that, we formed a corporation with other villagers to organise our fishing. Because the economic circumstances of the corporation's members were not the same, methods differed.

1. We pooled our capital to buy a boat, and divided the catch equally,
2. If someone in the partnership took the boat out, he got 2 parts of the catch, and the others all got 1 part. For example, if their were 8 in the partnership and one took the boat out, the catch would be divided into 9 parts of which 2 would go to the one who had done the fishing.

The corporation had only a few members, generally between 4 and 8.

As for me, my economic situation was worsening, so to find a way out, in 1927 I sailed together with a broker from a neighbouring village to Hong Kong, where we stayed for 3 or 4 days. Around 100–200 new guests left Hong Kong aboard a ship bound for Deli. Once we arrived in

Deli, we were assigned to the Delitai Plantation owned by the Five Companies.

When I sold myself into indenture in 1927, I received f60. This sum was taken back to my brother by the broker, but only after I myself had arrived at the plantation. The brokers in those days had themselves worked as indentured labourers in the past. They went home to recruit new workers, but rarely managed to recruit more than 10, and usually just 3 or 4.

The basic unit of organisation of the Chinese labourers on the Delitai Plantation was the company. Each company normally had just over 30 workers, and at most just over 50. Apart from the Chinese, there were also Javanese, who were in the majority.

During the first year, while I was a new guest, I grew 15,000 plants, and there was little money left at the big reckoning, but after that I received more than fl00. During picking and storing, apart from what I needed for living expenses, I had enough extra to remit to my family. But I became a gambling addict, so I had to sign on as a coolie again and again, until the sixth winter. I didn't leave the plantation until 1933, when I went out to do casual labour in a gang.

The work consisted mainly of reclaiming land and digging ditches on the rubber plantations. Between 1933 and 1942, when the Japanese advanced south, I was all along in work, moving between different places all over North Sumatra.

After the Japanese surrender, I grew vegetables on a market garden in Qishalan. After Indonesian independence, I continued doing casual labour, right through until the eve of my repatriation in 1960.

Interview with Huang Yada, a "piglet" on a tobacco plantation in East Sumatra

Interview by Wu Fengbin, May 1963, Zhize Farm, Yinjiang County

Huang Yada, originally called Huang Zhaohu, from Jialong Village in Luchuan County in Guangxi, is now 62. In 1927, he was tricked into selling himself into indenture, after which he grew tobacco for 10 years (1927–1937) on the Bulaleng Plantation. He then left the plantation and engaged in business for 4 years near Medan (1938–1941). He then grew vegetables for 4 years (1942–1945), and finally he went back to running a business (1946–1960). He returned to China in August 1960.

1. Leaving China under indenture

Before I left China, my family farmed 15 dou of land. I myself farmed 3, the rest was jointly owned. The rent was split 3:7, I was responsible for 7, they for the rest. One dou yielded more than 15 dou of grain, so 15 dou of an early-harvested crop yielded 200 dou, with 300 dou for a late harvest. There were four brothers, of which I was the youngest, brother number 12 [sic]. Then there were our parents and two sisters-in-law, eight people altogether. My eldest brother was a mason, fourth brother [sic] was a primary-school teacher, and eighth brother [sic] ran a business. I managed household affairs. During the busy season, I farmed the land, and during the idle season I helped out with the business. We had enough to eat. We didn't need to take loans.

Of the village's more than 1000 inhabitants, not one wanted to go to the Nanyang. In the past one had gone to Singapore, but we never heard back from him, so if anyone started talking about the Nanyang, people became uneasy.

My fellow-villager Huang Biguang was my father's pupil. He was 31, and ran a cloth business in the village. On one occasion, he asked me to help him to go to Hong Kong to handle the purchase of goods. He said he had a cousin who was a descendant of Shijiaoshui and we could stay with him. I thought he was intimately acquainted with my family and that he often used to make purchases in the Zhanjiang-Hong Kong region and needed help, so I could see no reason not to help him. It was the start of the third month and no longer the busy season, so I had little to do at home. Although I had no intention of joining in his business activities, I still wanted to go travelling with him, and if I helped I wouldn't have to pay travel costs, so I agreed to go.

When we set out, Huang Biguang got 4 or 5 of his brothers and cousins from the Huang lineage to come along, and after 3 days we reached Zhanjiang. We stayed in a hostel for 2 nights, and then got the train to Hong Kong. Huang paid the fares and accommodation. In Hong Kong we stayed in a hostel near the sea.

The hostel was 4 storeys high and full of people. We stayed there for a month, at 10 cents a day. We ate well, had fun, and looked round Hong Kong, which was nice.

At first I didn't realise what was going on, but after a while I began to think, and to ask myself where the money was coming from. I asked Huang. He said vaguely, "The hostel provides it, there'll be a bill at the end." He told his brothers to go and make some purchases, but I never saw that anything had been bought. Huang seemed anxious, because he said he'd given all his money to his cousins.

After we'd been there for three weeks, Huang said he'd been tricked by his cousins and they'd run off with the money and we'd been left behind in the hostel. Unless we got some money, we wouldn't be able to return home. He asked me what we should do. Everyone immediately started shouting. Huang made out that he was really to be pitied. He said, "I can't go home either. The only thing is to go to the Nanyang, the Dutch are currently recruiting people for their tobacco plantations." I said no, since I was in charge of things at home and they needed me there. Another of the Huangs also said no, since he had 9 brothers in his family and he was the eldest, and even though there were a lot of people in the family, they were always short of food, and he didn't want to go to the Nanyang. But resistance was pointless. Huang insisted that we were penniless and that the hostel boss was pressing for payment, otherwise they'd stop feeding us. The three of us talked about it and eventually decided that the only thing to do was sell ourselves into indenture.

But things weren't over yet. During the indenture process it turned out that Huang Biguang apparently had a problem with his eye, so even though they'd already taken his photo, he couldn't go to the Nanyang. What was he up to? We didn't understand. When we reached the Nanyang plantation, there were even some one-eyed workers there.

Huang bewailed his fate: "How can I go home? How can I face your parents?" He said he would go to Singapore, but pointed out that he was all alone without a cent to his name. When we signed up, we had received 10 yuan each, for daily needs. So we gave it all to him. We had nothing left for our journey to the Nanyang. I don't even know whether he went to Singapore.

So who had cheated us? I think it was Huang Biguang's cousins, but that he was in on it too. He was a rich peasant and a businessman, and his elder brother peddled opium and was earning lots of money. Huang not only sold us but fleeced us out of everything into the bargain.

Three months after arriving in the Nanyang I wrote a letter home. Only then did I realise that my father was worried and had sent my brothers to Hong Kong to look for me. But how could they find me? Even my name had been changed, from Huang Zhaohu to Huang Yada. Because of this incident, my father took ill and died. In 1931, my elder brother died, and in 1932 fourth brother died too, so the family became scattered and extinct.

In Hong Kong, first they took my photo, with a board in front of my chest with my name on it and my number. Then I had a physical examination. I had to lift a block of wood, my knees were tapped, and my vision was checked. Then they asked questions: "Do you want to go?" I didn't really, but I had no alternative than to say "Yes." "Do your parents know?" "Yes." Then they took my fingerprints, and while concluding the contract they explained that you could be released after growing tobacco for a year, or after three years in the case of unskilled labourers. The strongest ones would be sent to Mentok and the less strong to Deli, but I agreed to everything. After concluding the contract, I was allowed to leave the hostel and enjoy myself.

None of us got indenture money. All we got was 10 yuan for purchases, we got nothing else, even though the Chaozhounese got 50–70 yuan for their indenture. But their wages were less than those paid to those of us from Gaozhou [in Guangdong near the Guangxi border]. They got f0.3 a day, whereas we got f0.42.

In 1922, the Dutch were still mainly recruiting Chaozhounese, but after 1927 they switched in large part to recruiting Gaozhounese from Maoming [near Zhanjiang], for unknown reasons.

Most of those under indenture from Lufeng near Chaozhou were voluntary, but most of those from Maoming in Gaozhou were tricked.

In 1926, [the warlords] Long Jiguang and Lu Yunting fought each other and Long lost. Many of his soldiers sold themselves into indenture in the Nanyang (and went to Mentok and Deli).

I left Hong Kong in April, along with lots of people from Gaozhou, Guangxi, and Chaozhou, but they'd all changed their names and places of birth [on their documentation].

The ship took 7 days to reach Wulaowan in North Sumatra. I was then assigned to the Bulaleng Plantation, which was more than 30 kilometres away. There were 48 of us, all of us from the Gaozhou-Maoming area.

2. Ten years' life on the plantation

There were 90 plantations in North Sumatra—Dutch, American, Japanese, and British, but mostly Dutch. The biggest plantations had 1500–2000 workers. Even the smaller plantations had more than 1000 workers. The General Company was in Medan, with branches in the localities.

When the plantation first opened, I don't know how many people died, you were lucky to stay alive. In those days, the jungle had not been opened up, and some of the trees were so big that 3–4 people couldn't span them with their outstretched arms. The jungle was full of wild animals and huge snakes capable of devouring monkeys. The atmosphere was pestilent, the water was toxic, and even the leaves on the trees were poisonous. If you drank unboiled water, you would die. Malaria was prevalent, and there was no treatment available at the time. The weather in those days was much worse than it is today. Moreover, it was hot during the day and cold at night. People scared of taking cold showers were likely to die within 3 months, you had to shower until your entire body generated heat.

The Bulaleng Plantation had more than 1000 workers, fifty-fifty Chinese and Indonesians. The Indonesians cleared the land, whereas the Chinese mainly grew the tobacco. The big boss was Dutch. The big overseer, Lu Yahe, had a bodyguard, an accountant, and 6–7 small overseers. One small overseer was in charge of 30–40 labourers. If you included unskilled labourers, one small overseer was in charge of 70–80 workers.

Growing tobacco began in the second month. You planted the plants about 1.5 feet apart in rows 3 feet apart. There was no mechanical fertilisation, you just put some calcium sulphate under each plant. After planting, you had to water the plant when it became dry. Normally, you only had to earth it up twice a day. Indonesians removed the insects. Three months later, the picking started, and the leaves were strung up and dried. If it rained, you had to smoke-dry them. Thirty days later, you threaded the leaves and tied them into bundles of 40 leaves and sent them to the storage barn. The barn was looked after by special workers who kept the temperature below 40 degrees centigrade. If it rose above 38 degrees, the leaves had to be turned.

After using the soil once for planting, it had to be left fallow for 5 years before it could be used again.

The working day was 5–11 am and 1–5 pm. The plantation operated a contract system. An individual contract applied from planting to harvest. The most you could grow was 25,000 plants, but most people grew 15,000–16,000. I grew 18,000. If a seedling died, you had to replace it. Every month, you got 2 days off (on the 15th and the 30th).

For picking, there were no prescribed hours of work. After picking, you had to do the selection (long, short, good, bad, coarse, tender, and by colour—green, red, yellow, tender green, tender red, tender yellow, etc., more than twenty sorts in all). Forty leaves made 1 bundle, and 100 bundles of good leaves brought in fl.2, while bad leaves brought in f0.6. A harvest of 18,000 plants (with 40–50 leaves each) yielded 15,000 bundles, of which good and bad were in a ratio of 7:3, meaning a total of fl40. After selection you had to string the leaves, back to back and front to front. A bamboo rod with two bundles of 80 leaves brought in 12 cents, so 100 rods brought in fl2. This was very hard work, which often went on throughout the night, until daybreak. If you did all the stringing yourself, you could get more than fl00 for 18,000 plants. After drying the leaves and stringing them into bundles, 100 bundles yielded f0.4, and 18,000 plants yielded 15,000 bundles worth f60.

When you first arrived, everyone got a loan of fl5 a month, but the loan stopped after 3 months, after which you were paid for the picking. Unskilled Chinese labourers were paid f0.42 a day, and Indonesians f0.3 a day, like the Chaozhounese. That was because the Chaozhounese had been paid at the point of indenture.

The overseers in charge of unskilled labourers received twice the wage of an unskilled labourer. Those in charge of tobacco workers received 0.5 percent of the total amount of leaves picked, paid specially by the Dutch.

The big overseers got 2 percent of the total, also paid specially by the Dutch.

The big overseer got money from running gambling and opium dens. Many labourers were seduced into gambling. The overseers also ran small shops in which they sold alcohol, gruel, sweet buns, etc. Opium was openly on sale, at f0.25 a portion. More than 1 in 10 labourers smoked opium. The Dutch and the big overseers did everything they could to encourage gambling, opium-smoking, and prostitution to get the labourers to spend their money. New guests easily fell into the trap.

The labourers lived in reed huts with wooden walls on camp beds, often under mosquito nets. You cooked your own 3 meals a day. You bought your own clothes in the market, for a guilder or more. You didn't need permission to leave the plantation.

If a labourer fell ill, the company provided treatment. Most of the illnesses were jungle fever. One hospital served 5 plantations, and it had many patients. My relative Huang contracted it and died (in 1935). If you got this illness, you became bloated and you were a goner within the week. He had worked as a coolie for 7–8 years and never married, and then he died such a tragic death.

Only labourers who had worked for 30 years or more were eligible for old-age pensions. They got f6 a month and could use the bus without paying.

Generally speaking, after release there were only three options: go back to China, which 1 in 10 did; carry on growing tobacco, which 8 in 10 did; and go away, which 1 in 10 did. I myself thought that to leave the plantation you needed capital, so I might just as well carry on working for a few more years, which I did for the next 10 years, signing on time and again, and receiving f35 each time.

3. Coolie resistance

Before I went, there were quite a few cases of the overseer beating up people. After I went, such cases did not stop altogether. For example, in 1927, at the Liulianmoluo Plantation, where Zhu Yahe was the big overseer, one of his fellow-villagers called Zhu something, in his thirties, was wrongly accused of slacking on the job. He was beaten up by Zhu Yahe, and suffered chest injuries and later died. There was no compensation. Another of Zhu's fellow-villagers was also killed on the pretext of being a bad worker. The big overseers did so many bad things—out of every ten overseers, not one is blessed with good descendants.

Some labourers' resistance was passive, some was active. Some who couldn't reconcile themselves to life as a coolie killed themselves, others ran away. Some killed themselves after running up gambling debts.

In 1923–1924, a middle-school student from Chaozhou was tricked into going to the Bulaleng Tobacco Plantation. He refused to work, even when the overseer and the big overseer cursed and beat him. The case went to the Dutch court, where he was personally interrogated, and he politely accused them. He said: "I am a middle-school student, and definitely didn't come to do a labouring job." Afterwards, the Dutch feared a scandal and brought their influence to bear to get him sent back to China.

In 1927, of the 48 new guests who had arrived together with me, many had originally been soldiers, and were then forced to live an animal existence at low wages and did not eat poorly or save much and were cruelly abused by the overseers, which aroused their extreme resentment. On one occasion, the overseer said that the trench they'd dug was not deep enough and they should immediately dig it again. They refused, and 12 of them (mainly soldiers) stood together and argued with the overseer and started hitting him, and the overseer ran away.

I'll end with a story about five brothers resisting the Dutch. A long time before, five members of a sworn brotherhood had started working at the Dutch plantation. On one occasion, a Dutchman used the excuse that a hole had not been dug properly to start beating those doing the digging. The five sworn brothers got together and hacked the Dutchman to death with their hoes. Far from running away after the incident, they reported to the Dutch authorities. The Dutch interrogated them, and asked who had done the killing. Each one of the 5 said he had done it. The cruel Dutch authorities then crucified them. According to what I was told, the 5 sworn brothers subsequently manifested the presence of their spirits [*xianle sheng*]. Later, a Five Ancestors' Temple was erected in Medan on their behalf. This story is an example of the resistance of indentured labourers to the cruel treatment accorded them by the Dutch colonialists.

Interview with Zhuang Panliang, a "piglet" on a tobacco plantation in Deli

Interview by Gui Guanghua, May 1963, Zhize Farm, Yinjiang County

Zhuang Panliang, from a village in Chaoyang County in Guangdong, born in 1909, is now 54. In 1929, he sold himself into indenture and became a tobacco worker on a plantation in Deli. Ten years later, in 1939, he left the plantation and started selling chickens. After the Japanese surrender, he hawked fruit, until his return to China in 1960.

Before 1929, my village had around 3000–4000 inhabitants who all lived from farming. Some villagers had gone overseas, mainly to Siam, and a few had gone to Singapore, but none had gone to Deli under indenture. Probably 1 in 4 families had members overseas.

Before I left to go abroad, my father had already died and my mother had remarried. I and my younger brother were raised by the wife of my father's elder brother. At the time of my father's death, the family had more than 10 mu of land. After his death, my uncle sold much of it, leaving just 5–6 mu.

When I was 13, I left home and went to Shantou to work in a shop opened there by a relative. At first I received 2 yuan a month, but by the age of 20, when I'd already been working there for 8 years, I felt the wage was too low, just 4 yuan a month, so I went home to resume farming. That was in 1929. In 1929, there was a severe drought and it was impossible to continue farming. I could have returned to Shantou, but the wage was too low, so I sold 2 dan of grain for 7.20 yuan and used it to travel to Hong Kong, where I got work in the docks.

I worked for a few months in Hong Kong, but the wages were poor. A group of 5 or 6 of my friends among the dock-workers had a discussion and we decided to sell ourselves into indenture on a tobacco plantation in Deli.

In 1929, Hong Kong was full of hostels. Almost all of them specialised in recruiting labour for Deli. I and my 5 friends got 25 Hong Kong dollars each from a broker and he took us to a steamer on which we sailed out of Hong Kong. (It was called Jinma [Golden Horse]. At the time, there was another steamer called Wan Fushi [Ten Thousand Happinesses] that also took new guests to Deli.) On board, all the new guests slept on the deck, which was covered by a piece of sailcloth. Apart from new guests, there were other passengers who were paying their own way.

The sea journey took 7 days. After disembarking in Wulaowan, we took the train to the Dutch Twelve Companies' Xiangjiaoba Plantation near

Medan. There our names were taken, we were measured, and we each got f10 to buy the everyday things we needed. I was in the company of more than 30 others from the ship. Later, I heard that we were the final batch of new guests arriving in Deli from Hong Kong.

There were more than 600 Chinese on the Xiangjiaoba Plantation, divided into 12 companies. Apart from Chinese, there were Javanese, in greater numbers than the Chinese and including a large number of women. They were in charge of killing insects, spreading fertiliser (guano), taking out the seedlings, spreading the liquid medicine, and storage activities, like selecting and stringing leaves.

After arriving on the plantation, I first did more than seven months' unskilled labour, for which I received f0.47 a day. Later, the big overseer transferred me to growing tobacco, and in the first year I grew 18,000 plants. Before the picking, grain was issued twice a month, together with 4.75, 10 times in all. We worked a ten-hour day. We had to water the plants. If plants died after transplanting, they had to be replaced. If you couldn't keep up with the tasks, you could ask a Javanese to help, but you had to him or her out of your own pocket, at the big reckoning, when it was deducted. If you were ill and couldn't work, the overseer found a Javanese to replace you—f0.47 a day was then deducted.

After the first year, I got f11 per 1000 plants at the big reckoning. However, deductions included indenture money, the loans provided on arrival at the plantation, tools, the 10 distributions of grain and cash, medical fees (more than f2), barber's fees (f1.40), and bunk fees.

After the big reckoning, some received f70–80, while others received just a few guilders. Afterwards, the big overseer invited everyone to an opera performance. There was also gambling, and the wages soon vanished as the losses mounted. When the big overseer started inviting people to sign on again, what could you do but return to being a coolie? But first you got f35, from which only 14 were to be deducted. So you continued under indenture.

Starting from the second winter right through until the tenth, I grew 19,000 plants a year. Because I never had enough to buy myself free, I carried on for 10 years as a coolie, until I finally decided to leave after the tenth year.

In the third and fourth years, I heard that many plantations were closing down and that labourers were being transferred to other plantations. Some came to Xiangjiaoba. When the Japanese invaded southwards, few tobacco plantations remained, but Xiangjiaoba stayed open until the Japanese occupation. After that, the labourers used the plantation to grow rice.

On the plantations, companies apparently had a rule that Chinese labourers who worked for 30 years could get a pension of f5 a month from the big overseer.

Nearly all the Chinese who left the plantations became casual labourers. They worked mainly in North Sumatra. Some dug ditches on the rubber plantations, some built roads. Casual labourers weren't under indenture, but if they liked they could seek out a *kapala* (headman). But there was no fixed term and you were free, you could do whatever you liked. If you were dissatisfied, you could roll up your bedding and go somewhere else, unlike on the plantation. Most of the *kapala* were from Lufeng.

In1939, after I had left the Xiangjiaoba Tobacco Plantation, I started hawking chickens. Each day I went to the *kampong* (village) where the Indonesians lived and made purchases, and then I cycled round the Medan bazaars selling them. It was always a cash transaction. I earned more than I would have growing tobacco.

On the eve of the Japanese southward invasion, I got married. I have 7 sons and daughters.

After the Japanese occupation, I hawked fruit round the Medan markets. In 1960 the entire family was forced to return to China.

Interview with Liu Ying, a “piglet” on a tobacco plantation in East Sumatra

Interview by Liu Yuzun, May 1963, Zhize Farm, Yinjiang County

Liu Ying, born in 1877 in Huiyang County in Guangxi, went to Indonesia as a “piglet” in 1907, and worked on a rubber plantation for 5 years and as a woodworker for 8 years, before switching to casual labour, in which he remained until his return to China in August 1960.

1. Family circumstances and emigration

I was born into a family of tenant farmers in a village in Huiyang County in Guangdong. There were 4 people in our family when I was small—my parents, my elder brother, and me. We had no land and we were very poor. After elder brother grew up, he went to a place in Guangzhou to break stones, and managed to send some money home. I studied for a few years in the village private school, but I had to stop when funds ran out. At the aged of 14, I went to Guangzhou to join my brother breaking stones.

In 1907, at the age of 30, a “piglet” boss invited me and 3 other stone-breakers for a cup of tea and a smoke. He said you could earn well in the Nanyang, and if you stayed there for a few years you could return to China and lead a life of leisure. The 4 of us were taken in by his honeyed words. We accompanied him to a hostel in town, where we stayed for 1 night, and then we moved to Hong Kong, where we stayed for a fortnight and received 30–40 cents a day to spend. In the hostel in Hong Kong, we could come and go at will. Later, when we boarded the ship, we each got some new clothes, a jar of fermented tofu (for the journey, to use with vegetables), and a small basket. Apart from that, we didn’t get a cent.

When the ship docked in Singapore, we were locked up in a hostel, where we stayed for a month. We weren’t allowed to go out.

While we were still in Hong Kong, we went to the Dutch company for a physical examination (lifting a 60-pound stone and walking around with it, jumping over a 2-foot wooden bench, etc.). In Singapore, the Dutch put us back on a ship to Indonesia, where we had another physical examination. The man in charge of recruitment said to us: It’s great in the Nanyang, each person has a cook (in fact, you cooked for yourself) and you can wear silk pants and a silk shirt (in reality you went practically naked). The Dutchmen standing by had sinister smiles on their faces. Only when we reached the plantation did we realise what those sentences really meant.

2. Life and labour

After my second examination in Singapore, I boarded the ship to Indonesia. The Dutch assigned me to the Qishalan Rubber Plantation and said that I could buy myself free after 3 years. My work was mainly cutting grass, removing undergrowth, and digging ditches, for which I received 33 cents a day, paid at the end of the month.

We worked naked, save for a loincloth. We ate 3 times a day, and cooked for ourselves—everyone had a small wok.

In August or September during the first 3 years, until 1910, the overseer forced us to continue working under indenture and seduced us into borrowing money from the company (I owed fl5). After lending us the money, the company did everything it could to persuade the "piglets" to visit prostitutes, gamble, drink alcohol, and smoke opium, so that the money was soon gone. In this way, the "piglets" had no choice but to continue to work under indenture. I did this too in the fourth year (when I got f30 for signing on).

The overseer was very fierce with us. If we didn't start work on time, he'd kick or beat us.

The company frequently got people to hawk snacks and soup round the plantation. It was expensive, for example, a bowl of gruel cost 5 cents and a small glass of milk cost 12 cents. In principle, you could buy them or not, but people didn't dare not buy, because we knew that if we didn't the overseer would resent it and find all sorts of ways of making us suffer, for example, we'd done this wrong, or this piece of work needed redoing. So to avoid trouble, we'd buy it, however much it cost. Our purchases were totted up and deducted from our wages at the end of the month. This was one of the ways that the overseer used to exploit us.

Often, our income was dissipated immediately. That's why I spent 5 years on the plantation as a "piglet."

3. Alliance members incite the "piglets" to abscond

While we were on our way from Hong Kong to Singapore, Wu Fugui, a colleague of the [Chinese Alliance leader] Wen Shengcai, was also on board. He was from Wuzhou in Guangxi. He wore very refined clothes, but he travelled in the hold together with us new guests. He told us about politics, and explained how the white men cheated and slaughtered us Chinese, and that in the Nanyang many Chinese had been persecuted to death. He said selling "piglets" was like selling cattle and horses, and we should try to escape. He told us that when we reached Singapore, when the hostels sent people to fetch us, we should try to escape along the way, because when they got us inside the hostel, we would be trapped. He pointed out that there were several hundred of us, and only a few dozen people escorting us. We should stand together and escape en masse, and the escorts would be powerless. In any case, in Singapore they wouldn't dare grab people openly on the streets. He said after escaping we should run to the Taishengtang Medicine Shop to hide, he often went there and he'd find a way of helping us.

He was very good to us "piglets." He shared his food with us. He said he was a member of Sun Yat-sen and Wen Shengcai's party, and that he was on a mission to Singapore to collect money for the struggle against the Qing and to buy weapons.

When the ship reached Singapore, and the hostels sent people to fetch us, no one dared try to escape, because we felt that we didn't know about anything or know anyone in Singapore and didn't have anywhere to run. Many of us still thought we should try to find good work in the Nanyang.

4. The effect on the "piglets" of the 1911 Revolution

When news arrived of the victory of the 1911 Revolution, everyone was very excited, and the "piglets" on each plantation donated a guilder each to support Sun Yat-sen's efforts to restore China to good fortune. We all helped each other cut off our pigtails. The Chinese associations (tongxianghui and huiguan) in the port organised big celebrations, and lots of us went down to join in.

5. The "piglets'" resistance

Many labourers on the plantations resented the overseers' persecution, and they often rose up in resistance. In 1911, several new guests on one of the plantations killed an overseer (because he had often beaten people for no reason and was especially fierce towards us). Later the ringleader of those "piglets" was arrested and paraded round the port, and afterwards he was banished and his whereabouts were unknown—probably he was killed.

6. Life after release

After my release in 1912, I got my papers and decided to learn sawing, which I did until 1919. The wages for sawing were as follows: 13 cents for sawing a plank 7.5 inches across and around 10 foot in length; 18 cents for a plank 1 inch thick and 1 foot across. I worked hard every day, and I could earn f80–90 a month, which left f70–80 after deductions for food and other necessities. Although my income from sawing was much higher than from working on the plantation, it was extremely exhausting and required an enormous expenditure of energy. The hard-earned money was soon used up. I worked for 8 years in the sawmill, but came away from it with nothing.

Early in 1920, I switched to casual work. I worked as a handyman and an odd-job man for the Nanqiang School, for Medan's Women's Association, and for the Xinda Minhua School, and I had various part-time jobs. In 1957 I joined the Xianda Old People's Home, and in August 1960 I returned to China.

Interview with Yan Shiyi, a "piglet" on a rubber plantation in North Sumatra

Interview by Huang Zhongyan, May 1963, Zhize Farm, Yinjiang County

Yan Shiyi, from Shanjiao Village in Wuzhou in Guangxi, was born in 1887 and is now 76. In 1908, he left Hong Kong for Indonesia, and worked for 4 years as a "piglet" on the Ashahanxingjiashan Rubber Plantation. After his release, he became a sawyer, until his return to China in 1960. His memory is poor, so what follows is a fragmentary record.

Before I left China, my family had no land whatsoever. We were tenant farmers, everything was rented. I can't remember how much we rented. The family comprised my parents and my elder brother and his wife, I was the main earner. Nearly all the villagers were tenant farmers. We didn't have enough to eat, so lots of people wanted to abroad. A villager took us to Beihai [south of Nanning], where we were handed over to a hostel and sent to Hong Kong, where we were delivered to a "piglets'" hostel. We stayed on the second floor. A few days later, after passing a physical test, the hostel gave each of us 2 Hong Kong dollars, as well as a piece of rug, a set of clothing, and a wicker suitcase, after which we boarded a ship bound for overseas.

We arrived in Singapore, where we stayed in a hostel. We weren't allowed out. A few days later, we were put on the boat to Deli, where we were sent to the Ashahanxingjiashan Rubber Plantation. The plantation had been set up by whites. When it was first formed, it was based on a pre-existing tobacco plantation, so there was no need for deforestation and the removal of trunks and roots. The main job was opening land, repairing roads, digging out soil, evening out the land, and weeding. The main tools required were rakes and sickles, and everything depended on human power. Nearly all the labourers doing the clearing were Chinese, with a small number of Javanese. Some of the labourers had previously grown tobacco.

The big boss was a white monkey. He had a Chinese big overseer. The big boss didn't appear at the plantation, but the big overseer sometimes came for an inspection. The labourers were controlled by small overseers, each of which was in charge of 40–50 people. The small overseers didn't do manual labour, they merely inspected and supervised. If they spotted a *salah* (mistake), you could end up immediately in solitary confinement. I never experienced it personally, so I can't really describe it.

The working morning was from 5–11, followed by a meal break and an afternoon shift from 1–4. The quotas were set and assigned every day by the small overseers. Usually you were told at the end of each day about the following day's requirements.

You got fl5 a month and a small grain distribution plus f2.5 on the 15th and a big distribution and a settling up at the end of the month, when the grain and cash was deducted, at a rate of f3 a month. The tools were supplied, without any deduction. Whenever there was one of the fortnightly distributions, you had the next day off and you could go to the port and buy provisions. You didn't need a pass. The big overseer ran a small shop where you could buy things like salted fish and salted vegetables. We were accommodated communally, a dozen or so in one dormitory, it was a bit crowded.

After you'd worked 300 days, you could be released. I knew no one outside the plantation and I was unable to find any other work, so after my release I signed on again as a coolie, for f30. After that, my wage was still fl5 a month. I signed on again twice after that, and each time I got f30 signing-on money, but I was still on fl5 a month. The signing-on was for a year. I worked 4 years in all on the Xingjiashan Rubber Plantation. And then a friend helped me get out, and found me a job as a sawyer deep in the jungle. I got more than f20 a month, which was more than on the plantation. You were freer to move about. I stayed on there until I became an old man, right up until when I returned to China.

I never got married in China, and I never got married overseas either.

I'm illiterate, I can't read or write. It's very difficult to depend on others to do my writing for me, and I have no money to send home. So I have gradually lost touch with my village and my relatives. I can no longer go home.

Interview with Huang Chengzhao, a "piglet" on a rubber plantation in East Sumatra

Interview by Liu Yuzun, May 1963, Zhize Farm, Yinjiang County

Huang Chengzhao, from Shikengxu Village in Longchuan County in Guangdong, born in 1884, is now 79. In 1910, he sold himself to a Dutch rubber plantation in Indonesia, where he worked for 3 years. After leaving the plantation, he went to work as a carpenter, and he ran a small market garden for 10 years. He managed a small sawmill for 8 years. In 1943, he switched to running a small shop, which he was forced to close in January 1960. He returned to China in August 1960.

1. Family circumstances before emigration and the process of emigration

Before I left China, Shikengxu was a big village. It had more than 4000 inhabitants, including four surnames—Huang, Guan, Yang, and Zou. The local moneybags, Huang Bingyi, counted as one of the biggest landlords in the area. He had more than 1000 dan of land, and the poor of all four lineages in the village were his tenants. He had more than a dozen shops, big and small, and he controlled the local rice market. He also ran two pawn shops, where you could pawn clothes and farm tools, at 25 percent monthly interest. Poor people on the verge of starvation queued up to pawn their things.

My family was very poor. We had no land, and rented 8 dou (mainly from Huang Bingyi). It yielded more than 40 dan a year. Half of it was rent, so life was precarious. If we hit a bad month, we went to pawn things at Huang Bingyi's shop.

There were 8 people in my family: my parents, me and my wife, and two younger brothers and their wives (both child brides). Apart from the two wives, who counted as half a unit of labour power each, the rest of us were all fit and strong.

When I was a boy, I studied for three years in the village private school, but when money became scarce I had to stop. At the age of 19, I went to work on a boat on the Han River, and stayed until I was 24. At the age of 25, I returned home to get married. The wife didn't get on with my mother, and mother insisted we split up, but I was afraid of getting a bad reputation and insisted that there would be no splitting up, and instead I would go overseas, and earn my livelihood that way. In May 1910, at the age of 26, I and 4 others travelled from Longchuan to Meixian and from there to Shantou.

In Shantou we stayed in a hostel opened by a Hakka from Dapu. It had two sections, each on two floors, and every time the boat sailed the hostel delivered 100–200 new guests, all of them Hakkas. (I never saw a Chaozhounese.)

I stayed in the hostel for 7–8 days. The hostel charged 20 cents a day for food, and another 20 cents for other expenses. One day in the hostel I met a returned Overseas Chinese from Medan. He asked me where I was going, and I said I was going to Indonesia as a coolie. He told me I could get 50–60 yuan for my indenture and urged me to pester the "piglet" broker for it, otherwise the money would go begging. I asked the "piglet" boss and there was lots of arguing, but eventually I got 35 yuan (I sent 10 yuan back to Meixian and paid the hostel). If you add to that the 5 yuan I got to signing on at the foreign firm and the 5 I got when boarding the steamer, in all I received 45 yuan. When the "piglet" boss handed me the money, he insisted that I keep quiet about it, lest the other "piglets" start demanding the same. The other "piglets" had just come down from the village. They were completely at a loss in their new surroundings, and didn't know about the "piglet" boss's tricks, so most of them only got 15–20 yuan. I even heard someone say that if you knew what you were doing you would go straight to the Dutch office and sign on there as a "piglet," and then you could get as much as 80 yuan.

The night before embarkation, the "piglet" boss took all the new guests to the Dutch office in the foreign firm in Shantou for a physical examination, an interview, and a photograph. We were all measured and weighed and had to jump across a two-foot high wooden bench, to see how fit we were. The recruiters asked me whether I was doing this of my own free will, and when I said yes, I had to make my mark and received 5 yuan.

The ship was called You An (Friendly Peace). On embarking, we got a further 5 yuan but nothing else—you had to buy your own clothes and things. There were more than 200 new guests on board. We reached Wulaowan in 7 days. I still had my 35 yuan with me. I changed it all into Dutch guilders, at a rate of 5 to 7.

After disembarking at Wulaowan, we went to Medan to be registered, and got f7. After that, the more than 200 of us were assigned to various Dutch companies. More than 40 "piglets" were assigned along with me to a Twelve Companies rubber plantation.

2. The rubber plantation and its administrative structure

The rubber plantation was called the Danrongxilamo Plantation. It had originally been a tobacco plantation, but now it had switched to rubber. When I first arrived, there were large numbers of rubber trees already in operation, and other newly planted saplings. There were more than 200 Chinese on the plantation (all of them "piglets") and more than 1000 Javanese (mostly women). The Chinese mainly did the hoeing, dug ditches, turned the soil, and cleared the undergrowth. The Javanese mainly took care of planting the saplings and tapping the rubber.

The organisational structure of the plantation was as follows. At the very top was the big boss, a Dutchman. Under him were 3 number-two bosses (also Dutch), who assisted him. The big boss rarely inspected the plantation—that was the job of the number-two bosses. Beneath the number-two bosses were two layers of organisation, to control the Chinese and the Javanese respectively. Regarding the Chinese, there were 5–6 small overseers, each responsible for 30–40 labourers. These small overseers did not themselves take part in production. Their main job was to assign work areas to the workers under their control, to assign tasks, and to supervise labour and various activities, and to report constantly to boss number two. Usually the small overseers were responsible to a big overseer, also a Chinese, but on our plantation there were relatively few Chinese, so there were no big overseers, and the small overseers reported directly to the number-two bosses.

As for the Javanese, they had a big *wanlü* (himself a Javanese) and more than a score of small *wanlü* whose job was similar to that of the small overseers.

There were also 2–3 accountants, who looked after accounts, and a very rudimentary *sakit* place (clinic), with a couple of basic hygiene officials.

3. Labour, wages, and living

When we first arrived at the Twelve Companies, we were told that indenture lasted 3 years. The labour we performed was very exhausting, such as reclamation, digging ditches, raking the undergrowth, turning the soil, etc. We worked 10 hours a day. I slaved away under the hot sun, burnt black, I don't know how many layers of skin I lost. If you arrived at work or left work outside the prescribed hours, or if you were a bit slack, the overseer would punish you harshly, and you could at the slightest pretext end up in solitary confinement. Once on our plantation seven Chinese labourers knocked off half an hour early and on the way back to the hut came across the big overseer riding in a horse-drawn cart. They tried to hide but he saw them. The big overseer interrogated them and took their names. The next day, the 7 were put in a Dutch prison in solitary confinement for a week. All they got was a handful of poor-quality food, and every day they had to perform backbreaking physical labour (such as breaking stones, carting mud, repairing roads, etc.).

The "piglets" got 33 cents a day, from which 16 cents were deducted for food. Beyond that, each "piglet" got a wage of one guilder from which, in the case of new guests, 7 cents were deducted. Not only was the basic wage low but there were all kinds of deductions, so that you ended up being paid very little. The poorest labourers got no more than f2–3 a month. At the end of my first month on the plantation I ended up with f2.5.

Thirty-three cents was the rate per day. The plantation also ran a piece-rate system. Strong workers could earn from 60 to even 80 or 90 cents a day. For example, for every 2 metres of soil raked and turned (to a depth of 1 foot), you could get 5–7 cents. I was quite a strong worker, so in my second month on the plantation my wage was f5.5 and by my third month it had risen to more than f10 and by the fourth month to f15. After 1 year, I was earning f20–28 a month.

There were fortnightly grain distributions that were deducted at the end of each month but not at year's end.

Everything was crude and simple on the rubber plantation—work, food, clothes, accommodation, and conduct.

Food: Every day we ate 3 times. We ate water gruel in the morning and rice at noon and in the evening, with very poor meat and vegetables. We ate 8 to a table, and shared a plate of stinking salted fish and rotten vegetables. Even so, f4.8 were deducted each month. Since the two meals were basically inedible, many people got food from outside. I spent f3–4 a month on extra food.

Clothes: The company provided no clothing, we had to buy it all ourselves. Because of the terrible heat, we almost never wore clothes to work, just a loincloth. We only dressed up when we went down to the port.

Accommodation: We lived in a big wooden building with a roof made of leaves. There were no walls inside. Even during the daytime it was like night. Twelve men lived in one room. The labourers working under a small overseer lived packed together in 3–4 houses, so the overseer could control them easily. The labourers had to provide their own curtains, rugs, and reed mats.

Conduct: We slaved away every day in the hills. We had very little contact with the outside world. The company prescribed a fortnightly day off, at the middle and start of the month. The day off was unpaid. The labourers were free to go to the nearby port, but they usually had to come back the same day.

Illness: If you fell ill, you normally worked on, but if you contracted serious illnesses, the clinic was unable to help. You weren't paid for time off when ill.

4. "Piglet" resistance

Even though the overseers kept the labourers on a tight rein, sometimes the labourers hit back. One day, although it was already past knocking-off time, the small overseer stopped us going back and insisted that we continue working. There were a dozen of us. We were furious, and we ganged on the overseer and gave him a beating, after which he ran off. Incidents of that sort were frequent. In some places, overseers were beaten to death.

While we were working, we often used to deliberately ignore company regulations and do things in a slapdash manner. For example, while raking away undergrowth or turning over the soil, we would only turn over a bit and leave the rest intact, and just spread a bit of new soil on the surface. It was hard to see that the soil had not actually been turned. Boss number-two and the small overseers were wise to this practice and used sticks that they carried to prod the soil. If they discovered that the work had not been done properly, they either beat the workers with their sticks or ordered them to do it again. They would later create all sorts of problems for the labourers concerned. Even so, they couldn't intimidate the labourers. The labourers had lots more ways of resisting.

5. Relations between Chinese and Javanese labourers

On our plantation, Chinese and Javanese worked, lived, and ate separately, but we didn't live far from each other. After work, there were often interactions, and we got on well together. There were never any fights. Some Chinese married Javanese women workers and built little shacks for themselves on the plantation.

6. Release

After entering into indenture, I wished my 3 years would fly past as quickly as possible. Not long afterwards, I met a fellow-villager at Mingli, Wu Yadong, who'd opened a hot-food shop in Mingli. He kept on telling me that after my release I could stay in his shop if I couldn't find other work. So during my 3 years I worked like crazy and was really frugal. I refrained from visiting prostitutes, gambling, drinking, and other vices, and did my best to save money for my future release from indenture. During those three years, I never once had a day off, and I nearly always worked full-out.

In that way I completed my three back-breaking years as a "piglet." I asked the company for my papers and went to stay for a while in Wu Yadong's hot-food shop.

7. Work after release

After staying for a few months with Wu Yadong, in 1914 I became an apprentice sawyer in a sawmill near Mingli. I stayed there for nearly 2 years. Life as a sawyer was relatively free, there were no restrictions on when you started work or knocked off. You could work as much as you liked, or take time off if you felt like it. It was piece-work, so the more you did, the more you earned. And the wages were quite high. If I worked every day, flat out, I could earn up to fl00 a month. But it was wearing on your health. It took a lot more out of you than plantation labour, so we sawyers had to spend a lot on food. After two years in the sawmill, I had only saved just over f200.

It seemed to me that I had no long-term future in the sawmill, because the job was too wearing. In 1916, I left, and decided to invest my savings in a small vegetable garden. I went to Xiandadanaiyaoya and reclaimed 3.5 mu of land (I hired several men to help with the reclamation). I planted green vegetables, peanuts, and sweet potatoes and raised more than 20 pigs and some chickens and ducks, and I built myself a small wooden house. That meant all my savings were gone. To find a good workmate, I married an Indonesian woman.

Raising pigs and growing grain often depends on luck. If the harvest is good, and prices for poultry and pigs are high, and there's no pestilence, you can make several hundred or even as much as fl,000, but if you're unlucky and your animals get sick, or prices fall, you might find yourself merely breaking even or even losing money. I depended on my smallholding right up to 1926, when I passed it on to someone else for more than f3,000. After paying off debts of f1,000, I still had nearly f2,000 left. I used the money to set up a sawmill where I employed 10 workers. We sawed 30–40 tons a month, for which we earned around f150.

I ran the sawmill for nearly 20 years, right up to the end of 1942, when I opened a shop (there was no much timber near my sawmill, and anyway the price of wood was by that time low). I built my shop on a small patch of land rented from an Indonesian landlord (I spent more than f50,000 building the shop), and I used another f50,000 for business capital. But because of the political turmoil and official corruption, the shop was impossible to sustain, and in less than 10 years I'd used up all my capital. When Indonesia started discriminating against Chinese, we took a particularly heavy blow. In January 1960, I was forced to sell the shop to the Indonesian landlord (for just f4,000). In August I went back to China aboard a ship sent by the ancestral country to rescue the Overseas Chinese.

8. Links with the ancestral country and my family

After I went to Indonesia, my tie to my family was broken. However, I continued to pay close attention to events in the ancestral country. My deepest memory is of hearing about Sun Yat-sen's overthrow of the Qing Dynasty in October 1911. Everyone was really excited and we vied with one another to chop our pigtails off. We bought lots of fish and meat and had a feast in celebration. After the outbreak of the Anti-Japanese War, I immediately contributed f25 (I was running the sawmill at the time), to support the resistance.

9. The "piglets'" folk songs

The Hakka "piglets" liked to sing, and we often sang back and forth to one another in a musical dialogue while working. Most of the songs expressed our longing for our villages and our wives, and our bitterness at the harshness of life in the Nanyang. I forget the songs we used to sing, but I can remember a few verses of one.

> We left in the first month, and here we are today.
> Our shirts and trousers are ragged.
> We're determined to earn enough to return home,

We don't know how much we still owe,

From Hong Kong we crossed oceans,
Amid wild storms at sea.
I should have believed my sister,
And then I wouldn't be in this desperate situation.

Life is desperate,
Day and night I think of my darling sister.
After 360 days I can buy myself free,
I paint my sister's portrait on the wall.

During the day and night I think of you,
I think of my sister all the time.
Chopping bamboo,
At each notch I think of my sister.

Interview with Deng San, a "piglet" on a rubber plantation in East Sumatra

Interview by Huang Zhongyan, 1963, Zhize Farm, Yinjiang County

Deng San, from Laotangzao Village in Yangjiang County in Guangdong, born in 1890, is now 73. In 1911, he went to Singapore as a stowaway on a ship from Hong Kong and sold himself into indenture in Alahan. He was sent to work as a labourer on a rubber plantation in Qishalan. In 1912, he purchased his release, left the plantation, and did casual labouring jobs. He returned to China once, in 1918. His experience after his release is particularly worthy of note.

Before I left China, we had little land, but because my village was on the coast and you could do salt-farming, the whole family had adequate food and clothing. I wasn't the main worker in the family. In 1911, when I was 21, I went to Hong Kong to learn business. I got a job as a service worker in a hostel. The hostel specialised in receiving guests who had returned from overseas and "piglets" bound for abroad. I worked there for 2–3 months, but I lost a lot of money gambling, and to escape my debts I stowed away on a "piglet" ship. When the ship docked in Singapore, I had no money, so I was forced to sell myself into indenture in East Sumatra. The price in Singapore was 18 yuan, with 1 yuan equalling fl.4.

When the ship reached Qishalan, I was assigned to a rubber plantation. The plantation was owned by North Americans, who had bought it from the Dutch. The big boss (the manager) on the plantation was Dutch and there was just one big overseer, a Chinese. There were 7–8 gangers under the big overseer, each in charge of 30–40 labourers. There were more than 1000 workers on the plantation, including more than 300 Chinese. There were more Javanese—rubber tapping was their work, and many of them were women. The Javanese were under a big *wanlü* and some small *wanlü*. The Chinese had very little to do with the Javanese.

The Chinese dug the land, repaired roads, and did weeding, for 10 hours a day. There was a daily quota. If the soil was hard, the quota was 5 by 10 yan, with 1 yan roughly equal to 2 metres. Since it had earlier been a tobacco plantation, there was no jungle to clear, so the quota could usually be achieved. If we sometimes failed to meet the quota, the overseer was unlikely to blame us, but if we missed it repeatedly, he would extend the work time until it was finished. If you missed the quota by a big amount, he'd beat you and accuse you of deliberately slacking.

The new guests got fl0 a month and the company fed them—rotten fish and vegetables. People started getting their own food. Every month you only got 16 kilos of rice, and if that was not enough, you had to buy your own. Every month you spent around f2.8 on rice. The amount you spent on other food depended on whether you were frugal or not. We lived in thatched huts separated by wooden boards, several men to a room.

I obtained my release after 10 months. Because I'd sold myself voluntarily into indenture, and moreover in Singapore, away from China, there was no intermediate exploitation in my case, so my indenture costs were small. The deductions were also manageable, so I was able to get early release. People brought over by brokers from China often had to work for 3 years before their release.

After my release, I worked in a shop opened in Qishalan by a man from southern Guangdong, and did some casual labouring. A few months after that, I was introduced to some business by a fellow-villager, running a gang of workers maintaining the railway line. You were paid by the job, and I found some capable workers skilled in digging tunnels. The deeper you dug, the more dangerous it became, and the pay was high, as high as f100–120 a month. As the ganger, I made several f1,000 in just a few years. In 1918, I took money back to China. I stayed for 2 months in the village, and returned to Indonesia after all the money had been spent. While I was away, I had asked a friend to take over temporarily as ganger. After I returned, I continued to work on the railway, all in all for a decade. After that, with the help of friends and by pulling a few strings and spending a bit of money, I got permission from the Dutch government to contract to repair the roads, and I employed a number of wooden junks to get sand for the roads from along the coast. Later, I became a ganger in a sawmill, and employed some sawyers. Within a few years, I had amassed tens of thousands of guilders. I was bursting with ambition at the time, so I decided to switch to inter-island transportation. I borrowed 7 boats from the big company and I first I made quite a profit, but later bad luck raised its head, and 3 boats sank in a typhoon. Apart from the goods lost, I had to pay for the boats, and I was left bankrupt. After that, my hopes were utterly dashed. I used what was left to buy a small plantation and built a wooden house on it and raised pigs and grew vegetables, as well as growing 700 rubber trees and 100 orange trees. I also took an Indonesian wife. After several years of peaceful living, when the rubber trees were ripe for tapping, a Dutch official came to extort money from me, saying that the land the government had leased to me was for growing vegetables and not for rubber trees. Only when I paid him off did he desist. In 1942, the Japanese moved south and carried out their predations everywhere. At the time, I was busy elsewhere, but on my return the Japanese had sealed off the road. When I managed later to return to my plantation after the Japanese had withdrawn their blockade, I discovered that my house had been burned down. After that, I built another one, and made a living by tapping rubber. After the Japanese surrender, I muddled through for a few years. When the Indonesians started discriminating against the Chinese, it was impossible for us to stay. In 1960, I returned to China.

Interview with Wu Yasan, a "piglet" on a rubber plantation in East Sumatra

Interview by Huang Zhongyan, May 1963, Zhize Farm, Yinjiang County

Wu Yasan, born in 1884 in Songshuxia Village in Gaozhou in [western] Guangdong, is now 79. In 1911, he went to Hong Kong and sold himself into indenture on a Yahshan rubber plantation, until his release and departure from the plantation in 1917. He is old and his memory is beginning to fail him. What follows are some fragments of my interviews with him.

Before I left China, we were tenant farmers. We rented all our fields from a landlord called Luo, I can't remember how many, all I remember is that after we had paid the rent we had 3 dan of grain left. We had no supplementary income. When I turned 20, I was unable to get married. Not long afterwards, my parents both died, as result of our destitution, and my elder sister had already been married for a long time. There was me, a bachelor, with no means of support and no land to till. I decided to go abroad in search of a livelihood. I heard that the Nanyang was a good place to go, and that in a couple of years you could get rich and return home. I also heard that in Beihai they were recruiting people to go to the Nanyang, so I sold all of family's stuff to finance my trip to Beihai. In a hostel I met a broker who gave me a bit over 10 yuan indenture money and took me to Hong Kong and delivered me to the "piglet" hostel. He then returned to Beihai. In Hong Kong I had a physical examination, and a week later I sailed overseas. I'd already gambled all the indenture money away.

When we reached Indonesia, I was assigned to work as an unskilled labourer on the Ashahan Rubber Plantation. In the same port there were tea plantations and coffee plantations that also employed Chinese labourers.

There were already rubber trees ready for tapping, but all the tappers were Indonesians, the Chinese only did digging, weeding, banking up earth, and other heavy work. We were supervised by Chinese overseers—each overseer was in charge of more than 40 of us. Anyone who slacked on the job or couldn't finish their assignments was beaten and abused. Some were even put in solitary confinement for a fortnight or a month. Then you had to do hard labour, and you got fed but no pay. You had to make up the days you'd missed during your punishment and complete your allotted number of working days—otherwise, they wouldn't release you. We worked a ten-hour day starting at 5 in the morning with a midday break. Everything was done manually.

We were accommodated collectively, 5–6 to a room. We showered with well water. We didn't need to cook for ourselves. We ate coarse rice, stinking fish, and rotten vegetables, provided by the plantation. I was broke, so I had to eat the company's food and make do with it.

When you sold yourself into indenture, there was an oral contract that you would be released after 300 working days, but you couldn't get your papers and go away unless you gave money to the big overseer. When I completed my 300 days, I had no money for my papers, so I had to sign on again as a coolie. Signing on was for a year, and you got f30. I signed back on 5 times, and finally I gave up gambling and got my release, in 1917.

When the rubber plantation was founded, digging the earth and building roads was nearly all done by Chinese. Javanese gradually increased in number, while there were fewer and fewer Chinese new guests.

The white monkeys lived on the plantation, and often came to inspect the work. If the work had been done badly, they hit or kicked you. Sometimes they wouldn't hit you themselves, they'd get the overseers to do it. They would stand to one side and watch.

There were no police or army on the plantation. I never saw anyone go on strike or engage in collective resistance.

After leaving the plantation, I went to the Qishalan port and earned a living working on a vegetable garden. The boss was a Chaozhounese. We could more or less do as we liked, we were relatively free. There was no one to beat or curse us. The wages were higher than on the plantation. I worked there for 10 years. After that I started working in a brick kiln, for another 10 years. After that I did casual labour, reclaiming land for people.

I never married in China, and I didn't in Indonesia either. I lived a lonely life. I always worked hard, and muddled through.

When Sun Yat-sen carried out his revolution [in 1911], I was working on the rubber plantation in Ashahan. Everyone was really happy. Some immediately chopped off their pigtails, though others waited 2–3 years. Personally, I thought my pigtail was too long. It was hard to dry after showers, and it was hot to work under a pigtail. So I quickly followed the crowd and lopped it off. Afterwards, because we were illiterate, the Dutch colonialists and the overseers never told us anything, so we knew almost nothing about events in the ancestral country.

Interview with Liu Tai, a "piglet" in an old Bangka tin mine

Interview by Liu Yuzun, May 1963, Zhize Farm, Yinjiang County

Liu Tai, born in 1898 in Zhuyaojing Village in Bobai County in Guangxi, is now 65. He is illiterate. In 1923, he sold himself into indenture in an Indonesian tin mine and 2 years later he was released, after which he hawked fish. He managed a small plantation until his return to China in December 1960.

1. Family circumstances and emigration

In our village, my family was a middle family. There were 10 people in our family, mother, sixth uncle, second uncle and his wife, and me (we were the main labour power), and three who were not yet adults (three younger brothers and two child brides for two of them). We had 3 dan of land, of which we farmed 2.5 dan. Each dan yielded more than 40 dan of grain over two harvests a year. We also rented 5 dou, half of the yield from which went in rent. So the family had enough to eat, and we were quite well off.

One day I went gambling and lost 3 dan of grain. My mother and my uncle were furious with me, and I lost my temper and decided to leave home. I walked twelve miles to Beihai and went to Sun Shiliu's hostel and asked him to send me overseas. Sun immediately let me in, and said I shouldn't tell anyone, to avoid unnecessary trouble. He said once we'd got a dozen men together we could go to Hong Kong. I stayed in his hostel for a fortnight. When he had recruited a dozen people, he took us to a hostel in Hong Kong, and he then returned to Beihai.

While we were in the Hong Kong hostel, we got 10–20 cents a day to spend. Food was provided, and it was very good. We could come and go at will. After we'd been there for a few days, the hostel owner took us to the Dutch foreign firm for a physical examination, a photo, and an interview. Before boarding the ship, I got 7 Hong Kong dollars, a thin rug, too shirts and trousers, a bamboo hat, and a wicker suitcase. Apart from that, we didn't get a cent.

The ship first went to Singapore (Huang Si was on board, he was also a "piglet," he went to Indonesia to work in a tin mine, and in December 1960 he was, by coincidence, on the same ship back to China, and now he's on this same farm). We stayed in a hostel in Singapore, but we were kept under complete control. All of us new guests were locked up and not allowed the slightest freedom. When the hostel owner took us for another physical examination, we went and returned by car.

While I was having my physical examination in Singapore, the recruiting official told me that if I went to Indonesia to work in a tin mine, the work would be easy and the pay good, and that each day a worker could knock off after carrying just 3 baskets of mud. We also believed at the time that 3 baskets was nothing. But after we got to the mine, we discovered that what the official really meant was 3 cubic metres of mud. Moreover, the quota grew and grew as time passed, and sometimes the overseer demanded 7–8 cubic metres of us.

2. Life and labour

We stayed in the Singapore hostel for two days and nights, and then sailed to Indonesia and disembarked at Mentok. I was sent to No. 5 Company in Wuliyang, where there were around 800 Chinese miners, most of them "piglets" under indenture. Every day we worked 9 hours, from 5.30–11 and 12–4.30, with a meal break in between and half-hour breaks on both shifts. At first we got 24 cents a day, rising to 36 cents after 160 days. I stayed with the company for 2 years before getting my release. I planned to return to China immediately, but I had no money (I'd earned more than fl00, but I'd lent it to other people). So I didn't go back. In April 1925, I went to Nanbang to work in a small mine.

3. Working in the small mine

So I needed to sign on again. You got quite a lot of money when signing on. On one occasion, I got f95 (20 of which were an advance, later deducted). The wages were also quite good—51 cents a day, paid monthly, but only 80 percent was paid out at the time, while 20 percent was retained for distribution at the annual reckoning.

There were more than 30 of us in our gang. There was an overseer, a small overseer, someone in charge of provisions, and us coolies. The labourers had all been released from the big mine. Our leader contracted to develop a small mine for the Dutch company. He was in charge of hiring, and he sold the output to the Dutch company. As for profit and loss, it was all his business, it affected no one else.

We labourers were also on contracts. Sometimes we even had to shift 12 cubic metres a day and carry it for 40–50 metres. If we failed to meet the quota, then we had to redouble our efforts. But the overseer treated us quite well, not like in the big mine, where they would beat and curse you as soon as look at you. The overseer also provided the food, which was much the same as in the big mine.

In the past, none of the small mines had been mechanised. The mine I worked in had a little train fuelled by firewood and rented from the big Dutch mine (which no longer used firewood on its trains).

4. Work after leaving the mining company

In early 1928, I left the small mine and started hawking fish (from a bicycle). I could earn about f30 a month, which was quite good, and I was much freer. I could go out whenever I wanted, I was my own master, I was no longer at the overseer's beck and call. After a few years, I gradually accumulated some savings. In 1930, I got married, and reclaimed a small plantation from the jungle on which I grew rubber and peppers. I didn't give up the fish hawking until the Japanese marched south in 1942.

After the Japanese surrender in 1945, I went back to the Dutch tin mine for 4 years. Later, as my little plantation began gradually to develop, I found myself particularly busy, so I stopped working at the mine. Before I returned to China, my little plantation was producing 30–40 pounds of rubber a day, and 400–500 kilos of peppers a year. When I returned to China in 1960, I took only my wife and children nos. 2, 3, and 4. My eldest son stayed in Indonesia to run the little plantation.

5. The "piglets'" resistance at the mine

When we new guests signed our contracts in Hong Kong, we were told that we would be eligible for release after 360 working days. Bu after we had worked 360 days, the company refused to let us go and held on to our papers. Thereupon, more than 700 new guests poured into the Wuliyang office and smashed the windows. The Dutch called in the military police, who arrested more than 30 of us. That infuriated the entire workforce, and more than 700 new guests all demanded to be put in solitary confinement with those arrested. What could the Dutch company do? They had no choice but to release those arrested. We new guests were forced to continue working, and did not get our release papers for another 2 years.

Interview with Huang Si, a "piglet" in a Bangka tin mine

Interview by Liu Yuzun, May 1963, Zhize Farm, Yinjiang County

Huang Si, born in 1902 in Yanshan Village in Beiliu County in Guangxi, is now 61. He is illiterate. In 1923, he sold himself into indenture in Indonesia, where he worked for 4 years in a tin mine. Later, he ran a stall and raised pigs. He returned to China in December 1960.

1. Family circumstances and emigration

Before I went abroad, my family comprised 5 people: mother, elder brother, his wife, and me and my wife. All of us worked. We had 5 dou that we farmed ourselves and 2 that we rented. One dou yielded 4 dan a year in the course of two harvests. We had enough to eat, and usually had a surplus that we could sell.

I developed a habit that my elder brother constantly berated me for. Because of that we didn't get on, so in 1923 I visited the famous Beiliu "piglet" boss Su Wenting and asked him to send me to the Nanyang.

He was a well-known criminal in Beiliu. He and his son ran a "piglet" business between Beiliu, Wuzhou, and Hong Kong. His bases were the Taian Hostel in Beiliu and the Shun'anxiang Hostel in Hong Kong. (Because of his evil reputation, Su was later arrested by the Guangxi government and sent to gaol for 2 years.)

Su took me and more than 30 other new guests from Beiliu to Wuzhou, on foot—it took 5 days. We stayed in the Taian Hostel. The following day we took the boat to Hong Kong. After Su had delivered us to the hostel in Hong Kong, he returned to Wuzhou. We stayed in the hostel for 2 nights. The hostel boss then took us to the Dutch office for a physical examination and an interview. Before that, he drilled us in how to answer: yes, I was coming voluntarily; yes, my parents agreed; yes, I was a peasant capable of hard work, not a trader. Otherwise, we wouldn't be able to go (the Dutch wouldn't want us). We did as we were told, and passed the test.

In the Dutch office each of us got 7 Hong Kong dollars, some clothes, and a small wicker suitcase—just that. We only found out later that Su had made at least 35 yuan on each of us. (At the time, the ship from Wuzhou to Hong Kong cost 2.2 yuan, which if you included food added up at most to 5 yuan.)

2. The organisation of the tin mine

We sailed from Hong Kong to Singapore and then to Bangka. I was assigned to No. 3 Tin Mine in Wuliyang to cart mud. The mine had a big boss and a big overseer. Under the big overseer were 2–3 overseers, and under them were 5–6 small overseers, each in charge of 30–40 coolies. The big overseer was known as the *guasha* and his underlings as *guasha* no. 2. Their jobs were the same, only their titles were different.

3. The "piglets'" life and labour in the mine

We had to work 9 hours a day until 4 pm, with a midday break. We usually had to carry 3 cubic metres of mud a day, that was the quota. But the overseer often raised it to 4–5 cubic metres. At first, the daily rate was 24 cents, but after working for 160 days it rose to 36 cents and to 41 cents after 3 years, 46 after 4 years, and 51 after 5 years, and then it stopped rising.

The company fed us, but the food was atrocious, just rotten fish and vegetables day after day, with very little oil in it. But the overseers feasted on fish and meat. By rights, the "piglets" should have got an extra meal on Sundays, with pork, but in reality the pork was cut down to just a few scraps.

In May 1925, after I'd completed 2 years and saved more than f40, I asked to be released so I could return to China. According to company regulations, I had the right to a return ticket to Hong Kong from the Dutch company and to stay in the Dutch office's hostel in Hong Kong. They gave me 7 Hong Kong dollars to spend on the journey back to Wuzhou (the company paid the fare). I also got some clothes.

Not long after I had returned home, my original wife died of illness. I stayed at home for more than a year, and then decided to return to Indonesia. In June 1926, I sold myself back into indenture for 50 yuan. After reaching Wuliyang, I transferred to Company No. 3. Having already worked for 2 years, I counted as an old guest, so my pay started at 36 cents a day. I worked as a coolie in my new company for another 2 years, until 1928, when I got my release and started working as a water-seller.

4. Oppression and resistance

The tin mine company used to beat and curse us, and if we showed the slightest resistance, we would be put in solitary confinement. If a worker didn't show up for 3 days in succession, the company doctor would examine him, and if the doctor said there was nothing wrong with him, the worker would be put into solitary confinement (near the Dutch office). In our company one new guest couldn't stand the hard work and ran away, but he was soon caught and brought back. The company sent him to the "hospital" where he was given electric shocks as torture.

However, when the overseer's oppression became too much, the workers regularly resisted. I remember 2 occasions:

1. In 1923, when we first arrived in Wuliyang as new guests, we were told that we would be eligible for release after 360 working days. But after I had worked for 360 days, the company unreasonably increased it to 720 days, and lots of new guests resisted. In April–May 1924, up to 2000 new guests at No. 5, No. 4, No. 22, No. 21, and No. 25 Mines stormed the Dutch company's offices in Wuliyang and demanded that it stick to its contract. I also joined in. The Dutch refuse to budge, and called in several hundred military police who arrested more than 100 labourers. After that, even though we still had to work the 720 days before becoming eligible for release, the arrested labourers were released.
2. In 1926, the 43rd Company's big overseer Zeng Yunlong, who was a very fierce man, provoked the labourers' extreme resentment by beating some labourers especially severely. Some of his victims conspired to hack him to death with their hoes on his next visit to the mine. Their "piglet" ringleader was sentenced to 18 years.

5. Work after release

After my release, I sold water for 5–6 years, and saved several hundred guilders. I then switched to grinding beans to make tofu and to raising pigs, and managed to make a living. In 1941, I got married. After the Japanese southward invasion, there were no soya beans left so I couldn't make tofu, and it was impossible to raise pigs. I and my wife and 2 daughters lived a pitiful existence.

In the years 1946–1954, I returned to Mine No. 5, and in 1955 I got a labouring job, right through until December 1960, when I returned to China.

Interview with Peng Jingchu, a "piglet" in a Bangka tin mine

Interview by Wu Fengbin, May 1963, Zhize Farm, Yinjiang County

Peng Jingchu, now 60, is from Dasong Village in Beiliu County in Guangxi. In 1923, he sold himself into indenture and first joined Mine No. 4 in South Bangka, where he worked for 3 years (1923–1925). After his release, he sold fish for 3 years, and worked on a pepper plantation in Mentok for 9 years (1926–1937). Finally, he got a labouring job on a tin dredger, where he stayed for more than 20 years (1938–1960). He returned to China in 1960.

1. Reasons for leaving

Dasong Village had 4 surnames (Li, Liang, Chen, and Peng) and 400–500 households. Around a dozen people left for overseas.

Before I left, in my family there were 5 people, my elder brother, my younger brother, my parents, and me. We rented more than 3 mu from a man called Tan. We divided the harvest 40–60 in the landlord's favour, and had to take the crop to his door. In the past, there were all sorts of disasters, mainly insects. In 1922, there was a small flood, and 2 mu of our land turned to sand, so there was no harvest on it and we starved. We lived by carrying (a little over 1 yuan for a return journey of 5 days, with food costing 15 cents a day). Elder brother did casual labour for people. As for me, when I saw that there was no work, I heard people saying you could get 3 meals a day if you went to the Nanyang, with 3 different dishes at every meal, including fish and beans, and on Sundays and festivals they stewed a pig. In the course of a day's work, you had to carry "three baskets of mud." I started getting ready to go to the Nanyang.

I slipped away secretly, with 5–6 other "piglets," and we went to Zhanjiang. Our "piglet" boss had several other recruits as well, around a dozen of us in all. We took the boat to Hong Kong, where we stayed in the 3-storey Cheng'an Hostel.

In the hostel, we were interviewed and told about the length of the indenture (2 years) and the pay. After giving our fingerprints, we had a physical examination, for which we had to strip down, lift wood, and have our knees tapped and our photos taken. Before embarking, we each received a set of clothes, a rug, a wicker suitcase, a bamboo hat, and a reed mat. Also, we each got 24 cents to spend on necessities. If you didn't use it or didn't use it all, you could change it into guilders before boarding the ship. If you went out, you to be escorted by the "piglet" boss.

I left Hong Kong on the fifth day of the fifth month according to the old calendar, and we reached Mentok on the eleventh.

2. Working conditions in the mining area

There were numerous mining companies in South Bangka, and each company employed 100–200 workers. Under the mine boss was an accountant, a bodyguard, a big overseer, a number-two overseer, two small overseers, three vegetable growers, a firewood-cutter, and a medical person.

I joined the No. 4 Mine, which had reached a depth of 15–16 metres and was propped up on the sides by planks. New guests found it hard to walk on the gangplanks, particularly when they were wet, and it was easy to fall if you didn't watch out. I fell, but I didn't injure myself badly. The work was either contracted or non-contracted. If you were on a contract, you could knock off early when you'd achieved your quota, otherwise you had to work until dark. The quota was supposed to be 3 cubic feet a day, but in reality it was 5–6, and even 7–8, and the soil it had to be taken from deep in the earth.

The working day was 6 am to 6 pm. You were woken by someone knocking on the wall at 4.30, after which you had a cold shower and some food. At 9 am you got half an hour off in which to eat gruel, and an hour at midday for food. You got another half hour off at 3 pm. The working day grew longer the longer you stayed in the mine. In the first week, you only worked 3 hours (6–9); in the second week, 6 hours (6–12); in the third week, 7 hours; and in the fourth week, 10 hours. If you worked 26 days in a month, you got one guilder extra, but only 6–7 out of 10 could manage that. The other 3–4 couldn't.

The big overseer had lots of hatchet-men, whom he personally employed. He used them to hurry the workers up. If you weren't prepared to beat people, you would never get to be an overseer. Once when a ditch turned out to be a bit too narrow, the overseer (Lan Yabing's son Lan Yahuang) lost his temper and beat everyone.

If a labourer couldn't stand the treatment, he could run away, but sooner or later he'd be caught and brought back, and he would be forced to make up the lost time after being duly punished. Some labourers "disappeared," and were recorded as having absconded, but in reality they had either been killed or committed suicide or gobbled up by the water tiger, only the company knew. The labourers were on someone else's territory, they couldn't escape and they had no weapons, so they had no choice other than to put up with their miserable existence. But there were cases of resistance.

In 1924, an Indonesian in the bazaar slaughtered a cow and sold the meat, but he cheated some new guests and overcharged them. The new guests wanted their money back, but the Indonesian refused, and started arguing. After the workers had back to their huts and told people what had happened, a decision was taken to go back the next day and negotiate. That morning, the entire workforce set out, carrying hoes, but were stopped along the way by military police, who had been alerted by telephone. The police fired on the workers, injuring 2–3 of them, and dispersed the rest.

3. Living conditions

I stayed in the mine for 3 years. The first year, I got 24 cents a day, rising in the second half of the year to 36; in the third year, I got 4 cents. I got my release after 2 years, and then signed on for a third. I got f55 in a year, 20 of which were deducted.

The labourers got 3 meals of coarse rice and salted fish and green vegetables a day. On Sundays we got a small amount of pork between 5 of us. We lived in a wooden building on wooden beds full of bed-bugs, against which we had no remedy. None of us had mosquito nets, and we all wore coarse clothing that started running with sweat immediately you began working. Only those in charge had white shirts and trousers.

The overseer ran a small shop where he charged high prices. A tin of fish that cost 50 cents in the market cost 55 cents in his shop, and the market was less than a mile away. Every Sunday he killed a pig, but if you ate any you paid through your deductions. He also ran gambling sessions and openly sold opium at the official price.

Workers mainly got ill with malaria and night blindness (you couldn't see your way in the mornings and the evening, and you couldn't see people). The labourers found being ill a big nuisance. The beriberi mantri deliberately created difficulties, if you said you were ill, he would tap your chest and tell you that you weren't, that you were fit to work. If you said you had a fever or were dizzy, he'd go through the motions of taking your temperature and give you any old medicine.

4. Changes after my release

After 2 years, I got my release. I could go home or switch to another mine. On release, all they gave you was an identity card. Six out of 10 labourers stayed on in the mine, while a minority went home and an even smaller number took other jobs.

Because I didn't have any money, I signed on for another year, but at the end of the year I simply devoured the cash or gambled it away. I felt work was burdensome and that I would never be able to earn any money, so I decided to leave the company. I sold fish for 3 years, and after that I worked on a pepper plantation. During the first 3 years, I earned f20 a month. Then the price of peppers collapsed, and I earned only f18. So I returned to the mine.

The mine operated a shift-work system, and continued to operate day and night. Each shift had 50–60 workers, and the pay was f30 a month.

During the Japanese occupation, the mine stopped working, and the workers had to live off cassava.

When the Dutch returned [in 1945], they mechanised the mines and production increased, at a rate of 3–4 tons of tin every 24 hours. The workers' food was distributed by weight. A tin miner got 18 kilos of rice, a woman 16 kilos. Children were divided into two categories: bigger ones, who received 14–16 kilos, and small ones (10 and under) who received 10–12 kilos. Tin miners got 3 kilos of beans a month, a kilo of oil, and f30.

After Indonesian independence, the daily rate for unskilled workers was f16. After 1957, it rose to f18. Together with family earnings (there were 5 people in my family), it amounted to f1,000*f* a month. But because of price fluctuations, it was still hard to make ends meet.

Interview with Yan Gui, a "piglet" in a Bangka tin mine

Interview by Wu Fengbin, May 1963, Zhize Farm, Yinjiang County

Yan Gui, born in 1899 in a village in Cenxi County in Guangxi, is now 64. He had one year's schooling. In 1924, he sold himself into indenture. He worked for 3 years in a tin mine (1924–1927) and then switched to another mine (1927–1929). After that, he grew vegetables and did casual labour for 26 years. Between 1948 and 1960, he returned to the mine and stayed there until his return to China.

1. Indenture and emigration

Before I left China, my family had 7 members, my parents, my elder brother and sister-in-law, my nephew, my younger brother, and me. We lived by farming. We rented 5 mu and a water buffalo from a man called Zhao. One harvest produced 12 dan of grain, which was divided fifty-fifty with the landlord. That wasn't enough to live off, so we depended on my elder brother's petty business activities (buying tea leaves in the hills and selling them in the market) to make ends meet. Although we never had to borrow cash or grain, life was hard. When I heard someone say that the Nanyang was good, the idea of emigrating began to take root in me.

In 1924, bandits began to rampage through the villages in their hundreds, and they robbed people in broad daylight (in 1925, they even burned down houses in our village), so people were unable to make a living. I began to think even more seriously about going abroad. Although not one of our more than 100 villagers had ever gone to the Nanyang, people from other villages had, and I really believed that it would be a good thing to do.

In early April 1924, I slipped away early one morning and hurried to Wuzhou, where I took the bus to Hong Kong and stayed in the three-storey Menfa Hostel.

I stayed in the hostel for a week, and I was allowed to go out and have fun. There were 20–30 others in the same hostel, which cost 20–30 cents a day. They held an interview: "Do your parents know?" "Are you doing this of your own free will?" But they didn't ask us one by one, we had to answer all together by putting our hands in the air, which I did too. They explained the work and the pay. At the physical examination, you had to lift a 50-pound piece of wood and have you knees tapped and your eyes tested. Then they put your name on a board with a number and took your photo.

Before embarking, we each got 7 yuan to spend, as well as clothes, a bamboo hat, a wicker suitcase, a rug, and a reed mat. There was a roll call as we boarded. The boat, Zhijialun, was specially used for transporting "piglets." There were no single beds. There were more than 300 of us in the hold. The windows were locked and it was very muggy. The food was horrible, and the rice tasted of coal ash. It was even harder for those who got seasick. The boat was overcrowded and it was difficult to use the water. People who weren't used to such conditions easily fell ill.

When we were near Mentok, a man in his twenties died, I don't know what of, and he ended up being thrown into the sea.

It took 7 days to reach Mentok. We stayed in a hostel for 2 nights, and there was another physical examination. The food was atrocious. When people saw how coarse the rice was, several of them threw away the bowl and uttered curses. There was nothing the hostel owner could do except try to explain.

After we'd been there for 2 days, 13 of us were assigned to Company No. 24 in Bingang.

2. Slave labour

The mine boss was Wen Yuanchang. Under him was a big overseer, a number-two overseer, 3 overseers, a bodyguard, an accountant, 2 mantris, two storemen, 2 vegetable growers, a swineherd, and an alcohol brewer. The company employed more than 100 labourers. It had 6 machines.

Even though it had machines, it could not dispense with manual labour, and raking was still done by hand. The labourers were roused at 3–4 am by someone knocking on the wall and had to take a cold shower, and if the new guests wanted a lie-in, they were disappointed. You had to hang a board round your neck with your name on it and go to work. Carting mud was back-breaking work, and you had to walk along a gangplank. Some of the work was by contract, some not. The quota was 3–4 or 5–6 cubic feet of soil. I didn't like contract work, even though you could knock off early—it was too wearing.

The working hours were 6–11 am with a 15-minute break at 9 o'clock and 12.30–5 pm, also with a break. If you worked 26 days in the month, you got one guilder extra. You were paid if you were injured at work, but not if you were ill.

In the past the overseers had been very brutal. Old guests told us that the overseers used to say: "If we beat one to death, 10 will come, if we kill

10, 100 will come, if we kill 100, 1000 will come." The Dutch used to use the Chinese to do the beating, while they themselves stood in the background pulling the strings. After the Chinese investigators visited the Nanyang, the beating became less, but there were still cases of beating and cursing.

When the new guests first arrived, the work was so hard that people couldn't bear it and quite a few ran away, but they were usually caught and brought back. Of the 13 who arrived at the same time as me, 5 thought of absconding when they saw how bad the conditions were (new guests were allowed a break of 3 days before entering the mine). They stole away at dead of night on a boat and cautiously rowed out to sea, desperate to escape this sea-bound prison. But unfortunately the navy spotted them and they were arrested and sent back. They were sentenced to a year's hard labour, and then they had to return to the mine as new guests.

The labourers didn't only engage in passive resistance, they also engaged in active resistance, but it was spontaneous rather than organised. For example, in 1934 Chen Weiying, the boss of No. 41 Company, deliberately made deductions from people's wages, and by the tenth day of the month had still not made any payments. When the labourers enquired, he said the money hadn't yet arrived, which was not true. The labourers were furious, and went on strike. That day, 1200 stopped working. The boss took fright, and paid out the money the following day, on the 11th. Only then did the strike come to an end.

3. Life as a "piglet"

The workers' wages differed from company to company. Twenty percent of the monthly pay was deducted and not paid until April 1 of the following year. That was the day the ship sailed back to China. Those who wanted to return took the ship, the rest signed back on.

The wages were low and the work was hard. To keep body and soul together, you sometimes had to buy extra food. The communal food was invariably salted fish and greens, if you ate too much you'd be sick. But the kitchen refused to cook the food that you yourself bought, you had to cook it yourself. It was different for the accountants and the bodyguards, they always received high-quality food. On Sundays the mine boss killed a pig, but only they were allowed to feast on it.

The labourers wore coarse clothing, a black shirt and trousers. The [Chinese] mine boss and the overseers also dressed in black, but not the office staff. The labourers used to say: "A white shirt and white pants—not a bodyguard but an accountant."

We lived in wooden huts, 8 to a room. The workers didn't have mosquito nets. We tried to kill the mosquitoes with disinfectant, but it didn't work. There were also hordes of bedbugs.

If you wanted to go out on Sundays, you needed a pass, or you might get arrested by the police. You weren't allowed to spend the night away from the mine. You could only stay away if you had a two-day pass.

I did 2 years before my release. In those days, if you did 2 years you could get a green card, which cost f3 (in 1930 it changed to 3 years). But I didn't have any money, so I had to continue working.

I worked hard all my life. During my time on the plantation I managed to send back 100 yuan, after that I didn't send any more, though I did write each year. When I was young I was never ill, but now I'm old, and I'm ill 2 days out of 3. I've got a small hernia. I'm thin and I don't look well. By rights, the mining company should have given me a pension, but instead I was kicked out of the country. If it weren't for the People's Government, I'd be dead and buried in an unmarked grave.

Interview with Xu Yaer, a "piglet" in a Bangka tin mine.

Interview by Wu Fengbin, May 1963, Zhize Farm, Yinjiang County.

Xu Yaer, now 58, from Boluo County in Guangdong, sold himself into indenture in 1925. Initially he worked for the Liegang No. 2 Company (Chen Guangtian) from 1925 to 1927, but after his release he worked for a year (1927–1928) in the new No. 4 Mine in Wuliyang. He also did casual labour for 3 years (1928–1931) in Wuliyang, repairing roads. After that he worked for Chen Jiasong in Wuliyang on a tin dredger, from 1931 to 1960, when he returned to China.

1. Leaving China and heading south

My family lived in Boluo City. I lost my mother at the age of 14 and my father at the age of 19. Two brothers remained—we farmed rented land on the outskirts of town. I was still young at the time. I don't know how much we paid in rent. When I was 19, [the political warlord] Chen Jiongming revolted and the situation in Guangdong became unstable. The countryside bore the brunt of it. Sadly, my elder brother was impressed into the army, and it was just me left. I had little choice other than to seek refuge in Hong Kong.

In Hong Kong, with the help of friends, I got an unskilled job on the docks repairing ships. I earned 30 cents a day, of which I spent 20 on food. Seven months later, I left the docks and got work doing cleaning and collecting scrap iron, for 30–40 cents a day. Five months later, I lost my job. I heard about work in the Nanyang and that life there was good there, so decided to go to the Nanyang.

I first went to the Wanxing Hostel, which specialised in selling "piglets." I stayed there for 6 days, and after I had signed a contract, I was no longer allowed out. There was an iron grill across the door. Before I signed the contract, I had to answer some questions: "Are you going of your own accord?" "Do your parents know?" I said, "My parents are already dead, and I'm going of my own free will." The red-haired [white] man also said: "After you've worked for 360 days, a ship will bring you back to China. Your pay will be f2.40 a day." I don't know if he made a mistake or was lying, for I discovered after my arrival that the pay was f0.24 a day. After the contract came the physical examination. I had to lift a 50-pound weight 3 times, and my knees were tapped. They took 3 photos with my name and number on a board round my neck, like livestock.

The hostel owner didn't pay me by the day, but he gave me 18 yuan when I boarded the ship. People got different amounts: 10, 7, 20—it's not clear why, perhaps it depended on how long you stayed in the hostel, the longer you stayed, the less you received. Also, we each got a bamboo hat, a bamboo suitcase, black cloths, and a reed mat.

At the end of the second month, I left Hong Kong aboard the Zhudali. When we boarded, a dozen Indian policemen observed us. There were 700–800 "piglets" crowded together on the ship. It was very stuffy, and we spent 7 uncomfortable days and nights before finally reaching Mentok.

We stayed in Mentok for about a fortnight, in a new hostel capable of accommodating several thousand people. After I passed the physical test, I was "assigned" to the Liegang No. 2 Mine.

2. Two years as a "piglet"

The Liegang mine had dozens of overseers, and around a dozen small overseers (it was privately run, and the tin was sold on to the Dutch).

The boss, Chen Guangtian, was in charge of 600 labourers. Under him were a big overseer, 2 overseers, 3 small overseers, 1 bodyguard, 1 accountant, 2 mantris 3 storage people, 4 swineherds, 3 alcohol brewers, and 10 vegetable growers. He had big carts and carts for the mud.

In mechanised mines, miners no longer carried soil on their backs and shoulders, but the work was still onerous. Clearing the ditches was hard work. The ore-bearing mud was removed by an 80-horsepower engine, equal to the labour of more than 100 workers, but where the machines didn't reach, human power was still needed for raking, hoeing, and other jobs. The engines worked night and day, so the work pace was hectic.Work was organised in 3 shifts, from 6 am-2 pm, from 2–10 pm, and from 10 pm-6 am. You had to be punctual, otherwise you'd be beaten and marked down for punishment. For the early shift, you had to get up at 4 am, have a shower and some food, and start getting ready for work at 5.30. So in effect it added up to 10 hours.

When the new guests first arrived, they didn't know the ropes. The good overseers would teach them, but the bad ones would shout and get angry. The new guests had to put up with this, and there was some beating. If you got sunburnt or you didn't turn up for work, you risked a thrashing. The beriberi manle would come to the hut to check up on you, and if you refused to go to work, they'd hit you.

To increase its profits, the Dutch government urged people to work harder. There were rewards and incitements: Sunday work counted double, and work on other holidays counted treble. If you worked 26 days in the month, you got one guilder extra. But the bosses constantly deducted money, and sometimes paid out as little as 50 cents or even nothing at all.

The intensity of the work increased and there were many accidents, especially to people's hands and feet. Some people were even electrocuted to death. People sometimes got their legs trapped in machines.

If you were injured at work, you got sick pay, but if you were off work because of a minor ailment, you got nothing. The hospital was a long way from the mine (it was in the port), so workers were usually only prepared to go if they had been ill for 2–3 days. To avoid losing money, sick people continued to turn up to work. Obviously, that prolonged the illness and could turn a small ailment into a major one. During my 2 years of indenture, I also fell ill on several occasions, with headaches and malaria.

3. Living conditions

The labourers' clothes were black and made of coarse cloth purchased in the mine shop or in the port. The bosses and the overseers, on the other hand, might have worn black shirts and pants in the mine, but when they went to the port they dressed in white, and wore a while hat or a bamboo hat. The Dutch wore silk, shoes and socks, and white hats. [...].

We had very little in our quarters. Only 2–3 out of 10 had mosquito nets, and 50 percent lacked quilts and 60 percent had no sandals. Two to three out of 10 had only a wooden pillow, or just 3 bits of boards piled up under their heads.

Very few labourers got a pension. You had to be over 55 and to have worked for 25 years. Labourers could rarely meet that condition, although those higher up could, including accountants and bodyguards.

There were next to no cultural activities, apart from a puppet show at New Year. The Dutch and the Chinese bosses ran an opium den and a gambling den to fleece the workers. The labourers' only enjoyment was gambling. Among them, 70–80 percent gambled. Labourers could borrow money from the boss, at 20 percent monthly interest. Even so, people borrowed.

After your release at the end of 2 years, you received papers that enabled you to work in a mine anywhere in Bangka or to return to China. If you wanted to go to another province, you needed evidence from the mining company and from the Dutch authorities, with a photo, which cost f3.

Two out of 5 got their release on time. In the case of others, including me, it was extended because of days off due to illness.

Fewer than 3 in 10 returned to China. The rest continued working in the mine. The mine was happy to keep them, and to see the bad labourers go. Fewer than 4 in 10 left to work in other mines.

Interview with Huang Xiang, a "piglet" in a Bangka tin mine

Interview by Wu Fengbin, May 1963, Zhize Farm, Yinjiang County

Huang Xiang is from Yangshan County in Guangdong. In 1925, he sold himself into indenture. He first joined Mine No. 3 in Wuliyang, where he worked from 1925 to 1926. After his release, he worked in another mine for 1 year, and after that he caught fish for 22 years, from 1929 to 1950. He returning to a mine in Wuliyang in 1950, and stayed there until his return to China in 1960.

In 1929–1933, during the world economic crisis, the small mines closed one after the other. In 1932–1933, the big mines closed too. There was no longer a market for tin—the US, which was the main customer, didn't want any. Only 3 companies remained in Wuliyang, and their workforce had been pared back to just over 100. Thousands were sent back to China. Some went to Singapore after their release, where some stayed only briefly before going home. Prices collapsed. For example, the price of fresh fish fell from 30 cents a kilo in 1930 to 10 cents in 1932 and 8 cents in 1933.

[In the mid 1920s], conditions were so bad that many labourers ran away. To stop the desertions, the Dutch only allowed you to leave the mine on Sundays if you had a pass—otherwise the police might arrest you. Even so, many ran away, from all the companies. If you were caught and brought back, you were gaoled and made to do hard labour. In my unit, a man from Guangzhou called Li Sen ran away before dawn, but was brought back several months later and spent a month in gaol. After his release from gaol, he ran away again. Later he died, I don't know how.

There were many instances of resistance against the Dutch. I only remember one occasion, in 1938–1939, when Li Yagui in Mine No. 14 beat a new guest to death. The other new guests banded together to resist. The Dutch army turned up and fired some blanks, but the labourers were not cowed. They hacked off a Dutch army officer's left hand with a rake. The Dutch charged, and arrested quite a few Chinese labourers. The Dutch treated the Chinese overseers as their puppets, using Chinese to control Chinese. The overseers were in the pay of the Dutch, but it was the Dutch who benefited most.

The labourers suffered all sorts of illnesses, particularly foot rot [beri-beri?] and malaria. Foot rot could lead to death in serious cases. In each company an average of 20–30 labourers a year fell ill with infectious diseases. The infections could last for a long time, 8 months in the worst case.

I got both beriberi and malaria. I was in hospital with foot rot for 37 days, of which I had to make up 7 after my discharge. I continued to get paid during my illness. In 1926, the mining company had no treatment for foot rot, just a few pills and a cursory examination. When I didn't recover, I was sent to a bigger hospital where I was put in a ward with 30–40 other patients. They were there for all sorts of reasons. The big doctor was quite good, but not the others. If you were the slightest bit slow to take your medicine, they'd shout at you and even hit you. I once got 3–4 slaps for not turning over quickly enough to take my medicine. No one cared if we were hurt. The big doctor only came round once a week to look at the serious cases, and ignored the rest. Those who died were carted off to the morgue.

[…]

Release was fixed at 2 years after the start of indenture for new guests. For example, if you started work on May 1, your release was scheduled for May 1 the year after next. But that was just generally speaking. It would be extended if you absconded, slacked, or committed a crime. Within the 2 years of your indenture, if you missed 30 days due to illness you did not need to make them up, but if you missed 31 days, then you were required to make up 1 day, and your indenture was extended by 1 day, and so on.

Most new guests got their release on time. Of the more than 120 who arrived together with me, only 4–5 had the period of their indenture extended due to illness. But after your release, you were generally broke, and despite your new wings you were still unable to fly, so most stayed on in the mine. After release, a little over 30 returned to China, and a dozen or so went to Singapore. A few opened vegetable gardens growing pepper (you could earn f0.60 a day—more than in the mine). But 70–80 stayed on in the mine

[…]

Mines were divided into big and small. Some people claimed the small mines were owned by private individual, but I never saw cases of that in Wuliyang. However, the gangs were privately run, and were different from the small mines.

The gangs were formed by groups of friends, all of them old guests. They ranged in size from less than a dozen to at most 20. They got permission from the Dutch to do mining, and sold them the resulting ore. The Dutch provided food and tools, but didn't initially grant loans, until after some tin had been produced (if you didn't produce any within

3 months, you got no loan). The food and tools were subsequently deducted.

The gangs did everything by hand, they had no machines. They mostly dug to a depth of 2–3 metres, at most 4. Their area of operations was outside the area of the mine. The price of the tin sold to the Dutch differed from year to year. The gang divided up the takings equally, there was no boss and no unequal distribution. In 1928–1929, most of the gangs made a loss, and the Dutch government had no more use for them.

I worked in a small mine for 2 years, from 1927 to 1928. The boss was Li Yazhao from Meixian. He had more than 20 labourers and 1 overseer. [...] All those in charge of the small mines were paid by the Dutch. The bosses got f27–28 a month, the overseers f25, and the labourers f15.

All the workers were old guests, and some were locally born Chinese. They received f25 at the annual signing on, which was not subsequently deducted. You got f0.51 a day and a bonus of f2.5 a month if you worked 26 days. The work was relatively light, just 5–6 hours a day, but with a quota, sometimes as high as 8–10 cubic feet of soil. We lived in reed huts, because the workforce in small mines was constantly on the move. The mines closed in 1929–1933, and more or less stayed shut.

Interview with Xu Shiwu, a "piglet" in a Bangka tin mine

Interview by Huang Zhongyan, May 1963, Zhize Farm, Yinjiang County

Xu Shiwu, born in Huangshan Village in Beiliu County in Guangxi in 1909, is now 54. He was tricked into selling himself into indenture in 1926, aged 17. He worked for 3 years in No. 3 Tin Mine in Wuliyang. After his release, he left to do various other jobs.

[…] I was assigned to No. 3 Tin Mine. It was owned by a company, which paid the wages. The lowest level of overseers were all released miners. The boss and the overseers were all locally born Chinese. The small overseers were trained in martial arts.

The mine's white doctor committed all kinds of outrages. He was always in cahoots with the overseers. They dragged off to clinic those among the new guests they viewed as "malcontents" and gave them electric shocks. You could hear them screaming pitifully.

Each miner had a small booklet in which his pay was recorded, the number of days he'd worked, and a column to note whether or not he'd done anything wrong, fallen ill, etc. If there were lots of negative comments, it would be difficult for him in future to find new employment. If you were injured on the job or died, you got no wages, and nor did your family. I heard that if you worked uninterruptedly in the mine, did as the company told you, didn't do anything wrong, and stayed until you were 50 or 55, the Dutch company would give you a pension of 30 kilos of rice a month and f3 to spend and a place to live, but I never witnessed any cases of that happening.

[…]

You Yashen, from Haikang County in Guangdong, born 1905, illiterate, sold himself into indenture in 1927 to a tin mine, remained a tunneller until 1960.

Lü Ying, Lufeng County in Guangdong, born 1904, sold himself into indenture in 1928 to a tin mine, became a firewood gather in 1939 on leaving the mine, and then a petty trader.

Luo Jie, born 1892 in Conghua County in Guangdong, sold himself into indenture in 1928 to a tin mine, became vegetable gardener after release.

Interview with Zhu Fuzhong, a "piglet" in a Bangka tin mine

Interview by Gui Guanghua, May 1963, Zhize Farm, Yinjiang County

Zhu Fuzhong, born in Wuchang in Hubei and now 55, left Hong Kong as a "piglet" in 1929 and went to work in a mine in Bangka, where he became a ganger. He returned to China in 1931 but set out again for Bangka in the same year and sold himself to another mine, where he again became a ganger. After Indonesia became independent, he became a small *guasha*, and the following year he was promoted to the rank of full *guasha*. He returned to China in 1960.

1. Situation before and at the time of emigration

Before I left China in 1929, I was a soldier. In 1929, oppressed by Chiang Kai-shek's reactionary Kuomintang, I and 17 others soldiers went to Hong Kong. The situation was unstable, but we came across a broker on the streets recruiting people, so 18 of us decided to go to the Nanyang as "piglets."

After my first year working on a tin dredger, I was promoted to ganger. After completing my second year in 1931, I returned to China, but in the same year I sold myself into indenture for a second time. Because I'd already sold myself once and knew the ropes, I knew a broker could get more than 200 Hong Kong dollars for a new guest, so when the broker offered me 7 dollars I pointed out the price should be a lot higher, and after some haggling I got 25 dollars. When we arrived at Mentok and they found out that I'd been there before, they reappointed me as a ganger on the tin dredger. In 1935 I was transferred to No. 3 Mine in Shaheng, also as a ganger.

2. The situation in the Shaheng mines and the division of labour on the tin dredger

In 1929 there were altogether 9 mines in Shaheng. The Chinese labourers called them by their numbers. No. 5 Mine used a tin dredger (from what I heard, dredgers were only introduced in Shaheng in 1925). It was located in the sea.

While using the dredger, 2 boats were positioned around it, one at the front and one at the back. The one at the front, which was smaller and had a crew of only 15, removed the earth, while the bigger one at the back, crewed by some 40 men, extracted the ore. There were also other workers to look after the dredger, the iron cables, and the engines, about 40 in all. That made 80 on the second boat.

The dredger was operated on a shift system, each shift lasting 8 hours. Unlike other workers, who could rest, the dredger workers were unable to stop working. The most you could produce in a single day was 30 tons and the least 2–3 tons, depending on the nature of the soil. The average yield was 8 tons.

3. The organisation of production in the mine

In No. 5 Mine, there was a mine boss, who supervised the entire operation. Under him were various overseers, gangers, and other labourers, as in other mines, as well as some who worked on provisions (including raising pigs and gathering firewood). All the bosses at the 9 mines in Shaheng were locally born Chinese, Hakka speakers from Guangdong. Most of the overseers had been promoted from among the workforce, with the consent of the Dutch mining company.

4. The pay system

The new guests received f0.24 a day for the first 180 working days, after which it rose to f0.36. In the third and fourth years it rose further to f0.46 and f0.51, at which point it stopped rising. There was another group known as "unoccupied," i.e., free workers, who were paid rather more, f0.75. They were not constrained by indenture and could come and go at their will. But if the company decided there were too many workers, they were the first to go.

5. Working hours

[...]

The working day was not invariable. For example, starting in 1935, Shaheng's No. 3 Mine extended its working day by an hour. That situation continued for the next two years. Because the work was burdensome and the hours were long, people started missing the quota and the ganger would give them a kicking. As a result, people started running away. Bangka is an island, so it was not easy to escape, and there were Dutch army patrols all over the place. As soon as an escape became known, a general alert was sounded. Once the overseers found the runaways, first they tried to talk them round, but if that didn't work, they got the police to arrest them. On their return, they were beaten, and some hanged themselves. This was by no means an unusual occurrence at the time. Others returned to China after their 2 years were up.

6. The length of indenture and related regulations

[...]

New guests who had become old guests, or those who were already old guests, would be asked at the start of each year by the mine boss whether they wished to stay on or not. If they did, they could sign on for an average of f50, but sometimes this figure fell to as low as f35. However, if labour was scarce and other mines were in competition for workers, the signing-on fee could rise to f80 and even f100. This sum was not subsequently deducted.

7. The division of labour and the establishment of quotas

The staff at No. 3 Mine numbered around 200, including more than 30 officers of various sorts and menials alongside 160 directly engaged in production. However, the quota of 3.3 baskets was set on the basis of the entire staff and workforce, which meant that the actual quota for each labourer was a little over 4 baskets. The quota also depended on the quality of the soil—if it was relatively loose, the quota rose, sometimes to as high 8–9 baskets; but if the soil was hard, the quota could fall to 3–4 baskets.

Every day at the start of work, quotas were announced. Ins some cases, 3–4 workers would join together in a partnership to complete the quota, and draw lots for their role. Once you had finished your quota, you were free to leave, but if you were unable to finish it, the first time you would get a telling off and the second time a beating. Some of the weaker labourers had to work an hour extra.

With the overseer watching, you were not able to slack. If you really couldn't finish the work, you could perhaps adjust it a little. I heard that in the past workers who were unable to stand the pressure hanged themselves.

Since there were 3 kinds of labourers (new, old, and "unoccupied"), the actual division of labour often took the form of giving the heavy tasks to the new guests, the light tasks to the old guests, and jobs like pig-raising and cleaning up to the "unoccupied" workers.

8. The 1933 mining crisis

In 1933, around half the 9 mines in Shaheng stopped producing, some for a year, some for 6 months. The tin dredger stopped working and was sent for repair. Some labourers were transferred to jungle clearance, others were transferred elsewhere, and new guests who had just completed their indenture were returned to China. The "unoccupied" workers were dismissed.

9. The miners' lives

The miners all lived in one place, 8 to a room. Sundays were free. New guests had to get permission to leave the mine, in the form of a pass, or they ran the risk of being arrested if challenged. Old guests who had been released from indenture but had not yet worked for a full five years merely needed the overseer's permission, and could use the green card issued by the Dutch authorities, they needed no special pass. Old guests who had worked for 5 years (including "unoccupied" workers) could come and go at will, using their yellow card, which allowed them to travel throughout Indonesia and to Singapore. [...]

There was also a provision that after working for 25 years, a labourer was eligible for free food and clothing from the mining company, but that happened only very rarely, for even though they had worked for 25 years, they preferred to continue working because the pay was better.

The Shaheng mine had a clinic and a hygiene officer, while people with more serious illnesses could go to the hospital in Shaheng. That was the only hospital in Shaheng, and it was not very good. It usually had 20–30 patients, sometimes as many as 50, but it only had 1 doctor. It was unable to handle patients with serious ailments, who had to be transferred to the general hospital in Bingang. Sometimes the hospital required the patients to do work in the neighbourhood, for example, cutting grass,

10. Pay and division of labour

As far as I know, pay in the Dutch mining company stayed stable from 1929 until the eve of the Japanese southward invasion. The mine boss received f125, the overseer f70, the small overseer f60, and the ganger f40. The Dutch authorities levied a 4 percent tax on this monthly income.

Apart from the monthly pay, the overseer received a red envelope (a bonus) from the Dutch company at year's end, the size of which depended on output. The mine boss never revealed the size of the bonus. But I heard it was distributed in the following proportions: mine boss, X shares; big overseer, 4 shares; small overseer, 3 shares, gangers, 1 share each; *wanlü*, 1 share each; accountant, 1 share.

11. Small mines and partnerships

Small mines: In Shaheng, apart from the 9 mines directly under the control of the Dutch companies, there were some small mines operated by private individuals. As their name implies, they were small in size, with 20–30 workers under a mine boss, an overseer, and an accountant. The labourers were paid by the day but at a higher rate (f0.80) than in the Dutch mines. However, the quota was higher—a daily average of 6 baskets. If you were ill and couldn't work, you weren't paid and you had to compensate your replacement. You didn't get any of the provisions provided by the Dutch in the formal mines.

The bosses in such mines were all seasoned labourers, relatively prosperous locally born Chinese. If they discovered a rich seam, they could earn well from it, after getting the Dutch company's agreement and signing a contract. The contract (1) specified the area to be mined; (2) set a price for the tin, which was to be sold in its entirety to the Dutch company (at a rate of f250 per 100 kilos); (3) and agreed to pay an advance in cash and provisions, to be deducted at the point of payment.

Apart from the advance, the mine boss had to provide his own capital and tools. The mine boss kept all the profit after wages and the money spent on providing food.

Some of the small mine bosses had ties with the Dutch mine bosses. During tin extraction by the big mines, some extracted less than their companies had envisaged, so others could later increase their income.

Most of the small miners depended on manual labour, but some used old machines discarded by the Dutch and rented out to the Chinese. Some of the small mines grew in extent and ended up becoming mines belonging to the Dutch company.

On the eve of the Japanese advance in 1942, most of the small mines were gradually closing.

Partnerships also existed in the Shaheng area. They were privately organised and smaller in scale than the small mines. They usually had 10 or fewer workers. There was no boss, just one of their number who was chosen to sign a contract with the Dutch company. After getting the necessary papers, the partners set to work and shared profit and loss equally.

Most members of these partnerships were free miners (so-called "unoccupied" people). They provided their own tools, had rudimentary equipment, and formed and dispersed rapidly, so they were generally of short duration. In Shaheng, there were more small mines than partnerships.

Li Bao (born in 1908 in a village in Haikang County, Guangdong), illiterate, went into indenture in 1931 in a tin mine in Indonesia where he worked for more than 10 years on and off.

Li Gui, from a village in Yulin County in Guangxi, went into indenture in 1933 in a tin mine in Bangka, where he worked until 1941. He continued working in other tin mines until his return to China in 1960.

Huang Jin, born in 1917 in Rongxian in Guangxi, sold himself into indenture in 1936, at the age of 19 (though he pretended to be 24) and worked in a tin mine in Wuliyang. He stayed in the mine until his repatriation in 1960.

The miners were mainly from Leizhou, Guangxi, and Hainan, and the lingua franca was Guangfu Cantonese. The mine bosses were all locally born Chinese, they could speak foreign languages and various sorts of Cantonese. There were very few who were not locally born.

The mine was partly mechanised but it also depended for some operations on manual labour.

After arriving, I sent a letter home, and I received a reply later. In 1937, I remitted f36, which was equal to the time to 100 fabi. In 1938, after the Japanese invasion of Guangdong, the tie was broken, and later I had no money to send back.

I continued to work at the mine under the Japanese, but they only gave you a bit of rice and gruel and stole the clothes off your back. They paid you in paper money once a week, just f2–3 each, enough to buy 1 kilo of cassava. Many labourers ran away, and up to 20 died of hunger, leaving just a little over 100 of us in the mine. I grew cassava and sweet potatoes in my spare time, and ate them.

Liao Hanquan, born in 1902 in a village in Zhaoqing in Guangdong, sold himself into indenture in 1939 and worked as a charcoal maker near a mine in Mentok. He left home at the age of 13 and became a vagabond in Guangzhou. He took part in the Guangzhou Insurrection in 1927, in the Workers' Third Battalion. After the defeat, he fled to Foshan and later to Hong Kong, where he was cheated into going abroad. There were 100–200 charcoal workers who chopped down trees and supplied charcoal for the engines in the mine. I obtained my release after 3 years, and became a transport worker. After 6 months, I was promoted to ganger. Later I became a hawker before returning to China in 1960.

Interview with Chen Shanfu, a "piglet" in a Bangka tin mine
Interview by Wu Fengbin, May 1963, Zhize Farm, Yinjiang County

Chen Shanfu, born in a village in Pingnan County in Guangxi and now 48, sold himself into indenture in 1937, aged 17. During his 2 years of indenture, he worked in 6 mines for varying lengths of time. After his release, he spent 1 more year in the mines (1939–1940). He then chopped trees in Liegang for 8 months (1948). He worked in various other mines and on a rubber plantation from 1949–1951. He spent his last 8 years at No. 17 Mine in Wuliyang for 8 years, from 1952–1960, when he returned to China.

1. Reasons for emigrating

At the age of 19, unable to earn a living, I became a soldier, for 20 cents a day. I then fell ill and got leave to return home, and I left the army to look after my family (my grandmother, my mother, and my younger brother).

Later, 7 of us left the village to go to the Nanyang, out of poverty. They included an uncle of mine.

2. The workers' resistance in No. 3 Company in Wuliyang

I was assigned to the No. 3 Company in Wuliyang, which employed more than 1000 people, including more than 300 new guests, and 2 tin dredgers. The mine boss Chen Jiasong behaved very fiercely towards the workers. He was a martial-arts practitioner, and would hit or kick you at the slightest provocation. On the whole, there was not much beating at the time, except in his mine, where it persisted.

On one occasion, a labourer knocked off early after completing his contract and Chen challenged him. He ignored Chen and walked off, and Chen grabbed him, but the labourer could also do martial arts. He grabbed Chen by the leg, and then walked off anyway. On another occasion, Chen ordered some workers to pick up some wood but they were exhausted and ignored him. The overseer reported the incident to the mine boss, who came down and kicked one of the workers, who subsequently needed treatment for his injuries.

The Dutch also behaved brutally towards the Chinese labourers and blatantly discriminated against them. As a result, in 1938, an anti-Dutch struggle broke out.

The incident was sparked by the introduction by the Dutch of a 3-shift system. The shifts were 8 hours each, and you had to turn up half an hour early. My uncle Chen Heqing was on the first shift, from 6–2. At 1.30 the next shift turned up and the bell sounded, so the labourers started preparing to knock off, but a Dutchman refused to let them go, and said it was not yet time. Chen Heqing objected, and two Dutchmen hit him on the nose, covering him with blood. The labourers were furious, and decided to deal with the Dutchmen that same evening.

We prepared to attack them along the road. However, the incident had been reported to the mine boss, who immediately jumped on his bike and went to tell the Dutchmen not to walk home but to take a car.

When they had driven half way along the road, they met a barricade formed from tables and benches. The car could not pass. The Dutch ran off, and the labourers surrounded the car and smashed the windows.

The mine boss phoned Wuliyang and reported on the attack, and requested troops. The authorities dispatched a motor bike and a vehicle and more than 20 soldiers tried to quell the unrest. Three other empty vehicles turned up in preparation for arrests.

It happened to be mid-month, so the labourers didn't need to go to work. The workers remained solid. They said: "If you're going to arrest anyone, arrest us all. we'll stand our ground until nightfall, the Dutch army won't dare start anything." The Dutch troops said to the Chinese: "Who saw Chen Heqing attacked, what's the evidence?" Two workers stood up and attested to what they had seen. Someone else joined in to say the same. Seeing how things were, the Dutch army realised that the Dutchmen were in the wrong, and withdrew at 11 pm.

The next day, the mine boss announced that the Wuliyang Garrison had phoned to say the witnesses should go the next morning for questioning. Large numbers of labourers accompanied them to Wuliyang.

The labourers proposed that the Dutchmen's transfer be negotiated, or they would refuse to work for the company. News of the incident spread to Liegang, where the authorities, under the workers' pressure, finally agreed to transfer the young Dutchman and fined him f100, and also fined the dredger overseer f50. Only then was the incident resolved.

3. A Japanese atrocity in Mentok

In 1943, at No. 4 Mine in Mentok, the mine boss Cao Jingrong opened a small shop to exploit the labourers. The workers were already deeply in debt and he was afraid he'd be unable to get his money back. He thought it would be difficult to deduct the debts from wages at the mine, so he summoned the workers to the port. The workers had long been dissatisfied with him, and this incident made them even angrier, and they planned to give him a beating. He got wind of it and drove to the port to ask the Japanese army to suppress the workers.

That evening at around 5 o'clock, 90 Japanese soldiers arrived at the mine in 3 vehicles. They immediately surrounded the mine and set up machine guns. The mine boss read out a list of names one by one, and all the workers on his list were tied up at the wrists. There were more than 30 of them. They were all bayoneted to death on the spot.

At 11 pm, after the Japanese had left, the big overseer told the workers: "The mine boss says don't start work tomorrow until you've buried the corpses. And don't ever resist again, or you'll end up in the same way."

The next morning, the workers buried the dead and hosed away the blood, and then trudged off with heavy steps to work.

4. One year in a small mine

In 1950, I worked for 1 year in No. 41 Mine in Wuliyang. The mine boss, Zhou Huachuan, was a locally born Chinese. Earlier, he'd opened a small shop, but business was not good, so someone got him a job running the mine.

The mine was privately owned. Zhou employed around 25 workers. He rented a 95-horsepower train from the Dutch, fuelled by firewood. The Dutch bought the tin and supplied provisions, and Zhou bought the rakes and wicker scoops.

The workers got their wages from Zhou. They worked an 8-hour day, and were paid f100–120 a month. Zhou hired 2 overseers who got f300–350 a month each. Zhou stopped running the mine after 2 years.

Interview with Qian Zhen, a "piglet" in a Bangka tin mine

Interview by Huang Zhongyan, May 1963, Zhize Farm, Yinjiang County

Qian Zhen, born in a village in Yangshan County in Guangdong in 1913, is now 50. He sold himself into indenture in 1938, and worked in a mine in Wuliyang until his return to China in 1960.

[…] When I was 10, the reactionary army killed my father and robbed us of everything, on the pretext of eradicating bandits. I and my 2 brothers (I was the middle one) were raised thanks to the hard work and frugality of our mother. We rented land and had virtually nothing to eat. We had no house, and lived in a reed shack in the hills. We had to borrow from the landlord, at 50 percent annual interest. […] In 1937, the landlord evicted us, so I decided to go to the Nanyang, where I'd heard that wages were high and work was easy to find.

Early in 1938, I was taken to Guangzhou and then to Hong Kong by a fellow-villager who was a broker. There were more than 70 of us in Hong Kong preparing to sell ourselves into indenture. Quite a few of them were old guests. At the physical test, some deliberately pretended they couldn't jump across the bench or lift the weight, so only 20 or so of us passed. […]

The company took care of the food. It was not deducted from the pay. There was fresh fish, and sometimes a white doctor turned up to check on hygiene. If the workers made negative comments about the food, the doctor would get the mine boss to carry out improvements. You could take as much food as you liked. You could go to the port for prostitutes, gambling, drinking, and opium. You could leave the mine for 2–3 days without permission.

After 2 years, I obtained my release. I was paid 24 cents a day, rising to 36 in the third year and 41 in the fourth—that's when the Japanese marched south. By the time of my release, the signing-on system had fallen into disuse, and there was no longer any signing-on money (in 1940). By then, the workers were comparatively free. The workers were also braver—if a ganger hit you, you were likely to hit him back, and leave the mine afterwards and get work elsewhere.

Many of the mine bosses in those days were locally born Chinese. I never heard of any small mines that ran a share system. Some women took part in rinsing the ore, but most of them were family dependants. The ore was all sold to the Dutch, or you'd be accused of theft. The workers weren't qualified to run small mines, but in many cases the locally born Chinese were the children of mine bosses. They had social status and culture, they knew how to handle social relations, they knew the ropes and had connections, the Dutch trusted them, they could obtain the necessary capital to open a mine, and it was easy for them to recruit workers. The organisation of the small mines copied that of the big mines, except in scale. But they were subordinate to the big mines.

When the Japanese came south, I was working in No. 3 Mine. I stayed on after the invasion. The mine boss was Chen Jiasong, who called himself "the big Japanese." He forced the workers to work. He beat and abused them. He was an accomplice in evil of the Japanese. He helped the Japanese slaughter 59 miners.

I was still at the mine when the Japanese surrendered, and I stayed there right through until my return to China in 1960.

Interview with He De, a “piglet” in a Bangka tin mine

Interview by Wu Fengbin, May 1963, Zhize Farm, Yinjiang County

He De, also called He Pushou, was born in a village in Enping County in Guangdong in 1913. In 1928, he went to Burma to work in a shop, and in 1934 he returned to China. In 1940, he sold himself into indenture to the No. 2 and No. 3 Mines in Shaheng. In 1945, he set up as a hawker. In 1958–1960, he worked in the propaganda section of the Indonesian Chinese Professional Association, after which he returned to China.

[…]

2. Life in the mine

Although the mine was mechanised, carrying was still done on the back and shoulder, and where the hose didn’t reach, human power was still used. […]

The overseer treated new and old guests differently. The new guests didn’t know the ropes, and were constantly abused and shouted at. The old guests could afford to be more relaxed. This was especially true of those who got on well with the boss and the overseer. By then, there were fewer cases of people being beaten, but it did happen, as I know from personal experience in 1940. In 1943, an incident occurred in which the Japanese devils collaborated with mine owners to beat workers. The worst incident was at No. 5 Mine in Mentok, where a dozen or so workers were massacred.

Su He, a Cantonese in his twenties at No. 3 Mine, was inexperienced and did not work well. The mine boss called him into the office and gave him a sound beating, breaking his hand. Despite injuring him, the overseer ignored his plight.

During the Japanese occupation, food was scarce, and many starved to death. I don’t know about other companies, but 6 of the 13 Chinese labourers in my company starved to death, almost 1 in 2.

3. Resistance

In 1940, 12 days after we 13 new guests had arrived at No. 2 Mine, I was shocked by how hard the work was and we started talking about it. Some said they’d been cheated, others vowed to stop working, and we decided by a show of hands that I and Lingwen (from Enping) would go to the mine boss and demand to be sent back to China. The boss, Wen

Rongde, beat the table with his fist and shouted: "You're rebelling! I'm going to gaol you." He berated us for a while, and then transferred me and Lingwen to No. 3 Mine, to put an end to our resistance.

Also in 1940, Kong Jin, a man from Enping who had gone to Indonesia together with me, and more or less my age, didn't want to carry on and shouted that he had been cheated. It's true, he couldn't do the work, and he continued to resist. The overseer shouted at him, but it made no difference. So they started to persecute him. They put him into solitary confinement, first for a week and then, when he still refused to work, for 3 weeks. After that, he still wouldn't work, so he was gaoled for 3 months. The Dutch mine owners were worried that they'd get into trouble, so they sent him back to Hong Kong.

Appendix B

G. Pastor, *De panglongs*, Batavia: Weltevreden, 1927

In 1927, the Labour Bureau (Kantoor van Arbeid) published this book, originally 151 pages long but greatly condensed in this translation, as part of its effort to investigate and reform labour relations in the Dutch East Indies. The book, written by a bureau inspector, reveals the atrocities and abuse extent to which indentured Chinese labourers were subjected on the panglongs and in the sawmills of East Sumatra.[1] *Most of the abusers in the case of these workers and most of the panglong owners and managers were themselves Chinese. The book ends on an optimistic note, but a careful reading suggests that the optimism was not entirely warranted.*

After the Labour Inspectorate for the Outlying Regions was made jointly responsible in January 1925 for ensuring compliance with the Panglong Regulations, the panglong companies and the Chinese woodcutters and charcoal burners became a focus of public attention. These companies can be found in great numbers in the almost inaccessible flood jungle along Sumatra's east coast, on the islands in the Bengkalis district, and in the Riau-Lingga archipelago, which was previously practically

[1] On the panglongs, see pp. 287-290.

G. Benton, *Chinese Indentured Labour in the Dutch East Indies, 1880–1942*, Palgrave Macmillan Transnational History Series,
https://doi.org/10.1007/978-3-031-05024-4

unknown. Shortly after the Labour Inspector in Tandjong Pinang (Riau) had handed in his initial reports regarding cases of assault, deprivation of liberty, and murder committed against Chinese coolies, the newspapers published a host of articles about the tragic circumstances in which these workers lived in the jungle and the often inhumane treatment they experienced at the hands of their bosses (kapalas).

Because of the shortage of information, the articles and reports were able to provide only a partial picture of the industry, the circumstances under which it was carried on, the abuses identified, and the measures taken by the Labour Inspectorate.

During the supervision exercised over the last two years by the Labour Inspectorate, with the help of Government officials, the police, and civil servants employed in the forestry sector, the information required for a more complete picture was gradually obtained, so that it is now possible both to provide a description of this particular industry and the conditions to be found in it and to report on a number of incidents that demonstrate the urgent need for enhanced supervision.

Before that, I will explain where the Chinese logging camps (*houtkapperijen*) are located, what a panglong is, and the different sorts of logging businesses.

Chapter 1. The Panglong Region

The panglong region consists of a strip of land around 10 kilometres wide on the east coast of Sumatra, starting in the north at Bagan Si Api Api and extending as far south as the Indragiri, which belongs to the Riau Residence; and the islands along the Sumatrawal, chiefly Roepat, Bengkalis, Padang, Merbau, Tebing Tinggi, Serapong, Mendol, and Rangsang, in addition to the around one thousand larger and smaller islands that form the Riau-Lingga archipelago. In August 1923, six Chinese logging companies were also found by a Labour Inspector in the Aceh area that worked according to the panglong system. There were no complaints of ill-treatment, but the accommodation and the lack of adequate medical care left much to be desired. The panglong region is located more or less opposite Singapore.

Where beams, firewood, and charcoal are transported exclusively by tongkang (an unmotorised cargo boat), permission to do the logging is only requested after the owner has located a suitable terrain as close as possible to Singapore. The need for a regular supply of labour for the panglongs and the way in which it comes about also means that the panglong owner will try to locate his business near the place whence he acquires his workers.

A licence for logging is granted for a terrain not exceeding 500 hectares in size. Such a licence is issued by the relevant head of the local administration for a term not shorter than one year and renewable for not longer than five years.

Only very rarely does the prospective owner himself enter the jungle to identify a site for his panglong. Usually he asks local inhabitants of the jungle where wood suitable for his purpose is best available. For this service, the orang-utan (jungle people) received a few Singapore dollars in payment. All the logs and charcoal are destined for the Singapore market, whence it is shipped to various places in the Malay Peninsula, Siam, British India, and Hong Kong.

Panglong owners (taukeh). With very few exceptions, the panglong owners or the people financing them are Chinese established in Singapore. They usually head up large sawmills, shipyards, or furniture workshops. Only a minority are located in the Dutch East Indies. As early as 1898, of the 131 panglong owners in the Bengkalis department, 128 were based in Singapore and one in Malacca.

These panglong owners put a Chinese in charge of their panglongs, usually a veteran of the trade. Things are then left completely in that person's hands. Although there has recently been some improvement in this respect, it is worth noting that the taukeh—the actual employer—never used to go anywhere near the panglong. He knew nothing of what went on there. He was mainly interested solely in the amount of wood that his panglong produced. On that depended the amount of money and food that he gave the captain (taikong) of the vessel sent to collect the timber, for the kapala panglong to use for house-keeping, etc. What the panglong manager did with the money mattered little to the owner, as long as the supply of wood continued without interruption.

This gave the kapalas, safe in their remote strongholds, unlimited power over the Chinese working under them. They did everything they could to profit to the greatest possible extent from those under their supervision, their so-called compatriots. That some did not flinch from the worst crimes will become clear in the following pages.

In very many cases the owner of a panglong was not even aware of its location. If the condition of the jungle and the quantity of timber on the panglong allowed, a firm might stay in the same place for a number of years. Otherwise, the kapala would seek out a better terrain. Once he had found one, he was obliged to ask the head of Local Administration for permission to move his panglong there. When the tongkang arrives from Singapore, the beams are loaded onto it first. Material necessary for the new coolie quarters (bangsal) are then stacked on top of the beams, together with food and a few sticks of furniture. The coolies find a place to perch in preparation for the voyage. Then off they sail to the new site, a big event in the otherwise monotonous coolie life. The captain of the ship is probably the only one who knows how to find his way from Singapore to a new panglong site.

These sailing ships, whose capacity ranges from 80 to 120 English tons, are the sole connection between the settlements of Chinese loggers in the inaccessible primeval jungle and the civilised world. They transmit messages to and from the panglong. If due to various circumstances and incidents, of which more anon, a labour shortage arises in the panglong, the taikong will inform the licence holder in Singapore. The licence holder would then get hold of the necessary workers and ship them south at the next opportunity. Many panglong licence holders own more then one tongkang: others hire them for a given number of voyages.

As I said earlier, the owners have begun to take steps to improve the supervision of their businesses and have shown ever greater interest in the way which they are managed. According to panglong regulations, the licence holder's local representative can be held jointly accountable for violations, so it has been possible to take measures against the kapalas, but the Labour Inspectorate nevertheless thought it desirable to concentrate on creating more interest in their businesses among the licensees. Such was the goal at meetings convened in Selat Pandjang (Bengkalis), Tandjong Balei (Karimoen), Prigi Radja (Indragiri Lowlands), and Penoeba (Lingga) with licensees and their representatives, attended by relevant officials. Several panglong owners now visit their loggers once or more a year. Some, for example, the owner of panglong no. 16 on the Kateman (Riau), a man called A Kong, often stays for several months at a time and manages his panglong himself. The owner of panglong no. 15, also on the Kateman, has been seen there a few times. A representative of the Siong Dim sawmill in Singapore, which owns or has a financial interest in a large number of panglongs, has also started visiting them occasionally.

Types of Panglong

"Panglong" means sawmill and is the Chinese word for a logging company where tree trunks are turned into planks. These sawmills used to be found in great numbers, especially in the Bengkalis department on the east coast of Sumatra, but they are rarely encountered nowadays. There are only a few left, and they are not very busy. This part of the industry has moved to Singapore. But although plank sawmills are few and far between, the name panglong continues to exist and is now used specifically, though improperly, for places that engage in:

(a) beam-manufacture.
(b) firewood-making
(c) charcoal-burning.

Beam-manufacture. The actual Chinese name is balalong. These balalongs have increased in number and largely replaced the old sawmills. The vast majority of beam-making takes place in Bengkalis, both on the Sumatra coast and on the islands of Tebing Tinggi, Padang, Serapong, and Mendol. In 1925 there were a dozen such on the north coast of the island of Rangsang. They were somewhat fewer in number in the Riau Residence, mainly in Karimoen and Lingga.

When setting up a balalong or moving one to another part of the jungle, you have to clear a space as close as possible to the coast or the river bank, where the coolie-quarters—the bangsal or kongsi house—are to be erected. The bangsal is by no means always built by the panglong residents themselves. The work is often outsourced to orang-utan.

The land, which can be completely submerged at high tide, turns into mud overgrown with trees and plants at low tide. This often means that the kongsi house must be situated deep in the jungle. The sledway, which provides the sole access from shore to coolie quarters, can, at low water, lie three to four metres above the mud.

On the coast or riverbank, a jetty is built on the same lines as a sledway, but wider. This jetty also serves as somewhere to stack the felled tree trunks, which are sawn into three or four pieces before being removed from the jungle. The tongkang cannot always reach this spot. When the logging posts are located on rivers that are relatively shallow, the sailing ships are moored at the mouth and the logs are floated down to it on rafts. Many of these rivers dry up completely at ebb tide. Other logging posts are located on shallow coastal mud banks and are only accessible once a day, at high tide.

While the jungle dwellers or some of the panglong coolies get started on setting up the bangsal, the rest of the workers begin under the leadership of the assistant kapala to cut a path through the jungle where a sledway can be laid. The kapala pays little attention to actual panglong work. He does not join in, and his role is restricted to looking after the food and ensuring "panglong discipline." The activities are managed by the assistant kapala or the mandur.

The sledway consists of large logs that are crisscrossed in the mud and stacked on top of one another until the desired height is reached. The logs on top, laid out longitudinally along the track, are indented with triangular notches into which the sleepers are slotted. The sledway, two to four metres wide, is best likened to a massive ladder laid flat on the ground. The sleepers are placed at intervals of approximately 65 centimetres. The main sledway sometimes stretches for several kilometres into the jungle. Smaller auxiliary sledways or tracks are constructed to transport timber from the jungle either side of this main thoroughfare. Once the timber has been cleared from the vicinity of this main sledway, a new main sledway is set up starting from the same point at the jetty but aimed in a different direction. In such cases, the kongsi house has to be moved elsewhere. Many logging stations are served by an entire network of such paths.

I mentioned earlier that the trunks are sawn into the desired dimensions at the spot where they are felled. They are then dragged on sledges to the drop-off point. These sledges consist of two heavy ribs, three to four metres long, which curve upwards at the end. The ribs are connected by cross-beams bound by steel wire.

The panglong coolies toiled from dawn to dusk, and suffered the worst abuse from the cruel and hardhearted kapalas and their henchmen. Working on a roller-bed sledway was no easy matter. It takes the workforce imported from China by way of Singapore a long time to acquire this skill. To make the sledges slide more easily, the middle part of the sleepers is heavily greased and must therefore be avoided. It is only possible to move along the sides. More often than one would wish, however, the sleeper on the opposite side of the sledway from a coolie flips loose of its notch and tilts upwards, causing the coolie with his unprotected feet, legs, and chest to scrape across the rough and smeared logs and end up in the mud, from which the stumps of trees protrude dangerously. As a result, infected leg wounds are extremely common. In the past, not the slightest concern was shown for such injuries, and workers' legs were a mass of festering wounds.

This often marked the start of great suffering for the *xinke*. Tormented by terrible pains, he was unable to walk, or found it very difficult to so. However, the mandur assigned to each team of log-haulers is incapable of pity. He knows that he must deliver the required number of loads to the jetty if he is to avoid incurring the displeasure of the chief mandur and the kapala. The injured log-hauler is urged to pull harder and the mandur uses whatever comes to hand to make his point. Often, as a result, the injured worker kept hauling until he dropped. Sometimes he was then taken to the bangsal, but more often than not he had to make his own way to the kongsi house along one of the supplementary sledways. He was given next to no time to recover. After one or two days, he was summarily ordered back to work. Some panglongs applied the rule "he who does not work shall not eat," and some unfortunates were driven out of the bangsal. A large number of the complaints made during inspections of the balalongs or visits by the Labour Inspector to hospitals concerning assault, murder, culpable death, etc. were found to relate to blows struck at or minor mistreatment of a worker at a time when he was unable to work due to injury or illness.

Usually each team of log-haulers has eight members. Some balalongs have two or three such teams. The lengths of wood are loaded onto the sledge and strapped to it, either singly or in sets of up to four, depending on their thickness and weight—each is about 16 foot long. Four workers walk on either side of the sledge, using belts made of bark and rope tied around their chest and shoulders to drag the heavy loads from the jungle. While they pull, they chant monotonously, to which rhythm they drag the sledge slowly forward. Because of the chanting, you often hear them approaching from a great distance. During the initial inspections, the coolies, who suffered greatly at the hands of their immediate superiors, said they preferred to meet us in the absence of the kapala and the mandur. It turned out that they did not dare to complain when their bosses were present, for they knew that the bosses would take revenge as soon as the officials had left for elsewhere. It was also important to make sure that accomplices and friends of the panglong bosses, for example the axe-man, the sawyer, the cook, and the sampan captain, were not able to find out who was making the complaints. After arriving at a panglong, as soon as we heard the song of an approaching team of log-men we asked the accompanying police officials to gather the panglong residents together in the bangsal and to wait there, while the kapala was invited to get the coolie list and the payroll and debt book. Meanwhile, the Labour Inspector headed off with his Chinese interpreter to meet the approaching haulers, who were able to present their complaints without hindrance, at a distance both from the kongsi house and from the place in the jungle where the others worked.

In general, conditions were worst in the balalongs. That is not to say, however, that nothing bad ever happened in the firewood or charcoal sections.

The Firewood Sections

These sections also had their own separate Chinese name, tjalong. The balalongs only provided material suitable for timber, while the tjalongs delivered another type of wood known as kajoe-bakau. Even the oldest trunks had a diameter of little more than a foot.

In the Bengkalis department, firewood is mainly found in the rivers and creeks on the islands. There is little of it on Sumatra. In the region of Riau and its surroundings it can be found everywhere. This firewood is in great demand in Singapore.

A tjalong is set up in the same way as a logging station. Mangroves—unlike the trees other than teak usually sought out by the loggers—are found on land newly washed together but submerged at high tide. In such places it is impossible to find anywhere free of mud and flooding on which to build a kongsi house. When the water level rises, an unpleasant smell often rises from the mud.

Jetties and sledges are made for the tjalongs in the same way as for the logging stations, but of lighter material and thinner wood. This is inevitable, for the thicker wood used on the balalongs cannot be found in the mangrove forests. However, firewood weighs less than heavy logs, so the sledways need not be so strong.

These stations have one or two permanent tree fellers. Most of the workers—who are often fewer in number than in the balalongs—are divided into two groups: the sawyers, who work in pairs using a pullsaw on the felled trunks at the spot where they have been chopped down to saw them into pieces, and the woodcutters who then chop them into firewood. This firewood is stacked together in the jungle on small sledges and transported along a sledway to the loading area.

However, firewood is not always cut in the same way. In some tjalongs, sections of the jungle are laid bare with the help of sledways. This method is similar in some respects to that used in the balalongs. Other companies dispatch workers on sampans on the rising tide to cut and saw suitable trees along the coast and the river banks and to take them on their vessels to the kongsi house, where they spend the rest of the day turning them into firewood.

Inspectors often found it difficult to meet up with the people working in such places. The best—often the only—time to reach such a tjalong is at high tide, which is precisely when the workers set out in all directions only to return several hours later, at the onset of the ebb. The Labour Inspectors were unhappy, and so too were the forestry officials, who saw this way of working as a form of plunder, for only the trees along the coast and the river banks were felled while the timber further away from the water was ignored. It also contravened article 2 (2) of the panglong regulations, which stipulates that a logging licence can only be granted for a site of no more than 500 hectares.

Workers hired to cut firewood usually work under contract and are paid by the amount of firewood they produce, so it is commonly assumed that the mandurs have no need to drive them on. In reality, inspections reveal that the opposite is true. Although workers are paid—in so far as payment actually takes place—for the quantity delivered, this quantity is set in advance and is often inordinately high. This frequently gives rise to discontent among the workers, which leads in turn to further maltreatment by the kapalas and mandurs.

c. Charcoal Kilns

The charcoal kilns or thoea-longs in Bengkalis are mainly found on the island of Roepat. They are scattered across most of the in the Riau-Lingga Archipelago, but not in the lower Indragiri region.

In companies that employ more than three or four workers, some are put in charge of the kilns while the others cut wood.

The number of kilns ranges from one to five. These kilns, made of clay shaped into an oval, are filled with pieces of wood about six feet long. The ovens have to burn for 20 to 25 days before the wood is ready. The kilns cannot be erected on the places along the shore that are flooded at high tide, so they are located on solid ground, where clay can be found for fashioning the kilns. The thoea-longs are therefore found almost exclusively on habitable land, often in the vicinity of large Malay kampongs. As a result, there are few of the abuses that tend to be the order of the day in many logging and firewood stations, since the charcoal workers come regularly into contact with the local Malays. These Malays, who live in kampongs under the supervision of the administration, are familiar by name with the Chinese employed by the companies. Crimes of the sort that might have been committed in the balalongs and were kept secret there could not be hidden long from the eyes of officials of the Native Administration office.

Unlike workers in the log-cutting and firewood-cutting sections, workers in the charcoal section, where hours are shorter, enjoy more freedom. After a day's work, they are allowed to go to one of the nearby kampongs. There were no complaints of abuse. In matters of housing, medical care, food, and payroll administration, however, violations were reported at almost all the kilns inspected under the panglong regulations.

In the immediate vicinity of the kilns, which are usually in more inhabited regions, the requisite bakau wood was not to be found. Here, too, the woodcutters take to their sampans to collect bakau wood from the narrow strips of bakau forest along the edges of the islands or on the river banks. They sometimes stay out for several days until their sampan is full—yet another reason why it was not always possible to gather all the workers together for inspection. Calling in a group of workers could, given the great distances over which they move, take two to three days, and even then you could never be sure, because of the slapdash way in which the coolie administration was conducted, that a couple of coolies had not been left behind in the bakau forest. However, this "swarming" method of collecting wood is applied only rarely. Most kilns employ one to four workers, who take care of the ovens and do everything that needs doing. In such circumstances, the wood is cut not by the panglong workers but by Malays. Only rarely are these Malays employed by the kiln owner. Usually they sell a quantity of wood to the kapala at very irregular intervals, at a price determined by the size of the sampan. In the case of the small number of workers on these thoea-longs, things were generally satisfactory even before the Labour Inspectorate was charged with their supervision. In the log and firewood cutting sections, only the kapalas and mandurs have their wives and children with them, by way of exception. Among the coolies working the charcoal ovens, on the other hand, several had formed families and lived together with them in separate houses. Some have even started building gardens and planting clumps of roembia (sago palms), etc. In the Bengkalis region in particular, there are many such sago palm developments.

Panglongs on Private Concessions

Until recently, panglongs were generally taken to mean logging companies that had received a licence under the provisions of the panglong regulations to fell timber within a given strip of land of no more than 500 hectares in extent (article 2, paragraph 2). Article l (2) c of the same issue of the Staatsblad stipulates that an enterprise cannot be seen as a panglong in the case of "the long-term exploitation of jungle forest complexes as regulated either in no. 6075 of the Supplement to the Staatsblad (jungle concessions) or by an agreement concluded with the relevant authorities (regarding large-scale logging companies)."

However, on a few jungle concessions or big logging enterprises in the Bengkalis region, panglongs seemed to be in operation. On these concessions(whether or not in conflict with the conditions regarding concessions), Chinese are, under certain circumstances, allowed by the concessionary or his authorised representative to cut wood in a specified section of the site. In one case, a taukeh licence was granted on payment of a certain sum of money each month to sell the wood elsewhere for the licensee's own benefit, while in other cases the panglong boss received compensation for the amount delivered by his panglong to the concession on which his sawmill was located. In that case, the concessionary acted in almost the same way as the government in the case of jungle belonging to the state. Both grant the Chinese panglong owner permission to harvest timber in a specific area under certain conditions.

The so-called government panglongs—the name, although somewhat inaccurate, has stuck—differ from the "pseudo-panglongs" on private concessions only in that the link created between the government and the panglong boss by the licence in the first case has, in the second case, been replaced by a lease or sale and purchase agreement or a labour contract between the concessionary and the panglong operator.

As for the manner of working, relations among the workmen, the recruitment of the workers, their housing, medical care, working hours, calculation and payment of wages, food, etc., there is no evident difference between "government panglongs" and "concessionary or long-lease panglongs." There was also no evident difference in the way in which the workers were treated. To judge by the volume of complaints brought before the police and the Labour Inspectorate, abuse and suchlike featured just as much on the concessionary panglongs as on terrains directly leased to Chinese by the government. The fact that one or more Europeans were appointed to supervise such concessions made no difference. The kapalas and mandurs were equally cruel to the workmen on the concessionary panglongs. The panglong bosses considered themselves lord and master of their enterprises and of those placed under them. They felt no affinity other than a purely commercial one with the European representative and the workers too see only the Chinese panglong boss as their employer. After all, he is the one who took them on and transported them to the panglong. The workman receives from him his orders, his opium, the customary beatings, and, if he is lucky, his wages. But although working conditions on the concessionary panglongs are not governed by the provisions of the panglong regulations and the workers, because they are not in the employment of the concessionary or his representative, are not governed by Stb.1911 no. 540, 1924, no. 250 (the so-called free workers' scheme), it is clear from the reports released by the Labour Inspectors, government officials, and police superintendents, who report all kinds of abuses and crimes, that proposals must be made to the Government in order to achieve better supervision. Stb. 1927 no. 198 (annex B) therefore proposes the adoption of a regulation regarding labour relations on those panglongs that are not covered by the provisions of the panglong regulations.

Number of Panglongs

Although panglongs have probably been in operation within our borders since the middle of the previous century, run by Chinese from Singapore, figures regarding the number of panglongs have been available only for the last few years, in reports delivered by officials. For the Bengkalis region, the first figures for the years 1893 and 1896 can be found in the Explanatory Memorandum attached to the draft panglong regulation of January 17, 1903, submitted by Inspector H. P. v. d. Horst. The figures for the year 1898 are derived from the report issued by the Van der Steenstraten Commission dated September 23, 1898. For the Riau Residence and surroundings, the only reliable figures available in the course of compiling this report were from 1925 onwards.

Sorts of panglong	Number of panglongs in the Bengkalis department in the years:							
	1893	1896	1898	1903	1913	1925	1926	1927
Plank sawmills	35	40	52	14	11	—	—	—
Beam cutting	18	37	34	86	97	76	69	80
Firewood cutting	—	—	30	29	46	28	25	16
Charcoal burning	4	7	15	41	62	69	70	72
Total	57	84	131	170	216	173	164	168

The above Table shows that plank-sawing first increased and then started to die off after 1898. A few panglongs continued sawing planks in 1925, but most of the wood was sent uncut to Singapore. The reason for the drop in number in 1926 is that 15 panglongs were closed down, ten of them as a result of adverse reports by the Labour Inspectorate.

In the Riau district, no panglongs were closed due to poor conditions in 1925 and just one was closed in 1926. However, eighteen licences were withdrawn mainly due to non-payment of taxes and unauthorised relocations.

Towards the end of 1925 and through 1926, the retail price of charcoal at Tandjong Pinang rose to between 3 and -4 Straits dollars ($1 = fl.40). Apparently this led many panglong owners to apply for new licences, which was also reflected in the figures for charcoal kilns in 1926 and 1927.

In early 1927, there were 31 panglongs on the concessions referred to in the previous section.

The following table shows the total number of panglongs:

Panglongs located	Total number of panglongs at start of 1927			
	Beam cutting	Firewood cutting	Charcoal burning	Total
in Bengkalis	80	16	72	168
on concessions	31	—	—	31
in Riau	20	21	194	234
	131	37	266	434

For all kinds of reasons, it used to be very difficult to estimate the number of logging companies. Regular inspections were not feasible due to a lack of sufficient and suitable vessels and an insufficient number of officials, all the more so because the panglongs, hidden away in the lush jungle, could only be reached along shallow creeks and rivers. In order to facilitate tracking down the panglongs, the regional prescriptions in the panglong regulations stipulate that a wooden board with the number of the panglong must be displayed at a visible place on the coast or the river bank. The regulations add that the holder of a panglong licence or his authorised representative must, "if a panglong be located on a tributary, place simple signposts on the branches, so that the panglong can easily be found." But the panglong bosses do not always follow the regulations to the letter, even though several reports have been drawn up regarding the matter. Some panglongs used the number board as a table in the bangsal! Looking after the panglong furniture has never been a priority for panglong managers. Also in 1898, the V. d. Steenstraten and Moll Commission found a number board being used as a canteen table in a kongsi house.

Chapter 2. The Initial Establishment of Panglongs

People have often asked when the first Chinese started up a panglong company in the East Indies. To answer this question, experts have examined the current state of the soil and of the trees and plants in the jungle. In his July–August 1923 travel report, Dr. Plassehaert, Inspector for the Outer Possessions of the Forestry Service, came to the conclusion that panglongs had been in existence for about forty years. This would seem to be confirmed by the fact that at the time of the Ordinance of December 24, 1882, which entered into force on February 1, 1883, "some temporary provisions were made regarding the levying of taxes on sawmills." More than two years later, the ordinance of February 5, 1885 (Stb. 1885 no. 33) laid down the conditions for establishing sawmills on the island of Bengkalis.

Mr. A. F. P. Graafland says in his "Sketch of the Chinese firms in the Karimoen Department" that the first panglongs most probably dated back to the 1860s and 1870s. The author is unable to specify the exact year, but he assumes with some certainty that there were some in Karimoen in 1888. Presumably the first panglongs were located on islands of the Bintan and Bantam group and in Karimoen, which are closest to Singapore and belong to the Riau archipelago. Nowadays, most of the Riau islands no longer have any exploitable forest. According to Mr. Graafland's estimate, we can assume that these islands were stripped bare in a period of 30 to 40 years. Probably the extensive gambier culture in this region has strongly contributed to the deforestation.

Gradually the Chinese loggers moved to larger islands further away from Singapore. Apparently Mr. Graafland regretted this. He said: "Finally they ended up on Lingga and Singkep, where nowadays nearly fifty logging companies and a tin mine are ruthlessly stripping away the beautiful jungle." Mr. Graafland's supposition that the panglongs started up roughly in the years 1866–1870 is apparently confirmed by the contract signed between the Netherlands Indies Government and the Sultan of Siak Sri Indrapoora on July 26, 1873, whereby the island of Bengkalis "was ceded in full and in perpetuity to the Government." The aim of the agreement was to give the Netherlands Indies Government the right to tax jungle land. A contract dated October 25, 1890, between the two parties determined that "except for the self-government already granted to native concessions, the right to tax the jungle timber is ceded to the Netherlands Indies Government on a broad strip of land along the coast from the border of Panei to Pelalawan and including all the islands belonging to Siak." Similar rights over other nearby regions were granted in a contract signed on February 4, 1879, and ratified on October 18 and another signed and ratified in April and June. The banks of the Kampar River for 50 kilometres upstream were deemed as coastal. The foregoing suggests, however, that even before July 1873, when negotiations were conducted regarding the transfer of taxation rights to the Government, logging companies were already present in the region. It can therefore be assumed that this Chinese logging company is already between 55 and 60 years old.

Panglong Legislation

As already noted, the first ordinance laying down provisions concerning taxation dates from 1882 (Stb. 1885 no. 322), while in 1885 (Stb. 1885 no. 33) the conditions were established for the opening of. sawmills. As mentioned, sawmills were initially in the majority, and the government publication made no mention of firewood cutting and charcoal burning.

Tax regulations. Every several years, the authorities tried to improve the panglong regulations, which were initially little more than tax schemes. The Government's income from the panglongs was calculated on the basis of the number of people employed on the panglongs and not, as is currently the case, the amount of timber felled. In order to prevent the panglong bosses from understating the number of their employees, Stb. 1882 no. 322 set the minimum number of workers at 25, not including the kapala. Stb. 1885 no. 33 kept the minimum at 25 but added the kapala, the cook, the clerk, and the barber to those exempted, since the legislator took the position that these people were not involved in actual logging. As far as barbers are concerned, it is striking that none was found on any panglong in the years 1925–1926. Instead, one of the workers cut hair in his spare time, to get some extra income. The minimum of 25 workers was again included in the regulations of 1893 (Stb. no. 115). There was no suggestion that permission would not be forthcoming if the minimum were not met but one can assume that in such cases the renewal of a licence would be refused. However, an ordinance in January 1894 (Stb. no. 7) authorised deviations in respect of the minimum number of workers.

This provision regarding a mandatory minimum had a fiscal aim, but it also ensured that a sufficient number of workers would be available for such heavy work. Even so, the provision was no longer included in panglong regulations after 1898. Recent inspections have often found an insufficient number of coolies on some panglongs, which creates the possible danger of an excessive workload for employees. In addition to a number of other changes to the existing panglong regulations, the Labour Bureau is therefore considering whether or not to reinstate the minimum, while lowering it in the case of firewood gatherers and charcoal burners.

Taxes. The way in which the tax was to be levied and the question of whether or not more benefit could be derived for the Government from the panglongs led officials to urge the Government on several occasions to amend existing arrangements. The amount of tax to be paid monthly per head changed more than once over the years.

A missive from the Bengkalis inspector dated August 22, 1893, carried an announcement that Mr. Van Akker, who rented all of the Sultan of Siak's panglongs, had initially demanded $1 a month for each logger. Later on, this amount was set at $0.75. Each kiln was taxed at the rate of $2 a month. Presumably, further discussions were held regarding the rate of payment.

As for taxes from territories over which taxation rights had been transferred to the Government, the Resident of Sumatra's East Coast set the rate at f2.50 per logger and f1.50 per sawer. Later a proposal was made to amend these amounts to f2.25 and f1. The logging rights were valid until 1893. A licence system was implemented in 1893.

Because the owners of the panglongs, their financiers, and their logging managers never came to Bengkalis and were not known to the administration, all kinds of difficulties arose regarding taxation. Checking out the panglongs was not easy—the licence never seemed to be available to inspect. Often the licences turned out to be kept by the Kapitein of the Chinese at Bengkalis and the Lieutenant of the Chinese at Tebing Tinggi. In order to facilitate the collection of taxes, in 1893 the Resident of Bengkalis proposed making the two Chinese officers responsible for this and compensating them with 3 or 4 percent of the panglong income.

It seems the requirement that the licence should always be available on every panglong was subsequently dropped. On almost every panglong one was informed during the first inspections in 1925 that the licence was not available and was in the possession either of the Chinese official administrators or of the panglong owner in Singapore. This question was taken up at meetings with the panglong bosses. As a result, the licences are now displayed behind glass in a frame in the bangsal.

Shortly after the promulgation of Stb. 893 no. 115, a serious decline in timber prices led to a big reduction in the number of panglongs. The monthly rent for a panglong on the islands in the Pelalawan region fell from f840 in 1884 to f180 in 1893.

In August 1893, the panglong concessionaries filed petitions asking the Sultan to cut the coolie tax to f1 a month in connection with the low timber prices. In the discussion of the Indies budget in the House of Representatives, a call went up to abolish the lease tax, given that the sawmills in Pelalawan seemed doomed.

During this panglong crisis, the coolies were left to their own devices by their employers. Since there was no profit to be made from the timber trade, the panglong owners stopped sending money and food for the coolies. These people then sold all the timber that had been cut and sawn and disappeared from the panglongs to take refuge elsewhere.

Complaints from the [British-ruled] Straits Administration concerning the mistreatment of workers. Apart from the fiscal interest in the panglongs as a source of income, the poor treatment of the panglong coolies gradually attracted attention. Controleur Van der Horst notes, in his above-mentioned memorandum, that initially only the interests of the tax authorities were taken into account and the workers were practically ignored. Complaints by the Straits Administration forced an intervention. Presumably escaping coolies had complained to the Protector of Chinese about conditions in the panglongs.

In his letter of December 11, 1896, the Dutch Consul- General in Singapore wrote:

> It is the intention of the Protector, if the conditions of the workers on Serapong Island do not improve, to ask the Governor of this colony to consider prohibiting emigration there.

The Protector had received the following complaints:

1. Twenty-three workers were transferred from one panglong to another without being consulted.
2. Workers complained of being detained on panglongs against their will.
3. Wages had not been paid.
4. Sick coolies were dragged from the bangsal to a cabin in the jungle and abandoned.
5. Sinkehs unfamiliar with the work were said to have been caned.
6. Workers who fled the panglongs were maltreated as a matter of course and often killed.

The Resident of the East Coast of Sumatra, after becoming aware of this, instructed the Assistant Resident at Bengkalis to deal with the coolie abuse.

First Government Inquiry. Meanwhile, on June 4, 1898, a commission was appointed to carry out a local investigation into conditions on the panglongs in Bengkalis and the reports of abuse. Assistant Resident H. A. van der Steenstraten and the Official for Chinese Affairs, A. E. Moll in Medan, were appointed to the Commission. On September 23 of that year, the said gentlemen submitted their report, details of which follow below.

The number of known panglongs in 1898 was 131. According to the then current regulation, these companies employed some 3400 coolies. Of the 83 panglongs visited by the Commission, 49 were sawmills and 34 were plank-cutting businesses.

The various complaints brought before the Protector of Chinese were investigated. The report said that Mr. Fernandez, an employee of the Chinese Protectorate, had already been to Bengkalis to hold talks. Of the 23 workers who had been sent to another panglong against their will, 16 could be found; the rest were missing.

In addition, the Commission commented that in the contracts concluded in the presence of the Protector in Singapore by the plank-cutters, provision had been made for them to continue working until they had cleared their debts.

It is clear that bringing those contracts to the attention of the authorities in Singapore was well intentioned. However, it turned out that the said authorities were not sufficiently familiar with actual conditions on the panglongs. With regard to the contracts, the Commission said: "It sometimes happened that the contract was withdrawn, a smaller wage was paid, and there were no dismissals if debts were cleared."

Sinkehs often worked simply for their keep. Everything—except the food—was recorded as debt. The worker only started getting wages after he had delivered, say, 1400 planks, which took about 18 months. By that time, however, he was so deep in debt that he could no longer get out of it. The wages varied between f3 and f6 a month. However, payment never happened. Wages were only settled on return to Singapore—for most workers, that meant never.

Advances, the Commission continued, were fiddled. The consumption of opium was vigorously promoted, for the kapala made a profit from it. The great majority of the workers fell deeper and deeper into debt. "They are cheated in every respect by the taukeh," said the two rapporteurs. "It is easy for the taukeh, since most coolies are incapable of managing their own accounts." The Commission concluded that non-compliance with contracts and deprivation of liberty were the coolies' most common and rightful grievances.

The coolies had also complained to the Protector about the actions of some kapalas. When the rapporteurs arrived in the panglong area, four kapalas had fled to China. Regarding the complaints, the report said: "Cases of abuse are rare; sinkehs do get a slap now and then, if they are clumsy or lazy, but once they understand their job, they are rarely beaten. Among the more than 2500 workers who appeared before us in the panglongs, only 10 showed traces of rattan blows. Only deserters are beaten. Repeat deserters are, according to some coolies, sometimes killed, but in general the rattan is certainly not used on panglongs any more than in companies under European management."

With regard to the fourth point, the Commission opined: "In one respect, those statements are false, i.e., the claim that the sick coolies are dragged off to a cabin in the jungle and left to their own devices. The rule is that the sick are kept in the panglong house, where they always have food and usually get medicines. However, there is no question of medical treatment."

Even so, the rapporteurs were able to establish—contrary to the above claim—that on Tjin A Tik's panglong, lepers and a blind coolie were ejected [into the jungle].

Although the Commission had apparently got the impression that serious abuse had not happened, the report stated that two workers had died as a result of their treatment.

It is not impossible that conditions on the panglongs have worsened since the Commission finished its research and that cases of serious assault have occurred more often. Later reports, including that by Mr. J. Snellen van Vollenhoven, Officer of Chinese Affairs, in 1918, and by the Labour Inspectorate in 1925 and 1926, give a different view of abuses committed in the panglongs from that in the report by Van der Steenstraten and Moll's Commission.

This Commission has also looked at the tax payable by the timber companies. In its opinion, approximately f20,000 more could be extracted from the panglongs annually.

Finally, the Commission concludes that conditions will only improve if there is constant checking. Such was not the case in earlier years. The then Assistant Resident of Bengkalis did not visit even twenty panglongs in almost five years, according to the Commission. The crew of the regional vessel in Bengkalis did not even know the location of the panglongs.

In order to improve supervision of the panglongs, the Commission proposed to the Government that it appoint a controleur at Tebing Tinggi. Furthermore, it considered it desirable to prevent coolies from working for more than three years in the panglongs, and recommended that each panglong deposit f200 with the board from which to pay wages or nursing costs in cases of sickness.

New Government measures. To combat apparent abuses, on May 7, 1901, the Government decreed, for the purpose of monitoring the panglongs, the appointment of a controleur at Tebing Tinggi and of a Chinese clerk and an interpreter for the Macao, Keh [Hakka], and Hokkien dialects.

Before the arrival of this Inspector, few penalties were imposed, presumably because of the lack of supervision. In 1896, ten violations and one crime were brought to court. In 1897, these figures were thirteen and one respectively. That far more intensive control was urgently needed is clear from the figures for convictions in the period from October 1901 to October 1902. In that year 105 criminal cases involving 242 defendants were brought before the Magistrate at Selat Pandjang on Tebing Tinggi Island. Twenty-eight people were ordered to take up employment; 214 fines were imposed to a total of fl1,624. These fines do not include those imposed for late payment of taxes.

However, the mere placement of a controleur and a clerk-interpreter in Selat Pandjang did not resolve the problem. The appointed officer had to be able to visit the panglongs, which could only happen once a vessel was made available.

Efforts were also made to improve things in various other ways. A small hospital was set up at Selat Pandjang. In January 1903, a Javanese doctor was employed and paid by the Government.

The Dutch Consul General in Singapore, in a letter dated October 6, 1903, mentioned the Po Ho Peng Timber and Firewood Society and asked the Protector of Chinese to press it to pay the wages of the panglong coolies regularly and provide decent housing and medical care, including the building of a new hospital at Tebing Tinggi.

However, these measures were directed exclusively at the panglongs in the Bengkalis department, whereas the Riau residence also had a large number of such companies. As a result, in 1903 Mr. Ezerman, the Officer for China Affairs in that region, was charged with investigating conditions on the panglongs. He came to the conclusion that, give or take a few local differences, the situation in Riau was much the same as in Bengkalis.

At the time, the panglongs in this administrative area were already under police supervision. This is evident from what Hadji Salim told the Volksraad in 1923:

> The Government Agent mentioned something else in connection with free labour, namely the panglongs, practically a legendary issue for the Volksraad. I don't believe there are many who could imagine what a panglong is and the dire conditions that obtain there.
>
> I've been to many panglongs myself. I paid visits to the panglongs because at the time, in 1904 and 1905, my father was sent out with an armed police escort to track down crimes on the panglongs. I went along because I knew from practical experience that letting my father accompany the armed police officers could result in disaster. I remember one armed policeman said: "Must I sell my life for fl3.50?" I knew he was right, so I went with my father. For me, it was more than a matter of fl3.50.
>
> On that occasion, I got to know the panglongs. These are sawmills located at the mouth of the Sumatran rivers south of Siak and on the islands

> opposite, all located in swampy areas. They are called panglongs in so far as they process timber into planks.
>
> It is interesting to visit these enterprises. Why? Because you can only get there after a lot of manoeuvring against a strong current, which runs regularly alongside the landing pier. This landing pier has no platforms and consists solely of unsawn trunks.
>
> The road to the panglongs, which are often a kilometre or more from the coast, can best be described as consisting of ladders lying on the ground, with logs laid lengthwise at a distance of two to three metres over which other logs are laid widthwise. Once you reach the panglong, you will find a kind of blockhouse behind a fence three metres high, housing a number of very angry dogs. In the panglong is the taukeh, who works with a number of coolies. The taukeh and the coolies belong to the same race [dialect group], but they are actually half savages; not one of them attaches much value to a human life, not even his own.
>
> They work together and eat together. Marriage is also so to say shared in common. After the tour with my father, I remember that he returned with evidence of seven murders and a much larger number of assaults.
>
> The coolies reach the panglongs on board tongkangs belonging to the taukeh and can only leave them in the same way; no other means of transport are available, there are no proas and certainly no steamers.
>
> Conditions on such a panglong are definitely not rosy.

The panglongs in the Lower House. The House of Representatives has been busy with the panglong issue since 1893. Back then, however, people were only concerned with the income that could be extracted for the Government. Working conditions in the sawmills in the Riau region only became an issue in 1907, following the publication of an article in *De Locomotief* on August 11, 1906.

Following a report by Mr. de Iongh regarding the fate of the Chinese coolies on Bangka, the editors of *De Locomotief* said: "these loggers, left to the mercy of their Chinese bosses, have to endure a fate that the Dutch Indies Government can in no way justify."

Apart from rock-bottom wages, a lot of cheating goes on with monetary advances, and there is a system of so-called "forced shopping" [having to buy from the company store at inflated prices]. The accommodation was filthy, shabby, and dismal. The atmosphere was stuffy and stank.

The editorial added that the coolies had been hired to go to Singapore to work in the gambier gardens but ended up instead on the panglongs. There was a system of punishments whereby all the coolies were obliged to join together to cane anyone who infringed "panglong discipline." If a worker refused to participate, he risked the same punishment.

Eventually, it was suggested that a Dutch-Indies Protector be appointed to oversee the treatment of Chinese workers, just as the British Protector of Chinese works to prevent vexation and deception in the matter of labour recruitment.

Mr. van Kol added that he had heard that workers had to sign on for seven or eight years. Sick coolies were supposed to be put ashore by their bosses on one of the islands in Karimoen. Finally, he mentioned the following incident:

> The captain of the English steamship Billiton rescued 7 Chinese workers at sea from a native dug-out [prauw]. They said that ten of them had fled thirteen days earlier from a panglong on one of the Natoena Islands. In the meantime, three of them had died. The captain took them on board and took care of them. He said that the boat in which he found the Chinese was suitable for a maximum of six and that it was highly dangerous "to roam the seas around the Riau archipelago, which are known for their perilous waters and the sudden emergence of storms and heavy waves."

Mr. van Kol suggested that the Minister should not wait long before mounting an investigation and should intervene immediately.

As a result, the Minister of Colonies wrote to the Governor-General on January 12, 1907, and thereby brought the attention of the Indies Government back to the matter.

Mr. D. C. Stibbe, Inspector of Labour, who in July 1907 had already visited some panglongs in the Bengkalis district, was charged with investigating the panglong situation in Riau. In his report of August 16, 1909, Mr. Stibbe recommended regular strict controls, to which end in his opinion a fast-moving steamship and a motorboat should be made available. He also suggested using a sailing boat with a sampan to keep watch, so that it could make unscheduled visits to the panglongs to carry out checks.

At the time, most of the sawmills in the Riau region were located in Kateman (Karimoen) and on the island of Lingga.

On November 6, 1909, the Resident of Riau was asked to set about founding a panglong hospital and to revise the Riau charter of May 1, 1907 (*Javasche Courant*, May 14–17, 1907) in order to make medical treatment compulsory for workers.

In response to the Stibbe report, the Resident of Sumatra's East Coast proposed in a letter dated February 4, 1910, setting up a means of controlling the panglongs. For this the following would be necessary:

(a) a fast-moving steamship,
(b) a motorboat,
(c) a sailing craft,
(d) a so-called sampan-pandjang.

Meanwhile, a new regulation was introduced in 1909 regarding the panglongs in the Bengkalis region. Although it did not set a minimum number of workers, the owners of such establishments or their representatives (a clerk, cook, or mandur) were declared exempt from taxation. Article 8 was especially important for ensuring a vigorous intervention. It authorised the Assistant Resident of Bengkalis to withdraw a licence "on the grounds of maltreatment of persons employed by the panglong."

Chapter 3. Extension of Supervision Desirable

The measures taken by the Government and the supervision carried out by officials was not yet enough to put an end to the abuse and misery to which workers found themselves subjected. Reports came in again and again of very severe beatings. The coolies' state of health left much to be desired. The enlarged panglong hospital in Selat Pandjang, which some concessionaries had financed to the tune of $700, received a constant stream of large numbers of sick workers. In 1913, there were 291 patients, including 58 with beriberi, of whom twelve died. The numbers in 1914 were 363, 103, and 22 respectively.

On May 24, 1915, there were 61 patients in the hospital in question, including twenty with beriberi, all from the panglongs.

In the 1910 panglong examination on the east coast of Sumatra, panglong licence holders were instructed to provide a sufficient stock of foodstuffs and medicines. Proper accommodation and medical care was to be provided at the expense of the panglongs. The coolies had to be given the opportunity in cases of illness or for any other valid reason to leave the panglong. However, little came in practice of these humane decisions.

During the discussion of the Indies budget in the Second Chamber in 1915, the question was posed as to whether or not it was desirable to put monitoring of the panglongs in the hands of Labour Inspectorate.

In response, the then Director of Justice pointed out that the Labour Inspectorate was only concerned with companies under the jurisdiction of the existing coolie ordinances and the so-called free-worker scheme (Stb. 1911 no. 540), which since 1902 had no longer been applicable to logging companies.

In 1911, in the regulation on free workers, no enterprises were specifically excluded, but it would have been contrary to the intentions of the legislator if panglongs had been included among "enterprises of a different kind." Panglongs were not covered by this arrangement, since they had always been regarded as small enterprises.

For Riau and the surrounding area, Stb. 1891 no. 219 had insisted that for statutory provisions to apply to a company, the company must be managed by Europeans. The panglongs therefore fell outside that regulation too. Moreover, extending the remit of the Labour Inspectorate to panglongs would be impossible unless the number of deputy inspectors was increased and vessels were made available.

All this stood in the way of an easy resolution of the difficulties that had arisen. However, conditions in the panglongs required decisive measures. Gradually, the atrocities practised in such places came to light. Mr. S. said in *Koloniaal Tijdschrift* 1915, II, pp. 1009 ff:

> The panglongs were indeed places of horror in which the wretched in body and spirit were forced to work by demons without mercy, where with merciless cruelty the workers were allowed just enough food and rest until the costs incurred [in recruiting them] had been amply repaid and the expected profit delivered.

According to this author, the Protector of Chinese in Singapore would have called the position of the panglong coolie "sheer slavery of the most brutal type."

A New Government Inquiry. Mr. J. Snellen van Vollenhoven, Officer for Chinese Affairs, was therefore commissioned in 1918 to produce a new study of conditions on the panglongs in Riau and Bengkalis. This study was done in two parts. From November 4 to December 15, 1918, the official visited Riau. He produced a report on around a dozen panglongs on January 9, 1919. In March and April 1919, he went to Bengkalis and completed his report on May 29.

In the first report, Mr. Snellen van Vollenhoven said that the situation on the panglongs, which he called "appendages of Singapore," were unacceptable. The coolies, who no longer sign a contract in Singapore, are cheated in many ways. They are told that they will be able to get a good job on one of the rubber estates on an island close to Singapore. However, they end up in inhospitable places in the swampy jungle. Lured from China to Singapore by recruiters, the sinkehs are sold on to the panglong owners.

In Riau at the time, the general rule seemed to be that no work was required on four days in every month. A full monthly wage was paid for 26 days of work. However, if only 25 days were worked, no matter what the reason, then only 25/30 of the monthly wage was paid. For every day less than 26 not worked, even due to illness, the wage was cut by $0.20 to pay for food consumed.

On the panglongs, Mr. Snellen van Vollenhoven found a Chinese regulation that stipulated that a worker who deserted and was recaptured was charged $3 for his reinstatement.

Opium consumption on the panglongs was greater than among Chinese labourers on the gambier estates.

The official then recounted a series of events from recent years, some of which are briefly summarised below.

The case was heard at a court on July 13,1915, of a mandur accused of tying a coolie to a stake and beating him so badly—even though, according to statements by the defendant and witnesses, the coolie was sick—that he died shortly afterwards.

Although this coolie had only been at the panglong for three months, he had already tried to flee on three occasions. The last time he had stolen a sampan. However, he never managed to reach an inhabited place. Probably because the mandur had paid a reward to the natives, on the last occasion he was returned to the panglong by two native sampan men.

On July 16, 1916, the court heard a case of a coolie beaten to death by an axe-wielding mandur in revenge for the coolie having abused him.

On October 10, 1916, two coolies who had fled their panglong because the work was too much for them were taken to court. They had managed to reach the shore, where they found a native in a sampan. They wanted to go to a kampong at the mouth of the Kateman River. However they could not agree a price with the native. In addition, they were afraid he would take them back to the panglong. A fight ensued in which the native was mistreated. During the investigation, the mandur said he had promised the Malays a reward of $3 a head.

On July 19, 1917, two coolies stood trial for murdering two mandurs. They explained that whenever officials arrived at the panglong, they [the coolies] were sent into the jungle to prevent them from voicing their complaints.

Conditions on the panglongs in the Bengkalis department were no better.

On panglong no. 33 in Bengkalis, Mr. Snellen van Vollenhoven found a leper and six coolies with serious untreated wounds. About a year and a half earlier, a worker was said to have been murdered.

When he arrived at panglong no. 214, fourteen of the thirty workers asked to be allowed to leave. Three complained of being beaten by the kapala and the mandur. Some traces of beatings were still visible.

In the jungle a very sick coolie was found under an awning. He had been transported there on a sled and left to his own devices.

A man exhausted by fever was found in the jungle. He subsequently died in hospital in Bengkalis.

The report also stated that in Selat Pandjang, the Fo Phin Kong So had been established. This was a refuge for poor and unemployed panglong coolies, under the supervision of an appointee of the Lieutenant Governor.

At the end of his report, Mr. Snellen van Vollenhoven asked why the Labour Inspectorate does not sort out the panglongs.

Economic considerations should, he said, be put to one side when it is a question of ending a state of slavery, a description that fits the bill.

It is undoubtedly true that Mr. Snellen van Vollenhoven's findings put the misery on the panglongs in a sharper light than earlier surveys ever had. The conditions sketched by him are not unlike those later established as crimes by the Labour Inspectorate.

It is must be assumed that by no means all the irregularities that take place on the panglongs can be put right and punished by the Board. The silence of the coolies who witness the torments endured by their comrades hindered many inquiries. They were all too afraid—even though they had been temporarily removed from the panglong in the course of the investigation—that they would later suffer a like fate. Only when despair had taken possession of the soul and left them indifferent to their fate, when they were suddenly animated by hope that the kapala and his henchmen would kill them in revenge and thus redeem their miserable lives or if they had the firm conviction that freedom awaited them, that they would they no longer return to that place of terrors, only then were they ready to bear witness.

It was often impossible to trace the whereabouts of missing coolies. Sometimes people claimed that they did not know them or could not remember them. In other cases, they said that the coolies had run off, been attacked by tigers, or been killed by a falling tree. Usually, people simply said that "they had returned to Singapore." But all too often it was clear that without further investigations no credibility could be attached to these claims.

The facts that emerged were so terrible that each time new measures had to be taken. In the roughly 36 panglongs located in Kateman in Karimoen department in the Riau region, there were nine cases of murder or manslaughter in 1917. In 1918, there were two known murders. In early 1919, a coolie from one sawmill ended up in another panglong. When this became apparent, the kapala of the first company went with some coolies to reclaim the deserter. A violent fight broke out, as a result of which four Chinese were injured.

To assist the administrative officers, in 1920 a Chinese interpreter from the Labour Inspectorate was stationed in Riau. He remained there until 1923.

The Labour Inspectorate is charged with supervision. Since the basis on which the levying of the panglong tax took place was not entirely satisfactory, the authorities considered whether or not to abandon it. Instead of a given amount per logger per month they wanted a monetary payment for the amount of timber cut and exported. In connection with this, a new panglong regulation was designed. The idea was also to take the abuses into greater account. A reorganisation of the forestry service in the panglong region was therefore deemed necessary. This began in 1923, and the new organisation was established in 1924.

A senior forestry official was sent to work in Tandjong Pinang (Riau), along with two foresters located in Bengkalis. Superintendents and wardens were later sent to Bengkalis, Seiat Pandjang, Penoeba, Karimoen, and Tambilahan (Indragiri). In addition to a number of mantris, some jungle surveyors were appointed, each of whom had 5 or 6 panglongs to supervise. Each was given a sampan and a rowing boat. A steam-propelled vessel and some motorboats meant that the head forester, the foresters, and the wardens were able to keep an eye on the lower staff as well as on the panglongs.

In October 1921, speaking of the new draft panglong regulation, the Governor of Oosthoek, Mr. Westenenk, had already suggested to the

Government that the Labour Inspectorate should take over the supervision of the panglongs.

The Governor reinforced his proposals by listing a large number of atrocities that had come to light, of the sort already mentioned in the report by Mr. Snellen van Vollenhoven. We read:

> Among the frightful figures of coolies clad in rags was one who had tied a piece of old felt around his shin to keep the flies off a wound. What it concealed defies description. Notwithstanding the express obligation imposed on the panglongs to provide medicines and bandages, nothing has been forthcoming.

In the new Panglong regulation promulgated in May 1923 much attention was devoted to counteracting the abuses and improving working conditions. The first paragraph of Article 6 reads:

> The relevant Head of Local Government is authorised to withdraw a licence:
>
> (a) if the licence-holder or his substitute has been convicted of mistreating people employed by the panglong, or if he or his personnel are found guilty of irregularities or of opposing the established order of things;
> (b) if the licensee is not, in the opinion of the head of local government, properly providing accommodation, food, or medical treatment for his employees or, through his actions or negligence, deprives them of their personal freedom;
> (c) if wages are paid late;
> (d) or if there are repeated or serious violations of these regulations.

In the first paragraph of article 8, violations of the regulations are punishable by imprisonment of not more than three months or a fine of not more than fl100.

The implementation of these regulations by the heads of the regional administration is governed by the following rules:

> The holder of a panglong licence or his representative is required to ensure:
>
> (a) that the residence of the workers and the surrounding areas are always kept in a good and clean condition;
> (b) that a list is posted containing the names of all those working in the panglong, with a notice in both Malay and Chinese stating the obligations of the panglong licensee or his authorised representative;

(c) that an accounts book (tsoentoe) be given to every worker and that it be updated daily by or on behalf of the manager and closed on a monthly basis, so that it is always clear how much a worker owes or is owed;
(d) that the company always has a sufficient amount of good food, good drinking water or tea, and medicines in stock:
(e) that accommodation is always provided at the company's expense (including the provision of mosquito nets), as well as nutrition and medical treatment and clothing for the workers;
(f) that the inspectors and officials are provided with all desired information relating to the enterprise, that they are given access to the records, and that all workers and—if required—all managers or their authorised representatives appear before officials;
(g) that workers who, due to dismissal, illness, or any other valid reason, wish to leave the company will be given the opportunity, if necessary, to get appropriate means of water transport;
(h) that workers who die at work are buried.

In his letter of October 5, 1921, Governor Westenenk told the Government that the new panglong regulations would make more intensive supervision even more necessary:

> That the new arrangement will reduce the exploitation of the coolies is not to be expected. The contrary is true: the sharper the fiscal control, the more heavily the company will be taxed. Obviously, it will inevitably backfire on the coolies, by increasing to the utmost the amount of work they do.

For control and supervision in order to improve working conditions in the panglongs, the Labour Inspectorate was the obvious designated body, by virtue of its experience in the field. In this connection, the Head of the Labour Bureau, in a letter of January 5, 1924, to the Government concerning Article 10 of the new panglong regulation (Stb 1923 no. 220), said that officials of the Labour Inspectorate for the Outlying Regions should be charged with attending to the regulations and the measures for implementing them adopted by the Heads of the Regional Administration. This was done by an Order that came into into force on January 1, 1925.

As a temporary measure, in accordance with the government decree, on January 1, 1925, the number of deputy inspectors employed by the Labour Inspectorate for the Outlying Region was expanded by one.

It soon became apparent that for a speedy adjudication of the many official summonses it was urgently necessary to appoint a Chairman to the court in Bengkalis. To this end, a proposal was sent out on June 17, 1925, by the Head of the Office of Labour.

Because of the large number of panglongs and their great spread, on June 19, 1925, the Government was urged to appoint an official of the Labour Inspectorate to be stationed in Bengkalis. In a letter dated July 3, 1925, from the Government Secretary, permission was given as of August 1 to add to the staff of the Labour Inspectorate a Deputy Inspector and a Chinese interpreter and clerk. At the end of November 1925, officials in Tandjong Pinang and Bengkalis were charged with supervising companies in their areas that were subject to the provisions of the Coolie Ordinance and Stb. 1911 no. 540. Given the vastness of the Riau region, a second Inspector was to be posted, starting on January 1, 1928.

The recruitment of workers for the panglongs. The workers needed for the panglongs are all recruited in Singapore. This happens in various places, but always in less favoured neighbourhoods, by way of the kedeh-nasi [rice shops], where Chinese waiting for employment, and having nothing but the set of clothes they wear, receive food and shelter. The settlement of their bills takes place as soon as the worker has found a job, i.e., once he has been sold to an employer.

That the employers were of the opinion that they had "bought" their workers was obvious from the following. In response to complaints made by coolies during an inspection on January 30, 1925, of panglong no. 23, in the Karimoen subdivision, the licensee's representative was reminded of his obligations to the workers. His answer was that the coolies had nothing to say, since they had been purchased (dibelih).

In Singapore there are separate institutions for the different Chinese tribes. The panglong owner knows where to go if he wants workers from Macau (Kongfu), Kehs [Hakkas], Hokkiens or members of other tribes. The owners of these coolie houses are—according to information obtained from their neighbours—known as *tucang jual orang orang* [human traffickers]. These traffickers receive a certain sum from the employer or his wharf agent for their efforts. Often it is agreed that the advance on the wages that the worker is promised is instead handed over to the manager of the premises on which accommodation and board has been provided for the coolie in the course of those few days. This is often the case with panglong coolies. Basically, they get an amount ranging from $10 to more than $100 advanced on their wages and leave without seeing a single cent of it. If the number of days spent in the accommodation does not justify withholding the entire advance, the man is told to take a few sets of clothing, a hat, a suitcase, a mat, a mosquito net, or some other item. The prices of these items are set so high that the advance passes entirely into the hands of the boarding-master, who anxiously prevents his guests from disappearing. Beyond this, the coolie has nothing. Moreover, he does not know what hangs over his head. Even if he did know, for the time being he is indifferent, since he is already satisfied with what he has received.

The young Chinese recruits are placed temporarily in such places, i.e., they are locked up there. Other Chinese who have become unemployed for all kinds of reasons are approached by recruiters on the street or at the dock and are also brought to these places. Dazzled by expectations, they are sent off to the panglongs. At best, they are informed beforehand that they will get a job in (say) carpentry. Often they are told that they will be put to work on a rubber estate or a gambier garden on one of the islands close to Singapore. During inspections, complaints are repeatedly heard about such deceptions. Many workers claim to have been cheated. For example, an unemployed Chinese hanging around in the port in Singapore was told that he can earn royally on the island, whose oil tanks can be seen gleaming in the sun a short distance away. The recruiter says he will take him to the island of Samboe, where the Batavia Petroleum Company has its tanks. However, the coolie ended up on panglong no. 263 on the island of Mendol.

Good craftsmen are sometimes found among the panglong coolies. Many times it turns out that a coolie used to work in Deli on one of the tobacco plantations but had fallen into the hands of professional recruiters in Singapore. Tricked into gambling their money away, they receive credit and opium. Awaking from their daze in the coolie hostel, they are informed that they are in debt. If they are unable to pay the debt, they are told to stay for a few days and the manager of the kedeh would try to get them work.

Naturally many of those destined for the panglongs have a sorry story to tell. Some of those who had been out of work had something on their conscience, which led them into trouble. Sacked workers or runaway prisoners along with jumped-ship sailors also ended up in the coolie houses.

The presence of such scum was not conducive to an improvement in conditions in the panglongs. Undoubtedly this is part of the explanation for the various kinds of misdeeds that over the years have come to light. Certainly it was not easy for the kapalas to keep these criminals under control. That serious beatings and murders should occur on panglongs where such individuals rise to the higher-paid positions such as mandur or even kapala goes without saying. Nevertheless, a stand must be taken against the opinion sometimes stated, that all panglong coolies belong to the scum of Chinese society. The experience of the latter two years suggests otherwise. The number of attacks on kapalas and mandurs committed by coolies is very small, and are usually in the form of revenge attacks for past acts of cruelty. Young sinkehs recently brought over are generally preferred on the panglongs. They are needed for the heavy work. They are stupid and simple-minded, but they are still unspoiled Chinese who are hungry and therefore much more likely to fall into the hands of recruiters. On the panglongs, they are introduced to opium, which they eventually use to try to forget their plight. They are beaten and tortured if they fail to meet the heavy demands put on them, so that the less strong are soon discarded. The physically stronger remain but, when they finally succumb to opium, they are no longer suitable for heavy work, so they have to switch to sledge-making, cooking, sampan loading, bark stripping, or looking after the pigs.

> Some weaklings cannot stand the work, but there are others, bent and bruised, who will never go home again, and carry out their work day in and day out in the jungle, work that no European would stand for a single hour and no native workman for a single day.

For some years now, Chinese bound for the panglongs no longer sign contracts with the Protector of the Chinese in Singapore. In his 1919 report, Mr. Snellen van Vollenhoven pointed this out. Officials of the Labour Inspectorate did not find a single contract anywhere.

Only in one part of the panglong region, in the Kateman, were panglong contracts concluded, and that was a few years ago. Moreover, the provisions of the contracts, which had been co-signed by the District Head of Kateman, were not kept to.

As a result of the Royal Decree in Stb. 1916 no. 47, all Foreign Orientals residing within the Dutch East Indies must be in possession of a so-called admission card, which currently costs f100. This is not applicable to Oriental Aliens in Tandjoeng Pinang and Lingga and in that part of the Karimoen in Riau beyond the Sumatrawal. As a consequence, admission cards have to be purchased for coolies in the panglongs on the mainland of Sumatra and on the islands in the Bengkalis department but not for the islands of the Riau Residence.

By asking, when coolies apply for admission card, about their age and whether or not they knew their destination and what wage they had been promised, officials of the Emigration Service in Samboe, Bengkalis, and Selat Pandjang have contributed greatly to improving conditions in the panglongs. In some cases, workers were too young or too weak to bear heavy loads and an admission card was refused. In other cases, it turned out that the worker had been deceived by false promises and lured away from Singapore. If the coolies indicated that they would rather be sent back, their transfer to the panglong was prevented.

The admission cards were paid for by the licence-holder and the amount was recorded as a debt in the form of an advance on wages. In the past, these admission cards were not handed over to the workers concerned, because the panglong bosses were worried that they might try to run away if they got the chance. In many cases, the cards were stowed away by the kapalas. Sometimes some of the panglongs handed them over to the Chinese Wijkmeesters for safe keeping. Inspecting the admission cards enabled the Labour Inspectors to establish a worker's identity and to determine which workers had vanished from the scene. All sorts of iniquities were uncovered. On July 11, 1925, on panglong no. 6 on the Soengei Batang in the Indragiri Lowlands, none of the 24 workers present was in possession of an admission card. Towards the end of the inspection, an employee of the Chinese Wijkmeester in Prigi Radja brought along 18 cards. Eleven lacked the prescribed photo, so it was not possible in all cases to establish people's identity. This was all the more regrettable because a certain Leong Heng had been accused of murder and assault. Although Leong Heng was no longer working as mandur on that panglong, that same afternoon—after more than four hours travel over water—he was arrested on another panglong by the mantri police, accompanied by the Labour Inspector. In the meantime, he had changed his name to Leong Fok.

I will illustrate the way in which admission cards are tampered with by means of a single example. On panglong no. 4 on the Soengei Tjontjong, also in the Indragiri Lowlands, the coolie Koh Fok Tjoeng was given a card without a photo in the name of Lim Djioe. Since then, he has always been known as Lim Djioe.

In consultation with the local administration, it was decided that the admission cards would always be kept in the panglongs and in the possession of the workers themselves. Officials also provided the cards, where necessary, with photos.

The large number of workers who turned out not to have admission cards had usually been smuggled into the panglongs They were either hidden away aboard a big tongkang or designated as part of the crew, thus managing to bypass the officials involved. The Labour Inspectors noted in their reports the details of those not in possession of an admission card.

Coolie administration. Lists of coolies were found in almost all coolie quarters. These listed the names of the coolies and how many days they had worked. Keeping track of these coolie lists left much to be desired, even though a clerk was charged with keeping them up-to-date on almost every panglong. Often for days on end no record had been kept of who had worked. That would lead later to differences of opinion. The number of registered workers on the list rarely accorded with the actual number. Workers for whom no admission card had been requested, the seriously ill, and those who had something on their conscience or who the kapala might suspect would try to complain to visiting officials were not listed and were ordered into the jungle for the duration of official visits. When, on March 17, 1925, the Labour Inspector, accompanied by the senior police officer Hass and the Forestry Superintendent Borgman, visited panglong no. 24 on the island of Padang, the sixteen coolies listed were led before him. Despite the police's best efforts, no other workers were found in the jungle. Yet there were all kinds of clues—including the number of sleeping places in the kongsi house—to indicate the presence of more than sixteen workers In the panglong. After checking the wage records and making a few remarks, the officials left the panglong, in the firm belief that they had been deceived. But the Labour Inspector decided to return unexpectedly the next day. In consultation with the accompanying officials, he chose a time when the water would be at its lowest. Admittedly, they had to make their way through a few hundred metres of thick mud, but it turned out to have been worthwhile. A total of sixteen more workers were found in the jungle and a subsequent investigation revealed a further three. So instead of the sixteen on the coolie list, there were in fact 35!

A similar thing happened in the worst of all the panglongs, no. 49 on the Soengei Deling on the island of Tebing Tinggi. The coolie list contained only 21 names on April 29, 1925, but Superintendent De Vries, of Bengkalis, kept on turning up other workers in the jungle, and in the end 45 Chinese coolies were identified.

It would undoubtedly be going too far to record all the facts in this report. Let these few examples suffice.

No record was kept of deaths, illnesses, hospitalisation, and return by workers to Singapore, or of those who ran away from the panglong. On several occasions, it was found that changes had been made to lists shortly before inspection, with the ink still wet on the page. This would happen when the kapala saw the vessel approaching, or if he was warned in advance. Such was the case on May 11, 1925, at panglong no. 223 in the Bengkalis region. The kapala ordered Jip Keh to write in Chinese characters under his own name and that of Liong Heng: "Ran away." Under the name Tju Tjong was written: "Returned to Singapore." However, these coolies were found by the police in the jungle. Jip Keh had very serious untended leg wounds and the kapala wanted him kept from sight. The other two had no admission card.

Especially at the start of the panglong inspections, the coolie lists presented numerous riddles that it was necessary to solve, not just to determine the correct number of workers. Often, the lists brought all sorts of sad stories to light.

At the meetings with the licence holders and their representatives, we always insisted on filling in the coolie lists accurately, as required under the panglong regulations. A new model coolie list was designed and given to the panglongs to be implemented.

Because of the large number of panglongs, it is not possible to visit each of them again and again in the course of just a few month, but it was highly desirable given the amount of suffering that if a premise could not be visited, we should at least be kept abreast of the changes and movements among the coolies. The licensees were therefore asked to deliver a monthly report on workers' deaths to the Labour Inspector. By late 1926, such reports were being submitted fairly regularly.

Number of workers and their nationality. The number of workers on a panglong differs greatly from place to place. In general, it can be assumed that there are at least twenty coolies in sawmills and at least ten firewood collectors. The number of charcoal burners would vary between one and twelve. Usually present would also be: one kapala, one mandur, one cook, one sampan man, one tree feller, one sawyer, one bark stripper, one clerk, four sledway makers, and five haulers.

In the firewood section, most of the workers are sawyers and woodcutters. Here too, however, one cannot dispense with a kapala, a mandur, a cook, a sampan man, and a tree-feller. The greatest number of workers found in a single sawmill was 45; on a firewood panglong, 35.

In 1903, the then Assistant Resident of Bengkalis proposed setting a minimum number of workers for the sawmill, firewood, and charcoal panglongs at (respectively) 25, 10, and 5. Apparently there have been periods in which the average number of workers per sawmill was higher. Mr. W. J. Beek speaks of panglongs with twenty to sixty coolies. A letter from the Resident of Riau dated September 10, 1906, reports one panglong with 120 coolies.

Wholly reliable figures for the total number of panglong workers are not yet available. As long as not all panglongs provide the necessary information, this will remain so.

The total number of panglongs in 1924 and 1925 was 392 and 379 respectively, with totals of 2476 and 2274 workers respectively. In the 110 enterprises inspected by the Labour Inspectorate in 1925, those employed included 1794 Chinese, 24 Malays, 10 Malay women, and 5 Malay children. In 1926, on the 147 panglongs inspected, there were 2084 Chinese and 56 Malays. Several Chinese workers were found who had worked on the panglong for 10, 15, 20, or more years consecutively. Most no longer had any desire to leave the panglong. As long as they could get enough opium every day, they were satisfied.

In 1925, a few young boys were found on some of the panglongs who did not work but served unspecified purposes. With the assistance of the administrative officers and the Consul-General of the Netherlands in Singapore, a couple of the boys were returned to their families; others claimed to have lost their parents or not to know where they were. In 1926, there were no longer any under-age Chinese on the panglongs.

Nearly all the workers employed on the panglongs are Chinese. They belong to the Kongfu [Guangfu], Keh [Hakka], and Hokkien tribes. They also come from Hainan, Chaozhou, and Luzhou. On panglongs where only Kongfu men worked, not much wrongdoing came to light during inspections and there were fewer complaints than on panglongs with workers from different tribes, or with kapalas of the Hokkien tribe.

On one sawmill in the Lingga department and on one firewood panglong on the Indragiri River, Malays were also found. These people—more commonly known as orang laut, "ocean people"—live in groups in oddly shaped sampans with high sterns. These nomadic people, who according to Mr. J. Beek are also known as pesukus and orang-mantang, are only 500 in number and live mainly by catching fish. Occasionally they agree for a certain sum of money to haul out the trees that the Chinese have felled. The women and children help in this work, although their participation is inappropriate. Some years ago, this Malay people carried out heavy hauling work on the panglongs in Lingga.

Mr. S. said of it:

> It is strange that a heathen fishing folk, uncivilised, living on sampans, in which they are born, marry, and die, are attracted to the idea of dragging heavy tree trunks out of the jungle and that women and children, driven by a sense of togetherness, cooperate in that work.

On the panglongs where Malays work alongside Chinese, Malay is gradually becoming the spoken language. On panglongs worked exclusively by Chinese, it is rarely the case that anyone can speak any language apart from one or two Chinese dialects. Malay will not get you work on a panglong. In the places where Chinese workers of different tribes are employed, it is often the case that, for example, a Hainanese cannot make himself understood to workers from another tribe. Only after a long time do they stitch together a mishmash of Chinese dialects that is intelligible to all.

Mutual relations on the panglongs. It is easy to understand that on many panglongs relationships cannot be called rosy. On panglongs where all the workers are from the same tribe, people get along. Usually, the workers are divided into three groups. The kapala needs a few helpers to maintain his authority. The mandur, the cook, the clerk, and the sampan man are often included among his friends. The activities of these people are such that they have much free time and can get together with the kapala in the kongsi house. At random times of the day, when everyone else is at work in the jungle, this group can often be found in the bangsal. The second group consists of the tree fellers, the sawyers, the bark removers, and the sledway runners. The haulers, who are immediately recognisable because of their youthfulness, shyness, and many leg wounds, make up the third group. The same division applies in the case of firewood collectors, with this difference: the third group is formed by the sawyers and tree fellers and the second group does not exist on the smaller firewood panglongs. These divisions are reflected in eating and sleeping arrangements.

So as not to interrupt the course of events in the panglongs with time-consuming inspections, inspections were deliberately suspended during meal breaks. As a result, the standard of nutrition could also be inspected.

The food is prepared in the same kitchen for one and all and by the same cook. However, it was clear from repeated careful inspections that the number of side dishes differed. The first group, consisting of 4, 5, or 6 men, received the same amount of fish or meat with the rice as the third group, which usually consisted of up to ten or more coolies. The kapala had access to chickens and pigs and sometimes to a vegetable garden. His friends were never short of anything. For the ordinary coolies, however, often no fresh vegetables were available. Their tea was of inferior quality.

As already mentioned, the sleeping-places of the kapala and his group are located in the middle of the bangsal in a closed-off area, with much of the character of a room. The kapala, mandur, cook, and sampan man each has his own separate bed. The other sleeping places are arranged on either side of the kongsi house along the thatched wall, where rain and wind can easily get in. The front section, which is easily accessible, belongs to the sledway makers and their friends. The beam haulers, sawyers, and tree fellers sleep towards the back of the bangsal. The sinkehs are confined to the least pleasant parts of the complex. Comradeship is found only among men from the same group and then, preferably, from the same tribe. It is striking that less abuse occurs among people of the same tribe.

Panglong discipline. Many panglongs have written regulations that are strictly enforced by the kapala and his accomplices. Violations are punished by fines and canings.

In the near past, one of the most general rules was that when a worker missed a day at work, for whatever reason, $0.20 of his wages were docked for each day's absence. For longer absences, the penalty increased: the supply of food ceased altogether and the man was sent into the jungle. In such cases, coolies of the same group sometimes kept some food from their own rations and took it out to him. If he was ill, sometimes his friends would make him a thatched shelter in the jungle.

Several workers complained that if the kapala or mandur thought someone had not worked hard enough, that person's wages would be cut as a punishment by an amount equal to the price of 2, 4, or 5 mata of opium [one-half mata = 193 milligrams]. The opium was then shared among the kapala's friends.

According to a note displayed in one bangsal, in Chinese characters, coolies were required to stack the firewood in designated places. If this rule was violated, the culprit was fined 2 mata of opium. In another panglong, the coolies had to store away their tools after returning home from work. Neglect of this rule led to a $5 fine. The same punishment—often equal to a whole month's wages—befell coolies who forgot to take tea into the jungle when it was their turn to do so.

In addition to these written regulations, $3, $5, or $10 were docked from the wages of those who ran away and were then brought back.

Much more serious, however, were the punishments that were not written down.

On panglong no. 1 on the Kateman River, the following drama unfolded. Two coolies had complained about a number of things to the Amir, the District Chief, when he visited the panglong. One evening, the two coolies were awakened by the licence holder Go Ghi—one of the few panglong owners who himself lived on the panglong, together with his brother, the kapala Go Long, and a mandur. The two coolies were told that they had to go to buy chickens. In the sampan, which was moored near the jetty, they were strapped onto bags of sand and thrown overboard a short distance from the panglong. Some of the coolies on the jetty saw this happen. One of them had heard the assault was being planned beforehand in the kapala's room. He had then gone to the place where the two unfortunates were sleeping and advised them to flee. The two coolies replied that they didn't know where to go. In the jungle they would die of hunger or be eaten by tigers. Fully aware of what awaited them, they accompanied their cruel bosses without resistance and were drowned in the Kateman River. This happened because they had dared to speak out. It was meant as a warning to the rest. None of the workers ever mentioned what happened. The coolie Jau Tiem only told the Labour Inspectors after he was certain that he would never have to return to the panglong. This sort of intimidation happens on many panglongs. The main culprit died in 1925 in prison in Tandjong Balei (Karimoen). The other two were sentenced to twenty years in jail by the Landraad.

I have already mentioned that returned deserters had to pay a certain sum by way of punishment. Attempting to escape also led to harsh corporal punishment. On April 29, 1925, Oei Tie, a coolie of panglong no. 49 in the Bengkalis region, revealed that a month earlier, in the morning, he had put on a jacket before going to work. This led the clerk A Tjoe to suspect that he was planning to flee. The clerk seized him and brought him before the assistant kapala Tang Wo, who had already behaved brutishly on this panglong on several previous occasions. While Tang Wo was beating him up, the krani A Tjoe fetched a piece of burning wood from the kitchen and prodded Oei Tie with it. During a subsequent inspection, the Labour Inspector counted 24 scars on the arms, back, chest, and shoulders of this worker. When runaway coolies were returned they were commonly beaten by the kapala or mandur. In the case of a repeated attempt to escape, it was customary in some panglongs for all the coolies to cane the would-be fugitive. Everyone joined in, because they knew that the same fate awaited them if they didn't. A third attempt to abscond from the panglong would often lead to a beating that left the victim unconscious or dead.

Before being beaten, "culprits" were often bound hand and foot to a pole. On some panglongs, they were hung up by ropes so that they could just touch the ground with their toes, with their hands tied behind their backs, and hoisted upwards, so that they were forced into a bowing posture.

In 1923, Ma Tjam of panglong no. 49 (in Bengkalis) fled for the third time. He had complained about his employer after arriving at Selat Pandjang. He was summoned to Selat Pandjang and the complaint was heard by the controleur. Then he and the controleur returned to the panglong. On the same day, Ma Tjam was called in by the assistant kapala, the clerk, and the sampan man, bound by his hands, and strung up. He was then beaten with sticks until he died. In February 1924, a certain Fong Sam was strung up by the same clerk and sampan man in the morning and left there until about 11 pm. Then he was hanged and beaten to death.

Many crimes have taken place on this panglong in the course of just a few years. The licensee Oei Tiau Hoat was present at some of these occurrences and had ordered the atrocities. The Labour Inspector was alerted to events on this panglong by a Chinese in Selat Pandjang on the evening of April 28, 1925. In the company of a forestry official from Bengkalis, Mr. Vincent, and the Police Overseer, Mr. De Vries, and some other police officers, the inspector made his way as quickly as possible to the sawmill. During the night, a vessel was made ready. On the morning of April 29, after a difficult trip, they reached the panglong, on the Soengei Djeling. The taukeh was present on the panglong and tried with the help of his clerk to mislead the officials. However, after a tireless search, the police found more and more coolies deep in the jungle.

Almost from the start, coolies said they were pleased that the Labour Inspector had come to the panglong. Until then, they said, no one had ever been there. They gave a lot of information about nutrition, location, wages, debts, medical treatment, etc.. They had much to say. While the coolies were sitting on the ground in the bangsal, suddenly Tan A Tjoi jumped up. Nervously, he asked permission in poor Malay to be allowed to say what he knew. He told of a large number of assaults and murders. At the end of his story, he begged to be allowed to leave the panglong—otherwise he would also be killed.

One of the witnesses mentioned by Tan A Tjoi recalled ten deaths, either murders or cases of sick coolies left to die in the jungle.

The search for workers hidden in the jungle went on for so long that it was not until dusk that the inspector departed. The taukeh, the assistant kapala, the clerk, and the sampan man were arrested and taken to Selat Pandjang together with witnesses.

The assistant kapala, the clerk, and the sampan man were taken to prison. The panglong owner was also imprisoned for several years. While in prison, he fell sick and was taken to the hospital, from where he managed to flee. He presumably went to China by way of Siam.

Although a connection cannot be proven, it is nevertheless worth noting that the Chinese who told the Labour Inspector about the panglong was axed to death a few days later in front of his home in Selat Pandjang.

Canes were not always used in beatings. Heavy pieces of wood, axe hafts, or pieces of iron were sometimes used. Preferably victims were beaten on the liver and in the spleen area.

When on March 22, 1925, the coolie Ma Khoe from panglong no. 263 ended up in hospital in Selat Pandjang, in a pitiful condition, he recounted what had happened to him on the panglong. He had been strung up from a beam in the roof of the kongsi house by a thick rope round his neck. He was then beaten with an iron rod while naked. His neck continued to show clear traces of the rope and his body was scarred all over.

In 1925, nearly all the panglongs visited by the Labour Inspectorate were places of ill repute or located in places that were hard to reach. The worst panglongs were in the Bengkalis region. The panglongs on private concessions were no exception to that rule. There were many allegations of deprivations of liberty, beatings, and murders

Results of inspections. Very rarely did coolies launch into complaints immediately the inspectors arrived. Only when it became clear to them what sorts of questions were being raised did they gain a certain confidence in the officials and their tongues begin to wag. From all that has been said, it will be clear that sawmill workers, haulers, and workers on the firewood panglongs suffered the most from the actions of their relentless and hard-hearted bosses. Experience taught the Labour Inspectorate how best to organise an inspection. Although there were some deviations from this routine, inspections were usually conducted in the following way.

To prevent the kapala and his cronies from taking measures to hide matters from the inspector, by telling workers what to say or hiding workers in the jungle and hiding the pay books and the admission cards of workers who had disappeared from the panglong, the vessel would anchor as far away as possible from the premises so that it could not be seen. The rest of the journey would be undertaken in a sloop. The police hurried as quickly as possible to the bangsal. The Labour Inspector started by asking questions about the number of workers and of the sick and deserters. Meanwhile, the bangsal was inspected and the stock of medicines and food was checked. The prices of articles that the coolies could buy from the kapala were also checked.

Sometimes a coolie was found asleep whose appearance or injuries attracted attention. A gesture in the direction of the kapala or mandur was often the point of departure for an investigation.

During the initial inspections, a special method was used to summon the coolies from the jungle. The kapala would fetch an empty bottle, smash the bottom off it, and call out a few times through it in the direction of the workers. Sometimes more than an hour passed before the first workers started trickling into the kongsi house. However, it soon became obvious time and again that not all the workers would turn up at the kapala's signal, so the method was discontinued. The police were asked to fetch the workers instead. A few native policemen stayed behind in the bangsal to keep an eye on those already gathered there. In the meantime, the Labour Inspector went with his interpreter to meet the coolies. If he came across a sledge along the way, he would ask how many loads its drivers had carried to the jetty that day and how many loads they had to transport in a single day. The aim was to make a rough calculation of the number of hours worked per day by the haulers. The answers they gave were vague and fearful. Yet the information was useful in regard to nutrition, working hours, the number of workers, and the number of sick.

When, on March 19, 1925, the Labour Inspector approached the bangsal on panglong no. 218, on the Soengei Duwa in Sumatra, the coolie Lok Jau stumbled out—already making sembah gestures from afar—to meet him. Lok Jau had a leg wound from his foot right up to his knee. He begged to be taken away. While the police were fetching the workers from the jungle, the Labour Inspector and his interpreter examined the stretch of jungle behind the bangsal. In a swampy spot under some nipa palms, the coolie Tjien Jie was found, almost incapacitated by a serious leg wound. He had been instructed by the kapala to hide in the jungle.

When the workers had all been brought together in the bangsal, they were told to fetch their payrolls, admission cards, and perhaps contracts. In that way, it soon became apparent who had the documents—the coolies, who would therefore be in a position to know the state of their wages, advances, and debts, or the kapala. The workers then gathered together in the front part of the coolie quarters. There were rarely enough chairs for them all, so they squatted on the ground. The interpreter of the Labour Inspectorate got the haulers, sawyers, and tree fellers to sit together. If the numbers did not tally, that was taken as an indication that workers were missing. Workers who shared sleeping places with one another were taken aside by the police and persuaded to point out where their comrades lay hidden or to tell the interpreter what had happened to them.

The kapala and his coolies were then informed of the officials' goal. The opportunity was also taken to explain the panglong regulations.

Each worker was asked how long he had been on the panglong, how many coolies he had come with, where they came from, and what their previous jobs had been. The pay books of all the workers present were checked. The coolies were asked what their wages were, what advance they had received, and what they owed. In the beginning, there were very few panglongs on which all the coolies knew the state of their debts and wages. Many were not in possession of a pay book. There were workers who had been working on the panglong for quite a few years but did not know what their pay was. In some cases one gained a strong impression that workers received no compensation for their labour other than board and lodging.

In the past, only total debts were recorded in the books, so it was impossible to find out how the debts had come about. Neither the workers nor the kapala were able to provide an adequate explanation. Finally, it transpired that there were quite a few cases of redemption fees paid by coolies who had escaped and been recaptured. The kapala confirmed that this was the case, as if it were the most logical thing in the world. In very many cases it cost little effort to discover from where and by whom a coolie had been brought back to the panglong. As soon as the labourer gained in trust and confidence, he would begin to explain why he had run away. Gradually complaints and grievances began to flood in. We found out how much opium the coolies consumed each day. Even coolies who did not themselves use opium had entries for opium in their pay books. This turned out to be the result of a fines system applied on the panglong.

Coolies' answers often prompted further questions, leading to an ever greater insight into the conditions prevailing on the panglongs. In this way, the following crimes came to light.

On panglong no. 235 on the island of Tebing Tinggi, the coolie Wang Lie Lie complained on March 20, 1925, that he was often beaten with a piece of wood by the mandur Oie Boen, and had scars on his back, stomach, chest, and head to prove it. He had last been assaulted on March 16, 1925, and had fresh scars on his back. Oei Boen confessed to having committed the assaults, and said he had done so every time Wang Lie Lie had stopped hauling logs.

The panglong bosses acted as their own judges in everything. On panglong no. 85, also located on Tebing Tinggi, the workers Tjan Tau and Lau A Fok were suspected of having stolen a ring. Instead of submitting a complaint to the competent authority, the kapala took things into his own hands. Three weeks before an inspection on March 19, 1925, the two suspects were beaten up on the orders of the kapala Lie Heng and the mandurs Lie Jie and Liong Kwai and tied with ropes. The sampan men An Beng and Lie Boen Liong were told to take the two coolies into the jungle. However, the sampan men thought it would be a good idea to take the two men to panglong no. 82 in the hope of selling them for "opium money." The kapala of the panglong didn't want to keep them, because it was clear that they would not be able to work for a while. Without offering them help or food, he dispatched them into the jungle. Although on the evening of the day of inspection searchers tried to find the two coolies, one of them was not found until the next morning, on panglong no. 140 on Soengei Keboelet. Lan A Fok was more dead than alive and seemed to be in a lot of pain, due to a large purulent wound in the middle of his chest. As for Tjan Tau, he was never heard of again.

Panglong no. 140 was therefore visited on March 20, 1925. There were eight young coolies, who were not in debt and had already on several occasions asked the owner to settle up. They wanted to leave the panglong. Each time the settlement was postponed. Because the licence holder lived in Selat Pandjang, these workers took their settlement books to the controleur. He provided all the assistance he could. The coolies managed to get off the panglong and received their money in Selat Pandjang.

On panglong no. 218, several coolies claimed to have been repeatedly beaten with canes by the kapala and the mandur. So Sieuw, who was about 15 years old, bore obvious scars. Liong Tjoi had also recently been beaten and had welts on his body and even grooves in his flesh. The rattan with which he had been beaten, and which had been wrapped around with pieces of string by the kapala, was shown as evidence. In October 1924 the worker Tjong Jie was beaten to death by the mandur Seng Tjung because he was too ill to work. The current kapala and one of the other coolies were given a reward of $1.50 for burying the corpse.

When on May 1, 1925, the coolies on panglong no. 139 (Padang Island) were asked whether any workers on the enterprise had died, it fell quiet in the bangsal. The question was repeated by the interpreter, but still there was no answer. Then the question was put to Lie Sim. He turned his head, hid his face in his arms. and began to weep. Then the question was put to Ng Hiat. He started shouting. The subsequent investigation brought to light the following information from the coolies.

In December 1924, the coolies Lian Wah and Tai Hak fell ill and died of neglect. In early 1925, Wong Man was maltreated and died shortly afterwards.

Afraid of beatings, the coolies dared not tell the judge what they knew. Trials were therefore made impossible. In the meantime, the panglong bosses were given the opportunity to make witnesses disappear, an opportunity that they did not waste.

A murder case was already under investigation at Selat Pandjang regarding panglong no. 15 on the island of Tebing Tinggi. The coolie Ng A Bie was heard as a witness, but made only minor statements and had been sent back to the panglong. On April 28, 1925, this panglong was inspected, and Ng A Bie begged to be allowed to leave the panglong. He then announced that he had not previously told the whole truth, because he had been threatened. He said that in June 1924 the coolie Lie Jong had run away from the panglong but had been brought back by one of the Malays called Momin, from Serapong. On his return he was tied up with a rope. That evening, at about 7 pm, he was beaten with axe hafts by Tjoei Lin, on his chest and belly. Lie Jong fainted and was taken by the three thugs to an abandoned Malay house. The three executioners went to the bangsal the next morning and told people that Lie Jong was dead.

The more the investigation on panglong no. 9 progressed, the more nervous the kapala Liong Jie became. At one point, he fled into the woods, where the police were unable to find him. He was arrested the next morning by two policemen. In its reports, the Labour Inspectorate noted the following regarding conditions on the panglong.

Two months before the inspection, Tjan Jie was kicked and beaten by the mandur Wong Tak with a piece of wood. He died the following day from his injuries. After hearing testimony from witnesses, Wong Tak said in the presence of the forestry official and the police superintendent that what the coolies said was true.

In late 1924, the son of the kapala, Liong Hok, beat the coolie Tjong Song to death. The perpetrator was said to have fled to Singapore. A few months later, the brute was tracked down to panglong no. 1 on the Kaleman River and handed over to the magistrate.

The coolies Wong Tjie and Tjan Pat accused the mandur Wong Tak of a terrible crime. In October 1924, he had he cut off Lau Sung's hand and Lau Sung had died as a result of the heavy bleeding. Wang Tak confessed.

Some twenty days before the inspection, Kwan Thong and Lie Tjoi were seriously ill. They were not given medicine and they died. Another sick coolie was taken into the jungle and also died. Two coolies on the panglong were ordered to bury the three corpses.

Just two days before the inspection, Wong Kie was struck on his buttocks with the blade of an axe. He had put a filthy plaster on the wound. No bandages were provided.

On panglong no. 248 on May 6, 1925, all kinds of complaints were heard. Lie Kiat said he was 67 years old and no longer able to perform heavy work. He had repeatedly requested to be allowed to leave the panglong. His requests were not met.

Lie Soen was punched and beaten with the handle of a knife by the kapala Koh Tjoan a month before the inspection. The kapala, becoming more and more agitated, finally struck him with the knife between the ribs on the left side.

Six workers reported that five coolies had been mistreated the previous year and had died immediately or soon afterwards. The main culprit was said to be the kapala Wong Boen, who no longer worked on the panglong. He was later arrested by the police superintendent De Vries on a nearby panglong on Tebing Tinggi Island.

The coolies on panglong no. 60 saw an opportunity during the inspection to whisper to the interpreter that Lie Fok and Loei Tjeng were hiding in the jungle. They had been mistreated and had fled in fear into the jungle. However, every evening they came into the bangsal to get food, which their comrades took for them.

In August 1924, Ng Tjan was tied up by the assistant kapala, strung up from a beam, and beaten with a piece of wood. Then he was taken into the jungle, from where he never returned.

The great number of beatings on this panglong led to further enquiries about Tjan Kai's whereabouts. On the coolie list under his name the kapala had written "run away." In response to questions, some of the coolies said that Tjan Kai had been beaten several times with a large stick by the mandur Wong Ka in March 1925. One afternoon, the abuse was repeated in the jungle. Tjan Kai was left at the place where this happened and was dead the next morning. Liong Kwai, who buried him, said that his chest, liver, and spleen were severely damaged.

These atrocities demonstrate what the workers on the panglongs had to endure from their bosses and the mandurs. That there are cases in which coolies took revenge on the panglong bosses and their friends for past assaults is hardly surprising.

On October 27, 1924, *Bataviaasch Nieuwsblad* carried a "Short Report from Riau" that made mention of a drama that arose on the night of July 18–19 of said year on the Tjiang Seng panglong in the Indragiri Lowlands. In a fight in the sawmill, three Chinese lost their lives and one was badly injured. An investigation showed that the coolies joined forces against the kapala and his cronies because they were constantly maltreated and forced to do hard labour. After the fight, they went to Prigi Radja in a sampan and told the Chinese Wijkmeester what had happened.

There were also occasions during the inspections when a coolie could contain himself no longer in front of the officials and would throw himself on his extortioner. On a panglong on the Kampar River, in the presence of the police superintendent, a coolie hit a mandur with an axe. The culprit was immediately arrested. The mandur was taken to hospital in Selat Pandjang, but soon died.

On panglong no. 3 on the Kateman River, while the Labour Inspector was busy checking the pay books, a fight broke out between two workers. When they had calmed down, they were asked the cause of the fight. It turned out that one of the sledge workers had been working on a panglong in Bengkalis department since the beginning of 1925 and returned to Singapore when the company closed due to bad market conditions. In Singapore, he had persuaded a young Chinese who was out of work to go with him to a panglong. Once they arrived at the panglong, the sinkeh was bitterly disappointed. At the inspection it turned out that that the recruiter had been familiar with conditions on the panglongs and had even worked in a sawmill that had to close due to serious crimes. It was clear to the sinkeh that his guide had known beforehand what misery awaited the sinkeh. He could not contain himself and fell upon the man who was the cause of his misfortune.

On panglong no. 14 during an inspection, a coolie grabbed a bamboo pipe and hit the mandur with it, wounding him in the head. He did this because he had been beaten by the mandur.

Apart from the improvements that were necessary in regard to employment conditions, the aim of the Labour Inspectorate was, with the help of the colonial Civil Service and the police, to put an end to such atrocities. Gradually the number of complaints regarding assaults decreased, while murders and misdeeds are now brought to light sooner as a result of the regular visits paid by officials of the government, the Forestry Commission, and the Labour Inspectorate.

In the first half of 1925, it became clear that an end had to be put to the recapture and return of fugitive workers. It is true that the coolies often gave information about the Malays who carried out the captures, but what they reported was often so vague that it was impossible to take measures on the basis of it. Moreover, witnesses could rarely be traced. The impression seemed to be that the Malay population was acting in good faith. All they knew was that the panglong coolies had a connection with their employers and therefore had to be returned to the company. Some lower-level officials in government service, sanpan men, jungle wardens, and customs men were also acting in good faith and saw nothing wrong with getting a reward for the return of panglong coolies. The panglong bosses had spread that idea over a number of years, and had offered rewards on all sides. The photos of runaway workers were shown around. The kapala of panglong no. 4 on Rangsang Island had managed to retrieve 25 runaway coolies.

Mr. Snellen van Vollenhoven mentioned in his report of May 1919 that the administration should try to get the Malays to stop bringing runaway workers back to the panglong and to hand them over to the authorities instead. This matter was raised by the Labour Inspectorate, with the result that the Resident of Riau, the Assistant Resident of Bengkalis, and the forestry officer in Tandjong Pinang took the matter in hand.

The matter was also raised at the meetings of licence holders and their representatives. It was pointed out that workers should not be kept on the panglongs against their will, and that workers who wished to leave the company due to dismissal, illness, or any other valid reason should be given access to an adequate means of transport by water back to the place where they had first been taken into service.

However, at the aforementioned meetings with panglong owners it became clear that some of the violations of the provisions of the panglong regulations were the result of unfamiliarity. To ensure that improvements on the panglongs—including on private concessions—were vigorously enforced, the heads of the Labour Bureau and the Labour Inspectorate toured Bengkalis in August 1925 and visited several panglongs, including the aforementioned panglong no. 9, where a few months earlier such terrible conditions had been discovered. Improvements in housing, nutrition, and medical care were in evidence. No complaints of abuse were heard.

Chapter 5. Working Hours

For the kapala, the mandurs, the tree fellers, the sawyers, the cooks, and the sampan rowers, there are no set working hours on the panglongs. The tree-fellers chop down some forest giants and the haulers do the rest of the work. The firewood men set to work under the eye of the kapala and the mandurs, while the tree fellers rest. The sledway builders, on the other hand, work as long as the sun is up.

The log haulers on the balalongs and the sawyers and hackers on the firewood panglongs used to have to work excessively long hours. Fellers were woken at 4 am, so that they could be in the jungle at the latest by daybreak, at the spot they had reached the evening before.

The coolies were often rudely awakened. On panglong no. 174 on the north coast of Rangsang Island, one coolie said in a report that a man who was not awake in the morning was pulled out of bed by his legs by the mandur so that he fell with his head on the ground and ripped his thumb open on a nail. As a result, he was unable to work for several days.

Work started at the latest at half past five in the morning and lasted until about 11 am or 12 noon, when there was a short break—usually half an hour—for the midday meal. Work then continued for at least 6 hours, often until 7, 8, and 9 pm. If the moon was full, they worked well into the night. This was especially the case on the firewood panglongs, where the sawyers and hackers were paid by result. Moreover, the kapalas promised the workers a reward if they exceeded the prescribed minimum. They were often beaten into submission.

Complaints were frequently heard about 12, 14, and 16-hour working days. When the tongkang sailed up to the front of the panglong and there was enough wood to fill it, even rest hours were ignored. Under normal circumstances, the haulers were told how many loads to take to the drop-off point. This depended on the distance from the felling site to the jetty. On some panglongs, one sledge of timber had to be transported between 10 and 14 times a day. There were cases where a distance of some three kilometres had to be covered twenty times a day, including ten times with a full load of timber.

If a tongkang was moored away from the jetty, the floaters, depending on the state of the water, had to float the timber over to the ship. As a rule, these people worked only a few days a month.

For the majority of coolies, there was no regulation regarding working hours in early 1925. The Labour Inspectorate attempted to improve the situation. During inspections and at meetings with the taukehs and kapalas, inspectors urged them to abolish night work and arrange for work to take place from 6 am to 11 am and again from 1 pm to 6 pm. The 10-hour working day is sometimes secretly exceeded, but it is now generally observed, at least in Riau.

During the early inspections, it became apparent that on the less bad panglongs it was customary to take half a day off every fourth day. In view of the hard work, that arrangement was considered preferable to one whole day off per week. This scheme was gradually introduced on all panglongs. No complaints were ever heard from charcoal burners about working hours.

Wages and debts. Before 1925, there was no question of a regular—and often even of irregular—payment of wages. Workers had been promised a certain wage per month, but payment almost never happened. On arrival at the panglong, the worker was deeply in debt to his employer. The costs of board and lodging while waiting in Singapore, transport to the panglong, and the cost of an admission card had all been charged to him. On panglong no. 52 on the Soengei Langkat on the island of Tebing Tinggi, visited on August 13, 1925, by the heads of the Labour Bureau and the Labour Inspectorate, three boys newly arrived from China were found who said when questioned that they had been abducted in the interior and then shipped from Hong Kong to Singapore. They were charged $55 for the transportation.

The aim was not so much to get the worker to repay all the expenses incurred as to keep him for as long as possible in debt, for it seemed generally accepted that as long as he remained in debt, he would not be allowed to leave the panglong. Given this intention, it is obvious that the employers or their representatives (the kapalas) would do everything possible to keep the coolies in debt. For the kapalas, this was also a welcome opportunity to sell provisions and thus increase their own income in various ways. They are after all the suppliers of clothing, mats, suitcases, sugar, milk, tobacco, cigarettes, biscuits, tins of fish, and opium. The cost of all these things was added as part of the so-called advance and deducted from the anyway low wages. So for one reason and another, the workers never got their hands on any money. They were usually not sufficiently educated to manage their own accounts. When the desire to get away from the panglong grew and they enquired about what was due to them, they were simply told the amount that they continued to owe their bosses. The kapala and the clerk knew how to draw maximum benefit from the advances and in recording the prices of purchased items. The workers were often unable to remember how much opium, sugar, or other items they had consumed. Such was most certainly the case when the kapala or his clerk failed to keep proper records for months on end.

Many workers were unable to say what their wages and debts were when asked. To the extent that there were pay books (tsoentoe) on the panglongs, only the totals were given, including of all the items bought by the coolies together with possible recapture fees (*opvatloon*) and fines. There was no way of knowing what and how much the worker had actually bought. It was equally difficult to keep track of the wages earned by the coolie, because bookkeeping was irregular and incomplete. If the kapala and the coolie succeeded in agreeing on the number of days worked by the latter in a given month, it often turned out that a certain amount was still deducted from the wages for food consumed on days when no work was done. If we add that in the case of haulers, sawyers, and hackers wages were initially almost never higher than $6 to $7 a month and that for days on which no work was done 20 or 25 cent were often withheld, it is obvious that in times of illness the coolies fell deeper and deeper into debt. For example, a worker who had not been able to work for 10 days received a wage of 20/30 x \$6 = \$4. If, on top of this, 10 times \$0.20 was withheld for food received during the period of illness, the amount left was only \$2, which was often not enough to pay for the opium consumed.

By strictly adhering to the regulations, whereby pay books had to be given to the worker rather kept by the kapala and had to be kept daily and settled monthly, a great improvement quickly came about in this matter. A statement would be made on the occasion of an initial inspection or meeting. If on a repeat visit to the panglong it was found that some workers were still without pay books, a summons would be issued against the licence holder or his representative. Now that a large number of panglongs have already been inspected more than once, the coolies themselves bring their pay books to the inspector, because they know that they will always be requested. Because of the system of daily updating of the books, the origin and course of debts can always be checked and it is also possible to prevent the kapala from charging excessively high prices for the articles he sells. To make checking even easier, the pay books on all panglongs have to conform to a model, already in use in the majority of companies.

Wages on panglongs are calculated in Straits dollars. The wages of the kapalas vary, from \$25 to \$75 a month. Once in a while the kapala gets a share of the profit. The wages of the assistant kapalas and the mandurs are from \$15 up to \$45 a month.

The wages of the tree fellers, sawyers, and tree trimmers are usually calculated according to the tonnage of timber delivered. They receive from \$0.12 to \$0.16 per ton. In general, they deliver at least 100 tons a month. A few tree fellers are on a fixed monthly wage, which rarely exceeds \$18.

Haulers' wages were initially low. In 1925, on the panglongs visited, 516 haulers were employed at 50 sawmills. They received the following monthly wages (in \$):

6.50	7.—	7.50	8.—	8.50	9.—	9.50	10.—	10.50	11.—	11.50	12.—	12.50	13.—	13.50	14.—	14.50	15.—	16.—	17.—	18.—
2	22	31	54	17	67	8	74	18	49	10	65	26	23	2	22	2	13	3	1	7

These wages have gradually increased. Wages less than $10 per month are no longer to be found.

The sledway workers were in a slightly more favourable position. The same 50 sawmills employed 232 trackway makers. They earned per month:

8.—	8.50	9.—	10.—	10.50	11.—	12.—	12.50	13.—	14.—	14.50	15.—	15.50	16.—	16.50	17.—	17.50	18.—	19.—	20.—	22.—	24.—	25.—	30.—
3	1	3	7	2	8	14	5	18	18	2	42	2	33	3	14	1	16	7	21	6	1	4	1

On firewood panglongs, wages are often based on the quantity of firewood delivered by other workers. A worker is paid $2 for 10,000 pieces of firewood. While this worker is dependent on the efforts of other coolies, he often helps the kapala carry out tasks of supervision.

The sawyers and tree fellers are on piece work. Two sawyers are usually paid $0.25 for 850 logs sawn per man. The loggers also receive $0.25, for 650 logs. These are the quantities that such workers can, under normal circumstances, deliver in the course of a 10-hour day. For larger quantities—usually above 20,000 pieces of firewood a month—a premium of $0.50 is often added.

In 1925, there were 152 sawyers and tree fellers on 17 firewood panglongs visited. The monthly wages were:

6.—	7.—	7.50	8.—	9.—	12.—	13.—	15.—	20.—	30.—
72	21	12	1	11	1	7	17	2	1

Incomes were especially low on firewood panglongs, where the workers—who depend on the tide—go looking for wood in sampans, in the course of which they lose much time. Some of these companies used to deduct $3 a month from wages for "sampan hire." On the insistence of the Labour Inspectorate, this no longer happens. The same applies to the $0.15 that sawyers had to pay every time their saw needed sharpening. The haulers use shoulder straps made of bark. Sinkehs are unable to make these straps, so it is always done by older coolies, who earn one or two matas of opium for this extra work. In the pay books, only the amount of opium is noted. These unlawful charges on workers' wages, including the amounts charged for recapture, were redressed during the inspections. It therefore often happened that instead of being in debt to the taukeh, the coolie could actually claim money back. On such occasions, often the coolie's first question was whether he could leave the panglong. Often, the kapala had too little money to make such payments. With the help of the Administrative Officers, such sums were recovered and given to the workers concerned. Sometimes, the coolies accepted rice and salted fish instead.

On several occasions, the accounts listed an amount — sometimes \$100 — sent to the coolie's relatives in China. However, there was never any evidence that this actually happened. There was never any acknowledgement from China that such an amount had been received.

The articles that the kapala sold to the coolies were over-charged. On some panglongs, the taukeh took care of the purchase of such goods in Singapore, for which the coolies placed an order with the taikong. The taukeh sent back the desired items on the next tongkang, together with a price list. The kapala often increased these prices, and relevant documents could never be found. Once, when the kapala claimed not to have documents in his possession, an armed police officer entered the bangsal holding the necessary papers, which the kapala had thrown through the window of the atap hall.

According to regulations, the employer was obliged, "in so far as is customary," to provide clothing for the workmen. However, this was nowhere mentioned in reports. The Labour Inspectors have so far not found a single panglong on which the workers receive free clothing. However, items of clothing were sent from Singapore at abnormally high prices.

Although nowadays almost all panglongs record wages appropriately, receipts and expenditures are given only as monthly totals and there is rarely any significant reduction in debt. Many coolies spend their whole wage—sometimes more than their wage—on opium, cigarettes, and tins of fish.

On some panglongs, debts were in excess of \$300, on others \$100–\$200. On only one panglong were the coolies not in debt. The coolies generally borrowed as much as possible. The bosses are—within limits—happy for this to happen, since it binds the workers to the panglong.

Only on one single panglong did the licence holder return to the workers the cost of their admission card after one year's work. After three years, the same taukeh wrote off his workers' debt so they could go to Singapore for a few weeks at their boss's expense.

On many occasions, workers complained that on arrival at the panglong they had had a ring, watch, chain, or the like and the kapala had taken it into "safe keeping." Usually this was denied by the panglong boss. In one case, there was a conviction for embezzlement—the kapala had taken a ring and sold it.

In general, the debts of workers who used opium were much higher than those of non-addicts. The situation on the private concessions was equally bad.

Average wages per month. Seven haulers on panglong no. 14 earned less than $10 a month. The pay books could not always be found. According to data from March 1927, panglong wages had gone up. Some panglongs could not be reached due to low water.

In June 1926, 20 panglongs run by the Sumatra Timber Company employed a total of 276 Chinese workers. The wages paid were between $11 and $50.

Workers employed on the charcoal ovens are often under contract. Most of these enterprises pay their workers from $0.70 to $1.20 per picul of charcoal. The workers who cut the wood receive a fixed monthly wage, which is usually low. At the request of the inspector, the wage was increased to $12 a month.

Some charcoal burners are paid by the number of times the furnace is filled. In 20–25 days, workers can earn between $28 and $40 or more. However, these people pay a certain amount—usually $2 a month—for the use of the oven. Unlike on all other panglongs, the workers take care of their own food. It is therefore necessary to take this into account when assessing wages.

The administration of wages on these panglongs left much to be desired. In early 1925, pay books were hardly anywhere in use. In that regard, an improvement can be seen. The debts on these panglongs are not as high as in the sawmills and the firewood sections.

Opium consumption. Opium consumption on the panglongs turned out after the first inspections to be greater than initially thought. While it was clear that opium was being smuggled in from Singapore, especially on the tongkangs, it was only after intensive inspection of wages and debts that the extent of the evil became generally known. On many occasions during inspections, illegally imported opium was discovered by the police.

In order to be able to trace the origins of the high level of workers' indebtedness, each worker was asked how much opium he used regularly. Having gained that information, tax administration improved and so did opium control, which resulted in a reduction in opium smuggling.

The vast majority of workers are addicted. The number of matas consumed per man per day varies from 1 to 6. As a rule, on arrival sinkehs are not yet addicted. However, they gradually become so. They are driven to it in all kinds of ways. The kapala has an interest in their addiction. Often they increase the official price by a few cents, for example, from 20 to 28 cents per mata. This price increase was prohibited by the Labour Inspectorate. Young Chinese who did not use opium were laughed at by their companions and urged to use it. It was never long before they gave in, in order to forget the misery around them for just a few moments. However, one mata a day was soon not enough. Many coolies spend more than their monthly wage on opium. The longer they stay on the panglong, the greater their debt, so that the prospect of a better life grows ever dimmer. They then seek their solace in the "Kraut Vergessenheit" (the herb of oblivion).

If you enter a bangsal on a day when the coolies have time off, you will find most of them on their beds preparing to preheat the pipe in the flame of a small lamp. They will not bestow on you even a second glance. Some are so addicted to opium that they skip meals. When workers were called in from the jungle for an inspection, they immediately started smoking. When coolies for some reason were arrested by the police, they first went to ask the kapala for opium. Conversely, opium can be used to buy silence from witnesses. The large number of matas given to coolies before burying their dead comrades sometimes suggested a clue to the direction that an investigation should follow, for burying a coolie who had died of a disease seldom yielded more than 3 or 5 matas of opium for those wielding the shovels.

Once when the kapala was arrested and he handed the supply of opium to the mandur who stayed behind on the panglong, the mandur was attacked by the coolies and a fight ensued while the officials were still in the bangsal. The police restored order.

Among younger Chinese, more and more people are gradually resisting the urge to smoke. Some coolies gave up altogether after spending time in hospital. In 1926–1927, seven panglongs were found to be opium-free.

Nutrition. In accordance with regulations, workers must be provided with free food. This is indeed what happens on most panglongs. There were only a small number of logging stations where the workers had to provide for themselves. You could usually purchase foodstuffs from the kapala, but for that the coolies had to pay a certain amount per month. Such was the case on panglongs where everyone was on borongan (piece work). On these sites, the coolies either cooked for themselves or paid a cook. On most panglongs, however, one of the coolies was appointed as cook; he received his wages from the licence holder.

Previously, a certain amount—usually 20 cents—was deducted from wages to pay for food on days off or while sick, i.e., in general on non-working days. Charging for food during illnesses was brought to an end by the Labour Inspectorate. All workers are now aware that this charge is contrary to regulations. Now very few panglongs deduct such a charge.

In normal circumstances, the quantity of food is acceptable. The cook prepares more than the workers need. Usually there is enough rice and vegetables to accompany the unsalted fish. Nevertheless, complaints were repeatedly made about a shortage of food. The reason was that the licence holders in Singapore always used to wait for the tongkang to fetch timber from the panglong before sending just enough food to last until the next boat left for the panglong. Sometimes, delays in Singapore or en route due to storms meant that the tongkang arrived late at the panglong, so that for a few days there was too little food to go round. The same happened when the licence holder lacked capital or ran into financial difficulties. The kapalas never had enough money to hand, and anyway it would be too much trouble to get money from the licence holder or to sail to Bengkalis or Selat Pandjang to buy provisions. Such a journey could take days, so they preferred to wait for the tongkang. On panglong no. 140, on one occasion the coolies had to wait two weeks for food to arrive. A storm had driven the tongkang back to Singapore. There was enough in stock for those on the panglong to hold out. However, it was often the case on inspections that the stock of food available was found to be insufficient. On one panglong there was not a single grain of rice. A general instruction therefore went out that enough food for one month should be available on the panglong.

If the quantity of food was sometimes a concern, its quality was even more so. Usually the rice was of poor quality, served with dried or salted vegetables. The very large number of coolies suffering from beriberi pointed to a vitamin deficiency. After consultations with doctors present in the panglong region, panglongs were instructed to provide katjang-idjoe (green beans) twice a week, on Wednesday and Saturday afternoon.

Coolies on all the panglongs now receive three meals a day, of which at least two are of rice with other food and one is porridge. Some of the better panglongs occasionally serve pork or chicken or duck. Even fresh eggs and tinned fish (sardines and salmon) is sometimes provided. Pork is served almost everywhere on Chinese holidays. Chickens, ducks, and pigs are raised on many panglongs.

In order to diversify and improve the provision of vegetables, the panglong bosses are encouraged to allow gardens. This has happened on several panglongs, but few crops thrive well in the acidic soil. Within the East Indies, import without prior inspection is allowed in the case of endives, beet, garlic, cabbage, lettuce, carrots, leeks, spinach, cress, onions, and sorrel.

On most panglongs, the drinking water is brackish and unusable. On some panglongs, rainwater is collected and stored in large barrels, which crawl with mosquito larvae. The provision of boiled tea is therefore mandatory.

Housing. With few exceptions, the coolie quarters do not meet even minimal expectations. Almost nowhere was there sufficient protection against rain and wind. Often the bangsals were in a state of imminent collapse. In general, more care had been taken with the sawmills than with the bangsals, whose furnishings were miserable beyond description. Many panglongs did not take into account when building bangsals of the possibility of high tides, and as a result bangsals frequently flood.

On one of the private concessions the water rose higher and higher during a panglong inspection. Insects of all kinds swarmed over the wooden floors looking for a dry place among the legs of those present in the bangsal. The sledway sleepers were lifted out of their notches by the rising water and drifted away. In such cases, inspectors insisted on a relocation or rebuilding of the kongsi house.

For better drainage, the kapalas were advised to dig gutters around the coolie quarters. Due to the proximity of a river or estuary, this was not always equally successful.

Throwing away rubbish in the vicinity of the bangsal had to be stopped. On many panglongs little thought had been given to the need for bathing facilities. Usually the sea or the river was the main repository of waste and sewage. On several occasions, coolies were attacked by crocodiles while bathing. In 1924, in one such instance on Selat Ringgit, between the islands of Tebing Tinggi and Merbau, a Chinese was bitten in both legs and died of his wounds.

Nor was much attention ever paid to the pathways to such places. There are now special regulations regarding toilets and bathing places. A simple enclosure is mandatory. So is a proper roadway.

The coolies on the panglongs on the mainland of Sumatra are taken by tigers according to reports. In one week there were four tiger attacks on panglongs on the Soengei Rawa concession. During one of them, three workers were sitting one evening at a table in the front part of the bangsal playing dominoes, one with his back to the entrance. He was snatched by a tiger. Two days after that, when the Labour Inspector arrived at the panglong, the animal's tracks could still be seen around the bangsal.

In early 1926, while returning from the jungle in Kateman, a tree feller was attacked by a tiger. He was rushed to hospital in Tandjong Balei but died shortly after admission. The tiger, which had been hit with an axe during the attack, was found dead in the jungle the next day.

To combat this danger, officers of the forestry commission demanded that fencing be placed around the bangsals. The front part of a bangsal, where people eat and take their rest, is generally completely open. The kitchens are usually under the same roof, to the right of the entrance. On some firewood panglongs, where the workers have to provide their own food, stoves are scattered all over the bangsals. Here, the situation was improved by requiring kitchens to be built outside bangsals.

Some companies were told to provide more tables and benches. One panglong boss decided to buy chairs. All bangsals are equipped with at least one clock.

The religious life of panglong coolies from China is limited to memorialising deceased relatives. At the middle of nearly all bangsals is a topekong, a sort of altar where incense is burned and offerings are made. Vases with paper flowers are often used for decoration.

Usually there are entrances on both sides of the topekong to the workers' sleeping quarters. The planks that lead to these quarters were replaced on the orders of the Labour Inspectorate by a wooden floor that extends up to and under the sleeping places. As a result, things are cleaner and less dirt gathers.

Usually the walls are made of palm fronds. After a relatively short time, not much is left of them. It was therefore decided that walls should be built of stronger material.

Usually, the kapala and the mandur sleep just behind the topekong, in a separate room. Behind it is a storage place for foodstuffs. If it was discovered that cooks, tree fellers, or sampan men were sleeping in such places, the practice was prohibited. The sampan men often have their own separate place on the coast or on the river bank, to stop would-be runaways from stealing the vessels.

Under existing regulations, mosquito nets must be provided free of charge. The account books often showed that a charge of $10 was levied for such a service. In such cases, the cost was restituted.

All too often the coolie houses were small for the number of workers or there were not enough sleeping places. The panglong coolies sleep with two to a single section of the long sleeping area, divided by mosquito nets.

It is often necessary to insist on the renewal of worn-out nets. Old, torn, and stinking of opium, because the workers wipe their pipes on them, the nets serve more as a shelter for vermin than for the purpose for which they are intended.

In the past, the passages in the sleeping quarters in many bangsals were very narrow. A single plank had been thrown down onto the swampy floor. The coolies had to walk along it to reach their sleeping mats.

One of the Labour Inspectorate's main concerns was to improve the accommodation in the panglongs. At meetings with the taukehs, officials clearly explained how improvements could be made. When it became known that a panglong was about to move location, the necessary requirements were once again made clear. In Bengkalis, where accommodation was generally worse than in Riau, a sketch was produced to indicate the preferred layout of a coolie house.

In 1925, 18 legal proceedings were instigated as a result of poor accommodation. In 1926, 38 percent of the accommodation on panglongs was found to be inadequate. Four cases went to trial.

Improving sleeping quarters went hand in hand with an extension of the entire building. There are currently some panglongs where the accommodation can indeed be called good. Some bangsals were shown to licence holders and kapalas as models.

The lighting on most panglongs is by petroleum lamps. Gasoline lighting has been installed in some sawmills.

To make the coolies' stay in the gloomy jungle more palatable, some bosses have provided gramophones. The coolies also enjoy a game of Chinese dice or dominoes. Women are rarely found on the panglongs. Just a few kapalas and mandur have their wives with them. Dancing girls—known as djogeds—come to give a performance now and then.

Charcoal burners who have their wives with them often live separately.

So accommodation on many panglongs has significantly improved. That the improvement is not confined to accommodation is apparent from the following quotation:

> Whoever gets to see the neatly kept coolie debt books, the meticulous registration of producers and products, the carefully maintained sleeping quarters and nutrition, the medicine chest, the timber mantris' inspection books, the number boards on the behtau's,[2] the work schedules, the railway tracks,[3] the panglong hospital in Selat Pandjang, the vessels being checked, the maps of the panglong region, the reports of the Labour Inspectorate, the registers produced by the forestry officials, the panglong regulations and the panglong charter, and the general observance of provisions will have to admit that much care has been devoted to the panglong system, and that some model panglongs have emerged that can serve as models for the rest.[4]

Medical care. The licence holders and their panglong managers did nothing about medical care. According to regulations, the panglongs must have a sufficient quantity of medicines to hand. However, most panglongs had nothing other than a few Chinese remedies. When kapalas are asked about the availability of medicines, a few dirty bottles are produced. Lizards, scorpions, and similar vermin are displayed in arrack bottles, but no connection is ever made. The licence holders and kapalas had no idea what sort of materials should be available. Steps were therefore taken, in consultation with physicians, to assemble first-aid kits. These have been purchased by a large number of panglongs, with money taken from the panglong medical fund and delivered to the panglongs free of charge. Hospital nurses now and then visit nearby panglongs to tend to minor illnesses on the spot.

The coolies in the panglong hospitals at Selat Pandjang (Bengkalis) and Soengei Goentung (Kateman) had in nearly all cases been brought there by officials rather than by their bosses.

From the stories heard during inspections, the impression was that sick coolies were simply not tolerated on the panglongs. Work had to be done!

[2] The landing stage.

[3] On some panglongs they have started using railways to make things easier for the haulers, while at the same time allowing a deeper exploration of the jungle.

[4] M. O. W., "De beruchte panglongs" (The infamous panglongs), *Eigen Haard*, March 5, 1927, pp. 159 ff.

No one could be allowed to take time off, for the number of workers was exactly enough to keep the business going. So they were often forced to continue working even when seriously ill, as the previous chapter showed. As a consequence, the sick person was dumped outside the community, more dead than alive. On many panglongs such workers were discovered in the jungle. Serious beriberi cases and lepers were invariably "removed" in this one way to the primeval forest, where in the best of cases fellow workers might knock together a place for them to sleep. On July 18, 1925, a coolie was found in the jungle behind panglong no. 34 on Tebing Tinggi Island. He had been given a few planks to sleep on, under a palm-frond roof. When this worker entered the bangsal, he told the following story. Some five years earlier, he had fallen on an axe and cut his stomach open, at the navel. This wound had grown into an artificial anus, through which he defecated. After the inspection, the man—a medical curiosity with natural resilience—had been brought on board the vessel and transported to the hospital in Selat Pandjang.

In 1925, 58 sick workers were taken to hospital from panglongs in the Bengkalis region and 22 in Riau. By 1926, these figures had fallen to 43 and 13 respectively. The panglong hospital in Selat Pandjang was the first such institution. Patients from panglongs closer to Bengkalis were often transported to the government hospital. In 1919, on the initiative of the administration, a small hospital was established at Soengei Goentung, at the mouth of the Kateman River.

In the course of 1925 this building was improved and better furnished. A house for a mantri nurse was also built.

Licence holders have to pay fl a month per coolie for hospital maintenance, so that their workers have access to free care.

In recent years, medical care has much improved. Civil servants from the forestry commission collect the hospital fees from the licence holders. In 1926, plans were laid for eight hospitals in the panglong area.

The number of workers who died in the hospitals in Bengkalis and Riau in 1925 and 1926 was 19 and 12 respectively. The main causes of death noted were beriberi, malaria, and general exhaustion. Notwithstanding the efforts of various officials, fourteen workers died on panglongs in 1926.

Conclusion. I can end this report by saying that conditions on the panglongs have changed for the better since 1925. The number of assaults and murders reported in 1926 was significantly lower than in 1925. With regard to the administration of wages, food, accommodation, and medical care, much has already been achieved, which is not to say that further improvements are not needed. Regular checks will undoubtedly lead to a gradual increase in the number of good panglongs.

In that regard, the article by M. O. W. that I quoted earlier has this to say:

> But it is a laudable fact that outsiders who visit panglongs nowadays will ask: "What is there to worry about here? The accommodation is good, the food is enough, there is a limit on hours worked: the coolies in general have no serious complaints. So where are those "notorious" panglongs? It sometimes happens that coolies with a vague idea of "getting help from outside" and a skewed notion of the support that they, as oppressed workers, can nowadays expect from the Government, suddenly vent an old wish for revenge or give voice to an indefinable wish for emancipation by murdering their mandur, preferably in the presence of an inspector. Such cases are rare, just as the old oligarchy is also disappearing; and panglong supervision has become significantly more intensive than in the past. Nowadays, on average just a dozen cases a year are brought before the courts! So the current state of the panglongs in general seems to give no cause whatsoever for alarm. Although life on the panglongs is by no means enviable and it remains difficult to achieve an improvement on every front, these enterprises no longer deserve the evil reputation that past circumstances rightly earned them.

Weltevreden, July 18, 1927. Inspector at the Labour Bureau, G. Pastor.

References

Adas, Michael. 1986. "From Footdragging to Flight: The Evasive History of Peasant Avoidance Protest in South and South-East Asia." *The Journal of Peasant Studies*, vol. 13 no. 2, 64–86.

Alexeeva, Olga V. 2021. "Between Scylla and Charybdis: Chinese Laborers under the French-American Supervision in France during World War I." In Robert B. McCormick, Araceli Hernández-Laroche, and Catherine G. Canino, eds, *An International Rediscovery of World War One: Distant Fronts*, Abingdon: Routledge, 139–158.

Allen, Richard B. 2012. "European Slave Trading, Abolitionism, and 'New Systems of Slavery' in the Indian Ocean." *PORTAL Journal of Multidisciplinary International Studies*, vol. 9, no. 1, Indian Ocean Traffic Special Issue, edited by Lola Sharon Davidson and Stephen Muecke, 1–21.

Allen, Richard B. 2014. "Slaves, Convicts, Abolitionism and the Global Origins of the Post-Emancipation Indentured Labor System." *Slavery & Abolition*, vol. 35, no. 2, 328–348.

Allen, Richard B. 2017. "Asian Indentured Labor in the 19th and Early 20th Century Colonial Plantation World." In *Oxford Research Encyclopedia of Asian History* (published online), 1 and 6.

Allen, Richard B. 2021. "The Poverty of Archival Riches: Reconstructing Eighteenth- and Nineteenth-Century Mauritian History." *International Journal of Historical Archaeology*, https://doi.org/10.1007/s10761-021-00639-y.

Allen, Richard B. 2022. "Introduction: Slavery, Slave Trading, and Bonded Labor Studies in Asia." In Allen, ed., 2022, 1–32.

G. Benton, *Chinese Indentured Labour in the Dutch East Indies, 1880–1942*, Palgrave Macmillan Transnational History Series, https://doi.org/10.1007/978-3-031-05024-4

Allen, Richard B., ed. 2022. *Slavery and Bonded Labor in Asia, 1250–1900.* Leiden: Brill.

Alleyne, Mervyn. 1988. *Roots of Jamaican Culture*. London: Pluto Press.

Amrith, Sunil S. 2009. "Tamil Diasporas across the Bay of Bengal." *The American Historical Review*, vol. 114, no. 3), 547–572.

Amrith, Sunil S. 2010. "Indians Overseas? Governing Tamil Migration to Malaya, 1870–1941." *Past & Present*, no. 208, 231–261.

Amrith, Sunil S. 2011. *Migration and Diaspora in Modern Asia.* Cambridge: Cambridge University Press.

Amrith, Sunil S. 2015. "Connecting Diaspora Histories: Indians and Chinese in Colonial Malaya." In Bhattacharya and Kripalani, eds, 13–24.

Andayani, Ambar, and D. Jupriono. 2019. "Representation of Nyi Roro Kidul in Myth, Legend, and Popular Culture." In *Anaphora: Journal of Language, Literary, and Cultural Studies*, vol. 2, no. 1, 28–36.

Andrade, Tonio. 2006. *How Taiwan Became Chinese: Dutch, Spanish and Han Colonization in the Seventeenth Century.* New York: Columbia University Press.

Arnot, D. B. 1929. "Timber Extraction in Johore." *Empire Forestry Journal*, vol. 8, no. 2, 233–237.

Arudsothy, Ponniah. 1986. The Labour Force in a Dual Economy. PhD, Glasgow University.

Baay, Reggie. 2015. *Daar werd wat gruwelijks verricht: Slavernij in Nederlands-Indië.* Amsterdam: Athenaeum-Polak and Van Gennep.

Bailey, Paul. 2011a. "'An Army of Workers': Chinese Indentured Labour in First World War France." In Santanu Das, ed., *Race, Empire and First World War Writing*, Cambridge: Cambridge University Press, 35–52.

Bailey, Paul. 2011b. "The Sino-French Connection and World War One." *Journal of the British Association for Chinese Studies*, vol. 1, 1–19.

Baines, Dudley.1994. "European Emigration, 1815–1930: Looking at the Emigration Decision Again." *The Economic History Review*, vol. 47, no. 3, 525–544.

Balachandran, G. 2011. "Making Coolies, (Un)making Workers: 'Globalizing' Labour in the Late-19th and Early-20th Centuries." *Journal of Historical Sociology*, vol. 24, no. 3, 266–296.

Balboa Navarro, Imilcy. 2021. "Las Recontratas de Coolies: A Medio Camino entre la Esclavitud y la Libertad Formal (Cuba, Década de 1860)." *Tzintzun. Revista de Estudios Históricos*, no. 74, 127–160.

Banerjee, Sukanya, Aims McGuinness, and Steven C. McKay, eds. 2012. *New Routes for Diaspora Studies.* Bloomington IN: Indiana University Press.

Banton, M. K. 2004. "The Colonial Office, 1820–1955: Constantly the Subject of Small Struggles." In Douglas Hay and Paul Craven, eds, *Masters, Servants, and Magistrates in Britain and the Empire, 1562–1955*, Chapel Hill: University of North Carolina Press, 251–302.

Bates, Crispin. 1992. "Tribal Migration In India and Beyond." In Gyan Prakash, ed., *The World of the Rural Labourer in Colonial India*, Delhi: Oxford University Press, 1992, 205–245.

Bates, Crispin. 2000. "Coerced and Migrant Labourers in India: The Colonial Experience." *Edinburgh Papers in South Asian Studies*, no. 13.

Bates, Crispin. 2003."Courts, Ship-rolls and Letters: Reflections on the Indian Labour Diaspora." In T. Awaya, ed., *Creating an Archive Today*, Tokyo University of Foreign Studies, 21st Century COE Programme, Centre for Documentation and Area-Transcultural Studies, 131–158.

Bates, Crispin. 2017. "Some Thoughts on the Representation and Misrepresentation of the Colonial South Asian Labour Diaspora." *South Asian Studies*, vol. 33, no. 1, 7–22.

Bates, Crispin, and Marina Carter. 2012. "Enslaved Lives, Enslaving Labels: A New Approach to the Colonial Indian Labor Diaspora." In Banerjee, McGuinness, and McKay, eds, 2012, 67–92.

Bates, Crispin, and Marina Carter. 2017. "Sirdars as Intermediaries in Nineteenth-century Indian Ocean Indentured Labour Migration." *Modern Asian Studies* vol. 51, no. 2, 462–484.

Bates, Crispin, and Marina Carter. 2021."Kala Pani Revisited: Indian Labour Migrants and the Sea Crossing." *Journal of Indentureship and Its Legacies*, vol. 1, no. 1, 36–62.

Bates, Crispin, Marina Carter, and Vishwanaden Govinden. 2017. The Abolition of Indian Indentured Migration to Mauritius. Unpublished paper.

Batsha, Nishant. 2017. The Currents of Restless Toil: Colonial Rule and Indian Indentured Labor in Trinidad and Fiji. PhD, Columbia University.

Baudet, Henri, and Meindert Fennema. 1983. *Het Nederlands belang bij Indië: Analyse van de politieke en economische gevolgen van de dekolonisatie van Indonesië. Hoe stelden overheid en bedrijfsleven zich op en wat was hun onderlinge relatie?* Utrecht-Antwerpen: Het Spectrum.

Behal, Rana. 2013. *Coolies, Recruiters and Planters: Migration of Indian Labour to the Southeast Asian and Assam Plantations during Colonial Rule*. Crossroads Asia, Working Paper series no. 9.

Behal, Rana. 2014. *One Hundred Years of Servitude: Political Economy of Tea Plantations in Colonial Assam*. New Delhi: Tulika Books.

Belle, Carl Vadivella. 2015. *Tragic Orphans: Indians in Malaysia*, Singapore: ISEAS.

Benton, Gregor. 1999. *New Fourth Army: Communist Resistance Along the Yangtze and the Huai, 1938–1941*. Berkeley CA: University of California Press.

Benton, Gregor. 2007. *Chinese Migrants and Internationalism: Forgotten Histories, 1917–1945*. London: Routledge.

Benton, Gregor. 2009. "Editor's Introduction." In García Triana and Eng Herrera, xi–xxxii.

Benton, Gregor. 2010. "China, Cuba, and the Chinese in Cuba: Emigration, International Relations, and How They Interact." In Zheng Yongnian, ed., 2010, 158–176.

Benton, Gregor. 2013. "San Fancón and the Goddess of Mercy: Two Chinese Folk Gods in Cuban Transfiguration." *Cutural & Social History: The Journal of the Social History Society*, vol. 10, no. 1, 93–108.

Benton, Gregor. 2016. "Chinese Migrants in China in a Labour-Movement Perspective." In *Auzhou paiHua zhengce de lishi zhongjie* (The end of the anti-Chinese policy in Australia: In commemoration of the victims). Edited by the Australian Chinese Workers' Association, Harbin: Heilongjiang renmin chuban she, 32–66.

Benton, Gregor, and Hong Liu. 2014. "The *Qiaopi* Project in Comparative Perspective." *China Qiaoxiang Studies*, Beijing: Overseas Chinese Press, 36–51.

Benton, Gregor, and Hong Liu. 2016. "The Qiaopi Trade and Its Role in Modern China and the Chinese Diaspora: Toward an Alternative Explanation of 'Transnational Capitalism.'" *The Journal of Asian Studies*, vol. 75, no. 3, 575–594.

Benton, Gregor, and Hong Liu. 2018. *Dear China: Emigrant Letters and Remittances, 1820–1980.* Oakland, CA: University of California Press.

Benton, Gregor, and Hong Liu. 2020. "*Qiaopi* and Charity: The Mechanisms and Impact of Diasporic Chinese Philanthropy." In John Fitzgerald and Hon-ming Yip, eds, *Chinese Diaspora Charity and the Cantonese Pacific*, Hong Kong: Hong Kong University Press, 51–71.

Benton, Gregor, Hong Liu, and Huimei Zhang. 2016c. "Letters sent home by Overseas Chinese in America and Australia." In Chen Jingzhun, ed. *Haibang Shengfu: Qiaopi Dang'an Yanjiu* (Archival research on qiaopi), Guangzhou: Ji'nan daxue chuban she, 34–43.

Benton, Gregor, Hong Liu, and Huimei Zhang. 2016a. Qiaopi and Politics. *The International Journal of Diasporic Chinese Studies*, vol. 8, no. 1, 1–36.

Benton, Gregor, Hong Liu, and Huimei Zhang, eds. 2016b. *The Qiaopi Trade and Transnational Networks in the Chinese Diaspora*, London: Routledge.

Benton, Gregor, Huimei Zhang, and Hong Liu. 2018. *Chinese Emigrants Write Home: A Dual-Language Anthology of Family Letters.* Singapore: World Scientific.

Benton, Gregor, and Terence Gomez. 2008. *The Chinese in Britain, 1800-Present: Economy, Transnationalism, Identity.* Houndmills: Palgrave Macmillan.

Bhagwanbali, Radjinder. 2010. *De nieuwe awatar van slavernij: Hindoestaansemigranten onder het indentured labour systeem naar Suriname, 1873–1916.* The Hague: Amrit.

Bhattacharya, Jayati, and Coonoor Kripalani, eds. 2015. *Indian and Chinese Immigrant Communities: Comparative Perspectives.* London: Anthem Press.

Bieber, Judy, ed., 2018. *Plantation Societies in the Era of European Expansion.* Abingdon: Routledge.

Blussé, Léonard. 1999. "Chinese Century: The Eighteenth Century in the China Sea Region." *Archipel*, no. 58, 107–129.

Blussé, Leonard, and Nie Dening. 2018. *The Chinese Annals of Batavia, The Kai Ba Lidai Shiji and Other Stories (1610–1795)*. Leiden: Brill.

Boeke, Julius Herman. 1942. *The Structure of Netherlands Indian Economy*. New York: Institute of Pacific Relations.

Bosma, Ulbe. 2009. "European Colonial Soldiers in the Nineteenth Century: Their Role in White Global Migration and Patterns of Colonial Settlement." *Journal of Global History*, no. 4, 317–336.

Bosma, Ulbe. 2011. "The Discourse on Free Labor and the Forced Cultivation System: The Contradictory Consequences of the Abolition of the Slave Trade in Colonial Java, 1811–1870." In Marcel van der Linden, ed., 2011, 387–418.

Bosma, Ulbe. 2014a. "The Economic Historiography of the Dutch Colonial Empire." *TSEG—The Low Countries Journal of Social and Economic History*, vol. 11, no. 2, 153–174.

Bosma, Ulbe. 2014b. "Migration and Colonial Enterprise in Nineteenth Century Java." In Jan Lucassen and Leo Lucassen, eds, *Globalising Migration History: The Eurasian Experience (16th-21st Centuries)*, Leiden: Brill, 2014, 151–179.

Bosma, Ulbe. 2019a. "Decolonization, Nation Building, and Migration Crises in Southeast Asia." In Cecilia Menjívar, Marie Ruiz, and. Immanuel Ness, eds, *The Oxford Handbook of Migration Crises*. New York: Oxford University Press.

Bosma, Ulbe. 2019b. *The Making of a Periphery: How Island Southeast Asia Became a Mass Exporter of Labor*. New York: Columbia University Press.

Bosma, Ulbe, ed. 2012. *Post-Colonial Immigrants and Identity Formations in the Netherlands*. Amsterdam: Amsterdam University Press.

Brandon, Pepijn. 2019. "Dutch Capitalism and Slavery." *Historical Materialism*, September.

Breman, Jan. 1985. *Of Peasants, Migrants and Paupers: Rural Labour Circulation and Capitalist Production in West India*. New Delhi: Oxford University Press.

Breman, Jan. 1987. *Koelies, Planters en Koloniale Politiek: Het arbeidsregime op de grootlandbouwondernemingen aan Sumatra's oostkust in het begin van de twintigste eeuw*, Dordrecht: Foris Publications.

Breman, Jan. 1988. "Het beest aan banden? De koloniale geest aan het begin van de twintigste eeuw." *Bijdragen tot de Taal-, Land- en Volkenkunde*, vol. 144, no. 1, 19–43.

Breman, Jan. 1989. *Taming the Coolie Beast: Plantation Society and the Colonial Order in Southeast Asia*. Delhi: Oxford University Press.

Breman, Jan. 1992. "Een advocaat van kwade zaken: Het koloniale milieu aan Sumatra's oostkust in de eerste decennia van deze eeuw." *De Gids*, no. 155, 476–492.

Breman, Jan. 1996. "The Village on Java and the Early Colonial State." In Hoadley and Gunnarsson, eds, 1996, 3–28.

Breman, Jan. 2020. "Colonialism and Its Racial Imprint." *Sojourn: Journal of Social Issues in Southeast Asia*, vol. 35, no. 3, 463–92.

Brown, Spencer H. 2004. "A Tool of Empire: The British Medical Establishment in Lagos, 1861–1905." *The International Journal of African Historical Studies*, vol. 37, no. 2, 309–343.

Buelens, Frans, and Ewout Frankema. 2016. "Colonial Adventures in Tropical Agriculture: New Estimates of Returns to Investment in the Netherlands Indies, 1919–1938." *Cliometrica*, no. 10, 197–224.

Burnard, Trevor. 2017. "Towns in Plantation Societies in Eighteenth-Century British America." *Early American Studies*, vol. 15, no. 4, 835–859.

Burton, Antoinette. 2015. *The Trouble with Empire: Challenges to Modern British Imperialism*, Oxford, Oxford University Press.

Campbell, Persia Crawford. 1923. *Chinese Coolie Emigration to Countries within the British Empire London*. London: Frank Cass.

Casimir, Jean. 1992. *The Caribbean: One and Divisible*. Santiago, Chile: Economic Commission for Latin America and the Caribbean.

Chakraborty, Subhas Ranjan. n.d. "Colonialism, Resource Crisis and (Forced) Migration."

Chan, Shelly. 2018. *Diaspora's Homeland: Modern China in the Age of Global Migration*. Durham: Duke University Press.

Chandra, Siddharth. 2000. "What the Numbers Really Tell Us about the Decline of the Opium Regie." *Indonesia*, no. 70, 101–123.

Chang Zengshu. 2008. "Aozhou taojin Huagong de 'yinxin'" ("The Australian Gold-miners' 'Silver Letters'"). In Wang Weizhong, ed., 2008, 455–460.

Chatterjee, Sumita. 1997. Indian Women's Lives and Labor: The Indentureship Experience in Trinidad and Guyana, 1845–1917. PhD, University of Massachusetts Amherst.

Chatterji, Joya, and David Washbrook. 2013. *Routledge Handbook of the South Asian Diaspora*. London: Routledge.

Chen Hansheng, ed. 1981–1985. *Huagong chuguo shiliao huibian* (A compilation of edited historical materials regarding going abroad by Huagong). Beijing: Zhonghua shuju, 12 vols.

Chen Jianbo. 2004. "Dui dangqian qiaopi wenhua yanjiu de sikao" (Some Thoughts on Contemporary Research into Qiaopi Culture). In Wang Weizhong, ed., 2004, 148–150.

Chen Lie. 2008. "Guanyu Chaoshan qiaopi wenhua ruogan wentide qiantan" ("Some Observations on Some Questions Concerning Chaoshan Qiaopi Culture"). In Wang Weizhong, ed., 2008, 225–236.

Chen Liyuan. 2008. "Qiaopi jingying wangluo de zuzhi xingtai yanjiu" ("Research into the Organizational Form of the Management of the Qiaopi Network"). In Wang Weizhong, ed., 2008, 185–194.

Chen Sanjing. 1975. *Huagong yu Ouzhan* (Huagong and the European War). Taipei: Zhongyang yanjiu yuan jindai shi yanjiu suo.

Chen, Ta. 1940. *Emigrant Communities in South China*. New York: Secretariat, Institute of Pacific Relations.

Chen Xiaogang, ed. 2009. *Huiwang Minnan qiaopi: Shoujie Minnan qiaopi yantao hui lunwen ji* (Looking Back on Minnan Qiaopi: Collection of Papers of the First Minnan Qiaopi Conference), Quanzhou: Huayi chuban she.

Chen Xunxian. 2004. "Shilun Qing dai Chao bang qiaopi ye dui wo guo yuanshi jinrong shichang de cujin yu gongxian" ("On the Chao Gang's Acceleration of and Contribution to Our Country's Primitive Financial Market in the Qing Dynasty"). In Wang Weizhong, ed., 2004, 187–192.

Chen Xunxian. 2010. "Lun 'yinxin hefeng' " ("On 'Silver and Letter in one Envelope'"). In Wang Weizhong, ed., 2010, 181–189.

Chen Yingqiu. 2004. "Huiyi baba sushuo de Huagong xuelei [blood and tears] shi" ("Recalling father's account of the Huagong history of blood and tears"). In Yang Tongling et al. 2004, 592–593.

Chen, Yong. 2000. *Chinese San Francisco, 1850–1943: A Trans-Pacific Community*. Stanford: Stanford University Press.

Chevaleyre, Claude. 2013. "Acting as Master and Bondservant: Considerations on Status Identities and the Nature of 'Bond-Servitude' in Late Ming China." In Stanziani, ed., 2013, 237–272.

Chevaleyre, Claude. 2022. "Human Trafficking in Late Imperial China." In Allen, ed., 2022, 150–177.

Chew, Daniel. 1990. *Chinese Pioneers on the Sarawak Frontier, 1841–1941*. Singapore: Oxford University Press.

Choi, Wai Kit. 2009. "Revolutionary Shanghai: Rethinking Class and the Politics of Difference through Chinese Communism." *Science & Society*, vol. 73, no. 2, 242–260.

Choi, Wai Kit. 2018. "Making Capitalism with Gangsters: Unfree Labor in Shanghai's Cotton Mills, 1927–1937." *International Labor and Working-Class History*, vol. 94, 107–132.

Claver, Alexander. 2014. *Dutch Commerce and Chinese Merchants in Java: Colonial Relationships in Trade and Finance, 1800–1942*. Leiden: Brill.

Claveyrolas, Mathieu. 2018. "From the Indian Ganges to a Mauritian Lake: Hindu Pilgrimage in a 'Diasporic' Context." In Simon Coleman and John Eade, eds., *Translating the Sacred: Pilgrimage and Political Economy in Transnational Contexts*, New York: Berghahn, 21–39.

Cohen de Boer, H. 1930. *Het Koelie-contract te Genève*. The Hague: D. A. Daamen's Uitgevers-Maatschappij.

Cole, G. D. H. 1923. *Labour in the Coal Mining Industry, 1914–21*. Oxford: Clarendon Press.

Colenbrander, H. T., compiler. 1920–1922. *Jan Pietersz. Coen, Bescheiden omtrent Zijn Bedrijf in Indië*. 4 vols. The Hague: Martinus Nijhoff.

Colombijn, Freek. 2010. *Under Construction: The Politics of Urban Space and Housing during the Decolonization of Indonesia, 1930–1960*. Leiden: Brill.

Compton Reeves, A. 1972. "Some of Humphrey Stafford's Military Indentures." *Nottingham Medieval Studies*, vol. 16, 80–91.

Coppel, Charles A. 2013. "Diaspora and Hybridity: *Peranakan* Chinese Culture in Indonesia." In Chee-Beng Tan, ed., *Routledge Handbook of the Chinese Diaspora*, Abingdon: Routledge, 2013, 345–358.

Curtin, Philip. 1998. *The Rise and Fall of the Plantation Complex: Essays in Atlantic History*. Cambridge: Cambridge University Press.

Damanik, Erond Litno. 2020. "Ethnicity Situation and Intolerant Attitudes in Multicultural Societies in the Medan City." *Humaniora*, vol. 32, no. 1, 39–50.

Darnell, Maxine. 1999. Responses and Reactions to the Importation of Indentured Chinese Labourers. Working Paper Series in Economic History, University of New England School of Economic Studies, no. 99-2, November.

Das, Anjan Kumar. 2019. The Health of Indian Migrant Plantation Workers: Malaya 1870–1939. Taylor's University, School of Medicine, Kuala Lumpur.

Davis, Kingsley. 1951. *The Population of India and Pakistan*. Princeton NJ: Princeton University Press.

De Bruin, A. G. 1918. *De Chineezen ter Oostkust van Sumatra*. Issued by Het Oostkust van Sumatra-Instituut. Leiden: Brill.

De Graaf, S., and D. G. Stibbe, with W. C. B. Wintgens, eds. 1918. *Encyclopaedie van Nederlandsch-Indië*, second edition. 2 vols. The Hague: Martinus Nijhoff.

De Groot, Cornelis. 1887. *Herinneringen aan Blitong, Historisch, Lithologisch, Mineralogisch, Geographisch, Geologisch en Mijnbouwkundig*. The Hague: H. L. Smits.

De Groot, Jan Jakob Maria. 1885. *Het kongsiwezen van Borneo*, The Hague: Martinus Nijhoff.

De Kat Angelino, A. D. A. 1931. *Colonial Policy*, vol. 2, *The Dutch East Indies*. Translated by G. J. Renier. The Hague: Martinus Nijhoff.

The Deli Coolie Question [1881–1882]. KIT BrRN – 40 KIT = 1953.

Deli Planters Vereeniging. 1929. *Regeling en Wenken*. Second revised edition.

Delius, Peter, and Stanley Trapido. 1982. "Inboekselings and Oorlams: The Creation and Transformation of a Servile Class." *Journal of Southern African Studies*, vol 8, no. 2, 214–242.

Deng Rui. 2004. "Cong Meizhou shi qiaohui de fazhan guocheng kan qiaopi ju xingshuai" ("Looking at the Rise and Fall of Qiaopi Offices from the Point of View of the Development of Overseas Remittances in Meizhou"). In Wang Weizhong, ed.., 2004, 57–64.

Deng Rui. 2010. "Qiantan qiaopi de zhongyao zuoyong ji kaifa liyong" ("On the Important Role and Uses of Qiaopi"). In Wang Weizhong, ed., 103–117.

Derks, Annuska. 2010. "Bonded Labour in Southeast Asia: Introduction." *Asian Journal of Social Science*, no. 38, 839–852

Derks, Hans. 2012. *History of the Opium Problem: The Assault on the East, Ca. 1600–1950*. Leiden: Brill.

Desai, Ashwin, and Goolam Vahed. 2015. *The South African Gandhi: Stretcher-Bearer of Empire*. Stanford: Stanford University Press.

Desmond, Matthew. 2019. "In order to understand the brutality of American capitalism, you have to start on the plantation." *The New York Times Magazine*, August 14.

Ding, Picus Sizhi. 2016. *Southern Min (Hokkien) as a Migrating Language: A Comparative Study of Language Shift and Maintenance Across National Borders*. Singapore: Springer.

Dodge, Nicholas N. 1980. "Population Estimates for the Malay Peninsula in the Nineteenth Century, with Special Reference to the East Coast States." *Population Studies*, vol. 34, no. 3, 437–475.

Douw, Leo. 2012. "Mainland Chinese Migrants in Taiwan, 1895–1945: The Drawbacks of Being Legal." In Barak Kalir and Malini Sur, eds, *Transnational Flows and Permissive Polities: Ethnographies of Human Mobilities in Asia*. Amsterdam: Amsterdam University Press, 2012, 189–206.

Dupuy, Alex. 1983. "Slavery and Underdevelopment in the Caribbean: A Critique of the 'Plantation Economy' Perspective." *Dialectical Anthropology*, vol. 7, no. 3, 237–251.

Emmer, Pieter C. 2011. "'As Always, the Trouble is with the French.' Britain, France, the Netherlands and the Colonial Labor Market in the 19th Century." In Van der Linden, ed., 2011, 263–283.

Entrikin, J. Nicholas. 1991. *The Betweenness of Place: Towards a Geography of Modernity*. Baltimore MA: Johns Hopkins University Press.

Erman, Erwiza. 1999. Miners, Managers and the State: A Socio-Political History of the Ombilin Coal-Mines, West Sumatra, 1892–1996. PhD thesis, University of Amsterdam.

Erman, Erwiza. 2017. "Chinese *Taukeh*, Labourer, and State Control: Case Study of *Panglong* in Eastern Region of Sumatra (1890–1930)." *Wacana*, vol. 18, no. 2, 514–539.

Extract from the Proceedings of the Imperial Legislative Council, India. March 1912. In *Speeches and Writings of Gopal Krishna Gokhale*, vol. 1, Asia Publishing House, 1962, 349–368.

Faruqee, Ashrufa. 1996. "Conceiving the Coolie Woman: Indentured Labour, Indian Women and Colonial Discourse." *South Asia Research*, vol. 16, no. 1, 61–76.

Fernando, M. R., and D. Bulbeck, eds. 1992. *Chinese Economic Activity in Netherlands India: Selected Translations from the Dutch*. Singapore: Institute of Southeast Asian Studies.

Fitzgerald, John. 2007. *Big White Lie: Chinese Australians in White Australia.* Sydney: UNSW Press.

Fix, Douglas. 2018. "Xiamen: Emigrants' Portal to a Broader World." *Chinese Studies Research Center Working Paper*, June.

Fokkens, F. 1896 [1992]. "A Plea for Tighter Controls on Chinese Revenue Farming and Immigration." In Fernando and Bulbeck, eds, 1992, 58–75.

Fox, Jefferson, et al. 2009. "Policies, Political-Economy, and Swidden in Southeast Asia." *Human Ecology: An Interdisciplinary Journal*, vol. 37, no. 3, 305–322.

Franke, Otto. 1923. "Gedächtnisrede des Hrn. Franke auf J. J. M. de Groot." In *Sitzungsberichte der Preussischen Akademie der Wissenschaften*, 1923, cxvii–cxxvi.

Frost, Mark Ravinder. 2005. "*Emporium in Imperio*: Nanyang Networks and the Straits Chinese in Singapore, 1819–1914." *Journal of Southeast Asian Studies*, vol. 36, no. 1, 29–66.

Fruin, R. 1923. "Immigratie van Java." Supplement to Deli Planters Vereeniging, Mededeling no, 14, *De Arbeidsregeling voor de Buitengewesten van Nederlandsch Indië*, Medan: Köhler, 54–76.

Furnivall, J. S. 1939. *Netherlands India: A Study of Plural Economy.* Cambridge: Cambridge University Press.

Galenson, David W. 1984. "The Rise and Fall of Indentured Servitude in the Americas: An Economic Analysis." *The Journal of Economic History*, vol. 44, no. 1, 1–26.

García Triana, Mauro, and Pedro Eng Herrera. 2009. *The Chinese in Cuba, 1847-Now.* Edited and translated by Gregor Benton. Lanham: Lexington Books.

Gedenkboek Billiton, 1852–1927. 1927. 2 pts. The Hague: Martinus Nijhoff.

Ginés-Blasi, Mònica. 2020. "A Philippine 'Coolie Trade': Trade and Exploitation of Chinese Labour in Spanish Colonial Philippines, 1850–98." *Journal of Southeast Asian Studies*, 1–27.

Ginés-Blasi, Mònica. 2021. "Exploiting Chinese Labour Emigration in Treaty Ports: The Role of Spanish Consulates in the 'Coolie Trade'." *International Review of Social History*, vol. 66, no. 1, 1–24.

Godley, Michael R., and Charles A. Coppel. 1990. "The Pied Piper and the Prodigal Children: A Report on the Indonesian-Chinese Students who went to Mao's China." *Archipel*, vol. 39, 179–198.

Gong Kai. 2016. "Wan Qing Zhongguo nüxing chuyang de lishi kaocha" ("Historical research into female overseas migration in the late Qing"). *Kaifeng jiaoyu xueyuan xuebao*, vol. 36, no. 7, 7–9.

Gonzales, Michael J. 1989. "Chinese Plantation Workers and Social Conflict in Peru in the Late Nineteenth Century." *Journal of Latin American Studies*, vol. 21, no. 3, 385–424.

Goodman, Bryna. 1995. *Native Place, City, and Nation. Regional Networks and Identities in Shanghai, 1853–1937.* Berkeley: University of California Press.

Gordon, Alec. 2004. "Dynamics of Labour Transformation: Natural Rubber in Southeast Asia." *Journal of Contemporary Asia*, no. 34, 523–546.

Gottschang, Thomas R., and Diana Lary. 2000. *Swallows and Settlers: The Great Migration from North China to Manchuria*. Ann Arbor: Center for Chinese Studies, University of Michigan.

Gouda, Frances. 2009. "Discipline versus Gentle Persuasion in Colonial Public Health: The Rockefeller Foundation's Intensive Rural Hygiene Work in the Netherlands East Indies, 1925–1940." Rockefeller Archive Center Research Report.

Gounder, Farzana. 2011. *Indentured Identities: Resistance and Accommodation in Plantation-Era Fiji*. Amsterdam: John Benjamins.

Groeneveldt, Willem Pieter, 1898. *De Nederlanders in China*. The Hague: Nijhoff.

Groenewoud, Margo. 1995. "Towards the Abolition of Penal Sanctions in Dutch Colonial Labour Legislation: An International Perspective." *Itinerario*, vol. 19 no. 2, 72–90.

Guilmoto, Christophe Z. 1993. "The Tamil Migration Cycle, 1830–1950." *Economic and Political Weekly*, January 16–23, 111–120.

Gunter, John.1939. *Inside Asia*. London: Hamish Hamilton.

Guowuyuan qiaoban qiaowu ganbu xuexiao, eds. 2005. *Huaqiao Huaren gaishu* (General situation of overseas and ethnic Chinese). Beijing: Jizhou chuban she.

Guowuyuan qiaogong shiwu ju, eds. [January] 1920a. *Nanyang He shu Wanlitong dao Huagong qingxing diaocha shu* (An Investigation into the Situation of Huagong on Dutch-ruled Belitung Island in the Nanyang). Beijing: Guowuyuan qiaogong shiwu ju.

Guowuyuan qiaogong shiwu ju, eds. [May] 1920b. *Nanyang He shu Wangjia dao Huagong qingxing diaocha shu* (An Investigation into the Situation of Huagong on Dutch-ruled Bangka Island in the Nanyang). Beijing: Guowuyuan qiaogong shiwu ju.

Hamashita Takeshi. 2015. "Comparison of Home Remittance System between India and Chinese Migrants in Southeast Asia: Nineteenth and Twentieth Centuries." In Bhattacharya and Kripalani, eds, 43–54.

Harris, Karen L 2010. "Sugar and Gold: Indentured Indian and Chinese Labour in South Africa." *Journal of Social Sciences*, vol. 25, nos. 1–3, 147–158.

Haynes, Douglas E., and Tirthanka Roy. 1999. "Conceiving Mobility: Weavers' Migrations in Pre-Colonial and Colonial India." *The Indian Economic & Social History Review*, vol. 36, no. 1, 35–67.

He Tianyi, ed. 1995. *Zhongguo laogong zai Riben* ("Chinese labour in Japan"). Beijing: Xinhua chuban she.

Heartfield, James. 2017. *The British and Foreign Anti-Slavery Society, 1838–1956: A History*. Oxford: Oxford University Press.

Heidhues, Mary F. Somers. 1991. "Company Island: A Note on the History of Belitung." *Indonesia*, no. 51, 1–20.

Heidhues, Mary F. Somers. 1992. *Bangka Tin and Mentok Pepper: Chinese Settlement on an Indonesian Island.* Pasir Panjang : Institute of Southeast Asian Studies.

Heidhues, Mary Somers. 1993. "Chinese Organization in West Borneo and Bangka: Kongsi and Hui." In Ownby and Heidhues, eds, 1993, 68–88.

Heidhues, Mary Somers. 1996. "Chinese Settlements in Rural Southeast Asia: Unwritten Histories." In Reid, ed., 1996, 164–182.

Heidhues, Mary F. Somers. 2003. *Golddiggers, Farmers, and Traders in the "Chinese Districts" of West Kalimantan, Indonesia.* Ithaca, NY: Cornell University, Southeast Asia Program Publications.

Heidhues, Mary Somers. 2007. "Poor Little Rich Islands: Metals in Bangka-Belitung and West Kalimantan." In Greg Bankoff and Peter Boomgaard, eds. *A History of Natural Resources in Asia: The Wealth of Nature.* Houndmills: Palgrave, 2007, 61–80.

Heidhues, Mary Somers. 2018. "When We Were Young: The Exile of the Republic's Leaders in Bangka, 1949." In Daniel S. Lev and Ruth T. McVey, eds, *Making Indonesia: Essays on Modern Indonesia in Honor of George McT. Kahin.* Ithaca, NY: Cornell University Press, 2018, 81–95.

Heijting, H. G. 1925. *De koelie-wetgeving.* The Hague: Van Stockhum.

Heinoldt, C. 1897. *Emigratie van Chineezen naar Banka.* N. p.: n. p.

Hess, Frank L., and Eva Hess. 1912. *Bibliography of the Geology and Mineralogy of Tin.* Smithsonian Miscellaneous Collections, vol. 58, no. 2, City of Washington: The Smithsonian Institution.

Hill, David T. 2020. "Cold War Polarization, Delegated Party Authority, and Diminishing Exilic Options: The Dilemma of Indonesian Political Exiles in China after 1965." *Bijdragen tot de Taal-, Land- en Volkenkunde*, no. 176, 338–372.

Hincapie, Luz Mercedes. 2010. "Pacific Transactions: Nicolás Tanco Armero and the Chinese Coolie Trade to Cuba." *Journal of Iberian and Latin American Research*, vol. 16, no. 1, 27–41.

Hirayama, Nagatomi. 2013. "Partifying Sichuan: The Chinese Youth Party in Sichuan, 1926–1937." *Frontiers of History in China*, vol. 8, no.2, 223–258.

Hjejle, Benedicte. 1967. "Slavery and Agricultural Bondage in South India in the Nineteenth Century." *The Scandinavian Economic History Review*, vol. 15 nos 1–2, 71–126.

Hoadley, Mason C., and Christer Gunnarsson, eds. 1996. *The Village Concept in the Transformation of Rural Southeast Asia: Studies from Indonesia, Malaysia and Thailand*, Richmond, Surrey: Curzon Press (Nordic Institute for Asian Studies, Studies in Asian Topics, no. 20), 1996.

Hoefte, Rosemarijn. 1998. "A Passage to Suriname? The Migration of Modes of Resistance by Asian Contract Laborers." *International Labor and Working-Class History*, vol. 54, 19–39.

Hoefte, Rosmarijn. 2012. "Plantations and Labour in the Caribbean in the Long Nineteenth Century." *International Review of Social History*, vol. 57, 257–268.

Hoefte, Rosemarijn. 2017. "Indentured Labor." In Karin Hofmeester and Marcel van der Linden, eds, *Handbook Global History of Work*, Berlin: De Gruyter, 363–376.

Hoi Ying Chen, Katherine. 2016. "The Transnational Journey of an Indonesian Chinese Couple in Hong Kong: The Story of One Family, Three Places, and Multiple Languages." In Li Wei, ed., *Multilingualism in the Chinese Diaspora Worldwide: Transnational Connections and Local Social Realities*, London: Routledge, 237–254.

Hong Sisi. 1985. *Yindunixiya Huaqiao shi* (History of overseas Chinese in Indonesia). Beijing: Haiyang chuban she.

Honig, Emily. 1983. "The Contract Labor System and Women Workers: Pre-Liberation Cotton Mills of Shanghai." *Modern China*, vol. 9, no. 4, 421–454.

Honig, Emily. 1986. *Sisters and Strangers: Women in the Shanghai Cotton Mills, 1919–1949*. Stanford: Stanford University Press.

Honig, Emily. 1992. *Creating Chinese Ethnicity: Subei People in Shanghai, 1850–1980*, New Haven, CT: Yale University Press.

Hou Weixiong. 2009. "Gulangyu yu Minnan qiaopi ye yizhi" ("Gulangyu and the Site of the Minnan Qiaopi Trade"). In Chen Xiaogang, ed., 2009, 136–141.

Houben, Vincent J. H. 1999. "The Quality of Coolie Life." In Houben and Lindblad, eds, 1999, 109–130.

Houben, Vincent J. H. 1999a. "Introduction: The Coolie System in Colonial Indonesia." In Houben and Lindblad, eds, 1999, 1–24.

Houben, Vincent J. H. 1999b. "Before Departure: Coolie Labour Recruitment in Java, 1900–1942." In Houben and Lindblad, eds, 1999, 25–42.

Houben, Vincent J. H. and J. Thomas Lindblad, eds. 1999. *Coolie Labour in Colonial Indonesia: A Study of Labour Relations in the Outer Islands, c. 1900–1940*, Wiesbaden: Harrassowitz Verlag.

Houben, Vincent, and Julia Seibert. 2013. "(Un)freedom: Colonial Labor Relations in Belgian Congo and the Netherlands East Indies Compared." In Ewout Frankema and Frans Buelens, eds, *Colonial Exploitation and Economic Development: The Belgian Congo and the Netherlands East Indies Compared*, Abingdon: Routledge, 2013, 178–192.

Hsu, Madeline. 1997. "Gold Mountain Dreams and Paper Son Schemes: Chinese Immigration under Exclusion." In Chinese Historical Society of America, eds. *Chinese America: History and Perspectives, 1997*. San Francisco: San Francisco State University, 46–60.

Huang Jiaxiang. 2010. "Zhaoan qiaopi ye liubian" ("Flow and Change in the Zhaoan Qiaopi Trade"). In Wang Weizhong, ed., 2010, 502–510.

Huang Qinlin 2012. "Guomin zhengfu shiqi Guangdong de liangci nanqiao jiuji huodong" ("Two movements to relieve the suffering of migrants in Guangdong under the Republican Government"). *Wuyi daxue xuebao (shehui kexue ban)*, vol. 14, no. 1, 55–59.

Huang Zijian. 2013. "Malaixiya qiaopi: Shehui shi ji qiaohui shi shiliao" ("Malaysian qiaopi: Historical materials for social history and remittance history"), in Zhongguo qiaopi shijie jiyi gongcheng guoji yantao hui zuwei hui, eds, *Lunwen ji* (Conference Papers Collection), Beijing: n.p., 131–141.

Hu-Dehart, Evelyn. 1994. "Chinese Coolie Labor in Cuba in the Nineteenth Century: Free Labor of Neoslavery." *Contributions in Black Studies*, vol. 12, 38–54.

Huff, Gregg, and Giovanni Caggiano. N. d. Migration and Elastic Labour in Economic Development: Southeast Asia before World War II. Unpublished paper.

Huff, W. G. 2001. "Entitlements, Destitution, and Emigration in the 1930s Singapore Great Depression." *The Economic History Review*, vol. 54, no. 2, 290–323.

Hui, Neha, and Uma Kambhampati. 2020. The Political Economy of Indian Indentured Labour in the 19th Century. Economics Discussion Papers 2020–16. Department of Economics, Reading University.

Hui, Yew-Foong. 2011. *Strangers at Home: History and Subjectivity among the Chinese Communities of of West Kalimantan, Indonesia*. Leiden: Brill.

Hui, Yew-Foong. 2013. "The Translocal Subject between China and Indonesia: The Case of the Pemangkat Chinese of West Kalimantan." In Siew-Min Sai and Chang-Yau Hoon, eds, *Chinese Indonesians Reassessed: History, Religion and Belonging*, New York: Routledge, 2013, 103–120.

Huzzey, Richard, and Henry Miller. 2022. "Colonial Petitions, Colonial Petitioners, and the Imperial Parliament, c. 1780–1918." *Journal of British Studies* http://dro.dur.ac.uk/34092/.

Indrayana, Denny. 2017. "*Pribumi*: Making Sense of a Troubled Term." *Indonesia at Melbourne*, October 24.

Ingleson, John. 1986. *In Search of Justice: Workers and Unions in Colonial Java, 1908–1926*. Singapore: Oxford University Press.

Ireland, Alleyne. 1905. *The Far Eastern Tropics: Studies in the Administration of Tropical Dependencies*. Boston: Houghton, Mifflin and Company.

Jackson, James C. 1969. "Towards an Understanding of Plantation Agriculture." *Area*, vol. 1, no. 4, 36–41.

Jain, Prakash C. 1989. "Emigration and Settlement of Indians Abroad." *Sociological Bulletin*, vol. 38, no. 1, 155–168.

Jany, Gregory. 2021. *Imperial Crossings: Chinese Indentured Migration to Sumatra's East Coast, 1865–1911*. Council on East Asian Studies, Yale University.

Jayawardena, Kumari, and Rachel Kurian. 2015. *Class, Patriarchy and Ethnicity on Sri Lankan Plantations: Two Centuries of Power and Protest*. Hyderabad: Orient Black Swan.

Jiang Bowei and Cai Mingsong. 2008. "Jinmen minxinju (piju) jingying moshi zhi tantao" ("Discussion of the Operational Model of the Jinmen Remittance Shop"). In Wang Weizhong, ed., 264–278.

Jiao Jianhua and Xu Cuihong. 2004. "Jindai pixin ju tese tanyuan" ("Origins of the Special Features of Modern Remittance Offices"). In Wang Weizhong, ed., 2004, 164–173.

Jomo Kwame Sundaram, 1988. *A Question of Class: Capital, the State and Uneven Development in Malaya*, Singapore: Oxford University Press.

Jones, Guno. 2012. "Dutch Politicians, the Dutch Nation and the Dynamics of Postcolonial Citizenship." In Bosma, ed., 2012, 27–48,

Kamp, A. F. 1960. *De standvastige tinnen soldaat, 1860–1960: N. V. Billiton Maatschappij*. The Hague: Billiton Maatschappij.

Karmakar, Krishna G. 2015. "Colonial Rule and Its Effects on India's Rural Economy." *Journal of South Asian Studies*, vol. 3, no. 3, 277–288.

Kartomi, Margaret J. 2012. *Musical Journeys in Sumatra*. Baltimore: University of Illinois Press.

Kaur, Amarjit. 2004. *Wage Labour in Southeast Asia since 1840: Globalisation, the International Division of Labour and Labour Transformations*. Houndsmill: Palgrave Macmillan.

Kaur, Amarjit. 2006. "Indian Labour, Labour Standards, and Workers' Health in Burma and Malaya, 1900–1940." *Modern Asian Studies*, vol. 40, no. 2, 425–475.

Kaur, Amarjit. 2013. "Indian Migrant Workers in Malaysia." *New Mandala*, 2 pts, February 20–21.

Kitamura, Yumi. 2007. "Museum as the Representation of Ethnicity: The Construction of Chinese Indonesian Ethnic Identity in Post-Suharto Indonesia." *Kyoto Review of Southeast Asia*, issues 8–9, 2007.

Kloosterboer, Willemina. 1960. *Involuntary Labour since the Abolition of Slavery A Survey of Compulsory Labour Throughout the World*. Leiden: Brill.

Knight, Roger.1988. "Peasant Labour and Capitalist Production in Late Colonial Indonesia: The 'Campaign' at a North Java Sugar Factory, 1840–70." *Journal of Southeast Asian Studies*, vol. 19, no. 2, 245–265.

Knight, Roger. 2011. "Indenture, Grand Narratives and Fragmented Histories: The Dutch East Indies, c. 1880–1940." In Van der Linden, ed., 2011, 419–432.

Kort historisch overzicht van de werving voor de Bankatinwinning buiten Banka, benevens van de maatregeln in verband met die werving getroffen, bijgewerkt tot 1 juli 1928. Arsip Nasional, Jakarta, Algemene Secretarie, Grote Bundel, TZG Agenda, file no. 8436, 1–3.

Kuhn, Philip A. 2008. *Chinese among Others: Emigration in Modern Times*. Lanham: Rowman and Littlefield.

Kuiper, Koos. 2017. *The Early Dutch Sinologists (1854–1900): Training in Holland and China, Functions in the Netherlands East Indies*. 2 vols. Leiden: Brill.

Kumar, Arun. 2019. “Letters of the Labouring Poor: The Art of Letter Writing in Colonial India.” *Past and Present*, https://doi.org/10.1093/pastj/gtz035.

Kumar, Ashutosh. 2014. “Indian Nationalists and the End of Indentured Emigration.” NMML, Occasional Paper, History and Society New Series, no. 48.

Kumar, Ashutosh. 2015. “Songs of Abolition: Anti Indentured Campaign in Early Twentieth Century India.” In Pratap Kumar, ed., *Indian Diaspora: Socio-Cultural and Religious Worlds*, Leiden: Brill, 2015, 38–51.

Kumar, Ashutosh. 2017. *Coolies of the Empire: Indentured Indians in the Sugar Colonies, 1830–1920.* Cambridge, Cambridge University Press.

Kynoch, Gary. 2005. “‘Your Petitioners are in Mortal Terror’: The Violent World of Chinese Mineworkers in South Africa, 1904–1910,” *Journal of Southern African Studies,* vol. 31, no. 3, 531–546.

Kwong, Peter. 2001. *Chinatown, New York: Labor and Politics, 1930–1950.* Revised with a new introduction. New York: The New Press.

Lal, Brij V. 1983. “Indian Indenture Historiography: A Note on Problems, Sources and Methods.” *Pacific Studies*, vol. 6, no. 2, 33–50.

Lal, Brij V. 2021. “Indian Indenture: History and Historiography in a Nutshell.” *Journal of Indentureship and Its Legacies*, vol. 1, no. 1, 1–15.

Lal, Vinay. 2017. “Indian Servitude in the British Empire.” In Radha Sarna Hegde and Ajaya Kumar Sahoo, eds, *Routledge Handbook of the Indian Diaspora*, Abingdon: Routledge, 17–27.

Lamb, Nicole. 2014. “A Time of Normalcy: Javanese ‘Coolies’ Remember the Colonial Estate.” *Bijdragen tot de Taal-*, Land- en Volkenkunde, no. 170, 530–556.

Landheer, Bartholomew. 1941. “Financial Policy of the Dutch East Indies.” *Far Eastern Survey*, vol. 10, no. 17, 195–200.

Lasker, Bruno. 1950. *Human Bondage in Southeast Asia.* Chapel Hill: University of North Carolina Press.

Le Moli, Ginevra. 2021. “‘Parity with All Nations’: The ‘Coolie’ Trade and the Quest for Recognition by China and Japan.” *Leiden Journal of International Law*, 1–19. https://doi.org/10.1017/S092215652100042X. Published August 19.

Lee Hock Guan. 2013. “Shades of Citizenship: Betwixt the Civic and the Ethnic.” In Daljit Singh, ed., *Southeast Asian Affairs 2013,* Singapore: ISEAS, 2013, 168–190.

Lee Kam Hing and Tan Chee-Beng, eds. 2000. *The Chinese in Malaysia*. Shah Alam: Oxford University Press.

Lee, Sharon M. 1989. “Female Immigrants and Labor in Colonial Malaya: 1860–1947.” *The International Migration Review*, vol. 23, no. 2, 309–331.

Leenarts, Ellen. 1999. Coolie Wages in Western Enterprises in the Outer Islands, 1919–1938.” In Houben, Lindblad, and others, eds, 1999, 131–155.

Leinbach, Thomas R. 1987. "Economic Growth, Development Planning and Policy Alternatives in Medan, Indonesia." *Journal of Southeast Asian Studies*, vol. 18, no. 1, 118–140.

Lewis, Hannah, Peter Dwyer, Stuart Hodkinson, and Louise Waite. 2015. "Hyper-Precarious Lives: Migrants, Work and Forced Labour in the Global North." *Progress in Human Geography*, vol. 39, no. 5, 580–600.

Li Anshan. 2000. *Feizhou Huaren Huaqiao shi* (History of overseas and ethnic Chinese in Africa). Beijing: Zhongguo Huaqiao chuban she.

Li, Huaiyin. 2005. *Village Governance in North China: Huailu County, 1875–1936*. Stanford CA: Stanford University Press.

Li Minghuan. 2012. "'Playing Edge Ball': Transnational Migration Brokerage in China." In Barak Kalir and Malini Sur, eds, *Transnational Flows and Permissive Polities Ethnographies of Human Mobilities in Asia*, Amsterdam: Amsterdam University Press, 2012, 207–228.

Li Xiaoyuan. 2008. "Qiaopi yu Chao Mei qiaoxiang diqu renmin shenghuo fangshi de bianqian" ("Qiaopi and Changes in Life-style of the People in the Chao and Mei Areas"). In Wang Weizhong, ed., 2008, 287–295.

Liem, Giok Kiauw Nio, and Patricia Tjiook-Liem. 2009. *De rechtspositie der Chinezen in Nederlands-Indië 1848–1942: Wetgevingsbeleid tussen beginsel en belang*. Leiden: Leiden University Press.

Lin Qingxi. 2010. "Chaoshan qiaopi zai renshi" ("Once Again Recognizing Chaoshan Qiaopi"). In Wang Weizhong, ed., 2010, 207–117.

Lin Sha. 2008. "Xiamen qiaopi ye de chansheng he fazhan" ("The Origins and Development of the Xiamen Qiaopi Trade"). In Wang Weizhong, ed., 2008, 354–357.

Lin Shuihao, He Guozhong, He Qiliang, Lai Guanfu, eds. 1998. *Malaixiya Huaren shi xinbian* (New history of Chinese in Malaysia). Kuala Lumpur: Malaixiya Zhonghua da huitang zonghui.

Lin Tengyun. 2008. "Cong qiaopi he piju shouju tan Meizhou Huaqiao yu Shantou bang de guanxi" ("Talking about the Relationship between the Meizhou Overseas Chinese and Shantou on the Basis of Qiaopi and Piju Receipts"). In Wang Weizhong, ed., 2008, 411–416.

Lindblad, J. Thomas. 1999. "Coolies in Deli: Labour Conditions in Western Enterprises in East Sumatra, 1910–1938." In Houben and Lindblad, eds, 1999, 43–78.

Lindquist, Johan, and Biao Xiang. 2019. "Space of Mediation: Labour Migration, Intermediaries and the State in Indonesia and China since the Nineteenth Century." *Revue Européenne des Migrations Internationales*, vol. 35, nos 1–2, 39–62

Lindsey, Tim, and Helen Pausacker, eds. 2005. *Chinese Indonesians: Remembering, Distorting, Forgetting*. Monash: ISEAS.

Liu, Andrew B. 2015. The Two Tea Countries: Competition, Labor, and Economic Thought in Coastal China and Eastern India, 1834–1942. PhD, Columbia University.

Liu Jin. 2009. *Wuyi yinxin* ("Wuyi silver and letters"). Guangzhou: Guangdong renmin chuban she.

Liu, Oiyan. 2014."Countering 'Chinese Imperialism': Sinophobia and Border Protection in the Dutch East Indies." *Indonesia*, no. 97, 87–110.

Liu Yuzun, Huang Zhongyan, Gui Guanghua, and Wu Fengbin, eds. 2016 [1963, 1978]. *"Zhuzai" Huagong fangwen lu* ("Transcripts of interviews with Chinese 'piglet' labourers"), Guangzhou: Guangdong renmin chuban she.

Liu Zhenggang and Wang Liwa. 2008. "Wan Qing Huaren nüxing bei youguai chuyang qianxi" ("Preliminary research on Chinese women abducted overseas in the late Qing"). *Wuyi daxue xuebao (shehui kexue ban)*, vol. 10, no. 4, 11–15.

Lockard, Craig A. 1971. "The Javanese as Emigrant: Observations on the Development of Javanese Settlements Overseas." *Indonesia*, no. 11, 41–62.

Lockard, Craig A. 1978. "Repatriation Movements among the Javanese in Suriname: A Comparative Analysis." *Caribbean Studies*, vol. 18, nos. 1–2, 85–113.

Loh, Kah Seng. 2022. "Coolies and Crisis in Singapore: The Great Depression in the 1930s and the Chinese Working Class." In Chi-cheung Choi, Tomoko Shiroyama, and Venus Viana, eds, *Strenuous Decades: Global Challenges and Transformation of Chinese Societies in Modern Asia*, Berlin: De Gruyter, 142–166.

Look Lai, Walton. 1989. "Chinese Indentured Labor: Migrations to the British West Indies in the Nineteenth Century." *Amerasia* vol. 15, no. 2, 117–138.

Look Lai, Walton. 1993. *Indentured Labor, Caribbean Sugar: Chinese and. Indian Migrants to the British West Indies, 1838–1918.* Introduced by Sidney W. Mintz. Baltimore: The Johns Hopkins University Press.

Look Lai, Walton. 1998. Imperialism, Indenture and Diaspora: The Origins of the West Indian Chinese Community. Paper for the UK Society for Caribbean Studies, Warwick University.

Look Lai, Walton 2009. "Asian Diasporas and Tropical Migration in the Age of Empire: A Comparative Overview." *Journal of Chinese Overseas*, no. 5, 28–54.

López, Kathleen. 2013. *Chinese Cubans: A Transnational History.* Chapel Hill: University of North Carolina Press.

Lovins, Christopher. 2022. "Korea: A Slave Society." In Allen, ed., 2022, 178–200.

Lu Wendi, Chen Zexian, and Peng Jiali, eds. 1981. *Guanyu Huagong chuguo de Zhongwai zonghexing zhuzuo* (Comprehensive writings from China and abroad concerning Huagong migration). In Chen Hansheng, ed., 1981–1985, vol. 4.

Lu Wendi, Chen Zexian, and Peng Jiali, eds. 1985a. *Zhongguo guanwen shu xuanji* (A selection of official Chinese documents). In Chen Hansheng, ed., 1981–1985, vol. 1, pt 1.

Lu Wendi, Chen Zexian, and Peng Jiali, eds, 1985b. *Zhongguo guanwen shu xuanji* (A selection of official Chinese documents). In Chen Hansheng, ed., 1981–1985, vol. 1, pt 4.

Lu Wendi, Peng Jiali, and Chen Zexian, eds. 1984a. *Guanyu Dongnan Ya Huagong de siren zhuzuo* (Private individuals' writings about Huagong in Southeast Asia). In Chen Hansheng, ed., 1981–1985, vol. 5.

Lu Wendi, Peng Jiali, and Chen Zexian, eds. 1984b. *Meiguo yu Jianada Huagong* (Huagong in America and Canada). In Chen Hansheng, ed., 1981–1985, vol. 7.

Lu Wendi, Peng Jiali, and Chen Zexian, eds. 1984c. *Da Yangzhou Huagong* (Huagong in the Pacific). In Chen Hansheng, ed., 1981–1985, vols. 8–10.

Luo Zeyang. 2004. "Qiaopi wenhua yu haiyang wenhua" ("Qiaopi culture and oceanic culture"). In Wang Weizhong, ed., 2004, 208–214.

Lutz, Jessie G. 2009. "Chinese Emigrants, Indentured Workers, and Christianity in the West Indies, British Guiana and Hawaii." *Caribbean Studies*, vol. 37, no. 2, 133–154.

Ma Chujian. 2008. "Chao bang pixin ju yu qiaohui liutong zhi fazhan chutan" ("Preliminary Research into the circulation of remittances by the Chao Gang remittance Ooffice"). In Wang Weizhong, ed., 2008, 21–32

Ma Huiyue. 2015. *Jindai qiyue Huagong falü* (Laws on modern Chinese indentured labour). Beijing: Falü chuban she.

Maassen, C. C. J. 1937. *De Javaansche landbouwkolonisatie in de Buitengewesten.* Batavia: Landsdrukkerij.

MacDonald, Andrew. 2008. "The View Across the Ocean: Indian Ocean Worlds and the Question of Power over the Long Nineteenth Century." *Journal of Natal and Zulu History*, vol. 26, no. 1, 108–129.

Macgregor, Paul, ed. 1995. *Histories of the Chinese in Australasia and the South Pacific.* Melbourne: Museum of Chinese Australian History.

MacNair, H. F. 1923. "The Chinese as Contract Laborers." *The Weekly Review*, June 2.

MacNair, H. F. 1924. "The Chinese in the Dutch East Indies." *The China Weekly Review*, September 20.

Maddison, Angus. 1989. "Dutch Income in and from Indonesia, 1700–1938." *Modern Asian Studies*, vol. 23, no. 4, 645–670.

Mahase, Radica. 2021. *Why Should We Be Called 'Coolies'? The End of Indian Indentured Labour.* Abingdon: Routledge.

Mahmud, Tayyab. 2012. Cheaper than a Slave: Indentured Labor, Colonialism and Capitalism. Seattle University School of Law Legal Paper Series # 12–34.

Manan, Tarmizi Abdul. 2019. "Legal Implication of Plantation Concessions during the Dutch Colonialism on the Contemporary Land Governance and Civil Rights." *Journal of Legal, Ethical and Regulatory Issues*, vol. 22, no. 2.

Mandle, Jay R. 1972. "The Plantation Economy: An Essay in Definition." *Science & Society*, vol. 36, no. 1, 49–62.

Manjapra, Kris. 2018. "Asian Plantation Histories at the Frontiers of Nation and Globalization." *Modern Asian Studies*, vol. 52, no. 6.

Manual of Netherlands India (Dutch East Indies). n.d. Compiled by the Geographical Section of the Naval Intelligence Division, Naval Staff, Admiralty. London: His Majesty's Stationery Office.

Martino, Enrique. 2016. Touts and Despots: Recruiting Assemblages of Contract Labour in Fernando Pó and the Gulf of Guinea, 1858–1979. PhD, Humboldt Universität.

Maul, Daniel Roger. 2007. "The International Labor Organization and the Struggle against Forced Labor from 1919 to the Present." *Labor History*, vol. 48, no. 4, 477–500.

Maul, Daniel Roger. 2012. "Prologue: Separate Worlds — The ILO and 'Native Labour,' 1919–39." In *Human Rights, Development and Decolonization: The International Labour Organization, 1940–70*, London: Palgrave Macmillan, 17–27.

McKeown, Adam. 2001. *Chinese Migrant Networks and Cultural Change: Peru, Chicago, Hawaii, 1900–1936*. Chicago, University of Chicago Press.

McKeown, Adam. 2004. "Global Migration, 1846–1940." *Journal of World History*, vol. 15, no. 2, 155–189.

McVey, Ruth T. 1965. *The Rise of Indonesian Communism*. Ithaca: Cornell University Press.

Mei Weiqiang and Zhang Guoxiong, eds. 2001. *Wuyi Huaqiao Huaren shi* ("A history of Wuyi's overseas and ethnic Chinese"). Guangzhou: Guangdong gaodeng jiaoyu chuban she.

Melbourn, G. Fraser. 1894. *The Planter's Manual: An English, Dutch, Malay and Keh Chinese Vocabulary*. Deli-Sumatra: n. p.

Metcalf, Thomas R. 1979. "Rural Society and British Rule in Nineteenth Century India." *The Journal of Asian Studies*, vol. 39, no. 1, 111–119.

Miles, Stephen. 2020. *Chinese Diasporas: A Social History of Global Migration*. New York: Cambridge University Press.

Mishra, Amit Kumar. 2015. "Sardars, Kanganies and Maistries: Intermediaries in the Indian Labour Diaspora During the Colonial Period." In Sigrid Wadauer, Thomas Buchner, and Alexander Mejstrik, eds, *The History of Labour Intermediation: Institutions and Finding Employment in the Nineteenth and Early Twentieth Centuries*, International Studies in Social History, vol. 26, New York: Berghahn, 368–387.

Misra, Maria. 1999. *Business, Race, and Politics in British India, c. 1850–1960*. New York: Clarendon Press.

Mo Zhen, ed. 2013. *Haibang chengfu: Guangdong qiaopi dang'an* (Fragrance from Abroad: Guangdong's Qiaopi Archive). Guangzhou: Lingnan meishu chuban she.

Mohapatra, Prabhu, and Rana Behal. 1991."'Tea and Money versus Human Life': The Rise and Fall of the Indenture System in the Assam Tea Plantations, 1840–1908." *Journal of Peasant Studies*, vol. 19, nos. 3–4, 142–172.

Mollema, J. C. 1922. *De ontwikkeling van het eiland Billiton en van de Billiton-Maatschappij*. The Hague: Nijhoff.

Moll-Murata, Christine. 2008. "Chinese Guilds from the Seventeenth to the Twentieth Centuries: An Overview." *International Review of Social History*, no. 53, 213–247.

Moll-Murata, Christine. 2016. "Tributary Labour Relations in China During the Ming-Qing Transition (Seventeenth to Eighteenth Centuries)." *International Review of Social History*, 61 (Special Issue S24, *Conquerors, Employers and Arbiters: States and Shifts in Labour Relations, 1500–2000*), 27–48.

Mongia, Radhika. 2018. *Indian Migration and Empire: A Colonial Genealogy of the Modern State*. Durham: Duke University Press.

Moore, Brian L. 1977. "The Retention of Caste Notions among the Indian Immigrants in British Guiana during the Nineteenth Century." *Comparative Studies in Society and History*, vol. 19, no. 1, 96–107.

Morton, Fred. 2005. "Female *inboekelinge* in the South African Republic, 1850–1880." *Slavery & Abolition*, vol. 26, no. 2, 199–215.

Nair, A. R. 1931. "British Malaya Owes Debt to Chinese Settlers." *The China Press*, September 26.

Narvaez, Benjamin Nicolas. 2010. Chinese Coolies in Cuba and Peru: Race, Labor, and Immigration, 1839–1886. PhD, The University of Texas at Austin.

Neale, Margaret. 1988. *We Were the Christmas Islanders: Reminiscences and Recollections of the People of an Isolated Island—the Australian Territory of Christmas Island, Indian Ocean, 1906–1980*. Chapman, ACT: N. p.

Ngai, Mae. 2017. "Trouble on the Rand: The Chinese Question in South Africa and the Apogee of White Settlerism." *International Labor and Working-Class History*, vol. 91, 59–78.

Nitisastro, Widjojo. 2006. *Population Trends in Indonesia*. Jakarta: Equinox Publishing.

Noa Siaosi, A. S. 2010. Catching the Dragon's Tail: The Impact of the Chinese in Samoa. MA thesis, University of Canterbury.

Northrup, David. 1995. *Indentured Labor in the Age of Imperialism, 1834–1922*. New York: Cambridge University Press.

Nugteren, Bastiaan. 2016. The Impossible Colonial Border: Chinese Migration and Immigration Policies in the Netherlands East Indies, 1880–1912. MA thesis, Leiden University.

Oekan Soekotjo Abdoellah. 1987. Transmigration Policies in Indonesia: Government Aims and Popular Response. https://doi.org/10.1111/j.2050-411X.1987.tb00501.x.

Om, Prakasch. 1998. "The Trading World of India and Southeast Asia in the Early Modern Period." *Archipel*, vol. 56, *L'horizon nousantarien. Mélanges en hommage à Denys Lombard*, vol. 1, 31–42.

Ong, Aihwa, and Donald Nonini, eds. 1997. *Ungrounded Empires: The Cultural Politics of Modern Chinese Transnationalism*. New York: Routledge.

Ownby, David. 1993. "Introduction: Secret Societies Reconsidered." In Ownby and Heidhues, eds, 1993, 3–33.

Ownby, David, and Mary Somers Heidhues, eds. *"Secret Societies" Reconsidered: Perspectives on the Social History of Modern South China and Southeast Asia*. Armonk, NY: M. E. Sharpe, 1993.

Pabottingi, Mochtar. 1991. Nationalism and Egalitarianism in Indonesia, 1908–1980. PhD, University of Hawaii.

Palmier, Leslie H. 1960. "The Javanese Nobility under the Dutch." *Comparative Studies in Society and History*, vol. 2, no. 2, 197–227.

Pan, Lynn, ed. 1998. *The Encylopedia of the Chinese Overseas*. Singapore: Archipelago Press.

Pande, Amba. 2013. "Conceptualising Indian Diaspora Diversities within a Common Identity." *Economic & Political Weekly*, December 7, 2013, vol. 48, no. 49.

Pantin, Dennis. 1980. "The Plantation Economy Model and the Caribbean." *Bulletin*, vol. 12, no. 1, Institute of Development Studies, Sussex, 17–23.

Parker, Edward Harper. 1902. *John Chinaman and a Few Others*. London: John Murray.

Pastor, G. 1927. *De panglongs*. Weltevreden: Landsdrukkerij.

Paulus, Jozlas, compiler. 1919. *Encyclopaedie van Nederlandsch-Indië*, second edition, 2 vols. The Hague: Martinus Nijhoff.

Pekelharing, N. R. 1924. *De groote cultures in Ned.-Indië en eenige naburige Koloniën* (The great cultures in the Neth. East Indies and neighbouring colonies). Weltevreden: Landsdruk, 1924.

Pelzer, Karl J. 1935. *Die Arbeiterwanderungen in Südostasien: Eine wirtschafts- und bevölkerungsgeographische Untersuchung*. Würzburg: Konrad Triltsch.

Pelzer, Karl J. 1938. "Present Day Labour Migration in India." In International Geographical Union, eds. *Comptes rendus du Congrès international de géographie*. Leiden: Brill, 65–75.

Pelzer, Karl J. 1957. "The Agrarian Conflict in East Sumatra." *Pacific Affairs*, vol. 30, no. 2, 151–159.

Perry, Elizabeth J. 1993. *Shanghai on Strike: The Politics of Chinese Labor*. Stanford: Stanford University Press.

Perry, Elizabeth J. 2008. "Reclaiming the Chinese Revolution." *The Journal of Asian Studies*, vol. 67, no. 4, 1147–1164.

Phoa Liong Gie 1936 [1992]. "The Changing Economic Position of the Chinese in Netherlands India." In Fernando and Bulbeck, eds, 1992, 5–18.

Pols, Hans. 2018. *Nurturing Indonesia: Medicine and Decolonisation in the Dutch East Indies*. Cambridge: Cambridge University Press.

Powell, Edward Alexander. 1921. *Where the Strange Trails Go Down: Sulu, Borneo, Celebes, Bali, Java, Sumatra, Straits Settlements, Malay States, Siam, Cambodia, Annam, Cochin-China*, New York: Charles Scribner's Sons.

Powell, Miles Alexander. 2016. "People in Peril, Environments at Risk: Coolies, Tigers, and Colonial Singapore's Ecology of Poverty." *Environment and History*, no. 22, 455–482.

Qin, Yucheng. 2016. *The Cultural Clash: Chinese Traditional Native-Place Sentiment and the Anti-Chinese Movement.* Lanham: University Press of America.

Rajasinghamsenanayake, Darini. 2017. "Precarious Citizens, Cyber-Nationalism: South-South Asia's Diasporas." *IIC Quarterly*, vol. 44, no. 2, 66–82.

Rankine, Wendy. 1995. "From Nauru to Nowhere: Pacific Island Chinese Evacuee Workers in Central Australian Wolfram Mines, 1942–43." In Paul Macgregor, ed., 1995, 152–158.

Ransmeier, Johanna S. 2017. *Sold People: Traffickers and Family Life in North China.* Cambridge MA: Harvard University Press.

Rapport betreffende Chineezen-Werving op Billiton. 1905. BrRG-33 = 16072 KIT.

Reddock, Rhoda. 2017. "South Asian Plantation Histories and their Enduring Legacies: Indian and Atlantic Ocean Connections." *Development and Change*, vol. 48, no. 1, 189–200.

Rediker, Marcus, Titas Chakraborty, and Matthias van Rossum, eds. 2019. *A Global History of Runaways: Workers, Mobility, and Capitalism, 1600–1850.* Oakland: University of California Press.

Reid, Anthony. 1970. "Early Chinese Immigration into North Sumatra." In Jerome Chen and Nicholas Tarling, eds, *Studies in the Social History of China and South-East Asia: Essays in Memory of Victor Purcell, 1896–1965*, Cambridge: Cambridge University Press, 1970, 289–320.

Reid, Anthony. 1979. *The Blood of the People: Revolution and the End of Traditional Rule in Northern Sumatra.* Kuala Lumpur: Oxford University Press.

Reid, Anthony. 1983. "Introduction: Slavery and Bondage in Southeast Asian History." In Anthony Reid, ed., *Slavery, Bondage and Dependency in Southeast Asia*, St Lucia, Brisbane: University of Queensland Press, 1–43.

Reid, Anthony. 1997a. "Introduction." In Reid, ed., 1997, 1–25.

Reid, Anthony, ed. 1996. *Sojourners and Settlers: Histories of Southeast Asia and the Chinese.* Sydney: Allen and Unwin.

Reid, Anthony, ed. 1997b. *The Last Stand of Asian Autonomies: Responses to Modernity in the Diverse States of Southeast Asia and Korea, 1750–1900*, New York: St. Martin's.

Rengasamey, Pushpavalli A., and Sivachandralingam Sunda. 2012. "Peranan dan Perkembangan Tabung Imigrasi Tamil di Tanah Melayu, 1907–1938" ("The

Role and Development of the Tamil Immigration Fund in Malaya, 1907–1938"). *Sarjana*, vol. 27, no. 2, December, 38–49.

Rengasamey, Pushpavalli A., and Sivachandralingam Sundara Raja. 2020. "A Critique on the South Indian Labour Fund and the Malaysian Indian Plantation Workers." *Kemanusiaan*, vol. 27, no. 1, 115–133.

Reviews. 2009. Kerry Ward, *Networks of Empire: Forced Migration in the Dutch East India Company*. With a Response by Kerry Ward. *International Journal of Maritime History*, vol. 21, no. 1, 297–340.

Report of Coolie Commission, Appointed to Inquire into the Condition of the Indian Immigrants in the Colony of Natal. 1872. Pietermaritzburg: Keith & Co.

Rhemrev, J. L. T. 1903 [1987]. Rapport van de resultaten van het mij bij Gouvernements Besluit van 24 Mei 1903 No. 19 opgedragen onderzoek. In Breman 1987, 315–408.

Rice, Richard. 1990. "Japanese Labor in World War II." *International Labor and Working-Class History*, no. 38, 29–45.

Richardson, Peter. 1977. "The Recruiting of Chinese Indentured Labour for the South African Gold-Mines, 1903–1908." *Journal of African History*, vol. 18, no. 1, 85–108.

Richardson, Peter. 1982. *Chinese Mine Labour in the Transvaal*, London: Macmillan.

Roopnarine, Lomarsh. 2006. "The Return of East Indian Indentured Servants from the Caribbean to India, 1838–1920." *Journal of Caribbean History*, vol. 40, no. 2, 308–324.

Roopnarine, Lomarsh. 2010. "The Indian Sea Voyage between India and the Caribbean during the Second Half of the Nineteenth Century." *Journal of Caribbean History*, vol. 44, no. 1, 48–74.

Rudner, David West. 1994. *Caste and Capitalism in Colonial India: The Nattukottai Chettiars*. Berkeley: University of California Press.

Ruzicka, Ivan. n.d. "Forest Exploitation in Indonesia: Past and Present." *Indonesia Circle*, vol. 6, no. 16, 3–15.

Sai, Siew-min. 2021. "Benevolent Technocracy: The Chinese Protectorate, Migration Control and Racialised Governmentality in Colonised Malaya." *Journal of Southeast Asian Studies*, 1–23. https://doi.org/10.1017/S002246342100059X.

Sandhu, Kernial Singh. 1993. "The Coming of the Indians to Malaysia." In K. S. Sandhu and A. Mani, eds, *Indian Communities in Southeast Asia*, Singapore: ISEAS, 1993, 151–89.

Sen, Samita. 2004a. "'Without His Consent?': Marriage and Women's Migration in Colonial India." *International Labor and Working Class History*, vol. 65, 77–104.

Sen, Samita. 2004b. *Women and Labour in Late Colonial India: The Bengal Jute Industry*. Cambridge University Press.

Sen, Samita. 2010. "Commercial Recruiting and Informal Intermediation: Debate over the Sardari System in Assam Tea Plantations, 1860–1900." *Modern Asian Studies*, vol. 44, no. 1, 3–28.

Shamsul Bahrin, Tunku. 1967. "The Pattern of Indonesian Migration and Settlement in Malaya." *Asian Studies*, vol. 5, no. 2, 233–257.

Shen Huifen. 2011. "Gudi qiucun: Taiping Yang zhanzheng shiqi Fujian de fanxiang nanqiao" ("Seeking refuge in one's native place: Refugee migrants who returned to the countryside in Fujian during the Pacific War"). *Shijie minzu*, no. 6 (2011), 59–68.

Shen Huifen. 2012. *China's Left -Behind Wives: Families of Migrants from Fujian to Southeast Asia, 1930s–1950s*. Singapore: National University of Singapore Press.

Shen, Jiaying. n.d. "A Great Convergence: The Mass Killing of Chinese in the 1923 Kantō Massacre." https://doi.org/10.1080/10371397.2020.1771175

Shih, Shu-mei. 2001. *The Lure of the Modern*. Berkeley: University of California Press.

Shimada, Ryuto. 2014. "Hinterlands and Port Cities in Southeast Asia's Economic Development in the Eighteenth Century: The Case of Tin Production and its Export Trade." In Tsukasa Mizushima, George Bryan Souza, and Dennis O. Flynn, eds, *Hinterlands and Commodities: Place, Space, Time and the Political Economic Development of Asia over the Long Eighteenth Century*. Leiden: Brill, 2014, 197–214.

Siddique, Sharon, and Leo Suryadinata. 1981. "Bumiputra and Pribumi: Economic Nationalism (Indiginism) in Malaysia and Indonesia." *Pacific Affairs*, vol. 54, no. 4, 662–687.

Siegel, Jeff. 1988. "Introduction." In Richard Keith Barz and Jeff Siegel, eds. *Language Transplanted: The Development of Overseas Hindi*. Wiesbaden: Otto Harrassowitz, 1–23.

Singh, Sandhu Kernial. 1969. *Indians in Malaya: Some Aspects of Their Immigration and Settlement (1786–1957)*. Cambridge: Cambridge University Press.

Singh, Sherry-Ann. 2019. "Indian Indentured Laborers in the Caribbean." In Steven Ratuva, ed., *The Palgrave Handbook of Ethnicity*, Singapore: Palgrave Macmillan, 1–17.

Singha, Radhika. 2020. *The Coolie's Great War: Indian Labour in a Global Conflict, 1914–1921. London:* Hurst.

Skinner, G. William. 1963."The Chinese Minority." In Ruth McVey, ed., *Indonesia*, New Haven, CT: Yale University Southeast Asia Studies, 1963, 97–117.

Snelders, Stephen, Leo van Bergen, and Frank Huisman. 2019. "Leprosy and the Colonial Gaze: Comparing the Dutch West and East Indies, 1750–1950." *Social History of Medicine*, vol. 34, no. 2, 611–631.

Southall, Roger. 1988. *Labour and Unions in Asia and Africa: Contemporary Issues*. London: Palgrave Macmillan.

Stanziani, Alessandro. 2014. *Bondage: Labor and Rights in Eurasia from the Sixteenth to the Early Twentieth Centuries*, New York: Berghahn Books.

Stanziani, Alessandro. 2018. *Labor on the Fringes of Empire: Voice, Exit and the Law*. New York: Palgrave Macmillan.

Stanziani, Alessandro, ed. 2013. *Labour, Coercion, and Economic Growth in Eurasia, 17th–20th Centuries*. Leiden: Brill.

Stenberg, Josh, and Minasny, Budiman. 2022. "Coolie Legend on the Deli Plantation: Tale, Text, and Temple of the Five Ancestors." *Bijdragen tot de taal-, land- en volkenkunde*, vol. 178, nos 2-3, 159–191.

Stewart, John R. 1940. "Chinese Migration to Manchuria Setting New Records." *Far Eastern Survey*, vol. 9, no. 18.

Stibbe, D. G., and C. Spat, with E. M. Uhlenbeck, eds. 1927. *Encyclopaedie van Nederlandsch-Indië*. Second edition. 8 vols. The Hague: Martinus Nijhoff, vol. 5.

Stokes, Eric. 1978. *The Peasant and the Raj: Studies in Agrarian Society and Peasant Rebellion*. Cambridge: Cambridge University Press.

Stoler, Ann Laura. 1985. *Capitalism and Confrontation in Sumatra's Plantation Belt, 1870–1979*. New Haven: Yale University Press.

Suryadinata, Leo. 2015. "China's Nationality Laws and the Chinese Overseas." In Bhattacharya and Kripalani, eds, 43–54.

Susanto Zuhdi. 2014. *Nasionalisme, Laut, dan Sejarah* ("Nationalism, the sea, and history"). Jakarta: Kobam.

Tan Chee-Beng. 2000 "Socio-cultural Diversities and Identities." In Lee Kam Hong and Tan Chee-Beng, eds, *The Chinese in Malaysia*, Shah Alam: Oxford University Press, 37–70.

Tappe, Oliver, and Ulrike Lindner. 2016. "Introduction: Global Variants of Bonded Labour." In Sabine Damir-Geilsdorf, Ulrike Lindner, Gesine Müller, Oliver Tappe, and Michael Zeuske, eds, *Bonded Labour: Global and Comparative Perspectives (18th–21st Century)*, Bielefeld: Transcript Verlag, 9–34.

Termorshuizen, Thio. 2008. "Indentured Labour in the Dutch Colonial Empire, 1800–1940." In Geert Oostindie, ed., *Dutch Colonialism, Migration and Cultural Heritage: Past and Present*, Leiden: Brill, 2008, 261–314.

Thampi, Madhavi. 2015. "Indian Soldiers and Policemen in China in the Colonial Period." In Bhattacharya and Kripalani, eds, 2015, 187–196.

Thompson, Edgar T. 1932. "Mines and Plantations and the Movements of Peoples." *American Journal of Sociology*, vol. 37, no. 4, 603–611.

Tian Yu. 1929. "Wulidong Huagong jinkuang" ("Recent situation of Huagong in Belitung"). *Nanyang yanjiu*, published by Jinan University's Nanyang Culture Department, vol. 2, no. 4, 282–293.

T'ien, Ju-K'ang. 1953. *The Chinese of Sarawak: A Study of Social Structure.* London: Department of Anthropology, London School of Economics and Political Science.

Tinker, Hugh.1974. *A New System of Slavery: The Export of Indian Labour Overseas 1830–1920.* London and New York: Oxford University Press.

Tirtosudarmo, Riwanto. 2005. The *Orang Melayu* and *Orang Jawa* in the "Lands Below the Winds." CRISE Working Paper, no. 14.

Tjandra, Surya. 2016. Labour Law and Development in Indonesia. Doctoral Thesis, Leiden University.

Trocki, Carl A. 1993. "The Rise and Fall of the Ngee Heng Kongsi in Singapore." In Ownby and Heidhues, eds, 1993, 89–119.

Trocki, Carl A. 2011. "Opium as a Commodity in the Chinese Nanyang Trade." In Eric Tagliacozzo and Wen-Chin Chang, eds, *Chinese Circulations: Capital, Commodities, and Networks in Southeast Asia*, Durham: Duke University, 2011, 84--106.

Tsai Chutung. 1910. "The Chinese Nationality Law, 1909." *The American Journal of International Law*, vol. 4, no. 2, 404–411.

Tucker, David. 2005. "Labour Policy and the Construction Industry in Manchukuo: System of Recruitment, Management, and Control." In Paul H. Kratoska, ed., *Asian Labour in the Wartime Japanese Empire: Unknown Histories.* New York: Routledge, 25–60.

Tumbe, Chinmay. 2012. "Migration Persistence across Twentieth Century India." *Migration and Development*, vol. 1, no. 1, 87–112.

Turnbull, C. M. 1977. *A History of Modern Singapore, 1819–2005.* Singapore: Singapore University Press.

Vahed, Goolam. 1995. The Making of Indian Identity In Durban, 1914–1949. PhD, Indiana University.

Vahed, Goolam. 2001. "Uprooting, Rerooting: Culture, Religion and Community among Indentured Muslim Migrants in Colonial Natal, 1860–1911." *South African Historical Journal*, vol. 45, no. 1, 191–222.

Vahed, Goolam. 2012. "Power and Resistance: Indentured Labour in Colonial Natal, 1860–1911." *Man in India*, special issue on Indian Indentured Labour, vol. 92, no. 2, 299–317.

Vahed, Goolam, and Ashwin Desai. 2012. "Indian Indenture: Speaking across the Oceans." *Man in India*, vol. 92, no. 2, 195–213.

Van Bergen, Leo. 2019. *The Dutch East Indies Red Cross, 1870–1950: On Humanitarianism and Colonialism.* Lanham MA: Rowman and Littlefield.

Van Blommestein, A. F. 1917. *De Nieuwe Koelie-Ordonnantie voor de Oostkust van Sumatra.* Amsterdam: Scheltema and Holkema.

Van den Berg, Jurrien. 1999. "Tin Island: Labour Conditions in the Billiton Mines in the Nineteenth and Early Twentieth Centuries." In Houben, Lindblad, and others 1999, 209–230.

Van den Brand, Johannes. 1903. *Nog Eens: De Millioenen uit Deli*. Amsterdam: Höveker and Wormser.
Van den Brand, Johannes. 1918. "Arbeidswetgeving." *Vrijzinning Weekblad*, no. 1, 687–689.
Van der Eng, Pierre. 2002. "Bridging a Gap: A Reconstruction of Population Patterns in Indonesia, 1930–61." *Asian Studies Review*, vol. 26, no. 4, 487–509.
Van der Linden, Marcel. 2016. "Dissecting Coerced Labor." In Van der Linden and Rodríguez García, eds, 2016, 293–332.
Van der Linden, Marcel, ed. 2011. *Humanitarian and Changing Labor Relations: The Long-term Consequences of the Abolition of the Slave Trade*, Leiden: Brill.
Van der Linden, Marcel, and Magaly Rodríguez García, eds. 2016. *On Coerced Labor: Work and Compulsion after Chattel Slavery*. Leiden: Brill.
Van Luijk, Eric W., and Jan C. van Ours. 1993. How to Control Drugs: The Lessons of the *Opiumregie* in the Dutch East Indies (1894–1940). Research Memorandum 1993–30, Vrije Universiteit Amsterdam.
Vandenbosch, Amry. 1931. "Colonial Labor Problems: The Labor Contract with Penal Sanction in the Dutch East Indies." *Pacific Affairs*, vol. 4, no. 4, 318–324.
Varma, Nitin. 2005. "Coolie Acts and the Acting Coolies: Coolie, Planter and State in the Late Nineteenth and Early Twentieth Century Colonial Tea Plantations of Assam." *Social Scientist*, vol. 33, no. 5–6, 49–72.
Viljoen, Russel. 2005. "Indentured Labour and Khoikhoi 'Equality' before the Law in Cape Colonial Society, South Africa: The Case of Jan Paerl, c. 1796." *Itinerario*, no. 29, 54–72.
Vleming, J. L., ed. 1992 [1926]. "The Chinese Business Community in Netherlands India." In Fernando and. Bulbeck, eds. 1992, 90–260.
Walden, Sue. 1995. "The Tin Fields of Northeast Tasmania: A Regional Variation?" In Macgregor 1995, 177–190.
Wang Cangbai. 2013. "*Guiqiao* as Political Subjects in the Making of the People's Republic of China, 1949–1979." In Biao Xiang, Brenda S. A. Yeoh, and Mika Toyota, eds, *Return: Nationalizing Transnational Mobility in Asia*, Durham: Duke University Press, 2013, 63–82.
Wang Gungwu. 1970. "Chinese Politics in Malaya." *The China Quarterly*, no. 43, 1–30.
Wang Gungwu. 2000. *The Chinese Overseas: From Earthbound China to the Quest for Autonomy*. Cambridge, MA: Harvard University Press.
Wang Gungwu. 2018. *Nanyang: Essays on Heritage*. Singapore: ISEAS.
Wang Linqian and Wu Kunxiang, eds. 2002. *Zaoqi Huaqiao yu qiyue Huagong (mai zhuzai) ziliao* (Early materials relating to overseas Chinese and indentured Huagong [piglet trade]). Chaoshan: Chaoshan lishi wenhua yanjiu zhongxin, Shantou shi wenhua ju, Shantou shi tushu guan.
Wang Qimin. 1982. "Qiyue Huagong zhi de lishi fenqi wenti" ("The issue of the historical stages of indentured Huagong"). *Fujian shida xuebao (zhenxue shehui kexue ban)*, no. 1, 95–101.

Wang Weizhong, ed. 2004. *Shou jie qiaopi wenhua yanjiu hui lunwen ji* (Papers from the First Qiaopi Cultural Symposium). Shantou: n.p.

Wang Weizhong, ed. 2008. *Di erjie qiaopi wenhua yantao hui lunwen xuan* ("Selection of Papers from the Second Qiaopi Culture Symposium"). N. p.: Gongyuan chuban youxian gongsi.

Wang Weizhong, ed. 2010. *Di san jie qiaopi wenhua yantao hui lunwen xuan* ("Third Symposium on Research into Qiaopi Culture"). Hong Kong: Tianma chuban youxian gongsi.

Ward, Kerry. 2009. *Networks of Empire: Forced Migration in the Dutch East India Company.* Cambridge: Cambridge University Press.

Warner, H. William. 2020. "The Kabuliwalas: Afghan Moneylending and the Credit Cosmopolis of British India, c. 1880–1947." *The Indian Economic & Social History Review*, April 2020.

Waters, Les. 1983. *The Union of Christmas Island Workers.* Sydney: George Allen and Unwin.

Wazar, R. M. 2004 [1956]. "Tinnen Munten van Bangka." *Erts: Maandblad der Billitonbedrijven*, October 1956, no. 10. Reprinted in Yang Tongling et al. 2004, 209–211.

Wertheim, Wim F. 1993. "Conditions on Sugar Estates in Colonial Java: Comparisons with Deli." *Journal of Southeast Asian Studies,* vol. 24, no. 2, 268–284.

Wickramasekara, Piyasiri. 2015. "Migration Regimes and their Linkages for Family Unity, Integrity and Development." In Marion Panizzon, Gottfried Zürcher, and Elisa Fornalé, eds, *The Palgrave Handbook of International Labour Migration: Law and Policy Perspectives,* Houndmills: Palgrave Macmillan, 146–180.

Williams, Michael. 1999. *Chinese Settlement in NSW: A Thematic History.* A Report for the NSW Heritage Office.

Williams, Michael. 2018. *Returning Home with Glory: Chinese Villagers around the Pacific, 1849 to 1949.* Hong Kong: Hong Kong University Press.

Willmott, W. E. 1998. "The South Pacific." In Pan 1998, 292–296.

Wilson, Jon. 2016. *India Conquered: Britain's Raj and the Chaos of Empire.* London, Simon and Schuster.

Wiseman, Roger. 2001. Three Crises: Management in the Colonial Java Sugar Industry, 1880s-1930s. PhD, University of Adelaide.

Wolf, Eric R., with Sydel Silverman. 2001. *Pathways of Power: Building an Anthropology of the Modern World.* Berkeley: University of California Press.

Wong Tze-ken, Danny. 2000. "The Chinese in Sabah: An Overview." In Lee Kam Hing and Tan Chee-Beng, eds, 2000, 382–405.

Wong Yee Tuan. 2015. *Penang Chinese Commerce in the 19th Century: The Rise and Fall of the Big Five.* Singapore: ISEAS.

Wu Fengbin. 1988. *Qiyue Huagong shi* (History of indentured Chinese labour). Nanchang: Jiangxi renmin chuban she.

Wu Hongli. 2008. "Chuxi Minnan qiaopi wenhua" ("Preliminary investigation into Southern Fujian's qiaopi culture"). In Wang Weizhong, ed., 2008, 358–369.

Wu Kuixin. 2004. "Qiaopi chuandi guandao de gengzu yu shutong" ("The blocking and dredging of the channels through which qiaopi were delivered"). In Wang Weizhong, ed., 200–207.

Xia Shuiping and Fang Xuejia. 2004. "Meizhou keshu diqude shuike ye shulüe" ("Discussion of the shuike trade in the Meizhou Hakka region"). In Wang Weizhong, ed., 2004, 179–186.

Xia Yuanming 2008. "Meizhou keshu diqu de shuike yu qiaopi ye shulüe" ("Short Account of the Shuike in the Meizhou Hakka Region"). In Wang Weizhong, ed., 2008, 370–390.

Xiao Jingliao. 2018. "Xianju gumiao zhen manbang: Lalü zhanzheng yu He Xiangu xinyang zai Yingshu Malaiya de kaizhan" ("Pacifying the wildland": The Larut Wars and the beginning of the He Xiangu cult in British Malaya"). *Zhongyang yanjiu yuan jindai shi yanjiu suo jikan*, no. 100, 47–84.

Xiao Wenping. 2004."Kejia shancun de shuike, qiaopi, yu qiaoxiang shehui" ("Shuike, qiaopi, and qiaoxiang society in the Hakka mountain villages"). In Wang Weizhong, ed., 2004, 253–263.

Xu Guanxi and Wu Zikai. n.d. "Shiliao cong: Zhongguo Yue xinan dao Heshu dong Yindu: Yifen zhuzai zhi xikuang laogong shi yuan cang" (Historical Materials: From Southwestern Guangdong Province to the Dutch East Indies: A Historical Record of Labour in the Tin Mines as Seen in a Piglet Identity Card"). *Guangzhouwan Historical Research Bulletin*.

Xu Guoqi. 2011. *Strangers on the Western Front: Chinese Workers in the Great War.* Cambridge MA: Harvard University Press.

Yacob, Shakila. 2007. "The United States Rubber Company in Southeast Asia,1910–1942." *Enterprise and Society*, vol. 8, no. 1, 136–174.

Yang Qunxi. 2004a. "Shilun Chao bang qiaopi ju jingying de tedian" ("On the special features of the management of the Chao Gang's remittance offices"). In Wang Weizhong, ed., 2004, 193–199.

Yang Qunxi, ed. 2004b. *Chaoshan diqu qiaopi ye ziliao* (Materials Concerning the Qiaopi Trade in the Chaoshan Region). Shantou: Shantou shi tushu guan.

Yang Tongling, Lin Zhang, Li Xinyun, Tan Enli, and Li Ensi. 2004. *Hunqian mengrao de guxiang—Bangjia dao* ("Lost in a reverie about one's native place: Bangka Island"). Beijing: Zhongguo youyi chuban gongsi.

Yap, Melanie, and Dianne Long Man. 1996. *Colour, Confusion and Concessions: The History of the Chinese in South Africa*. Hong Kong: Hong Kong University Press.

Yen Ching-hwang. 1985. *Coolies and Mandarins: China's Protection of Overseas Chinese During the Late Ch'ing Period (1851–1911)*. Singapore: Singapore University Press.

Yong Chen. 2000. *Chinese San Francisco, 1850–1943: A Trans-Pacific Community.* Stanford: Stanford University Press.

Young, Elliot. 2015. "Chinese Coolies, Universal Rights and the Limits of Liberalism in an Age of Empire." *Past & Present*, vol. 227, no. 1, 121–149.

Yuan Li and Chen Dazhang. 1991. *Haiwai Huaren ji qi juzhu di gaikuang*. (Survey of overseas Chinese and their settlements). Beijing: Zhongguo Huaqiao chuban gongsi.

Yun, Lisa. 2008. *The Coolie Speaks: Chinese Indentured Laborers and African Slaves in Cuba*. Philadelphia, PA: Temple University Press.

Yuniarti, Dewi Santoso, Jasmine Amelia Ulfah, and Iman Prihandono. 2020. "Buyer's Role in Improving BHR Practices in Indonesian Mineral Mining Industry." *Advances in Economics, Business and Management Research*, vol. 130, 285–299.

Zhang Beiyu. 2020. "A Bright Moon Roaming in Nanyang: Li Jinhui and the Chinese Song and Dance Troupe." *Paan*, no. 1, 134–150.

Zhang Shuoren. 2013. "Minguo shiqi Hainan qiaohui wenti shulun" ("On Some Questions Regarding Hainan Overseas Remittances in the Republican Period"). In *Hainan yimin lunwenji* (Collection of Essays on Hainan Emigration), edited by Hainan wenhua yanjiu zhongxin, Singapore: Xinjiapo Hainan wenhua zhongxin, 2013, 204–221.

Zheng He. 1933. "Taiwan Huagong gaikuang" (The general situation of Huagong in Taiwan). *Laogong yuekan*, vol. 1, no. 6, 107–110.

Zheng Yongnian, ed. 2010. *China and International Relations: The Chinese View and the Contribution of Wang Gungwu*. London: Routledge.

Zhou Nanjing, Chen Wenxian, Lin Liushun, and Zheng Min, eds. 1996. *Yindunixiya Huaren tonghua wenti ziliao huibian* (Materials on the assimilation of Indonesian Chinese). Beijing: Beijing daxue Yatai yanjiu zhongxin.

Zhou, Taomo. 2019. *Migration in the Time of Revolution: China, Indonesia, and the Cold War*. Ithaca: Cornell University Press.

Zhu Jieqin. 1984. "Shijiu shiji zhongqi zai Yindunixiya de qiyue Huagong" ("Indentured Huagong in Indonesia in the mid nineteenth century"). In Chen Hansheng, ed., 1981–1985, vol. 5, 217–243.

Zhuang Guotao. 1998. "Relations with China." In Pan, ed., 1998, 98–103.

Zondervan, Sjoerd. 2016. Patients of the Colonial State: The Rise of a Hospital System in the Netherlands Indies, 1890–1940. PhD, University of Maastricht.

Zou Qiudong and Su Tonghai. 2009. "Shuo 'huipi'" ("About 'huipi'"). In Chen Xiaogang, ed., 2009, 70–74.

Zurndorfer, Harriet T. 2022. "Economic, Social, and Legal Aspects of Slavery and Indentured Labor in Late Ming China (1550–1645): What the Huizhou Documents Tell Us." In Allen, ed., 2022, 131–149.

INDEX[1]

[1] Note: Page numbers followed by 'n' refer to notes.

G. Benton, *Chinese Indentured Labour in the Dutch East Indies, 1880–1942*, Palgrave Macmillan Transnational History Series, https://doi.org/10.1007/978-3-031-05024-4

T

www.ingramcontent.com/pod-product-compliance
Lightning Source LLC
Chambersburg PA
CBHW071934140126
38115CB00072B/61
* 9 7 8 3 0 3 1 0 5 0 2 3 7 *